GW01220402

BIG BOOKS

To dear Arnold
Many thanks for
adding more light
to the Yakar family.

"אף אור"
בונה פרפר חולף
(ברכה מאת.)

כסלו תנש"ד

Ramban

Commentary on the Torah

רמב״ן

Ramban
(Nachmanides)

Commentary on the Torah

ספר שמות

EXODUS

Translated and Annotated with Index
by Rabbi Dr. Charles B. Chavel, PH.B., M.A., LL.B., D.H.L., D.D.

Shilo Publishing House, Inc.
New York, N.Y. 10002

© Copyright 1973

by Shilo Publishing House, Inc.

Library of Congress Catalog Card No. 73-82961

Standard Book No. 088328-007-8

All Rights Reserved
No part of this book may be reprinted without permission in writing
from the publisher

Preface:

The publication of Ramban's commentary on the Book of Exodus to a certain extent may be accredited to the Torah-studying public. When I completed the translation of the commentary on the Book of Genesis, I had no intention of continuing the work. However, the spontaneous and warm response from the English-speaking public that concerns itself with the study of Torah, induced me to continue this sacred project.

As on the Book of Genesis, I am indebted first and foremost to Mr. Henry Petzenbaum and Mr. Joseph Salomon of Shilo Publishing House for their sincere and whole-hearted devotion to this great venture. No obstacles were too difficult for these two dedicated men in producing a book which bespeaks glory to the name of Ramban, as well as to all Torah. I am also grateful to Mr. Alan Augenbraun and Mr. Berel Berkovits for their valuable assistance in reading the manuscript.

I have already written on the nature of Ramban's commentary in my Preface to the Book of Genesis. May I add at this point: Whereas the Book of Genesis primarily deals with the origin of the world, of man and of our earliest ancestors, the Book of Exodus traces more specifically the history of Israel — its emergence as a people, its miraculous achievement of eternal freedom, the Revelation at Sinai, the ordinances which bestow the uniqueness of life upon our people, the building of the Tabernacle, etc. Ramban in his commentary rises to these occasions in his breadth of vision, profundity of thought, and thoroughness of scholarship. There is none comparable to him in the field of Biblical exegesis.

The Torah-loving and the Torah-studying student — surely, these two are synonymous — will do well to remember a saying of our Sages, of blessed memory, that a true knowledge of Torah is not acquired until one has gone over a text one hundred and one times. Ramban's commentary on the Torah is surely one of texts that our Sages would include in this category.

C. B. Chavel

Rosh Chodesh Nisan, 5733
April 3, 1973.

Contents

Preface	V
The Book of Exodus	3
The portion of:	
Shemoth	6
Va'eira	63
Bo	100
Beshalach	176
Yithro	249
Mishpatim	338
Terumah	434
Tetzaveh	471
Ki Thisa	510
Vayakheil	595
Pekudei	609
Additional Note	627
Index	631

COMMENTARY ON THE TORAH
BY OUR MASTER
RABBI MOSHE THE SON OF NACHMAN
THE GERONDITE

The Book of Exodus

'V'EILEH SHEMOTH' (AND THESE ARE THE NAMES OF...)[1]
In the Book of Genesis, which is the book of Creation, the Torah completed the account of how the world was brought forth from nothingness and how everything was created, as well as an account of all the events which befell the patriarchs, who are a sort of creation to their seed.[2] All the events that happened to them were symbolic occurrences, indicating and foretelling all that was destined to come upon their seed. After having completed the account of creation, the Torah begins another book concerning the subject that had been alluded to in those symbolic events [recorded in the Book of Genesis].

The Book of V'eileh Shemoth was set apart for the story of the first exile,[3] which had been clearly decreed,[4] and the redemption therefrom. This is why He reverted and began [this second book of

---

(1) The Hebrew names for the books of the Bible are generally taken from the first words in the Hebrew text. Thus the name *"V'eileh Shemoth"* for this second book of the Torah, or just *"Shemoth,"* as it is now known. In the Talmud it is known as *Chomesh Sheini*, the "Second Fifth" of the five books of the Torah (Sotah 36 b). The English name Exodus stems from the Septuagint, the first Greek translation of the Bible, and is based on the fact that the first fifteen chapters deal with the exodus from Egypt. (2) In his commentary on the Book of Genesis, Ramban develops this theme at great length. See Index to Vol. I, p. 618, Patriarchs. (3) Four exiles were decreed. The first one was in Egypt. See Index to Vol. I, p. 613, Exile. (4) Genesis 15:13.

the Torah] with the names of those persons who went down to Egypt, and mentioned their total number,[5] although this had already been written.[6] It is because their descent thereto constituted the beginning of the exile, which began from that moment on.[7]

Now the exile was not completed[8] until the day they returned to their place[9] and were restored to the status of their fathers. When they left Egypt, even though they came forth from the house of bondage, they were still considered exiles because they were *in a land that is not theirs*, [10] entangled in the desert. [11] When they came to Mount Sinai and made the Tabernacle, and the Holy One, blessed be He, caused His Divine Presence to dwell again amongst them, they returned to the status of their fathers when the *'sod eloka' (counsel of G-d) was upon their tents* [12] and "they

---

(5) In Verse 5 here: *And all the souls ... were seventy souls.* (6) Genesis 46:8-27. (7) The exile thus did not begin with the actual enslavement of the Israelites by the Egyptians; rather it started with their very descent into Egypt. Hence here at the beginning of the book of the exile, the Torah uses the same verse found in the Book of Genesis where the actual account of the descent is given, in order to indicate that the exile began at that point. See also Ramban on Genesis 46:2 (Vol. I, p. 553), where he alludes to this thought. Ramban makes further reference to it here in Verse 1. (8) Ramban is now aiming to explain why the second book of the Torah, which as explained above is the book of the first exile and the redemption therefrom, does not close with the actual exodus or with the Revelation on Sinai, but instead proceeds with the account of the building of the Tabernacle. Ramban's answer is most illuminating and inspiring. (9) See Hosea 5:15. (10) Genesis 15:13 . (11) See further, 14:3. (12) See Job 29:4, and Ramban's commentary thereon, (in my Kithvei Haramban: Vol. I, p. 90), where he interprets the verse as follows: "Job is saying that *sod eloka* — the counsel of G-d - was known in his tent, as if He foretold all future events. Thus Job and all who were with him were guarded from mishaps and troubles. It may be that *sod eloka* is a reference to the angels of the Supreme One and the host of the heavens that dwelled upon his tent to guard him from all evil, etc." Ramban is thus intimating here that the complete redemption of the Israelites from their first exile was not achieved until they were restored to the same position held by the patriarchs. Whereas the Divine Presence rested upon the tents of the patriarchs — see Shabbath 55b, where

were those who constituted the Chariot of the Holy One." [13] Then they were considered redeemed. It was for this reason that this second book of the Torah is concluded with the consummation of the building of the Tabernacle, and the glory of the Eternal filling it [14] always. [15]

Rashi clearly states that before the building of the Tabernacle, the Divine Presence was to be found upon the tents of the righteous — so Israel regained its original status only when the Divine Glory came to rest upon the Tabernacle at the time of its completion. See end of Book of Exodus. It is for this reason that the second book of the Torah — devoted as it is to the first exile and the redemption therefrom — continues with the account of the building of the Tabernacle. (13) Bereshith Rabbah 47:8. See Vol. I, p. 224. (14) Further, 40:35. (15) Numbers 9:16: *So it was always: the cloud covered it...*

Shemoth

1 1. AND THESE ARE THE NAMES OF .... The meaning [of the connective *vav* — *v'eileh*, ('and' these are) — when it would have sufficed to say, "These are the names of ...,"] is that Scripture desires to reckon the subject of the exile from the time they went down to Egypt. It was then that they were *the first of the exiles to go into exile,* [16] as I have explained. [17] It is for this reason that He returns to the beginning of the subject [stated in the Book of Genesis], which is the verse, *And all his seed he [Jacob] brought with him into Egypt.* [18] There it is written afterward, *And these are the names of the children of Israel, who came into Egypt,* etc. [19] This is the very same verse that He repeats here. Even though they are two separate books, the narrative is connected with subjects which follow one another successively. Here, once He mentioned the children of Jacob, He adopted a concise approach to his children's children and all of his seed [and did not mention them by name as He had done in the Book of Genesis]. Rather, He alluded to them only generally, just as He had said there, *All the souls of the house of Jacob, that came into Egypt, were threescore and ten.* [20]

A similar case is found in the Book of Chronicles and the Book of Ezra. The Book of Chronicles finishes with the verse: *Now in the first year of Cyrus king of Persia, that the word of the Eternal by the mouth of Jeremiah might be accomplished, the Eternal*

---

(16) Amos 6:7. (17) See Note 7 above. (18) Genesis 46:7. (19) *Ibid.,* Verse 8. (20) *Ibid.,* Verse 27. In the same way He said here in Verse 5: *And all the souls that came out of the loins of Jacob were seventy souls.*

EXODUS I, SHEMOTH

stirred up the spirit of Cyrus king of Persia, that he made a proclamation throughout all his kingdom, and put it also in writing, saying: Thus saith Cyrus king of Persia, etc.[21] The author repeated the very language of these two verses at the beginning of the Book of Ezra in order to connect the narrative. However, since they were indeed two books, he completed the first book, [i.e., the Book of Chronicles], with the events that transpired before the building of the Second Sanctuary, and he devoted the second book, [i.e., the Book of Ezra], to the events that happened from the time of the building [of that Sanctuary].[22] The same thing occurs in these two books, Bereshith and V'eileh Shemoth.

Rabbi Abraham ibn Ezra said that because He mentioned at the end of Bereshith [50:23] that Joseph *saw children of the third generation* to his children, this is why He mentioned [here in the second book] that his brethren likewise were at first few and then were fruitful and multiplied. But this is not correct.[23]

---

(21) II Chronicles 36:22-23. (22) Ramban's thesis apparently is that Ezra himself completely authored the two books, Chronicles and Ezra. See, however, Baba Bathra 15a, where it is stated, "Ezra wrote his book and the genealogy of Chronicles up to himself." This would seem to indicate that only the first chapters of the Book of Chronicles, which deal with the genealogical tables, were written by Ezra, but not the other parts of the book. The key to the understanding of Ramban's words must lie therefore in grasping his intent, i.e., that Ezra connected the Book of Chronicles with his own book by using the restoration-edict of Cyrus as the linking material, with the object of bringing out the continuity of the events during the two Sanctuaries. (23) Ramban did not explain the reason for his rejection of Ibn Ezra's interpretation. I found this in Isaac Abarbanel's (1437-1508) Commentary on the Torah, where he offers the following explanation for Ramban's rejection: "The reason for it is that in the Book of Genesis, the Torah has already mentioned each one of the twelve tribes, their children, and their children's children, who went down into Egypt. And this is far more than the mere names of the tribes He mentioned here. Besides, it would have sufficed to say here, *And the children of Israel were fruitful, and increased abundantly*, thus informing us of their great increase, and not just mentioning the names of the tribes. Moreover, in my opinion, if Ibn Ezra's interpretation be correct, it would not have been necessary here to include Joseph as it did in Verse 5, since he had been mentioned already at the beginning of this topic, [i.e., at the end of the Book of Genesis]. Moreover, the division of the chapters refutes Ibn Ezra's opinion."

Rashi wrote: "Although Scripture had already enumerated them whilst they were living, it again enumerates them by name, following their death, in order to show how they were beloved by G-d. They are compared to the stars which G-d also brings out by number and brings in by number, [24] as it is said, *He bringeth out their host by number, He calleth them all by name.*" [25] These are words of homiletic exposition, [26] and insofar as they indicate the love of G-d for the tribes — how the Holy One, blessed be He, loves them and repeats their names always — they are words of truth. But the matters of the connection of the verses and how they are joined by the *vav* — [*v'eileh shemoth* — *('And' these are the names of...)*] — is as I have explained.

10. COME, LET US DEAL WISELY WITH HIM. Pharaoh and his wise counsellors [27] did not see fit to slay them by the sword, for it would have been a gross treachery to smite without reason a people that had come into the land by command of a former king. The people of the country also would not give the king consent to commit such perfidy since he took counsel with them, [28] and all the more so since the children of Israel were a numerous and mighty people and would wage a great war against them. Rather, Pharaoh said he would do it wisely so that the Israelites would not feel that it was done in enmity against them.

It is for this reason that he placed a levy upon them, as it was customary that strangers in a country contribute a levy to the king, as it is mentioned in the case of King Solomon. [29] Afterwards he secretly commanded the midwives to kill the male children upon the birthstool [30] so that even the mothers should not know

---

(24) In our text of Rashi: "Which G-d also brings out and brings in by number and name." (25) Isaiah 40:26. "It is for this reason that He mentions the names of the tribes always and repeats them, all for the sake of showing how dear they are to G-d" (Bachya). (26) Shemoth Rabbah 1:3. (27) See Isaiah 19:11. (28) As it says in Verse 9: *And he said unto his people...* (29) II Chronicles 2:16-17. (30) Verse 16.

EXODUS I, SHEMOTH

it. Following that, *he charged all his people, Every son that is born, ye — yourselves — shall cast into the river.* [31] Essentially, Pharaoh did not want to charge his executioners to slay them by the decree of the king or to cast them into the river. Rather, he said to the people that whoever would find a Jewish child should throw him into the river. Should the child's father complain to the king or to the master of the city, they would tell him to bring witnesses and then they will exact vengeance [for the crime]. Now once the king's restriction was removed, [32] the Egyptians would search the houses, entering them at night, and indifferent [to the cries of the parents], would remove the children therefrom. It is therefore said, *And when she could no longer hide him.* [33]

It appears that this [decree to drown the Israelite children] lasted but a short time, for when Aaron was born [three years before Moses], [34] the decree was not yet in existence, [35] and when [shortly after] Moses was born, it appears that the decree was revoked. Perhaps it was through Pharaoh's daughter, who, in her compassion for the child Moses, said to her father that he should not act in that way. It may be that when it became known that this decree was enacted by the king, he revoked it, or again it may be that it was revoked on account of the astrologers, as is the opinion of the Rabbis, [36] since it was all done dexterously by them in order that the crime not be known. This is the meaning of the complaint made to Moses our teacher [by the officers of the children of Israel], *Ye have made our savor to be abhorred in the eyes of Pharaoh, and in the eyes of his servants, to put a sword in their hand to slay us,* [37] meaning, "Now they will increase their

---

(31) Verse 22. (32) Literally, "And when the king's strap was untied." In other words, when the government's restraint against murder was removed, the Egyptians, etc. Ramban thus traces through the verses the gradual disintegration of the Israelites' right to life in ancient Egypt. (33) Further, 2:3. (34) *Ibid.*, 7:7. (35) This would explain why his mother did not have to seek a way to preserve his life. (36) "When Moses was thrown into the waters, the astrologers said to Pharaoh, 'Their deliverer has already been cast into the waters.' Immediately, they voided the decree" (Shemoth Rabbah 1:29). See also Rashi to Verse 22 here. (37) Further, 5:21.

hatred of us and find justification for saying that we rebel against the government, and they will then openly slay us by the sword without the necessity of doing it slyly."

AND HE WILL GO UP 'MIN' (OUT OF) THE LAND. "I.e., 'against our will.' Our Rabbis explained that they spoke like a person who is pronouncing a curse against himself but assigns the curse to others. Thus it is as if Scripture wrote, 'And *we* shall have to go up out of the land, and they will possess it.' " These are the words of Rashi. But if the explanation is as the Rabbi has it, [i.e., that the Israelites will go up to wage war against the Egyptians], Scripture would have said, "And he will go up *al* (against) the land," [instead of saying *min ha'aretz (out* of the land)]. Such is the correct expression concerning warriors: *Nebuchadnezzar king of Babylon came up 'al' (against) all the fortified cities of Judah, and took them*[38]; *Rezin the king of Aram... went up to Jerusalem to war 'aleha' (against it).*[39] Perhaps [Rashi will explain it by] saying that the meaning is that "he will come up against us from the land wherein he dwells," meaning the land of Goshen.

It is possible to explain that Pharaoh is saying that "if wars will occur, the Israelites may join forces with our enemies *to take the spoil, and to take the prey.*[40] They will get themselves up out of this land to the land of Canaan with all our belongings, and we will not be able to wreak our vengeance on them nor to war against them." This is similar to the verses: *that brought us up out of the land of Egypt;*[41] *that brought up and that led the seed of the house of Israel out of the north country, and from all the countries whither I had driven them.*[42] Similarly, the verse, *And they shall appoint themselves one head, and shall go up out of the land,*[43] means they shall appoint over themselves a captain and they shall go up to their land out of the country in which they had been exiled.

(38) Ramban here combined two verses: II Kings 24:1 and 18:13. (39) Isaiah 7:1 . (40) *Ibid.*, 10:6. (41) Further, 32:1. (42) Jeremiah 23:8. (43) Hosea 2:2.

11. 'SAREI MISIM' (OFFICERS OF THE TRIBUTE) TO AFFLICT THEM. Pharaoh imposed a tribute upon the Israelite people to take men from them for the king's projects. He appointed Egyptian officers over the tribute to take men at will in turns to serve for a month or more in the royal building-projects and the rest of the days [they remained] at home. These officers commanded the Israelites to build cities for Pharaoh, and the people built storage-cities for Pharaoh through this levy. When the Egyptians saw that this forced labor did not harm the Israelites, they were in dread for their own lives [44] on account of them. They decreed that all Egyptians force the Israelites to serve them, [45] so that any Egyptian who needed work done had the authority to take from them men to do his work. This is the meaning of the verse, *And the Egyptians made the children of Israel to serve with rigor.* [45]

They furthermore decreed against them that they do hard work *in mortar and in brick.* [46] Whereas at first the officers would give them the bricks and the men of the forced labor would erect the buildings, they now conscripted the entire Israelite people into the work, commanding them to bring the earth, make the mortar with their hands and feet while only the straw was given to them from the king's house, and give the bricks to the men of the forced labor engaged in the construction of the buildings. Every other manner of hard service in the field for Pharaoh and the Egyptians — such as excavations and the removal of dung — were all imposed upon them. In addition, they subjugated them, pressing them not to rest while beating and cursing them. This is the sense of the expression, *in all their service, wherein they made them serve with rigor.* [46]

---

(44) Verse 12. (45) Verse 13. (46) Verse 14. Ramban now proceeds to show how *all* the Israelites — not only those forced into labor for the king's building-projects — were afflicted. It is necessary to recall the full text: *And the Egyptians made the children of Israel to serve with rigor. And they made their lives bitter with hard service, in mortar and in brick, and in all manner of service in the field; in all their service, wherein they made them serve with rigor* (Verses 13-14). Ramban understands the term "Egyptians" here as referring to the whole population. Further in the text, Ramban will suggest another interpretation.

The king supported them with *sparing bread*,[47] as is customary for those who work in his service. This is the purport of those lusting persons[48] who said, *We remember the fish, which we were wont to eat in Egypt for nought; the cucumbers,* etc.[49] Fish are very abundant in Egypt, and by command of the king, the Israelites would obtain them from those who caught them. They would also take cucumbers and melons from the vegetable-gardens,[49] no one putting them to shame, for such was the king's command.

But our Rabbis have said:[50] "The Israelites were servants to kings, but not servants to servants." If so, the verse, *And the Egyptians made the children of Israel to serve with rigor,*[45] alludes to Pharaoh's officers of the tribute, [mentioned above in Verse 11].

2 1. AND THERE WENT A MAN OF THE HOUSE OF LEVI. Our Rabbis have said[51] that he went after the advice of his daughter.[52] Rabbi Abraham ibn Ezra said that the Israelites dwelled in many cities, and this woman Jochebed lived in another city. [This would explain the term "went" in the above verse, i.e., he *went* to another city for his wife.] But what need is there for Scripture to mention this?

---

(47) Isaiah 30:20. (48) Numbers 11:4. (49) *Ibid.,* Verse 5. (50) Mechilta, Bachodesh, end of Chapter 5. (51) Sotah 12 a. (52) Amram and Jochebed, Moses' parents, had been married previously. The children of that union were Miriam and Aaron. "When Pharaoh decreed that the male children of the Hebrews be killed, Amram separated from his wife, and his example was followed by all of the Israelites. Miriam then told her father that his decree is worse than that of the king. 'Pharaoh decreed only against the male children, while you include the girls as well. It is doubtful if the decree of wicked Pharaoh will persist, while you are a righteous man and your enactment will surely be upheld by G-d.' Upon recognizing the justice of her plea, Amram remarried his wife, and the men who had previously followed his example also remarried" (Sotah 12 b). It is this episode which the verse suggests by saying, *And there went a man,* i.e., "went" after the advice of his daughter and remarried his divorced wife. See also further on in the text for a reference to a prophecy Miriam made at that time.

In my opinion Scripture uses the term "went" because this man paid no heed to Pharaoh's decree and took to himself a woman to beget children. Such is Scripture's way of speaking of anyone who prompts himself to do something new. Thus: *And Reuben went and lay with Bilhah;* [53] *So he went and took Gomer the daughter of Diblaim;* [54] *Come, and let us sell him to the Ishmaelites;* [55] *Come, and let us smite him with the tongue;* [56] *Come now, and let us reason together.* [57] Similarly this man Amram alerted himself and married a daughter of Levi.

The reason Scripture does not mention the name of the man nor the name of the woman he married is to avoid tracing their genealogy and mentioning who their fathers and their fathers' fathers were up to Levi. At this point, Scripture desires to shorten the subject until the birth of the redeemer takes place, and after that, in the second *seder,* [58] He traced the genealogy even of other tribes [59] on account of Moses.

In line with the simple meaning of Scripture, i.e., that this was a first marriage [and not a remarriage as stated above], there is no significance in its being mentioned earlier or later in the chapter. This marriage took place before Pharaoh's decree [that all male Hebrew children be killed], and she gave birth to Miriam and Aaron. After that, Pharaoh decreed, *Every son that is born, ye shall cast into the river,* [60] and then she gave birth to this goodly son Moses. Scripture did not mention the birth of Miriam and Aaron inasmuch as there was nothing new about them. However, in the opinion of our Rabbis, [51] this was a remarriage, since Amram separated from his wife in consequence of Pharaoh's decree and

---

(53) Genesis 35:22. (54) Hosea 1:3. Since she was a harlot, it required self-prompting on his part to perform the novel act of marrying her. (55) Genesis 37:27. (56) Jeremiah 18:18. (57) Isaiah 1:18. (58) I.e., in *Seder Va'eira.* (*A seder* is the weekly portion of the Torah read in the synagogue at the Sabbath morning services.) Specifically, Moses' genealogy is found in *Seder Va'eira,* Chapter 6, Verses 16-20. (59) Reuben and Simeon. (*Ibid.,* Verses 14-15). (60) Above, 1:22.

then took her back on account of his daughter's prophecy.[61] He made her a wedding and placed her in the litter, while Miriam and Aaron danced about them in their joy[62] because through this marriage, Israel would be redeemed [from Egypt]. Even though Aaron was young[63] [at that time], G-d put gladness in his heart for this occasion, or possibly his sister Miriam taught him.

2. AND WHEN SHE SAW HIM THAT HE WAS GOODLY SHE HID HIM. It is a known fact that all mothers love their children, goodly or ungoodly, and all of them would hide them [from harm] with all their might. There is thus no need for Scripture to explain *that he was goodly*. But the meaning of this goodliness is that she saw in him some unique quality which, in her opinion, foreshadowed that a miracle would happen to him and he would be saved. Therefore she applied herself and thought of ways to save him. When she saw that she could hide him no longer, she thought of saving him by another device. She made him an ark of bulrushes [and put him among the reeds at the side of the river], and his sister placed herself at a distance[64] — so that the Egyptians would not recognize her — *to know what would be done to him.*[64] All this is support for the words of our Rabbis who expounded,[51] "*That he was goodly,* namely, that the whole house became filled with light," and for what the Rabbis have said,[61] i.e., that Miriam prophesied, "Mother is destined to bear a son who will deliver Israel."

5. TO BATHE 'AL' (BY) THE RIVER. "Transpose [the order of the words in] the verse[65] and then explain it: the daughter of Pharaoh went down by the river to bathe in it." Thus the language of Rabbeinu Shlomo [Rashi]. If so, *al haye'or (by* or *upon the*

(61) Miriam prophesied, "My mother is destined to bear a son who will deliver Israel" (Sotah 13 a). (62) So clearly stated in Sotah 12 a. (63) He could have been no more than two years old since he was but three years older than Moses, and Moses was born after the second marriage. (64) Verse 4. (65) The order of the Hebrew words is: *And the daughter of Pharaoh came down to bathe by the river.* Rashi explains it to mean: "And the daughter of Pharaoh went down by the river to bathe in it."

river) is like *el haye'or* (to the river). Similarly, *And Elkanah went to Ramah 'al beitho' (upon his house)* [66] [is like *el beitho* (to his house)]; *Thus shall ye say every one 'al rei'eihu' (upon his neighbor) and every one to his brother* [67] [is like *el rei'eihu* (to his neighbor)].

It is possible that there were steps upon the bank of the river and that she went down from the royal palace to bathe upon the first step by the river, but did not enter into the river's stream. [In this case, the expression *al haye'or* would be completely understandable, as it would mean that she came down to bathe "*upon* the step near *the river*"], *and* then *she saw the ark among the reeds* far from her and she sent her handmaid to fetch it. It may be that to bathe *'al haye'or'* is like "to bathe *baye'or* (in the river)." Similarly, *And thou shalt put them 'al' one basket* [68] [is like *b'sal echad* ('into' one basket)].

6. AND BEHOLD IT WAS A WEEPING LAD. "His voice sounded like that of a grown lad." [69] Thus the language of Rabbeinu Shlomo. Now the Rabbis have already rejected this opinion, saying,[70] "If so, you have made Moses our teacher appear as having a blemish [and being unfit for Levitical service in the Tabernacle]."[71] Besides, what reason is there for Scripture to mention his unnatural voice?

---

(66) I Samuel 2:11. (67) Jeremiah 23:35. (68) Further, 29:3. (69) This interpretation is based on the change of reference to Moses within the same verse: *And she opened it, and saw it, even 'hayeled' (the child), and behold it was a weeping 'na'ar' (a young lad).* Hence, in accordance with Rabbi Yehudah's opinion in Sotah 12 b, Rashi construed that he was a child with the voice of a young lad. (70) This is the opinion of Rabbi Nechemya (*ibid.*). (71) Part of the Levitical services in the Tabernacle — and later in the Sanctuary in Jerusalem — consisted of the chanting of the services. A Levite who had no sweetness of voice was disqualified for this service. (See Maimonides' The Commandments, Vol. I, pp. 32-3, Soncino.) Now if as an infant, Moses, who was a Levite, already had a voice like that of a young lad, as he grew older his voice must have thickened. After the building of the Tabernacle when he was past eighty, his voice naturally could no longer be a singer's voice, as it would have been greatly out of proportion to his age.

And Rabbi Abraham ibn Ezra said that his limbs were developed as that of a young lad. Perhaps Scripture mentioned this in order to denote the child's beauty. It was due to his exquisite beautiful appearance that she [the princess] had compassion for him since she recognized that he had been recently born and yet his limbs were well-developed like those of a lad.

A more correct interpretation is that his was a strong and unrelenting cry like that of a lad, and therefore she had compassion for him. A homiletic exposition has it:[72] *"A weeping lad.* He was a child whose behavior was that of a lad [who is not prone to crying]. At that moment, the angel Gabriel came and struck him so that he would cry and she would be compassionate towards him."

In my opinion there is no need for all this. From the day of his birth, a child is called *na'ar* (lad) [in Scripture], as it is said, *What shall we do 'lana'ar' (to the lad) that shall be born?* [73] Similarly, *And David besought G-d for 'hana'ar' (the lad).* [74] Conversely, Scripture calls a grown lad *yeled* (child), as it is said in the case of Ishmael.[75] Similarly, *'v'hana'ar na'ar' (and the lad was young),* [76] meaning that he [Samuel] was a young child of twenty-four months. As soon as she [his mother, Hannah] had weaned him, she brought him up to Shiloh, as it is written, *And she gave her son suck until she weaned him. And when she had weaned him, she took him up with her.*[77]

---

(72) Shemoth Rabbah 1:28. (73) Judges 13:8. (74) II Samuel 12:16. The subject there is a child, not a grown lad. (75) *And she cast 'hayeled' (the child)* (Genesis 21:16). At that time, Ishmael was seventeen years old. (See Ramban, Vol. I, p. 270, and Note 329, *ibid.*). Yet he is called *yeled*. (76) I Samuel 1:24. That Samuel was but a child at that time is explained by Ramban in the text, and yet Scripture refers to him as a *na'ar*. (77) *Ibid.*, Verses 23-24.

AND SHE SAID, THIS IS ONE OF THE HEBREWS' CHILDREN. [She came to this conclusion because] contemplating what happened, she said [that his mother had done it] in order to save him or that she had placed him there so that she might not look upon the death of her child, and why should an Egyptian do that? Some Rabbis say [78] that [she knew he was a Hebrew because] she saw that he was circumcised. If so, [we must assume that] she removed his clothes and examined him. But there is no need for this. [79]

11. AND WHEN MOSES WAS GROWN UP HE WENT OUT UNTO HIS BRETHREN. This is to be understood that he grew to manhood. It has already been said, *And the child grew*,[80] which means that it was no longer necessary to wean him, and then the mother[81] *brought him to Pharaoh's daughter, and he became her son*,[80] for he was to stand in the presence of kings.[82] After that, he grew to manhood in maturity of mind.

AND HE WENT OUT UNTO HIS BRETHREN. This indicates that they told him he was a Jew,[83] and he desired to see them because they were his brethren. Now he looked on their

---

(78) This opinion, found in Sotah 12 a and in Shemoth Rabbah 1:29, is ascribed to Rabbi Yosei the son of Rabbi Chanina. (79) Ramban's intent seems to be that since Pharaoh's decree to cast the male children into the river applied only to Hebrew children — as the simple meaning of Scripture indicates — there was no need for the princess to seek to establish his identity. There is, however, a Midrashic tradition mentioned in Rashi (above, 1:22) that for one day the aforesaid decree applied to all children. The astrologers had said to the king, "Today the deliverer of the Hebrews has been born, and we do not know whether he is born of an Egyptian father or of an Israelite." Therefore the decree on that day applied to all children. In accordance with that opinion, it is logical to assume that she examined the child, and only then did she come to the conclusion that he was a Hebrew. This is the basis of the opinion of Rabbi Yosei the son of Rabbi Chanina (see preceding Note), i.e., that she knew he was a Hebrew because she saw that he was circumcised. (80) Verse 10. (81) Verses 8-9: *And the maiden went and called the mother of the child,* etc. (82) See Proverbs 22:29. (83) See Esther 3:4.

burdens and toils and could not bear [the sight of his people enslaved]. This was why he killed the Egyptian who was smiting the oppressed Hebrew.

14. WILT THOU SPEAK TO KILL ME? "From here we learn that Moses had killed the Egyptian by merely pronouncing the Tetragrammaton."[84] Thus the language of Rashi, and it is also a Midrash of our Rabbis.[85]

But I wonder. If so, who told *the wicked one* [86] that Moses killed him? Perhaps Moses placed his hands upon the Egyptian and cursed him in the Name of G-d,[87] [and the Hebrew who was now quarrelling with Moses saw him doing that]. This would explain the term *vayach ('and he smote' the Egyptian)*.[88] It may be that because the Egyptian had fallen dead before him [after he had pronounced the Tetragrammaton over him], Moses feared that they may report him and so he buried the Egyptian in the sand. The Hebrew who saw him doing that reckoned that Moses had caused [the Egyptian's death somehow, even though he did not know that he had killed him by pronouncing the Tetragrammaton]. Perhaps he thought Moses had killed him by the sword, as he saw only the burial.

In line with the plain meaning of Scripture, scholars say [89] that the expression. *wilt thou 'omer' (speak),* means "think," since we

---

(84) The Tetragrammaton (*Shem Hamphorash* or *Shem Hamyuchad*) is the Proper Name of G-d. It consists of four Hebrew letters, the utterance of which is now forbidden. It is translated here as the Eternal. By pronouncing this Name, Moses needed no weapon to accomplish his purpose of bringing about the deserved death of the Egyptian.   (85) Shemoth Rabbah 1:35.   (86) "The wicked one" — so called by the Torah in Verse 13: *and he* [Moses] *said to the wicked one, 'Why do you smite thy fellow?'*   (87) See II Kings 2:24.   (88) A similar use of the term is found in the case of the Assyrian army that was smitten outside Jerusalem by the angel of G-d. It says there, *And it came to pass that night, that the angel of the Eternal went forth 'vayach' (and smote) in the camp of the Assyrians* (II Kings 19:35). Now just as in that case *vayach* does not signify a physical act of striking by hand but rather the inflicting of defeat by supernatural power, so also here in the case of Moses. (Bachya.)   (89) Ibn Ezra in his commentary here, and R'dak in his Book of Roots, under the root *amar.*

find *amirah* (speaking) referring to the thought of the heart. *I said in my heart;* [90] *I say, that an untimely birth is better than he.* [91] But here there is no need for this, for [the intent of the Hebrew's words to Moses] is as follows: *"Who made thee a ruler and a judge over us? Is it because thou dost desire to kill me as thou didst kill the Egyptian that thou reprovest me and sayest, 'Why smitest thou thy fellow?' "*[92]

16. NOW THE PRIEST OF MIDIAN HAD SEVEN DAUGHTERS. Scripture does not mention him by name for he is not known [to the reader], but rather epithetically mentions that he was the honored one in his priesthood. This was Jethro, for after he became related to Moses it is written, *And Moses went and returned to Jether his father-in-law,*[93] and there it is written, *And Jethro said to Moses: Go in peace.*[93] [This proves that Jether and Jethro are the same person], just as Eliyah and Eliyahu,[94] Yirmiyah and Yirmiyahu.[95] After he became a proselyte to Judaism, he was called Hobab, as it is written, *from the children of Hobab the father-in-law of Moses,*[96] for it is the way of all who become converts to Judaism that they be called another name in Israel. And he [Jethro or Hobab] was the son of Reuel, for it is written, *And Moses said unto Hobab, the son of Reuel the Midianite.*[97] The verse here stating, *And they came to Reuel their father,*[98] means "their father's father," just as [Jacob had said], *O G-d of my father Abraham,*[99] [and Abraham was his father's

---

(90) Ecclesiastes 2:1. (91) *Ibid.*, 6:3. It is obvious that Ramban's intent in selecting these two verses from the Book of Ecclesiastes is to show that the term *amirah* (saying) as such is equivalent to *amirah b'leiv* (speaking in one's heart). Hence the Book of Ecclesiastes uses them interchangeably. (92) In other words, Ramban is saying that the expression *atah omer (thou sayest)* alludes to that which Moses had said in Verse 13: *Why smitest thou thy fellow?* The Hebrew thus said to Moses: "Is it because you desire to kill me as you killed the Egyptian that you reproved me by saying, 'Why do you smite your fellow?'" (93) Further, 4:18. (94) Eliyah (II Kings 1:3), Eliyahu (I Kings 17:1). (95) Yirmiyah (Jeremiah 27:1), Yirmiyahu (*ibid.*, 1:1). (96) Judges 4:11. (97) Numbers 10:29. (98) Verse 18. (99) Genesis 32:10.

father], and [when speaking of Belshazzar, king of Babylon, Scripture says], *Nebuchadnezzar his father,*[100] [while he was his father's father].[101] Similarly: *Know ye Laban the son of Nahor?*[102] *And Mephibosheth the son of Saul.*[103] There are many other such verses.

[Jethro's daughters came and told Reuel their grandfather of how Moses came to their aid — as is related in Verses 18-19 — and did not tell Jethro] because the priest was not found in the house since he was preoccupied with the ministry in his temple, and so they came to the grandfather. It is possible that the verse, *And Moses was content to dwell with the man,*[104] refers to the priest mentioned above [in Verse 16 — namely, Jethro][105] — for it was he who gave Moses Zipporah his daughter.

AND THEY CAME AND DREW WATER. Every day, the practice was that the shepherds drew water, filled the troughs and watered their flocks first, and then these women watered their flocks. It happened that on this day, the women preceded the men *and they came and drew water,* thinking to water their flocks before the shepherds came. But then *came the shepherds and drove*

---

(100) Daniel 5:2. (101) Evil-merodach, king of Babylon, ruled after Nebuchadnezzar (see II Kings 25:27), and he was followed by Belshazzar (see Megillah 11 a). Nebuchadnezzar was thus Belshazzar's grandfather, and yet Scripture (Daniel 5:2) speaks of him as his father. (102) Genesis 29:5. But Laban was really the son of Bethuel, for he was the brother of Rebekah (*ibid.*, 24:29), and of Rebekah it is written that her father was Bethuel (*ibid.*, Verse 15). Bethuel's father was Nahor (*ibid.*, 22:20-22). Yet Jacob asked, *Know ye Laban the son of Nahor?* It is because a grandfather is called "father." (103) II Samuel 19:25. Mephibosheth was the son of Jonathan (*ibid.*, 4:4), who was the son of Saul. (104) Verse 21. (105) The intent of Ramban's words is as follows: According to the above-mentioned interpretation that Jethro was not to be found in his home and that consequently his daughters told Reuel, his father, what had happened (as stated in Verses 18-20), it should follow that the expression, *And Moses was content to dwell with 'the man'* (Verse 21) refers to Reuel, and it was Reuel who gave Moses Zipporah his granddaughter as a wife. But, continues Ramban, it is possible that "the man" in Verse 21 refers back to "the priest" in Verse 16, and so it was Jethro who gave Moses his daughter in marriage.

them away [106] from the troughs, insisting on watering their own flocks first as they had always done. Moses' anger was aroused because of this injustice, and he saved them, for since they had filled the troughs, the water belonged to them. Moreover, he drew water for them [107] as the troughs did not suffice for all their flocks. This is the purport of the question, *How is it that ye are come so soon today?* [108] [which Reuel their grandfather asked them]. And they answered, *An Egyptian delivered us out of the hand of the shepherds,* [107] meaning that "they had always driven us away when we came to the troughs first."

23. AND IT CAME TO PASS IN THE COURSE OF THOSE MANY DAYS. Scripture uses the expression "in those days" or "on that day" only when alluding to a brief current event, but of a past event it says, *and it came to pass afterward.* [109] In that case then, it should have said here, "and it came to pass afterward that the king of Egypt died." It is for this reason that our Rabbis have said [110] that because they were days of suffering [for Israel], Scripture calls them "many" although alluding to a brief current event. [111] So also have the Rabbis said [112] in connection with the above-mentioned verse, *And it came to pass in those days when Moses was grown up,* [113] that his growth was unnatural, meaning, sudden and fast. [114] Under all circumstances, the period [covered in the verses], *and the king of Egypt died,* and the children of Israel cried out *and their cry came up unto G-d,* was [altogether] a brief period of time.

---

(106) Verse 17. (107) Verse 19. (108) Verse 18. (109) As in Judges 16:4. (110) Shemoth Rabbah 1:40. (111) In other words, Scripture is really referring here to a specific current event, namely, the death of the king, and yet it uses the term "many" — *and it came to pass in the course of those 'many' days* — instead of saying "in those days." To a suffering people — as Israel was at that time — even a brief period appeared as a long one. (112) Shemoth Rabbah 1:32. (113) Above, Verse 11. (114) Ramban is thus confirming what he stated above, i.e., that the Scriptural expression *in those days* alludes to a brief current event. Hence when it says in the case of Moses' growth, *and it was in those days and Moses was grown up,* the Rabbis interpreted it to mean that his growth was brief and sudden.

However, we might also explain that *in the course of those many days* refers to the days of suffering and hard labor which were exceedingly many, as the exile became very prolonged. It was this [long period of suffering and hard labor] which caused them to cry out, *and their cry came up unto G-d*. Similarly, the verse, *And it came to pass after many days, the word of the Eternal came to Elijah, in the third year*,[115] means that there were many days [of famine] and afterwards this event, [related there in the Book of Kings], occurred.

In my opinion, the purport of this verse, [*And it came to pass in the course of those many days*], is to allude to those days when Moses was a fugitive from Pharaoh. Indeed he was but a youth when he fled, as the verse said, *And when Moses was grown up he went out unto his brethren*,[113] suggesting that immediately when he grew up and became self-conscious and they told him that he was a Jew, he longed to see the burdens, toils and oppressions of his brethren. On that [first] day on which he went out, he smote the Egyptian, and on the second day, they denounced him [to the authorities] and he fled. He was thus at that time approximately twelve years of age, as our Sages have mentioned,[116] and at any rate not twenty,[117] and when he stood before Pharaoh he was eighty years old.[118] In that case, he was a fugitive from Pharaoh for about sixty years, [and it is with reference to those sixty years that Scripture speaks of *those 'many' days*].

It is likely that at the end of that period, Moses came to Midian and married Zipporah, since when this word [of G-d that he return to Egypt] came to him, he had begotten of her only his firstborn son Gershom[119] [while Eliezer, his second son, was born during his journey to Egypt].[120]

Scripture however mentions nothing of [the entire period of] his flight excepting, *And he dwelt in the land of Midian, and he*

---

(115) I Kings 18:1. (116) Shemoth Rabbah 5:1. (117) *Ibid.*, 1:32. (118) Further, 7:7. (119) Verse 22. (120) See Rashi further, 4:24. This proves that Moses' arrival and marriage in Midian were towards the end of his sixty-year absence from Egypt.

EXODUS II, SHEMOTH

sat down by a well, [121] since nothing happened to him in those other days which Scripture found necessary to relate. And it is logical. He who flees from the reach of a government does not tarry in a settled place or its environs. Instead, he flees from place to place in remote regions. Thus he stayed away for a long time, hiding himself and feigning to be a stranger, going about *from nation to nation, from one kingdom to another people,* [122] and at the end of that time he came to Midian and stayed there. This is the meaning of the verse, *And he dwelt in the land of Midian.* [121] It would have been fitting for Scripture to say, "and he went to the land of Midian," but instead it implies that he did not dwell in any city until the end [of the period], when he came to the land of Midian and there he dwelt.

Now due to the fact that Scripture mentions his flight from Pharaoh and his dwelling in Midian, and it immediately relates that he was made to return to Egypt by command of the Holy One, blessed be He, it alludes to this entire period by saying, *And it came to pass in the course of those many days,* meaning [those days] when Moses fled from before Pharaoh and during part of which time he stayed in Midian. At the end [of that period], the king of Egypt died, and the Divine Revelation concerning it came to Moses and he was returned to Egypt and redeemed the children of Israel. It is for this reason that Scripture does not say, "and it came to pass *after* many days," for the purport of that would have been that [the death of the king of Egypt] occurred long after Moses dwelt in Midian. But that is not so, for the expression *those many days* refers to all that is related above.

AND THE KING OF EGYPT DIED, AND THE CHILDREN OF ISRAEL SIGHED BY REASON OF THE BONDAGE. "He was stricken with leprosy [and hence may be considered as dead], and he was wont to slaughter Israelitic babes and bathe in their blood." Thus the words of Rashi. This is a Midrash of the Sages. [123]

(121) Verse 15. (122) Psalms 105:13. (123) Shemoth Rabbah 1:41.

In line with the plain meaning of Scripture, [it is to be explained that] the custom of all subjects of a wicked tyrant is to hope for and look forward to the day of his death. But when the Israelites saw that the king died, they wailed bitterly lest *a godless man may come to reign,* [124] who will be more wicked than the preceding king. They said, *Our bones are dried up, and our hope is lost,* [125] and thus they chose death rather than life.[126] This is the sense of the word *na'akatham (their groaning),* [127] for they groaned *with the groanings of a mortally-wounded man.* [128]

25. AND G-D SAW THE CHILDREN OF ISRAEL. Rabbi Abraham ibn Ezra explained this as meaning that G-d saw the violence which the Egyptians overtly did to them, *and G-d knew* what was done to them secretly. And Rashi explained: "*And G-d knew.* He directed His heart to them and did not hide His eye from them." This is correct in line with the plain meaning of Scripture. At first He hid His face from them and they were devoured,[129] but now G-d heard their groaning and He saw them, meaning that He no longer hid His face from them; He knew their pains and all that was done to them, as well as all that they required.

Now Scripture gives a lengthy account of the many reasons for their redemption: *And G-d heard their groaning, and G-d remembered His covenant with Abraham, with Isaac, and with Jacob;* [127] *And G-d saw the children of Israel, and G-d knew; For I know their pains.* [130] This is because even though the time [of bondage] decreed upon them was completed, they were not worthy of redemption, as was explained by the prophet Ezekiel;[131] it was only on account of the cry [132] that He in His mercies accepted their prayer.

(124) Job 34:30.   (125) Ezekiel 37:11.   (126) See Jeremiah 8:3. (127) Verse 24.   (128) Ezekiel 30:24.   (129) See Deuteronomy 31:17. (130) Further, 3:7.   (131) Ezekiel 20:6-10.   (132) *And we cried unto the Eternal, the G-d of our fathers, and the Eternal heard our voice* (Deuteronomy 26:7). See also Numbers 20:16.

EXODUS III, SHEMOTH

By way of the Truth, [the mystic lore of the Cabala], there is in this verse one of the great mysteries of the Torah, suggesting that their afflictions came up to the light of His countenance, which brought them [their afflictions] near the Knowledge [of G-d], just as is implied in the verse, *In midst of the 'shanim' (years) make it known; in wrath remember compassion.* [133] It is for this reason that Scripture gives this lengthy account — [*And G-d saw the children of Israel, and G-d knew*] — after already having mentioned, *And G-d heard... and G-d remembered.* [127] This verse, [*And G-d saw...,*] has been explained in the Midrash of Rabbi Nechunya ben Hakanah.[134] From there you will understand the verse.

3   2. AND THE ANGEL OF THE ETERNAL APPEARED UNTO HIM IN A FLAME OF FIRE. Because Scripture originally states, *And the angel of the Eternal appeared,* and then it goes on to say, *And when the Eternal saw that he turned aside to see, G-d called unto him,* [135] Rabbi Abraham ibn Ezra explained that *elohim* mentioned here [in the second verse] is the angel mentioned [in the first], as in the verse, *For I have seen 'elohim' face to face.* [136] The expression, *I am the G-d of thy father,* [137] is a case of the deputy speaking in the name of Him Who sent him. [138] But this is not correct. Moses the greatest in prophecy, would not have hidden his face from an angel [as is related in Verse 6].

---

(133) Habakkuk 3:2. Shem Tov ibn Gaon, (a Spanish Cabalist of the pupils of Rashba — printed in Ma'or V'shamesh, Livorno, 1839), explains that Ramban's intent in mentioning this verse is that the word *shanim* (years) should be understood as *sh'nayim* (two), a reference to the two Divine attributes, justice and mercy. When they unite, Israel is remembered for help and redemption. This is explicitly referred to in the second half of the verse: *in wrath remember compassion.* (134) Also called Sefer Habahir. Ramban's reference is found there in paragraph 76 (Margoliot ed.). See Vol. I, p. 24, Note 42. Ramban was the first author to quote from this classic of Jewish mystic thought in an open and extensive manner. See the learned work of Israel Weinstock, B'maglei Haniglah V'hanistar (Mosad Harav Kook, Jerusalem) on various aspects of this book. (135) Verse 4. (136) Genesis 32:31. The reference there is to an angel. See Ramban on Verses 26 and 30, there. (137) Verse 6. (138) See Vol. I, p. 260, for a similar instance.

Our Rabbis have said in Bereshith Rabbah: [139] *"Angel.* This refers to the angel Michael. Wherever Rabbi Yosei Ha'aruch [140] was seen, people would say, 'There is Rabbeinu Hakadosh.' Similarly, wherever the angel Michael appears, there is also present the Glory of the Divine Presence." The Rabbis intended to say that at first, the angel Michael appeared to Moses, and there was also the Glory of the Divine Presence, but Moses did not see the Glory, as he had not duly prepared his mind for prophecy. When he duly prepared his heart for it *and he turned aside to see,* then the vision of the Divine Presence revealed itself to him, *and G-d called unto him out of the midst of the bush.*[135]

AND, BEHOLD, THE BUSH 'BO'EIR' (BURNED) WITH FIRE. [The word *bo'eir*] has the same meaning as *doleik* (burning), [141] i.e., [the bush] was in the midst of a burning fire, and it is like the verse, *and the fathers 'm'va'arim' the fire,* [142] meaning, "kindling" and burning the wood with fire. But the expression, *why the bush is not 'yiv'ar'?* [143] means, "why is it not consumed and wasted?" Similarly, *As flax that was 'ba'aru' with fire* [144] means "consumed." And so is the opinion of Onkelos, who translated the first [*bo'eir*] as *bo'eir* (burning), and the second one [*yiv'ar*] as *mitokad,* [the Aramaic word for "consumed"]. It may be that *yiv'ar* has the same meaning as in the verses, *'Uvi'arta' (So shalt thou put away) the evil from the midst of thee;* [145] *Then a man useth it 'l'va'eir' (for fodder).* [146] Such is the style of the Sacred Language to use [one term in the same instance with two

---

(139) Bereshith Rabbah 97:4. The complete quote mentioned here by Ramban is found in Shemoth Rabbah 2:8. (140) Literally: "Rabbi Yosei the tall one." He was an outstanding pupil of Rabbeinu Hakadosh, or Rabbi Judah the Prince, redactor of the Mishnah. (141) Ramban's intent is to solve this difficulty: In the verse before us it says, *and, behold, the bush 'bo'eir',* and in Verse 3 it says that Moses asked, *why the bush is not 'yiv'ar'?* Ramban explains that in the first case, *bo'eir* has the same meaning as *doleik* (burning), while *yiv'ar* means "consumed." (142) Jeremiah 7:18. (143) Verse 3. (144) Judges 15:14. (145) Deuteronomy 17:7. (146) Isaiah 44:15. The expression "for fodder" suggests destruction and annihilation. See R'dak, (mentioned in my Hebrew commentary, p. 288), who so interprets this verse. Here then the sense of the verse would be: "why does the fire not *remove* or *eat up* the bush altogether?"

EXODUS III, SHEMOTH

different meanings], as in the verse: *They rode on thirty 'ayarim' (ass colts) and they had thirty 'ayarim' (cities).* [147]

5. APPROACH NOT HITHER. Moses had not yet reached the highest degree of prophecy, for at Mount Sinai *he drew near unto the thick darkness where G-d was.* [148] This also accounts for the hiding of his face [in this instance], for he had not yet reached that high [degree of prophecy of] which it was said of Moses, *and the similitude of the Eternal doth he behold.* [149]

FOR THE PLACE WHEREON THOU STANDEST IS HOLY GROUND. Even though Moses was far from the bush, the angel warned him [not to approach], for the whole mountain became sanctified when the Divine Presence came down upon the mountain–top, just as it did at the time of the Giving of the Torah. [150] Now Moses was on the mountain for he had ascended thereto, as it is said, *and he came to the mountain of G-d, unto Horeb,* [151] and the bush was on the top of the mountain. [152] Thus the entire site became holy and therefore the wearing of sandals was forbidden. A similar case is found in Joshua. [153] Likewise, the priests ministered in the Sanctuary only while barefoot.

6. I AM THE G-D OF THY FATHER. In accordance with the plain meaning of Scripture, this is equivalent to saying, "the G-d of thy fathers." However, He mentions the singular instead of the plural, for the intent is "the G-d of each one of your ancestors,"

---

(147) Judges 10:4. Thus the word *ayarim* has two separate meanings in the same verse. In the instance before us here, the Hebrew root *bo'eir* is used with two separate meanings: burning, and consuming or removing. (148) Further, 20:18. (149) Numbers 12:8. (150) Further, 19:20. (151) Verse 1. (152) Accordingly we must understand that before the burning of the bush began, Moses had already gone up on the mountain but not to its top. It was later when he desired to approach the top of the mountain to see *this great sight, why the bush is not burnt,* that he was warned not "to approach." Had he not been on the mountain at all, the warning should have been not "to come up." (153) Joshua 5:15.

since people refer to all ancestors as fathers. Similarly: *the G-d of thy father;* [154] *this is my G-d, and I will glorify Him; my father's G-d, and I will exalt Him,* [155] meaning "the G-d of my fathers."

Rabbi Abraham ibn Ezra said [that the word "father" in the phrase], *the G-d of my father,* refers to Abraham since he was the first who began to call upon the name of the Eternal. [156] After that, He mentioned Abraham by name and then joined the rest of the patriarchs to him. [157] In the opinion of our Rabbis, [158] ["father" in the phrase] *The G-d of thy father,* means Amram. This is just as if He had said, "I am thy G-d," [i.e., Moses' G-d], but He desired to associate His Name with that of a righteous man who had already died - [namely, Amram] - rather than with that of one yet alive, [i.e., Moses]. [159] After that, [He mentioned] *the G-d of Abraham, the G-d of Isaac, and the G-d of Jacob,* meaning that He is the G-d of all Israel.

The reason for His mentioning "the G-d of" with each one [of the patriarchs] instead of saying "the G-d of Abraham, Isaac, and Jacob" is that He referred to His Name and His memorial, [160] [thus alluding to the special attributes by which He was associated with each of the patriarchs], [161] blessed and magnified be He. I will explain yet more on this point in the chapter. [162]

---

(154) II Kings 20:5. These words were spoken by the prophet Isaiah to King Hezekiah. Now since David was not Hezekiah's father, it proves that people call an ancestor "father." (155) Further, 15:2. (156) Genesis 12:8. See Ramban there, Vol. I, p. 172. (157) The verse before us reads: *I am the G-d of thy father, the G-d of Abraham, the G-d of Isaac, and the G-d of Jacob.* (158) Shemoth Rabbah 3:1. (159) The reason for it is stated by Rashi in Genesis 28:13: "Because it is said, *Behold He putteth no trust even in His holy ones*" (Job 15:15). As long as a person lives, the evil inclination in him is still present. (160) See further, Verse 15. (161) "It is with reference to them [the separate attributes associated with the patriarchs] that Moses mentioned, *the great G-d, the mighty, and the feared* (Deuteronomy 10:17). 'The great' alludes to Abraham, as it is said, *and of great kindness* (Psalms 145:8); 'the mighty' to *the Fear of Isaac* (Genesis 31:42); and 'the feared' to Jacob, as it is said, *For with Thee there is forgiveness, that Thou mayest be feared*" (Psalms 130:4). (Ricanti in his work here on the Torah). (162) Further in Verse 15.

7. AND THE ETERNAL SAID. Scripture mentions Him in the attribute of mercy since it is in connection with His compassion for the people [in bondage], even though the entire chapter mentions Him by the name of *Elokim* (G-d), [a name signifying the attribute of justice].

8. AND I AM COME DOWN TO DELIVER THEM. That is, "for I have revealed Myself in fire on this mountain." This has the same meaning as in the verses: *And the Eternal came down upon Mount Sinai;* [163] *Because the Eternal descended upon it in fire.* [164] It may be that [the expression *come down* has the same meaning here] as in the verse, *I will go down now, and see whether they have done altogether according to the cry of it, which is come unto Me.* [165] I have already explained its secret there.

UNTO A GOOD AND LARGE LAND, UNTO A LAND FLOWING WITH MILK AND HONEY; UNTO THE PLACE OF THE CANAANITE, AND THE HITTITE, AND THE AMORITE, AND THE PERIZZITE, AND THE HIVITE, AND THE JEBUSITE. He mentions here six nations and omits the seventh.[166] Perhaps this was because his land was not *flowing with milk and honey* as were these [lands of the six nations mentioned]. Similarly, He mentions these six only in the verse, *For Mine angel shall go before thee.* [167] It may be because He alluded here [to a future event], i.e., that they will conquer these six nations first, for it is these six nations who assembled to fight Joshua, [168] and G-d gave them into his hand. Our Rabbis have said [169] that the Girgashite arose and emigrated of his own accord. This is why he is not mentioned together with those destined for

---

(163) Further, 19:20.   (164) *Ibid.*, Verse 18.   (165) Genesis 18:21. See Ramban there (Vol. I, p. 245) where he explains that the meaning is, "I will go down from the attribute of mercy to the attribute of justice." Here the meaning would be: "and I am come down from attribute to attribute." (166) The Girgashite, mentioned among the seven nations that Israel was to inherit (Deuteronomy 7:1).   (167) Further, 23:23. *And bring thee in unto the Amorite, and the Hittite, and the Perizzite, and the Canaanite, the Hivite, and the Jebusite.*   (168) So clearly stated in Joshua 9:1-2. (169) Yerushalmi Shebiith VI, 1.

destruction, as it is said concerning them, *and I will cut them off.* [167] I will discuss this matter further, [170] with the help of G-d.

The sense of the expression, *a land flowing with milk and honey,* is that He first praised the land as *a good land,* meaning that its climate is good and beautiful for people and that all that is good is found in it, *and as a large* land, meaning that it will afford all Israel to be established *in a broad place.* [171] It may be that *r'chavah* (large) means spaciousness, referring to [the extensive lands of] the lowland, the valley and the plain, large and small, and is not confined mostly to mountains and valleys. He then began to praise the land as being a land for cattle, having good pasture and good water which cause the cattle to have abundant milk, for healthy and good cattle with abundant milk are to be found only where the climate is good, with plenty of vegetation and good water. But since these are found only in the marsh-lands, [172] while on the height of the mountains fruits are not very fat and good, He further states that this land is so fat that its fruits [all over] are fat and sweet, even to the extent that it all flows with the honey that comes from them. Thus He has praised the land for all its *goodness of the Eternal, for the corn, and for the wine, and for the oil, and for the young of the flock and of the herd.* [173] This is the meaning of the verse, *It is the beauty of all lands.* [174]

The reason that He said, *unto the 'place' of the Canaanite,* and not "unto the 'land' of the Canaanite" as He said in all other places, [175] is to allude to the fact that they will inherit [the Canaanite, etc.], and will destroy them and settle in their places, and not dwell among them as their fathers had done.

9. AND NOW, BEHOLD, THE CRY OF THE CHILDREN OF ISRAEL IS COME UNTO ME. Even though He has already said, *and I have heard their cry,* [176] He says again that it has *come unto*

---

(170) Further, 23:25.   (171) See Psalms 31:9.   (172) The Hebrew: *ba'achu.* See Ramban, Genesis 41:2 (Vol. I, p. 495) for his explanation of that term.   (173) Jeremiah 31:11.   (174) Ezekiel 20:6.   (175) E.g., see further, 13:5.   (176) Verse 7.

Me, thus stating that "their cry has come to the Throne of My Glory, and I will no longer pardon [177] Pharaoh, for the Egyptians are oppressing them exceedingly." It is similar in sense to the expression, *a rage which hath reached up unto heaven.* [178]

By way of the Truth, [the mystic lore of the Cabala], *the cry of the children of Israel* is a reference to *Knesseth Yisrael,* [179] similar to the verse, *according to the cry of it which is come unto Me.* [180] I have alluded to it there.

The meaning of the verse, *moreover I have seen the oppression,* is that He will punish Pharaoh and his people because by oppressing Israel so exceedingly, they perpetrated more than had been decreed against them, as I have explained in *Seder Lech Lecha.* [181]

12. AND HE SAID: BECAUSE I WILL BE WITH THEE; AND THIS SHALL BE THE TOKEN UNTO THEE, THAT I HAVE SENT THEE: WHEN THOU HAST BROUGHT FORTH THE PEOPLE OUT OF EGYPT, YE SHALL SERVE G-D UPON THIS MOUNTAIN. Explanations of this verse are numerous. The correct interpretation in line with the simple meaning of Scripture is that the Holy One, blessed be He, had said two things to Moses. [First], He would come down *to deliver them out of the hand of the Egyptians.* [182] This might mean that He will deliver them out of their hands while they will remain in the land of Goshen itself or in some place nearby. Therefore, He further promised *to bring them up out of that* entire *land to the place of the Canaanite.*[182]

But Moses was fearful of both [promises], saying, *"Who am I, that I should go unto Pharaoh?* [183] I am but a humble person, a keeper of the flock, and he is a great king. If I will tell him to let the people go altogether, he will kill me." This is similar in

---

(177) According to another reading: "permit Pharaoh to enslave." (178) II Chronicles 28:9. (179) "The Congregation of Israel." Here understood in a Cabalistic sense, an allusion to the attribute of justice. (180) Genesis 18:21. (181) *Ibid.,* 15:13 (Vol. I, pp. 203-8). (182) Verse 8. (183) Verse 11.

meaning to that which Samuel said. *And if Saul hear it, he will kill me.* [184] And Moses said further, "*Who am I ... that I should bring forth the children of Israel out of Egypt,* [183] as Thou didst tell me to bring them up to the land of Canaan. *Surely this great nation is a wise and understanding people,* [185] and they will not hold me in sufficient esteem to go after me to the land of nations greater and mightier than they, [186] as Thou hadst said, *to bring them up ... unto a good and large land ... unto the place of the Canaanite.* [182] The delivery from the hand of Pharaoh — whether he will listen and lighten his yoke from upon them and thus deliver them [from bondage], or *drive them out of his land* against their will [187] — is not dependent on them. Besides, they themselves will listen to any one on this matter — for what man is there who would not want to go out from unparalleled cruel bondage — but they will not give heed to go up to the land of Canaan." Such indeed was the case. The war against those nations [in the land of Canaan] was hard on them from beginning to end, and they feared it while still in Egypt and later when they were in the desert. This then was the fear of Moses our teacher, of Pharaoh, and his apprehension of the children of Israel.

And the Eternal answered him on both matters. He said to him: "Do not fear Pharaoh for *I will be with thee* to save thee. *And this shall be the token unto thee* for the people *that I have sent thee* to them, for *when thou hast brought forth the people out of Egypt, ye shall serve G-d upon this mountain.* From then on, they will take upon themselves the worship of G-d and walk in His commandments, [188] *and they will also believe in thee forever,* [189] and they will run after thee [190] wherever thou shalt command them [to go]. Now I have revealed Myself to thee on this mountain *in a flame of fire,* for so it will be in front of all the people when they will serve Me on this mountain."

(184) I Samuel 16:2. (185) Deuteronomy 4:6. (186) See *ibid.*, Verse 38. (187) Further, 6:1. See also Rashi there. (188) See II Chronicles 17:4. (189) Further, 19.9. (190) See Song of Songs 1:4.

Thus in that which he saw, there was a sign for Moses that he should not fear Pharaoh since G-d assured him his deliverance. For Israel it was to be a sign that they should not fear the nations upon their coming to Mount Sinai, for to go out from Egypt — with Pharaoh's consent — to a nearby place *a three days' journey,* [191] they would surely give heed and do so whether willingly or unwillingly. [192]

By way of the Truth, [the mystic lore of the Cabala], *'V'zeh' (And this) shall be the token unto thee,* is like the verse, *'Zeh li' (I have now been) twenty years in thy house,* [193] thus alluding to the verses, *Because I will be with thee,* and behold *there is a sign unto thee,* the sign of the covenant that "I will be with thee always," just as it is intimated in the verse, *As for Me, behold, My covenant is with thee.*[194] "It is I who send you that you should serve G-d upon this mountain, and then I too will go up in the midst of this people *into the place which I have prepared."* [195]

13. AND THEY SHALL SAY UNTO ME: WHAT IS HIS NAME? WHAT SHALL I SAY UNTO THEM? This verse calls aloud for an explanation. It is incomprehensible that Moses should say, *And they shall say unto me: What is His name?* meaning that this will be a sign to them to believe in him. The asking for His Name and Moses' telling it to them are no sign to anyone who did not believe in Moses to begin with. If Israel knew that Name, Moses likewise knew it, and thus his knowledge thereof was equivalent to theirs and it would be no sign or wonder at all. If they had not heard of it previously, what proof would that be that they should believe in his words altogether? And now even after He informed him of the Great Name, Moses still said, *But, behold,*

---

(191) Further, Verse 18. See also Ramban further, 19:1. (192) In the Tur's rendition of Ramban: "they will surely listen and not ask for a sign." (193) Genesis 31:41. Literally: *"this* to me is twenty years." Rabbeinu Bachya ben Asher here intimates that Ramban's intent is to be understood in the light of the verse, *'Zeh' (This) is my G-d, and I will glorify Him* (further, 15:2). See my Hebrew commentary here on Ramban, p. 290. (194) Genesis 17:4. (195) Further, 23:20.

they will not believe me, [196] and then He gave him the various signs! [197]

Rabbi Abraham ibn Ezra said that Moses asked which of G-d's Names he should mention to Israel, for the Name of *E-il Sha-dai* (G-d Almighty) does not signify the performance of miraculous signs; only the Great Name, [i.e., the Tetragrammaton], indicates that. But this interpretation does not appear correct to me. Moses had not yet been told that He would make great and wondrous signs and portents at the going forth from Egypt. Rather, he was told that He would save them from the hand of the Egyptians and bring them up to the land of Canaan, and for that — to strike at the heart of Pharaoh, as well as to be victorious over the seven nations — the name *E-il Sha-dai* suffices. Sarah was taken out from Pharaoh's house *with great plagues,* [198] and Abraham alone subdued the great kings [199] — all with the help of *E-il Sha-dai,* the Divine Name known to the patriarchs, [200] and so likewise He would do to their descendants. Moreover, Jacob had said, *And 'Elokim' (G-d) will be with you, and bring you back unto the land of your fathers* [201], and Joseph also said, *'Elokim' (G-d) will surely remember you.* [202] Thus the remembrance is by *Elokim!*

In my opinion, Moses even at that time was already the father of wisdom, great in achievement of the heights of prophecy, and inherent in his question was the request that He inform him Who is sending him, that is to say, by what Divine attribute is he sent to the Israelites, just as Isaiah said, *And now the Eternal G-d hath sent me, and His spirit.* [203] Thus Moses said: "They will ask me concerning my mission whether it is with the attribute of *E-il Sha-dai* which stood by the patriarchs, or with the high attribute of mercy with which You will do signs and wonders which will be new phenomena in creation." [Moses was obliged to ask] this question because He had said to him, *I am the G-d of thy father,*

---

(196) *Ibid.,* 4:1.   (197) *Ibid.,* Verses 2-9.   (198) Genesis 12:17.
(199) *Ibid.,* 14:14-15.   (200) Further, 6:3.   (201) Genesis 48:21.
(202) *Ibid.,* 50:25.   (203) Isaiah 48:16.

EXODUS III, SHEMOTH

the G-d of Abraham, [204] and He did not elucidate to him at all any of His sacred Names. Moses then heard that He assured him of the Revelation on Mount Sinai and the Giving of the Torah, and he knew that the Torah would not be given with the Name of *E-il Sha-dai* mentioned in connection with the patriarchs, but would be given with the Great Name with which the world came into existence. Therefore he asked, *What shall I say unto them?*

Our Rabbis have alluded to this interpretation. Thus they said:[205] *"And Moses said unto G-d, Behold, when I come unto the children of Israel."* Rabbi Shimon related in the name of Rabbi Simon that Moses said: 'I am destined to become the agent between Thee and them when Thou wilt give them the Torah and say unto them, *I am the Eternal thy G-d.*' [206]

"And I shall say unto them: The G-d of your fathers hath sent me unto you. At that moment, Moses desired to be elucidated concerning his activities, for he feared lest the children of Israel ask him, *What is His name? What shall I say unto them?* At that moment Moses desired that the Holy One, blessed be He, inform him of the Great Name, [i.e., the Tetragrammaton]." This was the purport of Moses' question.

And G-d answered him, " 'I WILL BE THAT WHICH I WILL BE. [207] I will be with you [208] in this sorrow, and I will be with you [208] in other sorrows.' [209] Thereupon Moses said to Him, 'Master of the universe! Sufficient is the evil in its time, [and why should I mention to them other sorrows in store for them in the future].' G-d replied to him: 'You have spoken correctly. *Thus shalt thou say unto the children of Israel:* I WILL BE *hath sent me unto you.*' " Thus the language of Rashi quoting the words of our

---

(204) Verse 6. (205) Shemoth Rabbah 3:6. (206) Further, 20:2. "And if I am worthy to become Thy agent at the Giving of the Torah, I request to be informed now of Thy Great Name" (Eitz Yoseph to Shemoth Rabbah). This conclusion is here implied and is so clearly stated at the end of the Midrash here quoted. (207) Verse 14. (208) "You." In our version of Rashi: "them." (209) "In other sorrows." In our version of Rashi: "In the subjection [they will suffer at the hands] of the other kingdoms."

Rabbis.[210] Their intent in this Agadah is as follows: Moses had said before Him, blessed be He. *And they shall say unto me: What is His name?*, meaning that G-d should tell him the Name which wholly teaches His existence and His providence. The Holy One, blessed be He, answered him: "Why should they ask for My Name? They need no other proof, for I will be with them *in all their affliction.*[211] They shall call, and I will answer them."[212] This is the great proof that there is a G-d in Israel near to us *whenever we call upon Him,*[213] and *verily there is a G-d that judgeth in the earth.*[214] This is a correct interpretation of this Agadah (homily).

In a similar way it is said in a Midrash Agadah:[215] "And what is the meaning of I WILL BE THAT WHICH I WILL BE? 'As you are with Me, so I am with you. If they open their hands and give charity, I also will open My hand, as it is said, *The Eternal will open unto thee His good treasure the heaven to give the rain of thy land in its season.*[216] And if they do not open their hands, what is written there? *Behold, He withholdeth the waters, and they dry up.*'"[217]

In a similar vein the Rabbis expounded:[218] "Rabbi Yitzchak said that the Holy One, blessed be He, said to Moses: 'I am He Who has been, Who is now, and Who will be in the future.' This is why *Eh'yeh* is written here three times." The explanation of Rabbi Yitzchak's opinion is that since with respect to the Creator, past and future times are conceived completely in terms of the present — for there is no host succeeding host with regards to Him, and nothing of His time has passed — hence all times with reference to Him are called by one name, signifying a Being Whose existence is absolute.[219]

---

(210) Berachoth 9 b. (211) Isaiah 63:9. (212) See Psalms 91:14. (213) Deuteronomy 4:7. (214) Psalms 58:12. (215) Sefer V'hizhir. See Torah Shleimah by Rabbi M. Kasher, paragraph 188. (216) Deuteronomy 28:12. (217) Job 12:15. (218) Shemoth Rabbah 3:6. (219) Or "a Being Who is necessarily existent." "G-d alone is that Being, for His existence is absolute — existence and essence are perfectly identical. He is not a substance to which existence is joined as an accident, as an additional element. His existence is always absolute, and has never been a new element or an accident in Him" (Moreh Nebuchim, I, 57, Friedlander's translation).

Now Onkelos translated the first two names, [i.e. *'Eh'yeh Asher Eh'yeh'*], as "I will be with him that I will be," [220] but he did not translate the third name *Eh'yeh* expressed in the verse, *Thus shalt thou say unto the children of Israel: 'Eh'yeh' hath sent me unto you.* It appears that Onkelos' opinion is that *the glorious Name* [221] of which He informed Moses was this four-letter Name of which He commanded him, *Thus shalt thou say unto the children of Israel: 'Eh'yeh' hath sent me unto you.* But He first informed him of the purport thereof, for Moses' request had been to know the ways of G-d through His Name, just as he was once again to request [later on]: *Let me know Thy ways, that I may know Thee.* [222] And just as He answered him then, *And I will proclaim the name of the Eternal before thee, and I will be gracious unto whom I will be gracious* [223] — meaning that with *this glorious Name* [221] which He will proclaim before him, He will be gracious and will show mercy, and no man can fathom the profundity of His ways — in the same vein He said to him now: "I will be with him that I will be," meaning, "with My Name that you will tell them, namely, *Eh'yeh*, with that Name I am gracious and show mercy to man."

And the Gaon Rav Saadia wrote [224] that its explanation is as follows: "[He is the Being] Whose existence has never ceased and will never cease, for He is the first and the last." The opinion of the Gaon is not far from the opinion of Rabbi Yitzchak, [i.e., that the name *Eh'yeh* indicates eternity, as explained above].

And the Rabbi [Moshe ben Maimon] has said in the Moreh Nebuchim (Guide of the Perplexed) [225] that the meaning of

---

(220) The meaning thereof is further elucidated by Ramban. In our version of Onkelos, these two Divine Names are also not translated and instead are retained in their original Hebrew form. (221) Deuteronomy 28:58. (222) Further, 33:13. (223) *Ibid.*, Verse 19. (224) In his Arabic translation of, and commentary on, the Torah. So clearly mentioned by Rabbi Abraham the son of Rambam in his commentary (Wiesenberg ed., London, 1958, p. 226). See Index in my Kithvei Haramban, Vol. II, p. 564, under *lashon*, for Ramban's extensive use of Arabic. In view then of the fact that Ibn Ezra does not mention this interpretation of Rav Saadia Gaon in his commentary, nor is it found in Saadia's philosophic work Emunoth Vehadei'oth, it may be assumed that Ramban saw it in the original Arabic. (225) Part I, Chapter 63. In Friedlander's translation: p. 239.

Eh'yeh Asher Eh'yeh is: "He is the existing Being which is the existing Being, that is to say, Whose existence is absolute. The proof which Moses was to give to the elders of Israel consisted in demonstrating that there is a Being of absolute existence, that has never been and never will be without existence."

Now according to these Sages, [226] it is necessary to explain that the Holy One, blessed be He, said to Moses that he should tell them this Name and teach them its import. That is to say, Moses was to inform them of this Name and show the rational proofs by which His eternal being or existence would be firmly established among their wise men. The mere mention of the Divine Name — be it whatever it may — is no proof in itself to eradicate the doctrine of the eternity [of matter] from among them, or the calculated heresy of denying the existence [of the Supreme Being] altogether. But this is not the sense of the verse! Rather, [it clearly implies] that the very mention of the Name to them will be the proof, sign and token on the matter they will have asked of Moses.

In my opinion, the elders of Israel never doubted the existence of the Creator, as the Rabbi [Moshe ben Maimon] said — Heaven forbid! But this Name does contain the answer to [Moses' question of G-d], as we have explained it to you. [227] He informed Moses that he is being sent to them with the attribute of justice, which is within the attribute of mercy, [suggesting that the miracles which will be done on behalf of their deliverance from the bondage will at the same time be acts of judgment against the Egyptians. This is the sense of *Eh'yeh Asher Eh'yeh*: *"I will be* in judgment *that which I will be* in mercy]." And then G-d said to Moses, *Thus shalt thou say unto the children of Israel: 'Eh'yeh' sent me unto you,* thus teaching the unity [of the two attributes, which explains

---

(226) Namely, Rabbi Yitzchak, Rav Saadia Gaon, and Rambam in his Moreh Nebuchim, all mentioned above. (227) Namely, that Moses asked by what Divine attribute is his mission to them, whether with the attribute of *E-il Sha-dai* which stood by the patriarchs, or with the high attribute of mercy with which signs and wonders, new phenomena in creation, will be done to speed their redemption — all as explained above.

why the Divine Name is not mentioned here twice]. It is for this reason that G-d commanded Moses yet further, *Thus shalt thou say unto the children of Israel: The Eternal... hath sent me unto you,* [228] for this Name, [i.e., the Tetragrammaton], indicates the attribute of mercy, and thus they will know *that He hath caused His glorious arm to go at the right hand of Moses* [229] and He will make new signs and wonders in the world. Thus G-d explained to Moses that the Name *Eh'yeh* which He commanded him to tell the children of Israel corresponds to this Great Name [the Tetragrammaton] and that they are alike in language, [as both signify eternal existence], and in letters, for the two final letters of the first Name [*Eh'yeh*] constitute the first ones in the Tetragrammaton. And may the Holy One, blessed be He, show us wonders in His Torah. [230]

15. AND THIS IS MY MEMORIAL UNTO ALL GENERATIONS. This refers back to *the G-d of Abraham, the G-d of Isaac, and the G-d of Jacob,* for the covenant [of G-d] with the patriarchs will never be forgotten, and throughout all generations whenever the children of Israel will mention [in prayer], "the G-d of Abraham, Isaac, and Jacob," *G-d shall hear and answer them.* [231]

By way of the Truth, [the mystic lore of the Cabala], *this is My name forever* refers to *the G-d of Abraham, the G-d of Isaac. And this is My memorial* refers to the expression, *and the G-d of Jacob.* This is the reason He added here the letter *vav — [v'zeh zichri ('And' this is My memorial)].* [232] This is the sense of the

---

(228) Verse 15. The Divine Name mentioned here is the Tetragrammaton.
(229) Isaiah 63:12. (230) See a similar ending in Vol. I, p. 553. Ramban evidently uses the expression in order to indicate that he has merely touched on only the surface of the mysteries here indicated in the text, and one must constantly pray to be shown new wonders that lie hidden in the Torah.
(231) Psalms 55:20. The verse here thus states: *"Thus shalt thou say unto the children of Israel.* Whenever you mention Me in prayer say thus: *'G-d of Abraham, G-d of Isaac...' This is My memorial unto all generations."*
(232) It is to indicate that this is the preponderant Name in the memorial (Bachya).

expression, *zichri l'dor dor,* [with the words *l'dor dor* written] defectively, [i.e., without a *vav* between the *dalet* and the *resh*]. The person learned in the mysteries of the Torah will understand.

18. AND THEY SHALL HEARKEN TO THY VOICE. "I.e., of their own accord. As soon as you will mention to them this expression, [namely, the double use of the word *pakod — pakod pakad'ti (I have surely remembered),* mentioned in Verse 16], they will immediately hearken to your voice for they have long had this sign as a tradition from Jacob and Joseph, that by use of this expression they will be delivered [from Egypt]. Jacob said to them, *and G-d will surely remember you,*[233] and Joseph said to them, *G-d will surely remember you."*[234] Thus the language of Rashi. Perhaps Rashi will explain that Joseph used this expression twice[235] in order to affirm that it was a tradition he received from his father.

And in Eileh Shemoth Rabbah, the Rabbis said:[236] "[As soon as you will say to them *pakod pakad'ti*], they will immediately hearken to your voice. Why? It is because they have a tradition of the words [wherein G-d will announce the approaching redemption], so that the redeemer who will come and mention to them this double *p'kidah* [remembrance] is the true redeemer." Thus the language of the Rabbis on this Agadah.

Now you may ask: Why should they listen to Moses? Perhaps he heard this tradition as well as they did. In reply it may be said that thus they received the tradition from Joseph, who heard it from their father the prophet: *the first person* who will come and announce the message with this expression [*pakod pakad'ti*] will be the one who will deliver them [from Egypt], it being revealed

---

(233) See Genesis 50:24, that it is Joseph who is speaking. But it is clearly implied there that Joseph is quoting a tradition given to him by his father. Hence Rashi here mentions it in the name of Jacob. Ramban will further stress the fact that it was Joseph who stated it twice. (234) *Ibid.,* Verse 25. (235) See Note 233 above. (236) Shemoth Rabbah 3:11.

EXODUS III, SHEMOTH

and known before the Holy One, blessed be He, that no man will come and deceive them. This He promised them.

But in another place in the Midrash I found: [237] "Said Rabbi Chama the son of Rabbi Chanina: 'When Moses was in his twelfth year, he was torn up from his father's house. Why? Had he grown up in his father's house, the children of Israel would not have believed in him when he came and told them these things.[238] They would have said that his father handed him over these words, as Joseph had handed them over to Levi, and Levi to Kohath, and Kohath to Amram. This was why he was torn up from his father's house, and when he came and told Israel all the words, they therefore believed him, as it is said, *And the people believed.*'" [239] The intent of the Rabbis' words that Joseph handed it over to Levi [and as to why Jacob did not reveal it directly to Levi] is that Jacob revealed the secret to Joseph because of his love for him.[240] With this very same language Joseph made all his brothers swear, and he revealed it to Levi. [241] He told them that he gave this [as a secret to Levi] on account of the tradition he received from his father [not to reveal it], and he commanded that the matter remain a secret. [242]

---

(237) *Ibid.*, 5:1. (238) The Hebrew is: *hama'asim* (the deeds). If this is the correct reading, it is obviously a reference not only to the words of the message, but also to all of the signs he did before the people. (See further, 4:1-9 and 30). However, from the concluding language of this Midrash quoted here further — *kol had'varim* ('all' the words) — it is clear that the sense here is also "words," and reference is to the wording of the message of redemption: *pakod pakad'ti.* (239) Further, 4:31. (240) Genesis 37:3. And see Ramban there, Vol. I, pp. 451-2. (241) On the basis of Genesis 50:25, Ramban's intent may be explained as follows: Joseph made all his brothers swear to bring his bones up from Egypt at the time of the redemption, and to Levi he revealed the secret of *pakod pakad'ti*, that with these words the true messenger will announce the approaching redemption. (242) Hence when Moses came and said the words *pakod pakad'ti*, the elders of Israel who now knew of the tradition confirmed him as the true redeemer, for they knew that he could not have heard these words from his father as he was torn up from his father's home when only twelve years old.

19. 'V'LO B'YAD CHAZAKAH' (AND NOT BY A MIGHTY HAND). "So long as I do not let him feel My mighty hand he will not let you go." Thus the words of Rashi. [243]

The correct interpretation in my opinion is: "*The king of Egypt will not give you leave to go* by plea, *and not* [even] *by a mighty hand*, until I will put forth My hand *with all My wonders which I will do in his midst*, [244] *by a mighty hand, and by an outstretched arm, and by great terrors, and by signs and by wonders.* [245] *And after that he will let you go.*" [244] Indeed, all these manifestations came upon him before he gave them leave to go.

4

1. AND MOSES ANSWERED AND SAID: BUT, BEHOLD, THEY WILL NOT BELIEVE ME, NOR HEARKEN UNTO MY VOICE. "At that moment, Moses spoke improperly. The Holy One, blessed be He, had told him, *And they shall hearken to thy voice*, [246] and he said, *But, behold, they will not believe me.* Immediately, the Holy One, blessed be He, answered him according to his opinion, [247] and gave him signs commensurate with his words." Thus the language of V'eileh Shemoth Rabbah. [248]

And Rabbi Abraham ibn Ezra said, by way of the plain meaning of Scripture, that G-d related to Moses that the elders will believe him, but He did not mention that the people will believe. Perhaps they may hearken to his voice but would not believe him wholeheartedly. But this does not appear to be correct. Rather, it is possible to say that *v'sham'u l'kolecha (and they shall hearken to thy voice)* does not constitute a promise but a command: "And

---

(243) The sense of the verse according to Rashi is thus: "except by a mighty hand." It is so translated in the J.P.S. translation. Ramban will suggest its meaning to be: "and not even by a mighty hand." (244) Verse 20. (245) Deuteronomy 4:35. In the verse there, the phrase "by trials and by wonders" is listed first. (246) Above, 3:18. (247) Since it was Moses' opinion that the people would not believe him, he was therefore in need of certain wonders which he was to do before them to convince them of the truth of his mission. Accordingly, G-d now gave him the wonders he was to do. The implication of the Midrash is thus clear: If Moses had not said that the people would not believe him, there would have been no need for him to do these wonders before them. (248) Shemoth Rabbah 3:15.

EXODUS IV, SHEMOTH 43

they must hearken to your voice" — for it is to their advantage to listen — *and thou shalt come, thou and the elders of Israel, unto the king of Egypt.* [246] A similar case is found in the verse, *When the Egyptians shall hear — for Thou broughtest up this people in Thy might from among them — they will say to the inhabitants of this land,* [249] meaning it is fitting that the Egyptians should say so. Similarly, the verse, *In this thou shalt know that I am the Eternal,*[250] means it is fitting that it be so, but not that it so happened. In a similar vein is the verse in this chapter, *and they will believe the voice of the latter sign,*[251] [which means it is fitting that they believe the latter sign], and many similar cases.

The correct interpretation appears to me to be that the expression *v'sham'u l'kolecha* means that "they will listen to you to come with you to the king and say to him, *The G-d of the Hebrews hath happened to meet us,* [252] for what will they lose by it?" Thus G-d informed Moses that the king of Egypt would not give them leave to go, and this was why Moses said, *But, behold, they will not believe me,* for after seeing that Pharaoh did not give them permission to go, they would no longer believe him at all, *for they will say: "The Eternal hath not appeared unto thee.* If you were G-d's messenger, Pharaoh would not have rebelled against His word." It may be that they will say that "G-d has not appeared to you by the Great Name with the attribute of mercy, to do for us signs and wonders as you have said, for you are not greater than the patriarchs. [253] This was why Pharaoh did not hearken, for if Pharaoh had believed your words, we would have gone out from Egypt under all circumstances, and it is not our iniquities that have separated between us and the G-d of mercies." [254]

3. AND HE SAID: CAST IT ON THE GROUND. AND HE CAST IT ON THE GROUND. I do not understand why G-d performed the signs before Moses. Moses believed that it is the

(249) Numbers 14:13-14. (250) Further, 7:17. (251) Verse 8.
(252) *Ibid.,* 5:3. (253) To whom He appeared as *E-il Sha-dai.* See Ramban above, 3:13, for a full explanation of this matter. (254) See Isaiah 59:2.

Holy One, blessed be He, Who speaks with him, and it would have been fitting for Him to say, "The staff that is in your hand you shall cast on the ground before them, and it shall become a serpent," and the same also with respect to the second sign, [i.e., his hand becoming leprous], just as He said at the third sign, *and thou shalt take of the water of the river, and pour it upon the dry land,* etc. [255] It is for this reason that the words of our Rabbis [256] can be relied upon, namely, that the first sign, [i.e., the staff turning into a serpent], was a hint to Moses that he had slandered the Israelites [when he said that they would not believe him], [257] and the second sign was for the purpose of punishing him. [258] And this is the sense of the expression, *and Moses fled from before it* [the serpent]. He feared lest he would be punished and the serpent would bite him, since every person naturally avoids danger, even though Moses knew that if it was indeed G-d's desire [to punish him], there was no one that could deliver him out of His hand. [259]

Perhaps even though He informed Moses of the Great Name with which the world was created and everything came into existence, [260] He wished to show him that with this Name signs and wonders would be done, changing the natural order of things, so that the matter would be firmly established in Moses' heart and that he should in truth know that with the Great Name he will perform new things in the world. The first two signs were sufficient for Moses, and therefore the third miracle of the water [turning into blood] was not done here. Instead, G-d commanded him to do the third sign in the sight of the people.

(255) Further, Verse 9. In other words, the third sign of the water turning to blood was not performed now, but only when Moses came before the people. The question thus arises: Why did He perform the first two signs — the staff turning into a serpent, and Moses' hand becoming leprous — before Moses now? (256) Shemoth Rabbah 3:16. (257) See Genesis 3:5, that the serpent was the first creature to slander when it said to Eve, *For G-d doth know that in the day ye eat thereof, ye shall be as G-d, knowing good and evil.* Thus it suggested to her that it was not because it may bring about her death that G-d forbade it, but out of a sense of jealousy. As Rashi puts it: "Every artisan detests his fellow-artisans." (258) See Numbers 12:1-10 that the punishment for slander is leprosy. (259) See Daniel 8:4. (260) See above, 3:13.

EXODUS IV, SHEMOTH

5. THAT THEY MAY BELIEVE THAT THE ETERNAL ... HATH APPEARED TO THEE. The interpretation of this verse is that "they may believe when you do the sign before them." Scripture, however, speaks briefly about this for it is self-understood that G-d showed Moses wonders with the intent that he perform them before the people in order that they believe him.

9. 'V'HAYU' (AND IT SHALL BE) THAT THE WATER WHICH THOU TAKEST OUT OF THE RIVER 'V'HAYU' (SHALL BECOME) BLOOD UPON THE DRY LAND. "The word *v'hayu* is mentioned here twice.[261] It appears to me that if He had said, *'V'hayu* (And it shall be) that the water which thou takest out of the river be blood upon the dry land,' I might understand it to mean that it would be turned into blood in his hand, and that also when it reached the ground it would remain in the same state. But now, [as the verse actually reads], the final *v'hayu* teaches us that it would not become blood until it reaches the dry land."[262] Thus the language of Rashi.

But the purport of this verse is not as the Rabbi [Rashi] has it, and there is no need for his Midrash, for the masters of language[263] have found in many places that it is the normal style of Scripture to repeat words for the purpose of emphasis and significance, or because of some lengthy phrase intervening between them. Such a case is the verse: *And if a Levite come from any of thy gates out of all Israel, where he sojourneth, and come with all the desire of his soul.*[264] Here Scripture repeats [the

---

(261) The literal translation of the Hebrew text is: "And it shall be that the water which thou takest out of the river, and it will be blood upon the dry land." (262) The significance of this point is explained by L'vush Ha'orah (see Preface in Vol. I, p. IX, Note 12): If the water had turned into blood while still in Moses' hand, skeptics could say that it was done through some secret art. But running or flowing water turning into blood upon reaching the ground was undeniably a miracle. (263) Found in R'dak's Sefer Hamichlal. The repetition of a verb occurs after a lengthy intervening phrase. (264) Deuteronomy 18:6.

verb] "come" because of the lengthy expression between [the parts of the verse]. Similarly: *And the king of Egypt spoke to the Hebrew midwives, of whom the name of the one was Shiphrah, and the name of the other Puah; and he said: When ye act as midwives,* etc.; [265] *And G-d spoke unto Israel in the visions of the night, and He said: Jacob, Jacob.* [266] There are many instances of such verses.

10. AND MOSES SAID UNTO THE ETERNAL: O LORD, I AM NOT A MAN OF WORDS, NEITHER YESTERDAY NOR RECENTLY NOR SINCE THOU HAST SPOKEN UNTO THY SERVANT; FOR I AM SLOW OF SPEECH AND OF A SLOW TONGUE. "This teaches us that for an entire period of seven days, the Holy One, blessed be He, sat [267] and urged Moses to undertake the mission. [The expressions], 'yesterday,' 'recently,' and 'since Thou hast spoken,' imply three days, and the three-fold word *gam* — [here translated 'neither' or 'nor,' but literally meaning 'also'] — points to a similar extension of time. Thus you have six days [that have passed], and it was now the seventh day [when Moses still refused to go on his mission]." Thus the language of Rashi.

In line with the plain meaning of Scripture, the purport of the verse is as follows: [Moses said,] "For I am slow of speech from heretofore and from time past, for I have been slow of speech from my youth on and all the more now that I am old, *and also now since Thou hast spoken unto Thy servant,* for Thou hast not removed the defect in my speech when Thou didst command me to go to Pharaoh to speak in Thy name. How then can I go before him?" Now Moses out of his great desire not to go [on the mission] did not pray before G-d, blessed be He, that He remove his defective speech from him, but he argued: "Since You have not removed my slowness of speech from me from the time You spoke to me to undertake this mission, do not command me to go, for it

---

(265) Above, 1:15-16. Here the verb "said" is repeated because of the identification of the midwives stated in the verse. (266) Genesis 46:2. (267) "Sat." This word is not found in our text of Rashi.

is inconceivable that the Master of everything should send a man *of uncircumcised lips* [268] to a king of the nations." And since Moses did not pray [for the removal of his defect], the Holy One, blessed be He, did not desire to heal him. Instead, He said to him, *I will be with thy mouth, and teach thee what thou shalt speak,* [269] meaning that "you will be able to correctly express the words which I will put in your mouth."

And in V'eileh Shemoth Rabbah, [270] the Rabbis said: "The Holy One, blessed be He, said to Moses: 'Do not mind it that you are not a man of words. Have I not made the mouth of all that speak, and him that I desire I made dumb? And have I not made the deaf and the blind, and opened their eyes to see and ears to hear? Now had I wanted that you be a man of words, you would have been so. But it is my desire that you continue to be so, and when you will speak [to Pharaoh] your utterance will be correct, for *I will be with thy mouth*.' [269] This is the sense of the verse, *Now therefore go, and I will be with thy mouth.*" [269]

According to this Midrash, it appears to me that the reason He did not desire to remove his defective speech from him was because a miraculous event, [271] as told by our Rabbis, happened to Moses when he was still before Pharaoh. [272]

(268) Further, 6:12. (269) Verse 12. (270) Shemoth Rabbah 3:20. (271) That such is the intent of Ramban — and not that Moses did not desire to have the defect removed — may be seen from the language of the Tur, who states: "Some scholars say He did not heal him because Moses' defective speech came through a miracle." (272) Ramban evidently refers to Shemoth Rabbah 1:31, wherein it is related that when Moses was still an infant and Pharaoh played with him on his lap, Moses took the crown from the king's head and placed it on his own. Terrified at what had happened, the magicians advised that he be slain. But Jethro, who was one of the counsellors of the king, advised that he be tested as follows: Two dishes were to be placed before him, one containing pieces of gold and the other live coal. If he would stretch out his hand for the gold, it would be known that his taking the crown was done consciously, and therefore he was to be slain. But it he would grasp the live coal, he was innocent. When the test was made, Moses began stretching his hand toward the gold, but the angel Gabriel made him take the live coal. Thereupon Moses put his hand with the coal into his mouth, which burnt part of his tongue. As a result, he became slow of speech and of a slow tongue for all his life.

The correct interpretation appears to me to be that G-d said to Moses, *"Who hath made man's mouth? or Who maketh a man dumb? ... Is it not I the Eternal* [273] *Who does all this?* I could heal you. *But now* since you did not want to be healed, nor have you prayed to me about it, *go and I will be with thy mouth,* [269] and I will cause you success in My mission." It is also possible that there is a hint in the verse, *And the anger of the Eternal was kindled against Moses,* [274] that He did not want to heal him, and that He sent him against his will.

11. WHO HATH MADE MAN'S MOUTH? This is a reference to man's power of speech because it resides in the mouth. Similarly: *Safa echad* [275] [literally: "one lip"] (*one language*); *that speak 's'fath' Canaan* [276] [literally: "the lip of"] (*the language of Canaan*).

OR WHO MAKETH A MAN DUMB? Scholars have explained [277] that this refers back to man, meaning: "Who maketh a man that is dumb?" That is to say, "Who has created a man without the capacity of speaking?" "The making" thus refers to the making of man, but as regards the absence of the power of speech, you cannot speak in terms of "making," for it is non-existence, the lack of the power of speech. Perhaps because man has a speaking soul, [278] and, for people who lack this capacity, it is due to some obstruction in the veins of the tongue, it is then possible to say, "Who made the dumbness?" [since the making of the obstruction required an act]. Now the Rabbi [Moshe ben Maimon] said in the Moreh Nebuchim [279] that it may

---

(273) Verse 11.   (274) Verse 14.   (275) Genesis 11:1.   (276) Isaiah 19:18.   (277) The difficulty presents itself: Since the absence of a property is nothing positive and dumbness is the lack of the property of speech, how can one speak of "the making" of dumbness when it is nonexistent? See Rambam's Moreh Nebuchim, III, 10, where the author discusses this problem. The answer, quoted here by Ramban, that it refers back to "the man," suggesting, "Who can create a man without the capacity of speech?" is mentioned there by Rambam.   (278) See Ramban on Genesis 2:7 (Vol. I, pp. 66-69) on the great significance of this point.   (279) Moreh Nebuchim, III, 10.

be said of him who removes a certain property that he produced the absence of that property, for they say of him who puts out the light that he has produced darkness. In accordance with this view, Rambam explains the verse, *I form the light and create darkness, I make peace and create evil,* [280] [for darkness and evil are non-existent things].

13. SEND, I PRAY THEE, BY THE HAND OF HIM WHOM THOU WILT SEND. "This means by the hand of him whom You are accustomed to send, and that is Aaron. Another explanation is: by the hand of some other person whom Thou wilt be pleased to send, for in the end I will not bring them into the Land, nor am I destined to be their deliverer in the future. Thou hast many messengers." Thus the language of Rashi. And Onkelos said: "by the hand of him who is fit to be sent." This means: "Send by the hand of him who speaks eloquently, who will be fit and proper for an honorable mission such as this. Do not send by the hand of one who is slow of speech and of a slow tongue and be with his mouth when he speaks before Pharaoh, since it is not a matter of respect and honor that Your messenger be one *of uncircumcised lips,* [268] and none of the people will heed him when he speaks before the king, since this will appear to them as a defect."

The correct interpretation appears to me to be that Moses said, *"Send, I pray Thee, by the hand* of anyone *whom Thou wilt send,* for there is not a person in the world who is not more fit for the mission than I." The reason for all this obduracy of Moses was his great meekness, *above all the men that were upon the face of the earth,* [281] as he could not see himself assuming importance and speaking to the king and [taking] glory in saying, "The Eternal sent me," nor [to speak] to Israel to bring them out from Egypt and be king [282] over them.

14. I KNOW THAT HE [Aaron] CAN SPEAK WELL. That is to say, "It is revealed before Me that, out of his love for you, Aaron

(280) Isaiah 45:7.   (281) Numbers 12:3.   (282) Deuteronomy 33:5.

will willingly speak on your behalf even if I were not to command him. *And also, behold, he cometh forth* of his own bidding *to meet thee, and when he seeth thee he will be glad in his heart,* and he will not be jealous over your distinction in this honorable mission." The reason that it was necessary that G-d tell Aaron, *Go into the wilderness to meet Moses,* [283] was in order to inform him of the road by which Moses was coming. It is possible that Aaron heard of Moses' departure from Midian, and on his own accord he went out to meet him. Afterwards, when he was already on the way, it was said to him, "Go into the wilderness to meet him, for there you will find him."

15. AND I WILL BE WITH THY MOUTH. I.e., "to teach you that which you are to speak to Pharaoh." G-d now told Moses that Aaron will speak on his behalf only to the people, as it is said, *And he shall be thy spokesman unto the people,* [284] but Moses himself was to speak to Pharaoh. It is possible that this was out of respect to the king. But in the end, Moses came back and said, *Behold, I am of uncircumcised lips, and how shall Pharaoh hearken unto me?* [285] G-d then permitted him that he should not speak even to Pharaoh. This [consent] was a distinction to Moses, and therefore He said there, *See, I have set thee in G-d's stead to Pharaoh,* and *Aaron thy brother shall be thy prophet.* [286] And the intent of the expression [here in the verse], *and I will be with his* [Aaron's] *mouth,* [287] is that his words will find favor with everyone that will hear them.

17. AND THOU SHALT TAKE IN THY HAND THIS ROD, WHEREWITH THOU SHALT DO THE SIGNS. Concerning the rod, only one sign — that it turn into a serpent — has thus far been mentioned. But the [plural] expression "the signs" means "the signs which I will tell you."

---

(283) Further, Verse 27.   (284) Verse 16.   (285) Further, 6:30.
(286) *Ibid.*, 7:1.   (287) I.e., why was this promise necessary since Aaron was not defective of speech?

It appears to me that when G-d said to Moses, *With all My wonders which I will do in his midst,* [288] He informed him of all the wonders in detail, but Scripture speaks briefly, and this is the intent of the expression here, *wherewith thou shalt do the signs.*

19. AND THE ETERNAL SAID UNTO MOSES IN MIDIAN: GO, RETURN UNTO EGYPT, etc. Rabbi Abraham ibn Ezra said, "There is no strict chronological order in the narrative of the Torah, [289] and the explanation thereof is, 'now the Eternal had said.' There are many similar cases."

But Ibn Ezra's interpretation here is not correct. The first Divine communication, [i.e., that Moses return to Egypt], was not in Midian but at Mount Sinai. [290] In Midian He spoke to him only at this time, [as mentioned in the present verse]. However, when Moses accepted the mission by word of G-d to go to Egypt and he returned to Midian to obtain permission from his father-in-law, it was his intention to go alone and disguised. It is for this reason that Moses said to Jethro, *Let me go, I pray thee, and return unto my brethren that are in Egypt, and see whether they be yet alive.* [291] That is to say, "I will see my brethren whether they be yet alive and I will return," for it was to be in the nature of a visit by one who is anxious to see his brethren. But then the Eternal said to him in Midian, *Go, return unto Egypt,* that is to say, "Arise, go out of this land and return to the land of Egypt and have no fear there, for all those who sought to harm you have died, and stay there with the people until you will bring them forth from there." Therefore Moses took his wife and children since it was the right way to bring them with him, insamuch as the children of Israel would have greater reliance on him because of it. [They would say]: "A free man in Midian who lives peacefully in his home with his children and with his wife, a son-in-law of the

---

(288) Above, 3:20. (289) In Verse 18 it says that Moses bid farewell to Jethro because he was ready to return to Egypt. Why then was it necessary now that G-d command him to return there? For this reason, Ibn Ezra renders Verse 19 as meaning: "now the Eternal *had* said." (290) Above, 3:10. *Come now therefore, and I will send thee unto Pharaoh.* (291) Verse 18.

priest of the land, would not have brought them to be with slaves and make their lives bitter with hard service if his heart were not steadfast. He is trusting that they will soon go out from Egypt and that he will go up with them to the land of Canaan, and that it will then not be necessary for him to return to Midian to take his wife and his children from there."

20. AND MOSES TOOK HIS WIFE AND HIS SONS. The intent thereof is like that of the verse, *And the sons of Pallu: Eliab.* [292] At that time, he had only Gershom, as Scripture mentions, [293] and his wife became pregnant with Eliezer on the way [to Egypt] or in Egypt, if she went there.[294]

It is possible that before the Divine communication came to him *on the mountain of G-d,* [295] only Gershom had been born. Zipporah however was already pregnant [with Eliezer], and when he returned to Jether his father-in-law, [291] she gave birth, but *because the King's business required haste,* [296] he did not circumcise him, nor did he give him a name. On the way when his mother circumcised him, [297] she did not give him a name, as Moses was met at that time by the angel. [298] It was after he came to Egypt and saw that he was saved from all those who sought his life that he then called him Eliezer, *for the G-d of my father was my help, and delivered me from the sword of Pharaoh.* [299] Our Rabbis have also stated [300] that the child that was circumcised [by Zipporah, as mentioned here in Verse 25], was Eliezer.

AND HE RETURNED TO THE LAND OF EGYPT. I.e., with those mentioned [at the beginning of the verse, namely, his wife and his sons]. Rabbi Abraham ibn Ezra said that the expression, *and he returned to the land of Egypt,* means that Moses alone

---

(292) Numbers 26:8. It states "sons" in the plural, but mentions only one son. A similar case is here, as Ramban explains. (293) Above, 2:22. (294) See Ramban further in this verse. (295) Above 3:1. (296) I Samuel 21:9. Ramban evidently understands here the word "king" as referring to G-d. (297) Verse 25. (298) Verse 24. And see Rashi: "and the angel sought, etc." (299) Further, 18:4. (300) Shemoth Rabbah 5:8.

EXODUS IV, SHEMOTH

returned. When he was met by G-d,[301] Eliezer was circumcised, and when he was healed, Zipporah together with her children returned to her father.

This [explanation of Ibn Ezra] is possible, for due to the fact that Eliezer was circumcised, Moses could not take him on the road until the child would become strong. At the same time, he did not want to delay the mission of the Holy One, blessed be He, and therefore he left them in the lodging-place and commanded Zipporah to return to her father's home when the child will become healed. This is the purport of the expression, *after he had sent her away*.[302] It is also probable that they all went to Egypt, and after they stayed there for some time, she longed for her father and so Moses sent her with the children. This then would be the sense of the word *shilucheha (after 'he had sent her away')*,[302] since Jethro feared that perhaps it was Moses' intent to divorce her.

And in V'eileh Shemoth Rabbah,[303] [the Rabbis have said]: *"And Moses went and returned to Jether his father-in-law.*[291] Where did he go? He went to take his wife and sons. Jethro said to him, 'Where do you take them?' Moses replied, 'To Egypt.' Jethro said to him, 'Now that those who are in Egypt wish to leave it, do you desire to lead them there?' Moses replied, 'Very soon [those held in bondage] are destined to go forth from there and stand at Mount Sinai and hear the words of the Almighty, *I am the Eternal thy G-d Who brought thee out of the land of Egypt.*[304] Should my children not hear it together with them?' Jethro said to Moses, 'Go in peace.'"[291] In accordance with the opinion of the Rabbis [in the above Midrash], it is proper that we explain that after Moses and Jethro agreed on Moses' returning to Egypt, the Holy One, blessed be He, commanded him thereon, thus confirming the word of His servant,[305] and he returned to Egypt with his sons and his wife, as I have explained.

---

(301) Verse 24. Ibn Ezra refers to the language of the verse: *and the Eternal met him*. See above, Note 298. (302) Further, 18:2. (303) Shemoth Rabbah 4:4. (304) Further, 20:2. (305) See Isaiah 44:26.

21. AND THE ETERNAL SAID UNTO MOSES: 'WHEN THOU GOEST BACK INTO EGYPT SEE ALL THE WONDERS,' etc. Rabbi Abraham ibn Ezra said that this was said to Moses when he was yet in Midian. G-d informed him that He would harden Pharaoh's heart and he would not let the people go because of all the wonders which he would see until the last wonder. Ibn Ezra's intent is thus to explain this verse as saying: "*See* that for *all the wonders which I have put in thy hand* and which you will do *before Pharaoh,* for all of these he will not let them go until you will tell him that I will slay his son, his firstborn. Then he will let them go."

This explanation is not correct for what sense is there for the expression, *when thou goest back into Egypt, see,* etc.? Rather, the purport thereof is as follows: When leaving Midian, Moses took the rod of G-d in his hand [306] *to mark the way with his footsteps.* [307] G-d forewarned him and said to him, "When you go on the way, *mark well and behold* [308] that all the wonders which I have put in your hand you should do before Pharaoh; do not forget to do anything before him. *And I will harden his heart,* but do not despair from doing them because of his obstinacy, and you will yet warn him again on the last plague which will cause him to let them go." The purport of the expression, *I have put in thy hand,* is that "in your hand I have put them; you are to do them, and not someone else." He had already informed him that He would perform many signs and wonders in Pharaoh's midst, as He said, *with all My wonders which I will do in his midst.* [309] All this was an encouragement to Moses, for since he was forced to go on the mission, G-d warned him before the action, and commanded him again at the time of the action before each and every wonder.

It is possible that the expression [concerning the smiting of his firstborn], *and thou shalt say unto Pharaoh,* [310] is but to inform Moses now that in the end He will so command him to say it to Pharaoh. Thus the purport of His words is as follows: "*I will harden his heart and he will not let the people go* in spite of all

(306) Verse 20.   (307) Psalms 85:14.   (308) Ezekiel 44:5.
(309) Above, 3:20.   (310) Verse 22.

EXODUS IV, SHEMOTH

the wonders, *and thou shalt say* to him on that day, '*Behold I will slay thy son, thy firstborn*,' and then he will let them go." We do not find that He informed Moses of the death of their firstborn except at this time, and thus [we must say] that not all of the Divine communication [here given to Moses was relayed to Pharaoh] now. [311]

It is possible to explain [the matter as follows]: "*See all* these three [312] *wonders which I have put in thy hand* to do before the Israelites, *do them* also *before Pharaoh* so that Pharaoh should know that the elders of the people who request of him to let them go say so according to the commandment of G-d, and he should not come with a pretext against them." And so did Moses do [these three wonders [312] before Pharaoh], even though it is not so written. The verse [further on] which states, *When Pharaoh shall speak unto you, saying: 'Show a wonder for you,'* [313] [which might indicate that the wonder of the staff turning into a serpent was done by a special command, and not because of the Divine communication here, as explained above], means that Pharaoh will want a sign for himself. G-d thus commanded Moses to throw the rod and it shall become a *tanin*, not a *nachash*, [314] as mentioned the first time. Thus He wanted to show Pharaoh that Aaron's rod would swallow up their rods, instructing him that He would vanquish them and that they would be destroyed forever by Him.

---

(311) The intent of Ramban is as follows: In Chapter 11, Verse 1, it is said concerning the final plague: *And the Eternal said unto Moses: Yet one plague more will I bring upon Pharaoh, and upon Egypt; afterwards he will let you go hence.* But nothing was mentioned to Moses about what that plague was. Ramban suggests that Verses 22-23 here concerning the final plague were said to Moses now with the understanding that later, before the tenth plague, he was to relay the warning to Pharaoh, but not that he said it to Pharaoh as soon as he came to see him. Hence it was not necessary for Scripture to say in Chapter 11, Verse 1, what that "one plague more" was. (312) The staff turning into a serpent, Moses' hand becoming leprous, and the waters turning into blood (Verses 3-9). (313) Further, 7:9. (314) Ramban thus distinguishes between the *nachash* mentioned here in Verse 3, and *tanin* mentioned further in 7:9. Rashi however explains there that *tanin* means *nachash*. In the J.P.S. translation, both terms are translated as "serpents." In other translations, *nachash* is translated as "snake," and *tanin* as "reptile." Some such distinction between the terms is to be made according to Ramban.

In the Midrash V'eileh Shemoth Rabbah,[315] I have seen mentioned: "[*And the Eternal said to Moses:* '*When thou goest into Egypt, see all the wonders,*' etc.] To which wonders does He refer? If you say that it is to [the staff turning into] a serpent, [his hand becoming] leprous, and [the waters turning into] blood, the Holy One, blessed be He, told Moses to do these only before Israel! Moreover, we find nowhere that Moses did these signs before Pharaoh. But what then is the meaning of *all the wonders which I have put in thy hand?* This refers to the rod upon which were written the initials of the ten plagues: '*D'tzach Adash B'achab.*' "[316] According to this Midrash, the explanation of the verse will be: "*See* and contemplate the writing on the rod *which I have put in thy hand,* for all wonders thereon you will perform before Pharaoh."

27. AND HE MET HIM IN THE MOUNTAIN OF G-D. Thus you learn that Mount Sinai is between Midian and Egypt.

AND HE KISSED HIM. Aaron kissed Moses, for Moses the humble one treated his older brother with respect. For this reason, it does not say that they kissed each other.

28. AND MOSES TOLD AARON ALL THE WORDS OF THE ETERNAL WHEREWITH HE HATH SENT HIM. This means that he told all the words which were spoken between him and the Holy One, blessed be He, and all the objections he had raised against undertaking the mission, and that he was sent against his own will. This is the intent of the word *kol* ('*all' the words of the Eternal*). In Midrash Chazit [317] [we find it stated]: "And the Rabbis say that Moses revealed to Aaron the Tetragrammaton

---

(315) Shemoth Rabbah 5:6. (316) They are: *Dam* (blood), *Tz'phardei'a* (frogs), *Kinim* (lice), *Arob* (beasts), *Dever* (murrain), *Sh'chin* (boils), *Barad* (hail), *Arbeh* (locusts), *Choshech* (darkness), *Makath-b'choroth* (slaying of the firstborn). (317) Another name for the Midrash Rabbah on the Song of Songs. The quote is found there, 4:12. See Vol. I, p. 292, Note 73, for the reason of the name Chazit or Chazita.

[which had been revealed to him]." The intent of their explanation is that Moses told Aaron the Divine Names mentioned above [318] by which He sent him, and the Name that is derived [from them], [319] and the explanation that is inherent in them. [319]

5   3. LEST HE FALL UPON US WITH PESTILENCE. "Moses and Aaron wanted to say [to Pharaoh], 'Lest He fall upon thee,' but they showed respect to royalty." Thus the language of Rashi. Rabbi Abraham ibn Ezra explained: " *'Lest He fall upon us;* that is, including us Israelites, also you Pharaoh and all Egypt.' Therefore when the Egyptians saw the slaying of the firstborn, they said, *'We are all dead men,'* [320] for the words of Moses now became clear to them when he said, *Lest he fall upon us with pestilence,* and therefore they drove them to go to sacrifice [to G-d]."

This explanation of Ibn Ezra is not correct, for Moses and Aaron were not commanded to say that Israel too would share in the punishment of pestilence or sword if they would not sacrifice [to G-d], [321] and Moses and Aaron would by no means change anything in the mission of G-d.

By way of the Truth, [the mystic lore of the Cabala], this is the secret of the offerings, [322] as they constitute a redemption from punishment, for *before Him goeth the pestilence.* [323]

Or with the sword, this means the harsh [attribute of justice]. Moses said this because the Holy One, blessed be He, had commanded them, saying, *And you shall say unto him: 'The Eternal, the G-d of the Hebrews hath met with us. And now let us go ... that we may sacrifice to the Eternal our G-d,'*[324] and they said to Pharaoh, *Thus saith the Eternal, the G-d*

---

(318) See above, 3:13. (319) See my Hebrew commentary for elucidation of this Cabalistic subject. (320) Further, 12:33. (321) Only the Egyptians were to suffer that punishment if they failed to permit the Israelites to go to worship the Eternal. (322) See Ramban on Genesis 4:3 (Vol. I, p. 88, and Note 423). (323) Habakkuk 3:5. This explains the verse here: *Let us go...and sacrifice... lest He fall upon us with pestilence.* Ramban then proceeds to explain the end of the verse: *or with the sword.* (324) Verse 1.

of Israel: 'Let My people go.'³²⁴ Now Pharaoh was indeed a very wise man. He knew [of the existence of] G-d and acknowledged Him, as he — or his predecessor ³²⁵ — said to Joseph: *Forasmuch as G-d had shown thee all this;*³²⁶ *a man in whom the spirit of G-d is.* ³²⁷ But Pharaoh did not know the Proper Name of G-d, [i.e., the Tetragrammaton], ³²⁸ and accordingly, he answered, *I know not the Eternal.* ³²⁹ Therefore they replied and said to him, as they were commanded, *The G-d of the Hebrews hath met with us,* ³³⁰ mentioning to him only *the G-d of the Hebrews,* which is equivalent to *E-il Sha-dai.* They said, *He hath met with us,* relating to Pharaoh the exact language of the message they were commanded to bring him, and they explained to him that in this meeting which they would have [with G-d], it would be necessary for them to sacrifice before Him, lest the meeting be *with pestilence, or with the sword.* In a similar vein did Scripture set forth in connection with Balaam, as it is said, *And G-d met Balaam, and he said unto Him: I have prepared the seven altars, and I have offered up a bullock and a ram on every altar.* ³³¹

4. WHEREFORE DO YE, MOSES AND AARON...? Pharaoh asked them for their names, and he mentioned them by name in a manner indicating respect.

'TAPHRI'U' THE PEOPLE FROM THEIR WORK. Onkelos translated: *t'vatlu* (you cause them to idle from their work). Similarly: *'porei'a' (refuseth) instruction;*³³² *'vatiphr'u' (and ye have set at nought) all my counsel.* ³³³

(325) This is a reference to the difference of opinion among the Rabbis of the Talmud (Sotah 11 a) regarding the verse, *Now there arose a new king over Egypt, who knew not Joseph* (above, 1:8). One Rabbi said that he was really a new king; the other said that it was the same king but he decreed new edicts, and comported himself as though he did not know him. (326) Genesis 41:39. (327) *Ibid.,* Verse 38. (328) See above, Note 84. (329) Verse 2. (330) In Verse 3 before us. (331) Numbers 23:4. (332) Proverbs 13:18. Now Rashi explained *taphri'u* as meaning: "taking them away." Ramban therefore calls attention to Onkelos, who interpreted it as meaning "idle," "making to nought all their work." (333) *Ibid.,* 1:25.

EXODUS V, SHEMOTH

GET YOU TO YOUR BURDENS. If we follow the simple interpretation of Scripture, reference here is to the work for the king,[334] since Moses and Aaron were part of the [Hebrew] people for at this time they came before him with all the people. But he did not listen to them and commanded them: "Return you all to the work." Later when Moses and Aaron returned before Pharaoh and he said to them, *Show a wonder for you,*[335] and they did so, they appeared to him like the magicians, sorcerers, and wise men, and he showed them respect. Still later, when the plagues began coming upon him, he was in dread fear of them.

It appears furthermore that not all the children of Israel worked all the time for Pharaoh *in mortar and in brick,*[336] for in that case they would have filled the whole land of Egypt with cities. Rather, they worked in levies, and he pressed his yoke upon them by taking many of the Israelites [into his labors].

Now Rashi explained: "*Get you to your burdens,* i.e., 'to your work which you have to do in your homes.' But [it cannot signify 'go to your labors as slaves,' for he was speaking to Moses and Aaron, who were of the tribe of Levi, and] the work of Egyptian slavery was not imposed upon the tribe of Levi. You may know that this was so because Moses and Aaron went and came as they pleased." This is correct. All man's work whether at home or in the field is so called [*sebel* (labor)], just as in the verse: *over all the 'sebel' (labor) of the house of Joseph.*[337] And it is customary among all people to have wise men who teach them their laws. Therefore Pharaoh did not impose slavery upon the tribe of Levi, who were the teachers and the elders of the children of Israel, and it was all caused by G-d.

I have seen in V'eileh Shemoth Rabbah:[338] "Rabbi Yehoshua ben Levi said that the tribe of Levi was free from servile labor.

---

(334) Rashi's interpretation, mentioned further on in the text, is: "Go to your work which you have to do at home, etc." Now although Ramban will later agree with this explanation of Rashi, his point here is that in line with the simple meaning of Scripture, "the burdens" are a reference to the labors imposed upon them as slaves.   (335) Further, 7:9.   (336) Above, 1:14.   (337) I Kings 11:25.   (338) Shemoth Rabbah 5:2.

Pharaoh said to them, 'It is because you are free [from the forced labor] that you therefore say, *Let us go and sacrifice to our G-d.* [339] *Get ye unto your burdens* for Israel.' [340] Another interpretation: Pharaoh said to Moses and Aaron, 'It is enough for you that you are free! Perhaps you are displeased because you are not doing this forced labor; [if so], *get ye unto your burdens.*' "

And Rabbi Abraham ibn Ezra explained the verse, *Get ye unto your burdens,* as meaning the burdens of the entire people, since Pharaoh spoke to them for all Israel.

22. 'ADO-NOY', WHEREFORE HAST THOU DEALT ILL WITH THIS PEOPLE? The Divine Name is here written *Aleph Dalet,* for through the Proper Name of G-d, [i.e., the Tetragrammaton], which is the attribute of mercy, no evil would befall the people. However, above [in Chapter 4, Verses 10 and 13], Moses twice mentioned the Divine Name written *Aleph Dalet* — [*Bi Ado-noy* (O G-d)] — since he was praying that the anger of G-d would not be kindled against him [for refusing to undertake the mission to go to Pharaoh]. Perhaps Moses was afraid to mention the Great Divine Name that was then being revealed to him and speaking to him.

WHEREFORE HAST THOU DEALT ILL WITH THIS PEOPLE? [It should be asked]: After G-d twice informed [341] Moses that the king of Egypt would not let them go, why did he complain? Rabbi Abraham ibn Ezra said that Moses had thought that from the moment he would speak to Pharaoh in the name of G-d, he would ease the burden from upon the children of Israel, and that G-d would begin to redeem them, but Pharaoh hardened and increased their woes. This is the sense of the expression, *Wherefore has Thou dealt ill...?* "It is the opposite of what Thou hast told me, i.e., *I have surely seen the affliction of My people.* [342] *And I am come down*

(339) Verse 8. (340) In other words, "attend to your work of teaching them their laws, but do not divert them from doing my work with such a plan as going on a journey." (341) Above, 3:19 and 4:21. (342) *Ibid.,* 3:7.

EXODUS V, SHEMOTH

to deliver them." [343] But this [explanation of Ibn Ezra] does not appear to me to be correct because [Moses said], *Neither hast Thou delivered Thy people at all,* [344] and "delivery" means only their going forth from exile. [345]

In my opinion, Moses our teacher thought G-d had told him that Pharaoh would not let them go immediately at his command, nor by sign and wonder until He would perform His many wonders among them. But Moses thought that G-d would bring them upon Pharaoh in uninterrupted succession in a few days. When Pharaoh said, *I know not the Eternal,* [346] He would immediately command him to execute the sign of the serpent before the king, and [if] the king would still not listen, He would smite him on that very day with the plague of blood, followed by all the rest of the plagues. But when Moses saw that three days passed and the king increased their woes every day and G-d did not rebuke him, nor did He reveal Himself to Moses to inform him what he should do, then Moses thought that [the captivity] is a long one. [347]

It is possible that there was a long period of time to this story recounted here by Scripture. When the officers of the children of Israel were beaten, [348] days passed until they spoke to Pharaoh himself, saying to him, *Wherefore dealest thou thus with thy servants?* [349] It is not every person that has a right to come into the inner chambers of the king's palace and speak to him face to face, and all the more the officers of those people abhorrent to him. Thus they suffered in their burden and oppression many days, and they would come *even before the king's gate* [350] until their outcry was heard before the king and he commanded that they come before him and speak with him. It is likewise possible that Moses returned to the Eternal and said, *Wherefore hast Thou dealt ill...,* many days after the officers of the children of Israel met him.[351]

The Rabbis have said in V'eileh Shemoth Rabbah:[352] "And the

(343) *Ibid.,* Verse 8. (344) Verse 23. (345) How then could Ibn Ezra explain that Moses' primary complaint was that he had thought G-d would merely ease their burden? (346) Above, Verse 2. (347) See Jeremiah 29:28. (348) Verse 14. (349) Verse 15. (350) Esther 4:2. (351) Verse 20. (352) Shemoth Rabbah 5:23.

taskmasters of the people went out, and their officers, and they spoke to the people, saying, Thus saith Pharaoh: I will not give you straw. [353] When this was decreed by Pharaoh, Moses went to Midian and stayed there six months while Aaron remained in Egypt. At that time, Moses took his wife and sons back to Midian." The Rabbis have furthermore said: [354] *"And they met Moses and Aaron.* [351] After six months, the Holy One, blessed be He, revealed Himself to Moses in Midian and said to him, *Go, return unto Egypt.* [355] Moses then came from Midian, and Aaron from Egypt, when they were met by the officers of Israel as they came forth from Pharaoh." I have furthermore seen a similar [tradition] in Midrash Chazit: [356] *"My beloved is like a gazelle.* [357] Just as a gazelle appears [and hides] and reappears, so did the first redeemer, [i.e., Moses], appear to the children of Israel, then he disappeared, and then he appeared to them again. For how long was he away from them? Rabbi Tanchuma said three months. It is this which Scripture says, *And they met Moses and Aaron.* [351] And Rabbi Yehudah Beribi [358] said that [he was away from them] for periods of time." That is to say, the word "meeting" — [*and they 'met' Moses and Aaron*] — indicates periods of time.

Thus many days passed between G-d's speaking to Moses and Moses' coming to Pharaoh. Therefore when Moses returned to G-d he said, *"Wherefore hast Thou dealt ill with this people,* hurrying to send me before the time [of redemption] had come? It was not fitting to send me until You wanted to deliver them, but now You have dealt ill with them and You have not delivered them. And if You deal thus with them, they will perish in the affliction that will come upon them." Therefore G-d answered Moses at this time: "Soon *shalt thou see what I will do to Pharaoh,* [359] for I will not prolong it for him to the extent that you thought, and his time is near to come, and his days shall not be prolonged." [360]

(353) Verse 10. (354) Shemoth Rabbah 5:24. (355) Above, 4:19. (356) Shir Hashirim Rabbah 2:22. See Note 317 above. (357) Song of Songs 2:9. (358) In the Midrash above: "Yehudah B'rabbi." In the Hebrew text of Ramban: "And Rabbi Yehudah Br'." But see Hyman's Toldoth Tannaim V'amoraim that the correct reading is: "Rabbi Yehudah Beribi" or "Yudan Beribi". (359) Further, 6:1. (360) See Isaiah 13:22.

Va'eira

6   2. AND G-D SPOKE UNTO MOSES. Rashi explains that He spoke to him harshly[1] because he had been critical when he said, *Wherefore hast Thou dealt ill with this people?*[2] AND HE SAID UNTO HIM: "I AM THE ETERNAL, Who am faithful to recompense reward to those who walk before Me wholeheartedly."[3] In this sense we find the phrase explained in many places, etc. 3. "AND I APPEARED UNTO ABRAHAM, etc., BY THE NAME 'E-IL SHA-DAI' (G-D ALMIGHTY). I made many promises to him,[4] and in all cases I said to him, *I am G-d Almighty*.[5] BUT BY MY NAME, THE ETERNAL, WAS I NOT KNOWN UNTO THEM." It was not written here, ["But My Name, the Eternal], I did not make known to them." Rather, it is written, [*But by My Name, the Eternal*], *was I not known unto them*, meaning: "I was not recognized by them in My attribute of keeping faith, by reason of which My Name is called Eternal, which denotes that I am certain to fulfill the words [of My promise]. Indeed I made promises to the patriarchs[4] but did not fulfill them [during their lifetime]."

(1) Rashi's interpretation is based either on the name *Elokim* (G-d) mentioned here, which signifies the Divine attribute of justice (Mizrachi), or on the two words *Va'yedabeir Elokim* (And G-d spoke), whereas the usual expression in the Torah is *Va'yedabeir Hashem* (And the Eternal spoke) (Gur Aryeh). (2) Above, 5:22. (3) "Whole-heartedly." This word is not found in our printed texts of Rashi. But see Genesis 17:2 and 25:27 where it is found in connection with Abraham and Jacob respectively. See also Rashi, *ibid.*, 26:2, where a similar expression is mentioned in connection with Isaac. All three patriarchs were thus whole-hearted in their worship of G-d. (4) "Him": Abraham. In our texts of Rashi: "Them," which refers to all three patriarchs, and so it is mentioned further on. (5) Genesis 17:4 (to Abraham), 35:11 (to Jacob).

All these are the words of Rashi. His intent is to explain that the fulfillment of His promise [to the patriarchs] had not taken place. Even though the time for the fulfillment had not arrived [in their lifetime, and consequently the absence of such fulfillment was no indication of a lack of His "keeping faith" since the time had not arrived], yet He was not known to the patriarchs in the fulfillment of His promise.

But with all this interpretation, Rashi has not properly explained the language of the text.[6] [According to his interpretation], it should be said, *lo hodati* ["and My Name, the Eternal, 'I did not make known' to them," instead of *lo nodati* (*I was not made known*), as the text reads]. Or it should have said, "and My Name, the Eternal, *lo noda* (was not known) to them." Perhaps according to Rashi's opinion, the sense of the verse is: "and My Name is the Eternal, *v'lo*[7] *nodati lahem*," meaning that "I was not made known to them by that Name."

And the learned Rabbi Abraham ibn Ezra explained that the letter *beth* of the words *b'E-il Sha-dai* (by the Name G-d Almighty) connected [with the ensuing words *ush'mi Hashem*, making it *ubish'mi Hashem*], which has the following meaning: "And I appeared unto Abraham, etc., by the Name *E-il Sha-dai* (G-d Almighty), but *by* My Name the Eternal I was not made known unto them."[8]

(6) The Hebrew text reads: *ush'mi Hashem lo nodati lahem* (literally: *and My Name the Eternal I was not made known to them*). Ramban's point is that according to Rashi's interpretation, the verse should have read either (a) *lo hodati* (I did not make known), or (b) *ush'mi Hashem lo noda lahem* (and My Name the Eternal was not known to them).   (7) Ramban adds here the letter *vav* to the word *lo* — *v'lo* — thus making it independent of the expression *ush'mi Hashem*. Accordingly, there are two separate thoughts expressed: "and My Name is the Eternal," which denotes that "I am certain to substantiate My promise," and "I was not made known to them by that Name since I made promises to them but did not fulfill them."   (8) Thus according to Ibn Ezra, the sense of the verse is as if it were written: "And I appeared into Abraham...*b'E-il Sha-dai ubish'mi* — [instead of *ush'mi*] — *Hashem lo nodati lahem* (and by My Name the Eternal I was not made known to them)."

EXODUS VI, VA'EIRA 65

The purport of the verse is that He appeared to the patriarchs by this Name [*E-il Sha-dai*], which indicates that He is the victor [and prevailer][9] over the hosts of heaven, doing great miracles for them except that no change from the natural order of the world was noticeable, [as was the case with the miracles performed through Moses our teacher]. In famine, He redeemed them from death, *and in war from the power of the sword,*[10] and He gave them riches and honor and all the goodness, just like all the assurances mentioned in the Torah [in the section dealing] with the blessings and curses.[11]

It is not [in nature] that man should be rewarded for performance of a commandment or punished for committing a transgression but by a miracle. If man were left to his nature or his fortune, his deeds would neither add to him nor diminish from him. Rather, reward and punishment in this world, as mentioned in the entire scope of the Torah, are all miracles, but they are hidden. They appear to the onlooker as being part of the natural order of things, but in truth they come upon man as punishment and reward [for his deeds]. It is for this reason that the Torah speaks at great length of the assurances concerning this world, and does not explain the assurances of the soul in "the World of Souls."[12] These [assurances mentioned in the Torah as recompense for the observance or transgression of the Divine Commandments] are wonders which go contrary to nature,[13] while the existence of the soul [after the death of the body] and its cleaving unto G-d are the proper way inherent in its nature that she *returneth unto G-d*

---

(9) See Vol. I, pp. 215-6 and 556-7, for further discussion of this theme. See also end of *Seder Bo* in this volume. (10) Job 5:20. (11) Leviticus 26:3-46 and Deuteronomy 28:1-69. (12) This is the world to which the soul goes following the death of the body. At the resurrection, body and soul will be reunited. That world, according to Ramban, is *Olam Haba* (the Coming World). Ramban thus distinguishes between *Olam Han'shamoth* (the World of Souls) and *Olam Haba*. The *Olam Han'shamoth* is concomitant with this world, and *Olam Haba* is the world of the future. (13) "For it is not by nature that the heavens become as iron because we have sowed our fields in the Sabbatical year, etc." (Ramban, Vol. I, p. 557.)

Who gave it.[14] I will yet explain it further[15] if G-d accomplishes it for me.[16]

Thus G-d said to Moses: "I have appeared to the patriarchs with the might of My arm with which I prevail over the constellations and help those whom I have chosen, but with My Name *Yod Hei* with which all existence came into being I was not made known to them, that is, to create new things for them by the open change of nature. And *Wherefore say unto the children of Israel: I am the Eternal*,[17] and inform them once again of the Great Name, [i.e., the Tetragrammaton], for by that Name I will deal wondrously with them,[18] and they will know that *I am the Eternal, that maketh all things.*"[19]

All the words of Rabbi Abraham ibn Ezra on this matter were thus correct except that he was as one who prophesies but does not know it.[20] Even according to his interpretation, the verse should have said, "And I made Myself *known* to Abraham, etc., by the name of *E-il Sha-dai*, but by My Name *Hashem*, [which describes My true essence], I did not make Myself known to them," or it should have said, "but by the Name *Hashem* I did not *appear* to them."[21] However, Ibn Ezra can answer this by saying that because the prophecy of the patriarchs came to them *in the visions of the night*,[22] He said here, *Va'eira (And I appeared)* to them, and because that of Moses was *face to face*[23] He said here, "*I made Me not known to them* [the patriarchs] as I made Myself known to you [Moses]."

---

(14) Ecclesiastes 12:7. (15) Leviticus 26:11. (16) See Psalms 57:3. (17) Verse 6. (18) See Joel 2:26. (19) Isaiah 44:24. (20) The source of this expression, "he prophesied but did not know what he prophesied," is in Sotah 12 b. Ramban uses the expression here to intimate that Ibn Ezra did indeed allude to the correct interpretation of the verse, namely, that the letter *beth* in *b'E-il Sha-dai* is connected also to *ush'mi Hashem*, making it *ubish'mi Hashem*, as explained above (see Note 8). But, suggests Ramban, there is still a question to be raised on Ibn Ezra's explanation, as explained further in the text. (21) In other words, why does the Torah use two separate terms: *va'eira (and I appeared)* and *nodati (made Me known)*? One term — "appear" or "made Me known" — should have sufficed in both cases. (22) Genesis 46:2. See also Ramban, *ibid.*, 15:1 (Vol. I, p. 193). (23) Deuteronomy 34:10.

By way of the Truth, [the mystic teachings of the Cabala], the verse can be explained in consonance with its plain meaning and intent. [24] He is saying: "I the Eternal appeared to the patriarchs through the speculum of *E-il Sha-dai*," just as is the sense of the verse, *In a vision do I make Myself known to him.*[25] "But Myself, I the Eternal did not make Myself known to them, as they did not contemplate [Me] through a lucid speculum so that they should know me," just as is the sense of the verse, *And there hath not arisen a prophet since in Israel like unto Moses, whom the Eternal knew face to face.* [23] The patriarchs did know the Proper Name of the Eternal, but it was not known to them through prophecy. Therefore when Abraham spoke with G-d, he mentioned the Proper Name together with the Name *Aleph Dalet*[26] or *Aleph Dalet* alone.[27] The purport thereof is that the revelation of the Divine Presence and His communication with them came to them through an ameliorated attribute of justice,[28] and with that attribute was His conduct towards them. But with Moses, His conduct and His recognition to him were by the attribute of mercy, which is indicated by His Great Name, [i.e., the Tetragrammaton — the Eternal], just as is denoted in the verse, *He caused His glorious arm to go at the right hand of Moses,*[29] and it is written, *So didst Thou lead Thy people, to make Thyself a glorious name.* [30] Therefore Moses does not henceforth mention the name *E-il Sha-dai*, for the Torah was given with His great Name, as it is said, *I am the Eternal thy G-d.*[31] This is the sense of the verse, *Our of heaven He made thee to hear His voice, that He might instruct thee; and upon earth He made thee to see His great fire.*[32] I have already alluded to the explanation of the word *hashamayim* (the heaven).[33] May the Holy One, blessed be He, open our eyes and show us wonders in His Torah.

---

(24) Ramban is suggesting that whereas in other places the mystic teachings of the Cabala do not reflect the plain meaning of Scripture, here "the way of the Truth" is in harmony with the plain meaning and import of the text. (25) Numbers 12:6. (26) Genesis 15:2. See Ramban, *ibid.*, 17:1 (Vol. I, p. 216). (27) *Ibid.*, 18:30. (28) See Vol. I, p. 543. (29) Isaiah 63:12. (30) *Ibid.*, Verse 14. (31) Further, 20:2. (32) Deuteronomy 4:36. (33) In Genesis 1:8 (Vol. I, p. 37).

4. AND I HAVE ALSO ESTABLISHED MY COVENANT WITH THEM ... AND MOREOVER I HAVE HEARD THE GROANING OF THE CHILDREN OF ISRAEL.[34] The meaning thereof is as follows: "I have appeared to the patriarchs *by the Name 'E-il Sha-dai' and I have also established* this covenant [by this Divine Name] before Me, *and moreover* with My Great Name *I have* now *heard the groaning of the children of Israel, and I have remembered My covenant* which I have established for them with Me." The student learned [in the mystic lore of the Cabala] will understand.

Now as regards what our Rabbis have expounded:[35] i.e., that [the Holy One, blessed be He, said to Moses], "Alas for those that are gone, [namely, the patriarchs], and are no more to be found! Many a time did I reveal Myself to Abraham, Isaac, and Jacob by the Name *E-il Sha-dai,* and I did not inform them that My Name is the Eternal as I have said it to you, and yet none of them cast aspersions upon My dealings with them, etc. Moreover, none of them asked Me what My Name is, as you asked. Right at the beginning of My mission, you said to Me, 'What is Your Name?'[36] And at the end you said, *For since I came to Pharaoh to speak in Thy name, he hath dealt ill with this people,* etc.[37] It is in connection with this [complaint] that G-d said to Moses, *And I have also established My covenant with them,* etc.[38] The purport of this Midrash likewise fits in with the text.[39] The Rabbis, of blessed memory, found it difficult to understand why G-d mentioned the prophecy of the patriarchs altogether, diminishing their accomplishment in prophecy and saying that He appeared to them only by the Name of *E-il Sha-dai.* What purpose did that serve? He could have said, "I am the Eternal, and wherefore say unto the children of Israel: 'I am the Eternal, and I will bring you

---

(34) Verses 4-5.   (35) Shemoth Rabbah 6:4, and mentioned by Rashi in Verse 9 with variants.   (36) Above, 3:13.   (37) *Ibid.,* 5:23.   (38) Verse 4. That is to say, "Not only did I promise them the Land but I also established My covenant with them on that, and yet they did not find fault with Me" (*ibid.,* Shemoth Rabbah).   (39) See Rashi on Verse 9 where he explains that this Midrash does not fit in with the text for several reasons. Ramban proceeds to show that it can be fitted in with the verses.

[from under the burdens of the Egyptians], and you shall know that I am the Eternal Who brought you out.'" Therefore the Rabbis explained that the message constituted a rebuke to Moses, telling him: "Behold, the patriarchs, whose accomplishment in prophecy was not as high as yours inasmuch as they contemplated Deity only through the Name *E-il Sha-dai,* believed in Me, *And I have also established My covenant with them,* and I have heard the groaning of their children for their sake. Surely you who have known Me by the Great Name and whom I have given My assurance [by that Name], you should have trusted in [My] mercies and assured Israel in My Name that I will do signs and wonders for them." This interpretation too is correct and fitting.

6. AND I WILL BRING YOU OUT FROM UNDER THE BURDENS OF THE EGYPTIANS. He assured them that He will take them out from the land of the Egyptians and that they will no longer suffer from their heavy burden.

AND I WILL DELIVER YOU FROM THEIR BONDAGE. The Egyptians will no longer rule over them at all, nor will they subject them to be *a servant under tribute*[40] wherever they live.

AND I WILL REDEEM YOU. He will bring such judgments upon them until the Egyptians will say: "Here You have the Israelites as a redemption for our lives." The meaning of the word *g'ulah* (redemption) is close to the subject of *mecher* (sale), [thus implying that "I will buy you from the Egyptians"]. And the meaning of the expression, *with an outstretched arm,* is that His arm will be extended over them until He takes them out from Egypt.

7. AND I WILL TAKE YOU TO ME FOR A PEOPLE. That is, when you will come to Mount Sinai and you will accept the Torah. There, [at Mount Sinai], it was said, *Then ye shall be Mine own treasure.*[41]

(40) Genesis 49:15. (41) Further, 19:5.

AND YE SHALL KNOW THAT I AM THE ETERNAL YOUR G-D WHO BROUGHT YOU OUT FROM UNDER THE BURDENS OF THE EGYPTIANS. The purport thereof, said Rabbi Abraham ibn Ezra, is that it was in the combined mighty power of the higher constellations that the children of Israel should yet stay in the exile. But this is not of the theme of the chapter. Rather He says: "When I will redeem you with an outstretched arm visible to all nations, you shall know that it is I the Eternal Who performs new signs and wonders in the world, and that I am your G-d and for your sake I had so acted, for you are *the portions of the Eternal.*" [42]

8. AND I WILL BRING YOU IN UNTO THE LAND CONCERNING WHICH I LIFTED UP MY HAND. "I have lifted it up to swear by My throne." Thus the language of Rashi. Rabbi Abraham ibn Ezra said that it is an idiom [denoting the exercise of power], just like a man who lifts his hand to the heavens and swears, such as: *For I lift up My hand to heaven* [43] [to take an oath of vengeance]; *And he lifted up his right hand and his left hand unto heaven, and swore.* [44]

By way of the Truth, [the mystic lore of the Cabala], *I lifted up My hand* means that "I have raised the strength of My arm to Myself that I will give them the Land." Similarly, *For I lift up My hand to heaven* [43] means that "I will lift up the great hand to the heavens since it abounds in eternal life." [45] But the verse, *And he lifted up his right hand and his left hand unto heaven,* [44] has no relevance here, for that was said concerning the angel *clothed in linen,* [46] who swore *by Him that liveth for ever.* [44]

9. BUT THEY HEARKENED NOT UNTO MOSES FOR IMPATIENCE OF SPIRIT, AND FOR CRUEL BONDAGE. It was not because they did not believe in G-d and in His prophet [that

(42) Deuteronomy 32:9. (43) *Ibid.*, Verse 40. (44) Daniel 12:7. (45) According to Meir Abusaula (see Preface, Vol. I, p. XII, Note 21) the thought suggested here is that His Name will forever be in Israel's midst, and thus He assured them eternal life. (46) Daniel 12:6.

they hearkened not]. Rather, they paid no attention to his words because of impatience of spirit, as a person whose soul is grieved on account of his misery and who does not want to live another moment in his suffering even though he knows that he will be relieved later. The "impatience of spirit" was their fear that Pharaoh would put them to death, as their officers said to Moses,[47] and the "cruel bondage" was the pressure, for the taskmasters pressed upon them and hurried them [in their daily task],[48] which gave them no chance to hear anything and consider it.

10. AND THE ETERNAL SPOKE UNTO MOSES 'LEIMOR' (SAYING). The commentators[49] said that throughout the entire Torah, the word *leimor* means "saying to Israel," the purport thereof being that G-d said to Moses, "Say these, My words, to Israel." Here the word *leimor* means "saying to Pharaoh." But the verse stating [Laban's words to Jacob], *The G-d of your father spoke unto me yesternight 'leimor' (saying): Take heed to thyself that thou speak not to Jacob either good or bad,*[50] does not fit in correctly with this explanation [since Laban was not commanded to relate these words to Jacob]. Similarly, there are many cases in Scripture where the term "saying" is repeated, [and it is not correct to say that it means "saying it to others"]. Thus: *And the Eternal spoke unto Moses, saying: Speak unto the children of Israel, and say unto them;*[51] *And the Eternal spoke unto Moses, saying: Speak unto the children of Israel, and say unto them;*[52] *And they* [Moses and Aaron] *spoke unto all the congregation of the children of Israel, saying;*[53] *And the children of Israel spoke unto Moses, saying: Behold we perish;*[54] *And I spoke unto you at that time, saying.*[55] There are many other such verses. Likewise in

---

(47) Above, 5:21. (48) *Ibid.*, Verse 13. (49) R'dak in his Book of Roots, under the root *amar* (saying). (50) Genesis 31:29. (51) Leviticus 18:1-2. (52) Numbers 15:37-8. (53) *Ibid.*, 14:7. Here the word "saying" could not mean "saying it to others," since Moses and Aaron were already speaking directly to the people. (54) *Ibid.*, 17:27. (55) Deuteronomy 1:9.

this *seder*[56] we find: *And the Eternal spoke unto Moses and unto Aaron, saying: When Pharaoh will speak unto you, saying,*[57] and the word "saying" cannot correctly mean "saying it to others."

The correct interpretation appears to me to be that in all places the word *leimor* indicates the clarification of a subject. The verse, *And the Eternal spoke unto Moses, saying,* means really explicitly, free from doubt or uncertainty. This is why this expression always appears in the Torah, for of Moses' prophecy it was said, *Mouth to mouth do I speak with him, even manifestly, and not in dark speeches.*[58] And Laban also said to Jacob: "*Yesternight G-d spoke unto me, saying*[50] clearly that I should not harm you; except for that, I would have done you evil." Similarly, the verse, *And the children of Israel spoke unto Moses, saying: Behold, we perish,*[54] means that they said so explicitly to Moses and Aaron, shouting to them brazenly. [In Hebrew], the infinitive is used for clarification of a subject. Occasionally, it comes before the verb,[59] and sometimes it comes after the verb, such as: *'omrim amor'* (*they surely say*) *unto them that despise Me.*[60]

12. BEHOLD, THE CHILDREN OF ISRAEL HAVE NOT HEARKENED UNTO ME because You have done nothing [for Israel] so that my words should be acceptable to them. AND HOW THEN SHALL PHARAOH HEAR ME? AND besides, I AM OF UNCIRCUMCISED LIPS, and I am not fit to speak before a great king.

It is possible to explain that Moses thought that due to his deficiency — for he was of uncircumcised lips — the children of Israel would not hearken to him, *for he could not frame* [words] *to speak*[61] kindly to them, words of good cheer and comfort, and all the more how could he speak to Pharaoh?

(56) The portion of the Torah assigned for reading on a particular Sabbath. See Vol. I, p. 15. (57) Further, 7:8-9. (58) Numbers 12:8. (59) Such as *sachor s'charticha* (*I have surely hired thee*), in Genesis 30:16. Here the infinitive *sachor* is written before the verb *s'charticha.* (60) Jeremiah 23:17. Here the infinitive *amor* is written after the verb *omrim.* (61) Judges 12:6.

EXODUS VI, VA'EIRA

Now the reason that Moses again broached this argument [of his speech-impediment, when he had already mentioned it above in Chapter 4, Verse 10], is that G-d did not originally command him that he was to speak before Pharaoh. He merely said, *And thou shalt come, thou and the elders of Israel, unto the king of Egypt, and ye shall say unto him.* [62] In that case it was possible that the elders should speak [before Pharaoh] and Moses would remain silent. Then Moses said that he was ashamed even to speak to the people, saying, *I am not a man of words.* [63] Whereupon the Holy One, blessed be He, answered him, *And he* [Aaron] *shall be thy spokesman unto the people.* [64] And so indeed Moses and Aaron did when they first came to the people, as it is said, *And Aaron spoke all the words which the Eternal had spoken unto Moses, and did the signs in the sight of the people.*[65] But now Moses himself was commanded, *Wherefore say unto the children of Israel: I am the Eternal,* [66] and he did speak to them as He commanded him, but they did not hearken to him.[67] Now when He again commanded Moses to speak to Pharaoh, [68] Moses said, "How can I speak to him, I who am of uncircumcised lips." Then the Holy One, blessed be He, associated Aaron with him, and gave both of them *a charge unto the children of Israel*,[69] that they should say to them whatever He will command them, *and unto Pharaoh*[69] to bring them forth out of his land. Now Rashi commented: "[*And He gave them a charge unto the children of Israel, and unto Pharaoh, king of Egypt*]. That is to say, He gave them a command with regard to the children of Israel and His mission on which He had sent them to Pharaoh." But there is no need for this. [70]

13. AND HE GAVE THEM A CHARGE UNTO THE CHILDREN OF ISRAEL. Rashi wrote: "The purport of this command is explained in the second section,[71] after the order of

(62) Above, 3:18. (63) *Ibid.*, 4:10. (64) *Ibid.*, Verse 16. (65) *Ibid.*, Verse 30. (66) Verse 6. (67) Verse 9. (68) Verse 11. (69) Verse 12. (70) According to Rashi, the command of His mission to Pharaoh was the one with regard to Israel. But according to Ramban, there was also a command with regard to Israel, as explained in the text. (71) Further, Verses 29-30.

genealogy. [It properly belongs here], but because Scripture mentioned Moses and Aaron here, it interrupted the subject-matter [with the narrative of their genealogy], informing us how each was born and with whom they are connected by descent. *And the Eternal spoke unto Moses in the land of Egypt, saying: I am the Eternal; speak thou unto Pharaoh king of Egypt all that I speak unto thee.*[72] This is the selfsame command which is mentioned here [in Verse 11]: *Go in, speak unto Pharaoh king of Egypt.* However, because Scripture broke off the subject-matter in order to record their genealogy, it reverts to it [further in Verse 29] and begins it anew. *And Moses said before the Eternal: Behold, I am of uncircumcised lips, and how shall Pharaoh hearken unto me?*[73] This is the selfsame statement Moses made here [in Verse 12]: *Behold, the children of Israel have not hearkened unto me,* etc. However, because Scripture broke off the subject-matter [for the abovementioned reason], it repeats it there [further in Verse 30]. Such indeed is a proper method, just as a person who says, 'Let us return to the previous subject.' " And so also is the opinion of Rabbi Abraham ibn Ezra.

But I do not agree with this.[74] Rather, [it is my opinion] that when G-d commanded Moses to speak to the children of Israel — as it is said, *Wherefore say unto the children of Israel* [66] — he did so and they hearkened not unto him.[67] Then He commanded him to go before Pharaoh and bid him to let them go out of his land,[68] and Moses answered: *Behold, the children of Israel have not hearkened unto me,* etc.[69] Then the Holy One, blessed be He, commanded both Moses and Aaron to speak to the people and to Pharaoh.[75] Moses thus thought that both of them — [he and Aaron] — are to take equal part in all the signs they are to do; both of them are to come to the children of Israel and to Pharaoh. But indeed [Moses reckoned that] it is sufficient that only one

(72) *Ibid.*, Verse 29. (73) *Ibid.*, Verse 30. (74) The reason is obviously that Rashi's and Ibn Ezra's interpretation necessitates the conclusion that one set of verses — either 10-12 or 29-30 — is redundant. (75) This is in Verse 13 before us.

should speak, for such is the customary way of all pairs of emissaries, that one speaks and the other is silent. This was consented to, and G-d then said to him: *"I am the Eternal,* [72] *Who revealed Myself to you only to speak in My Great Name. Speak thou unto Pharaoh king of Egypt all that I speak unto thee,* [72] for it is to you that all communications are given, not to Aaron [primarily] and to you. It is you that I made the emissary to Pharaoh." Then Moses answered once again: *Behold, I am of uncircumcised lips,* etc. [73] And G-d said to him: *"See, I have set thee in G-d's stead to Pharaoh, and Aaron thy brother shall be thy prophet.* [76] You will go before Pharaoh with Aaron, and there [in Pharaoh's presence] you will command Aaron while Pharaoh will not hear your words, and Aaron as your emissary will make your words heard." This is just as G-d commands a prophet and the prophet makes His words audible and chastises [the people] with them. This was a great achievement for Moses,[77] which he merited by his humility since he was ashamed to speak because of his speech-impediment. And so Scripture says, *Moreover the man Moses was very great in the land of Egypt, in the sight of Pharaoh's servants, and in the sight of the people.*[78] It was measure for measure. He had been afraid lest he be despised in their eyes [on account of his defective speech, but Scripture testifies to the Egyptians' admiration of his greatness].

Now Rashi commented: *"Thou shalt speak* [79] each and every message once, just as you heard it from My mouth, *and your brother Aaron* shall express it in eloquent language and explain it in Pharaoh's hearing." This is not correct at all.

14. THESE ARE THE HEADS OF THEIR FATHERS' HOUSES: THE SONS OF REUBEN.... Scripture did not wish to

---

(76) Further, 7:1.   (77) Moses had thought that his speech impediment would be a handicap. It now turned out to be to his honor, for on account of it he was to state to Aaron every Divine message as it reached him, and Aaron was to address it to Pharaoh, just as G-d commands a prophet and the prophet addresses the message to the people.   (78) Further, 11:3. (79) *Ibid.*, 7:2.

begin with the statement, *And these are the names of the sons of Levi according to their generations,* [80] so that it should not appear that henceforth in honor of Moses, Levi is first in genealogy. Instead, [Scripture therefore] mentioned Levi's elder brothers, [i.e., Reuben and Simeon], and that Levi is counted third.

Now Scripture mentioned the sons of Levi *according to their generations* [80] because in the case of Reuben and Simeon, it mentioned only those who went down to Egypt with them, but in the case of Levi it mentioned his children, the number of years of his life, the birth of the fathers of the prophets — [namely, Kohath the grandfather, and Amram the father of Moses and Aaron] — and the number of years of their lives,[81] all in honor of the prophets. Besides, they themselves — [Kohath and Amram] — were the pious ones of the Most High, worthy to be spoken of as the fathers of the world.

23. AND AARON TOOK HIMSELF ELISHEBA, THE DAUGHTER OF AMMINADAB, THE SISTER OF NACHSHON TO WIFE. Just as Scripture mentioned the mother of the prophets, [namely, Jochebed],[82] in their honor, saying that she was the daughter of Levi, a righteous man, and alluding to the fact that a miracle occurred to her,[83] it also mentioned the mother of priesthood, i.e., that she was related to the seed of royalty, being the sister of the great prince [Nachshon of the tribe of Judah].

Scripture mentioned the mother of Phinehas,[84] for he too was a priest, a reward which he earned himself.[85] Now if this name Putiel — [Phinehas' maternal grandfather] — is a proper name, it is

---

(80) Verse 16.   (81) Verses 18 and 20.   (82) Verse 20.   (83) See Ramban to Genesis 46:15 (Vol. I, pp. 554-9).   (84) Verse 25: *And Eleazar, Aaron's son took him one of the daughters of Putiel to wife, and she bore him Phinehas.*   (85) See Numbers 25:6-13. Originally when Aaron and his four sons - Nadab and Abihu, Eleazar and Ithamar — were anointed as priests, this prerogative extended only to them and their offspring born after the anointment. Phinehas the son of Eleazar and grandson of Aaron who was alive at the time of the anointment was thus not included. Priesthood was later bestowed upon him as a reward for being zealous for G-d.

EXODUS VI, VA'EIRA

not clear why Scripture [suddenly] mentions the name of a person whose identity we do not know. It is for this reason that our Rabbis have said [86] that Phinehas was of the family of Joseph, who conquered his passion,[87] and of the family of Jethro, who fattened [88] calves for idolatrous sacrifice, and he is mentioned for praise [here together with Aaron and his sons], who for their righteousness were worthy to be endowed with everlasting priesthood.

In line with the plain meaning of Scripture, we will say [that the mothers of Moses and Aaron, of Aaron's sons, and of Phinehas are mentioned here because] in the case of kings, it is the customary way of Scripture to mention the names of their mothers: *And his mother's name was Maacah the daughter of Abishalom;* [89] *And his mother's name was Azubah the daughter of Shilhi;* [90] and so in all cases. It may be that [Scripture does not relate more about Putiel because] he was an honorable and known person in his generation, and it [sufficed just to] mention him in praise.

Scripture says, *of the daughters of Putiel,* [84] and not "the daughter of Putiel," because Putiel had many daughters and Eleazar chose one of them. It may be that she was not his daughter but his daughter's daughter who related herself to him on account of his distinction, and therefore Scripture did not mention her name.

28. AND IT CAME TO PASS ON THE DAY WHEN THE ETERNAL SPOKE UNTO MOSES IN THE LAND OF EGYPT. It

---

(86) Sotah 43 a, and mentioned here by Rashi. (87) Genesis 39:7-12. The Hebrew word *pitpeit* (conquered) is suggested by the name Putiel. (88) *Piteim* (fattened) is also suggested by the name Putiel. Phinehas was thus descended on his mother's side not only from Joseph but from Jethro also. (89) I Kings 15:10. Mentioned in the case of Asa, king of Judah. (90) II Chronicles 20:31. She was the mother of Jehoshaphat, king of Judah.

is possible to explain that the verse refers to the one above.[91] Scripture is thus stating: "And it came to pass that *it was they* — [Moses and Aaron] — *who spoke to Pharaoh, king of Egypt*[92] at the time *when the Eternal spoke unto Moses in the land of Egypt.*" For since Scripture said, *These are that Aaron and Moses, to whom the Eternal said: Bring out the children of Israel from the land of Egypt,* [93] it might have appeared that the communication came to both of them equally. Therefore it now explains [in Verse 28] that the communication came to Moses, and the command to bring them forth from Egypt was to both of them. This is why Scripture closed the chapter [of the genealogy of Moses and Aaron with this subject].

3. AND I WILL HARDEN PHARAOH'S HEART. The Rabbis said in Midrash Rabbah:[94] "G-d revealed to Moses that He was destined to harden Pharaoh's heart in order to bring judgment upon him for he caused them to work in cruel bondage." It is also stated there [in Midrash Rabbah]:[95] *"For I have hardened his heart.*[96] Rabbi Yochanan said, 'This provides a pretext for the heretics to say that G-d did not allow Pharaoh to repent.' Rabbi Shimon ben Lakish said, 'The mouths of the heretics be closed! Only, *if it concerneth the scorners, He scorneth them.*[97] When He warns one on three occasions and he does not turn from his ways, He closes the door of repentance on him in order to punish him for his sin. Such was the case with wicked Pharaoh. After the Holy

---

(91) Rashi and Ibn Ezra explain that Verse 28 here is connected with the following Verses 29-30: *And the Eternal spoke unto Moses, saying....* Ramban finds this difficult to accept since the plain meaning would seem to indicate that Verses 29-30 constitute an independent section not connected with the preceding verse. Therefore he interprets Verse 28 as being connected with the preceding verse, as explained in the text. (92) Verse 27. (93) Verse 26. (94) Shemoth Rabbah 5:6. (95) *Ibid.,* 13:4. (96) Further, 10:1. (97) Proverbs 3:34.

One, blessed be He, sent him five times [98] [the request to let His people go] and he paid no attention to His words, the Holy One, blessed be He, said to him: You have stiffened your neck and hardened your heart; I will double your defilement.' " [99]

The Rabbis [in the above Midrash] have thus discussed the question which all ask: [100] "If G-d hardened his heart, what then was Pharaoh's sin?" For this there are two explanations, and both of them are true. One is that Pharaoh in his wickedness had unjustifiably perpetrated such great evils against Israel that justice required that the ways of repentance be withheld from him, as is so indicated in many places in the Torah and in the Writings. [101] He was judged according to his wickedness which he had originally committed of his own will. The second explanation is that half of the plagues came upon him because of his transgressions, for in connection with them it is only said: *And Pharaoh's heart was hardened;* [102] *And Pharaoh hardened his heart.* [103] Thus Pharaoh refused to let the children of Israel go for the glory of G-d. But when the plagues began bearing down upon him and he became weary to suffer them, his heart softened and he bethought himself to send them out on account of the onslaught of the plagues, not in order to do the will of his Creator. Then *G-d hardened his spirit and made his heart obstinate,* [104] so that His name may be declared [throughout all the earth]. [105] Similar in meaning is the verse, *Thus will I magnify Myself, and sanctify Myself, and I will make Myself known in the eyes of many nations, and they shall know that I am the Eternal.* [106] And that which He said before the

---

(98) "In the case of the first five plagues, it is not stated, 'The Eternal hardened Pharaoh's heart,' but 'Pharaoh's heart was hardened' " (Rashi). That is, it was hardened by his own stubborness. (99) Literally: "I will add defilement to your defilement." (100) See Ibn Ezra here, and Rambam in his Shemonah Perakim, Chapter 8, and in his Mishneh Torah, Hilchoth Teshubah 6:3, where this problem is discussed. (101) See Rambam in Mishneh Torah, *ibid.*, where he quotes from the Prophets and Writings to substantiate this point. (102) Further, Verses 13 and 22, and 8:15. (103) *Ibid.* , 8:28 and 9:7. (104) Deuteronomy 2:30. (105) Further, 9:16. (106) Ezekiel 38:23.

plagues, *And I will harden his heart, and he will not let the people go,* [107] was merely His warning to Moses of that which He was destined to do to Pharaoh in the last [five] plagues, it being similar to that which He said, *And I know that the king of Egypt will not give you leave to go.* [108] This then is the meaning of the verse [before us], *And I will harden Pharaoh's heart, and multiply My signs.* That is to say, "I will harden his heart so *that My wonders may be multiplied in the land of Egypt,*" [109] since in the last five plagues, as well as at the drowning in the sea, it is said, *And the Eternal hardened the heart of Pharaoh,*[110] for *the king's heart is in the hand of the Eternal; He turneth it whithersoever He will.*[111]

11. AND THEY ALSO, THE MAGICIANS OF EGYPT, DID IN LIKE MANNER 'B'LAHATEIHEM' (WITH THEIR SECRET ARTS). Our Rabbis have said [112] that these are deeds of sorcerers who perform their arts through angels of destruction,[113] the word *b'lahateihem* being derived from the expressions: *eish loheit (flaming fire);* [114] *the flame 't'laheit' (burned up) the wicked.*[115] The purport [of the saying of the Sages] is that these deeds of sorcery are done by means of "the flaming ones," angels of a fire that burns in man, and he does not know that the fire burns in him and pays no attention to it. It is similar in sense to the expression, "And the Eternal opened the eyes of the young man of Elisha, and behold there were horses of fire and chariots of fire." [116] Perhaps these are identical with the angels that dwell in the atmosphere of the spheres of the [four] elements,[117] which are called *sarim*

---

(107) Above, 4:21. (108) *Ibid.,* 3:18. (109) Further, 11:9. (110) *Ibid.,* 14:8. (111) Proverbs 21:1. (112) Sanhedrin 67b. (113) A term found in Kiddushin 72a, and designating a supernatural being holding destructive power. (114) Psalms 104:4. (115) *Ibid.,* 106:18. (116) The verse, II Kings 6:17, reads: *And the Eternal opened the eyes of the young man, and he saw, and behold, the mountain was full of horses and chariots of fire round about Elisha.* (117) The four elements — fire, air, earth and water — are the basic components of all created things that are beneath the firmament, which is below the lunar sphere. See Rambam, Hilchoth Yesodei Hatorah 3:11 and 4:1.

(lords).[118] I will explain this theme again [in the Book of Leviticus 17:7] with the help of the Rock.

But the word *b'lateihem*, [mentioned further in 8:3 — *And the magicians did in like manner 'b'lateihem'*] — is explained [by the Rabbis] as meaning *sheidim* (demons) — the word being derived from the Hebrew word *lat* (secret): *Speak with David 'balat'* (*secretly*) — since the demons come quietly inasmuch as they are ethereal bodies whose presence is not felt. This is why Scripture states [in Verse 11 before us] that Pharaoh called *for the wise men and the sorcerers,* for the wise men who knew [the art of] incanting and assembling the demons were the leaders and elders of the Egyptians.

The term *chartumei mitzrayim* (the magicians of Egypt) includes both of them, [i.e., the wise men and the sorcerers]. We do not know the root of the word *chartumei*. Now Rabbi Abraham ibn Ezra says that it is either an Egyptian or Chaldean word since we find it only mentioned in their accounts.[119] The more likely explanation is that of Rashi, who said [120] that it is an Aramaic compound-word: *char tami* (those who excite themselves by means of the bones [of the dead]). It is known that the greater part of this craft is one with the bones of dead persons or the bones of animals, just as they mentioned in the case of the *yid'oni*.[121]

16. AND, BEHOLD, HITHERTO THOU HAST NOT HEARKENED. Because this was one of the [ten] plagues and henceforth He will begin to smite him, He therefore said to him that it was his wickedness which was responsible for the bringing of the punishment upon him since he hearkened not to the

---

(118) See my Hebrew commentary, p. 310, that it is possible there is another reading here. Instead of *sarim* (lords), the word should be *sheidim* (demons). The first reading seems to be more correct here. (119) Here, and in the Book of Daniel 2:2, and other places there. (120) Rashi's interpretation is found in Genesis 41:8. (121) Leviticus 19:31. "The *yid'oni* takes the bone of a bird [or a beast] called *yido'a*, puts it into his mouth, burns incense, recites certain prayers, performs a certain ritual until he is in a condition akin to fainting, and falls into a trance in which he predicts the future" (Maimonides;"The Commandments,"Vol. II, p. 10).

command of his Creator. Now at this time, [i.e., when the warning about the first plague was given to him], Pharaoh did not declare to Moses and Aaron that he will neither hearken to G-d's words nor let the people go. It was only at the first time [when they came before him] that he said, *I know not the Eternal, and moreover I will not let Israel go.* [122] At present, he did not rebuke them; he only heard their words and remained silent, for since they performed the wonder of the serpent before him and Aaron's rod swallowed up their rods, [123] he was already afraid of the plagues, except that during the first plagues he attempted that the magicians do likewise, that is, by means of deeds of sorcery. Thus he was afraid, and yet he hardened his heart. This is the sense of the expression, *And Pharaoh's heart was hardened.* [124]

20. AND HE LIFTED UP THE ROD, AND SMOTE THE WATERS THAT WERE IN THE RIVER IN THE SIGHT OF PHARAOH. That is to say, Aaron lifted up the rod and stretched out his hand over the land of Egypt in all directions,[125] and afterwards *he smote the waters that were in the river, in the sight of Pharaoh.* In Pharaoh's sight, *all the waters that were in the river turned to blood, and the blood was* furthermore *throughout all the land of Egypt.* [126] And Rabbi Abraham ibn Ezra said that Scripture mentioned the smiting of the river but found it unnecessary to mention the stretching out of the hand [in all directions] over the entire land of Egypt.[127]

---

(122) Above, 5:2. (123) Verse 12. (124) Further, Verse 22. (125) Ramban's intent is to state that the lifting up of the rod, mentioned here in Verse 20, is identical with "stretch out thy hand," mentioned in G-d's command in Verse 19. Ibn Ezra, as stated further in the text, differs with this opinion. (126) Verse 21. Ramban thus explains that the waters that were in the river turned to blood by reason of the smiting of the rod, while the waters in all other places turned into blood by reason of Aaron's stretching forth his hand in all directions (Bachya). (127) Thus according to Ibn Ezra, Scripture merely shortened its account here and did not mention the stretching out of Aaron's hand, but not, as Ramban has it, that the stretching out of the hand is already included in the act of the smiting of the waters of the river.

23. NEITHER DID HE SET HIS HEART TO THIS ALSO. I.e., to the wonder of the rod turning into a serpent,[128] nor to that of the waters turning into blood. [Thus the language of Rashi.] A more correct interpretation would appear to be that *to this also* means "to this also which was indeed a plague," [as distinguished from the wonder of the rod turning into a serpent, which was not a plague at all], and he should have feared lest the power of G-d be upon him from now on. [129]

And seven days were fulfilled after that the Eternal had smitten the river.[130] This is connected with the verse above, and the purport thereof is as follows: And with this[131] — namely, the Egyptians' digging round about the river *for they could not drink of the water of the river,* [as stated in Verse 24] — with this was filled the seven days after the river had been smitten.

8

5. 'L'MATHAI' (AGAINST WHAT TIME) SHALL I ENTREAT FOR THEE? Rashi commented: "If the text said *mathai* (when) — [not *l'mathai*] — *shall I entreat,* it would signify 'when shall I pray?' But now that it said *l'mathai,* it means 'Today I will pray for you that the frogs be destroyed by the time which you will set for me. Say then by what day you wish that they shall be destroyed.' "

In line with the plain meaning of Scripture, the removal of the plagues took place at the time of Moses' prayer, as it is written,

---

(128) Above, Verse 10. (129) See Ramban above in Verse 16, where he explains that beginning with the wonder of the rod, Pharaoh already began fearing the coming of the plagues. It is this then which Scripture says here: In spite of his fear which he already had then even before the plagues came, "also" now that the first plague did come and he should have feared the coming of other plagues, yet he did not set his heart to it. (130) Verse 25. (131) The verse states, *'Vayimalei' (And it was fulfilled) seven days,* using a singular verb when the verb actually required is a plural: *vayimal'u* (and they were fulfilled). Rashi explained it by adding the word *minyan* (number) in the singular, explaining it thus: "and *the number* of seven days was fulfilled." Ramban suggests that the verse is connected to the preceding one and is to be understood with the additional word of *bazeh* (with this), thus rendering the sense of the verse: "and with this activity — i.e., with the Egyptians' digging, etc., as stated in the above Verse 24 — was filled (or completed) seven days."

And Moses cried unto the Eternal, etc., *and the Eternal did according to the word of Moses* [132] and it is not written "and the Eternal did so tomorrow." The letter *lamed* in the word *l'mathai* is no proof that Moses prayed immediately, for the word *l'mathai* is equivalent to *mathai,* there being many verses where the *lamed* occurs [just for elegance of language], thus: *'l'min' (from) the day that thou didst go forth out of the land of Egypt;* [133] *until 'l'minchath' (the offering) of the evening;* [134] *the wing of the one cherub was five 'l'amoth' (cubits).* [135] There are many other such cases.

THAT THE FROGS BE DESTROYED. This is an allusion to their death, just as the expressions: *that soul shall be cut off;* [136] *and I will cut off from Ahab every man-child.* [137]

The intent of Moses' repeating the promise to Pharaoh, *And the frogs shall depart,* etc., [138] was to state that as soon as he will have prayed, the frogs will all be removed, and that Pharaoh should not fear that when these frogs die, others will come up from the river. Rather, the plague will be completely removed even though some of them will remain in the river. [138] All this was to inform Pharaoh that the plague came from G-d for the sake of Israel alone.

6. AND HE SAID, FOR TOMORROW. It is a known fact that it is man's nature to pray that his misfortune be removed from him at once. [The question then arises: Why did Pharaoh say that the frogs were to be removed tomorrow?] In the name of the Gaon Rav Shmuel ben Chophni, [139] they have explained that Pharaoh thought that perhaps some heavenly constellation brought the frogs

---

(132) Verses 8-9. (133) Deuteronomy 9:7. The *lamed* in the word *l'min* is superfluous. (134) Ezra 9:4. There the *lamed* in *l'minchath* is a superfluous style. (135) II Chronicles 3:11. Here the *lamed* in *l'amoth* is superfluous. (136) Further, 12:19. (137) I Kings 21:21. (138) Verse 7. (139) The father-in-law of Rav Hai Gaon, the last of the Gaonim. See Vol. I, p. 97, Note 477. Rav Shmuel, who was the Gaon of the Academy of Sura, wrote extensively in Arabic on Biblical exegesis as well as on Halachic themes. Only fragments of his work are now extant. He is quoted by Ibn Ezra (as in this case) and R'dak. In Biblical commentary, his method generally was that of the rationalist.

upon Egypt, and that Moses [by his knowledge of astrology] knows the time when they will disappear, and therefore Moses had said to him, *Have thou this glory over me*,[140] thinking that Pharaoh will now tell him to destroy them immediately. Therefore Pharaoh extended the time until the morrow.

The correct interpretation appears to me to be that because Moses had said, *Against what time shall I entreat for thee*,[140] Pharaoh thought that Moses was desirous for time, and so he fixed the shortest time limit, *And he said, For tomorrow*. Moses answered him, "*According to thy word*, let it be so, for since you did not ask that they be removed immediately, they shall not be removed until tomorrow."

14. AND THE MAGICIANS DID SO WITH THEIR SECRET ARTS TO BRING FORTH GNATS. The purport of the expression, *and the magicians did so*, [when it immediately says afterwards, *but they could not*], is that they hit the dust of the earth and incanted the demons and performed their secret arts, as they used to do at other times, in order *to bring forth the gnats, but they could not*. It is possible that the expression, *and the magicians did so*, teaches that they did indeed do the correct things which do bring forth the gnats, but they were not successful this time, [for G-d thwarted their plans]. The learned magicians knew what they could do and they had tried to do so at other times [and succeeded. Hence they tried to do it now, but they failed "because it was now the will of the Holy One, blessed be He, to remove that power from them henceforth]."[141]

15. AND THE MAGICIANS SAID UNTO PHARAOH: THIS IS THE FINGER OF G-D. Rabbi Abraham ibn Ezra commented that because the magicians had done as Aaron did with the serpent and also with the plagues of blood and the frogs and now they could not do so, they therefore said to Pharaoh: "This plague of gnats has not come through Aaron for the sake of Israel. Rather it is a plague of G-d due to the particular [evil] stars under which the

---

(140) Verse 5.   (141) From Ramban's sermon on *Torath Hashem T'mimah*. See my Kithvei Haramban, I, p. 146.

land of Egypt found itself at the time." Pharaoh did not deny the existence of the Creator [142] but only the Divine Name which Moses mentioned to him. This is similar in sense to the verse, *It was not His hand that smote us; it was a chance that happened to us.*[143] Therefore Pharaoh's heart was hardened. And Ibn Ezra brought proof for his explanation from the fact that Scripture does not state that the magicians said, "This is the finger of the Eternal," which would have been a reference to the G-d of Israel, just as Pharaoh said to Moses and Aaron, *Entreat the Eternal.* [144] Another proof [which Ibn Ezra brought for his explanation] is that in the case of the smiting of the river, Moses had forewarned Pharaoh, [145] but he mentioned nothing to him about the plague of gnats. [Therefore the magicians felt justified in saying that it was not a plague for the sake of Israel but merely due to the evil stars.]

Ibn Ezra's interpretation does not appear to me to be correct. "A chance" is not called "the finger of G-d." Only a plague which comes directly from Him as a form of punishment is called *the hand of the Eternal* [146] and *the finger of G-d,* just as it is written in the verse which [Ibn Ezra] mentioned: *It was not His hand that smote us.*[143] And it is furthermore written: *And Israel saw the great hand;*[147] *And the hand of the Eternal shall be against you;*[148] *the hand of G-d was very heavy there.* [148] Moreover, in the next plague of swarms, as well as in the following ones, Pharaoh no longer called upon the magicians to stand before Moses to do the same things, even though there had been a forewarning of their coming! [149]

(142) See Ramban above in *Seder Shemoth* 5:3. (143) I Samuel 6:9. (144) Verse 4. (145) Above 7:17-18. And so also was there a forewarning in the case of the frogs (*ibid.,* Verses 27-29). (146) I Samuel 5:9. (147) Further, 14:31. (148) I Samuel 12:15 and *ibid.,* 5:11. (149) How then could Ibn Ezra say that because Moses had not forewarned Pharaoh of the coming of the gnats, the magicians said that the plague came through the evil stars and not from the Eternal? In the following plagues when Pharaoh was forewarned of their coming, why did he not call upon the magicians to do likewise? The answer must be, as Ramban explains, that in the case of the plague of the gnats, the magicians already admitted that it was from the Eternal and therefore they could not do likewise. There was thus no need for Pharaoh to call upon them in the following plagues of which he was forewarned, since those were surely from the Eternal, the G-d of Israel, before Whom the magicians were helpless.

But the subject, in accordance with the simple explanation of Scripture, is as follows: When the magicians saw that they could not bring forth the gnats, they admitted Aaron's deed to be through an act of G-d, and this is why Pharaoh no longer called upon them from that time on. They [the magicians] said, *This is 'the finger' of G-d,* and not "the hand" of G-d [as is the customary way of the Scriptures to refer to plagues, as e.g., *It was not His 'hand' that smote us*][143] in order to minimize the plague, that is to say, it is but a small plague from Him [which we can easily endure].[150] They did not, however, say to Pharaoh, "This is the finger of 'the Eternal,' " [but instead they said, *"This is the finger of 'G-d' "*]. Pharaoh and his servants would not mention the Proper Divine Name except when speaking to Moses because he mentioned that Name to them. [In addressing Pharaoh, however, the magicians would not use that Name since that would be an open recognition on their part of His existence and power. Therefore they said to Pharaoh, " *This is the finger of 'G-d,'* " although their intent was to say, "This is the finger of 'the Eternal.' "] That the magicians could not bring forth the gnats was [not because they really could not do it, but it] was by reason of the fact that G-d so caused it to happen to them. He confounded their counsel in accordance with His Will, for everything is His and it is within His power to do all.

It appears to me further that in the first two plagues — in the one of blood, where the water naturally [151] changed into blood, and in the one of the frogs, which consisted of bringing them up from the river — since they did not involve the creation of some new phenomenon out of nothing or some act of new formation,[152] the magicians could do [as Aaron did]. Scripture does not say, "and the frogs came into existence," but only, *and*

---

(150) In his Discourse "The Law of the Eternal is Perfect," Ramban adds: "Nevertheless the magicians [thereby] admitted [that it was an act of G-d], and thus they became apprised of the fact that Moses' deed was effectuated by the Lord of the universe." (151) Since water and blood are both liquids, the change of the one into the other may be spoken of as in "the nature" of things inasmuch as both are classified under the element of water. See above, Note 117, on the four elements. (152) The Hebrew text reads: *bri'ah o yetzirah.* See Vol. I, p. 23, that only the term *bara* (or *bri'ah*) signifies "bringing forth something from nothing."

the frogs came up; [153] they assembled and came up. In the plague of gnats, however, there was an act of creation, for it is not in the nature of dust to turn into gnats. Therefore He said, *that it may become gnats.* [154] The verse, *And the magicians did so with their secret arts to bring forth gnats,* [155] is similar in intent to: *Let the earth bring forth the living creature,* etc., *and it was so.* [156] But only the Creator, praised and magnified be He, can perform such a [new] act of creation. The verse, *And the magicians did so...but they could not,* [155] means they incanted the demons to do their command, but they were powerless.

Confirming me in my opinion concerning the frogs, [i.e., that there was no new act of creation there], is the following text [of the Talmud]:[157] 'Rabbi Akiba said that there was only one frog [158] which swarmed and filled the whole land of Egypt. Rabbi Eliezer [159] ben Azaryah said to him: 'Akiba, what have you to do with Agadah (homily)? Turn from these matters and go instead to [delve in the difficulties of] Negaim [160] and Oholoth. [161] It was only one frog croaking to all other frogs, and so they gathered.' " Rabbi Eleazar ben Azaryah could not accept the opinion [of Rabbi Akiba] that the magicians should have been able to bestow a new nature upon the frog, i.e., that one frog should give birth to so many, which is contrary to its nature, but rather they gathered them in order to bring them up. In the opinion then of Rabbi Akiba, the verse *And the river shall swarm with frogs,* [162] means that the river should swarm with them more than its due. But according to Rabbi Eleazar ben Azaryah, the sense of that verse is

---

(153) Verse 2. (154) Verse 12. The word "become" suggests a new act of creation. (155) Verse 14. (156) Genesis 1:24. In other words, the expression here, "to bring forth the gnats," means a new act of creation, just as in the Book of Genesis. (157) Sanhedrin 67 b. (158) As Verse 2 has it: *'Vata'al hatz'phardei'a'* *(and the frog came up),* in the singular. (159) "Eliezer." In our text of the Gemara, "Eleazar," and so also further in Ramban. (160) Negaim (Leprosies) is the name of a treatise in the Mishnah dealing with the laws of leprosy. It is considered a very difficult subject. (161) Oholoth (Tents) is one of the most difficult treatises of the Mishnah. It deals with the laws regarding the uncleanness of a corpse as affecting a house and its vessels, as well as human beings. (162) Above, 7:28.

EXODUS VIII, VA'EIRA

like, *'shirtzu' in the earth*, [163] which connotes movement, as I have explained in *Seder Bereshith*, [164] and here its meaning is that the frogs gather and move about in the river and from there go up upon Egypt.

Now with regard to the gnats, our Rabbis have said [165] that the demon [through whose power this was to be done by the magicians] is powerless in the case of a creature that is smaller than a lentil. [166] The expression, *but they could not*, must therefore mean that they could not assemble gnats from their [breeding] places and bring them.

In Midrash Rabbah, the Rabbis have further said: [167] "Perceiving that they cannot bring forth the gnats, the magicians at once recognized that [Aaron's deed] was an act of G-d and not an act of the demons. From that moment on, therefore, they were no longer anxious to liken themselves to Moses by bringing forth the plagues."

Now with regard to Rabbi Abraham ibn Ezra's statement that Moses did not inform them of the coming of the plague of gnats, it appears to me that Aaron struck [the dust of the earth] with the rod *in the sight of Pharaoh*, just as he did in the case of the soot of the furnace. [168] However, there was no forewarning here, since the Holy One, blessed be He, warned Pharaoh only of those plagues which entailed the death of people. In the case of the frogs, [there was also death involved], as it is written: *And [He sent among them] frogs, which destroyed them,* [169] which is an

---

(163) Genesis 9:7. Said to Noah and his sons. (164) *Ibid.*, 1:20 (Vol. I, pp. 47-48). (165) Sanhedrin 67 b, and mentioned by Rashi here in Verse 14. (166) "Lentil." In our text of the Gemara, as well as in Rashi here: "a barley-corn." At any rate, it was completely unnecessary for Scripture to inform us that the magicians could not bring forth gnats, as these are creatures smaller in size than a barley-corn. The expression, *but they could not*, must hence mean as explained in the text. Such is Ramban's intent as explained by Rabbeinu Bachya. See my Hebrew commentary, p. 313. (167) Shemoth Rabbah 10:7. (168) Further, 9:8. In other words, just as in the case of boils it is said that it was done in the sight of the king, so also in the case of gnats, where the verse reads, *And Aaron stretched out his hand with his rod and smote the dust of the earth* (Verse 13), it was done in the sight of the king. (169) Psalms 78:45.

allusion to death or to the kind of destruction mentioned by our Rabbis,[170] i.e., that the frogs made them impotent. Similarly, [He warned him of] the locusts, [which destroyed the crops], because it would cause the Egyptians to die of hunger, for they ate up *the residue of that which escaped, which remaineth unto you from the hail.* [171] All this reflects His mercies towards man, just as it is said, *Nevertheless, if thou warn the wicked of his way to turn from it, and he turn not from his way; he shall die in his iniquity, but thou hast delivered thy soul.* [172] Therefore, He did not warn Pharaoh of the plagues of gnats, boils, and darkness, [as these did not entail the loss of human lives]. He warned him[173] only of the pestilence of cattle because it involved death which should have taken effect also on man, as He told him afterward, *For now I might have stretched out My hand and I might have smitten thee and thy people with pestilence. But in very deed for this cause have I raised thee up,* etc.[174] Therefore He informed him of what was to happen.

In the case of certain plagues, [i.e., blood, swarms, and hail], G-d said to Moses, *Rise up early in the morning ... lo he cometh forth to the water.*[175] In line with the plain meaning of Scripture,[176] this was the time when the kings were wont to go forth in the morning to enjoy themselves in the waters, and the Holy One, blessed be He, commanded Moses to go there. The reason for it is that since the plague of blood was the first one [of the plagues], He wanted Moses to do it in the sight of the king

---

(170) Shemoth Rabbah 10:4. (171) Further, 10:5. (172) Ezekiel 33:9. (173) Further, 9:3-4. (174) *Ibid.,* Verses 15-16. (175) The three verses are mentioned by Ramban more fully later in the text. Here he mentions the text in a general way although it is based on Verse 16 here. (176) Rashi commented (above, 7:15): "*Lo, he goeth forth unto the water* to ease himself. Pharaoh claimed to be a god and asserted that [because of his divine powers], he did not need to ease himself. Therefore he would rise early and go forth to the Nile to ease himself in secret." This interpretation of Rashi which is based upon a Midrash (Tanchuma Va'eira, 14) is alluded to by Ramban's words that his own explanation is "in line with the plain meaning of Scripture," thus implying that there is a Midrashic or homiletic interpretation of the verse, namely, that of Rashi mentioned above.

and without fear of him. This is the sense of the expression, *and thou shalt place thyself towards him.* [177] Similarly, in the plague of swarms it is said, *Rise up early in the morning, and stand before Pharaoh; lo, he cometh forth to the water,* [178] and also in the case of hail it is said, *Rise up early in the morning and stand before Pharaoh,* [179] which likewise took place when the king went forth to the water. He wanted these two plagues to be wrought [at that particular time] because since swarms and hail brought death and punishment upon the people, the Holy One, blessed be He, wanted the warning to be given in the sight of all people. When the king went forth to the water, a multitude of people followed him, and when Moses will then forewarn him in their sight, perhaps they might plead with their master to return from his evil way. In case they do not do so, they will deserve punishment. But in the case of the other plagues, the warning given to the king alone was sufficient, and therefore in connection with them it is said, *Go in unto Pharaoh,* [180] meaning that Moses was to go into the palace. In the case of gnats and boils, it does not say [that Moses was to go into the palace] because Aaron had to strike the dust of the earth [to bring on the plague of the gnats], and in the king's palace there is no dust, as it has *a pavement of green and white marble.* [181] In the case of boils, Moses had to throw the soot of the furnace heavenward. [182] Thus [we must say that] these two plagues, [i.e., gnats and boils], were done in the sight of Pharaoh when he was *in the court of the garden of the king's palace,* [183] or some similar place.

18. AND I WILL SET APART IN THAT DAY THE LAND OF GOSHEN. Due to the fact that the first plagues were not migratory in nature, it was no wonder that they were confined to the land of Egypt and were not to be in the land of Goshen,

---

(177) Above, 7:15, in the case of the first plague. (178) Here in Verse 16. (179) Further, 9:13. (180) Above, 7:26 (in the plague of frogs); further, 9:1 (pestilence), and 10:1 (locusts). (181) Esther 1:6. (182) Further, 9:10. (183) Esther 1:5.

[Israel's habitation]. [184] But this [plague of swarms] was a migratory plague. Thus when the wild beasts came up *from the lions' dens, from the mountains of the leopards,* [185] and brought ruin upon the whole land of Egypt, it was natural that they also come into the land of Goshen, which contained some of the best of the land of Egypt. [186] Therefore it was necessary for Him to say, *And I will set apart in that day the land of Goshen,* so that it would be completely saved [from the wild beasts] because *My people dwell in it,* as the majority of its inhabitants were Israelites.

And I will put 'p'duth' (a division) between My people and thy people. [187] The intent thereof is that even in the land of Egypt, if the beasts will find a certain Jew, they will not harm him. Instead they will devour the Egyptians, as it is written: *He sent among them swarms of beasts, which devoured them.* [188] This is the sense of the word *'p'duth' between My people and thy people,* which is similar to the verse, *I have given Egypt as thy ransom, Ethiopia and Seba for thee.* [189]

I AM THE ETERNAL IN THE MIDST OF THE EARTH. Rabbi Abraham ibn Ezra explained it as being a figure of speech, emblematic of the nature of kings to establish their seat of government in the center of the kingdom in order to be near to the remote corners thereof. This explanation makes no sense. Rather, its intent is to state that He rules and supervises *in the midst of the earth,* and not, as some think, that *thick clouds are a covering to Him, that He seeth not; and He walketh in the circuit of heaven.* [190] It is possible that the sense of the expression is similar to the verse, *For My name is in him,* [191] and the secret thereof is sublime and recondite. [192]

---

(184) Genesis 47:15. (185) Song of Songs 4:8. (186) See Genesis 47:6, where the land of Goshen is referred to as *the best of the land* of Egypt. (187) Verse 19. (188) Psalms 78:45. (189) Isaiah 43:3. (190) Job 22:14. (191) Further, 23:21. (192) See my Hebrew commentary, p. 314, that the allusion here is to the Cabalistic term of "the upper earth." See Ramban to Genesis 1:5 (Vol. I, pp. 35-38).

25. AND MOSES SAID: BEHOLD, I GO OUT FROM THEE, AND I WILL ENTREAT THE ETERNAL THAT THE SWARMS WILL DEPART FROM PHARAOH, FROM HIS SERVANTS, AND FROM HIS PEOPLE, TOMORROW.[193] Just as Pharaoh, during the plague of the frogs, had asked that it be removed tomorrow,[194] so did Moses want to do it in this case as well; he would pray that the swarms [of beasts] shall depart tomorrow. And then G-d *removed the swarms,*[195] and they vanished completely, unlike the case of the frogs, [where Scripture states that they died].[196] This was for the reason, as stated by our Rabbis,[197] that the Holy One, blessed be He, desired to afflict them with plagues from which they would derive no benefit.[198] Now Moses guarded himself when he spoke to Pharaoh, saying *to destroy the frogs,*[199] which alludes merely to their death, as I have explained there,[199] [while here in the case of swarms, he said *that the swarms will depart*].

3. BEHOLD, THE HAND OF THE ETERNAL IS UPON THY CATTLE WHICH ARE IN THE FIELD. Scripture speaks of the ordinary custom that most cattle are in the field, but the plague was also upon the cattle in the houses, just as it is said, *And all the cattle of Egypt died.*[200] It is possible that because *every shepherd is an abomination unto the Egyptians,*[201] the Egyptians removed the cattle from the cities except for the use of horses for riding and asses for loading. Thus the cattle were located far from Egypt, grazing in the fields bordering upon Goshen, and in those pastures the cattle of the Egyptians and of the Israelites would intermingle. Therefore it was necessary that it be said, *And the*

---

(193) The question here arises: Why did Moses say that he will pray that the removal of the plague be tomorrow, when Pharaoh had just said to him, *Entreat for me* (Verse 24)? Ramban proceeds to answer this question. (194) Above, Verse 6. (195) Verse 27. (196) Above, Verse 9. (197) Shemoth Rabbah 10:6. (198) If the beasts had died in the land of Egypt, the Egyptians would have made use of their skins. Hence they just disappeared. This of course was not the case with the frogs. (199) Above, Verse 5. (200) Verse 6. (201) Genesis 46:34.

Eternal shall make a division between the cattle of Israel and the cattle of Egypt.[202] It may be that the division was necessary because since the pestilence was caused by the change of air, it should naturally spread over the whole district, [affecting the cattle of the Israelites as well], but G-d dealt wondrously with them.[203]

9. AND IT SHALL BECOME SMALL DUST OVER ALL THE LAND OF EGYPT. According to the opinion of our Rabbis,[204] [the small quantity of] soot [in the hands of Moses] became the dust which settled over the whole land of Egypt, and that dust, coming *upon man and upon beast,* caused them to break forth with boils and blains *throughout all the land of Egypt,* since it was a burning hot dust. Perhaps the wind caused the dust to enter the homes as well, and there was thus no escape from it. This is a correct [conjecture]. Many times during a drought, the fall of the dew is accompanied by a sort of dust, and it is furthermore written, *The Eternal will make the rain of thy land powder and dust.*[205]

It is also possible to say, in line with the plain meaning of Scripture, that the purport of the expression, *And it shall become small dust,* is that the dust which will be produced in that place from the soot will bring the boils *over all the land of Egypt,* as He infected the air to do so, it being a decree of the Supreme One.[206]

11. AND THE MAGICIANS COULD NOT STAND BEFORE MOSES. *They were ashamed, and confounded, and covered their*

---

(202) Verse 4.   (203) See Joel 2:26.   (204) Shemoth Rabbah 11:6. (205) Deuteronomy 28:24.   (206) According to this interpretation, the miracle entailed was thus greater than the one in consonance with the first interpretation, which had the dust throughout the land of Egypt causing the boils and the blains. According to the second interpretation, the soot of the furnace became dust only over the place where the miracle was wrought, which in turn caused the whole atmosphere over Egypt to effect the boils.

heads [207] since they were full of boils and could not rescue themselves. Therefore they made no appearance in the royal palace, nor did they appear before Moses in the streets. And so they were imprisoned in their homes.

12. AND THE ETERNAL HARDENED THE HEART OF PHARAOH. It is possible that during the first plagues, the magicians hardened Pharaoh's heart in order to pride themselves in their wisdom. But now that they did not come before him and there was none to help him and none to uphold him [208] in his folly except his iniquities that ensnared him, [209] [it was G-d Who hardened his heart]. It is possible that Scripture is alluding to that which our Rabbis have explained, [210] i.e., that during the first plagues, the hardening of Pharaoh's heart was his own doing, [211] and now it was [rightfully] caused by G-d, as I have explained above. [212] This is the true explanation.

In view of the fact that Scripture states, *A very grievous hail, such as hath not been in Egypt since the day it was founded,* and repeats it again, *Very grievous, such as had not been in all the land of Egypt since it became a nation,* [213] there is an allusion that there are other places in the world where such hail did come down, such as is mentioned in the verse, *And the Eternal cast down great stones from heaven upon them,* [214] or as is mentioned in connection with [the destruction of] Sodom, *brimstone, and salt, and fire.* [215] But in the land of Egypt, where there is no rain or hail, this was a great wonder.

I have not understood what is said in Midrash Rabbah: [216] "The verse does not say, 'as hath not been in Egypt like it,' but instead

---

(207) Jeremiah 14:3. (208) See Isaiah 63:5. (209) See Proverbs 5:22. (210) Shemoth Rabbah 11:7. (211) And not, as stated before, that it was caused by the magicians, who were proud of their arts. (212) Above, 7:3. (213) Further, Verses 18 and 24. (214) Joshua 10:11. (215) Deuteronomy 29:22. (216) Shemoth Rabbah 12:2. In our Midrash, there is a different version of this text. See also my Hebrew commentary, p. 316.

it says, 'as hath not been like it in Egypt,' which means there has neither been like it in the world nor in Egypt."²¹⁷ And the expression, *since the day it was founded,* is equivalent to saying: "Your fathers and your grandfathers have never seen the like of it." But it is not possible to say that it suggests that the like of it occurred before the world was founded or before the inception of nations. Perhaps because this hail came as a punishment upon the inhabitants of Egypt and was not in the natural order, [the verse] is saying that nothing like it has ever occurred because of the sins of the fathers, for before the inception of Egypt as a nation, surely there was no [reason for] such hail to come.

18. BEHOLD, TOMORROW ABOUT THIS TIME I WILL CAUSE IT TO RAIN A VERY GRIEVOUS HAIL, etc. 19. NOW THEREFORE SEND, HASTEN IN THY CATTLE. All this is G-d's word to Moses, and it is self-understood that Moses came and told Pharaoh all the words of G-d that He sent him to speak, and there was no need to prolong the account [of Moses' going to Pharaoh and so telling him]. Scripture only states, *He that feared the word of the Eternal among the servants of Pharaoh made his servants and his cattle flee into the houses,* ²¹⁸ from which it is clear that Moses had told them [G-d's words]. This advice was on account of G-d's being merciful to them, since the plague of hail was sent only against the produce of the earth and not against man, *therefore doth He instruct sinners in the way* ²¹⁹ to save them from the plague.

26. ONLY IN THE LAND OF GOSHEN, WHERE THE CHILDREN OF ISRAEL WERE, WAS THERE NO HAIL. Because Moses had stretched forth his hand toward heaven and brought

---

(217) This Midrash is in clear contradiction to that which Ramban stated above, i.e., that such hail has come down in other places. Therefore Ramban preceded the Midrash by saying that he does not understand it. Since Ramban's opinion is based upon the verses mentioned above, he cannot revoke his opinion as being incorrect.   (218) Verse 20.   (219) Psalms 25:8.

EXODUS IX, VA'EIRA

down the hail, [220] it should have followed that it came down also upon the land of Goshen, as the air thereof and that of Egypt are the same. Therefore Scripture explained that the air over the land of Goshen was saved [from the hail] because the children of Israel were there.

27. I HAVE SINNED THIS TIME. The explanation thereof is: "This time I will acknowledge the Eternal, [221] for I have sinned against Him, and He is the righteous One, *and I and my people are wicked,* for we have rebelled against His word from then until now."

29. AS SOON AS I AM GONE OUT OF THE CITY, I WILL SPREAD FORTH MY HANDS UNTO THE ETERNAL. In line with the plain meaning of Scripture, it is possible to say that [on other occasions] Moses prayed in his house, [which was within the city]. However, this time He saw fit that his hands be spread heavenward so that the thunders and the hail cease immediately, and that was impossible to be done in the city [because it was replete with idols]. Hence he said, *As soon as I am gone out of the city.* And so it is said further on, *And Moses went out of the city from Pharaoh, and spread forth his hands.*[222] But at first, [i.e., during the plague of swarms], Moses said to Pharaoh, *Behold, I go out from thee, and I will entreat the Eternal,*[223] [for as soon as he left the palace he went to his house in the city and prayed].

But our Rabbis have said [224] that Moses "did not pray within the city because it was full of idols, and all the more He did not converse with him except outside the city." If so, we must say that since Pharaoh now pleaded with Moses that he remove the hail immediately, [225] Moses found it necessary to explain to him

---

(220) Verse 23. (221) See Ramban above, 8:15, that throughout, Pharaoh did not acknowledge the Eternal, the G-d of Israel. Ramban points out that this was the first time Pharaoh did acknowledge Him. Ramban transposes the words, *chatathi hapa'am Hashem hatzadik,* and explains them as follows: "*This time* I acknowledge *the Eternal,* for *I have sinned* against Him, etc." (222) Verse 33. (223) Above, 8:25. (224) Mechilta Introduction, and quoted further on (12:1) by Rashi. (225) Verse 28.

that he must go out of the city first and after that he will spread forth his hands to the Eternal, and He will remove it on account of his prayer. This is the true explanation.

30. I KNOW THAT 'TEREM' (NOT YET) [226] WILL YE FEAR THE ETERNAL G-D. Rabbi Abraham ibn Ezra correctly criticized Rashi [for explaining that wherever the word *terem* occurs in Scripture, it signifies "not yet" and does not mean "before"]. It is the opposite: it does not mean "no," but rather it means "before." And Ibn Ezra explained that the verse here is missing one word, [namely, *zeh* (this), making it read]: *terem zeh tir'un*. That is to say, "Before I will spread forth my hands and the thunders and hail will cease, ye do fear G-d, for after the removal of the plague you will return and rebel against Him."

It is furthermore correct to explain [227] that Moses is also alluding to the first occasions, saying: "I know from your [former actions] that before [I pray on your behalf] you fear G-d, and in the end, [after I pray], you rebel against Him. Before the plagues are removed from you, you fear G-d as you did in the plague of frogs and of swarms, and then you returned *and ye rebelled against the commandment of the Eternal,* [228] and so will you continue to be forever." It was for this reason that when Pharaoh recanted [his promise to let the people go], Moses no longer warned him of that but instead knowingly prayed on his behalf during the plague of the locust, [229] in order that he continue to sin.

31-32. AND THE FLAX AND THE BARLEY WERE SMITTEN, etc. Scripture narrates what happened, but I do not know why these two verses were entered in this place before the subject of Moses' prayer and the removal of the hail was completed. In the

(226) This translation accords with the interpretation of Rashi. Ibn Ezra's explanation as well as that of Ramban will differ, as explained further. (227) Ramban now proceeds to explain in a manner where it is not necessary to posit the absence of a word in the text of the verse. It thus has an advantage over that of Ibn Ezra. (228) Deuteronomy 1:47. (229) Further, 10:18.

name of Rav Saadia Gaon,[230] the commentators have said that these [two verses are also part of] Moses' words to Pharaoh. He said to him: "Before you had feared G-d and said, *The Eternal is the righteous One,* [231] the flax and the barley were already smitten and these can no longer be saved. *But the wheat and the spelt were not smitten* yet, and henceforth you will no longer suffer damage."

I find no sense in this explanation. *The hail smote every herb of the field* [232] and broke every tree,[232] and the wheat and the spelt were saved only because they had not sprouted at all or because they were so tender that they were not destroyed completely by the hail since they could sprout again. That being the case, even if the hail had continued for days more to come down upon them, there would not be a loss. There was thus no need for Moses to inform Pharaoh of what he lost and what he did not lose, for when the hail will be removed, he will himself see!

In my opinion, these are Moses' words to Pharaoh. Moses said to him: "I know that before the plagues are removed, you fear G-d, and afterward you repeat your folly.[233] Now the flax and the barley were smitten while the wheat and the spelt which are your livelihood were not smitten in this plague, but it is within G-d's power to destroy them if you return and sin again before Him." Thus Moses alluded to them that which G-d said later [of the locust], *And they shall eat the residue of that which escaped.* [234]

---

(230) Mentioned by Ibn Ezra here. One of the greatest Jewish personalities of all times, Rav Saadia (892 or 882-942) was Gaon of the Academy of Sura. He wrote extensively on every aspect of Jewish learning: Bible, Talmud, grammar, philology, philosophy, polemics against the Karaites, etc. His work, Ha'emunoth Vehadei'oth, the first of its kind in the field of Jewish religious philosophy, exercised a great influence on Jewish thought. He translated the Scriptures into Arabic and wrote extensive commentaries in Arabic on the books of the Bible, which influenced the later commentators. Ramban's knowledge of his commentaries, as indicated here, seems to have been mainly through a secondary source. See, however, Note 224 in *Seder Shemoth* that there is some proof indicating that Ramban may have seen the Gaon's commentary in the original Arabic. (231) Verse 27. (232) Verse 25. (233) See Proverbs 26:11. (234) Further, 10:5.

Bo

10   1. AND THE ETERNAL SAID UNTO MOSES: GO IN UNTO PHARAOH; FOR I HAVE HARDENED HIS HEART AND THE HEART OF HIS SERVANTS. The Holy One, blessed be He, informed Moses that it is He Who has hardened their hearts in spite of their fear of Him during the hail and their confession of sin.[1] And He explained to him: "The reason I hardened their hearts is that I might set in their midst these signs that I wish to do among them so that the Egyptians will know My power, but not in order that I can punish them more on account of this hardening of heart, and also that you and all Israel should recount during the coming generations the power of My deeds, *and you shall know that I am the Eternal*,[2] and whatsoever I please, I do in heaven and in earth."[3]

2. 'HITH'ALALTI.' "*I have mocked* him, for it is I Who hardened his heart and exacted punishments of him." This is similar in intent to the verse: *He that sits in heaven smiles, the Eternal mocks them.*[4]

The Holy One, blessed be He, now informed Moses of the plague of locusts, [although this is not stated here in Scripture], and that he should tell it to Pharaoh, for what sense was there that

---

(1) Although Scripture above (9:27) mentions only Pharaoh confessing his sin, it is apparent from Verse 30 there that the king's servants also made this confession, since Moses said to all of them, *But as for thee and thy servants, I know that ye will not yet fear the Eternal G-d.* This is a clear indication that the servants too had joined the king in admitting their guilt. Ramban is thus correct in writing here in the plural: " *their* confession of sin."   (2) Verse 2.   (3) See Psalms 135:6.   (4) *Ibid.*, 2:4.

100

he be commanded, *Go in unto Pharaoh*,⁵ and not say something to him, the plague being mentioned only in the words of Moses to Pharaoh,⁶ as Scripture spoke succinctly of this. So also was the case above with the plague of hail, where Scripture told of the words of the Holy One, blessed be He, to Moses, *Stand before Pharaoh, and say unto him*, etc.,⁷ but did not at all mention that Moses said so to Pharaoh, as I have explained.⁸ The reason for it is that Scripture does not want to elaborate on it in two places, [i.e., when G-d said it to Moses, and when Moses relayed it to Pharaoh], and so it shortens the narrative sometimes at one point and other times at another.

In Eileh Shemoth Rabbah,⁹ I have seen it stated: "*And that thou mayest tell in the ears of thy son.* The Holy One, blessed be He, informed Moses what plague He is about to bring upon them, and Moses wrote it down with a hint: *And that thou mayest tell in the ears of thy son, and of thy son's son,* which is an allusion to the plague of locusts, just as it is said [of the locusts in the days of the prophet Joel], *Tell ye your children of it, and let your children tell their children,* etc." ¹⁰

3. AND MOSES AND AARON CAME IN UNTO PHARAOH. Rabbi Abraham ibn Ezra commented: "We know that Moses never came to Pharaoh without being accompanied by Aaron, who was the interpreter.¹¹ Scripture here makes a point of mentioning Moses and Aaron in order [to make clear] that Pharaoh's command that both of them be brought again before him ¹² and his final act of driving them out ¹³ — something he had not done previously — [applied to the two brothers alike]."

---

(5) Verse 1. (6) Verses 4-6. (7) Above, 9:13. (8) *Ibid.*, Verse 18. (9) Shemoth Rabbah 13:5. (10) Joel 1:3. This was said by the prophet during the terrible plague of locusts and drought. See Ramban further, Verse 14. The Midrash thus confirms Ramban's explanation that within G-d's command to Moses, as stated in the Torah, there was also included the oral communication concerning the locusts. The Midrash however added that the plague is alluded to in the expression, *And that thou mayest tell*, etc., which is a reference to the locusts. (11) Above, 7:2. (12) Further, Verse 8. (13) *Ibid.*, Verse 11.

4. BEHOLD, TOMORROW WILL I BRING LOCUSTS. Commentators [14] have said that there was a long interval between the plague of hail and that of locusts, as is suggested by the expression, *and* [the locusts] *shall eat every tree which groweth for you out of the field.*[15] In my opinion, the interval between these plagues was not a long one but rather was very brief. It is known that the judgment of the Egyptians did not last more than a year, this being so established through our knowledge of the years of Moses our Teacher,[16] just as we have been taught in Tractate Eduyoth:[17] "The judgment of the Egyptians in Egypt endured twelve months." And so it is indicated by Scripture when saying, *and they shall eat the residue of that which is escaped, which remaineth unto you from the hail.*[18] And it is further written, *even all that the hail had left,*[19] thus indicating that it was in that very same year. If so, [we must say that] the hail came down that year during the month of Adar, not before, *for the barley was in the ears*[20] [and therefore smitten by the hail], but the wheat had not grown up [21] and therefore its tender sprouts could not be completely destroyed by the hail, as they would grow back again. Then too the vine had not yet budded, and the trees were not in flower. It is for this reason that Scripture states, *and* [the hail] *broke every tree of the field,*[22] meaning that it broke the branches and boughs. Then, in one month's time, in the month of Nisan, the wheat and the spelt grew, these being *the residue of that which is escaped, which remaineth unto you from the hail,*[18] and the trees began to blossom and the flowers appeared. This then is the purport of the word *hatzomei'ach*

(14) Ibn Ezra (Verse 5) in the name of another commentator. (15) In the present verse. Since we have been told that the hail broke every tree of the field (above, 9:25), a long interval must have passed to allow the trees to grow back. (16) Moses was eighty years old when he stood before Pharaoh (above, 7:7). Add the forty years of the desert, and you have the one hundred and twenty years he lived (Deuteronomy 34:7). Thus, the elapsed time of all the ten punishments decreed for Egypt could not possibly have been more than a year. (17) Eduyoth 2:10. (18) Verse 5. (19) Further, Verse 12. (20) Above, 9:31. (21) *Ibid.*, Verse 32. (22) Above, 9:25.

EXODUS X, BO

(which groweth),[18] since the locusts came and ate their blossoms and thus destroyed everything since they did not leave them a blossom or flower. And in this very month, the children of Israel were redeemed [from Egypt]. The verse which states [that the locusts consumed] *all the fruit of the tree,*[23] [which would indicate that there were fruits already on the tree and, therefore, that a long interval must have passed between the plagues of hail and locusts], is to be understood as referring to the flower which produces the fruits, similar to the expression, *every herb on the tree,* [23] [which cannot be understood literally, since herbs do not grow on trees. Consequently, it must be understood as Rashi has it: "any green leaf on the tree." Here too then, "the fruit of the tree" is not to be taken literally, but should be understood as "the flower of the tree"].

6. AND HE TURNED AND WENT OUT FROM PHARAOH. Due to the fact that the Egyptians were in a state of trepidation during the plague of hail, Moses thought that now too they would fear lest they die from famine if they lose *the residue of that which is escaped,*[18] which remained to them. Therefore he went out without the king's permission before they accepted or rejected his request, so that they might take counsel on the matter. This was indeed correct, for so the servants did and said to Pharaoh, *Knowest thou not yet that Egypt is destroyed?*[24] In the words of our Rabbis: [25] "Moses saw the servants turning to each other, believing in his words, so he went out from there in order that they may take counsel to do repentance."

The correct interpretation appears to me to be that Moses did so every time he came to Pharaoh's palace; he warned him and went out. Scripture found it necessary to mention it only here because of the sequel: *And Moses and Aaron were brought again unto Pharaoh.* [26]

---

(23) Verse 15. (24) Verse 7. (25) Shemoth Rabbah 13:5. (26) Verse 8.

8. BUT WHO ARE THEY THAT SHALL GO? Pharaoh desired that their leaders, elders, and officers [27] should go, *men that are pointed out by name*.[28] Moses answered him that also the sons and daughters will go, *"for we must hold a feast unto the Eternal*,[29] and it is mandatory upon us all to take part in the feast." Pharaoh's anger was then kindled on account of the sons and daughters, and he said that under no circumstances will he send the little ones, for they take no part in the offerings. Instead he would send all the adult males because of the feast which Moses mentioned, while the little ones and the women will remain [in Egypt].

10. SEE YE THAT EVIL IS BEFORE YOUR FACE. "The intent of the verse is as the Targum [Onkelos] explained it." Thus the language of Rashi. Now how commendable it would have been if Rashi had written out [the text of Onkelos he referred to], since there are variant texts of this Targum! In some texts, it is written: "See, the evil you are about to do is set against you." [30] According to this text, it appears that Onkelos intended to explain: "the evil you are contemplating to do is set before you, bearing witness against you that it is your desire to escape altogether." This is similar to the verse, *And set two men, base fellows, before him* [Naboth], *and let them bear witness against him, saying*, etc.[31] It is also similar to [the expressions]: *And they sat down to eat bread*,[32] which the Targum translates *v'istacharu* (and they sat down), [the same as the term *istacharat* that appears to be in the Targum here]; *Arise, I pray thee, sit*,[33] which the Targum translates *istachar* (sit).

And there are versions of [Targum Onkelos] in which it is written: "will turn against yourself." [34] The purport thereof is

---

(27) See Deuteronomy 29:9. (28) Numbers 1:17. (29) Verse 9. (30) This is not the text found in our version of Targum Onkelos. Ramban will later mention two other variants of Onkelos' text here. See Note 34 for the text found in our version of the Targum. (31) I Kings 21:10. (32) Genesis 30:25. (33) *Ibid.*, 27:19. (34) This text appears in our version of Targum Onkelos.

EXODUS X, BO

thus: "Behold, this evil you are about to do is destined to turn against you, for it will pass upon you." This is similar to the expression, *So shall no inheritance of the children of Israel pass from tribe to tribe,* [35] which the Targum translates: *lo tistachar* (not pass), [similar to the Targum here, *l'istachro*]. This explanation finds authority in the Midrash of the Sages, who said in Eileh Shemoth Rabbah: [36] "[Pharaoh said]: 'It is the custom of young men and the elders to offer sacrifice, but is it the custom of children and the little ones to do so? He who says so intends only to escape. See that which you want to do, namely to escape, will turn against you, that you will not go forth from here,' " a kind of measure for measure.

And I have found yet another version in the Targum: "your countenance does not bear witness to the absence of this evil," meaning that "your countenance does not bear witness to the removal of the evil in your hearts. On the contrary, the show of your countenance bears witness against you."

In line with the plain meaning of Scripture, [the intent of the verse is to be understood as follows]: "Know that evil is before you, ready and imminent to come upon you from me, for I will requite you evil when I see that you want to escape."

14. NEITHER AFTER THEM SHALL BE SUCH [LOCUSTS]. Scripture informs us by way of prophecy that after them, there would never be such [locusts]. Now Rashi commented: "[The plague of locusts] which occurred during the days of Joel, of which it is said, *There hath not been ever the like,* [37] teaches us that it was greater [38] than that in the days of Moses. The one that happened in the days of Joel was caused by many species together: locust, caterpillar, canker-worm, palmer-worm. [39] But the one which occurred in the days of Moses consisted only of one species, the like of which there never was and never will be."

---

(35) Numbers 36:7.   (36) Shemoth Rabbah 13:5.   (37) Joel 2:2.
(38) "Greater." In our text of Rashi: "more grievous."   (39) Joel 2:4.

I have found difficulty in understanding the explanation of the Rabbi [Rashi]. It is written [of the plague which happened in the days of Moses], *He also gave their produce unto the caterpillar,* [40] and it is also written, *He spoke, and the locust came, and the canker-worm without number.* [41] Perhaps the Rabbi [Rashi] will answer by saying that in the days of Moses, locust proper was greater than that in the days of Joel, but all other species of locusts in the days of Joel were greater than those in the days of Moses. But these are useless arguments. [42] Instead, [we must say that the expression], *in all the borders of Egypt,* is connected with the end of the verse: *before them there were no such locusts as they, neither after them shall be such* there [in Egypt, but in other places there may be]. [43] It is possible that because the land of Egypt is exceedingly moistened by the river, locusts are not abundant there, for these naturally come in years of drought, as is mentioned by the prophet Joel. [44]

Now Rabbeinu Chananel [45] has written in his commentary on the Torah: "From the time that Moses our teacher prayed [for the removal of the locusts] till now, the locusts have not caused

---

(40) Psalms 78:46.   (41) *Ibid.*, 105:34. Thus it is clear that in the plague which occurred in the days of Moses, there were also many species of locusts involved, unlike Rashi's explanation above.   (42) It is illogical to say that the Torah here attached such importance to the plague just because one of the species involved was greater than that in the days of Joel, although in the number of species, the plague of locusts which occurred in the days of the prophet was unparalleled. (Mizrachi in explanation of Ramban's intent.) (43) There is thus no contradiction to the prophet Joel's words. That plague of locusts did not occur in the land of Egypt.   (44) *For the water brooks are dried up* (Joel 1:20).   (45) A Rabbi of Kairwan, North Africa, who flourished in the first half of the eleventh century, just when the Gaonic period in Babylon was about to come to a close. Rabbeinu Chananel's commentaries on the Talmud are among the most important works in Rabbinic literature. He also wrote a commentary on the Torah, which has been lost in the course of time, except for important extracts from it which are found mostly in the commentary of Bachya ben Asher. Some extracts are found in the works of Ramban and in the Sermons of Yehoshua ibn Shuib, a pupil of Rashba. An edition of mine of these collected explanations of Rabbeinu Chananel has recently appeared through the Mosad Harav Kook, Jerusalem, and they indicate a wide spectrum of interests on the part of the author in Biblical themes.

damage to the entire land of Egypt, and if an attack of them does occur in the Land of Israel and they proceed to enter within the border of Egypt, they do not devour the produce of the land. People say that this is known by all. Come and see! In the case of frogs, Moses said, *Only in the river they will remain,* [46] and therefore the *altamtzach* — [the Arabic word for frogs] — have remained in the river till now. However, in the case of the locusts it is written, *There remained not one locust in all the border of Egypt.* [47] It is of a phenomenon of this kind that Scripture says, *Speak ye of all His marvellous works."* [48] Thus the language of the Rabbi.

In my opinion, the plain meaning of the verse, [*neither after them shall be such*], is that because the plague of locusts is known to come in all generations, and moreover since this one [in the days of Moses] came in a natural way, it having been the east wind that brought the locusts, [49] [and there was thus reason to believe that such a plague would again come upon Egypt in a natural way], Scripture therefore states that such locusts were the greatest that ever occurred in the natural order of things. Neither before them were there such locusts as they, nor after them shall be such. Through the magnitude of the plague, the Egyptians thus knew that it was a special act of G-d, since the like never happened before. [The plague] that occurred in the days of Joel was likewise a special act of G-d, [and hence Scripture also describes it by saying, *There hath never been the like*].[37]

17. NOW THEREFORE FORGIVE, I PRAY THEE, MY SIN. This is an expression of respect to Moses [on the part of Pharaoh] since Moses was *in G-d's stead to Pharaoh,* [50] *and very great in the land of Egypt.* [51] [Hence Pharaoh addressed this appeal to Moses alone, as the singular verb *sa* (forgive) indicates, for the king knew of the extraordinary position of Moses, as explained.] *And entreat ye the Eternal your G-d.* He addressed this appeal to both Moses

---

(46) Above, 8:5. (47) Further, Verse 19. (48) Psalms 105:2. (49) Verse 13. (50) Above, 7:1. (51) Further, 11:3.

and Aaron. He respectfully spoke thus every time [that he asked for prayer on his behalf][52] although Pharaoh knew that Moses alone was the one who prayed, for so he told him: *Against what time shall I entreat for thee;*[53] *And I will entreat the Eternal;*[54] *I will spread forth my hands to the Eternal.*[55] Moses did not say it in the plural, [i.e., "we shall entreat"], so that he should not utter a falsehood, [but Pharaoh nevertheless addressed himself to both as an expression of respect].

23. THEY SAW NOT ONE ANOTHER, NEITHER ROSE ANY FROM HIS PLACE. The meaning thereof is that this darkness was not a mere absence of sunlight where the sun set and it was like night. Rather, it was *a thick darkness.*[56] That is to say, it was a very thick cloud that came down from heaven. It is for this reason that He said, "*Stretch out thy hand toward heaven*[57] to bring down from there a great darkness which would descend upon them[58] and which would extinguish every light, just as in all deep caverns and in all extremely dark places where light cannot last [as it is swallowed up in the density of the thick darkness]." Similarly, people who pass through the Mountains of Darkness[59] find that no candle or fire can continue to burn at all. It is for this reason that *they saw not one another, neither rose any from his place,* for otherwise they would have used the light of fire. This is the intent of the verse, *He sent darkness, and it became dark.*[60] It was not the usual absence of daylight above but an extraordinary

---

(52) Above, 8:4 (in the case of frogs), 8:24 (swarms of beasts), and 9:38 (hail). In each case, Pharaoh said *ha'tiru* (pray ye) in the plural. (53) *Above,* 8:5. *(54) Ibid.,* Verse 25. (55) *Ibid.,* 9:29. (56) Verse 22. (57) Verse 21. (58) See Genesis 15:12. (59) The name is found in the Talmud (Tamid 32a) in connection with Alexander the Great, who told the Sages of the south: "I wish to go to the country of Africa," whereupon they answered him, "you cannot go, for the Mountains of Darkness intercede." It would seem then that these were mountains somewhere in the heart of Africa, a dim knowledge of which reached the outer world. Considering the fact that the heart of central Africa was not penetrated by European explorers till the end of the nineteenth century, it is no wonder that not much was known in Medieval Europe about this region. (60) Psalms 105:28.

EXODUS X, BO

darkness as well. It is possible that it was such a very thick cloud that there was something tangible in it, as our Rabbis have said,[61] and as indeed it happens on the Atlantic Ocean, as Rabbi Abraham ibn Ezra testified.[62]

24. ONLY LET YOUR FLOCKS AND YOUR HERDS BE STAYED. Since the Israelites *were keepers of cattle,*[63] and all their wealth and belongings consisted of cattle, Pharaoh thought that they would not leave all their possessions and flee from the country. Even if they were to flee, he would be left with their great wealth, as they were very rich in cattle.

25. THOU MUST ALSO GIVE INTO OUR HAND SACRIFICES AND BURNT-OFFERINGS. Moses did not make this a condition, neither did Pharaoh. Rather, these are words to impress Pharaoh. In effect Moses was saying to him that G-d's power will be so heavy upon him and his people that even sacrifices and burnt-offerings *and all that he hath will he give for his life.*[64] Indeed, when Pharaoh said to Moses and Aaron [at the time that he gave the people permission to go], *And bless me also,*[65] he would willingly have given all his cattle in atonement for his sin [of rebelling against G-d's command till then]. Moses however had no intention to do so, for *the sacrifice of the wicked is an abomination,*[66] as *it pleased the Eternal to crush him,*[67] not to forgive him but instead to punish him and to overthrow him with all his host in the midst of the sea.

Now our Rabbis have said[68] that Pharaoh's expression [to Moses and Aaron], *Take both your flocks and your herds, as ye*

---

(61) Shemoth Rabbah 14:1. (62) "It often happens on the Atlantic Ocean that it is impossible to distinguish day from night, and this sometimes lasts for five days. I have personally experienced it many times" (Ibn Ezra). A native of Spain, Ibn Ezra was born in the city of Tudela in the year 1093. In search of knowledge, he journeyed throughout the European countries and the Near East, where he made the acquaintance of the greatest luminaries of his time. Sometime after 1150, he visited London, where in the course of his journey he most likely experienced the density of fog he describes. (63) Genesis 46:32. (64) Job 2:4. (65) Further, 12:32. (66) Proverbs 21:27. (67) Isaiah 53:10. (68) Mechilta d'Rabbi Shimon ben Yochai, on the Verse further, 12:32.

have said, [65] refers to their saying to him, *Thou must also give into our hand sacrifices and burnt-offerings.* Perhaps the Rabbis intended to say that Pharaoh hinted to Moses and Aaron that he is ready to give them whatever they say, but not at all that they took anything from him. It may be that he supplied them with sacrifices and burnt-offerings for their use so that the Israelites would fulfill their own obligation [in the observance of G-d's feast]. But this also is not correct. [69]

29. AND MOSES SAID: THOU HAST SPOKEN WELL; I WILL NOT SEE THY FACE AGAIN ANY MORE. That is, "I will not see you again after I leave you." After the plague of the firstborn, Moses did not see Pharaoh. The meaning of the verse, *And he called for Moses and Aaron,* [70] is [not that he called them to come to see him, but instead] that he himself went to the entrance of their home and shouted in the darkness, *Rise up, get you forth from among my people.* [70] Perhaps he sent the message to them by Egyptians, of whom it is said, *And the Egyptians were urgent upon the people to send them out of the land in haste.*[71]

It is possible that the verse, *I will not see thy face again any more,* means "in your palace," namely, "I will not come to you any more." And so the Rabbis have said in Eileh Shemoth Rabbah: [72] "You have spoken well in saying, *See my face no more.* [73] I will not come to you again; you will come to me." [74]

---

(69) Since permission for their own cattle for sacrifices was specifically made a condition by Moses [here in Verse 26 — *Our cattle shall also go with us... for thereof must we take to serve the Eternal our G-d*] — it could not be correct to say that they later took sacrifices for themselves from Pharaoh. We must therefore conclude that Pharaoh only hinted to them that he was ready to give them whatever they demand, but actually they took no animals from him for sacrifice.   (70) Further, 12:31.   (71) *Ibid.,* Verse 33.   (72) Shemoth Rabbah 14:4.   (73) Verse 28.   (74) According to this Midrash then, Moses did see Pharaoh later, but the king came to him. According to the first explanation, however, after he left the palace this time, Moses no longer saw Pharaoh at all.

11

1. AND THE ETERNAL SAID UNTO MOSES: YET ONE PLAGUE MORE WILL I BRING UPON PHARAOH. "This [prophecy] was spoken to him while he was still standing before Pharaoh, for after he left him he did not see his face again." Thus the language of Rashi.

Our Rabbis have similarly said:[75] "G-d sprung upon Moses. He, as it were, entered Pharaoh's palace, [which was replete with abominations], for the sake of Moses — who had said, *I will see thy face again no more* —[76] so that Moses might not be branded a liar. Now you find no other occasion on which the Holy One, blessed be He, spoke to Moses in the royal palace except this moment. Whence may we deduce this? From the verse, *As soon as I am gone out of the city, I will spread forth my hands unto the Eternal.*[77] But now the Holy One, blessed be He, sprang upon Moses and said to him, *Yet one plague more,* etc."

Now here too [78] there is a shortening of narrative. G-d said to Moses, *Yet one plague more will I bring upon Pharaoh,* and He informed him of the nature of that plague, saying to him, *At midnight I will go out into the midst of Egypt,* as well as the whole communication stated in this section, [further in Verses 5-8, as Moses' address to Pharaoh in the Name of G-d]. But Scripture did not want to lengthen the account by first narrating what G-d said to Moses, it being sufficient to state what Moses said to Pharaoh, i.e., *Thus saith the Eternal,*[79] just as I have explained in the case of the locusts.[78] There are many such sections in the Torah. In this *Seder* (section of the Torah), in the segment, *Sanctify unto Me all the firstborn,*[80] Scripture shortens the subject which the Holy One, blessed be He, communicated to Moses, and it prolongs the account of Moses' words to the people, i.e., *Remember this day,* etc.,[81] and so on to the end of that entire segment. [82] They really are G-d's words to Moses, which he said to Israel in the very language with which he was commanded.

---

(75) Shemoth Rabbah 18:1.   (76) Above, 10:29.   (77) *Ibid.,* 9:29. And see Ramban there.   (78) See Ramban above, 10:2.   (79) Verse 4. (80) Further, 13:2.   (81) *Ibid.,* Verse 3.   (82) I.e., to the end of Verse 16 there.

2. SPEAK NOW IN THE EARS OF THE PEOPLE. I.e., after you depart from Pharaoh.

3. AND THE ETERNAL GAVE THE PEOPLE FAVOR IN THE SIGHT OF THE EGYPTIANS. The purport thereof is that the Egyptians did not hate them because of the plagues. Instead, they conceived affection for them, and the Israelites found favor in their eyes, the Egyptians acknowledging, "we are the wicked ones. There is violence in our hands, and you merit that G-d be gracious to you."

MOREOVER, THE MAN MOSES, who brought the plagues upon them, WAS VERY GREAT IN THE ENTIRE LAND OF EGYPT, IN THE SIGHT OF PHARAOH'S SERVANTS — his opponents — AND IN THE SIGHT OF THE PEOPLE, Israel.[83] After [the officers of the children of Israel] had said to Moses and Aaron, *The Eternal look upon you, and judge,*[84] after *they hearkened not unto Moses for impatience of spirit,*[85] he now became very great in their sight when they saw *that he was established to be a prophet of the Eternal.*[86] And some scholars[87] say that the expression, *in the sight of the people,* means the Egyptians.

The reason Scripture does not state [that Moses was very great] "in the sight of Pharaoh and in the sight of his servants," [but instead mentions only Pharaoh's servants], is that G-d made Pharaoh's heart obstinate towards Moses because he [Pharaoh] had twice spoken to him improperly,[88] and He desired that Pharaoh come to Moses and bow down to him as one comes before his enemy, all this being a sign of the power and achievement of Moses.

Now it is impossible to explain the expression, *And the Eternal gave the people favor in the sight of the Egyptians,* as referring to

---

(83) Unlike Ibn Ezra, who explains *in the sight of the people* as referring to the Egyptians. Ramban will refer to this explanation further on. (84) Above, 5:21. (85) *Ibid.*, 6:9. (86) I Samuel 3:20. (87) Ibn Ezra. (88) Above, 10:10 (*So be the Eternal with you, as I will let you go*), and *ibid.*, Verse 28 (*Get thee from me*).

the favor they found in the eyes of the Egyptians at the time of the borrowing, [mentioned further, 12:36]. In that case, the verse there relates that G-d later fulfilled the promise He made here.[89] If the verse here were establishing the Divine promise, [i.e., that the people will find favor in the sight of the Egyptians and that they will let them have what they asked], the verse here should not have said, *And the Eternal gave;* it should have said, "And I will give the people favor." [Hence we must conclude that the intent of the verse here is to be explained as above, i.e., that the Egyptians bore no grudge against the Israelites because of the plagues.] It is further on at the time of the actual event that Scripture says, *And the Eternal gave the people favor in the sight of the Egyptians, so that they let them have what they asked.* [90]

4. AND MOSES SAID: THUS SAITH THE ETERNAL: ABOUT MIDNIGHT WILL I GO OUT INTO THE MIDST OF EGYPT. Moses said this to Pharaoh and to his servants, as he mentioned at the end of his words, *And all these thy servants shall come down unto me.*[91] Now he did not explain on what night this plague will take place, since this Divine communication to Moses and the transmission thereof to Pharaoh happened before the first of Nisan,[92] and when he said *about midnight,* he did not yet know on which night it would be. Thus Moses did not inform them of

(89) The explanation refuted now by Ramban is that of Ibn Ezra [in Verse 3 before us]. (90) Further, 12:36. (91) Verse 8. (92) In view of the fact that Ramban wrote above (10:4) that the plague of the locusts occurred in the month of Nisan, it is difficult to understand his statement here that the Divine communication to Moses and the transmission thereof to Pharaoh concerning the plague of the firstborn happened *before* the first of Nisan. In my opinion, this is to be explained on the basis of that which Ramban wrote in *Seder Shemoth* (4:21), that at the very first time that Moses came before Pharaoh, he warned him of the *last plague* which will force him to let the people go. In that case, the Divine communication to Moses and the transmission of it to Pharaoh did indeed take place before the first of Nisan. The verse here, *yet one plague more will I bring upon Pharaoh,* must then be understood in the sense that G-d told Moses that the time had come for the final plague of which He had told him in the beginning and which Moses had related to Pharaoh. See also my Hebrew commentary, p. 323, for further discussion of this problem.

the specific night on which this plague would take place, but instead he said in kindled anger, *"I will see thy face again no more."* [93] It is you who will call upon me at about midnight to go out from your country, and your servants will bow down to me." [91] In the second section He elucidated to Israel, *And I will go through the land of Egypt in that night,* [94] and in the third section Scripture states, *And it came to pass at midnight,* [95] i.e., the night mentioned when they were eating the paschal lamb.

9. AND THE ETERNAL SAID UNTO MOSES: PHARAOH WILL NOT HEARKEN UNTO YOU. It was to be expected that Pharaoh and his servants should dread the plague of the firstborn and be in consternation thereof moreso than for anything that had happened to them — indeed they had previously seen all the words of Moses fulfilled. G-d therefore informed Moses that it is He Who is hardening his [Pharaoh's] heart, so that His wonders would be multiplied through the plague of the firstborn in both man and beast and the judgments He will execute against their gods. [94]

Rashi commented: *"So that My wonders may be multiplied.* This refers to the slaying of the firstborn, the division of the Red Sea, and the overthrowing of the Egyptians in it." This explanation is not possible, because of the verse after that which states, *And the Eternal hardened Pharaoh's heart, and he did not let the children of Israel go out of his land.* [96]

10. AND MOSES AND AARON DID ALL THESE WONDERS. These are the wonders mentioned above. Scripture states this now because it completes [the narrative of] all the deeds they did

---

(93) Above, 10:29. (94) Further, 12:12. (95) *Ibid.,* Verse 29. (96) Verse 10. This indicates that the expression, *that My wonders may be multiplied,* which was mentioned in Verse 9, refers only to those wonders which took place *before* the exodus, as Verse 10 clearly indicates that on account of the hardening of Pharaoh's heart he did not let the people go. It thus cannot refer to the division of the Red Sea and the overthrowing of the Egyptians in it, as these wonders happened *after* the exodus (Mizrachi).

[before Pharaoh], including the decree of the plague of the firstborn of which they already informed Pharaoh, for in the actual slaying of the firstborn, Moses and Aaron had no part.

12 2. THIS MONTH SHALL BE UNTO YOU THE BEGINNING OF MONTHS. This is the first commandment which the Holy One, blessed be He, commanded Israel through Moses. Therefore it says here [that the Eternal spoke unto Moses and Aaron] *in the land of Egypt,* [97] for the rest of the commandments of the Torah were given to him on Mount Sinai. It may be that the intent of the expression, *in the land of Egypt,* is to exclude the city of Egypt, just as our Rabbis have said: [98] *"In the land of Egypt.* This means outside the city."

Now Scripture should have first said, *Speak ye unto all the congregation of Israel, saying:* [99] *This month shall be unto you the beginning of months,* and so on to the end of the chapter. [Why then is the verse, *Speak ye,* etc., mentioned after the verse, *This month,* etc.?] It is because Moses and Aaron — [as mentioned in Verse 1: *And the Eternal spoke unto Moses and Aaron in the land of Egypt, saying: This month,* etc.] — are in the place of Israel. Saying it to them is equivalent to saying it to Israel in all their generations. In the following verse, however, He repeats by saying, *Speak ye unto all the congregation of Israel,* in order to command them something which is not binding for all time, namely, the buying of the paschal offering in Egypt on the tenth day of Nisan. [100]

---

(97) Verse 1. (98) Mechilta, Introduction. (99) Verse 3. (100) In subsequent generations, the paschal offering may be purchased at any time (Pesachim 96a). Ramban's thought is thus clear. With the commandment, *This month shall be unto you,* etc., applying as it does for all time, it is sufficient for Scripture to mention only Moses and Aaron in connection with it, since they are in place of Israel for all times. But since the command mentioned in Verse 3, *In the tenth day of this month they shall take to them every man a lamb,* applied only to the paschal offering in Egypt, He therefore preceded it again by saying, *Speak ye unto all the congregation of Israel,* the Israel of that time.

According to the Midrashic interpretation,[101] *lachem* (unto you) [in the verse, *This month shall be unto you*], means that "the Sanctification of the New Moon"[101] is to be performed only by a Court of experts [as Moses and Aaron were]. And this is the reason it does not say at the beginning [of Verse 2], *Speak ye unto all the congregation of Israel,* since "the Sanctification of the New Moon" can be performed only by Moses and Aaron and their like.

Now the purport of the expression, *This month shall be unto you the beginning of months,* is that Israel is to count this as the first of the months, and from it they are to count all months — second, third, etc., until a year of twelve months is completed — in order that there be through this enumeration a remembrance of the great miracle, [i.e., the exodus from Egypt, which occurred in the first month]. Whenever we will mention the months, the miracle will be remembered.[102] It is for this reason that the months have no individual names in the Torah. Instead, Scripture says: *In the third month;*[103] *And it came to pass in the second year, in the second month ... that the cloud was taken up from over the Tabernacle of the Testimony;*[104] *And in the seventh month, on the first day of the month,* etc.,[105] and so in all cases. Just as in counting the weekdays we always remember the Sabbath-day since the weekdays have no specific name of their own, but instead are called "one day in the Sabbath," "the second

---

(101) Rosh Hashanah 25 b. The process involved witnesses who saw the appearance of the new moon. After their testimony was heard and examined, the chief of the Court then said, "It is hallowed!" and all the people answered him, "It is hallowed! It is hallowed!" This established that day as being the first of the month, and the occurrence of all festivals of that month were accordingly determined. With the Great Court or Sanhedrin no longer functioning in the Land of Israel, the first of the month is established only by calculating when the new moon appears. For a more detailed discussion of this important topic, see my translation of "The Commandments," Vol. I, pp. 159-163. (102) Thus everytime a person says, for example, "the third month," he implies that it is the third in the order of the months which begins with Nisan, when the exodus occurred. (103) Further, 19:1. (104) Numbers 10:11. (105) *Ibid.,* 29:1.

EXODUS XII, BO

day in the Sabbath," as I will explain,[106] so we remember the exodus from Egypt in our counting "the first month," "the second month," "the third month," etc., to our redemption.

This order of the counting of the months is not in regard to the years, for the beginning of our years is from Tishri, [the seventh month], as it is written, *And the feast of ingathering at the turn of the year,*[107] and it is further written, *And the feast of ingathering, at the end of the year.*[108] If so, when we call the month of Nisan the first of the months and Tishri the seventh, the meaning thereof is "the first [month] to the redemption" and "the seventh month" thereto. This then is the intent of the expression, *it shall be the first month to you,* meaning that it is not the first in regard to the year but it is the first "to you," i.e., that it be called "the first" for the purpose of remembering our redemption.

Our Rabbis have already mentioned this matter when saying, [109] "The names of the months came up with us from Babylon," since at first we had no names for the months. The reason for this [adoption of the names of the months when our ancestors returned from Babylon to build the Second Temple], was that at first their reckoning was a memorial to the exodus from Egypt, but when we came up from Babylon, and the words of Scripture were fulfilled — *And it shall no more be said: As the Eternal liveth, that brought up the children of Israel out of the land of Egypt, but: As the Eternal liveth that brought up and that led the children of Israel from the land of the north*[110] — from then on we began to call the months by the names they were called in the land of Babylon. We are thus reminded that there we stayed [during our exile] and from there, blessed G-d brought us up [to

---

(106) Further, 20:8.   (107) *Ibid.,* 34:22. Now the feast of ingathering is in the seventh month (Leviticus 23:39) and yet Scripture calls it here *at the turn of the year,* which means the beginning of the new year. Thus we learn that Tishri is the beginning of the year, although in the order of the counting of the months it is the seventh month.   (108) *Ibid.,* 23:16.   (109) Yerushalmi Rosh Hashanah I, 2.   (110) Jeremiah 16:14-15. The expression *and that led* is found *ibid.,* 23:8.

our Land].[111] These names — Nisan, Iyar, and the others — are Persian names and are to be found only in the books of the prophets of the Babylonian era[112] and in the Scroll of Esther.[113] It is for this reason that Scripture says, *In the first month, which is the month of Nisan,*[114] just as it says, *they cast 'pur,' that is, the lot.*[115] To this day, people of Persia and Media use these names of the months — Nisan, Tishri, and the others — as we do. Thus through the names of the months we remember our second redemption even as we had done until then with regard to the first one.

3. THEY SHALL TAKE TO THEM EVERY MAN A LAMB, ACCORDING TO THEIR FATHERS' HOUSES. The reason for this commandment is that the constellation of Aries (the Ram) is at the height of its power in the month of Nisan, it being the sign of the zodiac which ascends the heavens.[116] Therefore He commanded us to slaughter the sheep and to eat it in order to inform us that it was not by the power of that constellation that

(111) From Ramban's "Sermon on Rosh Hashanah," where he discussed the same topic (Kithvei Haramban, Vol. I, p. 215), it is crystal clear that the author's intent here was not that the memorial of the redemption from Babylon will thrust aside the memorial of the redemption from Egypt. Rather, the one of Babylon will be added to that of Egypt, so that the names of the months will be reminiscent of the two redemptions together. See Note 114 further, for example. Joseph Albo's position in his book Ikkarim (Roots), III, 16, that Ramban's intent here was that after the return from the Babylonian exile, the first memorial was to give way altogether to the second, is thus not correct. For further discussion of this problem see the note in my Hebrew commentary Vol. II, p. 520.   (112) See Zechariah 1:7, etc.; Ezra 6:15; Nehemiah 1:1.   (113) Esther 3:7, etc.   (114) *Ibid.* Thus both memorials are mentioned simultaneously: *the first month* to our redemption from Egypt, *which is the month of Nisan*, a name which is reminiscent of our Babylonian exile from which we have also been redeemed.   (115) *Ibid.* In this case too Scripture explains the Persian word *pur* as meaning lot, just as it explained the name Nisan as being "the first month."   (116) There are twelve signs or constellations in the zodiac, an imaginary belt encircling the heavens, revolving around the sun. Each month, another constellation begins the procession of the signs in their course around the heavens. The Ram is the first sign of the zodiac in the month of Nisan.

we went out from Egypt, but by decree of the Supreme One. And according to the opinion of our Rabbis [117] that the Egyptians worshipped it as a deity, He has all the more informed us through this that He subdued their gods and their powers at the height of their ascendancy. And thus the Rabbis have said:[118] *"Take you lambs and slaughter* [119] *the gods of Egypt."*

6. 'BEIN HA'ARBAYIM' (AT EVENTIDE). "The period beginning at the sixth hour and onward, [counted from the beginning of the day, which in Torah-law is always divided into twelve hours], is called *bein ha'arbayim* (at eventide), because the sun inclines in the direction of its setting there to become darkened. It appears to me that the expression *bein ha'arbayim* denotes those hours which are between the beginning of the darkening of the day and the final darkening at night. The darkening of the day is at the beginning of the seventh hour of the day, from the time *the shadows of the evening are stretched out,* [120] and the darkening of the night is at the beginning of the night. The word *erev* (night) is an expression of gloom and darkness, just as in the verse, *All joy is 'arbah' (darkened)."* [121] Thus the language of Rashi.

Rabbi Abraham ibn Ezra refuted [this explanation of Rashi] by pointing to the verse which says, *And when Aaron lighteth the lamps 'bein ha'arbayim'* [122] ['There is no doubt that he lights the lamps at sundown"], as it is written there, *Aaron and his sons shall set it in order from evening to morning.* [123] [Thus it proves that *bein ha'arbayim* does not begin with the seventh hour of the day as Rashi would have it, but at sundown near night.] Besides,

---

(117) In translating the words of Moses to Pharaoh, *Lo, if we sacrifice the abomination of the Egyptians before their eyes,* etc., (above, 8:22), Onkelos translated: "if we sacrifice that which the Egyptians worship." In his Moreh Nebuchim (III, 46), Rambam also writes: "Scripture tells us, according to the version of Onkelos, that the Egyptians worshipped Aries, etc." (118) Shemoth Rabbah 16:2. (119) Further, Verse 21. (120) Jeremiah 6:4. (121) Isaiah 24:11. (122) Further, 30:8. (123) *Ibid.*, 27:21.

the verse regarding the paschal offering itself states: *There thou shalt sacrifice the Passover-offering at even, at the going down of the sun, at the time thou camest forth out of Egypt*,[124] and "the going down of the sun" occurs at sunset. [How then could Rashi explain *bein ha'arbayim* mentioned here as commencing at the seventh hour of the day?]

But this is no refutation of the Rabbi's [Rashi's] explanation. Our Rabbis have already said [125] that the meaning of the verse is as follows: "*At even*, you slaughter [the Passover-offering]; *at the going down of the sun*, you eat it; *at the time thou camest forth out of Egypt*, [i.e., in the morning of the fifteenth day of Nisan, it becomes *nothar*] [126] and you burn it." The Rabbi [Rashi] has already so commented [in his commentary to Deuteronomy 16:6].

The correct interpretation on this matter appears to me to be that the night is called *erev*, as it is said, *'ba'erev' ye shall eat unleavened bread*.[127] and this is at night, as it clearly states, *And they shall eat the flesh in that night, roast with fire, and unleavened bread*.[128] Similarly, *And there was 'erev' and there was morning*,[129] means the beginning of night when the stars do come forth. The same applies to the verse, *In the twilight, 'ba'erev' of the day, in the blackness of night and the darkness*,[130] [where the word *ba'erev*, coming after "the twilight," must signify the night]. Now the end of the day is also called *erev*, as the verses indicate: *And the two angels came to Sodom 'ba'erev,' and Lot sat in the gate of Sodom;*[131] *And it came to pass 'ba'erev' that the*

---

(124) Deuteronomy 16:6. (125) Berachoth 9 a. (126) Literally, "left over." Portions of sacrifices left over after the prescribed time within which they are to be eaten must be burnt. See "The Commandments," Vol. I, pp. 103-4. Now since the Passover-offering is to be eaten only on the night of the fifteenth day, whatever is left by the morning of that day is to be burnt. The actual burning, however, takes place on the morning of the sixteenth day, since it is not permissible to burn *nothar* on a Festival day. (127) Further, Verse 18. (128) *Ibid.*, Verse 8. (129) Genesis 1:5. (130) Proverbs 7:9. (131) Genesis 19:1. In view of the fact that Lot surely did not sit in the gate at night, *ba'erev* must mean at the end of the day.

EXODUS XII, BO   121

quails came up,[132] and the quails did not come at night.[133] There are many other such cases.

It is further written: *'Erev,' and morning, and at noonday, I will sigh and moan.* [134] Now these three periods include the whole day [of twenty-four hours. Therefore, if we interpret *erev* as meaning actual night, the hours from noonday to night will be missing here. We must] thus conclude that [the period] immediately after noonday is called *erev*, [which lasts from the latter part of the day till morning. Thus the verse encompasses the whole day of twenty-four hours].

Morning is so called from sunrise and thence onward as long as the sun remains in the east. This period lasts four hours, just as the Rabbis testified [135] that the morning Daily Whole-offering [for the entire congregation of Israel] may be offered in the [first] four hours of the day [but not later].

After morning, the time is called *tzohorayim* (noonday), just as it is said, *from morning until 'tzohorayim' (noon).*[136] It consists of two hours: the fifth and the sixth hours of the day. The word *tzohorayim* is of the root *'tzohar' (A light) shalt thou make to the ark,* [137] and implies brightness. It is written in the plural [*tzohorayim*] because it is the two [brightest parts of the day] which, so to speak, make two *tzohorayim*. It may be that it is written in the plural because light is then disseminated on all sides. In the morning the light is centered in the east, and towards evening it is in the west, but in the middle of the day when it is high in the sky, it gives light on all sides.

When *tzohorayim* (noonday) passes and the sun departs from shining upon two sides, the time of the day is called *arbayim* —

---

(132) Further, 16:13.   (133) *Ibid.*, Verse 12: *At eventide ye shall eat flesh.* This clearly indicates that the quails came before the night. The word *ba'erev* in the verse, *And it came to pass 'ba'erev' that the quails came up*, must therefore mean at the end of the day.   (134) Psalms 55:18.   (135) In Tractate Eduyoth 6:1. This testimony is attributed to Rabbi Yehudah ben Baba.   (136) I Kings 18:26.   (137) Genesis 6:16.

[from the root *erev* (darkness)] – because the sun has darkened from [its state of shining on] those two sides. This period [of *arbayim*] lasts as long as the sun shines in the sky [and is permissible for the slaughtering of the Passover-offering]. But beginning with sundown, which is about an hour and a quarter [before the day terminates with the coming out of the stars], it is no longer the time for the slaughtering thereof according to the opinion of our Rabbis,[138] for that period of time is no longer *arbayim* but rather *erev yom* (the evening of the day).[139]

The reason it is called *bein ha'arbayim* [in the Torah, and not just *arbayim*], is not that the word *bein* signifies here "between," [as Rashi above explained that the expression *bein ha'arbayim* denotes that time-period which is "between" the beginning of those hours, etc.], but it is something like "in their midst," similar to these verses: *Let there now be an oath 'beinotheinu beineinu ubeinecha';*[140] *A piece of land worth four hundred shekels of silver, what is that 'beini ubeincha'?;*[141] *And her stature was exalted 'al bein' (among) the thick branches;*[142] *Take fire 'mibeinoth' the wheelwork,*[143] which means from "within their midst"; *Take up their fire-pans 'mibein' the burning,*[144] which means "from the midst thereof," similar to the expression, *She rises also 'be'od' night,*[145] which means in the midst of the night. And so is the expression *bein ha'arbayim,* [which signifies "in the midst of that part of the day called *arbayim*,"as explained above]. It does not state *ba'arbayim,* for that might have indicated the *erev*

---

(138) Mechilta Pischa, 5: "*At eventide.* I might understand this to mean at the evening twilight. Scripture therefore says, etc." (139) *In the twilight, 'b'erev yom' (in the evening of the day)* (Proverbs 7:9). (140) Genesis 26:28. It is generally translated: *between us, even between us and thee.* But according to Ramban, the meaning thereof would be: "let there be an oath in our midst, even in us and in thee." (141) *Ibid.,* 23:15. It is generally translated: *between me and thee.* Ramban understands it: "in the midst of me and you, the value of the land is not worth discussing." (142) Ezekiel 19:11. Ramban would explain it: "her stature was exalted in the midst of the thick foliage." (143) *Ibid.,* 10:6. It is generally translated: "from 'between' the wheelwork." (144) Numbers 17:2. (145) Proverbs 31:15. It is generally translated: "she rises also 'while it is yet' night."

of many days. Thus Scripture is saying that we should slaughter the Passover-offering in the midst of the *arbayim*, since the time prescribed by the Torah for the slaughtering of the Passover-offering is from after the sixth hour of the day till the commencement of sunset. And Scripture also says, *In the first month, on the fourteenth day of the month 'bein ha'arbayim' (at eventide) is the Passover of the Eternal*,[146] which refers to the time of the slaughtering [of the Passover-offering]. Similarly, the verse, *In the fourteenth day of this month 'bein ha'arbayim' ye shall observe it*,[147] refers to the beginning of the observance, which is the slaughtering, [while the eating of the Passover-offering takes place on the following night]. The verse stating [in connection with the quails], *'bein ha'arbayim' ye shall eat flesh*,[148] also refers to the hours mentioned, [i.e., from after the sixth hour of the day till the start of sunset], since they had extensive time for the eating of meat. The following verse there which states, *And it came to pass 'ba'erev' (at even), that the quails came up*,[149] is [so stated] because on the first day, the quails came up for one hour within that period called *erev*.[150] [Therefore it does not say, "and it came to pass *bein ha'arbayim* that the quails came up," for that would have signified that the quails came up during the whole stretch of time from after the sixth hour of the day till sundown.]

It is possible to explain the expression *bein ha'arbayim* in accordance with the explanation of Rashi,[151] i.e., that there are

---

(146) Leviticus 23:5. (147) Numbers 9:3. (148) Further, 16:12. (149) Ibid., Verse 13. (150) In other words, Scripture is stating that during the part of the day called *erev* which, as explained above, extends from immediately after *tzohorayim* until the end of the day — making a period of six hours — the quails came up for a time. See my Hebrew commentary, p. 327, for further discussion of this text. (151) The plural form of *arbayim* suggests two kinds of *erev*, and the word *bein* signifies "between." Thus *bein ha'arbayim* denotes those hours which are between the darkening of the day and the darkening of the night. Thus is the explanation of Rashi. Ramban proceeds to confirm Rashi's explanation that the word *bein* means "between," but adds that the plural form of *arbayim* denotes two different periods of the day, unlike Rashi who wrote that it is between the darkening of the day and the darkening of the night, as will be explained.

two kinds of *erev*, an *erev* of the morning and an *erev* of the day, for Scripture so calls them: *the 'minchah' of the morning,* [152] and *the 'minchah' of the evening,* [153] as it is said, *And it came to pass in the morning, about the time of making the 'minchah',* [154] and it further says, *And I sat appalled until the 'minchah' of the evening. And at the evening 'minchah' I arose up from my fasting.* [155] Now the word *minchah* is an expression denoting the resting of the sun and the diminution of its great light, just as the Targum rendered [*l'ruach hayom*] *l'manach yoma* (where the day comes to rest). [156] And the plural form of *arbayim* connotes the two afternoons: "the greater afternoon," [i.e., the time from six and a half hours after the beginning of the day], and "the smaller afternoon," [i.e., from nine and a half hours after the start of the day until sunset], which the Sages have mentioned. [157] Now during this entire period [of *bein ha'arbayim*], it is permissible to kindle the lamps of the candelabrum [in the Sanctuary] [158] and to burn the incense, both of which are not permissible to be done at night but only at the time of the Daily Whole-offering of the eventide, and in fact their performance precedes the actual offering of the sacrifice upon the altar.

Onkelos' opinion seems to incline towards this explanation [that the plural form of *arbayim* denotes two different parts of the day], for he translated *bein ha'arbayim* as *bein shimshaya* (between the suns), meaning the times when the sun is in the east and the sun is in the west. The verse stating, *Aaron and his sons*

---

(152) Further, 29:41. Ramban will explain the word *minchah*. (153) II Kings 16:15. (154) *Ibid.*, 3:20. (155) Ezra 9:4-5. (156) In Genesis 3:8, we read: *And they* [Adam and Eve] *heard the voice of the Eternal G-d walking in the garden of Eden 'l'ruach hayom,'* which Rashi interpreted: "in that direction towards which the sun travels, which is the west." Onkelos rendered it: *l'manach yoma,* "in the afternoon," or literally, "when the day comes to rest." Thus it is seen that the word *minchah* denotes rest. (157) Berachoth 26 b. (158) Unlike the opinion of Ibn Ezra mentioned above, i.e., that the kindling of the lamps of the candelabrum in the Sanctuary was done at sundown.

EXODUS XII, BO

shall set it in order from evening to morning,[159] means [that it be given its due measure of oil] so that it may burn a whole night [although the actual kindling thereof could be done anytime in the *bein ha'arbayim*. It does not mean, as Ibn Ezra explained, that this verse teaches that the kindling of the candelabrum took place at sundown].

Thus we can explain the verse, *There thou shalt sacrifice the Passover-offering 'ba'erev' (at even),*[160] to mean at the above-mentioned time, [i.e., the afternoon], for that is called *erev* [as explained]. The following expression there, *at the going down of the sun*, is connected with the following verse, *And thou shalt roast and eat it.*[161] There are many such cases in Scripture [where an expression in one verse is connected with the following verse].[162]

In my opinion however, the verse, *There thou shalt sacrifice the Passover-offering*, does not at all refer to the time of the slaughtering thereof, [which took place on the afternoon of the fourteenth day of Nisan]. Rather, the purport thereof is to state *that at the place which the Eternal thy G-d chose to establish His name in, there thou shalt* observe [the commandment concerning] the Passover-offering at night, *at the going down of the sun*, which is *the time thou camest forth out of Egypt*. It is concerning this performance that Scripture says [in the following verse], *And thou shalt roast and eat it in the place*[161] mentioned. The sacrifice

---

(159) Further, 27:21. From this verse, Ibn Ezra had proven at the beginning of this discussion — see at Note 123 — that the lamps of the candelabrum are kindled at sundown. Ramban proceeds to explain that the purport of the verse is that the priests are to put into the lamps their due measure of oil so that they will burn from evening to morning, but not that it mattered that they were kindled only at sundown. As explained above, that could be done anytime during "the greater afternoon" and "the smaller afternoon." Thus Ibn Ezra's strictures on Rashi are removed. (160) Deuteronomy 16:6. See above at Note 124 how Ibn Ezra brought this verse in proof against Rashi's explanation. Ramban already refuted it above on the basis of the teaching of the Rabbis. Here he refutes Ibn Ezra on the basis of the plain meaning of what he has shown, i.e., that *erev* also means the afternoon, etc. Ramban's own explanation of this verse is yet to follow. (161) *Ibid.*, Verse 7. (162) See Vol. I, pp. 437-8.

itself is called *zevach*, [163] as Scripture says, *Thou shalt not offer the blood of 'zivchi' (My sacrifice) upon leaven,* [164] which means "My Passover-offering."

This then is the purport of the whole chapter [in Deuteronomy]: *Observe the month of Aviv, and observe the Passover unto the Eternal thy G-d; for in the month of Aviv the Eternal thy G-d brought thee forth out of Egypt by night,* etc. *Thou shalt eat no leavened bread with it.* [165] Thus He mentioned the observance of the Passover-offering and the night, [clearly indicating that in those verses, He refers only to the time of the eating of the Passover-offering, which occurs on the night of the fifteenth day, and not to the slaughtering thereof which takes place in the afternoon of the fourteenth day]. Commanding how they are to eat it, He then mentioned that [we must eat no leavened bread] for seven days.[166] But in this entire chapter, there is not a single reference to the fourteenth day of Nisan on which the slaughtering of the Passover-offering takes place. Similarly He said there, *Neither shall any of the flesh which thou sacrificest the first day at even, remain all night until the morning,* [167] Now the expression, *the first day at even,* [definitely] means the fifteenth day of Nisan, the first of the seven days mentioned,[166] since the fourteenth day is not mentioned here at all. So also, the verse stating, *On the fourteenth day of the month at even, ye shall eat unleavened bread,* [168] means the night of the fifteenth day. Thus the intent of the expression, *which thou sacrificest the first day at even,* [167] is that neither shall

---

(163) Ramban's intent is to clarify that the word *tizbach* — *There thou shalt 'tizbach' the Passover-offering* — does not mean "slaughter," in which case it would necessarily be referring to the afternoon of the fourteenth day of Nisan. Instead, Ramban proceeds to show that the word *zevach* refers to the sacrifice itself, and the verse therefore refers to the eating thereof which takes place on the following night of the fifteenth day. All this, however, is from the standpoint of the plain meaning of Scripture. Ramban has already noted that the Rabbis in the Talmud (see Note 125), as well as Rashi in his commentary to Deuteronomy 16:6, have explained *tizbach* as "slaughter." (164) Further, 34:25. (165) Deuteronomy 16:1-3. (166) *Ibid.,* Verse 3. (167) *Ibid.,* Verse 4. (168) Further, Verse 18.

EXODUS XII, BO

any of the flesh of the offering which you are eating on the night of the first day [of the seven-day festival] remain until the morning.

8. AND UNLEAVENED BREAD, 'AL' (WITH) BITTER HERBS THEY SHALL EAT IT. The purport of the verse is as follows: *And they shall eat the flesh in that night, roast with fire,* and with unleavened bread with bitter herbs, they shall eat it. [The word *al* here thus means "with," and not "upon," as it generally does.] Similarly: *'al' unleavened bread and bitter herbs* [169] means "with"; *And they came both men 'al' women* [170] [means "with" the women]; *its head 'al' its legs 'v'al' the inwards thereof* [171] [means its head "with" its legs "and with" the inwards thereof]. Scripture does not say *im* (with) [but instead uses *al*] in order to instruct that it is not obligatory to wrap them together, [i.e., insert the paschal meat and the bitter herbs between the unleavened bread], and eat them. [172] Thus [the word *umatzoth (and unleavened bread)*] is missing the letter *beth*, [which would make it *ubematzoth* (and with unleavened bread)], similar to the expressions: *they shall wash 'mayim'* (water) [173] [the word missing a *beth*, which would make it *b'mayim*, (with water)]; *And Seled died 'lo' (no) children,* [174] [the word *lo* missing a *beth*, which would make it *b'lo* (without) children]. Thus Scripture teaches that there is no commandment for eating the bitter herbs alone, but only with the eating of the flesh of the Passover-offering. [175] Concerning unleavened bread, however, Scripture repeated it by

---

(169) Numbers 9:11. Mentioned in connection with the Second Passover-offering. (170) Further, 35:22. (171) Verse 9. (172) Hillel in fact did wrap them together and eat them. The Sages, however, differed with him and held it not to be obligatory to eat them in that way (Pesachim 115a). As is known, nowadays at the performance of the *Seder* on the night of Passover, the wrapping together of unleavened bread and bitter herbs is observed "according to the custom of Hillel." (173) Further, 30:20. (174) I Chronicles 2:30. (175) Thus nowadways when we have no Passover-offering, we are not obligated by law of the Torah to eat bitter herbs. It is by law of the Rabbis that we are now obligated to eat bitter herbs at the *Seder* (Mishneh Torah, Hilchoth Chametz Umatzah, 7:12).

commanding, *At even ye shall eat unleavened bread*,[176] even by itself [when there is no Passover-offering], as is the opinion of our Rabbis.[177]

A more correct interpretation is that we say that the word, *umatzoth* (and unleavened bread), is connected with the earlier part of the verse: *And they shall eat the flesh ... and unleavened bread.* The verse then continues to command that the flesh mentioned be eaten with bitter herbs. Thus He commanded the eating of the flesh with the eating of the unleavened bread, but He did not command the eating of bitter herbs, except by saying that they should eat the meat with bitter herbs, thus hinting that there is no [separate] commandment regarding the bitter herbs. It is only that the meat must be eaten with them, and when there is no Passover-offering there is no specific commandment [of the Torah] regarding the eating of the bitter herbs. It also teaches us that the bitter herbs do not invalidate the meat. Thus, if one ate the meat of the Passover-offering and did not eat bitter herbs, he has [nevertheless] fulfilled his duty of eating the Passover-offering, since the commandment concerning the eating of the Passover-offering is like the commandment of eating unleavened bread, each one an independent commandment in itself.[178]

9. EAT NOT OF IT RAW, NOR SODDEN AT ALL WITH WATER. This commandment applies for all generations [and not merely for the Passover at the time of the exodus], for all commandments here relate to the body of the Passover-offering and therefore apply for all times. But the commandments concerning those that eat thereof — such as *your loins girded*, etc.,[179] and the blood which is to be on the lintel[180] — apply only to the Passover of Egypt. And so Scripture says concerning the second Passover-offering: *They shall eat it with unleavened bread and bitter herbs; They shall leave none of it unto the*

---

(176) Verse 18. (177) Pesachim 120 a. (178) For further discussion of this topic, see "The Commandments," Soncino, Vol. I, pp. 65-67. (179) Verse 11. (180) Further, Verse 22.

morning, nor break a bone thereof; according to all the statute of the Passover they shall keep it.[181] [The expression, *according to all the statute,* etc.], refers to the law of roasting with fire, and that it is not to be eaten either raw or sodden.[182]

12. AND AGAINST ALL THE GODS OF EGYPT WILL I EXECUTE JUDGMENTS. The idol of wood rotted, and the one of metal melted.[183]

Now Scripture did not elucidate the nature of these judgments because *the vanities by which they are instructed are but timber.*[184] Similarly, at the time when this actually took place, it is written, *And the Eternal smote all the firstborn ... and all the firstborn of cattle,*[185] but does not mention the judgments executed against their gods. Their apprehension [on that night] concerned the death of the firstborn, as it is said, *And Pharaoh rose up in the night, he, and all his servants, and all the Egyptians,*[186] whereas the judgments executed against their idols did not come to be known till the morning when they went to the house of their abominations. And it is written, *And the Egyptians were burying them that the Eternal had smitten among them, even all their firstborn, and upon their gods the Eternal executed judgments.*[187]

In my opinion, Scripture alludes here to the lords on high, the gods of Egypt, something like the verse, *The Eternal will punish the host of the high heavens on high, and the kings of the earth*

---

(181) Numbers 9:11-12. (182) These strictures not clearly mentioned in connection with the Second Passover-offering are netheteles included within the expression, *according to all the statute of the Passover they shall keep it.* (183) This is the language of Rashi. The Mechilta here has it: "the metal idols corroded." (184) Jeremiah 10:8. In other words, Scripture finds it inappropriate to speak at length about these hollow and worthless abominations. (185) Further, Verse 29. (186) *Ibid.,* Verse 30. The verse there clearly states that "the great cry" was due to the death of the firstborn. (187) Numbers 33:4. The verse clearly hints that on the morning [of the fifteenth day of Nisan], when the Egyptians were burying the dead, they discovered that judgments had also been executed against their idols.

upon the earth.[188] Thus He subdued the power of the Egyptians and that of the lords over them. But Scripture hints and deals briefly with hidden matters.

I WILL EXECUTE JUDGMENTS: I AM THE ETERNAL. "I Myself and not by means of the [189] messenger." Thus the language of Rashi. But the Midrash of the Sages is not so. Instead, the Midrash reads:[190] *"And I will go through the land of Egypt* — I, and not an angel. *And I will smite all the firstborn* — I, and not a seraph. *And against all the gods of Egypt I will execute judgments* — I, and not the messenger. *I am the Eternal* — I am He, and no other." The purport of the Midrash is as follows: Since this chapter contains the words of Moses to Israel,[191] it would have been proper for the verse here to say, "And the Eternal will go through the land of Egypt and He will smite all the firstborn," [instead of saying, *And I will go through*]. It is for this reason that the Rabbis interpreted the expression, *and I will go through the land of Egypt,* as meaning "I Myself" and not a messenger sent by Him in plagues, as in the days of David [192] and Sennacherib. [193] *"And I will smite all the firstborn* — I, and not a seraph," means that the striking of the plague will be done by the Holy One, blessed be He, and not like a king who wreaks vengeance on his enemies through his executioners, their counterparts on high being the seraphim from whom the fire comes forth consuming His enemies, as in the case of Elijah and the captain of the fifty.[194] *"And against all the gods of Egypt I will execute judgments,* and not by means of the messenger" sent by Him, blessed be He, for whatever is to be done upon the earth. This is the great angel, who on account of it is called Mattatron, the meaning of the word being "the guide of the road." Thus the

(188) Isaiah 24:21. (189) "The messenger." In our text of Rashi: "a messenger." Ramban's version will be explained further on in the text. (190) Mentioned in the Hagadah recited on the night of Passover. (191) As indicated in Verse 3 above: *Speak ye unto all the congregation of Israel, saying....* (192) II Samuel 24:16. (193) II Kings 19:35. (194) *Ibid.,* 1:10.

EXODUS XII, BO

Rabbis have said in the Sifre: [195] "The Holy One, blessed be He, was the *mattatron* (guide) for Moses, and He showed him the entire Land of Israel." And in the [Midrash] Yelamdeinu [196] we find: "*And Balak heard that Balaam came* [197] for Balaam sent his *mattatron* before him." And it is furthermore written there: [198] "*Behold, I have begun to deliver up Sihon and his land before thee.* [199] Do not let it worry you. I am your *mattatron*. And be not surprised at this for I am even to be the *mattatron* before an uncircumcised person, i.e., before Cyrus [king of Persia], as it is said, *I will go before thee.* [200] Before a woman — Deborah and Barak — I will lead on the way, as it is said, *Is not the Eternal gone out before thee.*"[201] [We find this word *mattatron*] also in many other places. I have also heard that in the Greek language, a messenger is called *mattator*. And [finally] the Rabbis interpreted [in the Midrash mentioned at the beginning of this discussion]: "*I am the Eternal* — I am He, and no other," meaning that He is one, and there is no other god beside Him to protest against His act. This is the purport of this Midrash.

16. NO MANNER OF WORK SHALL BE DONE IN THEM. Rashi commented: "Even by the agency of others."

I do not understand this. If these "others" are Israelites, they themselves are commanded not to work on the Festival, and I am not bound to ensure that my work is not done through them. It is only where one deceives another in a matter which is prohibited —

---

(195) Sifre, *Ha'azinu*, 338. (196) Literally: "May [our master] teach us." This was a Midrash which contained homilies that opened with the expression *yelamdeinu rabbeinu* (may our master teach us) i.e., about some matter of *Halachic* (legal) content. The Rabbi answered the question briefly and then turned to elaborate on the moral and ethical aspects connected therewith. This Midrash is now practically lost except for some sections found in the Tanchuma. The particular Midrash Ramban mentions here is found in the Aruch, under the root *mattator*. (197) Numbers 22:36. (198) This Midrash too is found in the Aruch, under the root *mattator*, which mentions it in the name of the Yelamdeinu. (199) Deuteronomy 2:31. (200) Isaiah 45:2. (201) Judges 4:14.

whether it be in the deceiver's work or in that of the deceived — that the deceiver transgresses the prohibition, *Before the blind do not put a stumbling-block.* [202] And if these "others" are non-Israelites, we are by law of the Torah not admonished at all against their working either on a Festival or on a Sabbath, except that there is a prohibition by the Rabbis if we tell him [the non-Israelite] to do the work, just as the Rabbis have said: [203] "Telling a non-Israelite [to do work on the Sabbath or Festival] is prohibited by law of the Rabbis," and this is a principle clearly established in the Gemara. [204] [How then could Rashi derive this principle of prohibiting telling a non-Israelite to do work for us on a Festival from a verse in the Torah, when it is only prohibited by Rabbinic law?]

However, I have found this text in the Mechilta: [205] *"No manner of work shall be done in them.* This means that neither you nor your fellow-Israelite shall do any work, nor shall a non-Israelite do your work. You so interpret it to mean that neither you nor your fellow-Israelite shall do any work, nor shall a non-Israelite do your work, but perhaps it rather means that neither you nor your fellow-Israelite shall do any work, and the

---

(202) Leviticus 19:14. For fuller discussion of this commandment see "The Commandments," Vol. II, pp. 277-8. (203) Shabbath 150 a. (204) The Gemara (literally: "teaching") is the collected discussions of the Rabbis centering around the Mishnah. The Mishnah and Gemara combined are known as the Talmud. After the Mishnah was compiled in the Land of Israel by Rabbi Yehudah Hanasi (about the year 200 of the Common Era), the Mishnah was studied in all academies of learning in Babylon and in the Land of Israel, and finally the teachings were gathered together in the Gemara. The teachings of the Rabbis of the Land of Israel on the Mishnah were assembled in the Jerusalem Talmud, while those of Babylon were gathered together in the Babylonian Talmud. To this day, Talmudic study is devoted almost exclusively to the Babylonian Talmud. This is because the Babylonian Talmud was compiled after the Jerusalem Talmud, and therefore its decisions were reached after having taken the teachings of the Palestinian Rabbis into consideration. (205) The Mechilta is a Tannaitic Midrash on the Book of Exodus, beginning with Chapter 12, Verse 1. It does not, however, cover the entire Book of Exodus. The text mentioned by Ramban is found here on the verse before us.

non-Israelite shall not do even his own work! Scripture therefore says, *Six days shall work be done.* [206] This teaches that neither you nor your fellow-Israelite shall do any work [on the Sabbath], but the non-Israelite may do his own work. These are the words of Rabbi Yashiya. Rabbi Yonathan says that there is no need for this proof. Has it not already been said, *Six days shalt thou labour, and do all thy work?* [207] Now by the syllogism of *kal vachomer,* [208] we proceed as follows: If on the Sabbath, in regard to which the Torah is so strict, you are not admonished against a non-Israelite's work as you are against your own work, [it is logical to assume that on a Festival-day, in regard to which the Torah is not so strict — inasmuch as preparation of food is permitted on a Festival-day but not on the Sabbath — you are surely not admonished against a non-Israelite's work as you are against your own work]." Thus far extends the text of this Beraitha. [209] Now surely this is but a case of a mere *asmachta,* [a Scriptural text used as a mere support for a Rabbinical enactment]. Since they aimed to prohibit, by law of the Rabbis, telling a non-Israelite to do our work [on a Sabbath or Festival], they used this verse as a support, [but it is actually a Rabbinical law]. It is however permissible for a non-Israelite to do his own work. And thus we incidentally learn that the Rabbinical enactment against telling a non-Israelite to do work applies only to doing our work, but one may tell him to do his own work and he

---

(206) Leviticus 23:3. The verse continues, *but on the seventh day is a sabbath of solemn rest, a holy convocation; ye shall do no manner of work.* See my Hebrew commentary, p. 330, for a detailed explanation of how the principle discussed is derived from the language of the verse. (207) Further, 20:9. (208) Literally: "a minor and major." This is a form of reasoning by which a certain stricture applying to a minor matter is established as applying all the more to a major matter. Conversely, if a certain leniency applies to a major matter, it must apply all the more to the minor matter. It is one of the thirteen rules by which the Torah is interpreted. (209) Literally: "outside." A teaching of the Tannaim that for some reason had not been included in the Mishnah by Rabbi Yehudah Hanasi. The teachings contained in the Mechilta on the Book of Exodus, Sifra on Leviticus, and Sifre on Numbers and Deuteronomy fall into the category of Beraithoth.

may do it. So did Rashi explain it in the Gemara [204] of [Tractate] Baba Metzia. [210]

There in the Mechilta it further says: [211] "I know only that work which can be regarded as labor is prohibited. Whence do we learn that activities which are prohibited by Rabbinical enactment [are also forbidden]? Scripture therefore says, *And ye shall observe this day,*[212] including all activities prohibited by Rabbinical law." Now Beraithoth [209] like these, [if not accompanied by a proper interpretation], may lead one into a mistaken opinion and should not be quoted literally, for this Beraitha too apparently is a mere *asmachta,* and I have a correct interpretation thereof. I will yet discuss it, with the help of G-d. [213]

SAVE THAT WHICH MAY BE EATEN BY EVERY BEING, [THAT ONLY MAY BE DONE FOR YOU]. "Even [the food eaten] by cattle [may be prepared on the Festival-day]. One might think that [food may be prepared] for non-Israelites too. Scripture therefore states, *for you:* [you are permitted to prepare food only for that which belongs to you and for which you have the responsibility of feeding]." Thus the language of Rashi. This too is not in accordance with the final decision of the law. Rather, [the word *lachem (for you)* signifies]: *for you* and not for non-Israelites, *for you* and not for cattle.

19. NO LEAVEN SHALL BE FOUND IN YOUR HOMES. "Whence do we know that this applies also to the borders? Scripture therefore says, *Neither shall there be leaven seen with thee, in all thy borders.* [214] Why then need Scripture say here, *in*

---

(210) Baba Metzia 90 a.   (211) Mechilta on Verse 17.   (212) Verse 17. (213) In *Seder Emor* (Leviticus 23:24). Ramban's interpretation there of this topic has been called by the Ritba (see Vol. I, Preface, x), "a gem which has come down to us from the teachings of our master Rabbi Moshe ben Nachman."   (214) Further, 13:7. The term "our borders" is to be understood as "our external properties" besides our homes.

all your homes, [since these are already included in the comprehensive term of *borders*]? It is to teach us that just as what is in your home is under your control, so also what is *in thy borders* must be under your control. Thus there is excluded [from this prohibition] leavened bread actually owned by a non-Israelite but deposited with an Israelite for which the latter has accepted no responsibility." This is the language of Rashi.

I do not find it correct. The purport of the term "under your control" is not to exclude leavened bread owned by a non-Israelite [which is deposited with an Israelite], since that is indeed under the Israelite's control. Homes and borders are both alike in this respect since both of them are under his control and the leavened bread belongs to others. [215] Moreover, the case of leavened bread owned by a non-Israelite [and deposited with an Israelite for which the Israelite] has accepted no responsibility, is not covered by this analogy, since the term "home" indicates permission no more than does the term "border." Instead, the term "home" implies prohibition, as is obvious from the language of this verse before us, *it shall not be found in your homes* [under any circumstance]. We derive the permission from the expression, *Neither shall there be seen leaven with thee*,[214] [i.e., that which actually belongs to you,[216] as the Rabbis commented upon it]: "You may not see [leaven or leavened bread] which is yours, but you may see that of others and that which belongs to the Temple-treasury. I know only that this principle applies to the borders, [since the expression *with thee* is stated in connection with the borders, as it says, *Neither shall there be leaven seen 'with thee' in all 'thy borders'*]. Whence do I know this applies also to the homes?

(215) In other words, what new principle could there be derived by this comparison, which Rashi mentioned, of the border to the home, since there is no difference between them regarding a case of this kind? (216) And not, as Rashi explained it, that the permission for this case, i.e., of leavened bread owned by a non-Israelite and deposited with an Israelite for which the Israelite assumed no responsibility — is derived from the expression "in your homes" in the verse before us.

Scripture therefore uses the identical word *s'or* (leaven) in the case of both home and border," [217] as is explained at the beginning of Tractate Pesachim. [218]

But this Midrash [mentioned by Rashi], which explains, "just as what is in your home is under your control, so also what is *in thy borders* must be under your control," is only intended to exclude [from this prohibition] an Israelite's leavened bread which is deposited with a non-Israelite. And thus it is taught in the Mechilta: [219] *"In your homes.* Why is this said? Because it is stated, *in all thy borders,* [214] which I might understand literally, [i.e., that we are not to leave our leavened bread in all our borders even if it is deposited with a non-Israelite]. Scripture therefore says, *in your homes*; just as what is in your home is under your control, so also what is *in thy border* must be under your control. Thus there is excluded [from this prohibition] an Israelite's leavened bread which he deposited with a non-Israelite. Even though the Israelite may destroy it, he could not do so because he does not have complete control over it. [Also] excluded [from this prohibition] is the leavened bread of a non-Israelite which is deposited with an Israelite, and [an Israelite's] leavened bread buried under debris, for although it is under the control of the Israelite [or in his territory], he has not the right to destroy it, [or in the case of debris, he does not have the physical ability of actually destroying it], etc."

(217) This principle of interpretation is known as *gzeirah shavah*, "an equal expression." Where a verbal congruity appears between two laws in the text of the Torah, it indicates that a law mentioned in one case applies equally to the other. In the case before us, the word *s'or* (leaven) appears here in Verse 19 where "home" is mentioned, and is also mentioned further, 13:7, where the border is mentioned. Now in the case of the border, the Torah clearly stated that the prohibition applies only where it actually belongs to the owner. On the strength of the *gzeirah shavah*, the same law applies to the case of the home. The *gzeirah shavah* is one of the thirteen rules by which the Torah is interpreted. One cannot establish, though, an analogy from congruent expressions of one's own accord; the application of the similarity of expression must be authorized by tradition. (218) Pesachim 5 b. (219) Mechilta on the verse before us.

EXODUS XII, BO

The explanation of this Mechilta is as follows: One might have thought that the intent of the verse, *Neither shall there be leaven seen with thee in all thy borders,* is to prohibit the leaving of our leavened bread in all our borders, even in the house of a non-Israelite. Therefore the Torah wrote *in your homes* to exclude [from this prohibition] the house of a non-Israelite. Thus we learn from this Beraitha [209] that by law of the Torah we are admonished only against keeping our leavened bread under our control, whether it be in our homes or in our borders. But if we have deposited it with a non-Israelite in his home, we do not transgress [the two prohibitions], *Neither shall there be leaven seen with thee,*[214] and *There shall no leaven be found in your homes.*[220] And it must necessarily be so. If you do not say thus, then it should follow that for his own leavened bread, an Israelite will transgress the commandments even if he deposited it with a non-Israelite who is beyond the sea, while for a non-Israelite's leavened bread, even though it be in the Israelite's home, the Israelite does not violate the prohibitions. If that is the case, why does Scripture say [in one place], *in your homes,* and in another, *in thy borders,* when there is no difference between our homes and our borders and the homes and borders of the non-Israelites! Instead, we must conclude that by law of the Torah, we are admonished [against keeping and seeing leaven or leavened bread] only when it is in our control.[221] But by enactment of the Sofrim, [the Rabbis of the pre-tannaitic period beginning with Ezra], we are obligated to destroy our leavened bread under all circumstances.

Accordingly, the Rabbis have said in the Gemara:[222] "If the Israelite singled out a room [to the non-Israelite and said to him,

---

(220) Verse 19 before us. See "The Commandments," Vol. II, pp. 197-8, where Rambam states that these are counted as two separate commandments.
(221) Hence by law of the Torah, an Israelite who deposited his leavened bread with a non-Israelite is not dutybound to destroy it. It is by law of the Rabbis, Ramban continues, that he is bound to destroy it in that case.
(222) Pesachim 6 a. See above, Note 204, for the word Gemara.

'This corner is for you to keep your leavened bread'], the Israelite does not violate [the prohibitions against keeping or seeing leavened bread in his possession]." This teaches us that for a non-Israelite's leavened bread for which the Israelite *has* accepted responsibility, even though it be deemed as belonging to the Israelite, it is forbidden only when it is under the control of the Israelite, but if it be under the control of the non-Israelite, it is permissible. [In this case where the Israelite singled out a room for him to keep his leavened bread, "it is as if the Israelite assumed responsibility for the non-Israelite's leavened bread which is in the non-Israelite's home"], and even by law of the Rabbis, nothing was decreed against it. The Rabbi [Rashi], however, is not of this opinion in his commentary on the Gemara Pesachim.[223]

It is this principle which is the purport of the Beraitha[209] we have cited: "Thus there is excluded [from this prohibition] leavened bread owned by a non-Israelite which is deposited with an Israelite." [It is excluded] on account of the analogy between the homes and the borders:[224] just as in the case of the borders it is permissible because it says *with thee*, meaning, "you may not see [leaven or leavened bread] which is yours, but you may see that of others and that which belongs to the Temple-treasury," so too in the case of the home it is also permissible. Excluded also is the case of an Israelite's leavened bread buried under great debris where it is impossible for him to clear away the ruin, and it is lost to him and everyone. It is permissible since it is no longer called "his."

(223) In his commentary (Pesachim 6 b), Rashi explains that the case of the Israelite who singled out a room for the non-Israelite to keep his leavened bread, applies only if the Israelite did not assume responsibility. If he assumed responsibility for it, he transgresses the prohibitions entailed. Ramban's position that the above case applies even if the Israelite assumed responsibility for the non-Israelite's leavened bread, coincides with that of Rabbeinu Tam, mentioned in Tosafoth there. (224) See Note 217 above. And not, as Rashi explained, that it is derived from the expression *in your homes*, as explained above.

EXODUS XII, BO

20. ANYTHING THAT IS LEAVENED YE SHALL NOT EAT. "This includes food with which leaven is mixed." Thus the language of Rashi.

This too is not in accordance with the final decision of the law, for the adopted opinion is like that of the Sages who say that the penalty incurred for eating leavened food is extinction, but for food with an admixture of leaven, there is no specific verse that includes it, [although it is nevertheless forbidden]. [225]

21 THEN MOSES CALLED FOR ALL THE ELDERS OF ISRAEL, AND SAID UNTO THEM: DRAW OUT, AND TAKE YOU LAMBS ACCORDING TO YOUR FAMILIES AND SLAUGHTER THE PASSOVER. This chapter shortens the account of how the laws which G-d had commanded Moses, as stated in the section above, [were communicated by him to Israel], as it is self-understood that Moses related all the laws to Israel in detail and taught them the matter involved, it being included in the verse, *As the Eternal hath commanded Moses and Aaron, so did they*. [226] Instead, Scripture mentioned this section in a general way, saying that Moses called for all the elders of Israel and they gathered together to him all the people. Then they [the elders] [227] said to the whole congregation of Israel, "*Draw out* the sheep from the flock to your homes, and keep it there from the tenth day of the month [till the fourteenth, when it is to be slaughtered as the Passover-offering]."

It is possible that Scripture used the word, *mishchu* (draw out), because their sheep were very far from them *in the land of*

---

(225) Why then did Rashi interpret the verse in accordance with the opinion of a single Sage — Rabbi Eliezer — when the Sages who are the majority differ with him? Commentators, however, have shown that the accepted final decision of the law in this case *is* in accordance with the opinion of Rabbi Eliezer. Maimonides and other scholars have all accepted the decision of Rabbi Eliezer. See my Hebrew commentary, p. 333. (226) Verse 28. (227) So explained later on in the text, and so clearly rendered in the Tur: "Moses called for all the elders of Israel and they gathered together to him all the people, and then they themselves said to the whole congregation of Israel, *Draw out, and take you lambs*, etc."

Goshen, for every shepherd is an abomination unto the Egyptians.[228] It said, *and take you,* meaning "take the lambs according to your families," *every man a lamb, according to their fathers' houses,*[229] *and slaughter the Passover lamb*[230] *at eventide,*[231] all in accordance with what has been explained above concerning this commandment.

Now we read in the Mechilta:[232] *"Then Moses called for all the elders of Israel.* This teaches us that he constituted them a court.[233] *And he said unto them.* The word came from the mouth of Moses, saying it to all Israel.[234] These are the words of Rabbi Yashiya. Rabbi Yonathan says that the word came out from the mouth of Moses saying it to the elders, and the elders saying it to all Israel." Thus according to Rabbi Yashiya, the expression, *Then Moses called for all the elders of Israel,* means that he told them to gather together to him all the people, [and he himself told the people all the laws of the Passover mentioned above], as I have explained. But according to the opinion of Rabbi Yonathan, the elders related it to the assembly. Accordingly, the verse stating, *Speak ye unto all the congregation of Israel,*[235] refers [not to Moses and Aaron mentioned in the two verses there above, but] to the elders that were assembled before [Moses and Aaron, and they — the elders — spoke to the congregation], as is also the purport of the verse, *Then it shall be, if it be done in error by 'the eyes of the congregation,'*[236] [which is a reference to the elders of the congregation, members of the Court].

---

(228) Genesis 46:34. (229) Above, Verse 3. (230) Verse 21 before us. (231) Above, Verse 6. (232) Mechilta on the verse before us. See above, Note 205. (233) The teaching is derived from the word *z'keinim* (the elders), "and *zakein* denotes only one who has acquired wisdom" (Kiddushin 32 b). See Ramban above, Verse 2, that "elders" are needed for the Sanctification of the New Moon, as mentioned in the section above, and hence Moses constituted them a court. (234) According to this opinion of Rabbi Yashiya, the court of the elders was constituted only for the Sanctification of the New Moon, and then after the elders gathered the people by command of Moses, he himself said to the people, *Draw out,* etc. (235) Above, Verse 3. (236) Numbers 15:24.

EXODUS XII, BO 141

This section adds an explanation to the putting of the blood [of the Passover-offering, mentioned above in Verse 7], i.e., that it be done with a bunch of hyssop and that it be dipped in the blood that is in the basin, [237] which was not explicitly mentioned above but in a general way, *And they shall take of the blood,* etc.[238] It teaches us that every undefined "taking" prescribed in the Torah must be with "a bunch," [239] and that all "taking" of the blood [prescribed in the Torah] must be in a vessel, [240] as our Rabbis have explained. [241]

And He further explained to them in this section, *and none of you shall go out of the door of his house until the morning,* [237] for on account of it they were commanded to put the blood [of the Passover-offering] upon the lintel so that they would be protected there, just as He said, *and there shall be no plague upon you to destroy you.* [242]

Now Rashi commented: "*And none of you shall go out.* This teaches us that once permission is given to the destroying angel, he does not discriminate between righteous and wicked, and night-time is the domain of the destroying messengers, as it is said, *Thou makest darkness, and it is night, wherein all the beasts of the forest do creep forth.*" [243]

I did not understand that which Rashi said, "and night-time is the domain of the destroying messengers, as it is said, ... *wherein all the beasts of the forest do creep forth.*" [243] Is a person forbidden on any night to go out of the door of his house until the morning, on the authority of this verse? Rather, Rashi should

---

(237) Verse 22. (238) Above, Verse 7. (239) Thus, in the case of the Red Heifer where the verse says, *And the priest shall take cedar-wood, and hyssop, and scarlet* (Numbers 19:6) it means a bunch of cedar-wood and hyssop tied with scarlet (Parah 3:10). (240) Thus, when Scripture says, *And the priest that is anointed shall take of the blood* (Leviticus 4:5), it means of the blood that is in the vessel. (241) Mechilta here on the matter of "the bunch". Concerning the principle of taking the blood in a vessel, I have not found a source deriving it from the verse before us. In Zebachim 97 b, it is derived from the verse, *And he* [Moses] *put it in basins* (further, 24:6). (242) Above, Verse 13. (243) Psalms 104:20.

have said, "for on *that night* permission to destroy was given the angel of destruction, and therefore He warned them against it." But the Rabbi [Rashi] did not find it correct to say so since the Holy One, blessed be He, in His Presence and in His glory, was the One who smote [the first-born]. [244]

This subject is taught in the Mechilta in another version: [245] *"And none of you shall go out of the door of his house until the morning.* This teaches us that once permission is given to the destroying angel,[246] he does not discriminate between righteous and wicked, as it is said, *Come My people, enter into thy chambers ... until the indignation be overpast.*[247] And it also says, *Behold, I am against thee, and will draw forth My sword out of its sheath, and will cut off from thee the righteous and the wicked.*[248] And it further says, *And it shall come to pass, while My glory passeth by, that I will put thee in a cleft of the rock.*[249] This is to teach you [250] that you are to come into a place only in the daytime [251] and leave it only in the daytime.[251] And thus you find that the patriarchs and the prophets observed this as a custom, as it is said: *And Abraham rose early in the morning;*[252] *And Jacob rose up early in the morning;* [253] *And Moses rose up early in the morning;* [254] *And Joshua rose up in the morning;* [255] *And Samuel rose early to meet Saul in the morning.* [256] Now is it not a *kal*

---

(244) Hence there was nothing unique about this night as far as the destroying angel was concerned since he had no special function that night, and yet the Israelites were warned against going out of the door of their homes until the morning! It must necessarily be that night-time is the domain of the destroying messengers. Now on every other night, if a person goes out and he is harmed by them, the profaning of G-d's Name is not entailed. But on the night of Passover, if an Israelite were to be harmed, the Egyptians would say that Moses was not a true prophet, and G-d's Name would be profaned. Hence they were forbidden to go out from their homes. (245) Mechilta on the verse before us (Lauterbach's edition, pp. 85-6). (246) "The destroying angel." In the Mechilta: "the angel." (247) Isaiah 26:20. (248) Ezekiel 21:8. (249) Further, 33:22. (250) In the Mechilta: *"Until the morning.* This is to teach you...." (251) Literally: "when it is good," a reference to the verse, *And G-d saw the light, that it was good* (Genesis 1:4). (252) *Ibid.,* 22:3. (253) *Ibid.,* 28:18. (254) Further, 34:4. (255) Joshua 3:1. (256) I Samuel 15:12.

EXODUS XII, BO

vachomer: [257] If the patriarchs and the prophets, who went to carry out the will of Him by Whose word the world came into being, observed this as a custom, how much more should all other people observe it! And thus it says, *Thou makest darkness, and it is night;* [243] *The young lions roar after their prey;* [258] *Thou givest it unto them, they gather it;* [259] *The sun ariseth, they slink away.* [260] From then on, *Man goeth forth unto his work, and to his labor until the evening."* [261] Thus far extends [the quotation from] the Beraitha. [262]

The purport thereof is to state that Scripture warned the Israelites in Egypt not to go out of the door of their homes on that night because the Holy One, blessed be He, was passing through Egypt like a king who passes from one place to another and whose guardsmen go before him so that people should neither meet him nor see him. This is similar to that which is said, *And the Eternal my G-d shall come, and all the holy ones with Thee;* [263] and also, *And it shall come to pass, while My glory passeth by, that I will put thee in a cleft of the rock,* [249] i.e., to protect him [Moses] from the seraphim and the heavenly agencies. And since we find that once permission is given to the destroying angel he does not discriminate between righteous and wicked, therefore a person has no right [264] to change from the customary way of the world and leave at night-time, since it is the time of the wild beasts when they go out for prey, and there is no way [for them] to distinguish between righteous and wicked.

23. AND HE WILL NOT SUFFER THE DESTROYER TO COME IN UNTO YOUR HOUSES. This means the angel that brings destruction in the world at the time of a plague, similar to

---

(257) See above, Note 208. (258) Psalms 104:21. (259) *Ibid.*, Verse 28. (260) *Ibid.*, Verse 22. (261) *Ibid.*, Verse 23. (262) See above, Note 208. (263) Zechariah 14:5. (264) Thus there appears a distinction between Rashi's explanation and that of Ramban. The conclusion drawn from Rashi's explanation would be that "it is forbidden" to go out on any other night, as Ramban argued. According to Ramban, one has "no right" to do it, since in going against the established order of nature, he may endanger his life, and this he has no right to do.

that which it says, *And He said to the angel that destroyed the people: It is enough; now stay thy hand.* [265] It is not, however, a reference to the One Who brought the destruction in Egypt, since it was the Holy One, blessed be He, Who smote them.

24. AND YE SHALL OBSERVE THIS THING. This refers to the Passover-offering itself, concerning which He had said above, *and slaughter the Passover lamb,* [266] even though it is removed [by two verses from here]. It does not refer to the putting of the blood [upon the lintel and on the two side-posts, mentioned above] in the verse nearby, since only in the Passover of Egypt were they commanded to do so, [i.e., to put the blood upon the lintel, etc.], as it is said, *For the Eternal will pass through to smite the Egyptians; and when He seeth the blood upon the lintel,* etc. [267] Similarly, the expression, *and ye shall keep this service,* [268] means the offering of the Passover. A similar case [of a Scriptural expression that is connected with one that is far removed and not with the one nearby], is the verse, *And also unto thy bondwoman thou shalt do likewise.* [269]

28. AND THE CHILDREN OF ISRAEL WENT AND DID SO; AS THE ETERNAL HATH COMMANDED MOSES AND AARON, SO DID THEY. That is, they departed from before Moses and

---

(265) II Samuel 24:16. (266) Above, Verse 21. (267) Verse 23. How then could we explain the end of the verse before us, which states that we are to observe *this thing* as an ordinance *forever*, when it applied only to the Passover of Egypt? Hence we must say that the expression, *this thing*, refers to the Passover-offering itself, mentioned above in Verse 21, which we are commanded to observe *forever*, i.e., whenever the Sanctuary is in existence. Verse 11, which states, *And thus shall ye eat it: with your loins girded*, etc., also applied only to the Passover of Egypt (Pesachim 96 a). (268) Verse 25.
(269) Deuteronomy 15:17. This is connected with Verse 14 there above, thus making it obligatory for the master to present a released bondwoman with valuable gifts, even as he must do to the bondman. But it is not to be connected with the expression in the first half of Verse 17 itself, which establishes the law of a bondman who refused to be liberated at the end of his six years of bondage, i.e., that his ear is to be pierced and he is to be a bondman forever. As regards this law, it does not apply to a bondwoman.

EXODUS XII, BO

went to the sheep and slaughtered the Passover-offering at eventide [of the fourteenth day of Nisan]. Now such is Scriptural custom to repeat and say, *so did they*, in order to explain that they did not omit anything from whatever they were commanded, as I have explained in the case of Noah.[270] A similar case is the verse, *And Moses saw all the work, and behold, they had done it; as the Eternal had commanded, even so had they done it.*[271]

Now our Rabbis have a Midrash on this verse, since it was not necessary for Scripture to mention that the children of Israel "went" [and did so]. Therefore they explained:[272] *"And the children of Israel went.* This indicates that reward is given for going [to perform a religious duty] as well as for actually performing it. *And they did so.* And had they already done so?[273] No, but once they undertook to perform these duties, Scripture accounts it to them as if they had done them. *As the Eternal hath commanded Moses and Aaron, so did they.* This is to make known the praiseworthiness of Israel, i.e., that they did exactly as Moses and Aaron told them. Another interpretation: What is the meaning of the words, *so did they*? It is to teach us that Moses and Aaron also did so."[274] The Rabbis thus expounded first that the repetition [of the phrase, *so did they*], was in praise of Israel, i.e., that they did not forget [all they were commanded], and that they did not omit anything of whatever was told to them. This is the customary way of the [Sacred] Language in many places.

---

(270) Genesis 6:22. See Vol. I, p. 114. (271) Further, 39:42. (272) Mechilta on the verse before us. (273) "Was not all this spoken to them at the beginning ot the month?" (Rashi). They were commanded to take the lamb on the tenth day and slaughter it on the fourteenth. Thus they could not actually have done it all at once. (274) Since one of the main purposes of the slaughtering of the lamb was a rejection of the belief in idolatry — see Ramban above, Verse 3 — one might have thought that Moses and Aaron, whose belief in the One True G-d was perfect, were not in need of taking part in this commandment. Scripture therefore informs us, according to this Mechilta, that they did as all Israel did, inasmuch as they so cherished G-d's commandment. (From the commentary Zeh Yenachmeinu on the Mechilta, mentioned in my Hebrew work, p. 335.)

30. **FOR THERE WAS NOT A HOUSE WHERE THERE WAS NOT ONE DEAD.** Rashi comments: "If there was a firstborn there, he died; if there was no firstborn there, the chief person in the house died because he is called *b'chor* (firstborn), as it is said, *I also will appoint him firstborn*.[275] Another interpretation: The Egyptian women led dissolute lives under their husbands and bore children from unmarried young men. Thus they had many firstborn sons, sometimes [as many as] five to one woman, each one being the firstborn to his own father."

In line with the plain meaning of Scripture, the firstborn that died in Egypt were the firstborn of their mothers, and this is why He sanctified in their place *all the firstborn, whatsoever openeth the womb among the children of Israel, both of man and of beast.*[276] *The firstborn of Pharaoh that sat on his throne*[277] was the firstborn to his mother. And such indeed is the custom among kings that the reigning mistress be a virgin, something like it is said in the case of Ahasuerus.[278] But in accordance with the opinion of our Rabbis [who say that the firstborn of a father also died], we shall explain that in Egypt, He smote all their firstborn. That is to say, the firstborn of the father, since he is the first-fruit of his strength,[279] and the firstborn of the mother, since he opened the womb, and also the chief person in the house. Yet it was His desire to sanctify in Israel in their place only the firstborn of the mother, because that is a matter more known and of open knowledge. In cattle, only the firstborn of the mother is known at all, and therefore He chose from among all of them only [the firstborn of the mother]. A sort of proof for this [statement of the Rabbis that the firstborn of the father was also smitten] is the verse: *And He smote all the firstborn in Egypt, the first-fruits of their strength in the tents of Ham,*[280] for such an expression, [i.e., the first-fruits of his strength], is said only of a male.

(275) Psalms 89:27.   (276) Further, 13:2.   (277) Verse 29.
(278) Esther 2:3.   (279) See Genesis 49:3.   (280) Psalms 78:51.

31. AND HE CALLED FOR MOSES AND AARON BY NIGHT. "This teaches us that Pharaoh went round to the entrances leading into the city, crying out, 'Where does Moses dwell? Where does Aaron dwell?' " Thus the language of Rashi. Now this happened because Moses and Aaron lodged [close to the vicinity of the palace] that night, [the city of] Egypt, so that Moses' words would be fulfilled, as he said, *And all these thy servants shall come down unto me, and bow down unto me, saying: Get thee out.* [281] And when Pharaoh came to them, they sent messengers to the land of Goshen where the children of Israel dwelled, giving them permission to leave, and they all assembled in Rameses. [282] By that time, it was already well into the day. From there they journeyed *with a high hand,* with Moses at their lead, as it is said, *And they journeyed from Rameses in the first month, on the fifteenth day of the first month; on the morrow after the Passover the children of Israel went out with a high hand in the sight of all the Egyptians.* [283] The verse stating, *The Eternal thy G-d brought thee forth out of Egypt by night* [284] [is no contradiction], since from the time Pharaoh gave them permission to go — [which was at night] — they are already deemed as "going forth" from Egypt.

And thus the Rabbis have said in the Sifre: [285] "Had they not gone forth out of Egypt only at daytime, as it is said, *On the morrow after the Passover the children of Israel went out?* [283] [How then does Scripture say that we were brought forth out of Egypt *by night?*] [284] Simply, this teaches us that the redemption [from bondage] took place at night [although the actual exodus took place during the day]." And in the Gemara of Tractate Berachoth we read: [286] "All Rabbis agree that the redemption took place at night, as it is said, *The Eternal thy G-d brought thee forth out of Egypt by night,* [284] but the actual going forth took place only at daytime, as it is said, *On the morrow after the Passover the children of Israel went with a high hand in the sight of all the Egyptians.*" [283]

---

(281) Above, 11:8.   (282) Verse 37.   (283) Numbers 33:3.
(284) Deuteronomy 16:1.   (285) Sifre, *Re'ei,* 128. See above, Note 209, on the word "Sifre."   (286) Berachoth 9 a.

And some scholars say [287] that they went out from [the city of] Egypt at night, and at daytime they went out from the land of Egypt, which is Rameses, for many of them dwelled in the city of Egypt, and they left at night and joined their brothers in Rameses. But this is not correct, since Scripture says, *And none of you shall go out of the door of his house until the morning.* [288] Thus they were forbidden to go out of their homes at all at night. And similarly the Rabbis have said in the Mechilta: [289] *"And he called to Moses, and Aaron by night, and said: Rise up, get you forth.* But Moses said to Pharaoh: 'Thus we have been commanded: *And none of you shall go out of the door of his house until the morning.* [288] Are we thieves that we should go forth at night? We shall go forth only *with a high hand in the sight of all the Egyptians.*' "

Now Onkelos explained [290] that the miracles which were done for the Israelites on that night make it proper to say that on that night G-d "brought thee forth," because on account of these miracles, they went forth from Egypt.

RISE UP, GET YOU FORTH FROM AMONG MY PEOPLE. The intent thereof is that it was a royal command that they go forth at once, "for I will not give you permission to tarry among my people at all, since they are being killed on account of you."

BOTH YE — [i.e., Moses and Aaron], who do the smiting [291] — AND THE CHILDREN OF ISRAEL. "All of you go out, and do not tarry here under any circumstance." This was to fulfill what G-d had said to Moses, *He shall surely thrust you hence.* [292]

(287) Mentioned by Ibn Ezra here. (288) Above, Verse 22. (289) Mechilta on the Verse before us, with changes. A Midrashic text closer to the one Ramban mentions appears in Midrash Tehilim 113:2. See my Hebrew commentary, p. 336. (290) The verse of Deuteronomy 16:1, *The Eternal thy G-d brought thee forth out of Egypt by night,* was translated by Onkelos thus: "The Eternal thy G-d brought thee forth out of Egypt and did miracles for you at night." (291) This is unlike Rashi who explained: "*Both ye,* the men; *and the children of Israel,* the little ones." (292) Above, 11:1.

EXODUS XII, BO   149

AND GO SERVE THE ETERNAL, AS YE HAVE SAID. Pharaoh said this by way of conciliation so that they would be willing to go forth and listen to him, "since you have been wanting to go to the desert to serve the Eternal."

32. AND BLESS ME ALSO. The purport of it is that "when you will sacrifice to the Eternal your G-d as you have said, and you will pray for yourselves that He should not strike you with pestilence or sword,[293] remember me also in your prayers together with yourselves."

Now Rashi commented: "Pray on my behalf that I should not die, for I am a firstborn." The plain meaning thereof is that they should bless him and his kingdom, for included within the blessing to a king is the state of peace of the whole kingdom. And in the Mechilta we read:[294] *"And bless me also.* Pray on my behalf that the punishment may desist from me," meaning that he should no longer be punished on their account.

39. AND THEY BAKED UNLEAVENED CAKES OF THE DOUGH. The meaning thereof is that they baked unleavened bread of the dough because of the precept which they were commanded: *There shall be no leaven found in your homes, for whosoever eateth that which is leavened, that soul shall be cut off from the congregation of Israel.*[295]

BECAUSE THEY WERE THRUST OUT OF EGYPT. The sense of it is that they baked the dough on the road because they had been driven out of Egypt, and could not wait to bake it in the city and carry the unleavened bread. Therefore they carried the dough, and *their kneading-troughs were bound up in their clothes upon their shoulders,*[296] and they hurried and baked it *before it was leavened*[296] on the road, or in Succoth,[297] where they arrived in a short while as our Rabbis have said.[298]

(293) See above, 5:3.   (294) Mechilta on the verse before us. (295) Above, Verse 19.   (296) Verse 34.   (297) Verse 37. (298) Mechilta here: "In the twinkling of an eye, the children of Israel travelled from Rameses to Succoth."

40. NOW THE TIME THAT THE CHILDREN OF ISRAEL DWELT IN EGYPT WAS FOUR HUNDRED AND THIRTY YEARS. "From the birth of Isaac till now there were four hundred years. [We must reckon from that event, for only] from the time that Abraham had a child [from Sarah] could the prophecy, *that thy seed shall be a stranger in a land that is not theirs,*[299] be fulfilled. And there had been thirty years since that decree made at the 'covenant between the parts'[300] until the birth of Isaac. And when you will reckon the four hundred years from the birth of Isaac, you will find that from the time they came into Egypt, until the time they left, it was two hundred and ten years." Thus the language of Rashi, and it is also the opinion of our Rabbis.[301]

The explanation, however, is not correct in every detail. It is written, *And Abram was seventy and five years old when he departed out of Haran,*[302] and the event of the "covenant between the parts"[300] took place a long time after that.[303] We must therefore explain the case satisfactorily in accordance with what we have been taught in the Seder Olam:[304] "Our father Abraham was seventy years old when G-d spoke to him at the 'covenant between the parts,' as it is said, *And it came to pass at the end of four hundred and thirty years ... that all the hosts of the Eternal went out from the land of Egypt.*[305] Then he returned

---

(299) Genesis 15:13. *And they shall serve them, and they shall afflict them four hundred years.* (300) *Ibid.,* Verse 18. (301) Bereshith Rabbah 44:21. *"That thy seed shall be a stranger in a land that is not theirs.* This means [that the four-hundred year period will begin] from the time seed will be seen by you." (302) Genesis 12:4. (303) And from the "covenant between the parts" until the birth of Isaac, as Rashi stated, thirty years elapsed. How then is it possible that Abraham was one hundred years old at the birth of Isaac (Genesis 21:5) if he was seventy-five years old when he left Haran, and the covenant took place long after his departure from Haran? (304) Literally: "Order of the World." This is an historical chronicle of events from the time of creation to the destruction of the Second Temple. It was authored by Rabbi Yosei ben Chalafta, a disciple of Rabbi Akiba. The text quoted here is found in Chapter 1. (305) Verse 41 here. "And you cannot find four hundred and thirty years unless the "covenant between the parts" took place thirty years before the birth of Isaac" (Yaakov Emden, in his commentary on the Seder Olam).

EXODUS XII, BO

to Haran and stayed there five years, as it is said, *And Abram was seventy and five years old when he departed out of Haran.*[302] The sense of the verse then is to state that when Abraham finally left Haran, his native land, never to return again to his father's house, he was seventy-five years old.[306]

In line with the plain meaning of Scripture, it is my opinion that G-d said to Abraham, "*Know of a surety that* before I give you this land, *thy seed shall be a stranger in a land that is not theirs* for a long time — *four hundred years.*" He did not care to mention the additional thirty years [307] to him [i.e., Abraham], because He told him further on, *And in the fourth generation they shall come back hither,*[308] thereby informing him that they will not come back immediately at the end of four hundred years until the fourth generation when the sin of the Amorite will be full.[308] Thus He alluded to these thirty years, for the Israelites' staying in the desert for forty years was not on account of the sin of the Amorite not yet being full, [since the four hundred and thirty years were completed at the time of the exodus; their stay in the desert was on account of their own misdeeds].

Accordingly, the purport of the verse [before us] is as follows: Now the time that the children of Israel dwelt in Egypt was until four hundred and thirty years, since they lived there in order to

---

(306) And the "covenant between the parts" accordingly took place five years before his final departure from Haran, since from the time of the covenant to the birth of Isaac, as Rashi stated, thirty years had passed. (307) Ramban thus introduced a new explanation to help solve the problem, which was as follows: Since in Genesis 15:13, the length of the exile was foretold to be four hundred years, how is it that Scripture mentions here in Verse 40 an additional thirty years? Rashi answered that the four-hundred year period represents the time from Isaac's birth till the exodus, and the additional thirty years represent the preceding years that elapsed between "the covenant between the parts" and the birth of Isaac. Accordingly, we were forced to say that the covenant took place five years before Abraham's final departure from Haran. Ramban suggests that the intent of the verse in Genesis 15:13 is also four hundred and thirty years, for although the additional thirty years are not clearly written in the verse, they are nevertheless alluded to, as is explained further on. In his commentary on the following verse, Ramban will revert to this theme for further elucidation. (308) Genesis 15:16.

fulfill the period of time set [for Abraham's seed] to live in a land that is not theirs. Thus Scripture informed us that now when they went forth from Egypt, the exile decreed upon them was completed. He brought them forth from servitude to [complete] freedom, and it was not that He took them out from Egypt and they were yet to be strangers in a land not their own. Now because He has already mentioned this matter and informed us thereof [in the section of the "covenant between the parts"], there was no need to prolong it [here], for this verse [here] is intended only to inform us of the thirty years that were added to [the four hundred years mentioned specifically to Abraham]. This is why He says it briefly, i.e., that in Egypt were completed the four hundred years mentioned to their father Abraham and known to them, and an additional thirty years. Then He reverts and says, *And it came to pass at the end of four hundred and thirty years* [309] of their exile, *they went out from the land of Egypt* to perpetual freedom.

A similar case is the verse, *And the days in which we came from Kadesh – barnea, until we were come over the brook Zered were thirty and eight years.* [310] This is to complete the reckoning. The journey from Kadesh–barnea to the brook Zered did not take thirty-eight years. Instead, they abode in Kadesh many years, [311] and then they journeyed from there and turned back by the way to the Red Sea, [312] and in the thirty-eighth year they went over the brook Zered. The purport of the verse is thus: *and the days in which we came from Kadesh-barnea, until we were come over the brook Zered were* until *thirty and eight years* had passed. Similarly: *Happy is he that waiteth, and cometh to the thousand three hundred and five and thirty days* [313] means [happy is he who waits and reaches] the end of those days, not the days themselves.

(309) Verse 41.   (310) Deuteronomy 2:14.   (311) *Ibid.*, 1:46.   (312) *Ibid.*, 2:1.   (313) Daniel 12:12.

42. IT WAS A NIGHT OF WATCHING UNTO THE ETERNAL FOR BRINGING THEM OUT FROM THE LAND OF EGYPT. The verse is stating that from the time He decreed the exile upon them, He observed the matter that He bring them out on that night once the end had come, for *I will hasten it in its time.*[314] It may be that the verse, *It was a night of watching unto the Eternal,* means that He was watching and looking forward to the night when He would bring them out from the land of Egypt, for the Holy One, blessed be He, looked forward to the time when they would merit to be brought out therefrom.

Now if we are to say [as Rashi did, quoted in the commentary on Verse 40], that the [period referred to in] the verse, *that thy seed shall be a stranger in a land that is not theirs,*[299] begins from the time that Abraham had seed, and that the reckoning [of the four hundred and thirty years] begins from the birth of Isaac, you will find that they stayed in Egypt two hundred and forty years, according to the explanation we mentioned.[315] But this too in my opinion is not correct according to the plain meaning of Scripture, since all the days of Abraham cannot be counted as exile with respect to his seed.

The correct interpretation is that He was saying to Abraham "*that thy seed shall be a stranger in a land that is not theirs ... four hundred years*[299] from this day on."[316] The purport thereof was to tell him: "your children will not immediately inherit this land which I give them, but instead they will be strangers like you

---

(314) Isaiah 60:22.   (315) Thus: Isaac was sixty years old when Jacob and Esau were born (Genesis 25:26). When he stood before Pharaoh, Jacob was one hundred and thirty years old (*ibid.*, 47:9). We thus have one hundred and ninety years since the birth of Isaac. Deduct them from the sum of four hundred and thirty, and you have two hundred and forty years remaining for the stay in Egypt.   (316) I.e., from the time of the "covenant between the parts." According to Ramban, who is now following the simple meaning of Scripture, this covenant took place after Abram had left Haran when he was seventy-five years old or thereabout. Thus at the time of the covenant, Abraham was about eighty years old, and not seventy, as we reasoned before according to Rashi. (See beginning of Verse 40.)

were, in a land not theirs [for a period of] four hundred years and more. They will not return here till the fourth generation [308] when four hundred and thirty years will be completed." But if so, then their stay in Egypt lasted about two hundred and twenty years or thereabouts.[317] Now if the numerical value of the word *'r'du'* (get you down) thither,[318] [which is two hundred and ten], be an established tradition in Israel, it is possible that [Jacob, by using the word *r'du*], alluded to those who arrived in Egypt that after Jacob's death they would stay there two hundred and ten years. With the seventeen years that Jacob lived in the land of Egypt,[319] their stay altogether totalled two hundred and twenty-seven years.

And I have already mentioned [320] the explanation of Rabbi Abraham ibn Ezra that the expression, *that thy seed shall be a stranger,* means "in servitude and affliction until the end of a four-hundred year period commencing from this day of the covenant." And Ibn Ezra further said that the thirty additional years [mentioned here in Verses 40-41] represent the time that elapsed between Abraham's departure from his country [321] [and the day of the covenant]. Accordingly, the explanation of the verse here is as follows: *"Now the time that the children of Israel*

(317) According to Ramban's interpretation, Abraham was about eighty years old at the time of the covenant. (See Note above). It was twenty years from then until Isaac's birth, since Scripture states that Abraham was one hundred years old when Isaac was born. Isaac was sixty years old when Jacob was born, and when Jacob stood before Pharaoh, he was one hundred and thirty. Thus we have two hundred and ten years. Deduct them from four hundred and thirty, and you are left with two hundred and twenty, which is the length of time they stayed in Egypt. (318) Genesis 42:2. These were Jacob's words to his sons upon sending them to buy food in Egypt. He did not use the word *l'chu* (go you), but *r'du* (get you down), because the numerical value of the word *r'du* is two hundred and ten. There was thus an allusion here to the time the Israelites would stay in Egypt. (319) Genesis 47:28. (320) *Ibid.,* 15:13 (in Vol. I, *Seder Lech Lecha,* p. 203). (321) I.e., his native country, Ur of the Chaldees. From there he went with his father to Haran, where they stayed five years, and then Abraham left for the land of Canaan. He was then seventy-five years old. Twenty-five years later when Isaac was born, the thirty year period, commencing from the time he left Ur of the Chaldees, was thus completed (Ibn Ezra).

dwelt in Egypt until the end of the period when they and their ancestors were strangers in a land not theirs, *was four hundred and thirty years."*

I maintain further that the most lucid explanation of all is that we say that the decree of the four-hundred year period, [as mentioned in Genesis 15:13], is to be reckoned from that day [of the "covenant between the parts]," as we have mentioned, and these thirty additional years — [in Verses 40-41 here] — were due to the sin of that generation. If exile and affliction are decreed upon a person for a year or two because of his sin and he will fully continue to add to his transgressions, exile and visitation of seven times [322] the original magnitude will be his lot; his first punishment is no guarantee against his being punished for the additional sin he committed. Now it had been decreed upon Abraham that his children would be strangers in a land not their own [for a period of] four hundred years, and that they will not return until the fourth generation, *for the iniquity of the Amorite is not yet full.* [308] Abraham was given no assurance [concerning the precise ending of the exile], except in the promise, *And afterward they will come out with great substance,* [323] and that ["afterward"] could be immediately [after the four-hundred year period] or some subsequent time. Even that promise was given conditionally, as He said, *And also that nation, whom they shall serve, will I judge; and afterward shall they come out with great substance,* [323] meaning that He will bring them to judgment to determine whether they did to Israel in accordance with their deeds and as was decreed upon them. [324] Besides, no assurance is immune to annulment because of subsequent sin unless it is accompanied by an oath. And it is a known fact that the Israelites in Egypt were wicked and exceeding sinners, having also done away with circumcision, as it is written, *And they rebelled against Me, and would not hearken unto Me; they did not every man cast away the detestable things of their eyes, neither did they forsake the idols of Egypt; then I said I would pour out My fury upon*

(322) See Leviticus 26:28. (323) Genesis 15:14. (324) For fuller explanation of this point, see Vol. I, pp. 204-205.

them in the midst of the land of Egypt.[325] Again it says, *And put away the gods which your fathers served beyond the River, and in Egypt, and serve ye the Eternal.*[326] It was for this reason that He prolonged their exile for thirty years.

In fact, it should have been prolonged even more, but on account of their cries and many prayers, [it was shortened to thirty years]. This is the sense of the verses: *And the children of Israel sighed by reason of the bondage, and they cried, and their cry came up unto G-d;*[327] *And G-d heard their groaning,*[328] *And now, behold, the cry of the children of Israel is come unto Me.*[329] And it further states, *And we cried unto the Eternal, the G-d of our fathers, and the Eternal heard our voice, and saw our affliction, and our toil, and our oppression,*[330] since they did not deserve to be redeemed on account of the end [of the four-hundred year period], but only because He accepted their cry and their groaning on account of the great agony they were in, as I have explained in *Seder V'eileh Shemoth.*[331] Why should the earlier scholars — [i.e., Rashi and Ibn Ezra] — find it difficult to explain that their exile was prolonged after the end [of the four-hundred year period] by thirty years, when on account of the sin of the spies their stay in the wilderness was later prolonged forty years![332] Those forty years were indeed an affliction to them, as Scripture states, *And thou shalt remember all the way which the Eternal thy G-d hath led thee these forty years in the wilderness, that He might afflict thee.*[333] And it further says, *And He afflicted thee, and suffered thee to hunger.*[334] Thus they were subject [in the wilderness] to complete exile in a land given over to *serpents, fiery serpents, and scorpions,*[335] and the promise, *And in the fourth generation they shall come back hither,*[308] was not fulfilled in them, since during those forty years, that generation surely passed away after the [fifth] generation was already born. Thus the sins caused all delays.

(325) Ezekiel 20:8. (326) Joshua 24:14. (327) Above, 2:23.
(328) *Ibid.,* Verse 24. (329) *Ibid.,* 3:9. (330) Deuteronomy 26:7.
(331) Above, 2:25. (332) Numbers 14:34. (333) Deuteronomy 8:2.
(334) *Ibid.,* Verse 4. (335) *Ibid.,* Verse 15.

EXODUS XII, BO

It is possible that this [delay of the thirty years] was on account of the children of Ephraim who went out [from the land of Egypt] thirty years before the coming of Moses our teacher, and as our Rabbis have mentioned. [336] They reckoned [the end of the four-hundred year period from the time it was declared to Abraham], and they made no error, *but his own iniquities shall ensnare the wicked.* [337] And may the Holy One, blessed be He, forgive us all sin and error.

THIS SAME NIGHT IS A NIGHT OF WATCHING UNTO THE ETERNAL FOR ALL THE CHILDREN OF ISRAEL THROUGHOUT THEIR GENERATIONS. The intent of this is "that this night set aside by G-d to bring Israel out of Egypt is *unto the Eternal.* That is to say, it is to be sanctified to His Name. [It is] *a night of watching for all the children of Israel throughout their generations,* meaning that they are to observe it by worshipping Him through the eating of the Passover-offering, the remembering of the miracles, and the reciting of praise and thanksgiving to His Name," just as He said, *And thou shalt keep this ordinance.* [338] And He further said, *Observe the month of Aviv, and keep the Passover.* [339]

Rabbi Abraham ibn Ezra explained that the intent of the expression, *It was a night of watching unto the Eternal,* is that G-d watched the Israelites and did not suffer the destroyer to come into their homes. This is not correct, since Scripture continues to state, *It was a night of watching... for bringing them out from the land of Egypt.*

---

(336) Sanhedrin 92 b. (337) Proverbs 5:22. In other words, the children of Ephraim were accurate in their reckoning. However, they failed to know that on account of the sins of the generation, thirty years had been added to the length of the bondage. (338) Further, 13:10. The Hebrew *v'shamarta (and thou shalt keep)* is of the same root as *shimurim (watching)* here. (339) Deuteronomy 16:1. Here too the word *shamor (observe)* is of the same root as *shimurim* in the verse before us. It thus proves that *leil shimurim (a night of watching)* means "a night of observance of the Passover service."

43. AND THE ETERNAL SAID UNTO MOSES AND AARON: THIS IS THE ORDINANCE OF THE PASSOVER. "This chapter was related to them on the fourteenth day of Nisan." Thus the language of Rashi. This is correct, since at the end of this chapter it is written, *Thus did all the children of Israel, as the Eternal hath commanded,* [340] attesting concerning them that they and their servants were circumcised, [as this is a prerequisite for eating the Passover-offering].[341] But if so, Scripture should have logically mentioned this chapter before the section, *And it came to pass at midnight.*[342] But the reason [*the section of the ordinance of the Passover* is placed here] is as follows: The chapter of *This month shall be unto you the beginning of months*[343] was said on the first of the month.[344] Immediately on that day, Moses fulfilled his mission, [as it states], *Then Moses called for all the elders of Israel, and said unto them,*[345] meaning that he commanded them concerning *the ordinance of the Passover* [mentioned here], and he assured them that they will be redeemed on the night of the fifteenth day [of Nisan]. They believed, *and the people bowed the head and worshipped.*[346] To this account Scripture adjoined the section, *And it came to pass at midnight,*[342] in order to state that He fulfilled the promise He made to them. On finishing this section, Scripture then reverts to the first theme in order to complete the ordinance of the Passover.

This chapter adds many commandments [concerning the Passover-offering]: the prohibitions of an alien or an uncircumcised Israelite eating thereof, the prohibitions of removing the flesh thereof from where it is eaten and of breaking any of its bones, and the law of the Passover-offering of a proselyte. These commandments applied immediately and for all generations.[347] Then Scripture completed the section by saying that the children of Israel did all this; *as G-d commanded... so did they.*[340] It uses the expression, *all the children of Israel,*[340] in order to explain

---

(340) Further, Verse 50. (341) Verses 44 and 48. (342) Above, Verse 29. (343) *Ibid.,* Verse 2. (344) Pesachim 6 b. (345) Above, Verse 21. (346) *Ibid.,* Verse 27. (347) Unlike certain other laws which applied only to the Passover-offering in Egypt. (See Ramban above, Verse 24 and Note 267).

EXODUS XII. BO

that there was not one person who transgressed the command of G-d concerning all these matters [mentioned here in the section beginning, *This is the ordinance of the Passover*], as well as all He commanded regarding the laws of the Passover mentioned in the sections above.

Rabbi Abraham ibn Ezra wrote that this chapter dealing with the Passover of the generations, [as distinguished from the Passover of Egypt], was said *after* the Passover of Egypt, and the verse, *Thus did all the children of Israel,* [340] refers to the Passover in the wilderness, which they observed in the second year after the exodus. [348] [Although it should logically precede the Passover in the wilderness, according to Ibn Ezra] it is written here because of the general commandment [on the Passover here], the case being similar [to that of the jar of manna which Aaron was to put up before the Testimony in the Tabernacle, of which Scripture says], *And Aaron laid it up before the Testimony, for a charge.* [349] [This account should logically follow that of the building of the Tabernacle, but instead it was mentioned in the chapter dealing with the manna in order to complete the subject.]

This opinion [of Ibn Ezra here] is a mistake. The commandments in all these chapters deal only with the Passover of Egypt and the Passovers which they were to observe in the Land of Israel, as it is said above, *And it shall come to pass, when ye be come to the Land,* etc. [350] The Passover in the wilderness, however, was a commandment only for that particular time. [351]

THERE SHALL NO 'BEN NEICHAR' (ALIEN) EAT THEREOF. "This means one whose actions are estranged from his Heavenly Father, and applies both to a non-Israelite and an Israelite." [352] Thus the language of Rashi quoting from the

---

(348) Numbers 9:1.   (349) Further, 16:34.   (350) Above, Verse 25. (351) I.e., only for the second year after the exodus. During all other years in which they were in the wilderness, they did not sacrifice the Passover-offering (see Joshua 5:5), although the other laws of the Passover were of course observed.   (352) In our Rashi: "an apostate Israelite."

Mechilta.³⁵³ The verse of course is needed only for the case of an [apostate] Israelite. And so did Onkelos translate: *"There shall no 'ben neichar' eat thereof*, i.e, any Israelite who has become an apostate," meaning he has estranged himself from his brethren and from his Heavenly Father through his evil deeds.

This is the word *neichar*, mentioned by the Sages in all places, which means estranged, and the purport thereof is *m'shumad*, one who is a known [opponent to the Torah]. The usage of the word is similar to the Aramaic expression, *'ve'isht'moda' (And) Joseph (knew) his brethren, but they 'isht'modei' (knew) him not.*³⁵⁴ In the case of the word *m'shumad*, it is missing the letter *ayin*, just as it is absorbed in many [Aramaic] words: *midam* (anything) in place of *mida'am; dor kati* in place of *dor katia* (a chopped generation), ³⁵⁵ *baki* in place of *b'kia* (expert). ³⁵⁶

45. 'TOSHAV' (A SOJOURNER) 'V'SACHIR' (AND A HIRED SERVANT) SHALL NOT EAT THEREOF. *"Toshav* is a resident non-Israelite [who has foresworn idolatry, but has not as yet been fully converted to Judaism]. A *'sachir'* is a non-Israelite. But why should Scripture mention all these? They are uncircumcised, [and an uncircumcised person may not eat of the Passover-offering]! However, it refers to a circumcised Arabian or a circumcised Gibeonite." ³⁵⁷ Thus the language of Rashi.

I do not know why the Rabbi [Rashi] wrote down matters which are rejected in the Gemara. ³⁵⁸ The Rabbis have objected to this explanation [that the verse refers to a circumcised Arabian or a circumcised Gibeonite], asking: "Are these considered circumcised?! Have we not been taught that he who vows not to have benefit from the uncircumcised is permitted to have benefit from the uncircumcised of Israel, but not from the circumcised of

---

(353) Mechilta on the verse before us. (354) Genesis 42:8. (355) Kethuboth 10 b. (356) Sanhedrin 5 b. (357) "I might think that since they are circumcised, they are qualified to partake of the Passover-offering. Scripture therefore says, *A 'toshav' and a 'sachir' shall not eat thereof*" (Mechilta here). (358) Yebamoth 71 a.

other nations, as it is written, *For all the nations are uncircumcised, but all the house of Israel are uncircumcised in the heart?"* [359] Instead, the Rabbis [there in the Gemara] [358] explained the verse as referring to a proselyte who was circumcised but who has not yet undergone immersion. [360]

51. AND IT CAME TO PASS THE SELFSAME DAY THE ETERNAL DID BRING THE CHILDREN OF ISRAEL OUT OF THE LAND OF EGYPT. Since Scripture said above, *It was a night of watching unto the Eternal for bringing them out of the land of Egypt,* [361] it reverted and explained that they did not go out at all of the land then, but that Pharaoh gave them permission [at night] to go out, and thus they became free men. Instead, it was in the glare of full daylight that they went out from all the borders of Egypt with all *their hosts* — the hosts of women and *the mixed multitude* [362] that attached themselves to them.

Rabbi Abraham ibn Ezra explained the purport of the verse as follows: "*And it came to pass the selfsame day* that *the Eternal did bring the children of Israel out of the land of Egypt* that He spoke to Moses, saying, *Sanctify unto Me.*" [363]

13   2. SANCTIFY UNTO ME. This means that they are to consecrate the firstborn at once so that the commandment be applicable in the wilderness. This chapter adds many commandments: that they remember the day [when they left Egypt] and that the month was Aviv, [364] and that they keep *this*

---

(359) Jeremiah 9:25. Thus it is clear that a circumcised Arabian, etc., is considered uncircumcised, and no special verse is needed to exclude him from eating the Passover-offering, as Rashi interpreted. (360) For a proselyte to be fully accepted into the Jewish fold, he must undergo both circumcision, and immersion in a body of water valid for that purpose. The verse before us thus teaches that the proselyte who underwent the rite of circumcision alone is still forbidden to eat the Passover-offering, notwithstanding the fact that he is already circumcised and has begun his entry into the faith. (361) Above, Verse 42. (362) *Ibid.*, Verse 38. (363) Further, 13:2. Thus according to Ibn Ezra, the verse before us is to be joined to the following chapter. (364) Verses 3-4.

ordinance in its season.[365] This is an allusion to the intercalation [of an extra month] in the lunar year, [366] since we are to observe the Passover only in the month of Aviv, [which is the spring]. On the subject of leavened bread, this chapter adds: *Neither shall there be leaven seen with thee, in all thy borders.*[367] At the conclusion, it adds the commandment of the frontlets.[368]

5. AND IT SHALL BE WHEN THE ETERNAL SHALL BRING THEE INTO THE LAND OF THE CANAANITE, AND THE HITTITE, AND THE AMORITE, AND THE HIVITE, AND THE JEBUSITE. "Although it enumerates here only five peoples, all of the seven nations[369] are implied. They are all included in [the generic term] Canaanite although there was one of the races which had no name other than that of Canaanite."[370] Thus the language of Rashi.

It is true that they are all included in [the generic term] Canaanite, for they were all his sons.[371] Therefore when Scripture says, *And it shall be when the Eternal shall bring thee into the land of the Canaanite,* it alludes to all of the seven nations, and thus everywhere does Scripture make use of the term, "the land of Canaan." But here, [according to Rashi's interpretation], there is no reason why Scripture should mention most of them and yet leave some of them included in the term Canaanite!

(365) Verse 10. (366) A lunar year — i.e., twelve lunar months — totals 354 days, 8 hours, 48 minutes and 36 seconds, as opposed to the solar year, which consists of 365 days, 6 hours and 48 seconds (Mishneh Torah, Z'manim, Hilchoth Kiddush Hachodesh, 9:2). There is a difference of nearly eleven days, and in order to exclude the possibility of the Passover being shifted from the spring, it is therefore necessary to interpolate an additional month about once every three years. (367) Verse 7. (368) Verse 16. (369) The five nations mentioned here and the Perizzite and the Girgashite. See Ramban above, 3:8. (370) Thus under the name Canaanite, one may understand either that particularly so-called nation or any of the other six nations who, besides bearing the generic name Canaanite, were also known as Hivites, etc. In the verse before us, *the Canaanite* thus refers to the particular nation and to the two other nations, i.e., the Perizzite and the Girgashite, which are not specifically mentioned here, since they are included in the generic name Canaanite. (371) Genesis 10:15-16.

EXODUS XIII, BO

In the opinion of our Rabbis, [372] the land of these five nations mentioned here was *a land flowing with milk and honey,* but not so the land of the remaining two nations [omitted here]. Therefore He gladdened them only with this land [of the five nations]. Thus the Rabbis taught in the Sifre with respect to first-fruits: [373] *"And He hath given us this land, a land flowing with milk and honey.* [374] Just as *the land flowing with milk and honey* mentioned elsewhere, [i.e., in the verse before us], refers to the land of the five nations, so also the *land flowing with milk and honey* mentioned here [in the case of the first-fruits] means the land of the five nations. Rabbi Yosei says that first-fruits are not brought from beyond the Jordan since it is not a land flowing with milk and honey." Thus the land of the two nations, [the Perizzite and the Girgashite], were excluded from the law of first-fruits because theirs is not a land flowing with milk and honey, and for the same reason, Rabbi Yosei also excluded the land beyond the Jordan, which belonged to the Amorite. [375] And the Amorite mentioned here [among the five nations whose land was flowing with milk and honey], is the Amorite who lived in the Land of Israel proper. A text similar [to the one in the Sifre] is found in the Mechilta on this chapter.

It is further taught in the Sifre: [376] *"And they,* [i.e., all the tribe of Levi], *shall have no inheritance* [377] — this refers to the inheritance of the five nations; *Among their brethren* — this refers to the inheritance of the two nations." The Rabbis [of the Sifre] thus separated these five nations as different, because theirs was the main land which He promised them, for that was the land flowing with milk and honey. And Rashi, in the section of *Shoftim V'shotrim,* experienced difficulty in explaining this Beraitha. [378]

---

(372) In the Sifre mentioned further on in the text. (373) Sifre, *Ki Thavo,* 300. (374) Deuteronomy 26:9. (375) Numbers 32:33. (376) Sifre, *Shoftim,* 164. (377) Deuteronomy 18:2. (378) Upon quoting the text of the Sifre — though with a different version — Rashi comments there: "I do not, however, know for certain what the Sifre means." Rashi then proceeds to suggest his interpretation, and then mentions still another version of the text of the Sifre in question. The intent of Ramban's words here that Rashi experienced difficulty in explaining this text in

Now according to this opinion [that only the land of the five nations mentioned here was flowing with milk and honey], Scripture stated above, [*And I am come down to deliver them... and to bring them up*] *unto a good and large Land, unto a Land flowing with milk and honey,*[379] [and then proceeds to mention the five nations listed here as well as the Perizzite]. However, it does not add the Perizzite there on account of its land flowing with milk and honey, but because it was part of the *good and large Land.*

These are the six nations mentioned everywhere, [380] for the Girgashite, [the seventh nation], emigrated of his own accord, and is not mentioned in the Torah except in the verse: *And He shall cast out many nations before thee, the Hittite, and the Girgashite, and the Amorite, and the Canaanite, and the Perizzite, and the Hivite, and the Jebusite, seven nations.*[381] This is why He said *many nations*, [i.e., because all seven are mentioned]. And it is also written: *But thou shalt surely destroy them: the Hittite, and the Amorite, the Canaanite, and the Perizzite, the Hivite, and the Jebusite,*[382] but He did not mention the Girgashite, thus alluding to the fact that he would not war against the Israelites but instead would emigrate of his own accord.

6. AND IN THE SEVENTH DAY SHALL BE A FEAST TO THE ETERNAL. This means that they are to bring their Festival-offering [383] on the seventh day [of Passover] and are not to delay it any longer, for after that, one can no longer make amends for it. However, as far as the Festival-offering [383] is

---

Deuteronomy 18:2 is thus clear. (See Note 209 above on the meaning of the word Beraitha.) (379) Above, 3:8. (380) See further, 23:23 and 34:11. (381) Deuteronomy 7:1. (382) *Ibid.*, 20:17. (383) Upon going up to the Sanctuary on the three Festivals of Pesach, Shevuoth, and Succoth, one is obligated to bring a Festival peace-offering. (See "The Commandments," Vol. I, pp. 60-61). That Festival-offering should be brought on the first day of the festival and not later than on the seventh day of Passover or on *Shmini Atzereth,* which is the eighth day of Succoth. The Festival of Shevuoth, though only one day, has a similar seven-day extension period (Chagigah 9 a).

concerned, amends can be made for the first day of the festival all seven days. Both [the first and seventh] days of Passover are alike with respect to the law of *a holy convocation*, as He said above, *And in the first day there shall be to you a holy convocation, and in the seventh day a holy convocation.* [384]

8. IT IS BECAUSE OF THAT THE ETERNAL DID FOR ME. This is equivalent to saying, "It is because of that *which* the Eternal did for me when I came forth out of Egypt." A similar case is the verse: *And thou shalt show them the way they are to go in,* [385] [which means "*wherein* they are to go"]. There are many such cases. The father is thus stating [to his son]: "It is because of that which G-d did for me when I came forth out of Egypt that I observe this service." It is similar to that which is stated further on: *Therefore I sacrifice to the Eternal all that openeth the womb.* [386]

The intent of the word *zeh* (that) [in the verse, *It is because of 'that'*], is: "tell him 'that' which you yourself see, i.e., what G-d did for you when you came forth out of Egypt." And our Rabbis have explained [387] that the word *zeh* (that) alludes to the unleavened bread and bitter herbs that are laid before him.

It is possible that the purport of the verse, *And thou shalt tell thy son... It is 'ba'avur' (because) of that the Eternal did for me when I came forth out of Egypt,* is equivalent to the verse's saying "such and such did G-d do unto me." The word *ba'avur* also serves to indicate something within a subject itself, [and it does not only convey the idea: "because" of some other subject]. This is as the case in the verse, *'ba'avur' the child that was alive thou didst fast and weep,* [388] [which means "while" the child was alive], and not "because". [David did not fast and weep "because" the child was alive; he fasted and wept "while" the child was alive so that it should get well.]

Rabbi Abraham ibn Ezra said that the purport of the verse is: "*Because of that* which I do and worship Him by eating the

(384) Above, 12:16.   (385) Further, 18:20.   (386) Verse 15.
(387) Mechilta on the verse before us.   (388) II Samuel 12:21.

Passover-offering and the unleavened bread, *the Eternal did for me wonders until He brought me forth out of Egypt.*" But it is not correct. I will yet explain this verse. [389]

9. AND IT SHALL BE FOR A SIGN UNTO THEE UPON THY HAND, AND FOR A MEMORIAL BETWEEN THINE EYES, THAT THE LAW OF THE ETERNAL MAY BE IN THY MOUTH; FOR WITH A STRONG HAND HATH THE ETERNAL BROUGHT THEE OUT OF EGYPT. To be interpreted [properly, the verse must be transposed]: "And it shall be for a sign unto thee upon thy hand and for a memorial between thine eyes, that with a strong hand hath the Eternal brought thee out of Egypt, that the law of the Eternal may be in thy mouth." The meaning thereof is that you are to inscribe the exodus from Egypt [in the phylacteries] upon your hand and between your eyes, and remember it always in order that G-d's law be in your mouth, [so that you will] observe His commandments and teachings, for He is your Master *Who redeemed thee out of the house of bondage.* [390]

11. AND IT SHALL BE WHEN THE ETERNAL SHALL BRING THEE INTO THE LAND OF THE CANAANITES. This is stated because the law of that which "openeth the womb" [mentioned in Verse 12], applied only from the time they came to the Land of Israel. [391]

In line with the plain meaning of Scripture, the verse, *Sanctify unto Me all the firstborn,* [mentioned in Verse 2 above] means all the firstborn living at that time. Since He redeemed them from

---

(389) Further, Verse 16, beginning with: "By way of Truth." See Ramban's discussion there which helps to explain why he did not find Ibn Ezra's — and incidentally, also Rashi's — explanation of the verse satisfactory. In Ramban's opinion, the delivery from Egypt, besides having the purpose of enabling Israel to fulfill G-d's commandments — as Rashi and Ibn Ezra so interpret the verse here — also served another very high purpose, as explained there. (390) Deuteronomy 13:6. (391) See my Hebrew commentary p. 344 for correctness of this reading as based on Ramban manuscript. It is also borne out by Ramban's statement further on in this section: "But the commandment... did not apply to the firstborn in the wilderness."

death when He smote in the land of Egypt, He commanded [in that verse above] that they be sanctified to Him to do the work of G-d, whatever He will command them to do. He did not command them at this time concerning the redemption of the firstborn, but only after He exchanged them for the Levites and He commanded the redemption of the firstborn that were over and above the number of the Levites.[392] But the commandment [as expressed in the verse, *Sanctify unto Me all the firstborn*], did not apply to the firstborn in the wilderness. Now, [in the verse before us], He commanded that when they shall come into the Land of Israel, the law should apply to the firstborn of both man and beast [393] and the firstling of an ass, [394] and then He commanded the law of their redemption for the generations.[394]

AS HE SWORE UNTO THEE AND TO THY FATHERS. The meaning of it is that "He swore to your fathers to give it to you," just as it is said above, *which He swore unto thy fathers to give thee.* [395] It may be that G-d's word by itself is called "an oath," for thus He said twice:[396] *And I am come down to deliver them out of the hand of the Egyptians, and to bring them up out of that land unto a good land,* [397] and again it says, *And I will bring you in unto the land concerning which I lifted up My hand.*[398]

12. 'V'HA'AVARTA' UNTO THE ETERNAL ALL THAT OPENETH THE WOMB. This is an expression of setting apart, i.e., that one is to remove the firstling from the flock and it is to be for the Eternal. Then He reverts and explains that this "setting apart" means that every first male offspring dropped by a beast, and every first offspring of an ass and every firstborn son of a man shall be the Eternal's. But Rashi commented: *"And thou shalt set apart unto the Eternal all that openeth the womb.* Scripture is speaking of the firstborn of man."

---

(392) Numbers 3:44-47. (393) Verse 12. (394) Verse 13. (395) Verse 5. (396) "And the repetition of an expression may be regarded as an oath" (Shebuoth 36 a, and see also Rashi to Genesis 8:21). (397) Above, 3:8. (398) *Ibid.*, 6:8.

16. 'ULTOTAPHOTH' BETWEEN THINE EYES. No affinity is known to this word. Linguists, [399] however, associated it with the expressions: *'v'hateiph'* *(And speak) to the south;* [400] *And my word 'titoph' (dropped) upon them.*[401] The figurative usage thereof is based on the verse: *And the mountains shall drop ('v'hitiphu') sweet wine.* [402] Thus the verse is saying that you should make the exodus from Egypt a sign upon your hand, and between your eyes a source for discourse distilling as the dew upon those that hear it. [403] Our Rabbis, however, have called an object which lies upon the head *totaphoth*, just as they have said: "[A woman] may not go out [on the Sabbath] with a *totepheth* or head-bangles." [404] Rabbi Abahu said: "What is *totepheth*? It is a forehead-band extending from ear to ear." [405] Now it is the Rabbis [of the Talmud] who are the [true Hebrew] linguists, as they spoke the language and knew it and it is from them that we should accept [the explanation of the word *ultotaphoth*].

Now Scripture says *totaphoth* [in the plural] and not *totepheth* [in the singular] because there are many compartments in the phylacteries, [406] just as we have received their form from the holy fathers [407] who saw the prophets and the ancient ones up to Moses our teacher doing so.

Now the fundamental reason of this commandment is that we lay the script of the exodus from Egypt upon the hand and upon the head opposite the heart and the brain, which are the pivots of

(399) Menachem ben Saruk, quoted in Rashi. See also Ibn Ezra. (400) Ezekiel 21:2. (401) Job 29:22. Ramban evidently understands it: "and to them I spoke my word," meaning "they followed my advice without question." (402) Amos 9:13. The figurative sense of the verse is that the mountains "will speak" of sweet wine. (403) See Deuteronomy 32:2. (404) Shabbath 57 a. (405) *Ibid.,* 57 b. (406) The phylactery of the head is divided into four vertical compartments, each compartment containing a scroll of one of the four Scriptural passages referring to this commandment. The phylactery of the arm contains one interior chamber which contains but one single scroll upon which all four sections of the Law are inscribed together. For fuller discussion of the subject, see "The Commandments," Vol. I, p. 18-19. (407) A reference to the Sages of the Talmud, who received the true Tradition of the Torah.

thought. Thus we are to inscribe [on parchment] the Scriptural sections of *Kadesh (Sanctify unto Me)* [Verses 1-10], and *V'haya ki y'viacha (And it shall be when the Eternal shall bring thee)* [Verses 11-16], and enclose them in the phylacteries because of this commandment wherein we were charged to make the exodus from Egypt for frontlets between our eyes. [We are also to inscribe and enclose in the phylacteries the sections of] *Sh'ma (Hear O Israel)* [Deuteronomy 6:4-9] and *V'haya im shamo'a (And it shall come to pass, if ye shall hearken)* [ibid., 11:13-21] because we are charged to have the commandments [of the Torah] also for frontlets between our eyes, as it is written: *And these words, which I command thee this day, shall be upon thy heart;*[408] *and they shall be for frontlets between thine eyes.*[409] This is why we also inscribe [on parchment] these two sections — [*Sh'ma* and *V'haya im shamo'a*] — for frontlets [even though the exodus is not mentioned in them], for they contain the commandments of the Unity of G-d, the memorial of all commandments, the doctrine of retribution, which states that the consequence of disobeying the commandments is punishment and that blessings come in the wake of obedience — and the whole foundation of the faith.[410] Now of the phylactery of the arm, Scripture says, *And it shall be for a sign unto thee upon thy hand,*[411] which the Rabbis explained[412] as referring to the left arm, which is opposite the heart.

(408) Deuteronomy 6:6. (409) *Ibid.*, Verse 8. (410) "The whole foundation of the faith." This may refer to the principle of the Unity of G-d which is indeed the root of faith, as Ramban describes it in Deuteronomy 6:4. However, in view of the fact that this principle has already been explicitly mentioned here by Ramban, the reference must be to some other doctrine. It is reasonable to assume that Ramban is here alluding to a point he has explained in many places — "a true principle, clearly indicated in the Torah... that in the entire scope of the Torah there are only miracles, and no nature or custom." (See Vol. I, pp. 556-7; see also his commentary above, 6:2, and on Leviticus 26:11.) The theme appears also in his introduction to the Commentary on the Book of Job (Kithvei Haramban, Vol. I, pp. 17-19). In his "Sermon on the Perfection of the Torah," (*Ibid.*, p. 153) as well as at the end of this *Seder*, he states clearly that "a person has no part in the Torah of Moses our teacher" unless he believes in this principle. It is thus logical to assume that "the whole foundation of the faith" mentioned here is a reference to the above principle. (411) Above, Verse 9. (412) Menachoth 36 b.

By way of the Truth, [the mystic lore of the Cabala], the verse, *It is because of 'zeh' (this) which the Eternal did for me,*[413] is similar to *'zeh' (this) is my G-d, and I will glorify Him.*[414] The verse here thus states that it was because of His name and His glory that He did for us and brought us forth out of Egypt. *And "this" shall be for a sign unto thee* on the arm of your strength,[415] just as it is written, *For Thou art the glory of their strength.*[416] Thus the sign [of the phylactery] is similar to the sign of circumcision[417] and the Sabbath.[418] And since all [emanations] are one perfect unity, which is alluded to in "the sign" on the arm, our ancestors have received the tradition from Moses, who received it from the mouth of the Almighty, that [all four sections of Scripture inscribed in the phylacteries, as described above], are encased in one compartment. This is something like Scripture says, *achothi kalah,*[419] because it is united and comprised of the thirty-two paths of wisdom[420] [with which the world was created], and it is further written, *His left hand is under my head.*[421]

Then Scripture says, *And it shall be for a memorial between thine eyes,*[411] meaning that we are to lay them at the place of remembrance, which is between the eyes, at the beginning of the brain. It is there that remembrance begins by recalling the appearances [of persons and events] after they have passed away from us. These frontlets circle around the whole head with their straps, while the loop rests directly over the base of the brain which guards the memory. And the expression, *between your eyes,* means that they are to be placed upon the middle of the head, not towards one side. It may be that in the middle of the head, there are the roots of the eyes and from these stems the power of sight.

---

(413) Above, Verse 8.   (414) Further, 15:2.   (415) See Psalms 89:11.   (416) *Ibid.,* Verse 18.   (417) Genesis 17:11.   (418) Further, 31:13.   (419) Song of Songs 5:1. Literally, "my sister, the bride," but here interpreted on the basis of the Hebrew roots which suggest "unity" (*achothi,* my sister — *echad,* one) and "totality" (*kalah,* bride — *kol,* all), as explained in the text. See also Vol. I, p. 292, where Ramban refers to this theme. (420) Sefer Yetzirah 1:1   (421) Song of Songs 2:6.

EXODUS XIII, BO

Similarly, the verse, *Nor make ye any baldness between your eyes for the dead,* [422] [means baldness adjoining the forehead. Thus the expression *between your eyes* mentioned here in the case of the frontlets also refers to the identical place]. It is to explain this point, [i.e., that the phylactery of the head is not to be placed between the eyes, as the literal meaning of the words might indicate, but that it is to be placed upon the middle of the head adjoining the forehead], that He reverts here [in Verse 16 and instead of using the expression, *and for 'a memorial' between your eyes,* as stated in Verse 9], and says *'ultotaphoth' between your eyes.* This is in order to explain that the commandment is not fulfilled by placing the phylactery between the eyes bottomward, but rather it is to be placed high on the head where it is to be there like *totaphoth,* [and we have seen above that the word *totepheth* was used by the Rabbis for an object which lies upon the head]. He uses the plural form [*totaphoth,* and not the singular *totepheth*], because the compartments in the phylactery of the head are many, as we have received the form by Tradition.

And now I shall declare to you a general principle in the reason of many commandments. Beginning with the days of Enosh [423] when idol-worship came into existence, opinions in the matter of faith fell into error. Some people denied the root of faith by saying that the world is eternal; *they denied the Eternal, and said: It is not He* [424] [Who called forth the world into existence]. Others denied His knowledge of individual matters, *and they say, How doth G-d know? and is there knowledge in the Most High?* [425] Some admit His knowledge but deny the principle of

---

(422) Deuteronomy 14:1. See Rashi, *ibid.,* that the expression *between the eyes* means on the head adjoining the forehead. See also Rashi to Leviticus 21:5. (423) Genesis 4:26. See also Rambam, Mishneh Torah, Hilchoth Akum, 1:1, where he traces the process of intellectual degeneration by which mankind fell into gross idolatry. Ramban primarily follows here the process of deterioration as affecting the three basic principles of faith: the existence of the Creator, His providence over the world, and the truth of prophecy. The chief purpose of the commandments of the Torah is to guard Israel against deviating from these principles. (424) Jeremiah 5:12. (425) Psalms 73:11.

providence *and make men as the fishes of the sea,* [426] [believing] that G-d does not watch over them and that there is no punishment or reward for their deeds, for they say *the Eternal hath forsaken the land.* [427] Now when G-d is pleased to bring about a change in the customary and natural order of the world for the sake of a people or an individual, then the voidance of all these [false beliefs] becomes clear to all people, since a wondrous miracle shows that the world has a G-d Who created it, and Who knows and supervises it, and Who has the power to change it. And when that wonder is previously prophesied by a prophet, another principle is further established, namely, that of the truth of prophecy, *that G-d doth speak with man,* [428] and that *He revealeth His counsel unto His servants the prophets,* [429] and thereby the whole Torah is confirmed. This is why Scripture says in connection with the wonders [in Egypt]: *That thou* [Pharaoh] *mayest know that I am the Eternal in the midst of the earth,* [430] which teaches us the principle of providence, i.e., that G-d has not abandoned the world to chance, as they [the heretics] would have it; *That thou mayest know that the earth is the Eternal's,* [431] which informs us of the principle of creation, for everything is His since He created all out of nothing; *That thou mayest know that there is none like Me in all the earth,* [432] which indicates His might, i.e., that He rules over everything and that there is nothing to withhold Him. The Egyptians either denied or doubted all of these [three] principles, [and the miracles confirmed their truth].

Accordingly, it follows that the great signs and wonders constitute *faithful witnesses* [433] to the truth of the belief in the existence of the Creator and the truth of the whole Torah. And because the Holy One, blessed be He, will not make signs and wonders in every generation for the eyes of some wicked man or heretic, He therefore commanded us that we should always make a memorial or sign of that which we have seen with our eyes, and

(426) Habakkuk 1:14. (427) Ezekiel 8:12. (428) Deuteronomy 5:28. (429) Amos 3:7. (430) Above, 8:18. (431) *Ibid.,* 9:29. (432) *Ibid.,* Verse 14. (433) Isaiah 8:2.

that we should transmit the matter to our children, and their children to their children, to the generations to come, and He placed great emphasis on it, as is indicated by the fact that one is liable to extinction for eating leavened bread on the Passover, and for abandoning the Passover-offering, [i.e., for not taking part in the slaughtering thereof].[434] He has further required of us that we inscribe upon our arms and between our eyes all that we have seen in the way of signs and wonders, and to inscribe it yet upon the doorposts of the houses, and that we remember it by recital in the morning and evening — just as the Rabbis have said: "The recital of the benediction *True and firm,* [which follows the *Sh'ma* in the morning and which terminates with a blessing to G-d for the redemption from Egypt], is obligatory as a matter of Scriptural law because it is written, *That thou mayest remember the day when thou camest forth out of the land of Egypt all the days of thy life.*[435] [He further required] that we make a booth every year[436] and many other commandments like them which are a memorial to the exodus from Egypt. All these commandments are designed for the purpose that in all generations we should have testimonies to the wonders so that they should not be forgotten and so that the heretic should not be able to open his lips to deny the belief in [the existence of] G-d. He who buys a *Mezuzah*[437] for one *zuz* [a silver coin] and affixes it to his doorpost and has the proper intent of heart on its content, has already admitted the creation of the world, the Creator's knowledge and His providence, and also his belief in prophecy as well as in all fundamental principles of the Torah, besides admitting that the mercy of the Creator is very great upon them that do His will, since He brought us forth from that bondage to freedom and to great honor on account of the merit of our fathers who delighted in the fear of His Name.[438] It is for this reason that the Rabbis have said:[439]

---

(434) Numbers 9:13. (435) Deuteronomy 16:3. (436) Leviticus 23:42. (437) Literally: "door-post." It is a scroll of parchment on which are written the two Scriptural portions, Deuteronomy 6:4-9 and 11:13-21, and which is fastened to the right-hand door-post. (438) See Nehemiah 1:11. (439) Aboth 2:1.

"Be as heedful of a light commandment [440] as of a weighty one," for they are all exceedingly precious and beloved, for through them a person always expresses thankfulness to his G-d.

And the purpose of all the commandments is that we believe in our G-d and be thankful to Him for having created us, for we know of no other reason for the first creation, [441] and G-d the Most High has no demand on the lower creatures, excepting that man should know and be thankful to G-d for having created him. The purposes of raising our voices in prayer and of the service in synagogues, as well as the merit of public prayer, is precisely this: that people should have a place wherein they assemble and express their thankfulness to G-d for having created them and supported them, and thus proclaim and say before Him, "We are your creatures."

This is the intent of what the Rabbis of blessed memory have said: [442] *"And they cried mightily unto G-d.* [443] From here you learn that prayer must be accompanied by sound. The undaunted one wins over the abashed one."

Through the great open miracles, one comes to admit the hidden miracles which constitute the foundation of the whole Torah, for no one can have a part in the Torah of Moses our teacher unless he believes that all our words and our events, [as dictated in the Torah], are miraculous in scope, there being no natural or customary way of the world in them, whether affecting the public or the individual. Instead, if a person observes the commandments, His reward will bring him success, and if he violates them, His

---

(440) Here understood in the sense of a commandment, the fulfillment of which does not entail a great expense, just like a *Mezuzah* that can be bought for one *zuz* and affixed to the door-post. (441) "The first creation." In his "Sermon on the Perfection of the Torah," where Ramban discusses the same topic (Kithvei Haramban, Vol. I, p. 152), the text reads: "for we know of no other reason for 'the creation of man.'" See, however, my Hebrew commentary, in the fifth edition, p. 557, where I suggest that the term "the first creation" may be a reference to the period from Adam to Abraham. (442) Yalkut Shimoni, Jonah 550. See also Yerushalmi Taanith, II, 1. (443) Jonah 3:8.

punishment will cause his extinction. It is all by decree of the Most High, as I have already mentioned. [444] The hidden miracles done to the public come to be known as is mentioned in the assurances of the Torah on the subject of the blessings and imprecations, [445] as the verse says: *And all the nations shall say: Wherefore hath the Eternal done thus unto this land? ... Then men shall say: Because they forsook the covenant of the Eternal, the G-d of their fathers.* [446] Thus it will become known to all nations that their punishment came from G-d. And of the fulfillment of the commandments it says, *And all the peoples of the earth shall see that the name of the Eternal is called upon thee.* [447] I will yet explain this, with the help of G-d. [448]

---

(444) See Vol. I, pp. 215-216 and 556-558.   (445) Leviticus 26:3-46; Deuteronomy 28:1-68.   (446) Deuteronomy 29:23-4.   (447) *Ibid.*, 28:10.   (448) Leviticus 26:11.

Beshalach

17. AND G-D LED THEM NOT BY THE WAY OF THE LAND OF THE PHILISTINES BECAUSE[1] IT WAS NEAR. "It would therefore be easy [for the Israelites] to return to Egypt by the same route. There are many Midrashic explanations, [but the above is the plain sense of Scripture]." Thus the language of Rashi. This is also the opinion of Rabbi Abraham ibn Ezra, who explained the purport of the verse to be that G-d led them not by the way of the land of the Philistines "because" it was near. They might therefore be filled with regret [when they experience war], and they would immediately return to Egypt.

In my opinion, if their explanations were correct, the expression *for G-d said* would have been mentioned in first place in the verse, in which case the verse would read: "and G-d led them not by the way of the land of the Philistines, for G-d said, 'Because it is near, lest peradventure the people repent!'"[2] But the correct interpretation is that [the expression in question does not state the reason for G-d's choice but merely] states that *G-d led them not by the way of the land of the Philistines* although *it was near* and it would have been advantageous to lead them by that route, for

---

(1) "Because." Thus Rashi and Ibn Ezra render the Hebrew word *ki*, as will be explained. Ramban will suggest further on in the text that the word *ki* should be understood here as "although." The J.P.S. translation follows Ramban's explanation. (2) But actually the verse reads: *and G-d led them not by the way of the land of the Philistines because it was near; for G-d said*, etc. In other words, Ramban argues that according to Rashi and Ibn Ezra, the reason for G-d's choice of the route by the wilderness and not by the land of the Philistines [*because it was near*], should have followed after the expression *for G-d said*.

G-d said: *Lest peradventure the people repent when they see war, and they return to Egypt.*

The reason they would experience war if they went by the way of the land of the Philistines, is that the Philistines would surely not have given them permission to go peacefully through their land, and thus they might return to Egypt. But by the way of the wilderness, they would not see war until they came to the lands of Sihon and Og, the kings of the Amorites,[3] which were given to them [i.e. to Israel]. At that time, they were already far from Egypt, [and there was thus no reason to fear that they would be tempted to return to Egypt because of war]. The war of Amalek in Rephidim[4] was no reason for the Israelites to return to Egypt, since they did not pass through the land of the Amalekites. Rather, Amalek came from his country and warred against them because of his hatred of Israel. Even if they were to take their own course to return to Egypt, it would be to no avail since Amalek would fight them on the way. Besides, they were already far from Egypt because of the circuitous route which they had followed, and they knew of no other route.

Now Rashi commented: "*When they see war.* For instance, the war of the Canaanite and the Amalekite.[5] If they had proceeded by the direct route, they would have then turned back. For after He had made them go round by a circuitous way they said, *Let us make a captain and go back to Egypt,*[6] and how much more so would they have said it had He led them by a straight road!"[7]

The purport of that which Scripture states, *and G-d led them not... But G-d led the people about, by the way of the wilderness,*[8] is that when they journeyed from Succoth,[9] a pillar of cloud[10] began to go before them. It did not go by the way of

---

(3) Deuteronomy 3:8. (4) Further, 17:8-13. (5) In Numbers 14:45 and so in Rashi here: *And the Amalekite and the Canaanite came down.* (6) *Ibid.,* 14:4. (7) Mechilta on the verse before us. (8) Verse 18. (9) Verse 20. (10) Verse 21.

the land of the Philistines but instead went by the way of the wilderness of Etham,[9] and the Israelites walked after it. The cloud then rested in Etham and they encamped there, and that was at the edge of the wilderness.[9]

18. AND THE CHILDREN OF ISRAEL WENT UP ARMED OUT OF THE LAND OF EGYPT. This means that even though G-d led them about by the way of the wilderness, they still feared lest the Philistines who dwelt in the nearby cities come upon them. Therefore they were armed, as are people who go out to war. Some scholars[11] say that Scripture is relating that they went out *with a high hand,*[12] deeming themselves redeemed from bondage, and they did not leave like slaves escaping [from their master].

21. AND THE ETERNAL WENT BEFORE THEM. The Sages have already said,[13] "Wherever the phrase *And the Eternal* is mentioned, it means He and His Celestial Court." The Holy One, blessed be He, went before them by day, and His Celestial Court by night.[14] If so, the explanation of the verse is that G-d[15] abode in the midst of the cloud, and He went before them by day in a pillar of cloud. By night, His Celestial Court abode in a pillar of fire to give them light. This is similar in meaning to that which the verse says: *Inasmuch as Thou Eternal art seen face to face, and Thy cloud standeth over them, and Thou goest before them, in a pillar of cloud by day, and in a pillar of fire by night.*[16]

I have seen in Eileh Shemoth Rabbah:[17] *"For ye shall not go out in haste, neither shall ye go by flight; for the Eternal will go*

---

(11) Found in Ibn Ezra. (12) Further, 14:8. "With a high hand carrying their arms and not like slaves who escape from their master" (Ibn Ezra). (13) Bereshith Rabbah 51:3. See Vol. I, p. 260. (14) This sentence is not part of the above Midrash. See my Hebrew commentary, p. 348, for a similar interpretation in the Zohar, the mystical commentary on the Torah. (15) Literally: "the Name," i.e., the Great Divine Name known by the attribute of mercy. (Ricanti, interpreting the meaning of Ramban.) See my Hebrew commentary, p. 348. (16) Numbers 14:14. (17) Shemoth Rabbah 19:7.

EXODUS XIV, BESHALACH

before you.[18] In the past, I and My Celestial Court went before you, as it is said, *And the Eternal went before them by day,* but in the World to Come,[19] I Myself will go before you, as it is said, *For the Eternal will go before you, and the G-d of Israel will be your rearward.*"[18] The secret of this Midrash is as I have mentioned, i.e., that at the first redemption, the Holy One, blessed be He, was with them by day and His Celestial Court by night, but in the World to Come,[19] the attribute of His Celestial Court will be elevated in mercy and the Eternal — the Tetragrammaton — will go before them, for the G-d of Israel will then assemble His people, *and the night will shine as the day, the darkness even as the light,*[20] as everything will then be united in the attribute of mercy.

Rabbi Abraham ibn Ezra commented that Scripture here speaks according to the language of men, since it was the power of G-d and His messenger that went with Israel, [thus, *and the Eternal went before them* would mean "and the angel of the Eternal went before them"], similar in meaning to the verse, *He caused His glorious arm to go at the right hand of Moses.*[21] Now it is true that the verse here is similar in meaning to the verse, *He caused His glorious arm to go at the right hand of Moses,*[21] but it is not as Rabbi Abraham ibn Ezra understood it.[22] And it is further written, *So didst Thou lead Thy people to make Thyself a glorious Name,*[23] [thus indicating that it was the Holy One, blessed be He, Himself that went before the people, and not, as Ibn Ezra explained, that the reference here is to an angel].

14 4. AND I WILL HARDEN PHARAOH'S HEART, AND HE SHALL PURSUE AFTER THEM. Because Pharaoh feared them at

---

(18) Isaiah 52:12.   (19) Here referring to the Messianic era.   (20) Psalms 139:12.   (21) Isaiah 63:12.   (22) See above, 6:2, for Ramban's understanding of the verse in Isaiah, and see also further, 14:29, which states: *And the angel of G-d, who went before the camp of Israel, journeyed.* It was this verse apparently that forced Ibn Ezra to arrive at his interpretation here. See Ramban, *ibid.*, for a fuller discussion.   (23) Isaiah 63:14.

the plague of the firstborn and he asked them *and bless me also*,[24] he was not disposed to pursue after the Israelites even if they were to flee, and he would rather have Moses do with them as he pleases. Therefore, it was necessary to state that G-d hardened his heart to pursue after them. Further on, it says once more, *And I, behold, I will harden the hearts of the Egyptians, and they shall go in after them*.[25] After the Egyptians saw that the sea had split before the children of Israel and that they walked in the midst of the sea upon dry land, which is the most outstanding wonder of all wonders, how could they be disposed to come in after them to harm them! This was indeed madness on their part. But it was He Who turned their counsel into foolishness[26] and strengthened their hearts to enter the sea.

5. AND IT WAS TOLD THE KING OF EGYPT THAT THE PEOPLE HAD FLED. "He sent guards with them, and as soon as they had reached the three days' journey that was fixed for them to go and return, and [these guards] saw that they were not returning to Egypt, they went and reported to Pharaoh on the fourth day. On the fifth and sixth days, the Egyptians pursued after them. On the night of the seventh day, they went down into the sea, and on the following morning, the Israelites uttered the Song, and this was the seventh day of Passover. It is for this reason that [during the Synagogue service] on the seventh day of Passover, we read [the Scriptural portion containing] the Song at the Red Sea." This is the language of Rashi. And so it is also explained in the Mechilta. [27]

---

(24) Above, 12:32. (25) Further, Verse 17. (26) See II Samuel 15:31. (27) Mechilta here on Verse 3. Ramban's intent is that the Mechilta states the order of events as mentioned by Rashi. The established custom of reading during the Synagogue service on the seventh day of Passover the Scriptural portion containing the Song at the Red Sea is of later origin, as is evidenced by the fact that in the Mishnah (Megillah 30b) and in Tractate Sofrim (17:5) another reading is indicated. The reading is mentioned in the Gemara of Tractate Megillah 31 a, quoting a Beraitha. The reason why Rashi at this point mentioned the Synagogue custom for the reading of the Torah on the seventh day of Passover, was to show that it is in keeping with "the event of the day."

In line with the plain meaning of Scripture, the verse here is to be understood in the light of that which G-d said, *And Pharaoh will say of the children of Israel: They are entangled in the land.*[28] When the children of Israel [indicated that this was] so, and they turned back and encamped before Phi-hahiroth before Baal-zephon,[29] this was reported to the king of Egypt. He said *that the people were fled* and entangled in the desert, and that they were not going towards a definite place to offer sacrifices for G-d. And this is the intent of the verse, *and the children of Israel went out with a high hand.*[30] This means that they made themselves a flag and a banner for display, and they went out *with mirth and with songs, with tabret and with harp,*[31] like people who are redeemed from bondage to freedom, and not like slaves who expect to return to their servitude. All this was told to Pharaoh.

10. AND THEY WERE SORE AFRAID; AND THE CHILDREN OF ISRAEL CRIED OUT UNTO THE ETERNAL. 11. AND THEY SAID UNTO MOSES: 'BECAUSE WERE THERE NO GRAVES IN EGYPT, HAST THOU TAKEN US TO DIE IN THE WILDERNESS'? It does not appear logical that people who are crying out to G-d to help them, should at the same time protest against the deliverance He performed for them, and say that it would have been better if He had not saved them! The correct interpretation therefore is that there were conflicting groups,[32] and Scripture relates what all of them did. Thus it narrates that one group cried to G-d [for help], and another denied His prophet and did not acknowledge the deliverance done for them. They said

---

(28) Verse 3.   (29) Verse 2.   (30) Verse 8.   (31) Genesis 31:27.
(32) As stated in the Mechilta here on Verse 13: "The Israelites at the Red Sea were divided into four groups, etc." In Rabbeinu Bachya's rendition of this text of Ramban, it clearly reads: "Therefore we can rely upon the words of our Rabbis who say that these verses represent different groups" (Bachya's Commentary on the Torah, Vol. II, p. 113, in my edition). Ramban, however, following the plain meaning of Scripture here, does not describe them as four groups but merely as 'conflicting groups' without enumeration.

it would have been better for them had He not saved them. It is with reference to this group that it is written, *They were rebellious at the sea, even at the Red Sea.*[33] This is why Scripture here repeats in the same verse the term, *the children of Israel,* [saying: *and 'the children of Israel' lifted up their eyes...*] *and 'the children of Israel' cried out unto the Eternal.* It thus indicates that it was the better ones among the people that cried out to G-d; the remainder rebelled against His word. This is why Scripture says afterward, *And the people feared the Eternal; and they believed in the Eternal, and in His servant Moses.*[34] It does not say "and *Israel* feared the Eternal, and they believed," but it says instead "the people," for the term *the children of Israel* signifies the outstanding ones, while *the people* is a name for the multitude. Similarly, the verse, *And the people murmured,*[35] [clearly indicates the usage of the term *people* in Scripture]. Our Rabbis have also mentioned it:[36] "*And the people began to commit harlotry.*[37] Wherever it says *the people,* it is an expression of reproach, and wherever it says *Israel,* it is one of praise."

Now the people did not say, "you have taken us away to die in war," but [they said], *hast thou taken us away to die in the wilderness,* and again they said, *that we should die in the wilderness.*[38] This was due to the fact that long before they feared war,[39] they already did not want to go out to the desert lest they die there from hunger and thirst.

It is possible that they said so to Moses upon their going forth from the country while they were still in the land of Egypt, when G-d led them about *by the way of the wilderness by the Red Sea.*[40] Perhaps they said so to Moses at the beginning: "Where shall we go? If by the way of the Philistines, they will war against

---

(33) Psalms 106:7. (34) Further, Verse 31. (35) *Ibid.,* 15:24. (36) Bamidbar Rabbah 20:22. (37) Numbers 25:1. (38) Verse 12. (39) The Tur renders this passage thus thus: "They said that even if they would not experience any war, they did not want to go out to the desert." (40) Above, 13:18.

us, and if by the way of the wilderness, *better for us to serve the Egyptians, than that we should die in the wilderness.*" [41]

It is also possible to say that the people did believe in G-d and prayed to Him to save them, but a doubt entered their hearts concerning Moses lest he took them out of Egypt in order to rule over them. Although they had seen the signs and wonders he did, they thought that he did them through some manner of wisdom. Perhaps G-d brought the plagues upon the Egyptians on account of their wickedness, [but not necessarily for the purpose of redemption of Israel, and Moses took them out of Egypt just to rule over them], for if G-d had desired their going out, Pharaoh would not have pursued after them.

And Onkelos here translated *vayitz'aku (and they cried out)* as *uz'aku*,[42] thus making its purport to be "complaint," meaning that they did not pray to G-d but that they complained to Him for having taken them out of Egypt. It is similar in usage to that in the verse, *'vayitz'aku' unto Pharaoh, saying, Wherefore dealest thou thus with thy servants?*[43] [which does not mean "and they prayed," but that they complained.] Similarly, *Then there was a great 'tza'akath' of the people and of their wives against their brethren the Jews,*[44] which means they were complaining against them with a great voice and outcry.

In the Mechilta we find;[45] "They seized upon the occupation of their fathers, [i.e., at first they conducted themselves properly in that they prayed to G-d as their fathers had done]. *And they said unto Moses: 'Because were there no graves,* etc.?' After 'they had added leaven into the dough,'[46] they came to Moses and said to

---

(41) Verse 12. (42) Elsewhere Onkelos translates it *v'tzalu* (and they prayed). See Deuteronomy 26:7, *vanitz'ak*, which Onkelos renders *v'tzaleinu* (and we prayed). The word *uz'aku*, on the other hand, means "complaint," as is explained in the text. (43) Above, 5:15. (44) Nehemiah 5:1. (45) Mechilta on the verse before us. (46) Ramban will explain further on that this is a euphemism for the *yeitzer hara* (the evil inclination). In other words, after doubts had entered their minds and excitement was stirred up, they came to Moses and said to him, etc.

him, *Is not this the word that we spoke unto thee in Egypt, etc.?*"[41] The "leaven in the dough" is a reference to the evil inclination. Thus the Sages in the Mechilta intended to say that at first the people prayed to G-d to instill in Pharaoh's heart the desire to turn back from pursuing them. However, when they saw that he was not turning back but instead was marching and drawing near them, they said, "Our prayers have not been accepted," and an evil thought entered their hearts to find fault with Moses as they had previously done.

13. FOR WHEREAS YE HAVE SEEN THE EGYPTIANS TODAY, YE SHALL SEE THEM AGAIN NO MORE. In the opinion of our Rabbis,[47] this is a negative commandment for all times. If so, Scripture is stating: "*Fear ye not, stand still* in your places, *and see the salvation of the Eternal* in that He will save you today from their hands. Concerning the Egyptians you see today, G-d commands you *to see them no more* of your own free will henceforth and *for ever.*" It is thus a commandment by the mouth of Moses to Israel, even though it is not mentioned above [that G-d had said so to Moses]. Similarly, the verse, *And he* [the king] *shall not cause the people to return to Egypt, to the end that he should multiply horses; forasmuch as the Eternal hath said unto you: Ye shall henceforth return no more that way,*[48] indeed constitutes a commandment, not just a promise.

15. AND THE ETERNAL SAID UNTO MOSES: WHEREFORE CRIEST THOU UNTO ME? Rabbi Abraham ibn Ezra commented[49] that Moses corresponds in function to all of Israel who were praying to G-d, as Scripture said, *And the children of*

---

(47) Yerushalmi Succah V, 1. See Maimonides' "The Commandments," Vol. II, pp. 44-46, in my translation. (48) Deuteronomy 17:16. (49) The difficulty is that there is no mention above of Moses' praying. Rashi therefore comments that this verse itself — *Wherefore criest thou unto Me?* — teaches by implication that Moses had been praying. Ibn Ezra's explanation is first in the text, and Ramban's interpretation follows it.

Israel cried out unto the Eternal.[50] But if so, why did G-d say, *Wherefore criest thou?* When it was indeed proper that they should pray! Perhaps [Ibn Ezra] will say that the sense thereof is: "Why do you let them pray? Speak to them so that they will go forward, for I have already told you, *And I will be honored through Pharaoh.*"[51]

And our Rabbis have said[52] that it was Moses who was crying and praying. This is the correct interpretation [and not, as Ibn Ezra said, that the reference here is to all of Israel]. Moses was at a loss concerning what he was to do. Although G-d had told him, *And I will be honored through Pharaoh,*[51] he did not know how to conduct himself at that moment when he was at the edge of the sea and the enemy was pursuing and overtaking [them]. He therefore prayed that G-d should instruct him in the manner that he should choose.[53] This then is the meaning of *Wherefore criest thou unto Me?* meaning: "You should have asked what to do, and there is no need for you to cry, since I have already informed you, *And I will be honored through Pharaoh.*"[51] Now Scripture did not relate that Moses was crying out to G-d, because he is included among Israel, [of whom it was already written above in Verse 10: *And the children of Israel cried out unto the Eternal*].

19. AND THE ANGEL OF G-D JOURNEYED. Rabbi Abraham ibn Ezra commented that the *angel of G-d* is the great prince [Michael],[54] who went in the cloud. It is to him that Scripture refers when it said, *And the Eternal went before them.*[55] When this angel, *who went before the camp of Israel, journeyed and went behind them,* the pillar of cloud journeyed with him. *And*

---

(50) Above, Verse 10. In other words, the name Moses is here equivalent to all Israel. But Ramban questions this explanation of Ibn Ezra: "If so, etc." (51) Above, Verse 4. (52) In the Mechilta on the verse before us. (53) See Psalms 25:12. (54) See Daniel 12:1. (55) Above, 13:21. See there towards the end, where Ramban mentions this explanation of Ibn Ezra, i.e., that the meaning thereof is that the angel of the Eternal went before them.

there was the cloud and the darkness[56] between the camp of Egypt and the camp of Israel, *but it gave light by night*[56] through the pillar of fire to Israel, as it did on other nights, in order to enable them to traverse the sea, for it was at night that they traversed it.

In my opinion, that which Scripture says, *And the angel of G-d journeyed,* occurred at the beginning of the night. *The angel of G-d, who went before the camp of Israel* alludes to the Celestial Court of the Holy One, blessed be He, which is known as the attribute of justice, [which is called][57] "angel" in certain places of Scripture. It was he who dwelled in the pillar of fire and went before them by night to give them light. Therefore Scripture here mentions [not the Tetragrammaton, which indicates the attribute of mercy, but] *ha'Elokim* (G-d), [the name which denotes the attribute of justice]. It is possible that [the word *malach* (angel)] is not in a construct state [meaning "the angel of"] but instead is in apposition.

Now I have seen in the Mechilta of Rabbi Shimon ben Yochai:[58] "Rabbi Yonathan the son of Yochai asked Rabbi Shimon the son of Yochai, 'Why is it that in all places it is written, *the angel of the Eternal,*[59] and here it is written, *the angel of 'Elokim'* (G-d)?' Rabbi Shimon answered him, *'Elokim* everywhere denotes "Judge" [literally: judgment], etc.' "[60] The Rabbis thus alluded to that which we have said.

---

(56) Verse 20. (57) So clearly rendered by Rabbeinu Bachya (Vol. II, p. 115, in my edition). (58) The standard Mechilta, a Tannaitic commentary of the Book of Exodus, is that of Rabbi Ishmael. There is another Mechilta, that of Rabbi Shimon ben Yochai, to which Ramban refers here. To distinguish it from the other, standard, work, Ramban therefore specifies it by name. For another example, see Vol. I, p. 603. The quotation mentioned here appears in Hoffman's edition of that work on p. 49. The essence of this particular Midrash is also found here in Rashi. (59) E.g., Genesis 16:7 and above, 3:2. (60) "The verse thus teaches us that Israel at that moment was arraigned in judgment, i.e., whether to be saved or to be destroyed with the Egyptians" (Mechilta quoted, and also mentioned in Rashi here).

EXODUS XIV, BESHALACH

Thus [the angel] now journeyed in the pillar of fire from *before the camp of Israel and went behind them, and the pillar of cloud from before them* also *journeyed and stood behind them.* Thus the two pillars were behind the camp of Israel. Scripture then reverts [in Verse 20] to explain that the pillar of cloud *came between the camp of Egypt and the camp of Israel,* that is to say, the pillar of cloud did not intervene between the pillar of fire and the camp of Israel, but rather it interposed between the camp of Egypt and the pillar of fire.[61] *And there was the cloud and the darkness* between the two camps, with the pillar of fire giving light to Israel, even though it was behind them, because it was high, [thus illuminating the way for them to pass through the sea, as explained above.] The pillar of cloud did not obstruct the illumination from reaching them as it did to the Egyptians. This is the meaning of the verse, *and it gave light by night,* since the pillar of fire illuminated the night for them.

This was not as on all other nights, when its function was *to lead them the way,*[62] for on that night it did not go before them, [but instead the pillar of fire remained stationary]. This was so because if the pillar of fire would have gone before Israel as on other nights [when they journeyed], and the pillar of cloud was between the two camps, then the Israelites would have passed through the sea quickly. Consequently, the Egyptians would not have seen them, and they would not have come after them. However, now [that the pillar of fire was stationary] the Israelites walked slowly, and since there was no great distance between the camps, the Egyptians saw the camp of Israel from the midst of the cloud, and they followed them. They saw the fire out of the midst of the cloud,[63] but they were not able to approach them because of the two pillars which interposed.

---

(61) Thus the order was as follows: First came the camp of Israel, followed by the pillar of fire. After that was the pillar of cloud, followed by the camp of Egypt. The two pillars thus intervened between the two camps (Bachya). (62) Above, 13:21. (63) "For he who sits in darkness can see light in the distance. But the Israelites did not see the Egyptians, for he who sits in an illuminated place cannot see one who sits in darkness" (Bachya).

This is the sense of the verse, *And the one* [camp] *came not near the other all the night.*[64] *And it came to pass in the morning-watch, that the Eternal looked forth upon the host of the Egyptians through the pillar of fire and of cloud,*[65] meaning: He removed the pillar of fire from the camp of Israel, as was customary on all days, and today He put it [in a position] overlooking the camp of Egypt. It was thus between the Egyptians and the pillar of cloud which served Israel by day.[66] *And He confounded the camp of Egypt*[65] by causing the pillar of fire to bear down upon them with its great heat reaching them, and *the flame burned up the wicked.*[67] Now I have already explained in the story of Creation[68] that the element of fire is called "darkness," and *the cloud and the darkness* [mentioned in Verse 20] accordingly mean the pillar of fire and the pillar of cloud. To all Israel, the pillar of fire had given light because of its high position [as explained above], but now it darkened for the Egyptians, because it came together with the pillar of cloud, which caused it to darken just as the sun when covered by a cloud. Thus He did everything by means of these two pillars. This is the correct interpretation of these verses.

21. AND MOSES STRETCHED OUT HIS HAND OVER THE SEA; AND THE ETERNAL CAUSED THE SEA TO GO BACK BY A STRONG EAST WIND ALL THE NIGHT. It was His will, may He be blessed, to divide the sea by a strong drying wind, making it appear as *if* the wind dried the sea, something like that which is written, *An east wind shall come, the wind of the Eternal coming up from the wilderness, and his spring shall become dry, and his fountain shall be dried up.*[69] He thus caused the Egyptians

---

(64) Verse 20. (65) Verse 24. (66) In other words, although the pillar of fire was between Israel and the pillar of cloud during the night, in the morning watch G-d took the pillar of fire and placed it between the camp of Egypt and the pillar of cloud. With the pillar of fire heating the Egyptians, they fell into confusion. (67) Psalms 106:18. (68) Genesis 1:1. See Vol. I, p. 26. There the reason is given why the element of fire is designated as *choshech* (darkness). (69) Hosea 13:15.

EXODUS XIV, BESHALACH

to err and then destroyed them,[70] for because of this, they thought that perhaps it was the wind which made the sea into dry land, but that it was not the power of G-d that did this for the sake of Israel. Although the wind does not split the sea into sections, they paid no attention even to this and they followed after the Israelites into the sea out of their desire to harm them. This is the intent of the expressions: *and I will harden Pharaoh's heart;*[71] *and they shall go in after them.*[72] He hardened their hearts [so that each one] would say: *"I will pursue my enemies and I will overtake them in the sea,*[73] *and there is none that can deliver out of my hand."*[74] They did not remember now [what they themselves had said], *for the Eternal fighteth for them against the Egyptians.*[75]

28. AND THE WATERS RETURNED, AND COVERED THE CHARIOTS, AND THE HORSEMEN, 'L'CHOL' (TO ALL) THE HOST OF PHARAOH. "[The word *l'chol* should really have been *kol* without the letter *lamed*. However], it is the normal manner of expression of many verses to write a redundant *lamed*, as for example: *'l'chol the instruments of the Tabernacle;*[76] *'l'chol' the vessels thereof thou shalt make of brass;*[77] It is only an elegance in Scriptural style." Thus the language of Rashi.

But it is not so in this place.[78] Instead its meaning is as follows: "And the waters covered the chariots and the horsemen *and all*

---

(70) See Job 12:23. The verse however reads, *masgi (He increases) the nations*, etc. Ramban interprets it in the sense of *mashgi* (He causes to err.) A similar usage of this verse appears in Rashi above, Verse 2. The source of this rendition of the verse is in the Mechilta, *ibid.* (71) Above, Verse 4. (72) Verse 17. (73) Psalms 18:38. See also further, 15:9. (74) Deuteronomy 32:39. (75) Further, Verse 25. (76) *Ibid.*, 27:19. Literally: *'to all' the instruments of the Tabernacle*, but the meaning is " 'all' the instruments." (77) *Ibid.*, Verse 4. Literally: *'to all' the vessels*, but the meaning is " 'all' the vessels thereof." (78) Ramban understood Rashi as explaining *the chariots and horsemen* as being in apposition to *all the host*. Therefore Rashi had written that the *lamed* of *l'chol* is redundant, since the expression *all the host* is added by way of explanation. But Ramban interprets *all the host* to mean the people Pharaoh took with him besides the chariots and the horsemen. Therefore the *lamed* is not an idiomatic form here and is a necessary part of the verse, as is explained further in the text.

the [79] host of Pharaoh that went in after them into the sea." *The host* is not identical with *the chariots and the horsemen,* [as is suggested by Rashi's explanation], but rather they are his people that Pharaoh took with him,[80] just as it is said above: *all the horses and chariots of Pharaoh, and his horsemen, and his host.*[81] A similar usage of the letter *lamed* in connection with the term "covering" is found in these verses: *As the waters cover 'la'yam;*'[82] *And thou shalt make a covering 'la'ohel.'*[83] The term "covering" also appears [in conjunction] with the word *al*, e.g., *The fat that covereth 'al' the inwards.*[84] There are many cases like this.

31. AND ISRAEL SAW THE GREAT HAND. "I.e., the great power which the hand of the Holy One, blessed be He, had exercised. There are many meanings that are appropriate for the word *yad* (hand), but all of them signify the actual hand, and the interpreter must adapt the meaning according to the theme of the subject discussed." Thus the language of Rashi. But Onkelos did not explain *the great hand* as referring to power, for he translated: "the might of the great hand." And Rabbi Abraham ibn Ezra commented that it means "the great blow." And so it also says, *Behold, the hand of the Eternal is upon the cattle,*[85] [which means that a great plague will overtake them]; *The hand of G-d was very heavy there,*[86] [which means that a great calamity befell the Philistines].

By way of the Truth, [the mystic teachings of the Cabala], the verse is stating that *the great hand,* which is the attribute of justice

---

(79) The letter *lamed* in the word *l'chol* thus indicates the object, and is as if it were written "*v'eth* (and the) host of Pharaoh." See my Hebrew commentary, p. 352. (80) Above, Verse 6. (81) *Ibid.*, Verse 9. Here it is clear that *the host* is separate from the chariots and horsemen, since it says "and the host." (82) Isaiah 11:9. Literally: *'to' the sea,* but the meaning is "the sea." (83) Further, 26:14. Literally: *'to' the tent,* but it means "and thou shalt make 'the tent' a covering of...." (84) Leviticus 4:8. Literally, *that covereth 'upon' the inwards,* but the word *al* is understood as *eth,* a word which indicates the direct object. (85) Above, 9:3. (86) I Samuel 5:11.

that G-d exercised upon the Egyptians, became revealed to them, since it was there inflicting punishment upon the Egyptians. This is like the verse, *And upon earth He made thee to see His great fire.*[87] This is the *right hand* which *dashes in pieces the enemy,*[88] and it is *the arm of the Eternal,* concerning which Scripture says, *Awake, awake, put on strength, O arm of the Eternal;*[89] *Art thou not it that dried up the sea?*[90]

15

1. 'AZ YASHIR MOSHEH'(THEN MOSES WILL SING).[91] Rashi comments: "[*Then*], when Moses saw the miracle, the thought came to his heart that he would sing a song,[92] and thus he actually did, [as it is said], *and they spoke, saying.* Similarly, *az yedabeir Yehoshua*[93] means that when he saw the miracle [mentioned there], his heart prompted him to speak, and thus he actually did, [as it is said], *and he said in the sight of Israel.*[94] The same interpretation applies to the Song of the Well, which begins with the words, *az yashir Yisrael,*[95] and Scripture explains after that, *Spring up, O well, sing ye unto it.*[96] Likewise: *az yivneh Shlomoh,*[97] which the Sages of Israel explained it as meaning[98] that he proposed to build but did not build it.[99] This explanation serves to clarify the literal meaning of the text."

(87) Deuteronomy 4:36. (88) See further, 15:6. (89) Isaiah 51:9. (90) *Ibid.,* Verse 10. (91) It is of course translated as a past tense: "Then Moses sang." Rashi and Ramban will discuss why the future tense is used here by the Torah. (92) According to Rashi, this explains why the future tense — *yashir* (he will sing) — is used here by the Torah, since the expression denotes Moses' thought that he should sing. Rashi thus interprets *yashir* to be a pure future. Ramban will differ with this interpretation. (93) Joshua 10:12. Literally: "Then Joshua will speak." (94) *Ibid.* (95) Numbers 21:17. Literally: "Then Israel will sing." (96) *Ibid.* This part of the verse shows that the preceding expression, *az yashir Yisrael,* denotes intent of heart to sing, thus: "Then, when they saw the miracle, their hearts told them that they should sing," and so they did, as is indicated by the expression *sing ye unto it,* which is the call to the people to sing. (97) I Kings 11:7. Literally: "Then Solomon will build [a high place]." (98) Sanhedrin 91 b. (99) "Thus we learn that the *yod* as a prefix of the imperfect verb, [i.e., the future tense of a verb], indicates an intent to do a thing" (Rashi).

But what will the Rabbi [Rashi] say concerning these verses: *'Ya'asu'* [literally: "They will make"] *a calf in Horeb;*[100] *How oft 'yamruhu'* [literally: "will they rebel"] *against Him in the wilderness, and 'ya'atzivuhu'* [literally: "they will grieve Him"] *in the desert!*[101] The entire psalm is so written [in the future tense]: *yaharog* [literally: "He will destroy"] *their vines with hail;*[102] *y'shalach* [literally: "He will send"] *among them swarms of flies*[103] — [when all of these verbs refer to past events]! Similarly: *And from whence 'yavo'u'* [literally: "shall they come"] *unto thee?*[104] *Of the wounds which the Arameans 'yakuhu'* [literally: "shall smite him"].[105] Likewise, *Now Moses 'yikach'* [literally: "will take"] *the tent*[106] does not denote a continuous event,[107] since he took it only once.[108] Instead, [we must conclude that] it is the way of Scripture to use the future tense in place of the past form, and in many places the reverse is quite usual. The reason for this is that it is a distinctive way of language for a narrator of an event to place himself at a certain point of time which he desires, and he then alludes to the event. At times, he places himself at the moment of the action, and he speaks of it in the present tense as if he is watching it from its very beginning. He would say, "Israel is singing," as if they were singing right before him, and so also in other cases. However, at times the narrator places himself after the event and says, "This has already been done." It is all a matter of conveying an event realistically. It is for this reason that this interchangeable use of the tenses occurs in matters of prophecy.

(100) Psalms 106:19. (101) *Ibid.*, 78:40. (102) *Ibid.*, Verse 47. (103) *Ibid.*, Verse 45. (104) II Kings 20:14. (105) *Ibid.*, 8:29. (106) Further, 33:7. (107) At this point, Ramban's intent is directed to another statement in Rashi's explanation, namely, that where an action is continuously happening, it is proper to use either the future tense or the past tense. Where the action is mentioned once and once only, the future cannot be used. However, Ramban points out, in the verse, *Now Moses 'yikach' the tent*, where the future tense "shall take" is used, the action is not one of continuous happening and still the future tense is used! (108) See Rashi further, 33:11, towards the end ("The Midrash explains, etc."), that Moses' removing his tent to pitch it outside the camp happened only once.

KI GA'OH GA'AH' (FOR HE IS HIGHLY EXALTED). "[He is exalted] high above songs, and however much I may praise Him, there still remain additional [splendor and praiseworthiness] in Him to be expressed." Thus the language of Rashi. [The Rabbi] thus interpreted *ga'oh ga'ah* as an expression of exaltation and supreme power. Perhaps this is so, such usage [of the word *ga'oh*] being found in the verses: *And here shall thy high ('big'on') waves be stayed;*[109] *For the waters were risen ('ga'u');*[110] *And if it exalt itself ('v'yigeh'), Thou huntest me as a lion*[111] — all of which are expressions of power and ascendancy.

But the correct interpretation is the opinion of Onkelos, who rendered it literally an expression of pride. The verse is thus stating that He was ennobled above the horse that proudly goes to battle together with its mighty rider, for He threw both of them into the sea. Similarly, the verse, *And in the greatness of Thy 'g'oncha',*[112] and all other such cases are all expressions of pride, for he who indulges in a feeling of pride elevates himself in importance.

2. THE ETERNAL IS MY STRENGTH AND SONG. Rabbi Abraham ibn Ezra explained that the word *ozi* (my strength) is connected with the following word [*v'zimrath* — and song], thus rendering its sense: "my strength and the song of my strength is the Eternal."[113] *This is my G-d 'v'anveihu':* I will make Him a habitation, [from the root *naveh* (habitation)]. *This is my father's G-d, and I will exalt Him,* i.e., by recounting His greatness.

Now this is surely the plain meaning of the verse. But [it should be noted that] Moses does not mention here the full Divine Name, [i.e., the Tetragrammaton, which consists of four letters], but instead mentions only the first two letters. In the entire Torah, it

---

(109) Job 38:11. (110) Ezekiel 47:5. (111) Job 10:16. (112) Further, Verse 7. (113) "That is to say, with this Name will I vanquish my enemies, and when I will sing of the victory, my song will be the song of the Eternal, for it is He who is my salvation" (Mishneh l'Ezra in his commentary on Ibn Ezra).

is the manner of Moses our teacher to mention the entire Great Name which He communicated to him, as it is said, *This is My Name for ever, and this is My memorial unto all generations.* [114] And the Rabbis have already explained the verse, *The hand is upon the throne of Y-ah,* [115] to mean that "the Holy One, blessed be He, swore that His throne will not be perfect nor will His Name be complete until the seed of Amalek will be entirely blotted out." [The question then arises: why is the full Divine Name not written here?]

By way of the Truth, [that is, the mystic lore of the Cabala], the whole deliverance at the sea came through the angel of G-d — the one of whom it is written, *for My Name is in him* [116] — just as it is said, *and Israel saw the great hand.* [117] The "hand" alludes to the attribute of justice, which is the great hand that executes the vengeance. It is by this attribute that the sea was divided, as the prophet explained, *Awake, awake, put on strength, O arm of the Eternal... Art thou not it that dried up the sea, the waters of the great deep?* [118] and as I have written above. [119] It is for this reason that Moses said that his strength and his song are this Name, [i.e., the first two letters of the Tetragrammaton, which allude to the attribute of justice], *For in Y-ah the Eternal is an everlasting Rock.* [120] And so did [the psalmist] explain: *What aileth thee, O thou sea, that thou fleest?... At the presence of the G-d of Jacob.* [121] And so the Rabbis have said in the Mechilta: [122] "When Israel went into the sea, the *Shechinah* (Divine presence) [123] was with them, as it is said, *And the angel of G-d journeyed.*" [124] And in Eileh Shemoth Rabbah, it is said: [125] "The word *oz* (strength) [or

---

(114) Above, 3:15. (115) Further, 17:16. Because only the first two letters of the Tetragrammaton are mentioned there, the Rabbis explained: "The Holy One, blessed be He, swore, etc." The explanation is found in Tanchuma, end of *Seder Ki Theitzei*, and is quoted by Rashi at the end of this *Seder*. (116) Further, 23:21. (117) Above, 14:31. (118) Isaiah 51:9-10. (119) Above, 14:31: "*The great hand* which is the attribute of justice... became revealed to them. (120) Isaiah 26:4. As translated in Singer's Daily Prayer Book. (121) Psalms 114:5-7. *The G-d of Jacob* alludes here to the attribute of justice. (122) Mechilta here on the verse before us. (123) See Vol. I, p. 551. (124) Above, 14:19. (125) Shemoth Rabbah 30:1.

ozi, "my strength," as is mentioned in this verse], alludes only to judgment, as it is said, *'v'oz' (And the strength) of a king is he who loveth justice.*" [126]

This is My G-d 'v'anveihu.' "I will elevate [the Great Name, i.e., the Tetragrammaton],[127] to the G-d of the most high *naveh* (abode), this being the G-d of my fathers, to whom He had appeared as *E-il Sha-dai.*[128] And now I shall exalt Him by the complete Name, for henceforth the Name will be *ish milchamah*, [literally, "man of war," but here alluding to the attribute of justice]. And *His Name* will be *the Eternal*, [meaning that the Name comprises justice with mercy],[129] similar in meaning to the verse, *Now will I be exalted; now will I lift Myself up.*[130] It is possible that the word *'zeh' (this)* alludes to the seven emanations in wisdom, this being associated with the verse, *'zeh' (this) is My Name for ever, 'v'zeh' (and this) is My memorial.*[131] And in the Mechilta we read:[132] *"My G-d.* He dealt with me according to the attribute of mercy, while with my fathers he dealt according to the attribute of justice. And whence do we know that *my G-d* signifies the attribute of mercy? Because it is said, *My G-d, my G-d, why hast Thou forsaken me?*[133] *Heal her now, O G-d, I beseech thee?*[134] *The Eternal is 'E-il' (G-d), and He hath given us light."*[135] If so, Scripture here says *'zeh E-ili' (this is my G-d)*, meaning that "with me He is *E-il* [G-d in His aspect of mercy] in this matter, since He was exalted with mercy to be compassionate in His justice."

---

(126) Psalms 99:4. (127) So clearly interpreted in Abusaula's commentary on Ramban. See Vol. I, p. XII, Note 21. (128) See Ramban above, 6:2, and also Vol. I, pp. 214-216. (129) Ramban is thus interpreting Verse 3, *The Eternal is a man of war, the Eternal is His Name*, to mean that Israel will henceforth exalt Him both in His aspect of justice and of mercy. I have followed Abusaula's interpretation of Ramban's text. (130) Isaiah 33:10. (131) Above, 3:15. (132) Mechilta here on Verse 2. (133) Psalms 22:2. "And surely one would not say to the attribute of justice, 'Why hast thou forsaken me?'" (Rashi further, 34:6). (134) Numbers 12:13. A supplication of this kind is naturally addressed to G-d in His aspect of mercy. (135) Psalms 118:27.

6. THY RIGHT HAND, O ETERNAL, GLORIOUS IN POWER, THY RIGHT HAND, O ETERNAL, DASHETH IN PIECES THE ENEMY. Rashi commented: "The literal sense of the text is as follows: 'Thy right hand that is glorious in power — what does it do? *Thy right hand, O Eternal, dasheth in pieces the enemy.*' There are many Scriptural verses that follow this form. *For lo Thine enemies, O Eternal, for lo Thine enemies shall perish;* [136] *Eternal, how long shall the wicked, how long shall the wicked exult?* [137] *The floods have lifted up, O Eternal, the floods have lifted up their voice.*" [138] In my opinion, however, this is not correct. Verses repeat words in order to indicate that such will always be the case, without identifying what they refer to until they mention it the second time. Had Scripture said here, "Thy right hand, thy right hand, dasheth in pieces the enemy" it would have been exactly like the other verses Rashi mentions. [But instead it says here, Thy right hand, O Eternal, 'glorious in power,' Thy right hand, O Eternal, dasheth... and consequently it is unlike the other verses mentioned.] Rabbi Abraham ibn Ezra said that the verse means: "Thy right hand, O Eternal, Thou Who art glorious in power, may Thy right hand dash in pieces the enemy." In that case, the verse here is similar in form to the verses mentioned [by Rashi].

A more correct interpretation would be to explain it thus: "Thy right hand, O Eternal, is glorious in power to humble all proud and lofty; Thy right hand, O Eternal, dashes in pieces the enemy with great power." It mentions *the right hand* both in the masculine and feminine forms, [139] just as in the verse, *Behold, a hand was put forth unto me; and lo, a roll of a book was therein,* [140] and is repeated as is customary in prophecies.

---

(136) *Ibid.*, 92:10. The meaning then would be: "*For lo Thine enemies, O Eternal,* what shall happen to them? *For lo Thine enemies shall perish.*" (137) *Ibid.*, 94:3. (138) *Ibid.*, 93:3. (139) *"Thy right hand... 'ne'edari' (glorious)"* is in the masculine gender; *"Thy right hand... 'tir'atz' (dasheth)"* is in the feminine. (140) Ezekiel 2:9. *Sh'luchah* (put forth) is a feminine form; *bo* (therein) is a masculine.

The student learned [in the mystic lore of the Cabala] will understand the way of the Truth in this verse from the first verses[141] I have explained. And so did the Rabbis say it:[142] "With the very same hand with which He sank the Egyptians, He delivered Israel,"[143] for it is "the power" that saves, as it is said, *And now, I pray Thee, let the power of the Eternal be great.*[144]

9. THE ENEMY SAID. "I.e., to his people, when he [Pharaoh] was persuading them with words: ' I will pursue them and I will overtake them, and I will divide the spoil with my captains and my servants.' "Thus the language of Rashi. Now I have seen in the Midrash Chazita:[145] "Thus did Rabbi Yishmael teach: *'The enemy said: I will pursue, I will overtake.* This should fittingly have been at the beginning of the Song, and why was it not written there? It is because there is no strict chronological order in the narrative of the Torah.' " Now Onkelos is of that opinion, for he translated, "the enemy had said," referring to the beginning of his plan to pursue after them.

In my opinion, by way of the plain meaning of Scripture, this is to be understood in connection with the preceding verses, [all of them together explaining how the destruction of the enemy came about.] First, Scripture said that they sank in the sea and that they went down into the depths.[146] This happened when *the waters returned, and covered the chariots, and the horsemen.*[147] After that, Scripture reverts to tell how this came about. *With the blast of Thy nostrils,* which is a reference to *the strong east wind,*[148] *the waters were piled up,* and *the deeps were congealed*[149] from the beginning. It was because of this that the

---

(141) See above, 14:31. (142) Shemoth Rabbah 24:1. (143) See my Hebrew commentary, p. 355, that it is so interpreted by Rabbeinu Bachya ben Asher. (144) Numbers 14:17. (145) I have not found this Midrash in Shir Hashirim Rabbah, (see above in *Seder Shemoth,* Note 317), but in Koheleth Rabbah 1:31 and also in the Mechilta of Rabbi Shimon ben Yochai on the verse here. (146) Verse 5. (147) Above, 14:28. (148) *Ibid.,* Verse 21. (149) Verse 8.

enemy thought that he would pursue and overtake them in the sea and divide their spoil, and that his lust would be satisfied upon them. But *Thou didst blow* [150] upon them *with Thy wind,* and *the sea covered them.*

Now Moses mentioned this for in this thought of Pharaoh too were discernible the wonderful causation of G-d, Who strengthened the hearts of the Egyptians and turned their counsel into foolishness to come after the Israelites into the sea, as I have explained above.[151] It is for this reason that following that verse, Moses said, *Who is like unto Thee, O Eternal, among the mighty,*[152] doing great and wondrous things in ways mutually opposed to each other, [such as was done here: with the same hand, He sank the Egyptians and delivered Israel, as mentioned above].

10. 'NASHAPHTA' WITH THY WIND. Rabbi Abraham ibn Ezra said that *nashaphta* is derived from the root *nesheph* (twilight), [153] for it was at twilight that He brought the wind which caused the water to return and drown the pursuers. Rashi explained it "as an expression for 'blowing,' similar in usage to the verse, *When 'nashaph' (He bloweth) upon them, they wither."* [154] Rashi has explained it well.

My opinion, furthermore, is that the purport of *nashaphta,* [written with the letter *phei*], is like [that written] with a *beth: Thou 'nashavta' (didst blow) with Thy wind.* The usage of the word is similar to: *Because the breath of the Eternal 'nashva' (bloweth) upon it;* [155] *'yasheiv' (He bloweth) His wind, and the waters flow.*[156] These two letters — [the *phei* or *pei* and the *beth*] — are of similar usage, just as in the verses: *'al gapei' (Upon) the highest places of the city,* [157] which is like *al gabei; 'im b'gapo'*

---

(150) Verse 10.   (151) Above, 14:21.   (152) Verse 11.   (153) "For there are two kinds of *nesheph* (twilight): the *nesheph* after sundown, and the *nesheph* before sunrise" (Ibn Ezra)! Here the *nesheph* before sunrise is referred to.   (154) Isaiah 40:24.   (155) *Ibid.,* Verse 7.   (156) Psalms 147:18.   (157) Proverbs 9:3.

EXODUS XV, BESHALACH

(if by himself),[158] which is like *im b'gabo*. Similarly: *And substance 'yivzor' (he shall scatter) among them;*[159] *'bizar' (He hath scattered) the peoples.*[160] These are expressions of *pizur* (scattering), [with the letter *beth* serving here as *phei*][161] In proper names, these letters also interchange, e.g., Shovach, and Shophach.[162] And our Rabbis say in the Mishnah:[163] "[If produce is proclaimed] *hevkeir* (ownerless) for the benefit of the poor [only], it is deemed *hevkeir* (ownerless)."[164] [The word *hevkeir*] is like *hephkeir* (ownerless). From the expression, *The grains 'avshu' (shrivel)*[165] comes the word *ipush* (musty). The term *ben p'kua,*[166] [an animal taken alive out of the slaughtered mother's womb], is used in place of *ben b'kua*, because the mother was "ripped open" and there was found in it a living offspring of nine months.

In my opinion also, *'hichpishani' in ashes*[167] is like *'hichbishani' (He presses me)* [or "He made me cower"] in ashes, the usage of the word being similar to: *And replenish the earth, 'v'chivshuha' (and subdue it);*[168] *'yichbosh' (He will subdue) our iniquities.*[169] In the language of the Rabbis we also find: "a measure which is *k'phushah,*"[170] meaning *k'vushah*, [a measure into which the contents have been "compressed", and which therefore contains more than its normal measure].

---

(158) Further, 21:3. (159) Daniel 11:24. (160) Psalms 68:31. (161) See Vol. I, pp. 505-506, for a similar interchange of letters between the *gimmel* and the *kuph*. (162) II Samuel 10:16; I Chronicles 19:16. (163) Peah 6:1. (164) If a person gives up his ownership of the produce of his field, he is free from the obligation of giving the Tithe. But if he proclaimed it ownerless only for the poor and not for the rich, the School of Shammai say it is deemed ownerless and is therefore Tithe-free. The Mishnah continues that the School of Hillel say that it can be deemed ownerless only if it is proclaimed ownerless equally for the rich. Ramban here is interested only in the language of the Mishnah using a *veth (hevkeir)* for a *phei*, and therefore he quotes only the beginning of the Mishnah. (165) Joel 1:17. (166) Chullin 69 a. Literally: "a child [of an animal] which is ripped open." (167) Lamentations 3:16. (168) Genesis 1:28. (169) Micah 7:19. (170) Yebamoth 107 b.

The purport of the verse is thus: "with Your strong and mighty wind, the waters of the sea were piled up, and when You blew the wind with which You control the sea, the sea covered them." This is the intent of the verse, *And the sea returned to its strength when the morning appeared*,[171] for He caused the wind to blow on it as He does at His strength when *He ruleth the proud swelling of the sea.*[172]

'TZALALU' AS LEAD. They went down into "the depths" (*m'tzoloth*) of the sea as lead. Now Moses mentioned this in the Song twice: *They went down into the sea like a stone*,[173] and *as lead*, [mentioned in the verse here], in order to emphasize that this too came upon them from the hand of G-d. There were many persons among the Egyptians who knew how to swim, and they were near dry land, and surely all those who rode on the horses could be expected to be saved since horses are accustomed to swimming in water. Similarly, *those that handle the shield*[174] can save themselves in water, and here not one of them escaped! This is the meaning of the verse, *And the Eternal overthrew ('vay'na'er') the Egyptians in the midst of the sea.*[171] He lifted them with *His rough blast*,[175] and He lowered them into the sea. The usage of the word is similar to that in the verses: *And the wicked 'v'yina'aru' (shall be shaken) out of it;*[176] *And the strong shall be 'lin'oreth' (as tow)*,[177] *'n'oreth'* being that which is separated and falls off from the flax when it is being prepared [for spinning].

11. WHO IS LIKE UNTO THEE, O ETERNAL, 'BA'EILIM'. "I.e., among the mighty ones, just as in the verses: *And 'eilei' (the mighty) of the land he took away;*[178] *'eyaluthi' (O Thou my strength), hasten to help me.*"[179] Thus the language of Rashi.

(171) Above, 14:27. (172) Psalms 89:10. (173) Verse 5. (174) Jeremiah 46:9. The shield can serve as a board for passing through the surf. See Yebamoth 121 a where Rabbi Akiba relates that once when his boat drowned "I chanced upon a board of the boat and every wave that came upon me I bent my head" and he was thus saved. (175) Isaiah 27:8. (176) Job 38:13. (177) Isaiah 1:31. (178) Ezekiel 17:13. (179) Psalms 22:20.

EXODUS XV, BESHALACH

Now it is true that the word *eilim* is an expression of power and strength, but *Who is like unto Thee 'ba'eilim'* is a reference to the angels who are called *eilim*, the usage of the word being similar to that in the verse, *This is 'E-ili' (my G-d), and I will glorify Him*,[180] and the Holy One, blessed be He, is called *E-il Elyon* (G-d the Most High)[181] above all powers. Similarly, *And he shall speak strange things against the G-d of 'eilim'* [182] is like the expression, *He is G-d of gods*.[183] Also, *Ascribe unto the Eternal, O ye 'b'nei eilim' (sons of might)* [184] is like the expression *b'nei ha'elohim*,[185] since they are at times called *eilim* or *b'nei eilim*, and sometimes also *ha'elohim* or *b'nei elohim*. Thus: *For the Eternal is greater than all 'ha'elohim';*[186] *And the 'b'nei ha'elohim' came to present themselves before the Eternal.*[187] Some scholars[188] say that the word *b'nei* is not in the construct state, nor are these expressions: *b'nei shileishim*,[189] *'anshei' (men) portrayed upon the wall*.[190] And this is the meaning of *Who is like Thee, 'ne'edar' (majestic) in holiness?* since there is no *adir* (lofty one) like Him in the celestial holy abode. And so we find in the Mechilta:[191] *"Who is like unto Thee* among those who serve before Thee in heaven, as it is said, *For who in the skies can be compared unto the Eternal, who among the sons of might can be likened unto the Eternal, a G-d to be feared in the great council of the holy ones?"*[192]

---

(180) Verse 2. (181) Genesis 14:18. (182) Daniel 11:36. (183) Deuteronomy 10:17. (184) Psalms 29:1. (185) Genesis 6:2. (186) Further, 18:11. (187) Job 1:6. (188) Reference is to R'dak, who mentions this point clearly in his Sefer Hamichlal, and quotes the verses mentioned here. If *b'nei* is not in the construct state, *b'nei eilim* will not mean "sons of the mighty ones," as it would if the word *b'nei* were in the construct state. Instaed, it means "the sons who are the mighty ones." (189) Genesis 50:23. In the construct state, it would mean "children of the third generation," i.e., the fourth generation. In the non-construct state, it would mean "children who were the third generation." (190) Ezekiel 23:14. The point here is that the word *anshei* (men) is vocalized with a *tzeirei*, as is the rule in the construct state. See Vol. I, p. 503. Yet it is not in the construct state. So also the word *b'nei*, although vocalized with a *tzeirei*, is not in the construct state. (191) Mechilta on the verse here. (192) Psalms 80:7-8.

'NORA TH'HILOTH' (FEARFUL IN PRAISES). "He is feared by those who recount His praises lest they enumerate fewer than there really are, [and thus fail to praise Him adequately], just as it is written, *To thee silence is praise.*"[193] Thus Rashi's language. Rabbi Abraham ibn Ezra also explained "that all who praise Him are fearful when praising His Name, for *Who can make all His praise to be heard?*[194] And they are duty-bound to praise His Name, for He alone does wonders."

In my opinion, *nora th'hiloth* means: "fearful with praises, for He does fearful things and He is praised for them, as when He wreaks vengeance on those who transgress His will and thereby helps those who serve Him. Thus He is [both] feared and highly praised." And because earthly kings are feared because of their *oppression and perverseness,*[195] Moses said that G-d is feared through the very things for which He is praised. Similarly, *To Thee 'dumiyah' is praise*[193] means, by way of the plain meaning of Scripture, "that hoping to Thee is praise, for all who hope to Thee obtain their wish, and they praise Thy Name in Zion and there they perform their vows[196] which they have vowed in the time of their trouble." The usage [of the word *dumiyah* as "hope"] is similar to that found in these verses: *Only to G-d 'dumi' (wait) thou, my soul, for from Him cometh my hope;*[197] *'vayidom hashemesh' and the moon stayed.*[198] Similarly, *Only to G-d 'dumiyah' my soul*[199] means: "only to G-d doth my soul hope." Thus it appears to me.

In the name of other scholars,[200] I have heard that it means: "to Thee, praise becomes silent, for no amount of praise can

---

(193) *Ibid.*, 65:2. (194) *Ibid.*, 106:2. (195) Isaiah 30:12. (196) See Psalms 65:2. (197) *Ibid.*, 62:6. One who hopes waits in expectation of something to happen. (198) Joshua 10:13. It is generally translated: *And the sun stood still.* Ramban obviously takes it to mean: "and the sun 'waited,'" a term akin to hoping, for he who hopes waits. (199) Psalms 62:2. (200) Mentioned by R'dak in his Sefer Hashorashim, under the root of *damah*, in the name of "some commentators."

fathom Thy great and fearful deeds." The usage is similar to the verse: *And at night there is no 'dumiyah' (respite) for me.*[201] Accordingly, the meaning of the expression, *O G-d, in Zion* [202] is "the G-d Who is in Zion." That is to say, the One Who dwells there. The correct interpretation is as we have said, [i.e., that *dumiyah* signifies "hope"].

12. THOU STRETCHEDST OUT THY RIGHT HAND — THE EARTH 'TIVLA'EIMO' (SWALLOWED THEM). The meaning is that "after you blew with Your wind and *the sea covered them,* You stretched out Your right hand and Your arm,[203] *and the earth swallowed them.*" The purport thereof is that after they drowned, the sea cast them out as is the custom of the seas, and so Scripture says, *And Israel saw the Egyptians dead upon the sea-shore.*[204] There, [on the sea-shore], their bodies decomposed and they returned to the dust upon the earth as they were,[205] and thus they were swallowed up and destroyed [by the earth]. The usage of the word *tivla'eimo* is similar to the expressions: *Together round about, 'vativla'eini' (Thou dost destroy me);*[206] *The Eternal 'bila' (hath swallowed up) unsparingly;*[207] *And the way of thy paths 'bileiu,'*[208] which means "they destroyed." Our Rabbis have said [209] that the earth opened her mouth and swallowed them, for they were privileged to be buried by virtue of having said, *The Eternal is righteous.*[210] [Thus, according to this Midrash of the

---

(201) Psalms 22:3.　(202) *Ibid.*, 65:2. The verse reads: *To Thee 'dumiyah' praise, O G-d in Zion, and unto Thee the vow is performed.* Now Ramban had first presented his own interpretation that the word *dumiyah* means hope, and the purport of the verse is that hoping to G-d is praise, for all who hope to G-d obtain their favor from Him and then they praise His name in Zion where they come to perform their vows. But according to the explanation of the other scholars, i.e., that *dumiyah* expresses a sense of silence, the verse means: "praise unto Thee becomes silent, O G-d Who dwells in Zion, for no amount of praise can fathom Thy deeds, and unto Thee the vow is performed."
(203) Verse 16: *By the greatness of Thine arm...*　(204) Above, 14:30.
(205) See Ecclesiastes 12:7.　(206) Job 10:8.　(207) Lamentations 2:2.
(208) Isaiah 3:12.　(209) Mechilta on the verse here.　(210) Above, 9:27.

Rabbis, the bodies of the Egyptians were not totally destroyed, for they even merited a place for burial.] But the expression of G-d's "outstretched right hand or arm," [as stated here. *Thou stretchedst out Thy right hand*], is used in Scripture only as indicating vengeance and destruction! Perhaps the Rabbis [of the above-mentioned interpretation] will explain the verse as follows: *"Thou stretchedst out Thy right hand* to slay them in the sea, and *the earth swallowed them up* after that," this being the burial which they merited.

13. THOU IN THY LOVE HAST LED THE PEOPLE THAT THOU HAST REDEEMED; THOU HAST GUIDED THEM IN THY STRENGTH TO THY HOLY HABITATION. Rabbi Abraham ibn Ezra explained that this is a past tense in place of the future, as is customary in prophecies. In my opinion, Moses is saying: *"Thou stretchedst out Thy right hand*[211] upon the enemy, and the earth swallowed them, but *Thou in Thy love hast led* — in a *pillar of cloud, to lead them the way*[212] — *the people that Thou hast redeemed,* and *Thou hast guided them* in the strength of Thy hands *to Thy holy habitation,"* for it is to that holy habitation that they were going, and so also, *And all nations shall flow unto it.*[213] *Thy holy habitation* is a reference to the Sanctuary [in Jerusalem], as Moses says again, *The Sanctuary, O Eternal, which Thy hands have established.*[214] And so the Rabbis have said in the Mechilta:[215] *"Habitation* is but a designation for the Sanctuary, as it is said, *Look upon Zion, the city of our solemn gatherings; thine eyes shall see Jerusalem a peaceful habitation."*[216]

14. THE PEOPLES HAVE HEARD, THEY TREMBLE. The purport thereof is: "when the people will hear [of Thy visitation upon the Egyptians], they will tremble from the blow of Thy hands, and pangs will take hold of the inhabitants of Philistia when

---

(211) Verse 12.   (212) Above, 13:21.   (213) Isaiah 2:2.   (214) Further, Verse 17.   (215) Mechilta on the verse here.   (216) Isaiah 33:20.

EXODUS XV, BESHALACH

they will hear [of those deeds]." It is possible that Moses is saying that the peoples have already heard all that G-d has done in the land of Egypt, and that they will always tremble from the disease He has put upon them.[217] Thus Moses continues to pray that He should let fall upon them terror and dread[218] so that they should not go out to war against Israel.

Rabbi Abraham ibn Ezra explained that the verse, *Horror and dread shall fall upon them,*[218] refers only to Philistia, [mentioned in Verse 14] and Edom and Moab, [mentioned in Verse 15], but not to the inhabitants of Canaan, [who are also mentioned at the end of Verse 15]. This is because Moses said afterward, [i.e., at the end of Verse 16 before us], *till Thy people pass over, O Eternal.* It was over them [Philistia, Edom and Moab] that the Israelites passed before they came into the land of Canaan, and these peoples really did not war against them. Even when Edom *came out against him with much people, and a strong hand,*[219] it was only so that the Israelites should not pass over his land, but he did not war against them. But were it not for the terror and dread that fell upon them, they would have wanted to battle against them out of their hatred of them. Now Moses did not mention Ammon, because Ammon and Moab are as one nation. It is possible that the dread of the Israelites fell on the Canaanite too, and he did not war against them until they had passed over [the Jordan], for *the Canaanite, the king of Arad, who dwelt in the south*[220] [and who warred against Israel when they were still in the wilderness], was not a Canaanite by descent, according to the opinion of our Rabbis.[221]

---

(217) See further, Verse 26. (218) Verse 16. (219) Numbers 20:20. (220) *Ibid.*, 21:1. (221) Tanchuma, *Chukath* 18. The explanation there is that this was Amalek, but he purposely changed his speech to the Canaanite language so that Israel might be misled and would pray that G-d should give the Canaanites into their hands. Since Amalek was actually not a Canaanite, their prayers would therefore be ineffectual. This interpretation is quoted by Rashi to Numbers 21:1.

18. THE ETERNAL SHALL REIGN FOR EVER AND EVER. Moses is saying that just as He has now shown that He is King and Ruler by having brought deliverance to His servants and destruction upon those that rebel against Him, so may it be His will to do so in all generations forever, that *He withdraw not His eyes from the righteous,*[222] nor hide them [His eyes] from the wicked ones who inflict evil upon others. There are many verses that are to be interpreted in this way, such as: *The Eternal will reign for ever, thy G-d, O Zion, unto all generations. Hallelujah;*[223] *Blessed be the Name of the Eternal from this time forth and for ever;*[224] *And the Eternal shall be King over all the earth.*[225]

Now Onkelos was apprehensive [of translating this verse literally, which is stated in a future tense], since G-d's sovereignty is [indeed] to all eternity [and no prayer for its continuance is possible]. Therefore he rendered it in the present tense: "The Kingdom of the Eternal endureth for ever and to all eternity," just as is expressed in the verse, *Thy Kingdom is a Kingdom for all ages.*[226] But I have not understood Onkelos' opinion in this matter, for it is written: *May the Glory of the Eternal endure for ever;*[227] *And let the whole earth be filled with His Glory;*[228] "Magnified and sanctified shall be [His great Name]";[229] *Yea, let it be established, and let Thy Name be magnified for ever.*[230] It is possible that the meaning of these [future tenses] is similar to the secret of the benedictions.[231]

---

(222) Job 36:7. (223) Psalms 146:10. (224) *Ibid.*, 113:2. (225) Zechariah 14:9. (226) Psalms 145:13. (227) *Ibid.*, 104:31. (228) *Ibid.*, 72:19. (229) From the beginning of the *Kaddish* prayer. In Ricanti's work on the Torah in quoting this text from Ramban, he writes clearly: "and in the *Kaddish* [we say], 'Magnified, etc.'" It is thus to be noted that the *Kaddish*-text is quoted by Ramban amidst Scriptural verses as authority for his thesis! The great sanctity of the *Kaddish* prayer is thus clearly indicated. (230) I Chronicles 17:24. (231) "Magnifying G-d's Name brings life and blessing to the world, thus assuring that His kingdom will be acknowledged in the world in the future. And so is the purport of the benedictions we make, which begin by referring to 'the Eternal, our G-d' and continue to mention 'King of the universe'" (Ma'or V'shamesh).

19. FOR THE HORSES OF PHARAOH WENT IN WITH HIS CHARIOTS AND WITH HIS HORSEMEN. Rabbi Abraham ibn Ezra said that this verse is also part of the Song, for Moses and the children of Israel were singing and saying: *For the horses of Pharaoh went in with his chariots and with his horsemen into the sea, and the Eternal brought back the waters of the sea upon them* while the children of Israel were walking *on dry land in the midst of the sea,* this being a miracle within a miracle.[232]

But this verse is not written in the style of the Song, nor is it in the style of prophecies! [Therefore, Ibn Ezra's interpretation is not correct.] Instead, the verse is to be interpreted [as dating the Song]: *Then sang Moses — when the horses of Pharaoh went in.* Immediately on that day — not the following day or at some later time — [he sang this Song]. It may be that the sense thereof is as follows: *Then Moses sang,* when *the horses of Pharaoh went into the sea and G-d brought back the waters of the sea upon them while the children of Israel were yet walking on dry land in the midst of it.* Thus the verse relates that they said the Song while they were walking in the midst of the sea on dry land. Scripture further tells[233] that it was then that Miriam the prophetess took the timbrel in hand and sang them the first verse of the Song that they, [i.e., the women], should sing after Moses and Israel.

20. AND MIRIAM THE PROPHETESS, THE SISTER OF AARON. The correct interpretation appears to me to be that because Moses and Miriam were mentioned in the Song and Aaron was not, Scripture wanted to mention him. It therefore said *the sister of Aaron* as a mark of honor to him, i.e., that he was her older brother and that his sister the prophetess connected her genealogy to him, since he too was a prophet and a holy man of G-d. It is possible that it is the custom of Scripture to trace the genealogy of a family through the oldest brother. Similarly it is

---

(232) *For* when *the horses of Pharaoh went in,* etc., *He brought the waters upon them.* and at the same time, *the children of Israel walked on dry land.* (233) Verses 20-21.

written, *And the sons of Caleb the brother of Jerahmeel,*[234] because he was the oldest brother, as it is said: *The sons also of Hezron... Jerahmeel, and Ram, and Chelubai.*[235]

25. THERE HE MADE FOR THEM A STATUTE AND AN ORDINANCE, AND THERE HE TRIED THEM. "At Marah He gave them some of the sections of the Torah so that they might engage in the study thereof, [such as]: the Sabbath, the Red Heifer,[236] and the laws of justice. *And there He tried them,* that is, the people."[237] Thus the language of Rashi, and it is the opinion of our Rabbis.[238]

But I wonder! Why does Scripture not explain these statutes and ordinances here, saying, "And the Eternal spoke to Moses: 'Command the children of Israel,'" as it says in the chapters mentioned above, *Speak ye unto all the congregation of Israel?*[239] Indeed, it does so with regard to all commandments given in the Tent of Meeting, on the plains of Moab,[240] and the Passover in

---

(234) I Chronicles 2:42. (235) *Ibid.*, 2:9. (236) Numbers, Chapter 19. The reason that Rashi singles out these three subjects — the Sabbath, the Red Heifer, and the laws of justice — is generally explained as follows: He mentions the Sabbath because it is referred to in the section on the manna (further, 16:23-30), as the means through which G-d tried Israel. The Red Heifer is the most outstanding example of a *chok* (a statute), the type of a commandment the reason for which we do not know. The laws of justice are the typical examples of *mishpat* (ordinance), which is a precept dictated by reason. Accordingly Rashi interpreted the verse before us — *a statute* etc. — as referring to these three subjects. (237) Rashi's intent is to explain the extra word *v'sham* ('*and there*' *He tried them*). It should have said, "There He made for them a statute and an ordinance and tried them," in which case it would have meant that He tried them with the statute and ordinance, i.e., to see if they would observe them. But since it says, *and there He tried them,* it must refer to something additional, namely, the preceding event when the people murmured against Moses instead of approaching him to pray that the bitterness of the waters be removed. It is to this event, according to Rashi, that the expression refers: "*And there He tried them, that is, the people*" (Sifthei Chachamim). Ramban, however, will explain that "the trial" was of another nature, as will be explained in the text. (238) Sanhedrin 56 b. (239) Above, 12:3. (240) Numbers 35:1.

the wilderness![241] Now Rashi's expression, "He gave them... sections of the Torah so that they might engage in the study thereof," indicates that Moses did inform them of these statutes and that he taught these statutes to them, [saying], "In the future, the Holy One, blessed be He, will command you so," in the same way as Abraham our father learned the Torah.[242] The purpose of it was to make them familiar with the commandments and to know if they would accept them *with joyfulness and with gladness of heart.* [243] This was "the trial" of which Scripture says, *and there He tried them,* and he [Moses] informed them that G-d would further command them the precepts of the Torah. This is the intent of the verse, *"If thou wilt diligently hearken to the voice of the Eternal thy G-d... and wilt give ear to His commandments,*[244] which He will command you [in the future]."

In line with the plain meaning of Scripture, when the Israelites began coming into *the great and dreadful wilderness... thirsty ground where there was no water,*[245] Moses established customs for them concerning how to regulate their lives and affairs *until they come to a land inhabited.* [246] A custom is called *chok,* this being associated with the expressions: *Feed me with 'chuki' (my customary) bread,*[247] *'chukoth' (the customary ways or laws) of heaven and earth.*[248] Custom is also called *mishpat* (judgment or

---

(241) *Ibid.,* 9:1-5. (242) See Vol. I, pp. 331-332. (243) Deuteronomy 28:47. (244) Verse 26. It is thus obvious that Ramban understands the word *vayomer* (and he said) as a reference to Moses, and not, as rendered in some translations, "and He said." (245) Deuteronomy 8:15. (246) Further, 16:35. — "*Moses* established customs." It should be noted that Ramban uses the expression *sam lahem* which could possibly be a reference to G-d, that "*He* established customs for them." But in Rabbeinu Bachya's commentary quoting Ramban he writes clearly: "In line with the plain meaning of Scripture, *statute and ordinance* are the customs how to regulate their lives in the desert, for Moses was king in Jeshurun, a leader who chastised his people and commanded them how to regulate their lives in the desert" (Bachya, Vol. II, p. 137 in my edition). On the basis of Bachya's interpretation I have translated here: "*Moses* established customs."

ordinance) because it is something measured out accurately. A similar usage [of the word *mishpat*] is found in these verses: *So did David, and so hath been 'mishpato' (his manner) all the while;*[249] *After the former 'mishpat' (manner) when thou wast his butler;*[250] *And the palace shall be inhabited upon 'mishpato'* [251] i.e., upon its ascertained dimension.

It may mean that Moses instructed them in the ways of the wilderness, namely to be ready to suffer hunger and thirst and to pray to G-d, and not to murmur. He taught them ordinances whereby they should live, to love one another, to follow the counsel of the elders, to be discreet in their tents with respect to women and children, to deal in a peaceful manner with the strangers that come into the camp to sell them various objects. He also imparted moral instructions, i.e., that they should not become like bands of marauders who do all abominable things and have no sense of shame, similar to that which the Torah commanded, *When thou goest forth in camp against thine enemies, then thou shalt keep thee from every evil thing.*[252] In the case of Joshua it is also said. *So Joshua made a covenant with the people that day, and set them a statute and an ordinance in Shechem.* [253] Here too the expression, [*a statute and an ordinance*], does not refer to the statutes and ordinances of the Torah, but rather to the customs and ways of civilized society, such as "the conditions which Joshua made [upon entering the Land]," which the Rabbis have mentioned,[254] and other such similar regulations. And Scripture says, *and there he tried them*, in order to inform us that he [Moses] led them by such a road on which there was no water, and he brought them to a place where the waters were bitter in order to test them, even as Scripture says, *And He afflicted thee,*

(247) Proverbs 30:8. (248) Jeremiah 33:25. (249) I Samuel 27:11. (250) Genesis 40:13. (251) Jeremiah 30:18. (252) Deuteronomy 23:10. (253) Joshua 24:25. (254) Baba Kamma 80 b-81 a: "Ten conditions did Joshua stipulate [with Israel when they came into the Land]: that all people have a right to pasture their cattle in forests [without the interference of the owner of the forest] etc." The customs established by Joshua were thus the norms of a functioning society.

and suffered thee to hunger;[255] *And that He might prove thee, to do thee good at thy latter end.*[256]

'VAYOREIHU HASHEM EITZ' (AND THE ETERNAL SHOWED HIM A TREE). The meaning thereof is that G-d showed Moses a tree and He told him, "Throw this tree into the waters, and they shall become sweet." Now due to the fact that I have not found the expression of *moreh*, [from which the word *vayoreihu* here is derived], except in the sense of instruction — [e.g., the verse], *'vayoreini' and said to me,*[257] which means "and he [my father] taught me," and so all other such expressions — it appears by way of the plain meaning of Scripture that this tree had a natural property to sweeten water, this being its uniqueness, and He taught it to Moses. Our Rabbis have said[258] that the tree was [naturally] bitter, but that this was a miracle within a miracle, [i.e., that He healed the bitter waters with something which was bitter], just as the salt which Elisha cast into the waters.[259] Now if so,[260] the word *'vayoreihu' (and He instructed him)* indicates that the tree was not found in that place, and the Holy One, blessed be He, taught him where it was to be found, or perhaps He made it available to him by a miracle. I found further in the Yelamdeinu:[261] "See what is written there: *Vayoreihu hashem eitz*. It does not say *vayar'eihu* (and He showed him) but *vayoreihu*, which means that He taught him His way." That is to say, He instructed him and taught him the way of the Holy One, blessed be He, i.e., that He sweetens the bitter with the bitter.

---

(255) Deuteronomy 8:3. (256) *Ibid.*, Verse 16. (257) Proverbs 4:4. (258) Mechilta on the verse here. (259) II Kings 2:21. "Now even if you put salt into good water, it immediately spoils. Here, Elisha put a thing that spoils [salt] into the waters that had already been spoiled, in order to perform a miracle, [i.e., to heal the waters], therewith" (Mechilta). (260) I.e., if, as this interpretation has it, the sweetening power of that tree was not a natural property thereof, the question again arises, why does Scripture say *vayoreihu* which indicates instruction? Ramban proceeds to remove this difficulty. (261) Tanchuma, *Beshalach* 24. For the name Yelamdeinu, see above in *Seder Bo*, Note 196.

26. IF 'SHAMO'A TISHMA' TO THE VOICE OF THE ETERNAL THY G-D. Rabbi Abraham ibn Ezra explained that "[*shamo'a tishma* here] means 'to understand'[262] the purport of that which He has commanded you to do. *And thou wilt do that which is right in His eyes* — this implies the positive commandments — *and wilt give ear to His commandments* — this implies the negative commandments." [Thus the language of Ibn Ezra.] And in the Mechilta, the Rabbis have said:[263] "*And thou wilt do that which is right in His eyes,* this means in business dealings. This teaches us that if a person is honest in his business dealings, and the spirit of his fellow creatures finds pleasure in him, it is accounted to him as though he had fulfilled the entire Torah." [264] I will further explain this when I come to the verse '*And thou shalt do that which is upright and good,*' if the good G-d will show me goodness. [265]

I WILL PUT NONE OF THE DISEASES UPON THEE, WHICH I HAVE PUT UPON THE EGYPTIANS; FOR I AM THE ETERNAL THAT HEALETH THEE. Rashi wrote: "*I will put none of the diseases upon thee,* and if I do place them [because you will not hearken to My voice], they will be as though they had not been placed, *for I am the Eternal that healeth thee.* This is the homiletic exposition. But according to the plain meaning of Scripture, the verse is to be understood in the sense of a person who says, 'I am the physician who warns you not to eat certain things which might bring a man back to his state of disease.'" Thus far the language of Rashi.

(262) Now ordinarily, *shamo'a tishma* would mean "surely listen" or "diligently hearken," but wherever this expression is followed by the letter *lamed* — as in this case, [*shamo'a tishma l'kol*] — or a *beth*, it means 'understanding.' This is why Ibn Ezra explained it here to mean "if you will have a full understanding of His commandments." (263) Mechilta on the verse here. (264) This is based upon the following phrases, *and thou wilt give ear to His commandments, and keep all His statutes.* The sense thereof is thus: "If you will do that which is right in G-d's eyes, meaning if you will be honest in your business dealings, it will be accounted to you as though you had given ear, etc." (265) See Ramban Deuteronomy 6:18.

But according to the plain meaning of Scripture, *rophecha* is not an adjective, [or more precisely, a noun-adjective, as Rashi would have it, meaning "Thy physician Who teaches thee how disease should not befall thee." Instead, the meaning of the verse is "that I am the One Who heals thee."] Besides, it is not customary that a master should assure his servants that "if you will do all my will and desire, I will not slay you with sore diseases." None of the Divine assurances of the Torah are expressed in that way! Rather, the verse here constitutes an admonition by which He warned them not to be among those that rebel against Him as the Egyptians had been. By hearkening to His voice, they will be saved from all sickness, since that sickness deservedly comes upon all those who rebel against His will, even as it befell the Egyptians when they did not hearken to Him. This is similar to that which He said that He will put *upon thee all the diseases of Egypt which thou wast in dread of, and they shall cleave unto thee.*[266] And He further said, *For I am the Eternal that healeth thee.* This constitutes a promise "that I will remove from you sickness that comes in the natural course of events, even as I healed the waters [at Marah]."

Rabbi Abraham ibn Ezra commented that this sign, [i.e., making the bitter waters sweet], which was the first one done for them in the wilderness, was in contrast to the first plague that came upon the Egyptians. The waters of the [Nile] river were sweet and He changed them to be of evil effect, while these waters of Marah were bitter and He healed them. Thus it was shown that G-d does things which are contrary to each other, and therefore you should fear Him and not rebel against Him so that He should not afflict you as He did [afflict] them. You should love Him for He will bestow goodness upon you, even as He healed the waters for you. [Thus far Ibn Ezra's comment.]

Now on the matter of Scripture making use here of two expressions, saying, "His commandments, His statutes," and

(266) Deuteronomy 28:60.

concluding, *I will put none of the diseases upon thee, for I am the Eternal,* [thus using the third-person and first-person pronouns in the same verse], I have already *written you three times*[267] on the explanation thereof. [Here] it can be understood from the word *'l'kol' (to the voice)* and the word *'ani' (I)*, which convey the thought that if we shall listen to the voice of our G-d to keep G-d's commandments and His statutes, the Glorious Name will be our healer. It is on the basis [of the verse] that the Sages instituted [the formula of] benedictions [which contain two different pronouns, thus: "Blessed art *Thou* O Eternal, our G-d, King of the universe,] Who hast sanctified us with *His* commandments and hast commanded us." The benedictions contain an expression of acknowledgment of G-d's Sovereignty, [saying as we do, "our G-d, King of the universe"], and the commandments have been given to us *from everlasting even to everlasting.*[268] The student learned [in the mystic lore of the Cabala] will understand.

And I will enlighten you [on this matter]. All benedictions which contain an expression of His Sovereignty are so formulated that they show respect to the Sovereign of the universe, Who has sanctified us [by His commandments] and Who has done [a certain deed] for us. But where a benediction follows another one, in which case the Sovereignty of G-d is not mentioned,[269] it is

---

(267) Proverbs 22:20, according to Jonathan ben Uziel's translation. Ramban uses the expression here in a figurative sense, meaning: "I have already elucidated this matter in other places." See Vol. I, pp. 260-261. See also further, 24:2. (268) I Chronicles 16:36. (269) Such is an established rule in the prayers. The opening benediction starts: *Baruch atah Hashem Elokeinu melech ha'olam (Blessed art Thou, O Eternal, King of the universe...),* the Sovereignty of G-d thus being acknowledged in the second person, i.e., as the One directly addressed. But the benediction concludes with a reference to that Sovereign in the third person, thus concluding, "Who has sanctified us by *His* commandments." The following benedictions do not open with a reference to G-d's Sovereignty, but instead continue throughout in the second person. For example, in the Grace after the meal, the first benediction begins: "Blessed art *Thou,* O Eternal our G-d, *King of the universe,* Who sustains the whole world with *His* goodness...

EXODUS XV, BESHALACH

formulated in the second-person, such as [the benedictions beginning]: "Thou art Mighty," "Thou art Holy,"[270] and so all the others. The prayer of *Aleinu l'shabei'ach* (" It is for us to praise the Lord of all things," a prayer which begins the three special sections of the New Year Additional Service], was designated in the third-person [even though it is not preceded by a benediction in which G-d's Sovereignty is mentioned], because we mention therein, "And we bend the knee and bow low and offer thanks before the Supreme King of kings." [271] Understand this.

27. AND THERE WERE TWELVE SPRINGS OF WATER, AND THREE SCORE AND TEN PALM TREES. It is not such a significant matter that seventy palm trees are found in a certain place. In the lowlands, a thousand and more palm trees can be found in one location, and springs of abundant water *are springing forth in valleys and hills*,[272] and Scripture does not mention them at all! [Why then are these springs and palm trees singled out here?]

He giveth food to all flesh....." The second benediction begins: "We thank Thee, O Eternal our G-d, for the goodly and ample land of our desire which Thou gavest....." It should be noted that this rule applies only where a number of benedictions relate to one unit of prayer, such as the Grace after the Meal, or the Morning *Sh'ma*, the Evening *Sh'ma*, etc. Where the benedictions consist of short unrelated statements, such as the blessings of thanksgiving with which the Morning Service begins, each benediction contains an expression of G-d as the Sovereign of the universe. (270) These are the second and third benedictions of the *Sh'moneh Esreh* [literally: the "Eighteen" Blessings — the central prayer around which the regular daily services are built]. They do not begin with a reference to G-d's Sovereignty, and therefore are formulated in the second person: "*Thou* art Mighty;" "*Thou* art Holy." It should be noted that in the first benediction of the *Sh'moneh Esreh,* although there is no reference to G-d as the Sovereign of the universe, the expression "G-d of Abraham" is deemed equivalent to "King of the universe," since Abraham was the first to acknowledge His Sovereignty over the whole universe. See my Hebrew commentary, p. 361. (271) When one stands in His very presence, it is not proper to address prayer to Him in the second person. Hence the *Aleinu* prayer is designated in the third person. (Ricanti). See my Hebrew commentary, p. 361. (272) Deuteronomy 8:7.

Now Rabbi Abraham ibn Ezra explained that Scripture narrates that they came to a good place which was unlike Marah. In Elim, there were many springs, and the waters were sweet and good, since palm trees cannot thrive in soil where the waters are bitter. It is for this reason that Scripture says here *and they encamped there,* because on account of it, they stayed there for more days than in the other places they passed through. In the section of *Eileh Mas'ei,*[273] however, Scripture does not relate anything about Marah, and yet it states, *And they journeyed from Marah, and came unto Elim; and in Elim were twelve springs of water, and three score and ten palm trees, and they encamped there,*[274] and a description of a place at such length is not found there about any of the places they traversed!

Now Rashi wrote: "*Twelve springs of water,* a number corresponding to the twelve tribes of Israel, were ready for them. *And seventy palm trees* — these corresponded to the seventy elders." But I do not know the nature of this preparation, i.e., whether it was done for them by a miracle just for that time. I have however, seen here in the Mechilta: "Rabbi Eleazar of Modaim said: 'On the very day that the Holy One, blessed be He, created His world, He created twelve springs corresponding to the twelve tribes of Israel, and seventy palm trees corresponding to the seventy elders.'" Scripture thus tells that each tribe encamped beside his spring and the elders sat in their shade praising G-d for them, because He had prepared for them [such a restful place] in a land of drought. Our Rabbis have yet another explanation in the

---

(273) Numbers 33:1-49. A detailed listing is given there of all the places through which Israel passed on the way from Egypt to the Promised Land.
(274) *Ibid.,* Verse 9. Accordingly Ibn Ezra's explanation that the springs and palm trees of Elim were mentioned here in order to contrast with Marah, where the waters were bitter, cannot be correct, because there in *Eileh Mas'ei,* Scripture states nothing about Marah and yet mentions the same about Elim as here.

EXODUS XVI, BESHALACH

Midrash of Rabbi Nechunya ben Hakanah[275] on this verse, which is wonderful in our eyes. [276]

16

1. AND THEY TOOK THEIR JOURNEY FROM ELIM, AND ALL THE CONGREGATION OF THE CHILDREN OF ISRAEL CAME UNTO THE WILDERNESS OF SIN. Scripture speaks briefly here, for when they journeyed from Elim, *they pitched by the Red Sea, and they journeyed from the Red Sea, and they pitched in the wilderness of Sin*,[277] since this great wilderness extended from Elim to Sinai. Thus, when they travelled from Elim, they camped beside the Red Sea in that wilderness. Then they journeyed from the edge of the sea and entered into the midst of the wilderness, making the stages of Dophkah and Alush,[278] and then *they journeyed from Alush*, which is in the wilderness of Sinai, *and they pitched in Rephidim*.[279]

In the opinion of our Rabbis,[280] the manna began falling in Alush. When the Israelites saw that they were journeying and camping in the wilderness — in Dophkah and Alush — and had not come out of it, they became frightened and began murmuring. This is the meaning of the verse, *And they murmured... in the wilderness*,[281] for they had not murmured when they came there but only after they were there in the wilderness [for an extended period of time].

---

(275) Sefer Habahir, 161. Another name for this Midrash of Rabbi Nechunya ben Hakanah is Sefer Habahir (Book of the Bright Light). It is one of the oldest books of the Cabala. See I. Weinstock, B'maglei Haniglah V'hanistar, pp. 15-20, on the origin of the names. (276) See my Hebrew commentary, pp. 361-2, for further elucidation on this mystic matter. (277) Numbers 33:10-11. (278) *Ibid.*, Verses 12-13. See Ramban further at beginning of *Seder Yithro* (Note 25) for how this explanation affects a major problem in Torah exegesis as to when Jethro came, i.e., before or after the Giving of the Torah. (279) *Ibid.*, Verse 14. (280) Shemoth Rabbah 25:5. (281) Verse 2.

THE WILDERNESS OF SIN WHICH IS BETWEEN ELIM AND SINAI. The reason for this [geographic description] is to distinguish between this wilderness of Sin and the other wilderness, Tzin, written with the letter *tzade,* where the Israelites came in the fortieth year [of their stay in the wilderness] *and Miriam died there.*[282] This is why Scripture mentions there, *And they pitched in the wilderness of Tzin — the same is Kadesh,*[283] in order to differentiate it [from the wilderness of Sin mentioned here].

2. AND THE WHOLE CONGREGATION OF THE CHILDREN OF ISRAEL MURMURED AGAINST MOSES. Scripture should have first narrated the nature of the complaint just as it did in Marah[284] and Rephidim,[285] and at all other complaints — and stated here first: "and there was no flesh to eat, nor bread for them to the full, and the people were famished for bread." Now Rashi explained that the reason Scripture specifically mentions [that the date of their arrival in the wilderness of Sin] was *on the fifteenth day of the second month*[286] is in order "to make this encampment unique. On that day, there came to an end the provision which the Israelites took along with them from Egypt, and they now needed the manna. It thus informs you that they ate sixty-one meals[287] of the remains of the dough [which they had baked in Egypt on the day of the exodus]."[288] [Thus far the language of Rashi.] This is a tradition received by our Rabbis,[289]

---

(282) Numbers 20:1.   (283) *Ibid.*, 33:36.   (284) Above 15:23-24, *And when they came to Marah, they could not drink of the waters of Marah, for they were bitter.... And the people murmured against Moses.*   (285) Further, 17:1-2. *And they encamped in Rephidim, and there was no water for the people to drink. And the people strove with Moses.*   (286) Verse 1. (287) The manna first came down on the sixteenth day of Iyar, the second month (see Verse 4), thirty-one days after the exodus. Since two meals are ordinarily eaten daily (see Verse 8), this period required sixty-two meals. The first meal, however, was taken in Egypt on the night of the fifteenth day of Nisan, thus leaving sixty-one meals, which were furnished by the provisions they brought out of Egypt.   (288) Above 12:39.   (289) Mechilta on Verse 1 here.

and the reason that Scripture did not [first] explain the nature of their complaint was that it had not elaborated on this miracle which was done for them secretively, [i.e., that the remains of the dough furnished sixty-one meals]. And it is as I have already written in *Seder Vayigash* concerning the reason [that Scripture is disposed to be silent on hidden miracles].[290]

Rabbi Abraham ibn Ezra wrote that Scripture records the date *on the fifteenth day of the second month* in order to explain that a month's time had already elapsed since their departure from Egypt. In the meantime, they consumed the bread they took out of Egypt as well as their cattle, since they were a great multitude of people. This was the reason for the murmuring.

In my opinion, the reason for their complaint is to be found in the Scriptural expression, *and they came... unto the wilderness of Sin.*[286] When they came to that wilderness far away from Egypt, they began saying: "What shall we eat? What will this great wilderness into which we have come supply us with?" It may be that at first they had thought that after a few days they would come to the cities round about them. Now that a month had gone by and *they found no city of habitation,*[291] they said, "We will all die in the great wilderness into which we have come." This then is the meaning of the verse, *And the whole congregation of the children of Israel murmured against Moses and against Aaron in the wilderness,* the murmuring being because of the wilderness. And so likewise the people said, *for ye have brought us forth into this wilderness, to put to death this whole assembly by famine.*[292] Thus they mentioned "the wilderness' and "the assembly," therein stating that a large assembly such as this will undoubtedly die of hunger in this great wilderness. The Holy One, blessed be He, hearkened unto them, and He now began *to prepare a table* for them *in the wilderness*[293] until they came to a land inhabited.[294]

(290) See Vol. I, pp. 556-558. (291) Psalms 107:4. (292) Verse 3. (293) Psalms 78:19. (294) Further, Verse 35.

4. BEHOLD, I WILL 'MAMTIR' (CAUSE TO RAIN) BREAD FROM HEAVEN FOR YOU. Rabbi Abraham ibn Ezra wrote that because the manna came down like rain from heaven, He said *mamtir,* [which is derived from the root *matar* (rain)]. But we find: *'yamteir' (He will cause to rain) coals, fire and brimstone;*[295] *And the Eternal 'himtir' (caused to rain) upon Sodom and upon Gomorrah brimstone and fire.*[296] [Brimstone and fire do not come down like rain, and yet Scripture uses the word *matar* with reference to them!] Perhaps in these cases they accompanied the rain of which the term "coming down" may properly be used. Onkelos' opinion is that *mamtir* just means "cause to bring down," for he translated: "behold, I will cause to bring down." [However, it has no connection here with rain, as Ibn Ezra would have it.]

It is possible that the word *mamtir* can be associated with the expression *'kamatarah' (as a mark) for the arrow,*[297] although they are of different roots.[298] Scripture makes use of both terms when speaking of every form of "falling from above." Thus it is called *matarah* (target) because they come down like arrows [on a target], and it says, *'vayamteir' (And He caused to rain) upon them flesh as the dust, and winged fowl as the sand of the seas.*[299] It may be that [Scripture does not use the term *mamtir* for every form of "falling from above," but only] for the fowl of heaven. [Therefore, the term, *vayamteir* in the above – mentioned verse refers only to the winged fowl] because they came down upon them as the rain.

BREAD. Because they made bread out of the manna — as it is written, *and they made cakes of it*[300] — [Scripture calls it *lechem* (bread)], for every form of bread is called *lechem,* not just those of wheat and barley. It says *cause to rain bread* [although it did

---

(295) Psalms 11:6. (296) Genesis 19:24. (297) Lamentations 3:12. (298) For the word *matarah* (target) is of the root *natar* (keep), since a target is kept in sight and watched. *Mamtir* however is of the root *matar* (rain). Yet, as Ramban concludes, they have a common association, as is explained in the text. (299) Psalms 78:27. (300) Numbers 11:8.

EXODUS XVI, BESHALACH

not come down in the form of bread, for the meaning thereof is] that He is causing it to come down for them to make it into bread. Similarly: *As for the earth, out of it cometh bread*,[301] [meaning: "out of it cometh the wheat from which bread is made"]. So also: *To bring forth bread out of the earth*,[302] which means that He brings forth the wheat from which people make bread. And some scholars[303] interpret: *Behold, I will cause to rain bread*, meaning food. Similarly: *'lechem' of the offering;*[304] *For he offereth the 'lechem' of thy G-d;*[305] *When thou sittest 'lilchom' with a ruler*[306] — all are expressions of food.[307] The correct interpretation is that *lilchom*[306] means "to eat bread," and *'lechem' of thy G-d*[305] is a euphemism, meaning that it is "the food" for G-d even as bread is for man, for we find it said, *Man doth not live by bread only.*[308]

THAT I MAY TRY THEM, WHETHER THEY WILL WALK IN MY LAW OR NOT. "I.e., whether they will observe the commandments associated with it, such as [the laws] that they should not leave [a remainder] of it until the morning[309] and that they should not go out on the Sabbath to collect it."[310] Thus the language of Rashi.

But this is not correct.[311] Rather, the intent [of the trial mentioned here] is as He said, *Who fed thee in the wilderness with manna, which thy fathers knew not; that He might afflict thee, and that He might try thee, to do thee good at thy latter end.*[312] [The manna itself] was a trial to them, since they had no food in

---

(301) Job 28:5. (302) Psalms 104:14. (303) Ibn Ezra, and R'dak in his Sefer Hashorashim, under the root *lechem*. (304) Leviticus 3:16. (305) *Ibid.*, 21:8. (306) Proverbs 23:1. (307) Thus is the opinion of Ibn Ezra and R'dak (see Note 303). But, continues Ramban, the correct interpretation is, etc. (308) Deuteronomy 8:3. (309) Further, Verse 19. (310) Verse 26. (311) Ramban's objection seems to be that the word *l'ma'an* ("that" or "for the sake of") — *'that' I may try them* — expresses causation in itself, namely, that the manna as such will be their trial, as will be explained, and not the precepts associated with it, as Rashi explained. (312) Deuteronomy 8:16.

the wilderness and were without recourse to any sustenance except the manna, which they knew not from before and had never heard of from their fathers. Each day's quantity came down on its day, and they were eagerly desirous for it. Yet with all this, they hearkened to walk after G-d to a place of no food. And so indeed He said to them again, *And thou shalt remember all the way in which the Eternal thy G-d hath led thee these forty years in the wilderness, that He might afflict thee, to try thee, to know what was in thy heart, whether thou wouldest keep His commandments, or no.* [313] He could have led them by way of *the cities that were round about them.*[314] Instead, He led them *through the wilderness wherein were serpents, fiery serpents, and scorpions,*[315] and each day's quantity of food would come to them only from heaven in order to try them and to do them good at the end so that they would believe in Him forever. I have already explained the matter of "trial" in the commentary on the verse, *And G-d tried Abraham.*[316]

The Rabbi [Moshe ben Maimon] has written in the Moreh Nebuchim[317] [on the verse before us, *That I may try them, whether they will walk in My law or not,* that it means] that "everyone capable of knowledge should know and determine whether there is usefulness in the service of G-d, and whether there is adequate satisfaction in it or not." But if so, it would have been proper for Him to say, "that *He* may try them to know!"

Now Scripture mentions here only the matter of manna, which was "the bread" which He caused to rain upon them, [and it does not refer to the flesh which He gave them]. However, from that which Moses told them, *This shall be, when the Eternal shall give you in the evening flesh to eat, and in the morning bread to the*

---

(313) *Ibid.*, Verse 2.   (314) Genesis 35:5.   (315) Deuteronomy 8:15. (316) Genesis 22:1 (Vol. I, p. 275).   (317) III, 24. Ramban is following Al Charizi's translation of the Moreh Nebuchim. In Ibn Tibbon's translation, (as rendered by Friedlander, III, p. 114): *"That I may prove them whether they will walk in My law or not;* i.e., let every one who desires try and see whether it is useful and sufficient to devote himself to the service of G-d."

EXODUS XVI, BESHALACH

full,[318] we know that everything was told to him. It is only that when a subject is mentioned twice, Scripture shortens it in the report of the command or the narrative, as I have mentioned to you many times.[319] At times, it omits one — [the command or the narrative] — altogether, such a case being the verse written in this section: *This is the thing which the Eternal hath commanded: Let an omerful of it* [the manna] *be kept throughout your generations,*[320] and the command [of G-d to Moses] is not recorded at all. This is also the case in many places. But in the opinion of those scholars[321] who say that *lechem* here means "all food," it is possible that by saying, *Behold, I will cause to rain 'lechem,'* the meaning refers to both the manna and to the quail, i.e., that He would fulfill their request for bread and flesh. Moses explained that the flesh would be [available] to eat in the evening, and the bread would be [available] in the morning to the full, as is the customary way.

6. AT EVEN, THEN YE SHALL KNOW THAT THE ETERNAL HATH BROUGHT YOU OUT FROM THE LAND OF EGYPT. "And it is not we. [i.e., Moses and Aaron] who have taken you out from there, as you have said, *for ye have brought us forth.*"[322] 7. AND IN THE MORNING, THEN YE SHALL SEE THE GLORY OF THE ETERNAL. This does not refer to G-d's Glory that appeared in the cloud, [mentioned further in Verse 10], for that occurred [later] in the day when Aaron spoke to them, *and they looked toward the wilderness and, behold, the Glory of the Eternal appeared in the cloud.*[323] "But," commented Rashi, "thus did Moses say to them: *At even, then ye shall know* that His hand has the power to give you your desire, and He will give you flesh. He will not, however, give it to you with 'a bright countenance,' since you were improper in asking for it, [inasmuch as one can

---

(318) Further, Verse 8. (319) See above, 10:2 and 11:1. (320) Further, Verse 32. (321) See above, Note 303. (322) Above, Verse 3. (323) Further, Verse 10.

exist without meat]. Besides, you asked for it out of a full stomach, [i.e., while still having cattle which you took along with you from Egypt]. But as regards the bread for which you properly asked out of necessity, when it falls in the morning, you will see the Glory of His countenance, as He will bring it down for you in a manner indicative of love, i.e., in the morning, while there is yet time to prepare it."[324]

But it is not correct to interpret the expression, *and in the morning, then ye shall see the Glory of the Eternal* as applying to the gift of the manna because He gave it to them early in the morning. What *Glory of the Eternal* is made manifest in this? Moreover, how does it logically connect with the phrase following it, *for that He hath heard your murmurings?* And this Midrash of our Rabbis, [which Rashi mentions, i.e., that there was a difference in the ways the manna and the quail were given to them], is not like a comment upon the expression, *then ye shall see the Glory of the Eternal.* Instead, the Rabbis said it [as an explanation of the fact] that He apportioned their sustenance twice a day and did not distribute all of it in the morning. Thus the Rabbis said in the Mechilta:[325] *"And Moses said: 'This shall be, when the Eternal shall give you in the evening flesh to eat, and in the morning bread to the full.'* From here, you learn that He gave them the quail with 'a dark countenance.' The manna, however, which they were justified in requesting, He gave them with 'a bright countenance.' "That is to say, in the morning.

Rabbi Abraham ibn Ezra wrote that the expression, *and in the morning*, etc., [beginning in Verse 7], is a continuation of the

---

(324) In the printed Rashi text, it concludes: "and there shall be dew above it and dew below it as though it were packed in a chest." The quail, on the other hand, came down *at even* (Verse 13) when there was not much time to prepare it. It was thus given, as the Mechilta — quoted by Ramban — said further on, *b'panim chasheichoth* (with a 'dark countenance'), or as Rashi puts it, *lo b'panim me'iroth* (not with a 'bright countenance').
(325) Mechilta on Verse 8.

previous verse. [It constitutes Moses' answer to] what the Israelites had said, *for ye have brought us forth* [326] from Egypt. Moses replied: "G-d will now show two signs for you so that you may know that it was He Who brought you out from there. One, [the quail] will come in the evening of this day, and the other, [the manna] will come tomorrow in the morning." And, [continued Ibn Ezra], it would have been proper for Scripture to say: "At even, and in the morning, then ye shall know that the Eternal hath brought you out from the land of Egypt." The expression *in the morning* is not connected with *then ye shall see the Glory of the Eternal,* since they saw the Glory [later] on that day [and not in the following morning].[327] But this interpretation too does not appear to be correct.[328]

The correct interpretation appears to me to be that the wonder inherent in the manna was extremely great, whereas He brought the quail in from the sea by a wind which came from Him.[329] The manna, however, was created for them now; [it was] a new creation in heaven, similar to the process of [the original] Creation. This is the intent of what the Rabbis have said with respect to the manna, i.e., that it was created on the sixth day of creation between sundown and nightfall.[330] This is why Scripture said: "By the sign He will perform for you on the coming night,

---

(326) Verse 3. (327) To grasp the boldness of Ibn Ezra's explanation, one must note the following sequence of language in the two verses: (6) *And Moses and Aaron said... At even, then ye shall know that the Eternal hath brought you out from the land of Egypt.* (7) *And in the morning, then ye shall see the Glory of the Eternal.* According to Ibn Ezra's interpretation, the expression of Verse 7, *and in the morning,* is to be understood together with *at even* (of Verse 6), thus: "at even and in the morning, then ye shall know that the Eternal hath brought you out from the land of Egypt." The phrase, *and in the morning,* cannot be connected with *then ye shall see the Glory of the Eternal,* for as narrated in Verses 9-10, the Glory of the Eternal appeared that very same day, and not in the following morning. Ramban will further refute this explanation of Ibn Ezra on the basis of the fact that after all, the verses are not written in the way Ibn Ezra would transpose them. His own exposition will then follow. (328) See end of above Note. (329) Numbers 11:31. (330) Aboth 5:6.

you will know that He brought you out from the land of Egypt, since He prepared *a table in the wilderness* for you.[331] But by the great wonder He will do for you in the morning, you will see the Glory of His kingdom, *for what god is there in heaven or on earth that can do according to* His *works and according to* His *mighty acts?*"[332] By the great and marvellous things that G-d does, He shows His Glory, similar to that which is written, *I will gather all nations, and all tongues, and they shall come, and shall see My Glory.*[333] It is further written [there], *and they shall declare My Glory,*[334] and there are many other verses similar to this effect. So also is the opinion of Onkelos who rendered [the verse here]: "and you will *see* the Glory of G-d." He did not translate it, "and [the Glory of G-d] will be made manifest." [335]

Know that the subject of the manna involves a great matter. [336] Our rabbis have alluded to it in Tractate Yoma:[337] " *Man did eat bread of 'abirim' (the mighty),*[338] i.e., bread which the ministering angels eat! These are the words of Rabbi Akiba. Rabbi Yishmael said to him, 'You have made a mistake. Do the ministering angels indeed eat bread? Has it not been said [by Moses], *I did neither eat bread nor drink water?*[339] Rather, *the bread of 'abirim'* means bread which was absorbed in the *eivarim* (limbs).' " [340]

The purport of Rabbi Akiba's words is that the existence of the ministering angels is sustained by the Divine Glory. And so the Rabbis interpreted:[341] *"And Thou 'm'chayeh' (preservest) them*

---

(331) See Psalms 78:19. (332) Deuteronomy 3:24. (333) Isaiah 66:18. (334) *Ibid.*, Verse 19. (335) Had Onkelos translated "and the Glory of G-d will be made manifest," it would have comprised Onkelos' effort to remove any implication of G-d's corporeality. But now that he translated, "and you will *see* the Glory of G-d," his reference is to the great and wonderful deed G-d will do for them through the manna. (336) "Matter." In the Ricanti quoting Ramban: "secret." (337) Yoma 75 b. (338) Psalms 78:25. A reference to the manna which the Israelites ate in the wilderness. The question arises about the meaning of the word *abirim*. (339) Deuteronomy 9:9. (340) See Vol. I, p. 76, on the fruits of the Garden of Eden. (341) Shemoth Rabbah 32:4.

EXODUS XVI, BESHALACH

all [342] [means] He gives food (*'michyah'*) to you all." It is with reference to this that it is said, *And the light is sweet,* [343] since through the Light, they perceive good discernment. Now the manna was a product of that Higher Light which became tangible by the will of its Creator, blessed be He, and thus [according to Rabbi Akiba], both the people who ate the manna and the ministering angels were sustained by the same substance. But Rabbi Yishmael criticized him, since the existence of the ministering angels is not dependent upon something tangible evolving from the Light. Their existence is by means of the Higher Light itself.

It was for this reason, [i.e., the heavenly origin of the manna], that the Israelites found in the manna every flavor they desired. The rational power of the soul causes it to cleave to the higher worlds, thus finding restful life and obtaining His favor. [344]

And thus the Rabbis have said in the Mechilta: [345] "Today, [i.e., in this world], you will not find it, but you will find it in the World to Come." This text [of the Mechilta] can support two explanations. We may say that among those [inheriting eternal life] in the World to Come, [346] there will be some who have not achieved that high status of sustaining themselves steadily by the Divine Glory. Their existence will be made possible by something tangible evolving from that Glory, like the status of the generation of the wilderness who attained [the beholding of] the Divine

---

(342) Nehemiah 9:6.   (343) Ecclesiastes 11:7.   (344) See Proverbs 8:35. (345) Mechilta on Verse 25: *Today ye shall not find it in the field.* This teaching is that of Rabbi Eleazar Chisma. Ramban will later refer to it by name.   (346) Ramban clearly uses the concept of *olam haba* (the World to Come) as referring to the life after the resurrection. It is the life to be in the far hereafter, as distinguished from the *olam haneshamoth* (the World of the Souls), which is the life in the hereafter immediately following the demise of the body. In *olam haba*, body and soul will be reunited, and the manner of how the body will sustain itself is here alluded to by Ramban. See also Note 12 in *Seder Va'eira*. An exhaustive discussion of this whole subject is found in Ramban's Torath Ha'adam, (Kithvei Haramban, Vol. 2, pp. 283-311).

Glory at the Red Sea, just as the Rabbis have said:[347] "A maidservant saw at the sea what the prophet Ezekiel[348] never saw." From that time onward, their souls were elevated to be able to exist by the product [of the Divine Glory], which was the manna.

A more correct interpretation is that in the word *today* — [Verse 25: *'Today' ye shall not find it in the field*] — Scripture is alluding according to the words of Rabbi Eleazar Chisma,[349] that those [inheriting eternal life in] the World to Come[346] will exist by the substance of the manna which is the Higher Glory, just as the Rabbis have said:[350] "[In the World to Come] there will be neither eating nor drinking. Rather, the righteous [of the World to Come] will sit with their crowns on their heads and enjoy the Divine Glory." [This means] that those [inheriting] the World to Come will exist by their enjoyment of the Divine Glory, which will cleave to the crowns upon their heads. "The crown" is the attribute so named by Scripture when it says, *In that day shall the Eternal of hosts be for a crown of Glory.*[351] And it is with reference to it that it is said, *Even upon the crown wherewith his mother hath crowned him.*[352] Thus [the verses] allude to the manner in which the righteous inheriting the World to Come will be sustained, the hint being to the substance of the manna.

Now Scripture says, *And He commanded the skies above, and opened the doors of heaven; and He caused manna to rain upon them for food, and gave them of the corn of heaven. Man did eat the bread of the mighty,*[353] and it further says, *And He gave them in plenty the bread of heaven.*[354] From this, it appears that this "corn" is in heaven, and He caused it to come down for them by opening its doors. The intent thereof is, as I have explained, that

---

(347) Mechilta 15:2. (348) Reference is to Ezekiel, Chapter 1. In our Mechilta it states, "Isaiah and Ezekiel." See Isaiah 6:1-6. Rashi (above. 15:2) just has: "prophets." (349) See above, Note 345. (350) Berachoth 17 a. (351) Isaiah 28:5. (352) Song of Songs 3:11. (353) Psalms 78:23-25. (354) *Ibid.*, 105:40.

the [Higher] Light was made tangible [and assumed the form of the manna], for it is of the Higher Light that Scripture speaks in this language, [such as]: *the heavens were opened, and I saw visions of G-d.*[355] It may be that the manna was already existing in the heavens [in the form in which it came down], just as the Rabbis have said [330] that it was created on the sixth day of creation between sundown and nightfall.

7. AND WHAT ARE WE, THAT YE MURMUR AGAINST US. Rabbi Abraham ibn Ezra explained it as meaning: "And what power to act is there in our hands? We have only carried out what we have been commanded." But this is not so. Rather, the sense of the verse here is similar to: *What is man, that Thou art mindful of him?*[356] *Eternal, what is man that Thou takest knowledge of him?*[357] *For how little is he* [man] *to be accounted!*[358] And this [verse here] is an expression of humility. "For what are we that you should attribute us with bringing you out from the land of Egypt? Behold we are nothing, and our work is vanity.[359] And *your murmurings are not against us, but against the Eternal.*[360] It is He Who has brought you out from the land of Egypt, not we." And in the Mechilta we find.[361] "[They said to them]: 'Are we so distinguished that you arise and murmur against us?' "[362]

8. AND MOSES SAID: THIS SHALL BE, WHEN THE ETERNAL SHALL GIVE YOU IN THE EVENING FLESH. Moses is explaining his first statement, [recorded above in Verses 6-7]: *When the Eternal shall give you in the evening flesh to eat, then ye shall know that the Eternal hath brought you out from the land of Egypt;*[363] and when *He shall give you in the morning bread to the full, then ye shall see the Glory of the Eternal.*[364]

---

(355) Ezekiel 1:1. (356) Psalms 8:5. (357) *Ibid.*, 144:3. (358) Isaiah 2:22. (359) See *ibid.*, 41:24. (360) Verse 8. (361) Mechilta on the verse here. (362) This bears out Ramban's interpretation that the expression, *and what are we?* is one of humility, as explained. (363) Above, Verse 6. (364) Verse 7.

12. I HAVE HEARD THE MURMURINGS OF THE CHILDREN OF ISRAEL. SPEAK UNTO THEM, SAYING: AT DUSK YE SHALL EAT FLESH. This communication [*at dusk ye shall eat,* etc.], had already been conveyed by Moses to Israel,[365] but it is repeated here only because of that which He said *I have heard the murmurings of the children of Israel.* At first, He had said, *Behold, I will cause to rain bread from heaven to you;*[366] He would willingly do it for them as an act of kindness or because of their merits. But now He said that [their murmuring] is accounted to them as sin, and yet because of the very nature of the murmuring, He will do such things for them so that they might know thereby *that I am the Eternal your G-d.* Until now *ye do not believe the Eternal your G-d;*[367] this is why you murmur against His prophets.

It is possible that at first He did not promise them the manna for all the time that they would be in the wilderness. Thus they thought that perhaps it would be for one day or two, as long as they stayed in that place, and that when they would leave it, they would come to a place of food. But now He said to them, "*At dusk ye shall eat flesh* always, *and in* every *morning ye shall be filled with bread* as long as you will be in the wilderness." And so also is the opinion of our Rabbis,[368] that the quail were with them from that day on, just like the manna. It is logically so, for they expressed discontent about the two things — [flesh and bread][369] — and He hearkened to their murmurings on both matters, *and He gave them that which they craved.*[370] What would He give them, and what more,[371] if He supplied them with meat for only one day or two?

The reason that the chapter [of the Torah] speaks at length about the matter of the manna is that everything about it was of a

---

(365) Above, Verse 8. (366) *Ibid.,* Verse 4. (367) Deuteronomy 1:32. (368) Arakhin 15 b, Tosafoth. See my Hebrew commentary, p. 366. (369) Above, Verse 3: ... *when we sat by the flesh-pots, when we did eat bread to the full.* (370) Psalms 78:29. (371) See *ibid.,* 120:3.

EXODUS XVI, BESHALACH

wondrous nature, whereas with reference to the matter of the quail, it just writes briefly, *And it came to pass at even, that the quail came up,* [372] because it came in a natural way. [373] [Although the quail were a daily occurrence], the subject of the second [incident of] quail at Kibroth-hata'avah [374] [is singled out for mention in Scripture] because right now [in the wilderness of Sin], they did not receive of them to the full, just as He always says here, *flesh to eat, and bread to the full.* [375]

It is possible that only the adults gathered the quail — or it may be that they were marked by chance for the pious ones — while the young craved and hungered for them, since Scripture does not relate concerning the quail, "and they gathered some more, some less," as it does concerning the manna. [376] It is for this reason that Scripture says there [in the narrative of the second quail]: *And the mixed multitude that was among them fell a lusting,* [377] and it further says, *and the children of Israel also wept on their part,* [377] meaning that some of the children of Israel were also weeping for it, but not all. He then gave them in great quantity, as it says, *He that gathered least gathered ten heaps,* [378] and out of that abundance, they ate for a month's time [379] and then the quail reverted to their first state.

In line with the plain meaning of Scripture, the whole affair with the quail happened only at intervals, but since the manna was their staple food, they always had it, for their chief murmuring concerned it, as it is written, *for ye have brought us forth into this wilderness, to put to death this whole assembly by famine.* [380]

14. 'DAK' (A FINE) 'MECHUSPAS' (PEELED THING). In the opinion of Onkelos, [who translated the word *mechuspas* as

---

(372) Verse 13. (373) See Ramban above, Verse 6, beginning with: "The correct interpretation." (374) Numbers 11:31-34. (375) Verse 8. And also in Verse 12 here: *At dusk ye shall eat flesh, and in the morning ye shall be filled with bread.* This clearly indicates that bread they had to the full, but not flesh. (376) Further, Verse 17. (377) Numbers 11:4. (378) *Ibid.*, Verse 32. (379) *Ibid.*, Verse 20. (380) Above, Verse 3.

meaning "peeled," the word] is associated with the expressions: *'machsoph'* (streaks making bare) the white,[381] *'chasaph hashem'* (the Eternal hath made bare) His holy arm.[382] The letter *sin* [in the words *machsoph* and *chasaph*] is interchanged for the letter *samach* [in the word *mechuspas*], and the second root-letter of the verb [*chasaph*][383] is doubled, [thus making it *mechuspas*].

'DAK' (FINE) 'KAK'PHOR' (AS THE HOAR-FROST). *K'phor* is the covering [of minute ice-particles] upon the ground in cold weather. It is similar in usage to the expression, *He scattered 'k'phor' (hoar-frost) like ashes*.[384] Now Onkelos rendered [the Hebrew *dak kak'phor al ha'aretz*] into Aramaic thus: *da'adak k'gir kig'lida al ar'a*. On this, Rashi wrote [as an interpretation of Onkelos, that the word *gir* occurs in the expression], *"as stones of 'gir,'*[385] which is a kind of black color. This is just as we say in connection with the covering of the blood [of a slaughtered wild animal or fowl, which the Torah specified must be done with earth.[386] The Rabbis enumerate amongst the kinds of earth that can be used]:[387] *'gir* (powdered chalk) and arsenic (or orpiment).' [Onkelos' Aramaic rendition *da'adak k'gir kig'lida al ar'a* thus means:] 'thin [and brittle] like powdered chalk, and lying congealed as frost on the ground.' And this is the meaning of the Hebrew *dak kak'phor:* spread out fine and connected like hoar-frost. *Dak* means that there was a thin incrustation on top.

---

(381) Genesis 30:37. (382) Isaiah 52:10. (383) "The second root-letter of the verb." Literally: "the *ayin* of the verb." Following the theory of Dunash ben Labrat, the great Hebrew grammarian of the tenth century, we call the three letters of the root of any verb by the names of the three letters of the Hebrew *'po'al'* (verb) [which is spelled *pei, ayin* and *lamed*]. Thus the first letter of any verb is called the *pei* of the verb, the second is called the *ayin*, the third is called the *lamed*. In the verb *chasaph* before us, the second root-letter is the *sin* or its interchange, the *samach*, as explained in the text. In the word *mechuspas*, the *samach* appears twice. This then is the meaning of Ramban's saying, "and the *ayin* (second letter) of the verb is doubled." (384) Psalms 147:16. (385) Isaiah 27:9. Translated: "chalkstones." (386) Leviticus 17:13. (387) Chullin 88 b. See further my Hebrew commentary, p. 367, Note 7.

EXODUS XVI, BESHALACH

And that which Onkelos translated, *k'gir* (as powdered chalk), is an addition to the Hebrew text, there being no word corresponding to it in the verse." [These are the words of Rashi.]

But all this is not correct. *Gir* [is not a kind of black color, as Rashi wrote, but instead it] is a white earth which sticks to stone, and when crushed, it is used as plaster upon walls. It is very white and is better for the plastering of walls than lime, [which does not have the admixture of that white earth]. And so it is written, *upon the 'gira' (plaster) of the wall of the king's palace*.[388] This is why the manna which was white and spread out upon the earth could be associated with that crushed white earth.

Onkelos then translated the Hebrew word *k'phor* in two ways. First, he derived it from the expression, *and thou shalt pitch it within and without 'bakopher' (with pitch)*.[389] Hence, he said *k'gir* (as the white earth) with which [the stones] are fastened and covered. Then he derived it also from the expression, *He scattered 'k'phor' like ashes*,[384] which is the covering of minute ice needles which form in a cold atmosphere, just as he translated [the Hebrew] *'v'kerach' (and the frost) by night*,[390] "*ug'lida* (and frost) came down upon me at night." [391] The word can be used in the plural [*g'lidin*],[392] while the singular is called *g'lid* (ice), just as we have been taught in the Mishnah in Mikvaoth:[393] "These are the things which only serve to fill up the immersion-pool [to its prescribed measure of forty *s'ah*] and do not render it invalid: snow, hail, hoar-frost, *v'hag'lid* (and ice)." And so indeed does Onkelos translate many Scriptural texts in two ways. But in

---

(388) Daniel 5:5. (389) Genesis 5:14. (390) *Ibid.*, 31:40. (391) Thus it is not necessary to say, as Rashi did, that the Aramaic word *k'gir* in Onkelos' translation has no corresponding word in the Hebrew text. According to Ramban, both Aramaic words, *k'gir* and *kig'lida* ("as powdered white earth" and "as frost"), are two renditions of the one Hebrew word *kak'phor*. Such was Onkelos' style, to give two translations of one Hebrew word. (392) Shabbath 152 a: *sacharuni g'lidin* (ices have sorrounded me), a metaphoric expression of a person describing that the hairs of his mustache and beard have turned gray (Rashi, *ibid.*) (393) Mikvaoth 7:1.

carefully-edited texts of Targum Onkelos, it is written, *da'adak d'gir* [394] *kig'lida al ar'a,* and the meaning thereof is that the manna was piled up in heaps as ice upon the earth. This is the truth, for if [the word *k'gir* in the Targum] were of the root *gir* (powdered white earth or plaster), as we assumed at first], the Aramaic translation should have been: *k'gira d'g'lida* (as the powdered flakes of the ice), [and not, as we have it, *k'gira 'kig'lida*], for such is the style of the Aramaic language.[395]

20. AND IT BRED WORMS, AND IT STANK. "This is a verse that is to be transposed, because [the manna that was left over until the morning] must have first stunk and afterwards become wormy, just as it is said, *and it did not stink, neither was there any worm therein,*[396] this being the way of all things that become wormy." Thus Rashi's language. Now if the manna had become wormy in a natural way, as is the way of all things that become wormy, Rashi's statement would be correct. But since the manna became wormy in a miraculous way, it is possible that it bred worms first, [397] and there is thus no need for inverting] the verse. Moreover, the verse which states [concerning the manna which they retained for Sabbath morning], *and it did not stink, neither*

---

(394) And not *k'gir*, as we have assumed the reading in Onkelos to be until now. The reading of *k'gir* had forced Ramban to interpret that Onkelos simultaneously used two different translations of the Hebrew word *kak'phor*, namely, "as powdered white earth" and "as frost," as explained above. This is clearly a difficult position. But with this present reading in Onkelos — *d'gir*, which means a heap — the Aramaic text leads to one unified thought: the manna was piled up in heaps as ice upon the earth. (395) In other words, since all readings in the Targum have *kig'lida* ("as" ice), and not *d'g'lida* ("of" the ice), it shows that the antecedent word is *d'gir* (a heap) and not *k'gir* (as powdered white earth). Thus the thought conveyed by the Targum is that the manna lay powdered in heaps as ice upon the ground. (396) Further, Verse 24. (397) For had it given off a stench first, they would have sensed it at night, and they would have disposed of it. This was why it became wormy first, and Dathan and Abiram, who left it until the morning, contrary to Moses' command, did not know it. In the morning it stank and it became known to all, and Moses was angry with them (Tur). The source of this reasoning is found in Shemoth Rabbah, mentioned further on in the text.

was there any worm therein,[396] proves that it was so, [i.e., that the manna left over by Dathan and Abiram bred worms first and then stank]. Had it not become wormy until it first stank, when Scripture says [concerning the manna left for the Sabbath], *and it did not stink,* it would thereby have already assured us that there was no worm therein. Why then should it repeat afterwards, *neither was there any worm therein?* If however, as the plain meaning of Scripture indicates, the manna that was left over until the morning by Dathan and Abiram became wormy first [in a supernatural way], it became necessary for Scripture to state that *this* manna [that was left over for the Sabbath] did not stink, nor did any worm come therein at all. Even things which become wormy in a natural way do not give off a stench unless they are warm and moist, but dry things only become wormy and do not give off an odor at all, just as wormy wood or fruits that become wormy when still growing or [immediately] afterwards. Thus Scripture relates that this manna [which Dathan and Abiram left over on a weekday, also stank [in the morning] by a miracle. And in Eileh Shemoth Rabbah we find that the Rabbis have said:[398] "Is there anything that first becomes wormy and then gives off a stench? It is only that the Holy One, blessed be He, wanting to expose the deeds [of Dathan and Abiram] to the people, therefore caused [the left-over manna] to give off no stench at night lest they throw it out. Instead, during the entire night, it formed rows upon rows of worms, *and* at once *Moses was wroth with them."*

23. BAKE THAT WHICH YE WILL BAKE. Rashi explained: "Whatever you wish to bake in the oven or boil in water, bake and boil today — all [that you require] for two days." If so, the purport of the verse is as follows: *"That which you would bake* of the two omers you have, *bake* today, *and that which you would boil* of the two omers, boil now, *and all that remaineth* for you after eating to the full today, *lay up for you to be kept until the*

(398) Shemoth Rabbah 25:14.

morning." In the morning [of the Sabbath-day], when the Israelites saw that it did not spoil, they came before Moses, since they did not want to eat the manna of yesterday even though Moses had permitted it to be kept until the morning. Then Moses permitted them to eat it on that Sabbath-day only "because it was for that purpose of which I said to keep it for a charge." He further informed them of the reason of the commandment, for *today ye shall not find it in the field*,[399] since G-d does it so because *it is a holy Sabbath unto the Eternal*.[400] It is possible that by saying *and all that remaineth over*, He did not set any measure for that. Rather, they could eat at will on the sixth day, as the remainder would suffice for the Sabbath, because *it is the blessing of the Eternal*.[401]

And Rabbi Abraham ibn Ezra explained: *"That which you would bake* ordinarily — namely, the [daily] omer known to you — *bake* for your use today; *and all that remaineth*, namely, the second omer, *lay up for you to be kept until the morning.* At that time, Moses did not tell them what to do with the second omer. It was on the following morning [the Sabbath], that he told them, *eat that today."*[399] But if so, they ate the manna on the Sabbath raw, without baking it or seething it in pots and making cakes of it as it was their custom to do.[402] The first interpretation, [that of Rashi], is more correct, and so is the opinion of Onkelos.[403]

17 1. AND ALL THE CONGREGATION OF THE CHILDREN OF ISRAEL JOURNEYED FROM THE WILDERNESS OF SIN,

---

(399) Verse 25. (400) Verse 23 before us. (401) Proverbs 10:22. (402) Numbers 11:8. (403) Onkelos translated: "That which you intend baking, etc." By adding the word *athidin* (intend), Onkelos intimated his understanding of the verse to be similar to that of Rashi: "that which you intend baking of the two omers, bake today, etc." This is unlike the explanation of Ibn Ezra, who interpreted the verse as meaning: "that which you would bake ordinarily — [i.e., one omer] — bake today, and the other omer leave over till the morning," thus resulting in their eating the omer on the Sabbath in an unprepared state.

BY THEIR STAGES, ACCORDING TO THE COMMANDMENT OF THE ETERNAL, AND THEY ENCAMPED IN REPHIDIM. Scripture is stating that they journeyed from the wilderness of Sin, where they were encamped after they had set out from Elim,[404] and covered various stages of their journey in accord with G-d's command. Afterwards, they encamped in Rephidim. Scripture thus relates briefly here that when they first journeyed from the wilderness of Sin, they pitched in Dophkah, and afterwards in Alush, and from Alush they came to Rephidim.[405] This is the meaning of the expression here, *by their stages,* since there were many stages by which they came from the wilderness of Sin to Rephidim, and they did not reach it on the first journey. Scripture, however, [omits all these various stages here] because its only concern is to explain their murmuring. At the beginning of their arrival in that wilderness [of Sin], they complained for bread, and now they quarreled [with Moses] over water, [as it is said], *and there was no water for the people to drink.* When they came to that place and did not find fountains of water, they at once quarreled with Moses. This is the meaning of the expression, *Wherefore the people did quarrel with Moses,*[406] for the murmurings mentioned in places where Scripture says, *and they murmured,*[407] mean complaints, i.e., that they were declaring their grievances about their condition, saying, "What shall we do? What shall we eat, and what shall we drink?" But *vayarev* (and he quarreled) means that they did actually make quarrel with Moses, coming to him and saying, "Give us water, you and Aaron your brother, for you are responsible, our blood is upon you." And Moses said to them, *"Why quarrel ye with me? Wherefore do ye try the Eternal?"*[406] This quarrel is to test G-d, that is whether He can give you water.[408] If you will hold your peace and let me alone and instead pray to Him, perhaps He will answer you." And indeed, it was their intent to try [G-d], as Scripture says, *And the*

---

(404) Above, 16:1. (405) Numbers 33:12-14. (406) Verse 2. (407) Such as above, 16:2. (408) See Psalms 78:30.

name of the place was called Massah (Trying) *and Meribah* (Quarrel), *because of the quarrel of the children of Israel and because they tried the Eternal, saying: Is the Eternal among us, or not?*[409] Then their anger against him relented,[410] and for a day or two, they were supplied by the waters in their vessels. But afterwards, *the people thirsted there for water, and the people murmured against Moses,*[411] something like the complaints they made whenever they wanted something, saying, *Wherefore hast thou brought us up out of Egypt?*[411] When Moses saw that they thirsted for water, he prayed to G-d and recounted before Him his distress when they first quarreled with him.[412]

Rabbi Abraham ibn Ezra said that there were two groups: one that quarreled [with Moses because they had no water to drink], and one [that had water which they brought from Alush, the place where they were encamped before coming to Rephidim,[413] but] who tested G-d [to see if He would give them water]. The correct interpretation is as I have explained.

3. TO PUT US AND OUR CHILDREN AND OUR CATTLE TO DEATH WITH THIRST. In their complaint, they mentioned the cattle too, thus telling Moses that they need a lot of water and it is therefore necessary to take counsel on the whole matter. This is why it says at the second time [when the incident at the waters of Meribah is recorded], *and water came forth abundantly, and the congregation drank, and their cattle.*[414] And our Rabbis have said:[415] "They made their cattle equal in importance to themselves. They said: 'A man's beast is as his life. If a man travels on the road and his beast is not with him, he suffers.'"

(409) Further, Verse 7. (410) See Judges 8:3. (411) Verse 3. (412) Verse 4. (413) Numbers 33:14. (414) *Ibid.*, 20:11. Now here it is not mentioned but it is self-understood that when the rock was turned into a pool of water, they drank and they watered their flocks (Ramban in Verse 5 further). In the instance of the waters of Meribah at Kadesh, it is mentioned on account of the mishap that resulted from the entire affair, as explained there; see also **Ramban** here in Verse 5 for another interpretation. (415) Mechilta on the verse here.

EXODUS XVII, BESHALACH

Now the reason they mentioned *us and our children* and did not say generally: "to put us to death with thirst" or "to put to death this whole assembly," [an expression] which would have included men, women and the little ones, as they said in other places, [416] is that by mentioning the children to him, they emphasized their murmuring against him so that he should make haste in the matter, since the young ones could not suffer thirst at all and they would thus die before the eyes of their parents. This is something like the expression, *The tongue of the sucking child cleaveth to the roof of his mouth for thirst.* [417]

5. AND THE ETERNAL SAID UNTO MOSES: PASS ON BEFORE THE PEOPLE. This is similar in usage to the following expressions: *he* [Joseph] *caused them to pass into cities;*[418] *and I will make thee to pass with thine enemies into a land which thou knowest not.* [419] Thus the meaning thereof here is: "go away from them to another place," [as will be explained further]. Perhaps this is similar to the expressions: *and he* [Ahimaaz] *overran the Cushite;*[420] *and he* [Jacob] *himself passed over before them,*[421] meaning that he [Jacob] went in the forefront of them.

The purport of this verse is that the people were in Rephidim, and the rock from which the waters were to come was in Horeb, [422] this being Mount Sinai, according to the opinion of the former ones,[423] or in my opinion, some city near the mountain, as I will yet explain. [424] Moses therefore had to go first before the people, to pass on from Rephidim to Horeb — a distance of one more *parsah* [a Persian mile] or more — from the camp before them. It was for this reason that G-d said to him, *Pass on before*

---

(416) Such as above, 16:3, *to put to death this whole assembly by famine.* (417) Lamentations 4:4. (418) Genesis 47:21. (419) Jeremiah 15:14. (420) II Samuel 18:23. (421) Genesis 33:3. (422) Verse 6: *Behold, I will stand before thee there upon the rock in Horeb.* (423) I.e., the Rabbis of the Talmud. See Shabbath 89 a: "Mount Sinai bears five names: the wilderness of Zin, Horeb, etc." (424) At the beginning of *Seder Yithro* (18:1).

the people, and take with thee of the elders of Israel... and go.
That is to say, "Go until you will see Me stand before you upon
the rock in Horeb." Now Moses hit the rock, and water came out
of it. Scripture however does not relate that the congregation and
their cattle drank, as it does in the second incident [at the waters
of Meribah],[425] for it is self-understood that they did so. It is
clear that the people did not go to Horeb to drink, since they did
not arrive in front of Mount Sinai until afterwards in the third
month.[426] Instead, they sent their young men and their cattle
there to draw water and bring it to them, as is customary in
camps.

It appears likely to me that the waters — *cold flowing waters*[427]
— came out from the rock in Horeb and flowed to Rephidim, and
there the people drank them. This is Scripture's intent in saying,
*He brought streams out of the rock, and caused waters to run
down like rivers,*[428] and it is further written, *He opened the rock,
and waters gushed out; they ran, a river in the dry places.*[429] The
verse stating, *Behold, He smote the rock, that waters gushed out,
and streams overflowed,*[430] also applies to the rock in Horeb, in
line with the plain meaning of Scripture.[431] The second rock in
Kadesh,[432] [instead of gushing forth water], became cleft with a
sort of spring welling forth waters, and therefore Scripture states,
That is 'the well' whereof the Eternal said unto Moses, etc.,[433]
and Israel said in the Song, *'The well,' which the princes
digged,*[434] for it was like a well that was dug. It is for this reason
that Scripture says there, *and the congregation drank, and their
cattle,*[435] which means that there they drank from it at that place
immediately, but here [in Horeb], overflowing rivers came from it

---

(425) Numbers 20:11. This took place in Kadesh. See also above, Note 414.
(426) Further, 19:1.   (427) Jeremiah 18:14.   (428) Psalms 78:16.
(429) *Ibid.*, 105:41.   (430) *Ibid.*, 78:20.   (431) According to the
Midrash, however, this verse (Psalms 78:20) was said with reference to Moses'
smiting the rock in Kadesh, or, as they are called, the waters of Meribah
(Bamidbar Rabbah 19:8).   (432) Numbers 20:1.   (433) *Ibid.*, 21:16.
(434) *Ibid.*, Verse 18.   (435) *Ibid.*, 20:11.

and they drank of it in their homes at their will. Now although according to the tradition of our Rabbis, it was all Miriam's Well,[436] it is possible that on the first occasion [in Horeb] and during all their forty years' wandering, the waters came gushing out from the rock like overflowing rivers. The second time, [in Kadesh], as a punishment for that which took place there, it became [only] like a dug well that was full of fresh water [not a gushing spring].

AND THY ROD, WHEREWITH THOU SMOTEST THE RIVER, TAKE IN THY HAND. This means "[the staff wherewith] you commanded Aaron [to strike the river]."[437] He mentioned the striking of the river, but He did not say, "and the rod which was turned to a serpent"[438] or "the rod wherewith you did the signs."[439] This was in order to call attention to the wonder in it, for at that time, the rod turned the waters into blood, thus removing from them their particular nature, and now the rod brought water into a flinty rock, [440] thus doing things of contrary effect.

6. BEHOLD, I WILL STAND BEFORE THEE THERE UPON THE ROCK IN HOREB. Since the wonder with the water in this place was now to become a permanent feature as long as they would be in the wilderness, as our Rabbis have said,[441] this was why the Divine Glory was revealed upon it at this place, just as it says concerning the manna, *And in the morning, then ye shall see the Glory of the Eternal,*[442] since it remained a continuous wonder.

---

(436) "That is to say, the rock which was in Rephidim (Horeb) is the same as the one in Kadesh, this being 'Miriam's Well,' which accompanied the Israelites on all their marches during the forty years' wandering" (Rabbeinu Bachya, Vol. II, p. 153 in my edition). The tradition is mentioned in Bamidbar Rabbah 20:2. This miracle was wrought for the merits of the prophetess Miriam. Ramban's intent is thus clear: If it was all Miriam's Well, how can you explain its different forms of activity, for in Horeb it was like a gushing stream, and in Kadesh it was like a well? (437) Above, 7:19. (438) *Ibid.,* Verse 15. (439) See above, 4:17. (440) See Psalms 114:8. (441) See above, Note 436. (442) Above, 16:7.

9. AND MOSES SAID TO JOSHUA. It would appear from here that from the day he came before him, Moses called him Joshua, and so it is also written: *And Joshua heard the noise of the people.*[443] Scripture which states in the case of the spies, *And Moses called Hoshea the son of Nun, Joshua,*[444] must then be referring to the beginning, [when Joshua first came to minister before him]. The verse informs us that this Hoshea the son of Nun, who was chosen to be among the spies, is the same one that Moses called Joshua. Our Rabbis commented[445] [that Moses gave him this name of Yehoshua, which is a compound of *Y-ah* (G-d) and *hoshea* (help), because] he in effect prayed for him, "May G-d help thee that thou mayest not follow the [evil] counsel of the spies." The intent of this comment is to state that because of this event of which Moses knew in advance, i.e., that Joshua was destined to go with the spies, he called him by that name [Yehoshua — Joshua] at the outset. We may also say that at that time [when the spies were chosen], Moses designated that name in front of the assembly, i.e., that his name henceforth be not Hoshea but Joshua.

The reason that Moses commanded Joshua to fight with Amalek was so that he [Moses] might pray with the raising of hands on the top of the hill.[446] He went up there so that he might see the Israelites engage in battle and train his sight on them to bring them blessing. They too, upon seeing him with his hands spread heavenward and saying many prayers, would have trust in him, and they would thus be endowed with additional valor and strength.

In Pirke d'Rabbi Eliezer,[447] we find additionally: "All Israel went outside of their tents, and they saw Moses kneeling on his knees, and they did likewise. He fell on his face to the earth and they did likewise. He spread his hands heavenward, and they also did so.

---

(443) Further, 32:17. (444) Numbers 13:16. (445) Sotah 34 b, and quoted by Rashi, *ibid.* (446) Verse 10. (447) In the middle of Chapter 44.

[From here, you learn the principle that] as the public reader of prayers [448] recites, so do all the people respond after him. [449] And thus the Holy One, blessed be He, caused Amalek and his people to fall by the hand of Joshua." But if so, [i.e., if Moses' hands were spread heavenward], the sense of the expression, *with the rod of G-d in my hand,* must be that when Moses went up to the top of the hill and saw Amalek, he stretched forth his hand with the rod to bring down [upon the Amalekites] strokes of pestilence, *the sword and destruction,* [450] just as it is said in the case of Joshua: *Stretch out the javelin that is in thy hand toward Ai, for I will give it into thy hand.* [451] From the moment Moses began to pray and his hands were spread heavenward, he held nothing in his hand.

Moses our teacher did all this because Amalek was an enduring nation [452] and very powerful. The Israelites, on the other hand, were not accustomed to battle and had never seen it, just as Scripture says, *lest peradventure the people repent when they see war.* [453] In addition they were *faint and weary,* as it is written in the Book of Deuteronomy. [454] Therefore, he [Moses] feared them, and it became necessary for all this prayer and supplication.

It is possible that Moses feared lest Amalek be victorious with the sword, for he was the nation that inherited the sword by virtue of the blessing of the patriarch [Isaac], who said [to Esau, Amalek's ancestor], *and on thy sword you shall live.* [455] The first and final wars against Israel stem from this family, as Amalek is of the descendants of Esau. [456] It is from him who stood at the head of the nations [in power] [457] that the [first] war came against us.

---

(448) Literally: "the deputy of the congregation." (449) See Berachoth 49 b: "After the fashion of his benediction, so do the others answer him." See my Hebrew commentary, p. 371, for further elucidation of this point. (450) See Esther 9:5. (451) Joshua 8:18. (452) See Jeremiah 5:15. (453) Above, 13:17. (454) Deuteronomy 25:18. (455) Genesis 27:40. (456) *Ibid.,* 36:12. (457) Numbers 24:20. *Amalek was the first of the nations.* See Ramban, *ibid.,* where he interprets it to mean: "Amalek is the 'mightiest' of the nations. This was why he dared to come to fight Israel," it is clear that Ramban's intent here is similar.

From Esau's descendants, [namely, Rome], [458] the [present] exile and the last[459] destruction of the Sanctuary came upon us, just as our Rabbis have said[460] that today we are in the exile of Edom. When he will be vanquished, and he together with the many nations that are with him will be discomfited, we shall be saved out of it [i.e., the exile] forever, just as [the prophet] said, *And saviors shall come up on Mount Zion, to judge the mount of Esau; and the kingdom shall be the Eternal's.*[461] Now whatever Moses and Joshua did with them [the Amalekites] at first, Elijah and Mashiach ben Yoseph[462] will do with their descendants. This was why Moses strained himself in this matter.

11. AND WHEN HE LET DOWN HIS HAND, AMALEK PREVAILED. By way of the plain meaning of Scripture, when Moses was compelled to lower his hands because of weariness, he saw that Amalek prevailed. He then commanded Aaron and Hur to support them, and thus he would not lower them again. Our Rabbis have said in the Midrash:[463] "Did Moses cause Amalek to prevail over Israel? It was merely because a person is forbidden to tarry three hours with his hands spread heavenward."[464]

---

(458) See Vol. I, pp. 445, 568-569. (459) Ramban pointedly uses the word "last" and not "the second" in order to indicate that the Third Sanctuary, for the restitution of which we pray, will never suffer destruction. The second destruction by the hands of the Romans was thus the "last" destruction. (460) Gittin 57 b. See also above, Note 458. (461) Obadiah 1:21. (462) Succah 52 b. See Ramban's Sefer Hag'ulah (Kithvei Haramban, Vol. I, pp. 255-295) for further elucidation of his views of the process by which the final redemption will come to pass. For the purpose of illuminating his language here, suffice it to say that Mashiach ben Yoseph — or as Ramban calls him there, "Mashiach ben Ephraim," since Ephraim was a son of Joseph — will first accomplish the ingathering of the exiles and fight their wars. Then Mashiach ben David will come. (463) Sefer Habahir, 138. (464) See my Hebrew commentary for a quote from the Cabalistic work of the Tziyoni for an explanation of this doctrine. In his commentary on the Sefer Habahir (p. 61, Note 4), Reuben Margoliot quotes from the Commentary of the Vilna Gaon on Proverbs (25:17) that "one must not pray [any given Service] more than three hours."

EXODUS XVII, BESHALACH

12. AND HIS HANDS WERE 'EMUNAH'. This means that they remained steadily uplifted. The usage of the word is similar to the expressions: *'va'amanah' (And a sure) ordinance concerning the singers, as every day required;*[465] *And yet for all this we make 'amanah' (a sure) covenant,*[466] meaning a provision "fixed" by covenant. Similarly, *a peg fastened in a place 'ne'eman'* [467] means [sure and] strong.

By way of the Truth, [the mystic lore of the Cabala], Moses lifted his ten fingers to the height of heaven[468] in order to allude to the ten emanations and to cleave firmly to Him Who fights for Israel.[469] Here is explained the matter of uplifting of hands during the blessing of the priests, and its secret.[470]

14. WRITE THIS FOR A MEMORIAL IN THE BOOK. Rabbi Abraham ibn Ezra commented[471] that "this was a known book, namely, *the book of the wars of the Eternal,*[472] which contained the history of the wars which G-d fought for those that fear Him, and it is possible that the history began from the time of Abraham." There is nothing in these words of his but an opportunity [to say something without due consideration].[473]

The correct interpretation appears to me to be that the word, *baseifer (in the book),* alludes to the Book of the Law, something

---

(465) Nehemiah 11:23. (466) *Ibid.,* 10:1. (467) Isaiah 22:23. (468) See Proverbs 25:3. (469) Deuteronomy 3:22, *For the Eternal your G-d, He it is that fighteth for you.* (470) By uplifting their ten fingers, which allude to the ten emanations, the priests point to the Most High One Whose beneficence is brought down through them to the world by the priestly benediction (L'vush Ha'orah explaining the Ricanti, who quotes the language of Ramban). (471) This quote from Ibn Ezra is found in his commentary to Numbers 21:14. Part of it is also found here. (472) Numbers 21:14. (473) It should be pointed out that in his commentary to the Book of Numbers *(ibid),* Ramban agrees with Ibn Ezra's comment, by way of the plain meaning of Scripture. This is because it distinctly says there, *the book of the wars of the Eternal.* Here, however, it just says *in the book.* Hence Ramban rejects Ibn Ezra's interpretation that here too it refers to that book of the wars of the Eternal, which is no longer extant, and he proposes his own interpretation, as explained in the text.

like that which is written, *Take this Book of the Law*.[474] He is thus stating: "Write this in the Book of My Law so that the children of Israel should remember what Amalek did, *for I will utterly blot out* his remembrance, and I will lay My vengeance upon him by the hand of My people Israel."[475] This is the commandment we find written in the Book of Deuteronomy: *Remember what Amalek did unto thee*.[476] He said, *and rehearse it in the ears of Joshua*, to command him to remind Israel of all the travail that had come upon them because of Amalek, for he [Joshua] knows and is witness.[477] G-d is thus hinting that after the conquest of the Land, they would blot out Amalek, for the first commandment upon them was to destroy the seven nations[478] and take possession of the Land. This is Scripture's intent in what is said there: *And it shall be when the Eternal thy G-d hath given thee rest from all thine enemies... that thou shalt blot out the remembrance of Amalek*.[479] Now had it been like this in the days of Joshua the son of Nun, he would have urged them on to blot out Amalek, but in his days, a good deal of the Land remained to be possessed,[480] and the time for the fulfilling of the commandment did not come until the reign of Saul.[481]

16. FOR THE HAND UPON 'KEIS Y-AH' (THE THRONE OF THE ETERNAL). "The hand of the Holy One, blessed be He, is raised to swear by His throne that He will maintain [a state of] war and enmity against Amalek forever. Now what is the significance of the word *keis*, and why does it not say *kisei* [as usual]? Furthermore, even the Divine Name is divided into half![482] [The answer is that] the Holy One, blessed be He, swore that the throne will not be perfect and the Name will not be full

---

(474) Deuteronomy 31:26. (475) See Ezekiel 25:14. (476) Deuteronomy 25:17. (477) See Jeremiah 29:23. (478) Deuteronomy 7:1-2. (479) *Ibid.*, 25:19. (480) See Joshua 13:1. (481) See I Samuel, Chapter 15. (482) The Tetragrammaton consists of four letters, while here only the first two letters are mentioned.

EXODUS XVII, BESHALACH

until He will blot out the name of Amalek the son of Esau.[483] And when his name will be blotted out, then will G-d's Name be full and the throne perfect, as it is said, *The foe — they are destroyed; perpetual ruins.*[484] [This refers to Esau,[485] of whom it is said, *And he kept his wrath for ever.*][486] *Their very memorial is perished.*[484] What is written after that? *And the Eternal is enthroned for ever.*[487] Thus you see [that after Amalek's memory has perished], G-d's Name is full. *He hath established 'kis'o' (His throne) for judgment.*[487] Thus you see that the throne will be perfect." Thus far the language of Rashi, and it is a Midrash of the Sages. [488]

Some scholars[489] explain the verse as meaning that "when there will be a 'hand,' [i.e., king, as explained further], *upon the throne of the Eternal,*[490] *the Eternal will have war with Amalek, and so shall it be from generation to generation.*" The purport of this is that when there will be a king in Israel sitting upon *the throne of the Eternal,*[490] he shall wage war against Amalek, thus alluding to Saul, the first king [of Israel]. And so shall it continue *from generation to generation,* that every king of Israel shall be duty-bound to fight with them until their name will extinct.

The following is also a Midrash of the Gemara,[491] as found in [Tractate Sanhedrin] in the chapter of the High Priest:[492] "By saying, *The hand upon the throne of the Eternal: the Eternal will have war with Amalek from generation to generation,* Scripture intimates that the Israelites must first appoint a king over themselves [before they are to annihilate the offspring of Amalek], for *the throne of the Eternal* refers only to the king, as it is said, *Then Solomon sat on the throne of the Eternal.*[493] In line with the plain meaning of Scripture, this is correct.

---

(483) Amalek was a grandson of Esau (Genesis 36:12). (484) Psalms 9:7. (485) In our Rashi: "Amalek." (486) Amos 1:11. (487) Psalms 9:8. (488) Tanchuma, *Ki Theitzei* 11. (489) Mentioned in Ibn Ezra in the name of Rabbi Yeshuah. (490) The expression found in this verse before us. (491) See *Seder Bo*, Note 204. (492) Sanhedrin 20 b. See also Maimonides' "The Commandments," I, pp. 202-203. (493) I Chronicles

And by way of the Truth, [that is, the mystic lore of the Cabala, the verse is to be understood as meaning] that *the Hand,* [i.e., the attribute of justice], which is *upon the throne of Y-ah,* and which is *the war from the Eternal,* will continue *with Amalek from generation to generation,* for the high attribute of justice will pursue his extinction forever from generation to generation. The Midrash of the Sages [mentioned above] concerning "the full Divine Name" and "the perfect throne" allude to this [interpretation by way of the Truth].

Now the reason for the punishment of Amalek, i.e., why punitive measures were meted out to him more than to all other nations, is that when all the nations heard [of G-d's visitation upon the Egyptians], they trembled. Philistia, Edom, and Moab and the inhabitants of Canaan melted away [494] *from before the terror of the Eternal, and from the Glory of His majesty,* [495] whereas Amalek came from afar as if to make himself master over G-d. It is for this reason that it is said concerning him, *and he feared not G-d.* [496] Besides, he was a descendant of Esau and related to us, [497] *a passer-by who meddles with a quarrel not his own.* [498]

29:23. Ramban thus brought proof to the opinion of those scholars mentioned above, who interpret this verse as containing a hint that the reckoning with Amalek is to be deferred until there will be a king in Israel. (494) Above, 15:14-15. (495) Isaiah 2:10. (496) Deuteronomy 25:18. (497) As a relative he was obligated to show kindness towards us. Instead, he behaved very cruelly: *he met thee by the way, and smote the hindmost, all that were enfeebled in thy rear, when thou was faint and weary (ibid.)* (498) Proverbs, 26:17. Amalek had no reason to fear attacks from Israel, as they were not bent on taking his land. Amalek's interposition was thus "meddling with a quarrel not his own."

Yithro

18 1. Our Rabbis have already differed concerning this section.[1] Some say that Jethro came to Moses before the Giving of the Torah, as the sequence of the sections of the Torah indicate, and some say that he came after the Giving of the Torah. Now this [latter] opinion [that he came after the Giving of the Torah] is certainly assisted by the verse [here] which states, *And Jethro, Moses' father-in-law, came with his sons and his wife unto Moses into the wilderness where he was encamped, at the mount of G-d.*[2] Thus Scripture states that Jethro came to Moses when he was encamped before Mount Sinai, the place in which the Israelites camped for one year,[3] this being the meaning of the expression, *where he was encamped.*[2] Moreover, Moses said to Jethro, *and I make them know the statutes of G-d, and His laws,*[4] [thus indicating that the Torah had already been given]. Besides, it says here, *And Moses let his father-in-law depart; and he went his way unto his own land.*[5] This had taken place in the second year when they journeyed from Mount Sinai, as it is said in the *parashah* (section) of *Beha'alothcha:*[6] *And Moses said unto Hobab, the son of*

---

(1) Zebachim 116 a, and Mechilta in beginning of this *Seder*. The difference of opinion is between Rabbi Yehoshua and Rabbi Eleazar of Modi'im, Rabbi Yehoshua maintaining that Jethro arrived before the Giving of the Torah, and Rabbi Eleazar saying that he came after the Torah had been given. (2) Verse 5. (3) They arrived before Mount Sinai on the first day of Sivan (further, 19:1), and they first journeyed from there on the twentieth day of the second month in the second year after the exodus (Numbers 10:11). They thus stayed there for twelve months less ten days. (4) Further, Verse 16. (5) *Ibid.*, Verse 27. (6) Numbers 8:1 – 12:16.

Reuel the Midianite, Moses' father-in-law: we are journeying[7] There it is written: *And he* [Hobab] *said unto him* [Moses] : *I will not go; but I will depart to mine own land and to my kindred,*[8] this being identical with the departure mentioned here, *and he went his way unto his own land.*[5]

They[9] have further brought proof [that Jethro came after the Torah had been given] from that which Scripture says, *The Eternal our G-d spoke unto us in Horeb, saying: Ye have dwelt long enough in this mountain; turn you, and take your journey.*[10] There it is said, *And I spoke unto you at that time, saying: I am not able to bear you myself alone... So I took the heads of your tribes, wise men,* etc.[11] This is the advice that Jethro [gave Moses on the morning after he arrived at the camp, as mentioned here further on in Verse 13]. There — [in Moses' narration of the account in the Book of Deuteronomy] — it is written, *And we journeyed from Horeb,*[12] for they journeyed immediately [after they appointed judges in accordance with Jethro's advice. All of this serves to prove that Jethro came to Moses after the Giving of the Torah]. And if this is so, we are in need of a reason for this section being written here before [the account of the Giving of the Torah]!

Now Rabbi Abraham ibn Ezra wrote that this was because of the affair of Amalek. Having mentioned the evil which Amalek inflicted upon us and how G-d commanded us to requite him accordingly, Scripture [by way of contrast], now mentioned the good which Jethro did for us in order to instruct us that we should show him kindness. When we will come to exterminate Amalek, as is mandatory upon us, we should warn the Kenites, [the descendants of Jethro], who dwelt near Amalek, and not

---

(7) *Ibid.*, 10:29. Hobab is identified as Jethro (Rashi). Now if all this happened before the Giving of the Torah, how could Moses say, *We are journeying,* etc.? (8) *Ibid.*, Verse 30. (9) I.e., the commentators. The proof is found in Ibn Ezra here. (10) Deuteronomy 1:6-7. (11) *Ibid.*, Verses 9-15. (12) *Ibid.*, Verse 19.

EXODUS XVIII, YITHRO

destroy them together with Amalek. This was indeed done by Saul when he so spoke to the Kenites.[13]

Yet with all this, I find it difficult to understand this opinion [that Jethro came after the Revelation, for the following reasons]: When Scripture says, *Now Jethro...heard of all that G-d had done for Moses, and for Israel His people, how that the Eternal had brought Israel out of Egypt,* why does it not say that he heard what G-d had done to Moses and to Israel by giving the Torah, which is among the great wonders that were done for them, as He said: *For ask now of the days past, which were before thee, since the day that G-d created man upon the earth, and from the one end of heaven unto the other, whether there had been any such thing as this great thing is, or hath been heard like it? Did ever a people hear the voice of G-d speaking out of the midst of the fire, as thou hast heard, and live?*[14] And when Scripture states, *And Moses told his father-in-law all that the Eternal had done unto Pharaoh and to the Egyptians for Israel's sake, all the travail that had come upon them by the way,*[15] on the basis of which Jethro said, *Now I know that the Eternal is greater than all gods,*[16] why did not Moses tell him about the Revelation [17] on Sinai? Jethro would thereby know that the Eternal is the true G-d and that His Torah is the truth, there being no other but He, as Moses said, *Unto thee it was shown, that thou mightest know that the Eternal He is G-d, there is none else beside Him. Out of Heaven He made thee to hear His voice,* etc.[18]

Perhaps we may say that while he was yet in his country, Jethro immediately heard that G-d had brought Israel out of Egypt,

---

(13) I Samuel 15:6, *And Saul said unto the Kenites: Go, depart, get ye down from among the Amalekites, lest I destroy you with them; for ye showed kindness to all the children of Israel, when they came up out of Egypt.* (14) Deuteronomy 4:32-33. (15) Further, Verse 8. (16) *Ibid.*, Verse 11. (17) Literally: "'the stand' (*ma'amad*) at Mount Sinai," or "the Revelation on Mount Sinai." It is based on Deuteronomy 4:10, *the day that thou 'stoodest' before the Eternal thy G-d in Horeb.* The expression *ma'amad har sinai* appears in Rambam's Mishneh Torah, Hilchoth Yesodei Hatorah 8:1. (18) Deuteronomy 4:35-36.

whereupon he left his country and reached Moses where he camped before Mount Sinai following the Giving of the Torah. Scripture, however, does not narrate that Moses related the matter of the Revelation [17] to him, for it had just happened and they were still at that site, and it is self-understood that he told him about it.

The most likely explanation seems to me to be to follow the sequence of the sections of the Torah, i.e., that Jethro came before the Giving of the Torah when the Israelites were yet in Rephidim, just as the Rabbis have said in the Mechilta:[19] "Rabbi Yehoshua says, '[*Now Jethro...heard.* What particular event did he hear of that he came?] He heard of the war of Amalek, as mentioned in the preceding passage, [20] and he came.'" He then journeyed with the Israelites from Rephidim to Mount Sinai. The purport of the verse which states [that Jethro came] *unto the wilderness where he was encamped, at the mount of G-d,* [21] is that Mount Sinai was on the way from Midian, near that country. Moses went there to feed the flock of Midian,[22] and in connection with Aaron's [going forth to meet Moses upon his arrival in Egypt], it is said, *And he met him in the mountain of G-d.*[23] Thus Jethro left Midian with his daughter and the children and came to Mount Sinai.

At that time, Moses was in Rephidim, which is a locale in the wilderness of Sin. Scripture says, *And they took their journey from Elim, and all the congregation of the children of Israel came unto the wilderness of Sin, which is between Elim and Sinai,*[24] thus stating that the wilderness of Sin stretches until Mount Sinai and includes the locales of Dophkah, Alush, and Rephidim.[25] Even

---

(19) Mechilta here in Verse 1. On the word "Mechilta," see *Seder Bo*, Note 205. (20) Above, 17:8. (21) Verse 5. Now this verse clearly states that Jethro came to Moses, not in Rephidim, but to where he was camped before Mount Sinai. But the true meaning of the verse is that Mount Sinai, etc. (22) Above, 3:1. (23) *Ibid.*, 4:27. (24) *Ibid.*, 16:1. (25) Numbers 33:12-14. See Ramban above, 16:1, where the same explanation is expounded briefly. Here, since it affects a major problem in the background - i.e., whether Jethro's arrival occurred before or after the Giving of the Torah — Ramban discusses his explanation at greater length.

EXODUS XVIII, YITHRO

though it says, *And they journeyed...from the wilderness of Sin...and encamped in Rephidim,*[26] [which would seem to indicate that Rephidim was not in the wilderness of Sin], it nevertheless also says, *And they journeyed from the wilderness of Sin, and pitched in Dophkah,*[27] [and from Dophkah they came to Alush, and from Alush to Rephidim, as stated in the following verses [28] there]. Alush and Rephidim are all part of the wilderness of Sin itself,[29] as the whole desert there was called "the wilderness of Sin," and the place before Mount Sinai was [also] called "the wilderness of Sin." A similar case is the verse, *And they returned unto the land of the Philistines.*[30]

Thus, the explanation of the verse here is: *And Jethro, Moses' father-in-law, came with his sons and his wife unto Moses unto the wilderness where he was encamped,* and he [Jethro] came to *the mountain of G-d.*[31] It was to the mountain that he [Jethro] came, and he stopped there, this being similar in meaning to the expression, *and he came to the mountain of G-d,*[32] [which means that he stopped there]. In a similar sense also is the verse, *Ye have sat long enough at this mountain,*[33] [which means "you have dwelt long enough at this place"]. From Mount Sinai, Jethro sent [a message] to Moses, [who was in Rephidim], saying, '*I thy father-in-law Jethro am coming unto thee,*'[34] and Moses went out[35] to meet him. In this case, it would not be necessary for us to say, [as Ibn Ezra did], that the expression, *And he* [Jethro] *said to Moses: 'I thy father-in-law Jethro am coming,'*[34] means

---

(26) Above, 17:1. (27) Numbers 33:12. (28) *Ibid.*, Verses 13-14. (29) And yet it says (above, 17:1) that they journeyed *from the wilderness of Sin* and came to Rephidim! But how could this be, for it says in the Book of Numbers that they journeyed *from the wilderness of Sin* and came to Dophkah and then to Alush and finally to Rephidim? It must be, Ramban concludes, that the name "wilderness of Sin" applies in general to an entire area, as well as to one particular locale, as explained in the text. (30) Genesis 21:32. See Ramban there (Vol. I, p. 274) that "the sense of the verse is that they [Abimelech and Phicol] returned to their city which was in the land of the Philistines." Here too "the wilderness of Sin" includes Dophkah, Alush, and Rephidim. Thus, the sense of the verse, *and they encamped in Rephidim* (above, 17:1), is that they encamped in Rephidim, which was in the wilderness of Sin. (31) Verse 5. (32) Above, 3:1. (33) Deuteronomy 1:6. (34) Verse 6. (35) Verse 7.

that he said so before [he arrived at the mount of G-d, as stated in the preceding verse].[36] Even if Rephidim was not in the wilderness of Sin, it was at any event in the desert, for Israel did not come to an inhabited land during all of the forty years.[37] Further, Rephidim was near Mount Sinai, as [is evidenced by the fact] that a great multitude of people like them came from Rephidim to the mount of G-d in one day,[38] and as has been explained in the matter of the rock from which they drank in Rephidim, as I elucidated the subject there.[39] Thus the explanation I have offered here is correct.

I have also seen this text in the Mechilta:[40] *"Into the wilderness where he was encamped.* Scripture thus expresses surprise at him. Here is a man who dwells in the midst of the glory of the world and yet desires to go out into a desolate wilderness which has nothing to offer." The Rabbis' intent was to explain the phrase, *unto the wilderness where he was encamped,* as referring to [that part of] the wilderness where the mount of G-d was, for the wilderness of Sin extended from Elim[24] until Mount Sinai. Thus, Scripture here relates that Jethro came to the edge of the wilderness where Moses was camped, this being the desert where the mount of G-d was, i.e., unto Horeb.[41] Scripture mentioned this in praise of Jethro, who left his country and came to the wilderness where Moses was, because he knew that this was the mount of G-d, for on it G-d had appeared to Moses. He [Jethro] had already heard of the entire affair, i.e., that Israel went out from Egypt in order to serve G-d upon this mountain,[42] and he came *for the Name of the Eternal, the G-d of Israel.*[43] This too is correct.

---

(36) But according to Ramban's interpretation, the verses are in chronological order. First, as stated in Verse 5, Jethro arrived at the mount of G-d, and from there, as stated in Verse 6, he sent Moses — who was in Rephidim — the message: *I thy father-in-law Jethro am coming to thee.* In order to show respect to him, Moses went out to meet him, as related in Verse 7. (37) Above, 16:35. (38) I have not found any source for this statement of Ramban that the journey from Rephidim to Sinai was accomplished in one day. (39) Above, 17:5. (40) Mechilta here on Verse 5. (41) See above, 3:1. (42) *Ibid.,* Verse 12. (43) II Chronicles 6:7.

It also appears to me concerning that which the verse states here, *And Moses let his father-in-law depart; and he went his way unto his own land,*[44] that this took place in the first year [of the exodus] and he betook himself to his own land and returned there. It is possible that he went there to convert his family and then returned to Moses while he was yet at Mount Sinai, since it was near to Midian, as I have mentioned. When they broke camp in Iyar of the second year,[45] and Moses said to him, *We are journeying... come thou with us,*[46] and he answered him, *I will not go; but I will depart to mine own land, and to my kindred,*[47] Moses in turn pleaded with him very much and said to him, *Leave us not, I pray thee... and thou shalt be to us instead of eyes. And it shall be, if thou go with us, yea, it shall be, that what good soever the Eternal shall do unto us, the same will we do unto thee.*[48] and he did not answer him at all. It would appear then that he accepted Moses' plea and did according to his will and did not leave them. However, in the days of Saul, we find Jethro's descendants with Amalek,[49] and [after they departed from the Amalekites], they came and attached themselves again to Israel. [We also find that] the sons of Jonadab the son of Rechab — [i.e., descendants of Jethro] — were in Jerusalem.[50] Perhaps Jethro or his sons returned to their land after the death of Moses. It is possible also that the Kenite that dwelled with Amalek were of the family of Jethro but not his direct descendants, and Saul showed kindness unto the entire family on account of Jethro, just as Joshua dealt kindly with the [whole] family of Rahab[51] [because of her]. The opinion of our Rabbis is thus that Jethro did go along with the Israelites [in the wilderness]. Thus they said in the Sifre[52] that [at the time they divided up the land], the Israelites

---

(44) Further, Verse 27. (45) Numbers 10:11. (46) *Ibid.*, Verse 29. (47) *Ibid.*, Verse 30. (48) *Ibid.*, Verses 31-32. (49) I Samuel 15:6. See above, Note 13. (50) Jeremiah, Chapter 35. (51) Joshua 6:23. (52) The Sifre is a Tanaaitic Midrash on the Books of Numbers and Deuteronomy. The text quoted is in *Beha'alothcha*, 81. The Sifre is to be distinguished from the Sifra, which is a work of a similar nature on the Book of Leviticus. The Sifra is also referred to as Torath Kohanim [literally: "the law of the priests"].

gave him the most fertile part of Jericho, and they [Jethro's descendants] used it until the Sanctuary was built four hundred and forty years later.[53] [It was then given as a substitute to him who gave up the land upon which the Sanctuary was to be built.] Rashi himself wrote this tradition in *Seder Beha'alothcha*.[54] Thus it is clear that Jethro returned to Moses, [as we have explained above, after he had returned to his land in the first year of the exodus]. In the Mechilta,[55] we also find: "Jethro said to Moses: 'I am going to my land to convert the people of my country, for I shall bring them under the wings of Heaven.' I might think that he merely went back and did not return; Scripture therefore says, *And the children of the Kenite, Moses' father-in-law, went up out of the city of palm-trees,* etc." [56]

ALL THAT G-D HAD DONE TO[57] MOSES, AND TO [57] ISRAEL HIS PEOPLE. The marvels He did for Moses were the kindness and goodness He wrought with him, i.e., that he should always be able to come before Pharaoh and not be afraid of him, and that he should inflict the plagues upon him until they went out from Egypt — he and the people with him — Moses being a king to them.

And Rabbi ibn Ezra wrote, *"l'Mosheh ul'Yisrael* means 'for Moses and Israel.' The intent is with regard to the plagues and the drowning of Pharaoh" [which G-d wrought for the sake of Moses and Israel, His people]. And so it appears from the opinion of our Rabbis, who said:[58] "Moses was equal to Israel, and Israel to Moses."[59]

(53) The building of the Temple was begun four hundred and eighty years after the exodus (I Kings 6:1). Subtract the forty years of the stay in the wilderness, and you have four hundred and forty. (54) Numbers 10:32. (55) Mechilta here on Verse 27. (56) Judges 1:16. (57) The Hebrew reads: *l'Mosheh ul'Yisrael*. Ramban first explains it as meaning " 'to' Moses and 'to' Israel." Hence he proceeds to mention the wonders that G-d did to Moses, etc. Further on, he will mention the explanation of Ibn Ezra, who interpreted the verse as meaning " 'for' Moses and 'for' Israel." (58) Mechilta on this verse. (59) Now this statement of the Rabbis can be understood only if the letter *lamed* in the words *l'Mosheh ul'Yisrael* means " 'for' Moses and 'for' Israel." The Rabbis could then comment upon this that

ALL THAT G-D HAD DONE... HOW THAT THE ETERNAL HAD BROUGHT ISRAEL OUT OF EGYPT. The reason [for the use of these two Divine Names] is that Scripture first mentions the Name *Elokim* (G-d) that Jethro knew from before, and then states *that the Eternal had brought Israel out,* for that was the Name that now came to be known through Moses and through which the signs were performed [before Pharaoh and Israel]

2. AFTER HE HAD SENT HER AWAY. Because Scripture had [previously] mentioned, *And Moses took his wife and his sons... and he returned to the land of Egypt,*[60] it became necessary to state here that she was in her father's house, as Moses had sent her there. It is possible that Scripture is stating that Jethro took [Zipporah, Moses's wife], to return her to him although he had sent her away. Having heard *all that G-d had done for Moses,*[60] he thought that it was now time for her to follow the king wherever he would go.

3. AND HER TWO SONS; OF WHOM THE NAME OF THE ONE WAS GERSHOM. Even though this is not the place where [the narrative of] their birth is told, Scripture here explains the names of the two sons [of Moses — Gershom and Eliezer —] because there was no opportunity to mention the name of Eliezer at his birth, as I have explained in *Seder V'eileh Shemoth.*[61] Here, Scripture wanted to mention the kindness that the Holy One, blessed be He, had shown to Moses, who was a stranger in a strange land. [When he named his second son], he gave thanks there to G-d for having delivered him from the sword of Pharaoh when he fled from before him,[62] [and for making him] now king over Israel, and [because] He drowned Pharaoh and his people in the sea.

---

all the wonders were done for the sake of Moses alone or Israel alone, for Moses alone is equal in importance to Israel, and Israel alone to Moses. But if they interpreted the verse to mean "to Moses and to Israel," the above statement is incongruous. (60) Verse 1. (61) Above, 4:20. See Ramban there regarding why Eliezer was not named at that time. Gershom's name, on the other hand, is mentioned in 2:22. (62) *Ibid.*, 2:15.

The sense of the expression *for he said, I have been a stranger,* etc. is connected with Moses, who is mentioned in the first verse, [and not with Jethro, who is mentioned in the second verse]. Similarly, the following verse, *And the name of the other was Eliezer: for the G-d of my father was my help,* [63] is connected with the expression *for he said,* [found in the verse before us. It thus reads: "*And the name of the other was Eliezer;* for he said: *for the G-d,* etc."] There are many cases like that.

6. AND HE SAID UNTO MOSES: 'I THY FATHER-IN-LAW JETHRO AM COMING UNTO THEE.' He sent him the message in a letter in which [the above words] were written. A messenger, [as Rashi would have it], could not say, *I thy father-in-law.* Instead, he would say, "Behold, Jethro your father-in-law is coming to you." It is also not possible that Jethro told him so mouth to mouth, for in that case he would have said, "Behold, I have come to you." Besides, it is not customary in such instances for the speaker to mention his name: "I, such and such a person," for upon seeing him, he would recognize him. A similar case is the verse: *Then Huram the King of Tyre said* [64] *in writing, which he sent to Solomon.* [65]

10. BLESSED BE THE ETERNAL, WHO HATH DELIVERED YOU OUT OF THE HAND OF THE EGYPTIANS, AND OUT OF THE HAND OF PHARAOH; WHO HATH DELIVERED THE PEOPLE FROM UNDER THE HAND OF THE EGYPTIANS. [66] "He has done a great miracle for you in that Pharaoh and his people did not kill you, for it was on account of you that great plagues came upon them in their land." This miracle was particularly great as far as Moses was concerned [because he

---

(63) Verse 4.   (64) Thus the word "said" can clearly apply to "saying in writing."   (65) II Chronicles 2:10.   (66) The text presents these difficulties: Why is *the hand of the Egyptians* mentioned twice? Why does Jethro first address himself directly to the people, saying, *Who hath delivered you,* etc., and then speaks of them in the third person, saying, *Who hath delivered the people,* etc.? Ramban first presents his interpretation, followed by that of Ibn Ezra.

frequently came to Pharaoh, as explained above at the end of Verse 1]. Therefore Jethro mentioned him [specifically] in the second person, together with everybody, saying, *Who hath delivered you,* meaning "you [Moses], and the people." And He did another miracle: *Who hath delivered the people from under the hand of the Egyptians,* since they were in Egypt and they went out of there to everlasting freedom.

Rabbi Abraham ibn Ezra said that Jethro first blessed G-d, *Who hath delivered you,* meaning Moses and Aaron, through whom the plagues came upon Pharaoh and the Egyptians. Afterwards, he blessed Him for how *He hath delivered the people from under the hand of the Egyptians* in Egypt and at the sea.

11. FOR IT IS IN THE THING THAT 'ZADU' UPON THEM. The meaning of this is that in the matter wherein the Egyptians premeditated[67] [their wickedness] against Israel, *I [Jethro] now know that the Eternal is greater than all gods.* And the purport thereof is as follows: Due to the fact that G-d had decreed upon Israel, *and they shall enslave them, and they should afflict them,* [68] there would have been no great punishment meted out to the Egyptians. But they acted presumptuously against them, and intended to eradicate them from the world, just as they said, *Come, let us deal wisely with them, lest they multiply.*[69] Pharaoh commanded the midwives to kill the male children,[70] and he decreed upon [all his people, saying], *Every son that is born* [unto the Israelites] *ye shall cast into the river.*[71] It was due to this that there came upon the Egyptians the kind of punishment which utterly destroyed them. It is this principle which is expressed in His words, *And also that nation that made slaves of them will I judge,*[72] as I have explained.[73] Now G-d saw their intentions, and He took vengeance upon them for the wickedness of their hearts.

---

(67) Ramban thus explains the word *zadu* on the basis of *zadon* (premeditated, conscious sin), as is explained further in the text. (68) Genesis 15:13. (69) Exodus 1:10. (70) *Ibid.,* Verse 16. (71) *Ibid.,* Verse 22. (72) Genesis 15:14. (73) *Ibid.* (Vol. I, pp. 203-205.)

And thus does Scripture say again, *And Thou didst show signs and wonders upon Pharaoh... for Thou knowest that they dealt insolently against them,*[74] for the punishment was because of the wicked plans they devised to carry out against the Israelites. Thus *the Eternal looketh on the heart,*[75] and *executeth justice for the oppressed,*[76] *avengeth and is full of wrath,*[77] and no one can deter Him.

Now Onkelos translated [the above Scriptural expression] thus: "for by that very thing with which the Egyptians thought to judge Israel, they themselves were judged." By this rendition, Onkelos meant to say that their punishment came because of the drowning of the [Hebrew] children in the river, which was not part of the Divine decree, *and they shall enslave them, and they shall afflict them.*[68] Therefore, He destroyed them by water.

12. AND JETHRO, MOSES' FATHER-IN-LAW, TOOK A BURNT-OFFERING AND SACRIFICES FOR G-D. All this took place before they came to Mount Sinai.[78] It is also possible to explain that Scripture arranged the entire narrative of Jethro [in one section] even though this particular event occurred after he had stayed with the Israelites a long time and, in the meantime, became converted through circumcision, immersion, and the sprinkling of the blood of a sacrifice, according to the law.[79]

---

(74) Nehemiah 9:10. (75) I Chronicles 16:7. (76) Psalms 146:7. (77) Nahum 1:2. (78) See above at the beginning of this *Seder*, where Ramban develops at length his explanation that Jethro, having arrived at the mount of G-d, sent a messenger to Moses in Rephidim, informing him of his arrival. Moses thereupon went out to meet him and brought him to Rephidim, where this feast took place. It was thus before Israel's arrival at Mount Sinai that all this took place. (79) Kerithoth 9 a. When the Sanctuary or Tabernacle was in existence, a proselyte entered into the covenant with G-d by means of circumcision, immersion, and the sprinkling of the blood of a sacrifice. Since the destruction of the Sanctuary, only circumcision and immersion are required. These three things were all present at the Giving of the Torah. Circumcision was performed already in Egypt, as is evidenced by the verse, *and no uncircumcised person shall eat thereof,* i.e., of the

EXODUS XVIII, YITHRO

AND AARON CAME, AND ALL THE ELDERS OF ISRAEL, TO EAT BREAD. That is, with Jethro *in the day of his espousals,* [80] [i.e., in the day of his entrance into the covenant with G-d], for he was then as a newly-circumcised child.

13. AND IT CAME TO PASS ON THE MORROW, i.e., on the morrow of the day on which they held the above-mentioned [feast], THAT MOSES SAT TO JUDGE THE PEOPLE. In the Mechilta, the Rabbis have said: [81] *"On the morrow.* That is, on the morrow after the Day of the Atonement." Now the intent of the Rabbis was not that *on the morrow* alludes to the Day of Atonement, for Scripture has not mentioned the Day of Atonement at all that it should now refer to it by saying *on the morrow* thereof. Nor is the term *on the morrow* to be understood literally, [i.e., the day after the Day of Atonement], for they did not eat on the Day of Atonement, that is, if they observed such a day in the first year before they were commanded concerning it. [82] Moreover, it was on the Day of Atonement that the second Tablets of the Law were given. On the following day, Moses came and he spoke to the children of Israel, *and he gave them in commandment all that the Eternal had spoken with him in Mount Sinai.*[83] It thus could not have been a day on which he sat to judge the people, when *the people stood about* him *from the morning unto the evening.* It is also impossible to say that this was on the morrow of the Day of Atonement of the second year, for after the Israelites journeyed [from Sinai on the twentieth day of Iyar in the second

---

Passover-offering (above, 12:48). Immersion is mentioned further (19:10), and so is the bringing of a sacrifice (24:5). At the time of the Sanctuary, immersion and a sacrifice were required of a female proselyte. Nowadays, immersion alone is the prerequisite to her entrance into the covenant. See Rambam, Mishneh Torah, Hilchoth Isueri Biah, Chapter 13, for further eludication of these principles. See also Ramban further, 19:10.   (80) Song of Songs 3:11.   (81) Mechilta on the verse here.   (82) "It is impossible to say that they observed the Fast of the Atonement in that first year, since the people were not commanded therein until Moses came down from Mount Sinai for the third time, which was on the Day of Atonement itself" (Mizrachi).   (83) Further, 34:32.

year (Numbers 10:11)], Hobab [i.e., Jethro], said, *I will depart to mine own land, and to my kindred.*[84]

Rather, the intent of this Beraitha, [i.e., the Mechilta quoted above, "on the morrow after the Day of Atonement"], is that it was some day after the Day of Atonement, since Moses had no free day on which to sit in judgment from the day they came to Mount Sinai until after the Day of Atonement of that first year.[85]

Scripture says, *a burnt-offering and sacrifices to G-d,*[86] because Jethro did not yet know the Eternal. It was Moses who said, *all that the Eternal had done unto Pharaoh and to the Egyptians for Israel's sake... and how the Eternal delivered them,*[87] but Jethro sacrificed to *Elokim* (G-d). You will not find this concerning any of the sacrifices in *Torath Kohanim* (the law of the priests) [i.e., the Book of Leviticus], as I will explain with the help of G-d.[88] Similarly, *Because the people come unto me to inquire of G-d... and I make them know the statutes of G-d,*[89] are the words of

---

(84) Numbers 10:30. And even according to what Ramban has written above on Verse 1, i.e., that Jethro listened to Moses' plea to stay with Israel and he did not leave them, it is nevertheless obvious that at that time, he intended to leave them. The narrative contained in this section concerning Jethro's advice to Moses on the delegation of power in the administration of justice, could thus logically not have taken place on the morrow after the Day of Atonement in the second year, some four and a half months after they journeyed from Mount Sinai (Kur Zahab). (85) Immediately after the Torah was given on the sixth day of Sivan, Moses ascended the mountain and remained there for forty days. When he descended on the seventeenth of Tammuz and found the people worshipping the golden calf, he broke the Tablets. On the next day, he again ascended the mountain to pray for G-d's forgiveness, and stayed there forty days, which terminated on the twenty-ninth day of Ab. On the following day, he was told to come up to the mountain to receive the second Tablets. He again spent forty days there. Consequently, this forty-day period terminated on the tenth of Tishri, which is the Day of Atonement. Thus, from the time the Torah was given till after the Day of Atonement in the first year, Moses had no free day on which to sit in judgment, as is described in this section of the Torah. For the sources on the above dates, see Rashi here, and in more detail, further, 33:11, and Deuteronomy 9:18. (86) Above Verse 12. (87) *Ibid.*, Verse 8. (88) Leviticus 1:9. (89) Further. Verses 15-16.

Moses to his father-in-law, [who did not yet know the Eternal]. It is possible that Moses spoke to him thus, [using the name *Elokim* and not the Tetragrammaton], because of the verse which states, *for the judgment is G-d's*, [90] just as our Rabbis always mention: [91] *"Elokim* (G-d): this is the attribute of justice."

15. FOR THE PEOPLE COME UNTO ME TO INQUIRE OF G-D. Moses answered his father-in-law: "They must stand about me a great part of the day, for they come before me for many things. *Because the people come unto me to inquire of G-d*, that is, to pray for their sick, and to inform them of the whereabouts of what they have lost," this being "the inquiring of G-d."

And thus the people did with the [later] prophets, just as it is said, *In former times in Israel, when a man went to inquire of G-d, thus he said: Come and let us go to the seer.*[92] Similarly, *Go meet the man of G-d, and inquire of the Eternal by him, saying: Shall I recover from this sickness?*[93] meaning that the prophet should pray for his recovery and that he should inform him if his prayer was accepted. This is also the meaning of the verse, *and she [Rebekah] went to inquire of the Eternal,*[94] as I have explained there.

"Moreover," [Moses continued], "I adjudicate matters between them, *when they have a matter, it cometh unto me, and I judge.*[95] And I also teach them Torah, *and I make them know the statutes of G-d and His laws."* [95]

19. AND G-D BE WITH THEE. "I.e., in this counsel. Jethro said to Moses, 'Go and consult with the Almighty.'" Thus Rashi's language. And Rabbi Abraham ibn Ezra wrote: "'Listen to me, and G-d will help you to succeed as I have counselled you.'

---

(90) Deuteronomy 1:17.　(91) Bereshith Rabbah 73:2.　(92) I Samuel 9:9. The matter there concerned the finding of Saul's lost asses. The prophet was Samuel.　(93) II Kings 8:8. The speaker is Ben-hadad, king of Aram, and he is sending Hazael to the prophet Elisha, who had come to Damascus. (94) Genesis 25:22 (Vol. I, p. 316).　(95) Verse 16.

Further, however, Jethro said, *'If thou shalt do this thing, and G-d command thee so,*[96] which means 'if you will do this thing — i.e., that you will consult with the Almighty — and He will command you to do it, then you will be able to endure.' And there is no doubt that Moses did so" [i.e., he first consulted with G-d and received His sanction and then proceeded to make this arrangement].

BE THOU FOR THE PEOPLE 'MUL' G-D. That is, " 'before' G-d." Jethro told Moses, "Be thou their intercessor before G-d, to pray to Him." This is like the verse, *I call by day; I cry in the night before Thee.*[97]

AND BRING THOU THE CAUSES — namely, which they will ask — UNTO G-D. Jethro conceded the first matter that Moses had said, i.e., *Because the people come unto me to inquire of G-d.*[98] It is possible that in this too there was counselling on his part. Jethro would thus be saying: "*Be thou for the people before G-d,* to sit in the Tent of Meeting before Him, ready to inquire of Him [on the matters they bring to you]. And this should not be at the place where you sit in judgment [to adjudicate their disputes]."

20. AND THOU SHALT TEACH THEM THE STATUTES AND THE LAWS, AND SHALT SHOW THEM THE WAY WHEREIN THEY MUST WALK. That is, "according to the law and the commandment with which you will strongly admonish them, and you will teach the law and the commandment." Thus Jethro also conceded to Moses on this matter, of which he had said, *and I make them know the statutes of G-d, and His laws.*[98] In this too there was counsel [on the part of Jethro], i.e., that Moses should strongly admonish them and warn them of the commandments and [Divine] punishments [in case of transgression], since he himself would not be involved in the execution of the law. "But in matters of judgment whereof you said, *and I judge between a man and his*

---

(96) Verse 23.   (97) Psalms 88:2.

neighbor,[98] designate judges to act with you, *for the thing is too heavy for thee.*[99] That is, the judging of disputes between them is heavier than all, and it would be good for you and for them to make it easier for you *and they shall bear the burden with thee."*[100] Now it is known that Moses had officers in charge of the people. [It was the duty of these officers] to bring before him the persons against whom claims had been made and to force them to comply with the verdict of the judges. He assigned many of these officers as these judges. This is why Moses said in Deuteronomy, *and I made them heads over you, captains of thousands... and officers, tribe by tribe.*[101] There was no need to mention them here since their appointment was not part of Jethro's counsel.

21. MEN OF 'CHAYIL.' This means men who are capable of leading a great multitude of people. Every assembly and gathering is called *chayil*, and it does not apply only to soldiers going forth to war. Thus it is said [of the dry bones that Ezekiel resurrected], *a great 'chayil' (host).*[102] Of the locusts it is said, *My great 'chayil' (army).*[103] Of wealth it is stated, *My power and the might of my hand hath gotten this 'chayil' (wealth);*[104] *they carry upon the shoulders of young asses 'chayaleihem' (their riches).*[105] Of fruits it is said, *the fig-tree and the vine do yield 'cheilam' (their strength).*[106] Thus an *ish chayil* in the administration of justice is one who is wise, alert, and fair; in war, an *ish chayil* is one who is strong, alert, and who knows the art of arraying forces in battle. A woman also is an *eisheth chayil (a woman of valor)*[107] when she is alert and knows how to conduct the management of a home.

---

(98) Above, Verse 16. (99) Verse 18. (100) Verse 22. The purport of Jethro's counsel to Moses, according to Ramban, was thus: "You are indeed correct in not delegating to others the inquiry of G-d on all matters they desire. So also in the matter of instructing the people in G-d's laws. But in judging their disputes, add other judges to join with you."
(101) Deuteronomy 1:15. (102) Ezekiel 37:10. (103) Joel 2:25.
(104) Deuteronomy 8:17. (105) Isaiah 30:6. (106) Joel 2:22.
(107) Proverbs 31:10.

Jethro thus spoke in general and in particular. [In general], he told Moses to select people with powers of leadership in the administration of justice for this great people. In particular, they should be *such as fear G-d, men of truth, hating unjust gain,* for it is impossible for them to be "men of *chayil*" in judgment, without these qualities. It was not necessary for him to mention that they must be wise and understanding, for it is clear that these qualities are included in the term "men of *chayil.*" Further on, when it says, *And Moses chose men of 'chayil,'* [108] everything is already included — i.e., that they were G-d-fearing, men who hated unjust gain, wise and understanding. Moreover, Scripture says [that Moses chose them] *out of all Israel,* [108] which means [that they were] the preferred of all Israel, being the ones who have all of these qualities. Since Scripture states that he chose them *out of all Israel,* [108] it is already stating that they were chosen in preference to all, for it is known that the better ones in Israel possess all good qualities. Jethro, however, not being familiar with them, found it necessary to explain in detail [that they be G-d-fearing, men of truth, etc.]

Some scholars [109] explain *anshei chayil* as men of physical strength and zeal, *such as have ability to stand in the king's palace.* [110] Similarly, *eisheth chayil* [107] is a woman of strength and industry in the work of the home, as Scripture explains there in that section. [111] Likewise, *Make them wander to and fro 'b'cheilcha,'* [112] which means "by Thy power." Also, *Neither doth it,* [i.e., the horse], *afford escape by its great 'cheilo,'* [113] [which means "by its great strength"]. The word [*chayil*] is associated with the Aramaic, as is evidenced by the [Hebrew] expression, *'yesh l'eil yadi' (It is in the power of my hand),* [114] which is rendered in the Targum: "there is *cheila* in my hand." And further on it says, *And Moses chose men of 'chayil' out of all Israel,* [108] which means the preferred ones of the entire nation and all qualities are included, as I have explained.

(108) Further, Verse 25. (109) Ibn Ezra here. Also, R'dak in Sefer Hashorashim, on the root *chayil.* (110) Daniel 1:4. (111) Proverbs 31:10-31. (112) Psalms 59:12. (113) *Ibid.,* 33:17. (114) Genesis 31:29.

HATING UNJUST GAIN. "Men who disdain their own money in a law-suit, just as we say:[115] 'Any judge from whom money is collected by a judgment is not qualified as a judge.'" Thus Rashi's language. By this, Rashi meant to explain that they disdain all money which they know can be collected from them by law, and return it themselves even though it is truly theirs, such as the case wherein one bought a slave without witnesses,[116] or a similar example.

But the text in the Mechilta is not so, [i.e., as Rashi commented]. Rather, this is the way it is taught there:[117] "*'Hating unjust gain.* I.e., those who, when sitting in judgment, disdain to accept money.' These are the words of Rabbi Yehoshua. Rabbi Eleazar of Modi'im says: '*Hating unjust gain.* I. e., those who disdain their own money. If they disdain their own money, how much more will they despise the money of their friends!'" The explanation [of this text of the Mechilta] is that Rabbi Yehoshua interprets the expression *hating 'botza'* as meaning "hating bribery," the usage of the word [*betza*] being similar to: *Every one is greedy for 'botza' (gain);*[118] *Each one 'l'bitzo' (to his gain), one and all.*[119] Rabbi Eleazar of Modi'im explained that *hating 'botza'* means that they despise abundance of money and have no desire to increase their silver and gold, something like the verse, *If I rejoiced because my wealth was great, and because my hand had gotten much.*[120] Money [or profit] is called *betza* [in Hebrew]: *What 'betza' (profit) is it if we slay our brother?*[121] *Is it any 'betza' (profit or advantage) to the Almighty that thou art righteous?*[122] *And thou shalt devote 'bitz'am (their gain) unto the Eternal, and their substance unto the Lord of the whole earth.*[123]

---

(115) Baba Bathra 58 b. (116) And the owner comes to reclaim him. Now even though the slave is rightfully the buyer's, the latter knows that because he has no witnesses who can attest to the sale, the original owner will regain possession of the slave in a law-suit. The buyer therefore voluntarily returns the slave to the original owner. See my Hebrew commentary, p. 381, as to why Ramban mentioned such a specific case. (117) Mechilta on the verse here. (118) Jeremiah 6:13. (119) Isaiah 56:11. (120) Job 31:25. (121) Genesis 37:26. (122) Job 22:3. (123) Micah 4:13.

Again, I have seen in the Yelamdeinu:[124] *"Hating unjust gain* [means] those who disdain their own money, and needless to say, they disdain the money of others. They are the ones who say, 'Even if this man will burn my stack, even if he will destroy my plants, I will render judgment correctly.'" This is the intent of Rabbi Eleazar of Modi'im, who said that they disdain their own money, meaning that they pay no regard to their property when sitting in judgment, that is, if they will suffer a loss of money on account of it. Moses further admonished them on this, saying, *Ye shall not be afraid of the face of any man.*[125] [Thus according to the Yelamdeinu], *betza* means money, as I have explained. Onkelos rendered it: "those who hate to receive money." But the word "money," [as Onkelos uses it], does not mean a bribe, [which of course is forbidden in itself]. It means rather that they should never accept money from people as a gift or loan, so that they should show them no favoritism at the time of judgment. It is similar to what the Rabbis have said:[126] "A judge who is in the habit of borrowing things [from his neighbors] is forbidden to act as judge in a law-suit involving them."

In line with the plain meaning of Scripture, *men of truth, hating 'botza'*, means those who love the truth and hate "oppression." When they see oppression and violence, they cannot tolerate them, their whole desire being only to *deliver the spoiled out of the hand of the oppressor.*[127]

22. AND LET THEM JUDGE THE PEOPLE AT ALL TIMES. The meaning thereof is that "when there will be many judges available, the oppressed one will go to the judge at any time he desires and he will find him ready [to listen to his grievance]. He cannot come near you [i.e., Moses] at any time because of the great multitude of people before you and on account of your many preoccupations. The result of this is that many of them will rather tolerate the violence committed against them because they

---

(124) See Sifre, *Devarim* 17. For the name Yelamdeinu, see *Seder Bo*, Note 196.   (125) Deuteronomy 1:17.   (126) Kethuboth 105 b.   (127) Jeremiah 21:12.

have no opportunity to tell it to you. They do not want to abandon their work and affairs to wait for a free moment when they will be able to approach you." This is the sense of the expression, each one *shall go to his place in peace.*[128] At present, because they cannot come near for judgment at all times, they will not rest in peace, since this opens a door for unjust people to commit violence and for oppressors to cause contention. And the meaning of the expression *to his place*[128] is that to whatever place they will come, [they will live in peace] as long as they are in the camp in the wilderness.

From the language, *And let them judge the people 'at all times,'* our Rabbis have derived the principle[129] that in civil cases, the verdict may be reached even during the night,[130] since it does not say here, "[and let them judge the people] the whole day."

19 1. IN THE THIRD MONTH. Scripture should have said, "And they journeyed from Rephidim and they encamped in the wilderness of Sinai, in the third month after their going forth from the land of Egypt," just as it said above concerning the wilderness of Sin.[131] But [Scripture's manner of expression here is] due to the fact that their coming into the wilderness of Sinai was an occasion for joy and a festival to them, and that since they left Egypt they had been yearning for it. They knew that they would receive the Torah there, for Moses had told them what was said to him, *Ye shall serve G-d upon the mountain.*[132] And to Pharaoh also he said, *Let us go, we pray thee, three days' journey, into the wilderness and sacrifice unto the Eternal our G-d.*[133] For this reason, Scripture begins the section with the statement that *in the third month... the same day* that the month began,[134] *they came*

---

(128) Verse 23. (129) Sanhedrin 34 b. (130) In capital cases, the verdict must be reached during the daytime (*ibid.*, 32 a). The trial itself, in both capital and non-capital cases, must be held during the daytime (*ibid.*) (131) Above, 17:1: *And all the congregation of the children of Israel journeyed from the wilderness of Sin... and encamped in Rephidim.* (132) Above, 3:12. (133) *Ibid.*, 5:3. (134) Mechilta on the verse here, and mentioned in Rashi.

there [as they had eagerly anticipated]. Following this opening, Scripture reverts [to the usual style] as in the other journeys: *And they journeyed from Rephidim.*[135]

Now here too Scripture should have said "and they journeyed from Rephidim *and encamped* in the wilderness of Sinai." Instead it writes, *and they came to the wilderness of Sinai.* This is because Scripture's intent is to state that as soon as they came to the wilderness of Sinai and saw the mountain in front of them, they encamped in the wilderness and did not wait until they would enter a spot better for encampment. Instead, they camped in the wilderness or in Horeb,[136] which was a waste land before the mountain. This is the purport of the verse; *and they encamped in the wilderness, and there Israel encamped before the mount.*[135]

It is possible that they separated from their midst all *the mixed multitude that was among them,*[137] and the children of Israel alone camped before the mountain while the mixed multitude was behind them. For the Torah was given to Israel, as He said, *Thus shalt thou say to the house of Jacob, and tell the children of Israel,*[138] and this is the meaning of the expression, *and there Israel encamped.*[135] It may be that [the name "Israel"] is mentioned as a mark of honor at the time of their acceptance of the Torah.

Now Rashi wrote: "*And they journeyed from Rephidim.* What need was there for Scripture to state again expressly from where they set forth on the journey? Is it not already stated that they were encamped in Rephidim[131] and it is thus evident that they journeyed from there? It [i.e., the intent of the verse] is to declare that their departure from Rephidim was like their encampment[139] in the wilderness of Sinai. Just as their encampment[139] [in the wilderness of Sinai] was with repentance,[140] so also was their

---

(135) Verse 2. (136) Deuteronomy 4:10. (137) Numbers 11:4. See also above, 12:38. (138) Verse 3. (139) "Encampment." In our Rashi: "coming." (140) The repentance is indicated by the word *vayichan*, which is in the singular, thus indicating that Israel encamped before the mountain as one man and with one mind, "while all other encampments were with murmerings and with dissension" (Rashi, quoting Mechilta).

departure [from Rephidim] with repentance."[141] Thus Rashi's language. But I have not understood this. It says in connection with all journeys: *and they pitched* [camp] *in Elim;*[142] *And they took their journey from Elim... and they came unto the wilderness of Sin;*[143] *And they journeyed from the wilderness of Sin... and encamped in Rephidim;*[144] and so the entire section of *Mas'ei* [145] is written [with the name of the place whence they set forth on the journey repeated after it had already been mentioned that they had encamped there]. The intent of the repetition by Scripture is that there were no other encampments between them.

In the Mechilta, we find the following text[146] [on the same theme that Rashi mentioned, but presented in such a form that the above difficulties are eliminated]: "*And they departed from Rephidim and came to the desert of Sinai.*[135] Has it not already been stated in the section of the Torah dealing with all stages of the journey [from Egypt to the Jordan]: *And they journeyed from Rephidim, and pitched in the wilderness of Sinai?*[147] And what need is there for Scripture to state here, *and they came to the desert of Sinai?* It [i.e., the intent of the verse] is to declare that their departure from Rephidim [was like their encampment in the wilderness of Sinai], etc." The purport of this text of the Mechilta is to explain why, on account of certain new details mentioned there,[148] Scripture repeated in the section of *Eileh Mas'ei*[145] all stages of the journey from Elim and Rephidim mentioned here, although this journey [from Rephidim to the wilderness of Sinai] is mentioned in identical language both here and there. It was for this reason that [the Mechilta] was compelled to interpret that [the Scriptural restatement] was on account of the above analogy: [Just as their encampment at Sinai was with repentance, so also etc.].

(141) See above, 17:7, for their sin in Rephidim. The present analogy between their coming into the wilderness of Sinai, which was surely in a spirit of repentance, as explained above, and their departure from Rephidim, thus teaches us that their departure was also with repentance. (142) See Numbers 33:9. (143) Above, 16:1. (144) *Ibid.*, 17:1. (145) Numbers 33:1-49. (146) Mechilta on the verse here. (147) Numbers 33:15. (148) *Ibid.*, Verses 9 and 14.

3. AND MOSES WENT UP UNTO G-D. From the day they arrived at Mount Sinai, the cloud covered the mountain and the Glory of G-d was there. It is with reference to this that Scripture says, *And the Glory of the Eternal abode upon Mount Sinai, and the cloud covered it six days,*[149] i.e., before the Giving of the Torah. It is for this reason that Scripture says here, *And Moses went up unto G-d,* meaning that he went up to the edge of the mountain to be ready for Him, but he did not penetrate *the thick darkness where G-d was.*[150] *And the Eternal called unto him from the top of the mountain, saying: Thus shalt thou say to the house of Jacob.*

And Rabbi Abraham ibn Ezra wrote that the expression, *and He called unto him,* is an antecedent, meaning that He had called him [to come up to the mountain] and he went up to Him. But this does not appear to me to be correct, for the calling [mentioned in Scripture after Moses ascended the mountain] was: *Thus shalt thou say to the house of Jacob.* Now Ibn Ezra explains the verse to mean as follows: "*And the Eternal called unto him to say*[151] to him, *Thus shalt thou say to the house of Jacob.*" But this is not correct.

The meaning of the expression, *he went up unto G-d, and the Eternal called unto him,* is that Moses went up towards the Glory of G-d, which was abiding on the mountain to declare the Ten Commandments to Israel, and with His Great Name [the Tetragrammaton] He would speak with Moses, as is the meaning of the verse, *If there be a prophet among you,* etc.[152]

4. AND I BROUGHT YOU UNTO MYSELF. I.e., "to the place of My Glory, namely, this mountain where My Presence abides

---

(149) Further, 24:16.   (150) *Ibid.*, 20:18.   (151) Thus Ibn Ezra here interprets the word *leimor,* which is generally taken to mean "saying," as meaning "to say." The sense of the verse is thus: And Moses went up to G-d, for He had called him out of the mountain to tell him, "Thus shalt thou say to the house of Jacob, etc."   (152) Numbers 12:6. *If there be a prophet among you, I the Eternal do make Myself known unto him in a vision... My servant Moses is not so... with him do I speak mouth to mouth, even manifestly, and not in dark speeches* (Verses 6-8). See also Ramban in this chapter, further, Verse 20.

EXODUS XIX, YITHRO

there with you." Now Onkelos translated: "and I brought you near to My service." [To avoid a literal translation], Onkelos adapted an expression of respect towards Him Who is on high.

5. AND YE WILL KEEP MY COVENANT. I.e., "the covenant which I have made with your fathers to be a G-d unto them and to their seed after them."[153] Rabbi Abraham ibn Ezra explained it as referring to the covenant which Moses was to make with Israel after the Giving of the Torah, as he said, *Behold, the blood of the covenant, which the Eternal hath made with you in agreement with all these words.*[154]

By way of the Truth, [that is, the mystic lore of the Cabala, the verse is to be understood as meaning] that "you should keep My covenant to cleave unto Me, for if thou shalt indeed hearken unto My voice and do all that I speak,[155] *then ye shalt be Mine own 's'gulah'(treasure) from among all peoples.*"[156] This means that "you will be a treasure 'in My hand,'" for a king does not hand over a precious object into the hand of another [for permanent possession]. The word *s'gulah* here is similar in meaning to the expression: *'us'gulath' (and treasure) such as kings and the provinces have as their own.*[157]

FOR ALL THE EARTH IS MINE. This is similar in meaning to the verses: *Which the Eternal thy G-d hath allotted unto all the peoples... But you hath the Eternal taken.*[158] And thus He said, *"And I have set you apart from the peoples, that ye should be Mine*[159] [own] treasure." It may be that the word *s'gulah* connotes "attachment." [The sense of the verse would then be: "and you shall be attached to Me from among all peoples], for unto Me is the earth called *kol (all)*," as I have explained on the verse, *And the Eternal had blessed Abraham 'bakol' (in all things).*[160] The student learned [in the mystic lore of the Cabala]

---

(153) Genesis 17:7. (154) Further, 24:8. (155) See *Ibid.*, 23:22. (156) Here in Verse 5. (157) Ecclesiastes 2:8. (158) Deuteronomy 4:19-20. (159) Leviticus 20:26. (160) Genesis 24:1 (Vol. I, pp. 290-292).

will understand. Similarly, *And ye shall be unto me*[161] means that "you will be Mine in a special sense, and not as the rest of the peoples." And so did the Rabbis interpret it in the Mechilta: [162] *"And ye shall be unto Me.* As though it were possible to say it, [He is stating], 'I shall neither appoint nor delegate [any power] to rule over you, but I Myself will rule over you.' And thus it says, *Behold He that keepeth Israel doth neither slumber nor sleep."* [163]

6. A KINGDOM OF PRIESTS. This means that you shall be a kingdom of My servants. AND A HOLY NATION. I.e., to cleave unto the Holy G-d, just as He said, *Ye shall be holy, for I the Eternal your G-d am Holy.* [164] Thus He has assured them [of life] in this world and in the World to Come.[165]

7. AND MOSES CAME AND CALLED FOR THE ELDERS OF THE PEOPLE, AND SET BEFORE THEM ALL THESE WORDS. This means that he said to them: "Behold, I have presented before you the words [of G-d]. *Choose you this day* [166] if you will do so." Therefore, they answered him, *All that the Eternal hath spoken we will do.*[167] This is similar in meaning to the verse: *See, I have set before thee this day life and good, and death and evil,*[168] and also: *And these are the ordinances which thou shalt set before them,* [169] meaning that they are to say if they choose to observe them and accept [them] upon themselves. It is for this reason that it says there, *And Moses came and told the people all the words of the Eternal, and all the ordinances; and all the people answered with one voice, and said, All the words which the Eternal hath spoken will we do.*[170] Similarly, *And this is the law which Moses set before the children of Israel* [171] means that Moses asked the generation that was to come into the Land whether they would accept the Torah upon themselves, for he was about to make a covenant with them in the plains of Moab, just as he had

(161) Verse 6. (162) Mechilta, *ibid.* (163) Psalms 121:4. (164) Leviticus 19:2. (165) See *Seder Beshalach,* Note 346. (166) Joshua 24:15. (167) Verse 8. (168) Deuteronomy 30:15. (169) Further, 21:1. (170) *Ibid.,* 24:3. (171) Deuteronomy 4:44.

done with their fathers in Horeb.[172] And the Gaon Rav Saadia[173] said that the expression, *and he set before them,* is similar in meaning to the expression, *put it in their mouth,*[174] [this being a reference to the Oral Law, which is the commentary to the Written Law]. But the correct interpretation is only as I have explained.

And all the people answered together.[175] This also means that Moses called together the elders of the people, who are their wise men and their judges, for theirs is [the power of] choice. *And he set before them all these words* in the presence of the whole congregation, since it was with reference to all the people that G-d had commanded, *Thus shalt thou say to the house of Jacob, and tell the children of Israel.*[176] But they did not wait for the counsel and decision [of the elders, but readily], *all the people answered together — both small and great*[177] — *and said, All that the Eternal hath spoken will we do.*[175] And so it says again, *and all the people answered with one voice, and said: All the words which the Eternal hath spoken will we do.*[178]

8. 'VAYASHEV MOSHEH' THE WORDS OF THE PEOPLE UNTO THE ETERNAL. This means that Moses returned[179] before Him to the mountain with the people's answer. Now everything is revealed to Him, and He did not inquire of him, "What did this people answer you?" It is similar in meaning to the verse: *And the Eternal heard the voice of your words, when ye spoke unto me.*[180] And when Moses came before Him, the Holy One, blessed be He, said, *Lo, I come unto thee in a thick cloud, that the people may hear when I speak with thee, and may also believe thee*

---

(172) *Ibid.,* 28:69. (173) Mentioned here in Ibn Ezra. On Rav Saadia Gaon, see *Seder Va'eira,* Note 229. (174) Deuteronomy 31:19. (175) Verse 8. (176) Above, Verse 3. (177) II Kings 23:2. (178) Further, 24:3. (179) Ramban thus interprets the word *vayashev* in the sense of "returning," and not of "reporting": "he returned to G-d with the words of the people." "And there was no need to mention that 'he went up to the mountain,' since Scripture speaks here briefly" (Ibn Ezra). (180) Deuteronomy 5:25.

forever.[181] Then Moses said before Him,[182] "Master of the universe, your children are people of faith, and they accept upon themselves whatever You will speak."

The above usage [of the word *vayashev* as meaning "returning" or "coming back"] is also found in the verse, *'vayashivu' unto them word... and they showed them the fruit of the Land,*[183] which means: "They [i.e., the spies] came back to them with the things which they saw." [It cannot mean that "they reported" to them], for afterwards Scripture says there, *And they told him, and said.*[184] [Hence, *vayashivu* in the preceding verse must mean that "they came back" with the things they had seen.][185] There is thus no need for Rabbi Abraham ibn Ezra's interpretation on this point.[186]

9. IN A THICK CLOUD. This is *the thick darkness where G-d was,*[187] and all the people saw it and recognized it as such, as it is

---

(181) Verse 9. (182) This is the sense of the conclusion of Verse 9: *and Moses told the words of the people unto the Eternal,* i.e., the words they had said, "Master of the universe, etc." On the significance of this interpretation of Ramban, see further, Note 186. (183) Numbers 13:26. (184) *Ibid.,* Verse 27. (185) Similarly, *vayashev Mosheh* here means that "Moses came back" with the words of the people to G-d. Actually, however, as Ramban continues to explain, he did not report them, as everything was revealed to Him. This differs with Ibn Ezra's interpretation, as explained in the following note. (186) Ibn Ezra asks the following question: Since it says in Verse 8, *'vayashev Mosheh' the words of the people unto the Eternal,* why does it say again at the end of Verse 9, *and Moses told the words of the people unto the Eternal?* To remove this difficulty, Ibn Ezra said that *vayageid Mosheh (and Moses told)* in Verse 9 means that "Moses had already told the words of the people to G-d." It is thus clear that Ibn Ezra explained *vayashev Mosheh* in Verse 8 as meaning that Moses "reported" the words of the people to G-d. Hence, Ibn Ezra's difficulty and his forced solution. Ramban, however, explains *vayashev Mosheh* as meaning that Moses returned to G-d to report these words. Actually, there was no need to report them, as explained above. Then G-d said to him, *Lo, I come unto thee,* etc. (Verse 9), and finally *vayageid Mosheh:* Moses told these words to G-d, i.e., that His children are men of faith and that they accept upon themselves whatever He will speak. "There is thus no need for Ibn Ezra's interpretation on this point," as Ramban succinctly puts it. (187) Further, 20:18.

said, *And the appearance of the Glory of the Eternal was like devouring fire on the top of the mount in the eyes of the children of Israel.*[188]

IN ORDER THAT THE PEOPLE MAY HEAR WHEN I SPEAK WITH THEE. Rabbi Abraham ibn Ezra commented that there were among the Israelites people who doubted the existence of prophecy. And even though it is written, *and they believed in the Eternal, and in His servant Moses,*[189] it is said there, *and 'Israel' saw,*[189] but not "all Israel." It is this which they said to him [after the Giving of the Torah], *This day we have seen that G-d doth speak with man, and he liveth,*[190] for at first they did not believe so. This is the meaning of the verse here, *in order that the people may hear when I speak with thee,* the Ten Commandments, *and also believe in thee forever,* i.e., "that you are My prophet," for henceforth the matter of prophecy will be confirmed to them. [Thus far the words of Ibn Ezra.]

This is not correct. The children of Abraham never doubted prophecy, as they had always believed in it since the time of their forefathers. Scripture already has stated so: *And the people believed, and they heard that the Eternal hath remembered the children of Israel;*[191] *and they believed in the Eternal, and in His servant Moses.*[189] Even though it does not say there, "and all the people [believed]" or "all Israel believed," neither does it say here "that 'all the people' may hear."

The correct interpretation appears to me to be that G-d said to Moses: "*I come to thee in a thick cloud,* so that you should draw near *to the thick darkness*[187] *in order that the people may hear when I speak.* They themselves will be prophets when I speak, not [necessitating] that it should be confirmed to them through others," just as it is said, *When the Eternal said unto me: Assemble Me the people, and I will make them hear My words, that they may learn to fear Me all the days.*[192]

(188) *Ibid.,* 24:17. (189) Above, 14:31. (190) Deuteronomy 5:21. (191) Above, 4:31. (192) Deuteronomy 4:10.

"*And they may also believe in thee forever,* i.e., through all the generations. And if there will arise among them *a prophet or dreamer of dreams* [193] to refute your words, they will deny him at once, for they have already seen with their own eyes and heard with their own ears that you have reached the highest stage in prophecy. Through you, will become clear to them that which is written: *If there be a prophet among you, I the Eternal make Myself known unto him in a vision, I do speak with him in a dream. My servant Moses is not so; he is trusted in all My house; with him do I speak mouth to mouth.*"[194] It is for this reason that He said, "*in order that the people may hear when I speak with thee,* for they will hear when I speak *out of the midst of the fire,*[195] and they will know that it is I the Eternal Who speaks to you. They will believe in My words and also in you forever." Similarly, that which the people said, *This day we have seen that G-d doth speak with man, and he liveth,*[195] was to state: "Now the thing has been confirmed to us with the sight of our own eyes, as was the wish of G-d [that we should all become prophets]. Henceforth, *Go thou near,*[196] for we know that you have reached the great stage in prophecy, *and hear all that the Eternal our G-d may say... and we will hear it* from you, *and do it,*[196] for your prophecy has been confirmed to be above that of all prophets."

Now I have seen the Mechilta where it is written:[197] "*In order that the people may hear when I speak with thee.* This teaches that the Holy One, blessed be He, said to Moses: 'Behold, I will call you from the top of the mountain, and you will come up,' as it is said, *and the Eternal called Moses to the top of the mount, and Moses went up.*[198] *And they may also believe in thee forever,* i.e., 'in you and also in the prophets who are destined to arise

---

(193) *Ibid.,* 13:2. (194) Numbers 12:6-8. (195) Deuteronomy 5:21. This verse had been used by Ibn Ezra to bring proof that before the Revelation there were some Israelites who still doubted the existence of prophecy. Ramban is now to interpret the true purport of the verse. (196) *Ibid.,* Verse 24. (197) Mechilta on the verse here. (198) Further, Verse 20.

EXODUS XIX, YITHRO

after you.' " The words of the Mechilta incline towards the opinion of Rabbi Abraham ibn Ezra.[199]

10. 'V'KIDASHTAM' TODAY AND TOMORROW. Rashi explained: "*V'kidashtam* means 'and thou shalt prepare them.' " And so is the opinion of Onkelos. A similar usage is found in the verse: *I have commanded 'lim'kudashai'* ("those who are prepared for Me" or "My consecrated ones"),[200] and also in the following verse: *'hithkadshu' (prepare yourselves) for tomorrow.*[201] Rabbi Abraham ibn Ezra explained it as meaning that they should bathe themselves in water. But if so, what is the sense of *today and tomorrow* when bathing was required only once? The correct interpretation is that they should sanctify themselves by separating from their wives, and from all uncleanness, for he who guards [himself] from being defiled by uncleanness is called *'m'kudash'* (consecrated), just as it is said with reference to the priests, *There shall none defile himself for the dead;*[202] *They shall be holy unto their G-d.*[203] And it is further written, *because the priests had not sanctified themselves,*[204] that is to say, they had not purified themselves. Similarly, *And David answered the priest, and said unto him: To a certainty women have been kept from us about these three days; when I came out, the vessels of the young men were holy.*[205] And it is known that [before the Giving of the Torah the people] bathed themselves in water, this being derived logically from the required washing of garments.[206] And so did the Rabbis

---

(199) Since the Mechilta states that "they may believe in you and also 'in all the prophets,' " it would indicate that prophecy itself was still doubted, as Ibn Ezra wrote. (200) Isaiah 13:3. (201) Numbers 11:18. (202) Leviticus 21:1. (203) *Ibid.*, Verse 6. (204) II Chronicles 30:3. (205) I Samuel 21:6. (206) In other words, it is not necessary to explain *v'kidashtam*, as Ibn Ezra did, as meaning that they shall bathe themselves in water, for that requirement can be derived from the express commandment, *and let them wash their garments* (here, Verse 10). Hence, *v'kidashtam* must mean as Ramban explained it. The reasoning for the requirement of bathing or immersion is found here in the Mechilta: "*And let them wash their garments.* And whence do we know that immersion was also required? I reason as follows: If immersion is required in cases where washing of garments is not required (see Leviticus 15:16), is it not logical that immersion is also required in this case where washing of garments is expressly mentioned?"

say in the Mechilta:[207] "There is no case where washing of garments is required in the Torah without the requirement of immersion [of one's body]."

11. THE ETERNAL WILL COME DOWN IN THE SIGHT OF ALL THE PEOPLE. I.e., so that all the people will behold His coming down, meaning that they will see *the appearance of the Glory of the Eternal like devouring fire on the top of the mount,* [208] but they will not see G-d, for it is written, *for man shall not see Me and live.* [209]

13. WHEN 'HAYOVEIL' (THE RAM'S HORN) SOUNDETH LONG, THEY SHALL COME UP TO THE MOUNT. "The Hebrew word *hayoveil* denotes a ram's horn, and the horn used here was that of Isaac's ram." [210] Thus Rashi's language. But I have not understood this, for Isaac's ram was burnt as a whole-offering,[210] and horns and hoofs were completely burnt in whole-offerings.[211] Perhaps the Holy One, blessed be He, shaped the ashes of the horn [of Isaac's ram] and restored it to what it was originally. But in my opinion, this Agadah (homily) contains a secret. Thus they [212] have said that this Voice [heard on Mount Sinai, as stated in Verse 16], was that of *Pachad Yitzchak (the Fear of Isaac).* [213] It is for this reason that Scripture says, *and all the people that were in the camp trembled.* [214] At this manifestation of *G'vurah* [215] they did not grasp the commandment itself but *only a voice.* [216]

14. AND MOSES WENT DOWN FROM THE MOUNT UNTO THE PEOPLE, AND SANCTIFIED THE PEOPLE. This verse

---

(207) Mechilta, *ibid*. (208) Further, 24:17. (209) *Ibid*., 33:20. (210) Genesis 22:13. (211) Leviticus 1:9 and 13. (212) Evidently, a reference to the masters of Cabala. The source of this statement, i.e., that the Voice heard on Mount Sinai was that of *Pachad Yitzchak*, is unknown to me. (213) Genesis 31:42.. See Ramban, *ibid*. (Vol. I pp. 388-389). And in Bachya's commentary here (Vol. II, p. 172 of my edition): "This is the *Pachad Yitzchak* which they perceived at Mount Sinai." (214) Verse 16. "Just as it says [in Genesis 27:33], in the case of Isaac: *And Isaac trembled"* (Bachya, *ibid*.) (215) Literally: "strength." But here it denotes one of the Ten Emanations, the one which is synonymous with *Pachad Yitzchak*. (216) Deuteronomy 4:12. See also Ramban further on Verse 19.

teaches that the command expressed in the [above] verse, *And the Eternal said unto Moses: Go unto the people and sanctify them,*[217] was also given to him on the mountain which Moses ascended everytime that he was about to speak to Him. In the Mechilta, the Rabbis have explained: [218] "This teaches that Moses did not turn to his personal affairs nor go to his house at all, but he went directly *from the mount unto the people."*

19. MOSES SPOKE, AND G-D ANSWERED HIM BY A VOICE. In the Mechilta, the Rabbis have said[219] that this verse refers to the time of the Giving of the Torah, when Moses was proclaiming the commandments to Israel, as Rashi has written.

By way of the plain meaning of Scripture, the verse here does not yet speak of this. It is rather [to be explained as follows] : *The Glorious Name*[220] came down upon the mountain[221] on the third day, and Moses *brought forth the people out of the camp to meet* the Glory which appeared to them, *and they stood at the nether part of the mount.*[222] Moses went up near to the head of the mountain, where the Glory was, in a place designated for himself, and he spoke with Israel, teaching them what to do. The Israelites heard the Voice of G-d answering Moses and commanding him, but they did not understand what He said to him. Thus He commanded Moses the precepts mentioned further on in this section: *Go down, charge the people;*[223] *Go, get thee down, and thou shalt come up, thou, and Aaron with thee,* etc.[224] This happened before the Giving of the Torah and also during the time when the Ten Commandments were given, for Moses did not go up to the top of the mount *unto the thick darkness where G-d was*[225] until after the Giving of the Torah. And so he said, *"I stood between the Eternal and you at that time, to declare unto you the word of the Eternal; for you were afraid because of the fire, and went not up*

---

(217) Above, Verse 10. (218) Mechilta on the verse here. (219) Mechilta here. The language is that of Rashi. (220) Deuteronomy 28:58. (221) Verse 20. (222) Verse 17. (223) Verse 21. (224) Verse 24. (225) Further, 20:18.

into the mount, saying[226] [that you will not ascend] as I did go up." Some scholars[227] explain that the Israelites were very much afraid of *the voice of the horn* which *waxed louder and louder,*[228] and Moses would say to them at first: "Direct your thoughts, for now you will hear the Voice in such a manner," and immediately *G-d answered* him *by a voice.*

20. AND THE ETERNAL CAME DOWN UPON MOUNT SINAI. If you will succeed in having insight into this section [of the Torah], you will understand that His Great Name, [i.e., the Tetragrammaton], came down upon Mount Sinai, and that He abode thereon in fire and spoke to Moses. The communication to Moses in the entire section was by this Proper Name of the Eternal. However, the ascent [of Moses — as mentioned in Verse 3: *And Moses went up unto G-d*] — and his bringing forth [the people out of the camp — as mentioned in Verse 17] — were towards the place of the Glory, as I have explained.[229] And He warned, *lest they break through unto the Eternal to gaze,* [230] because even *the nobles of the children of Israel*[231] did not see Him, and all Israel heard the Voice of G-d *out of the midst of the fire.*[232] It is this which Scripture says, *And 'Elokim' (G-d) spoke all these words,*[233] just as our Rabbis have said:[234] "*Elokim* designates the Judge."[235] And they have also said [with reference to the first two commandments]:[236] "We have heard them from *Hagvurah* (the Almighty Himself)." In Deuteronomy it is written: *These words the Eternal spoke unto all your assembly.*[237] That is because Scripture explains there [in the same verse] that He spoke *out of the midst*

---

(226) Deuteronomy 5:5. (227) I have not been able to identify them. See my Hebrew commentary, p. 387, Note 5. (228) Verse 19 before us. (229) Above, Verse 3, also in Verse 19. (230) Verse 21. (231) Further, 24:11. (232) Deuteronomy 5:21. (233) Further, 20:1. (234) Mechilta, *ibid.* (235) "The Judge who is just in meting out punishment and faithful in giving reward" (Mechilta, *ibid.*) (236) Makkoth 24 a. See Maimonides' "The Commandments," Vol. I, p. 1. The term *Hagvurah* (the Almighty) is analogous to "the Judge." (237) Deuteronomy 5:19. And according to the above explanation, it should have said, "*Elokim* spoke." That is because, etc.

of the fire.[238] And this is the sense of the verse, *The Eternal spoke with you face to face in the mount out of the midst of the fire.*[238] And this is why it is said, *I am the Eternal thy G-d.*[239] Now do not find a difficulty in what the people said to Moses, *For who is there of all living flesh, that hath heard the Voice of the living G-d speaking out of the midst of the fire?*[240] They did not say "that they heard G-d speaking out of the midst of the fire," but they said *the Voice of G-d,* referring to what they perceived. This is why they said, *Go thou near, and hear all that the Eternal our G-d may say.*[241] And so did Moses say to them, *Did ever a people hear the Voice of G-d speaking out of the midst of the fire?*[242] The word "speaking" here is referring to "the Voice," something like the verse, *and he heard the Voice speaking unto him.*[243]

From this you will understand what the Rabbis have always said in Midrashic homilies, i.e., that the Torah was given in seven voices.[244] They are the ones to which David alluded in the psalm: *Ascribe unto the Eternal, O ye sons of might.*[245] This is also the number of times [that the Voice] is alluded to in this section of the Torah.[246] The verse, *And there were 'koloth' and*

---

(238) *Ibid.,* 5:4.   (239) Further, 20:2. "This alludes to the verse [in Deuteronomy 5:4, mentioned above]: *Face to face,* etc." (Abusaula). The allusion is to the two Divine Names — the Tetragrammaton and *Elokim* — mentioned together here in 20:2.   (240) Deuteronomy 5:23. This would indicate that they heard *Elokim chayim* speaking (Abusaula).   (241) *Ibid.,* Verse 24.   (242) *Ibid.,* 4:33.   (243) Numbers 7:89.   (244) Shemoth Rabbah 28:4, "Rabbi Yochanan said: 'The One Voice was divided into seven voices.'"   (245) Psalms 29:1. This psalm was considered by the Sages of the Talmud as referring to the Giving of the Torah (Sifre, *V'zoth Habrachah,* 343). The voice of the Eternal appears seven times in this psalm: *The voice of the Eternal is upon the waters* (Verse 3); *The voice of the Eternal is powerful; the voice of the Eternal is full of majesty* (Verse 4); *The voice of the Eternal breaketh the cedars* (Verse 5); *The voice of the Eternal heweth out flames of fire* (Verse 7); *The voice of the Eternal shaketh the wilderness* (Verse 8); *The voice of the Eternal maketh the hinds to calve* (Verse 9).   (246) 1. *And there were 'koloth' and lightnings* (Verse 16). Since the word *koloth* is written defectively without the letter *vav,* it signifies the singular: "and there was a voice." 2. *And the voice of a horn* (ibid.) 3. *And the voice of the horn* (Verse 19). 4. *And G-d answered him by a voice* (ibid.) 5. *And all the people perceived 'hakoloth'* (Verse 15). Here too the Hebrew *hakoloth* is written

lightnings,[247] is written defectively and therefore counted as one; likewise, the verse, *And all the people perceived 'hakoloth,'*[248] is missing the *vav* which signifies the plural, [and thus refers to only one voice]. Thus there are six ['voices' mentioned here in the section], and [in addition] it clearly says, *And G-d spoke.*[249] In Deuteronomy, Scripture likewise mentions seven 'voices' in connection with the Giving of the Torah.[250] In Tractate Berachoth,[251] however, the Rabbis have said in the Gemara[252] that the Torah was given in five 'voices.' That is because they counted only the voices which are concealed, while the two — i.e., *I am the Eternal thy G-d* and *Thou shalt have no other gods before Me*][253] — are explained in Scripture. The purport of this is that Moses our teacher was given the Torah in seven 'voices,'[254] and he was the one who heard them and contemplated them. The Israelites, however, heard one voice, as it is said, *a great voice, and it went on no more,*[255] and it is said again, *Ye heard the voice of words, but ye saw no form; only a voice.*[256] Here also Scripture alluded thereto in saying, *And all the people perceived 'hakoloth,'*[257] with one *vav* missing, [thus making it singular, 'the voice'], for all voices appeared as one. By way of the Truth, [the mystic lore of the Cabala], this is Scripture's intent in saying, *G-d hath spoken once, twice we have heard this.*[258] The sections of the Torah are thus explained, without anything being changed with another.

defectively and therefore refers only to one voice: "and all the people perceived the voice." 6. *And the voice of the horn (ibid.)* 7. *And G-d spoke* (20:1). Thus there are seven voices mentioned in this section of the Torah (Abusaula). (247) See Note 246, number 1. (248) *Ibid.*, number 5. (249) *Ibid.*, number 7. (250) 1. *Ye heard the voice of words* (Deuteronomy 4:12). 2. *Only a voice (ibid.)* 3. *A great voice* (5:19). 4. *The voice out of the midst of the fire* (5:20). 5. *And we have heard His voice* (Verse 21). 6. *If we hear the voice of the Eternal our G-d* (Verse 22). 7. *The voice of the living G-d speaking* (Verse 23). (251) Berachoth 6 b. (252) For the meaning of the word Gemara, see *Seder Bo*, Note 204. (253) So interpreted by Abusaula. See my Hebrew commentary, pp. 387-388. (254) "This is an allusion to the seven [lower of the Ten] Emanations" (Bachya). (255) Deuteronomy 5:19. (256) *Ibid.*, 4:12. (257) See above, Note 246, number 5. (258) Psalms 62:12. The verse actually reads: *'I' have heard this.*

22. AND THE PRIESTS ALSO, THAT COME NEAR TO THE ETERNAL. I.e., who offer the sacrifices to *the Glorious Name*[259] and who come near to Him with them. [They also must sanctify themselves and not go outside of their designated place.]

20   2. I AM THE ETERNAL THY G-D. This Divine utterance constitutes a positive commandment.[260] He said, *I am the Eternal,* thus teaching and commanding them that they should know and believe that the Eternal exists and that He is G-d to them. That is to say, there exists an Eternal Being through Whom everything has come into existence by His will[261] and power, and He is G-d to them, who are obligated to worship Him. He said, *Who brought thee out of the land of Egypt,* because His taking them out from there was the evidence establishing the existence and will of G-d, for it was with His knowledge and providence that we came out from there. The exodus is also evidence for the creation of the world, for assuming the eternity of the universe, [which precludes a Master of the universe Who is in control of it], it would follow that nothing could be changed from its nature.[262] And it is also evidence for G-d's infinite power, and His infinite power is an indication of the Unity, as He said, *that thou* [i.e., Pharaoh] *mayest know that there is none like Me in all the earth.*[263] This is the intent of the expression, *Who brought thee out,* since they are the ones who know and are witnesses to all these things.

---

(259) Deuteronomy 28:58. (260) See my Hebrew commentary, p. 388. on the position of the Hilchoth Gedoloth on this point. Ramban thus sides with Rambam, who, in his Sefer Hamitzvoth, counted this as the first commandment. See my translation, "The Commandments," I, pp. 1-2. (261) The universe is thus a result of design, and not merely of necessity. See Guide of the Perplexed, II, 18. (262) "If you believe in the eternity of matter, it leads to the conclusion that if G-d should desire to shorten a fly's wing or lengthen an ant's foot, He would not be able to do it" (Ramban, in his sermon, "G-d's Law Is Perfect," Kithvei Haramban, I, p. 146). The miracles preceding the exodus, in which G-d's mastery of the powers of nature was demonstrated, thus refuted the doctrine of the eternity of matter and established that of Creation. (263) Above, 9:14.

The meaning of *out of the house of bondage* is that they stayed in Egypt in a house of bondage as captives of Pharaoh.[264] He said this to them [in order to indicate] that they are obligated [to accept] *this* Great, *Glorious and Fearful Name*[259] as their G-d, and to worship Him, because He redeemed them from Egyptian bondage. It is similar in meaning to the verse, *They are My servants whom I brought forth out of the land of Egypt.*[265] I have also already alluded to above[266] by way of the Truth, [the mystic lore of the Cabala], to the reason why the two sacred Names — [the Tetragrammaton and *Elokim*] — are mentioned here.

This commandment, in the words of our Rabbis,[267] is called the obligation "to take upon oneself the yoke of the Kingdom of Heaven," for these words, [i.e., *the Eternal your G-d*], which I have mentioned, indicate a King addressing His people. Thus the Rabbis have said in the Mechilta:[268] *"Thou shalt have no other gods before Me.*[269] Why is this said?[270] Because it says, *I am the Eternal thy G-d.* This can be illustrated by a parable: A king invaded a country, and his attendants said to him, 'Issue decrees to us.'[271] He, however, refused, saying: 'No! When you have accepted my sovereignty, I will issue decrees to you, for if you do not accept my sovereignty, how will you carry out my decrees?' Similarly, G-d said to Israel: '*I am the Eternal thy G-d, thou shalt have no other gods.* I am He Whose sovereignty you have accepted in Egypt.' And when they said to Him: 'Yes,' [He continued]: 'Now, just as you have accepted My sovereignty, so you must also accept My decrees.'" That is to say, "Since you have accepted upon yourselves and have admitted that I am the Eternal, and that I am your G-d from the [time that you were yet in the] land of Egypt, then accept all My commandments."

---

(264) This accords with the interpretation of the Mechilta here: "*Out of the house of bondage.* They were slaves to kings." And as Rashi puts it, "from the house of Pharaoh where ye were slaves to him." (265) Leviticus 25:55. (266) Above, 19:20. (267) Berachoth 13 b. (268) Mechilta on Verse 3 here. (269) Verse 3. (270) Since it says, *I am the Eternal thy God*, etc., it already means, "I, am not another." Why then does He state again, *Thou shalt not have other gods before Me?* (271) "Us." In the Mechilta: "them," i.e., the people.

Now all the [Ten] Commandments are expressed in the singular — *the Eternal thy G-d, Who brought 'thee' out* — and not, as He began to say, [before the Giving of the Torah] : *'Ye' have seen;*[272] *if 'ye' will hearken.* [273] This is because His intent is to warn that each individual is subject to punishment for [transgression of] the commandments, since He addresses Himself to each one individually, commanding him that he should not think that He will judge according to the majority and that the individual will be saved with them. This intent was explained to the people by Moses at the end of the Torah, in the section of *Atem Nitzavim.*[274]

3. THOU SHALT HAVE NO OTHER GODS BEFORE MY FACE. Rashi wrote: "*Thou shalt have no other gods.* Why is this said? [270] It is because it says, *Thou shalt not make unto thee a graven image.*[275] From this I would only know that it is forbidden to make an idol. Whence do I know that one may not keep an idol that has already been made? Scripture therefore says, *Thou shalt have no other gods.*" This is indeed a Beraitha[276] taught in the Mechilta. [277] But if this is so, this verse would constitute a negative commandment in itself, being a prohibition against a person who retains an idol on his premises. [The violation thereof] does not make one liable to the death-penalty by the court. So [the question arises] : Why did He state the prohibition against keeping an idol, which makes one liable to whipping, before [He stated] the prohibition against bowing down to idols or worshipping them,[278] which makes one liable to extinction [if done intentionally but with no witnesses present], or death by the court [if there were witnesses] ?

In my opinion, the final decision of the Law is not in accordance with this Beraitha,[276] for it represents the opinion of a single Sage [against the opinion of the majority]. Thus we find it taught in the Sifra:[279] "*Nor make ye to yourselves molten*

---

(272) Above, 19:4. (273) *Ibid.*, Verse 5. (274) Deuteronomy 29:17-19. See Ramban there on Verse 17. (275) Verse 4. (276) See *Seder Bo*, Note 209. (277) Mechilta on the verse here. (278) In Verse 5. (279) Sifra, beginning of *Seder Kedoshim* (Leviticus, Chapter 19). On "Sifra," See above, Note 52.

gods.[280] I might think that others may make it for you. Scripture therefore says, *Nor... to yourselves.* From this I know only that [others may not make it] for you, but I might think that you may make it for others. Scripture therefore says, *Nor make ye*: not for you by others, and not by you for others. It is from here that the Rabbis have derived the principle that he who makes an idol for himself, transgresses two negative commandments: *Nor make ye,* and *Nor... to yourselves.* Rabbi Yosei says, 'He transgresses three negative commandments: *Nor make ye, Nor... to yourselves,* and also *Thou shalt have no other gods.*'" Thus you see that Rabbi Yosei's opinion is that of one against a majority, for it is he who says that the verse *Thou shalt have no other gods* constitutes a prohibition against retaining an idol [in one's house]. However, according to the opinion of the first Sage, [which is that of the majority of the Rabbis], it is not so.

The correct interpretation even according to the literal meaning of Scripture is that the usage of the language of the verse here is similar to the expressions: *and the Eternal shall be my G-d;*[281] *to be your G-d.*[282] The verse here thus states that excepting the Eternal only, we are not to have others as gods, neither from all the angels above nor from all the host of heaven who are called *elohim.* This is something like that which is said, *he that sacrificeth 'la'elohim' (unto the gods) save unto the Eternal only, shall be utterly destroyed.*[283] It is thus a prohibition against believing in any of these beings, accepting them as gods, or saying to them, "thou art my god."[284] This is also the opinion of Onkelos, who translated: "[thou shalt have no] other gods excepting Me."[285]

Know that wherever Scripture says *elohim acheirim,* the meaning is "others besides the Glorious Name." It uses this expression with reference to accepting G-d or worshipping Him, thus saying: "Do

---

(280) Leviticus 19:4. (281) Genesis 28:21. (282) Leviticus 11:45. (283) Further, 22:19. (284) See Psalms 140:7 and Sanhedrin 60 b. (285) Ramban's intent is evidently as follows: Since Onkelos always translated *elohim acheirim* as *ta'avath am'maya* (the deceptions of the nations) — see e.g., further, 23:13 — and here he translated, *ela acharan* (other gods), it shows that he referred to the angels of above, etc.

not accept them upon yourselves as G-d, with the exception only of the Eternal." But when Scripture speaks of making idols, it will never say *acheirim* (others) — ["other gods"] — Heaven forbid! [286] Instead it says, *Nor make to yourselves molten gods;*[280] *Molten gods do not make unto thee.*[287] They are called [gods] because they were made with the intent of serving their makers as gods, but in reference to them, Scripture says, *For they were no gods, but the works of men's hands, wood and stone; therefore they have destroyed them.* [288]

Thus in the second commandment, He admonished us firstly that we should not accept upon ourselves a master from among all gods excepting the Eternal. He then said that we should not make a graven image or any manner of likeness, [and we are not] to bow down to them or worship them in any manner whatsoever. It is for this reason that He said, *Thou shalt not bow down unto them,*[289] since it is connected with the making [of idols — mentioned in the preceding verse] — which He prohibited the people from bowing down to them. Thus all [of the first three verses in this second commandment] constitute prohibitions against worshipping idols, and their violations all entail death by the court. This verse, [i.e., *Thou shalt not make unto thee a graven image,* etc. (Verse 4)], is thus not a prohibition against making

---

(286) "When speaking of accepting or worshipping G-d, Scripture could say, 'Do not accept or worship any other god besides the Eternal.' But when Scripture warns against making an idol, how could it say [that we are] not to make 'other gods' when it is G-d Who has made everything and Who was not made!" (Tur.) (287) Further, 34:17. (288) Isaiah 37:19. (289) Verse 5. The intent of Ramban's words is as follows: According to his own interpretation that this entire second commandment is directed against worshipping idols, we can understand why it says here in Verse 5, *Thou shalt not bow down 'to them'* and it does not say 'other gods,' because the purport of that verse is to be understood in connection with the preceding verse: "do not make a graven image, etc., to bow down 'unto them.'" But according to Rashi, who interpreted *Thou shalt have no other gods* (Verse 3) as being a prohibition against keeping an idol, and *Thou shalt not make unto thee,* etc., (Verse 4) as being a prohibition against making idols, Verse 5 should have said, "Thou shalt not bow down 'to other gods,'" since the subject of worshipping the idols as gods is here mentioned for the first time.

idols which one does not worship oneself, [as Rashi would have it]. Further on [in Verse 20], He indeed warns against this, as it is said, *gods of silver, or gods of gold, ye shall not make unto thee.* Similarly, *Thou shalt not make unto thee molten gods,*[287] *Ye shall not make unto thee idols.*[290]

'AL PANAI' (BEFORE MY FACE). This is similar in meaning to these expressions: *Surely 'al panecha' (to Thy face) he will blaspheme Thee;*[291] *Now therefore be pleased to look upon me; for surely I shall not lie 'al p'neichem' (to your face).*[292] He thus admonishes here: "Do not make unto yourselves other gods, for they are before My face, as I look and gaze at all times and in all places at those who make them." A thing which is done in the face of a person when he is aware thereof is called *al panav* (before his face). Thus: *So the present passed over 'al panav' (before him).*[293] So also: *And Nadab and Abihu died... and Eleazar and Ithamar ministered in the priest's office 'al p'nei' (in the presence of) Aaron their father,*[294] meaning that Aaron their father saw it and was aware thereof. In the Book of Chronicles it is written: *And Nadab and Abihu died 'liphnei' (before) their father, and had no children.*[295] Thus the purport of the verse here is: "Do not make other gods unto yourselves, for I am present with you always and see you in private and in public."

By way of the Truth, [the mystic lore of the Cabala], you will understand the secret of *panim* (face) from that which we have written[296] that Scripture warned concerning the Revelation: [297] *'Panim b'phanim' (face to face) did the Eternal speak with you.*[298] And you will know the secret of the word *acheirim*

---

(290) Leviticus 26:1. (291) Job 1:11. (292) *Ibid.,* 6:28. (293) Genesis 32:22. (294) Numbers 3:4. (295) I Chronicles 24:2. Since in the above verse (Numbers 3:4), it says that Nadab and Abihu died *before the Eternal,* Ramban therefore also quotes the verse from Chronicles, where it is stated that they died before their father. Hence the significance of the statement that he saw the remaining two sons performing the Divine Service in his presence. (296) Above, 19:20. (297) See above, Note 17. (298) Deuteronomy 5:4.

(others), and then the entire verse will come [to light] in its plain meaning and purport. And so did Onkelos say it.[299] It is this which is said, *Ye shall not make with Me.*[300] *"For I the Eternal thy G-d am a jealous G-d,*[301] i.e., to be worshipped alone, and it is not fitting that you join others to Me. And I am *E-il,*[302] the Mighty One, [303] Who has the power in My hand; [304] and I am, furthermore, *kana,* avenging from the one who gives My glory to another and My praise to graven images."[305]

Now in no place in Scripture is an expression of 'jealousy' found in reference to the Glorious Name except in the matter of idol-worship. Thus the Rabbi [Moshe ben Maimon] wrote in the Moreh Nebuchim [306] that in the entire Torah and in all the books of the Prophets, you will not find the term *burning anger,* wrath, or jealousy [applied to G-d] except in reference to idolatry. But of the holy ones of the Supreme One it is written: *And the anger of the Eternal was kindled against Moses;*[307] *And the anger of the Eternal was kindled against them* [i.e., Aaron and Miriam] *and He departed!*[308] And it is further written, *My wrath is kindled against thee* [i.e., Eliphaz the Temanite] *and against thy two friends, for ye have not spoken of Me the thing that is right, as My servant Job has.*[309] However, as far as the term 'jealousy' is concerned, [Rambam] is correct [in maintaining that it is not applied to G-d except in reference to idolatry]. And so did the Rabbis say in the Mechilta:[310] "I zealously exact punishment for idolatry, but in other matters, I am gracious and merciful."

---

(299) Onkelos translated *al panai* as *bar mini* (outside of Me). Thus the sense of the verse is as follows: "Do not worship *elohim acheirim,* since they were all created, excepting G-d, Who is eternal and has not been created by any being." See also Note 285 above. (300) Verse 20. And as Rashi explains it: "Do not make any likeness of My ministers that serve Me." (301) Verse 5. (302) Ramban now continues to explain the two Hebrew words in the above Verse: *E-il kana (a jealous G-d).* (303) See Ramban on Genesis 17:1 (Vol. I, pp. 214-215). (304) See *ibid.,* 31:29. (305) See Isaiah 42:8. (306) Guide of the Perplexed, I, 36. (307) Exodus 4:14. (308) Numbers 12:9. (309) Job 42:7. (310) Mechilta on Verse 5 here.

In my opinion, jealousy is mentioned only with reference to idolatry in Israel. The reason for the jealousy is that Israel is the treasured possession of the Glorious Name, which He has separated to Himself, as I have explained above.[311] Now if His people, His servants, turn to other gods, G-d is 'jealous' of them even as a man is jealous of his wife when she goes to other men, and of a servant who makes another master for himself. But Scripture uses no such term of jealousy with reference to other peoples to whom He has allotted the hosts of heaven.[312]

At this point, I make mention of what Scripture teaches concerning idolatry. There were three kinds of idol-worship. The first [group of idol-worshippers] began to worship the angels, who are the Separate Intelligences,[313] because it is known that some of them have rulership over the peoples, something like it is written, *the prince of* the kingdom of *Greece*,[314] *the prince of the kingdom of Persia.*[315] They thought that [these angels] have power over them to do good or to do evil, and so each people began to worship the prince appointed over them, as the first [peoples] knew how to identify them. Now these are referred to in the Torah and in all the Writings as *other gods, the gods of the peoples,*[316] for angels are called *elohim,* as it is said, *He is G-d of gods;*[317] *Bow down to Him, all ye gods;*[318] *For the Eternal is greater than all gods.*[319] They worshipped the angels even though they admitted that supreme strength and infinite power belonged only to G-d the Most High. Thus did the Rabbis say,[320] [with reference to the peoples of the world], that they call G-d the Most High "G-d of gods." Regarding this kind of idol-worship, Scripture has said, *He that sacrificeth 'la'elohim' (to the gods) shall be*

---

(311) Above, 19:4. (312) See Deuteronomy 4:19. (313) "For the angels are not material bodies but only forms distinguished from each other... All these forms live and realize the Creator, and their knowledge of Him is exceedingly great" (Rambam, Mishneh Torah, Hilchoth Yesodei Hatorah 2:3-8). For Rambam's version of the development of idolatry, see his first chapter in Hilchoth Akum. See also Guide of the Perplexed I, 49, on figurative expressions applied to angels. (314) Daniel 10:20. (315) *Ibid.,* Verse 13. (316) Deuteronomy 6:14. (317) *Ibid.,* 10:17. (318) Psalms 97:7. (319) Above, 18:11. (320) Menachoth 110 a.

utterly destroyed.[321] It thus mentioned them by the name with which they were known.

The second kind of idolatry appeared when people began worshipping the visible hosts of heaven, some worshipping the sun or the moon, and others worshipping one of the constellations. Each of the nations knew the power of the constellation according to the dominion thereof in their land,[322] and they thought that by worshipping them, the constellation would be strengthened and it would help them, something like it is written, *or the sun, or the moon, or any of the host of heaven, etc.*[323] And it is further written, *And they shall spread them before the sun, and the moon, and all the host of heaven, whom they have loved, and whom they have served, and after whom they have walked, and whom they have sought, and to whom they have bowed,*[324] and as it is said in the Torah with reference to the prohibition of idolatry: *And lest thou lift up thine eyes unto heaven, and when thou seest the sun and the moon and the stars, even all the host of heaven, thou be drawn away and worship them and serve them, which the Eternal thy G-d hath allotted unto all the peoples under the whole heaven.*[312] That is to say, because G-d allotted them to all the peoples and gave each people a star or constellation, you should not let yourself be allured to worshipping them. Now these are the people who began making the many forms of graven images, *Asheirim and the sun-images.*[325] They would make the forms of the constellations in the hours of their strength according to their rank, and in the opinion of the people, it bestowed power and success upon them. It appears likely to me that this [form of idolatry] began in the Generation of the Dispersion,[326] when G-d

---

(321) Further, 22:19. (322) See Job 38:33. (323) Deuteronomy 17:3. (324) Jeremiah 8:2. (325) Isaiah 27:9. (326) See Ramban, Genesis 11:2 (Vol. I, pp. 154-155). In describing the beginnings of this second stage of idolatry, Rambam introduces it with this statement: "In the course of time, there arose among men false prophets who said that G-d commanded them, saying 'Worship that particular star'" (Mishneh Torah, Hilchoth Akum 1:2). Ramban here is more specific and suggests that the beginnings of this kind of idolatry took place in the age of the dispersion of the nations. This would seem to be the intent of Ramban's words, "It appears likely to me..."

scattered the nations to various countries and the stars and the constellations began holding sway over them according to their divisions. The builders of the Tower had declared their intention to make themselves a name [327] and not be scattered, as I have hinted in its place.[326] Now all these groups had false prophets who foretold them future events and informed them through the arts of sorcery and divination some of the things that were to come upon them. The constellations also have lords who abide in the atmosphere as the angels do in the heavens, and know the things that are to come.

Closely related to this kind of idolatry was the worship of human beings. When people of a country saw that a certain individual — such as Nebuchadnezzar — had great power and that his star was very much in the ascendancy, they thought that by accepting his worship upon themselves and directing their thought towards him, their star would also ascend together with his. He would also think that by their attaching their thoughts to him, his success would be augmented on account of the power of their souls directed towards him. This was the opinion of Pharaoh, who, according to the words of our Rabbis, [looked upon himself as a god],[328] and of Sennacherib, concerning whose ideas Scripture says, *I will ascend above the heights of the clouds; I will be like the Most High*,[329] and of Hiram[330] and his companions [331] who made themselves gods. They were wicked, but they were not absolute fools.

---

(327) Genesis 11:4. (328) Shemoth Rabbah 9:7. (329) Isaiah 14:14. It is to be noted though that this prophecy was said with reference to the king of Babylon (*ibid.*, Verses 4, and 22). Accordingly, it is difficult to understand why Ramban here mentions Sennacherib who was king of Assyria, and not Nebuchadnezzar, king of Babylon. See however, in Sefer Hage'ulah (Kithvei Haramban I, p. 274) where Ramban writes that Scripture sometimes "interchanges from the name of the king of Babylon to the king of Assyria" and he quotes various verses to prove it. In this sense it may be understood here that Ramban mentioned "Sennacherib" when his intent was really to the king of Babylon. (330) Ezekiel 28:2. (331) Such as Nimrod. See Chullin 89 a.

The third kind of idolatry appeared afterwards when people began worshipping the demons which are spirits, as I will explain with G-d's help.[332] Some of them too are appointed over the peoples to be masters in their lands and to harm their beleagured ones and those who have stumbled, as is known of their activity through the art of necromancy, as well as through the words of our Rabbis.[333] It is with reference to this [third kind of idolatry] that Scripture says, *They sacrificed unto demons, no-gods, gods that they knew not, new gods that came up of late, which your fathers dreaded not.*[334] Scripture ridicules them, [i.e., the Israelites], saying they sacrifice also to the demons who are no gods at all. That is to say, they are not like the angels who are called *eloha.* Instead, they are gods that they knew not, meaning that they found in them no trace of might or power of rulership. Furthermore, they are new to them, having learned only lately to worship them from the Egyptian sorcerers, and even their wicked forefathers such as Terach and Nimrod[335] did not dread them at all. Of this [kind of idolatry] Scripture warns, *And they shall no more sacrifice their sacrifices unto the demons, after whom they go astray.*[336]

Thus in this second commandment, the Torah prohibited all [kinds of] worship, *save unto the Eternal only.*[337] It is for this reason that He first admonished, *Thou shalt have no other gods 'al panai' (before My face),* which is a reference to the first kind of idolatry, namely, the worship of the angels. This is the intent of *al panai,* whose secret I have alluded to. Then He further admonished against graven images and *any manner of likeness of any thing that is in heaven above,*[338] which also alludes to mental images of spiritual phenomena, something like it is written, *It stood still, but I could not discern the appearance thereof; a form was before mine eyes.*[339] And so have the Rabbis said:[340] "That is in

---

(332) In *Seder Acharei Moth* (Leviticus 17:6). (333) Berachoth 6 a. See my Hebrew commentary, p. 393. (334) Deuteronomy 32:17. (335) Genesis 10:9. See Ramban there (Vol. I, p. 147). (336) Leviticus 17:7. (337) Further, 22:19. (338) Verse 4. (339) Job 4:16. (340) Rosh Hashanah 24 b.

heaven. This includes the sun, moon, stars, and constellations. *Above.* This includes the ministering angels." Of them, too, [the worshippers] would make figures representing the Separate Intelligences[313] which are the souls of the constellations, as happened in the case of the [golden calf], as I am prepared to explain there with the help of G-d.[341]

4. ALL THAT IS IN THE WATER UNDER THE EARTH. This expression includes the demons *beneath the waters and the inhabitants thereof.*[342] And so the Rabbis have said,[343] *"All that is in the water under the earth:* this includes the reflected images [which appear in the water]." Of all of them He said, *Thou shalt not bow down unto them, nor serve them*[344] in any manner of worship whatsoever, even if the worshipper's intent is not to remove himself from the authority of the Holy One, blessed be He. Thus He has ordered all these services to be devoted to the Proper Name [of the Eternal], blessed be He.

5. 'POKEID' (VISITING) THE INIQUITY OF THE FATHERS UPON THE CHILDREN UNTO THE THIRD AND FOURTH GENERATION OF THEM THAT HATE ME. Rabbi Abraham ibn Ezra said that the meaning of the term *p'kidah* is similar to that of *z'chirah* (remembrance), just as in the verse, *And the Eternal 'pakad' Sarah,*[345] which is like: "and the Eternal remembered her." The purport [of the verse here, according to Ibn Ezra], is that G-d will postpone [punishment] of the wicked person because perhaps he will repent and beget a righteous son. But if the son walks in his father's ways, as also the third and fourth generations, their memories will be destroyed, for G-d will 'remember' [to visit punishment upon them for] what the parents have done, and He will no longer postpone their punishment. All the commentators have similarly interpreted [the above Scriptural expression]. But if this be so, the sins of the fathers will not be visited upon their

---

(341) Further, 32:1.   (342) Job 26:5.   (343) Mechilta on the verse here.
(344) Verse 5.   (345) Genesis 21:1.

children nor upon the third generation, but only on the fourth. It would have been proper then for Scripture to say that He will visit the iniquity of the fathers and their sons and of the third generation upon the fourth generation! Perhaps these commentators will say that the sense of the verse is that He remembers the iniquity of the fathers upon their sons, saying [to them], "You and your fathers have sinned." He does thus with the third and fourth generations, and then takes vengeance upon them, and never again does He visit it upon them, for He destroys them all in their iniquity.

But their explanation is not correct. Scripture mentions G-d's remembrance of all of them equally, and it does not specify that the vengeance is exacted [only] in the end, i.e., on the fourth generation. Besides, the term *p'kidah* in conjunction with the word *al* — [as it occurs here: *'pokeid' avon avoth 'al' banim*] — is not used in connection with remembrance, but rather signifies vengeance [or punishment]. Thus: *And on the day 'pokdi upakad'ti' (that I do punish, I will punish) them for their sin;*[346] *In that day 'yiphkod hashem' (the Eternal will punish) with his sore and great and strong sword leviathan the slant serpent, and leviathan the tortuous serpent, and He will slay the dragon that is in the sea;* [347] *'yiphkod hashem' (the Eternal will punish) the host of the high heaven on high.* [348] All of these are expression of vengeance and punishment.

The correct interpretation thus appears to me to be that Scripture is stating that He visits the iniquity, which the father perpetrated, upon his children, and excises them on account of the iniquity of their father, something like it is said, *Prepare ye slaughter for his children for the iniquity of their fathers.*[349] Similarly, He visits it upon the third generation if the sin of the two generations is not yet full, something like [it is said], *for the iniquity of the Amorite is not yet full.*[350] Sometimes He visits the iniquity of all three generations upon the fourth one when their

---

(346) Further, 32:34. (347) Isaiah 27:1. (348) Ibid., 24:21. (349) Ibid., 14:21. (350) Genesis 15:16.

measure [of iniquity] is filled and then he excises them. But in the fifth generation, no one is punished for the iniquity of his ancestor in the first generation. Now in the Book of Deuteronomy, [where the Ten Commandments are restated], He added a *vav* [to the expression *'al shileishim'* (unto the third generation), thus making it] *'v'al' shileishim v'al ribei'im l'sonai*.[351] But the meaning of the *vav* [there is not the usual "and"] but "or" — [" 'or' unto the third generation 'or' unto the fourth generation of them that hate me" — as explained above].

Now Rabbi Abraham ibn Ezra wrote that children's children are called "children." This is why He used the briefer term.[352] You can understand this from the terms *shileishim* (the third generation) and *ribei'im* (the fourth generation).[353] But this is not so. *Shileishim* means the third generation in that sin. [Hence, it includes only the father, his children, and his children's children.] Likewise, *ribei'im* means the fourth generation in that sin, totalling four sinners. And the verse stated in connection with the thirteen attributes of G-d, *visiting the iniquity of the fathers upon the children, and upon the children's children, unto the third generation and unto the fourth generation*,[354] is to be

---

(351) Deuteronomy 5:9. (352) Ibn Ezra tried to answer this question: Since Scripture uses the terms *shileishim* and *ribei'im* to signify the third and fourth generations, why does it not say *shni'im* for the second generation instead of using the term *banim* (children)? For this reason, Ibn Ezra interpreted *banim* as meaning "children and children's children," for they are both called *banim*. Hence, Scripture could not use the term *shni'im*, for that would have meant only the second generation after the sinner, who is the first generation. However, in fact the second *and* third generations also need to be included here. For this reason, Scripture used *banim*, which includes the children's children as well, i.e., the third generation after the sinner. Accordingly, in Ibn Ezra's opinion, *shileishim* will mean the children of the third generation, who are the fourth generation after the sinner, and *ribei'im* will mean the children of the fourth generation, who constitute the fifth generation. Ramban will differ with this entire interpretation. (353) Ibn Ezra's intent is that when you consider the words *shileishim* and *ribei'im*, this question will occur: Why does Scripture not use the term *shni'im* instead of *banim*? You must then conclude as explained in the preceding note. (354) Further, 34:7.

explained[355] as "the children's children, *who are* the third and fourth generations." It is for this reason that Moses, [when invoking the thirteen attributes] in the case of the spies, turned back [to this specific attribute as expressed here in the Ten Commandments] and said, *visiting the iniquity of the fathers upon the children, upon the third and upon the fourth generation.*[356] He did not mention "children's children," for it is all one, [i.e., "children's children" is the same as *shileishim*].

Now Scripture states [that this attribute of punishment applies only to] *those that hate Me.* That is, if the children hate G-d. If the sinner begot a righteous son, he does not bear the iniquity of the father, as [the prophet] Ezekiel has explained.[357]

From the words of our Rabbis,[358] there appears a proof to the explanation I have presented above, [i.e., that *'pokeid' the sins of the fathers,* etc., is to be understood in the sense of "visiting" or "punishing"]. From here, they have derived the principle that the [Divine] measure of good is greater than the measure of punishment, for the measure of punishment is for four generations [while that of reward is for thousands]. But if it were as the first explanation has it, [namely, that of Ibn Ezra, that *pokeid* means "remembers," thus signifying that He postpones the punishment of the sinner until the fourth generation in the hope that perhaps he will beget a righteous son], then "the measure of good" would have been greater if He postponed punishment even to the tenth generation![359]

---

(355) The Hebrew text possibly lends itself to this translation: "He — [i.e., G-d, Who is proclaiming these thirteen attributes] — is explaining that *al b'nei banim* (upon the children's children) is the *shileishim* (the third generation) and *ribei'im* (the fourth generation)." In other words, *al b'nei banim* is in apposition to *al shileishim v'al ribei'im*. (356) Numbers 14:18. (357) Ezekiel 18:20. (358) Toseph'ta Sotah 4:1. (359) According to Ibn Ezra, the phrase in question represents a measure of G-d's mercy. He does not punish the sinner immediately but "remembers" it until the third and fourth generations because perhaps he will repent and beget a righteous son. But, asks Ramban, if that were the interpretation, "the measure of Divine good" would be increased if such "punishment" were withheld even to the

It is possible that this strict measure [of punishment that is imposed on a sinner and which is felt up to the fourth generation] applies only to idolatry, for it is with regard to this prohibition that He is warning here. However, in the rest of the commandments, [the rule applies that] *every one shall die of his iniquity*.[360] You will find the hidden secret of *visiting the iniquity of the fathers upon the children* in the Book of Ecclesiastes.[361] I have already written concerning it.[362]

6. AND HE SHOWETH MERCY UNTO THE THOUSANDTH GENERATION OF THEM THAT LOVE ME AND KEEP MY COMMANDMENTS. It appears from the sense of the verse that this Divine assurance is with respect to the subject-matter of the commandments that He mentioned. He is thus saying that to those that love Him, He will show mercy to their thousandth generation. These are the ones who sacrifice their lives for Him, for they are the ones who acknowledge only the Glorious Name and His G-dship and deny all strange gods, refusing to worship them even if they are in mortal danger. They are called "the lovers [of G-d]," for this is the kind of love that we have been obligated to observe even at the sacrifice of life, just as He has said, *And thou shalt love the Eternal thy G-d with all thy heart, and with all thy soul,*

---

tenth generation! Why then did the Rabbis in the above-mentioned text speak of the Divine measure of good being manifested in punishment only to four generations when that Divine manifestation would apply even if it were extended to the tenth generation? But according to Ramban, who asserts that this verse represents a measure of G-d's *judgment* — for *pokeid* means "punishing," and the verse declares that the effects of the punishment are felt up to and including the fourth generation — that question cannot be asked. If punishment were extended to the tenth generation, it would no longer represent "a measure of good." On the contrary, it would be a harsher judgment. (360) Jeremiah 31:30. (361) The allusion is to the verse, *One generation passeth away, and another generation cometh* (Ecclesiastes 1:4), upon which the Sefer Habahir commented: "that hath come already." This means that the generation that passes away had come into the sins of the father "that had come already" in a previous generation, and the sins of the father are now visited upon the son, etc. (Ma'or V'shamesh). The mystic doctrine of the transmigration of souls is thus alluded to here. (362) Genesis 38:8 (Vol. I, pp. 469-470).

and with all thy might,[363] meaning that you should give your very life because of your love of Him, that you should not alter Him for another god, nor join Him together with a strange god. It is for this reason that [the prophet] said of Abraham, *the seed of Abraham my friend,*[364] since he risked his life in order not to worship the idols in Ur of the Chaldees.[365] The rest of the righteous are called *those that keep My commandments.*

Now many scholars[366] have explained that "His lovers" are those who worship Him without the intention of receiving a reward, just as our Sages have mentioned.[367] But I have found in the Mechilta that it is said:[368] *"Of them that love Me.* This refers to Abraham and those like him. *And those that keep My commandments.* This refers to the prophets and the elders. Rabbi Nathan says that the verse, *of them that love Me and keep My commandments,* refers to those who dwell in the Land of Israel and give their lives for the commandments.[369] 'Why are you being led out to be executed?' 'Because I have circumcised my son.' 'Why are you being led out to be burned?' 'Because I read the Torah.' 'Why are you being led out to be hanged?' 'Because I ate the unleavened bread.' 'Why are you being lashed with the whip?'[370] 'Because I took the *lulav.*'[371] And it says, *Those with which I was wounded in the house of my friends.*[372] These are the wounds which have caused me to become beloved of My

---

(363) Deuteronomy 6:5. (364) Isaiah 41:8. See Maimonides' "The Commandments," Vol. I, p. 4. (365) See Ramban on Genesis 11:28 (Vol. I, pp. 156-161). (366) So it appears from Rashi's commentary to Sotah 31 a, and from Rambam's introduction to the tenth chapter of Sanhedrin. See my Hebrew commentary here, p. 395. (367) Aboth 1:3, "Be not like servants who minister to their Master with the intention of receiving a reward; but be like the servants who minister to their Master without the intention of receiving a reward." (368) Mechilta on the verse here. (369) The reference is obviously to the persecutions by the Roman emperor Hadrian (117-138 Common Era), when the Jews in the Land of Israel were forbidden the practice of Judaism, including the study of Torah. Their determination to remain in the Land of Israel and practice their faith instead of emigrating to more peaceful lands such as Babylon, was at those times constituted as a special manifestation of their love of G-d. (370) In our Mechilta: "Why are you whipped with a hundred lashes?" (371) "The Palm-branch." See Leviticus 23:40. (372) Zechariah 13:6.

Father in heaven." Thus Rabbi Nathan explained that the love [of G-d, which is referred to in the verse before us], meant the sacrifice of life for the sake of the commandments. Now the verse here certainly refers to idolatry, for it is with reference to it that we are obligated at all times forever to suffer death rather than transgress [the law].[373] But [Rabbi Nathan] broadened the matter to include all the commandments, [such as circumcision, the study of Torah, the eating of unleavened bread on Passover, the taking of the *lulav*[371] on Succoth — as mentioned above] — because in the time of religious persecutions, we are obligated to suffer death for any of the commandments[373] [rather than transgress them], as derived from the other verse, *And ye shall not profane My holy Name*.[374] And it would also be incorrect to say of the first Sage [in the above Mechilta] — i.e., who said that [*those who love Me*] refers to Abraham, while [*those who keep My commandments*] refers to the prophets — that he is of the opinion that the prophets kept the commandments with the intention that they receive a reward! [Thus the explanation of "the many scholars"[366] mentioned above is refuted by the Mechilta.] However, there is a secret in this [Mechilta]: Abraham risked his life in love[375] — something like it is written, *mercy to Abraham*[376] — and the rest of the prophets in *g'vurah* (might).[375] Understand this.

7. 'LO THISA' (THOU SHALT NOT TAKE) THE NAME OF THE ETERNAL THY G-D IN VAIN. This verse has already been explained in the words of our Rabbis.[377] He prohibits [here] swearing by the Glorious Name in vain, such as swearing that

---

(373) Sanhedrin 74 a. See Rambam, Mishneh Torah, Hilchoth Yesodei Hatorah 5:2-3.   (374) Leviticus 22:32. For full discussion of this topic, see my translation of Maimonides' "The Commandments." Vol. II, commandment 63, pp. 61-63.   (375) Abusaula, in his commentary on the mystic passages in Ramban, explains this as follows: "Abraham's power revealed itself in mercy, while that of the rest of the prophets in the ameliorated Divine attribute of justice." See Ramban, Genesis Vol. I, p. 543.   (376) Micah 7:20. "Know that mercy is love" (Ma'or V'shamesh).   (377) Shebuoth 21 a. Maimonides' "The Commandments," Vol. II, commandment 62, pp. 60-61.

EXODUS XX, YITHRO   303

which is contrary to facts known to man, or swearing to [the truth of] a self-evident fact. For example: if one swears that a pillar of marble is of gold, or that it is of marble, and the pillar is right before them and they recognize it as such [that it is of marble].

By way of the plain meaning of Scripture, the verse also prohibits the taking of the Glorious Name in vain upon one's lips [even without an oath], the usage of the term [*lo thisa*] being similar to these expressions: *'Lo thisa' (Thou shalt not utter) a false report;* [378] *Nor 'esa' (do I take) their names upon my lips.* [379] Speaking is called *thisa*, [which literally means "lifting"], because the speaker thereby lifts up his voice. Similarly: *'masa' (The burden) of the word of the Eternal;* [380] also, *In that day 'yisa' (shall he swear), saying: I will not be a healer,* [381] which means that he will lift up his voice to say so. And in truth, this — [i.e., just taking G-d's Name in vain even without an oath] — is also forbidden, and in the language of the Sages, [382] it is called "pronouncing the Name of Heaven to no purpose." Thus our Rabbis have already said: [383] "Whence do we know that [in dedicating a beast for a sacrifice] a man should not say, 'Unto the Eternal this is a whole-offering,' or 'Unto the Eternal this is a sin-offering,' but instead he should say, 'This is a whole-offering unto the Eternal,' 'This is a sin-offering unto the Eternal'? [384] Scripture therefore says, *an offering unto the Eternal.* [385] And must we not reason by using the method of *kal vachomer*? [386] If the Torah said of him who is about to dedicate [something to Heaven], 'Let My Name not rest on it until [he has first said] *korban* (sacrifice)', is it not logical [that we must not pronounce the Name of Heaven to no purpose]!"

---

(378) Further, 23:1.   (379) Psalms 16:4.   (380) Zechariah 9:1. (381) Isaiah 3:7.   (382) Temurah 3 b.   (383) Sifra, *Vayikra* 2. (384) The reason for the prohibition is that if he mentions the Name of G-d first and he immediately changes his mind about bringing the beast as an offering, he will have taken the Name of Heaven for no purpose (Nedarim 10 b, Rashi).   (385) Leviticus 1:2. Here the word "offering" is mentioned first and then the Name of G-d follows.   (386) See *Seder Bo*, Note 208.

He has placed this commandment after the prohibition of idolatry, because just as it is proper to fear the Great and Fearful Name by not giving His Glory to another,[387] so it is fitting to give glory to His Name. He who takes it in vain profanes it, similar to that which is written, *And ye shall not swear by My Name falsely, so that thou profane not the Name of thy G-d.*[388] Just as He was stringent in the case of idolatry and wrote the punishment [for transgression], i.e., that He is *a jealous G-d, visiting the iniquity of the fathers upon the children,*[389] so did He record here the punishment *that He will not hold him guiltless.* He used this expression instead of saying that He will visit his sin upon him, [as He did in the case of idolatry], because people who swear [in vain] do not consider it a real sin, and they think it is proper that He forgive them. Therefore He said that *whosoever toucheth that shall not go unpunished.*[390] Rabbi Abraham ibn Ezra has written appropriately on this verse. [391]

Now the language of this verse, *the Name of the Eternal thy G-d,* implies that it is as if Moses was speaking, and so also in the case of all the following commandments, whereas in the first two verses[392] G-d is speaking: *I; Who brought thee out; before Me; For I; Of them that love Me and keep My commandments.* It is for this reason that our Rabbis of blessed memory have said:[393] "We heard the two commandments — *I am the Eternal thy G-d* and *Thou shalt have no other gods* — from the Almighty Himself," for they are the root of everything. But Rabbi Abraham ibn Ezra asked [concerning this tradition of the Rabbis] that Scripture says, *And G-d spoke all these words,*[394] and still more clearly it is

---

(387) See Isaiah 42:8. (388) Leviticus 19:12. (389) Verse 5. (390) Proverbs 6:29. (391) The purport of Ibn Ezra's explanation is as follows: When one swears by the Name of G-d, his intent is to imply that just as G-d is true, so is his word true. When he fails to fulfill it, it is thus tantamount to denying Him. The same reasoning applies to an oath taken in vain. (392) "First two verses." When the Ten Commandments are read in public, all the five verses contained in the first and second commandments are read as if they were one verse. Ramban's language must then be understood as: "the first two commandments." (393) Makkoth 24 a. (394) Above, Verse 1.

EXODUS XX, YITHRO

written [following the Ten Commandments], *These words the Eternal spoke unto all your assembly*,[395] and again it is written there, *And He wrote them down upon two Tablets of stone*,[396] meaning that as He said the Ten Commandments *to all your assembly,* so He wrote them down upon the Tablets![397]

I will explain to you the tradition of our Rabbis [that we heard the first two commandments from the Almighty Himself]. Surely all Israel heard the entire Ten Commandments from the mouth of G-d, as the literal meaning of Scripture indicates. But in the first two commandments, they heard the utterance of speech and understood their words even as Moses understood them. Therefore He spoke to them directly [in the first person], just as a master speaks to his servant, as I have mentioned. From then on, in the rest of the commandments, they heard a voice of speech but they did not understand it, and it became necessary for Moses to explain to them each and every commandment until they understood it from Moses. And so [the Rabbis] explained:[398] *Moses spoke, and G-d answered him by a voice.*[399] Therefore [the rest of the Ten Commandments] were addressed by G-d to Moses so that he should tell them thus. The reason [that the first two commandments were spoken to the people directly by G-d] was so that they should all be prophets in the belief of G-d, [His existence, and His Unity], and in the prohibition of idolatry, as I have explained.[400] Those are the root of the whole Torah and the commandments, just as He said, *Assemble Me the people, and I will make them hear My words, that they may learn to fear Me all the days.*[401] But in the rest of the Ten Commandments, they

---

(395) Deuteronomy 5:19. (396) *Ibid.*, 4:13. (397) According to Ibn Ezra, all these verses apparently stand in contradiction to that which the Rabbis have said, i.e., that we heard only the first two commandments from the Almighty Himself. Ramban proceeds to remove the difficulty. (398) Guide of the Perplexed, II, 33: "*Moses spoke, and G-d answered by a voice.* In explanation thereof, the Sages said in the Mechilta that Moses brought to them every commandment as he heard it." I have not been able to identify the exact quotation in the Mechilta. (399) Above, 19:19. (400) *Ibid.*, 19:9. (401) Deuteronomy 4:10.

received their explanation from the mouth of Moses after having heard *a voice of words*,[402] while in all other commandments [of the whole Torah], they believed in Moses completely.

8. REMEMBER THE SABBATH DAY, TO KEEP IT HOLY. After He commanded that we believe in the Proper Name of G-d, blessed be He — i.e., that He exists, that He is the Creator, that He understands [and watches over all that happens to man], and that He is the All-powerful[403] — and [after commanding] that we should direct both our faith in all these matters and all honor towards Him alone,[404] and He further commanded that the remembrance of His Name be done in a manner of respect,[405] He now commanded that we make in this matter a sign and perpetual remembrance to let it be known that He created everything. This is in the commandment of the Sabbath, which is a remembrance of the creation.

Now He said here, *'Remember' the Sabbath-day, to keep it holy;* and in the Book of Deuteronomy it is written, *'Observe' the Sabbath-day, to keep it holy.*[406] Our Rabbis have said with respect to these verses:[407] *"Remember* and *Observe* were both spoken with one utterance." Now the Rabbis were not so particular as to comment on the other changes of language [between the Ten Commandments written here and those in the Book of Deuteronomy. They commented only on the above-mentioned change] because their intent is to point out that *zachor* (remember) constitutes a positive commandment, i.e., that He commanded that we remember the Sabbath-day to keep it holy and that we do not forget it, [as will be explained further on]. [They considered] *shamor* (observe), on the other hand, as a

---

(402) *Ibid.*, Verse 12. (403) All these principles of truth were made evident through expressing the first commandment. See Ramban above, Verse 2. (404) This was the theme of the second commandment. (405) As opposed to taking His Name in vain, as was stated in the third commandment. (406) Deuteronomy 5:12. (407) Mechilta on the verse here. Also Shebuoth 20 b.

negative commandment, just as they have said,[408] "Wherever Scripture says *take heed ('hishamer')*, or *lest ('pen')*, or *do not ('al')*, there is a negative commandment." It warns us that we should watch it [i.e., the Sabbath] to keep it holy and that we should not profane it, [thus clearly implying both a positive commandment and a negative one with respect to the Sabbath]. It would not have been proper for Moses to change G-d's words from a positive commandment to a negative commandment. [Therefore the Rabbis were careful to point out that both *remember* and *observe* were spoken by G-d in one utterance.] However, the change in the second commandment from *'and' any manner of likeness*[409] to *any manner of likeness*,[410] omitting the *vav* (and), and then adding it [to the expression *al shileishim (unto the third generation)*, which is found here in Verse 5, rendering it there in Deuteronomy], *v'al shileishim ('and' unto the third generation)*,[411] and all such similar changes in the rest of the Ten Commandments, do not matter, for it is all one. This explanation [of why the Rabbis were particular to comment only on the change from *remember* to *observe*] will not be entertained by one who is not used to the ways of the Talmud.[412] And the Rabbis have expressly said:[413] "Women are obligated by law of the Torah to proclaim the sanctity of the Sabbath,[414] because it is said, *remember* and *observe*, thus equating them so that all those who are obligated to *observe* the Sabbath are obligated also to

---

(408) Erubin 96 a, etc. (409) Verse 4. (410) Deuteronomy 5:8. (411) *Ibid.*, Verse 9. (412) See my Hebrew commentary, p. 398, that this is a veiled criticism of Ibn Ezra, who, in his commentary on Verse 1, continued to raise difficulties on this saying of the Sages and finally concluded that "reason does not bear out all these words." To this came the retort of Ramban: "this explanation, etc." In a Ramban manuscript, I found this remark expressed in a positive manner: "This explanation will be entertained by him who is used to the ways of the Talmud." Thus Ramban avoids casting a direct aspersion on Ibn Ezra's knowledge of the ways of the Talmud. (413) Berachoth 20 b. (414) The proclaiming of the sanctity of the Sabbath is one of the six hundred thirteen commandments of the Torah. See "The Commandments," Vol. I, pp. 164-165.

remember it.[415] And since women are obligated in the observance [of the Sabbath] — for women are obligated in the observance thereof, since the observance of all negative commandments is incumbent on women, [and *shamor* (observe) the Sabbath, as was mentioned above, constitutes a negative commandment] — they are obligated also to *remember* the Sabbath. Now women would not have been bound to remember the Sabbath — for it is a positive commandment that is dependent on time and is [therefore] not incumbent on women — were it not for this analogy [of *remember* and *observe*, i.e., that all who are obligated to observe are bound to *remember*], which does make it incumbent on them.[416]

But I wonder! If *remember* and *observe* were both said by the Almighty, why were they not [both] written in the first Tablets? It is possible that in both the first and second Tablets, [only] *remember* was written, and Moses explained to Israel that *observe* was [also] said with it. This is indeed the true intent [of the saying of the Rabbis that "*remember* and *observe* were both spoken with one utterance]". And in the Midrash of Rabbi Nechunya ben Hakanah,[417] the Sages have mentioned also a great secret in this matter of *remember* and *observe*.[418] Generally, [in

---

(415) The general rule is: "The observance of all *positive* commandments that depend on time is incumbent on men but not on women, but the observance of all the *negative* commandments, whether they depend on time or not, is incumbent both on men and women" (Kiddushin 29 a). Now proclaiming the sanctity of the Sabbath is naturally dependent on time — i.e., the arrival of the Sabbath — and one would therefore say that women are not obligated to observe that commandment. But '*shamor*' (observe) *the Sabbath-day to keep it holy*, as was explained in the text, constitutes a negative commandment, and therefore applies to women as well. Now since the Torah equated *zachor* (remember) with *shamor* (observe), it follows that women are also obligated in the positive commandment of proclaiming the sanctity of the Sabbath. (416) Ramban thus brought proof to his original point that the reason the Rabbis were particular about this change from *remember* to *observe* and not about the other changes in the Decalogues, is that here, the change represents a reclassification from a positive to a negative commandment. Hence it became necessary for them to point out that both words were spoken with one Divine utterance. (417) Sefer Habahir, 182. See Vol. I, p. 24, Note 42. (418) See my Hebrew commentary, p. 399.

EXODUS XX, YITHRO

the mystic lore], remembrance is at daytime and observance is at night, and this is the intent of what the Sages used to say on the Sabbath-eve at twilight [when welcoming the Sabbath]:[419] "Come, O Bride; Come, O Bride; Come, let us go forth to meet the Sabbath, the Queen, the Bride."[420] And the Sages call the blessing that is recited [over the *Kiddush*-cup] on the Sabbath-day "the great *Kiddush*,"[421] for it is the sanctification of the Great One.[422] Understand this.

It is also true that the attribute of "remembering" is alluded to in a positive commandment and issues forth from the attribute of love to that of mercy, for he who does his master's command is beloved of him and his master shows him mercy. But the attribute of "observing" is alluded to in a negative commandment, which goes to the attribute of justice and issues forth from that of fear, for he who guards himself from doing anything which does not please his master does so out of fear for him. It is for this reason that a positive commandment is greater than a negative commandment,[423] just as love is greater than fear, for he who

---

(419) Baba Kamma 32 b. (420) "The Queen, the Bride." In our Gemara: "the Bride, the Queen." — These words of welcome constitute to this day the official reception of the Sabbath in the Synagogue service as the worshippers bid "the Sabbath bride" come in peace. (421) Pesachim 106 a. (422) Ma'or V'shamesh. (423) The question arises: Since, as Ramban writes, a positive commandment is greater than a negative one, why are all punishments for violation of the precepts specified in the Torah only for the negative commandments? This would indicate that the negative commandments are stricter than the positive ones, and indeed, the Rabbis in the Talmud do speak of the negative commandments as being stricter than the positive. Why then did Ramban write that the positive ones are greater? See my Hebrew commentary, p. 399, for lengthy discussion of this problem. In conclusion, the answer presented is as follows: Ramban did not write that a positive commandment is "stricter" than a negative one; he wrote only "greater." Fulfillment of a Divine positive commandment represents an act of "doing good," while observance of a negative precept is an expression of one's "departing from evil." Between the two — doing good and departing from evil — the former indeed represents "a greater" expression of man's active dedication to the Divine service. Hence Ramban's statement above. As for the stricter punishment of the negative commandments, see further in text and also Note 427.

fulfills and observes the will of his master with his body and his possessions is greater than he who guards himself from doing that which is not pleasing to him. This is why the Rabbis have said [424] that a positive commandment overrides a negative commandment. And it is for this reason that punishment for violation of the negative commandments is great, — the court punishing the transgressor with whipping or death — whereas no punishment at all is meted out in the case of failure to fulfill the positive commandments, excepting when one is in brazen rebelliousness, such as when he says, "I shall not take the *lulav*,[371] I shall not make fringes [on my four-cournered garment],[425] I shall not make a tabernacle."[426] In these cases, the Sanhedrin would whip him until he accepts upon himself to do them, or until he dies. [427]

In explanation of the word *zachor* (remember) — [*remember the Sabbath-day*] — Rashi wrote: "Take care always to remember the Sabbath-day, so that if a food of good quality happens to come your way, you should put it away for the Sabbath." This is a Beraitha [428] taught in the Mechilta[429] in the following way: "Rabbi Eleazar the son of Chananyah the son of Chizkiyah the son of Garon says: '*Remember the Sabbath-day, to keep it holy*, and remember it from the first day of the week, so that if a good portion happens to come your way, prepare it for the Sabbath.'" But this [Beraitha in the Mechilta] is taught in the name of a

---

(424) Shabbath 132 b, etc. (425) Numbers 15:38. (426) Leviticus 23:42. (427) This rule applies only if the time of the performance is still applicable, but if, for example, the festival of Tabernacles has passed, he is not to be punished for his failure to observe the commandment. See Maimonides', "The Commandments," Vol. II, p. 423, where it is clearly so explained. Ramban's intent is obvious: The violation of a negative commandment entails an act on the part of the sinner, which goes in direct opposition to the King's command. Hence the punishment is "stricter" than in the case of a violation of a positive commandment, which entails only failure to act in accordance with the King's desire. Hence if the time for fulfillment of the positive commandment has not yet passed and he is in open defiance of the law, the court may act against him, but if the time for fulfillment has passed, no punishment is to be imposed on him. (428) See Note 209 in *Seder Bo*. (429) Mechilta on the verse here.

single Sage and is not the final decision of the law. In the Gemara,[430] we find that the Rabbis have said: "We have been taught [in the Beraitha]: They have told about Shammai the Elder that all his life, he ate in honor of the Sabbath. How so? If he found a beautiful animal to buy, he would say, 'This one will be in honor of the Sabbath.' On the following day, if he would find a more beautiful one, he left the second one for the Sabbath, and ate the first.[431] But Hillel the Elder was guided by another principle. All his deeds were for the sake of Heaven, as it is said, *Blessed be the Eternal, day by day He beareth our burden.*[432] We have also been so taught [in another Beraitha]: The School of Shammai say that on the first day of the week, you should begin preparing for your Sabbath. And the School of Hillel say: *Blessed be the Eternal, day by day He beareth our burden.*"[432] And in another Mechilta[433] we find: "Shammai the Elder says: 'Remembering' — [*Remember the Sabbath-day*] — means remember it before it comes; 'observing' — [*Observe the Sabbath-day*][406] — means observe it when it comes. It was told of Shammai the Elder that the memory of the Shabbath never left his lips. If he bought a good article he would say, 'This is for the Sabbath;' a new garment, he would say 'This is for the Sabbath.' But Hillel the Elder was guided by another principle, for he would say, 'Let all thy deeds be done for the sake of Heaven.' " And the accepted decision is like that of the School of Hillel. [Thus it is clear that Rashi's explanation is like that of Shammai the Elder, or of the School of Shammai, while the accepted decision of law is like that of Hillel or that of the School of Hillel.][434]

---

(430) Beitza 16 a. For the word "Gemara," see Note 204 in *Seder Bo*. (431) His eating the first one thus entailed something on which the honor of the Sabbath had rested (see Rashi in Beitza 16 a). Thus all his life he ate in honor of the Sabbath. (432) Psalms 68:20. Hillel was thus confident that before the Sabbath, G-d would provide him with his proper needs (Rashi, Beitza). (433) This is the Mechilta of Rabbi Shimon ben Yochai (Hoffman edition, p. 107). For the significance of the expression *"another* Mechilta," see Vol. I, p. 603, Note 245. (434) See my Hebrew commentary, p. 400, for Mizrachi's defense of Rashi's explanation.

In line with the plain meaning of Scripture, the Rabbis have said[435] that this verse commands us that we should always remember the Sabbath on every day, so that we should neither forget it nor confuse it with the other days.[436] By always remembering the Sabbath, it will at all times remind us of the creation, and we will forever acknowledge that the universe has a Creator, and that He commanded us regarding this sign, [i.e., the Sabbath], as He has said, *for it is a sign between Me and you,* [437] this being a fundamental principle in the belief of G-d. The meaning of *l'kadsho* (to keep it holy) is that our remembrance of it should be to the end that it be holy to us, just as He said, *and call the Sabbath a delight, the sacred of the Eternal honorable.* [438] The purport of this is that the resting thereon should be ours because it is a holy day, [which enables us] to turn away from our mental preoccupations and the vanities of the times and instead to give delight to our souls in the ways of G-d, and go to the Sages and to the prophets to hear the words of G-d. This is just as it is said, *Wherefore wilt thou go to him* [the prophet] *today? it is neither New Moon nor Sabbath,*[439] for such was their custom. And so did our Rabbis of blessed memory say:[440] "From this you learn that on the New Moon and on the Sabbath one must go [to the prophet]." This is the reason [that the Torah commanded us concerning the resting of cattle on the Sabbath], i.e., in order that we should harbor no thought of it in our hearts. And it is for this reason that the Rabbis, of blessed memory, have said[441] that the Sabbath is equal in importance to all the commandments in the Torah, just as they have said with reference to idolatry, [441] because on the Sabbath we testify to all the fundamentals of the faith — creation, providence, and prophecy. And in the Mechilta

---

(435) In the Mechilta quote further on. See Note 442. (436) If each of the days of the week were to have a name of its own — such as Sunday, Monday, etc. — then the Sabbath-day is confused with the other days. But if we refer to the days of the week in relation to the Sabbath — "the first day after the Sabbath," etc. — then the Sabbath-day stands unique. (437) Further 31:13. (438) Isaiah 58:13. (439) II Kings 4:23. (440) Rosh Hashanah 16 b. (441) Chullin 5 a. See also Vol. I, p. 332.

EXODUS XX, YITHRO 313

we find:[442] "Rabbi Yitzchak says: 'You should not count [the days of the week] as others count them. Rather you should count them with reference to the Sabbath.'" The meaning of this is that other nations count the days of the week in such a manner that each is independent of the other. Thus they call each day by a separate name or by a name of the ministers [in heaven, such as Sunday, which means "sun's day," Monday which means "moon's day," etc.], or by any other names which they call them. But Israel counts all days with reference to the Sabbath: "one day after the Sabbath," "two days after the Sabbath." This is of the essence of the commandment which we have been obligated always to remember the Sabbath every day [of the week]. This is the literal meaning of the verse, and so did Rabbi Abraham ibn Ezra interpret it.

And I say further that this is the intent of Shammai the Elder's interpretation [mentioned above],[433] who explained the command *remember* as meaning "[remember the Sabbath] before it comes." That is to say, we should by no means forget it. [By counting the days of the week with reference to the Sabbath, forgetting it will thus be impossible.] But in the Beraitha [quoted above], they also mentioned a degree of his piety, i.e., that he would remember the Sabbath even in his eating, for all his life he ate in honor of the Sabbath. Now Hillel himself agreed to the interpretation of Shammai [that we are to count the days of the week with reference to the Sabbath], but in food-matters he followed another principle, for all of his deeds were for the sake of Heaven, and he trusted in G-d that He would provide him with a better portion for the Sabbath than that of all the other days of the week.

However, our Rabbis have yet another Midrash on the word *l'kadsho* (to keep it holy),[443] namely, that we are to sanctify it by utterance of words. This is similar in usage to the verse, *And ye shall hallow the fiftieth year,*[444] which requires the sanctification

---

(442) Mechilta on the verse here. (443) In the Mechilta mentioned further in the text. (444) Leviticus 25:10.

of the court, i.e., that they say of the Jubilee year, "It is hallowed! It is hallowed!"[445] Here too He commanded that we remember the Sabbath-day by proclaiming its sanctity.[446] And so the Rabbis have said in the Mechilta:[442] *"To keep it holy.* Sanctify it by reciting a blessing. Based on this verse, the Rabbis have said: 'On its entrance, proclaim the sanctity of the Sabbath over wine. But from this verse, I know only the sanctification for the day. Whence do we know that this applies also for the night? [We know it] from the words of Scripture, *And ye shall keep the Sabbath."*[447] This is "the sanctification of the [Sabbath-] day" [to which the Rabbis refer].[448] It is incumbent upon us by law of the Torah, and is not a mere *asmachta.*[449] Thus the Rabbis have said:[448] "Women are obligated by law of the Torah to proclaim the sanctity of the day." Now this really refers to the sanctification recited at night, for all things requiring sanctification need to be done only once at the time of their entrance, such as the sanctification of the New Moon and the sanctification of the Jubilee year. However, the duty to recite it on the day itself is but an *asmachta,*[449] and [the *kiddush* at daytime] contains no reference to the holiness of the day — [since only a benediction over the wine is recited] — because it is sufficient that we proclaimed the sanctity of the Sabbath once at its entrance. So also is the recital [of the sanctity of the Sabbath] over wine only an *asmachta*[449] and is not at all a fixed part of the commandment itself.

And in the Gemara Pesachim,[450] the Rabbis have said: *"Remember the Sabbath-day, to keep it holy.* That is, remember it

---

(445) Rosh Hashanah 8 b, Rashi. (446) See Maimonides', "The Commandments," Vol. I, pp. 164-165. (447) Further, 31:14. Since the word "day" is not mentioned in this verse, as it is in the verse before us, *Remember the Sabbath-'day' to keep it holy,* it indicates that the proclamation of the Sabbath is to be observed at its entrance at night. See also further in the text here for a more correct version of this Mechilta as Ramban explains it. (448) Berachoth 20 b. (449) Literally: "Support." Where a law is actually of Rabbinic origin but a Scriptural text is quoted as a support, it is called an *asmachta.* (450) Pesachim 106 a.

over wine at its entrance. From this, I know only that it be done at daytime. Whence do we know that it must be done at night? It is from the Scriptural words, *the Sabbath-'day.'* [On the version of the Beraitha, the Sages of the Gemara asked] : 'This Tanna[451] is seeking to find a basis for the sanctification at night, and he mentions a verse which speaks of the day! Besides, the main sanctification is at nighttime!' Rather, you must learn [the above Beraitha] in this way: *'Remember the Sabbath-day, to keep it holy.* That is, remember it over wine at its entrance. From this, I know only that the Sabbath is to be sanctified at night.' Whence do we know that it must be done at daytime? It is from the Scriptural words, *the Sabbath day."* In a similar way we will explain the Mechilta [mentioned above to make it read as follows] : "From this, I know only that the sanctification of the Sabbath is to be done at night, which is the main *kiddush.* Whence do we know that it must be done at daytime, etc.," this being but a mere *asmachta.*[449] And from there you will learn that this commandment [of proclaiming the sanctity of the Sabbath] is derived from the word *l'kadsho* (to sanctify it), while the expression, *Remember the Sabbath-day,* constitutes the commandment to remember it continually every day, as we have explained. However, in the number of two hundred and forty-eight positive commandments that we have been commanded to observe, both aspects are included in the one commandment of remembering the Sabbath. Know this.

9. SIX DAYS SHALT THOU LABOR, AND DO ALL THY WORK. The term "labor" applies to work which is not for the needs of the body, such as cooking and the like, something like it is said: *and in all manner of labor in the field;*[452] *when thou tillest the ground;*[453] *and ye shall be tilled and sown,*[454] and as I will yet explain with the help of G-d.[455] It is for this reason that He said: "Six days you shall work the ground *and do all thy work*

---

(451) A Rabbi mentioned in a Mishnah or Beraitha. (452) Above, 1:14. (453) Genesis 4:12. (454) Ezekiel 36:9. (455) Leviticus 23:7.

which is for your physical needs and your benefit, something like, *bake that which you will bake*.[456] But on the Sabbath, you shall not do any kind of work, *thou, thy son, nor thy daughter* — i.e., the minors." Thus He has warned us against our minor children doing work on the Sabbath with our knowledge and consent. *Nor thy manservant, nor thy maidservant* means the servants who have undergone circumcision and immersion,[457] who are obligated to observe all laws of the Sabbath just as Israelites, even as He said in the Book of Deuteronomy, *that thy manservant and thy maidservant may rest as well as thou*.[458] In all [other] commandments of the Torah, observance is incumbent upon them as it is upon women, as is explained in the words of our Rabbis.[459] Now it would have been proper that He warn them directly, for they themselves are duty-bound to observe the Sabbath. Scripture, however, speaks to us because the servants are in our possession, thus telling us that their resting is incumbent upon us and that if they are not hindered from doing work, we will be punished on account of them. Besides, it is with Israel that G-d speaks in all of the Ten Commandments, [and for this reason, the command is not given directly to the servants].

10. NOR THY STRANGER THAT IS WITHIN THY GATES. In line with the plain meaning of Scripture, "the stranger of the gate" is always the *geir toshav*,[460] who came to dwell in "the gates of our cities" and has taken upon himself the Seven Laws of the Noachides.[461] It is he who is called "the stranger who eats the unlawfully-slaughtered animal," of whom Scripture says, *thou mayest give it to the stranger that is within thy gates, that he may eat it*.[462] Therefore, the commandment [prohibiting work on the Sabbath] was not directed to him so that Scripture would be

---

(456) Above, 16:23. (457) And are thus *b'nei b'rith* (children of the covenant). See Mechilta here. See also above, Note 79. (458) Deuteronomy 5:14. (459) Chagigah 4 a, etc. And see Note 415 above. (460) Literally: "resident alien," so called because he was permitted to dwell within the Land of Israel. The conditions under which he becomes a *geir toshav* are described here in the text. (461) See Vol. I, p. 417, Note 148, and see also in index there under "Noachides." (462) Deuteronomy 14:21.

saying: "Do not do any work on it, the home-born or the stranger." Instead, it is we who are commanded that he do no work for our benefit, just as [we are commanded about] our minors and the cattle, but this commandment is not incumbent upon him and he may do work for himself on the Sabbath. The verse which states, *so that the son of thy handmaid, and the stranger, may rest,*[463] speaks of the righteous proselyte who has become Jewish and embraced our Torah, which has commanded him concerning the Sabbath and all the rest of the commandments as well, as He has said, *One law and one ordinance shall be both for you, and for the stranger that sojourneth with you;*[464] *both for the stranger, and for him that is born in the land.*[465]

However, we have found in the words of our Rabbis that they have interpreted it in the opposite manner. Thus they have said[466] that by way of the plain meaning of Scripture, *thy stranger that is within thy gates* means the righteous proselyte, and ceasing from work [on the Sabbath] is incumbent upon him as it is upon us. The verse, *so that the son of thy handmaid, and the stranger, may rest,*[463] includes the uncircumcised *geir toshav.*[460] The Rabbis' intent in so explaining the verses is that first, [i.e., right here in the Ten Commandments], "the stranger" warned is the proselyte who has been circumcised, who is obligated in the observance of the Sabbath as we are. The second verse — [further, 23:12] — includes the uncircumcised [*geir toshav*]. Therefore, he is likened there to the cattle, as the verse says, *that thine ox and thine ass may have rest, and the son of thy handmaid, and the stranger, may rest.*[463] Thus He commanded us concerning the resting of all of them alike that they should not work for us, but they may do [work] for themselves if they so wish. Similarly, the servant and the stranger mentioned in the Ten Commandments are alike, being obligated in the observance of all laws of the Sabbath as we are, even as He has said, *that thy manservant and thy maidservant may rest as well as thou.*[458]

(463) Further, 23:12. (464) Numbers 15:16. (465) *Ibid.*, 9:14. (466) Mechilta on the verse here.

11. THE ETERNAL BLESSED THE SABBATH-DAY, AND SANCTIFIED IT. The verse is stating that the Sabbath-day will be blessed and hallowed because He has commanded to bless it and glorify it by remembering it. Therefore, He commanded us to rest thereon so that the day will be sacred to us, and that we should not do any work on it. And Rabbi Abraham ibn Ezra wrote that G-d blessed this day and sanctified it by endowing it with a greater capacity to enable the soul to receive additional wisdom than on all of the other days. I have already written concerning this matter by way of the Truth, [the mystic lore of the Cabala], on the verse in *Vayechulu*.[467] From there, you will succeed in understanding that the expression *ki sheisheth yamim asa hashem* — [literally: "for six days the Eternal made"][468] — is not missing the letter *beth*, [which would make the verse read: "for *in* six days the Eternal made"]. Rather, the sense of the verse is that G-d made six days[469] *and on the seventh day He ceased from work and rested.*[470]

12. HONOR THY FATHER. Having finished all that we are obligated towards the Creator Himself and His glory, He turns now to command us about those matters which concern created beings. He begins with the father, for in relation to his offspring, he is akin to a creator, being partner with Him in the forming of the child.[471] G-d is our first Father, and he who begets it [i.e., the child] is our last male parent. This is why He said in the Book of Deuteronomy, [*Honor thy father... as the Eternal thy G-d*

---

(467) Genesis 2:1. Ramban's discussion of the mystic nature of the blessing of the Sabbath is found there on Verse 3 (Vol. I, p. 60). (468) Here in the verse before us, which is generally translated: "for *in* six days the Eternal made." (469) Ramban is hinting here to what he wrote on Genesis 2:3, i.e., that the six days of creation allude to the six thousand years which are "all the days of the world." See Vol. I, pp. 61-64. Thus the sense of the verse here is clearly, "for G-d made six days," and not, "for *in* six days G-d made." The six days represent the six milleniums of world-history, while the seventh millenium "will be wholly a Sabbath and will bring rest for life everlasting" (*ibid.*, p. 64). (470) Further, 31:17. (471) Kiddushin 30 b: "There are three partners in man: the Holy One, blessed be He, his father and his mother."

commanded thee].[472] That is, "just as I have commanded you concerning My honor, so do I command you concerning the honor of those who have joined Me in your formation." Now Scripture has not explained [the nature of the honor we are to give our parents], for it may be derived from the honor mentioned above that we owe to our first Father, blessed be He. Thus, one is to acknowledge [his male parent] as his father and not deny him, saying of another man that he is his father. Nor should he serve him because of his estate or any other benefit he hopes to derive from him. Nor should he take his father's name and swear "by the life of my father" in vain or falsely. There are other matters which are included within the term "honor," for we are commanded in every aspect thereof, and they are explained in the words of our Rabbis.[473] The Sages have already said[474] that honoring parents has been likened to honoring G-d.

Now since this commandment refers to creatures on the earth, He has designated its reward to be prolongation of life on earth which He will give us. But in the opinion of our Rabbis,[475] the purport of the verse is *"that thy days may be long* and *upon the Land."* [It thus expresses two declarations]: He promises that our lives will be prolonged by observing this commandment — i.e., that G-d will fulfill our days in this world and they will be prolonged in the World to Come, which is unending — and that our dwelling will forever be on the good earth[476] which He will give us. And in the Book of Deuteronomy, He expressly stated it: *that thy day may be long, and that it may go well with thee, upon the Land which the Eternal thy G-d giveth thee.*[472] Thus they are two promises.

13. THOU SHALT NOT MURDER. THOU SHALT NOT COMMIT ADULTERY. THOU SHALT NOT STEAL. He is stating: "Now I have commanded you to acknowledge in thought and in

---

(472) Deuteronomy 5:16.   (473) "What is honoring [one's parents? It entails] providing them with food and drink, raiment and warmth, and guiding their footsteps [when they are old and infirm]" (Kiddushin 31 b). (474) *Ibid.,* 30 b.   (475) *Ibid.,* 39 b.   (476) A reference to eternal life.

deed that I am the Creator of all, and to honor parents because they joined [Me] in your formation. If so, guard against destroying the work of My hands and spilling the blood of man, whom I have created to honor Me and acknowledge Me in all these matters.[477] And do not commit adultery with your fellow-man's wife, because you will thereby destroy the principle of honoring parents, [causing the children] to deny the truth and acknowledge falsehood. They will not know their fathers and will thus give their honor to another, just as the idol-worshippers do, *who say to a block of wood, 'thou art my father,'*[478] and they do not know their Father who created them out of nothing." After that, He warned against stealing a human being,[479] for that too brings about a similar [disintegration of values].[480]

With respect to their stringency and penalties, the order of the commandments is as follows: after idolatry comes bloodshed, and after that adultery, and then stealing of a human being and false testimony and robbery;[481] and he who does not covet, will never harm his neighbor. Thus, He completed all obligations that a person owes towards his neighbor. After that, [in the *Seder* of *Mishpatim* which follows], He will explain the ordinances in detail, for he who has been found guilty in any suit to pay his neighbor will pay the amount he is so obligated if he does not covet or desire that which is not his.

Rabbi Abraham ibn Ezra wrote[482] [of the commandment, *Thou shalt not covet thy neighbor's house... thy neighbor's wife, nor his manservant, nor his maidservant,* etc.], that Scripture adopted a normal course of life. First, it mentioned the neighbor's house, for an enlightened person will first acquire a house, and then marry a woman to bring her to his house, and only afterwards will he acquire a manservant or a maidservant. But in the Book of

---

(477) See Ramban at end of *Seder Bo*. (478) Jeremiah 2:27. (479) Mechilta on the verse here. (480) See Ramban further, 21:15. (481) Since coveting also relates to action by robbery, Ramban mentions here "robbery" although the tenth commandment speaks of coveting. (482) In his introduction to the Ten Commandments.

Deuteronomy,[483] it mentions the wife first, because young men desire to marry first [before they acquire a house]. It may be [484] that because the coveting of a neighbor's wife is the greatest sin of all things mentioned in that verse, [it is listed first].

Thus, of the Ten Commandments, there are five which refer to the glory of the Creator and five are for the welfare of man, for [the fifth commandment], *Honor thy father,* is for the glory of G-d, since it is for the glory of the Creator that He commanded that one honor one's father who is a partner in the formation of the child. Five commandments thus remain for the needs and welfare of man.

In some commandments, He mentioned their recompense, and in others He did not. Thus, in the second commandment, He mentioned *a jealous G-d;*[485] in the third, *for the Eternal will not hold him guiltless;*[486] in the fifth, *that thy days may be long.*[487] But in the others, He mentioned neither punishment [for transgression], nor reward [for fulfillment]. The reason for this is that the last five commandments deal with the welfare of man, and *behold, His reward is with Him, and His recompense before Him.*[488] But in the case of idolatry, a warning of punishment is needed because of its great stringency, involving as it does the glory of the Creator.

It appears to me that His saying *a jealous G-d*[485] refers to the commandment, *Thou shalt have no other gods,*[489] and that His saying, *And He showeth mercy*[490] refers to *I am the Eternal,*[491] for punishment comes for [transgressing] the negative commandments, and reward for [fulfillment of] the positive commandments. [He did not mention the reward immediately in the first commandment because] the acceptance of the Kingdom of G-d, [as mentioned in the first commandment], and the

---

(483) Deuteronomy 5:18. (484) This is Ramban's own comment. (485) Verse 5. (486) Verse 7. (487) Verse 12. (488) Isaiah 40:10. In other words, the recompense for the last five commandments is self-evident. If man observes them, his society will prosper, and if not, the whole fabric of society will collapse. (489) Verse 3. (490) Verse 6. (491) Verse 2.

admonition against the worship of anything besides Him, constitute one subject. Therefore, He first finished that entire matter and then warned the idol-worshipper of punishment, and then He assured reward for he who fulfills the commandments.

He warned of punishment in case of a vain oath, *the Eternal will not hold him guiltless,*[486] but He mentioned no reward [for observing it]. For profaning the Sabbath, He mentioned neither excision [492] nor any other punishment, neither did He mention a reward for him *that keepeth the Sabbath from profaning it.* [493] This is because it is included in the first two commandments. He who observes the Sabbath testifies to the Creation and acknowledges his belief in the commandment, *I am the Eternal,* while he who profanes the Sabbath denies the Creation and admits the eternity of the universe, thereby denying the commandment, *I am the Eternal.* Thus, [the punishment for profaning the Sabbath] is included in: *a jealous G-d, visiting the iniquity,*[485] while [the reward for he who keeps the Sabbath] is included in the verse, *And He showeth mercy unto the thousandth generation.* [490] In the fifth commandment, which concerns the honor due to parents, He mentioned the reward because it is a positive commandment, [and as mentioned above, reward is for fulfillment of the positive commandments].

With reference to the writing on the Tablets of law, it would appear that the first five commandments were on one Tablet, for they are for the glory of the Creator, as I have mentioned, and the second five commandments were on another Tablet. Thus there were five opposite five, something like the Rabbis mentioned in the Book of Creation:[494] "With ten emanations,[495] intangible, as is the number of ten fingers, five opposite five, and the Covenant of the Unity placed directly in the middle." From this it will be made clear to you why there were two Tablets, for up to *Honor*

---

(492) Further, 31:14. (493) Isaiah 56:2. (494) Sefer Yetzirah 1:3. This is one of the earliest books on the Cabala. Saadia Gaon was among the first great scholars to write a commentary on it. It is written in profound symbolic language. (495) In our version of Sefer Yetzirah: "Ten Emanations"; the word "with" is not present.

thy father, it corresponds to the Written Torah, and from there on it corresponds to the Oral Torah. It would appear that it is this that our Rabbis, of blessed memory, have alluded to in saying [496] that the two Tablets correspond to heaven and earth, [497] to a groom and bride, [498] to the two friends [of the groom and bride], and to the two worlds [this world and the World to Come]. All these constitute one allusion, and the person learned in the mystic lore of the Cabala will understand the secret.

15. AND ALL THE PEOPLE PERCEIVED THE THUNDERINGS... 16. AND THEY SAID UNTO MOSES. In the opinion of the commentators, [499] this happened after the Giving of the Torah. It is with reference to this that Scripture says, *And ye came near unto me, even all the heads of your tribes, and your elders, and ye said: Behold, the Eternal our G-d hath shown us His Glory,* etc. *If we hear the Voice of the Eternal our G-d any more, then we shall die.* [500]

But such is not my opinion, for it says here, *but let not G-d speak with us,* [501] and it does not say "any more." Besides, Moses said here to the people, *Fear not,* [502] and there it is said, *They have well said all that they have spoken.* [503] Moreover, here it is told that they feared only the thunderings, the lightnings, and the smoking mountain, and there it is said that they feared the speaking of the Divine Presence, for they said, *For who is there of all flesh, that hath heard the Voice of the living G-d, speaking out of the midst of the fire, as we have, and lived?* [504] Again, here it is said, *And Moses drew near unto the thick darkness,* [505] but it does not say that "he entered into it." [If the events narrated in this

---

(496) Shemoth Rabbah 41:7. (497) Since the Torah was the instrument with which the world was created, the first Tablet containing our duties towards G-d thus corresponds to heaven, while the second Tablet which states our duties to man corresponds to earth (Eitz Yoseph, *ibid.*) (498) The symbol is that of the bestower and the bestowed. Heaven is the bestower and earth is the bestowed. So also is the relationship between G-d and man. (499) Ibn Ezra in Verse 16. (500) Deuteronomy 5:20-22. (501) Verse 16. (502) Verse 17. (503) Deuteronomy 5:25. (504) *Ibid.*, Verse 23. (505) Verse 18.

section of the Torah happened after the Revelation, it should have said that he came "into the midst of the cloud," as it says further on in 24:18.]

The correct interpretation regarding this section of the Torah and the [entire] order of events pertaining to the Revelation appears to me to be as follows: *And all the people perceived... And they said unto Moses* — all this happened before the Revelation. Now at first, [in Chapter 19], Scripture mentioned in sequence all the words of G-d that were commanded to Moses regarding the setting of a boundary to Mount Sinai and the admonition given to the people.[506] This is followed [at the beginning of Chapter 20] by the Ten Commandments, and now Scripture refers back and mentions the words of the people to Moses, relating that from the moment they had perceived the thunderings and the lightnings, they moved backwards and stood afar off, further away from the boundary of the mountain that Moses had set for them.

The order of events [on the day of the Revelation] was thus as follows: In the morning, there were thunderings and lightnings and the loud voice of the horn,[507] but the Divine Presence had not yet come down on the mountain, something like it is written, *And a great and strong wind rent the mountains, and broke in pieces the rocks before the Eternal; but the Eternal was not in the wind.*[508] *And the people that were in the camp* — i.e., in their place of encampment — *trembled.*[507] But Moses encouraged them and brought them forth *towards G-d... and they stood at the nether part of the mount.*[509] While they were standing there at the nether part of the mount in anticipation, *the Eternal descended upon the mount in fire and the smoke thereof ascended*[510] *unto the heart of heaven, with darkness, cloud, and thick darkness.*[511] The mountain itself trembled[510] and quivered as mountains do in an earthquake called *zalzalah,*[512] or even more

---

(506) Above, 19:24. (507) *Ibid.,* Verse 16. (508) I Kings 19:11. (509) Above, 19:17. (510) *Ibid.,* Verse 18. (511) Deuteronomy 4:11. (512) An Arabic word meaning earthquake. In another Ramban manuscript, the reading is *chalchalah.*

than that. And so it is written, *What aileth thee... ye mountains, that ye skip like rams; ye hills, like young sheep?*[513] This is not a figure of speech, just as the preceding verse — *The sea saw it, and fled; the Jordan turned backwards*[514] — is not a mere figure of speech. Meanwhile, the voice of the horn waxed louder and louder.[515] Then the people saw what was happening, and they moved backwards and stood further away from the boundary [that Moses had set for them]. They all said to Moses that G-d should not speak with them at all lest they die, for *by reason of the vision,* their pains came upon them and they retained no strength,[516] and if they would hear the Divine utterance, they would die. Moses, however, encouraged them, and he said to them, *Fear not.*[502] And they heard him, *and the people stood from afar off*[505] at their positions, for in spite of all his words, they did not want to come near the boundary [he had set for them]. *And Moses drew near unto the thick darkness*[505] but did not come into it, and then G-d uttered the Ten Commandments. Now following the Ten Commandments, Scripture did not mention here what the elders said to Moses, for it wanted to explain the commandments and the ordinances in succession. But in the Book of Deuteronomy, Moses mentioned that after the Ten Commandments [were given], all the heads of the tribes and their elders approached him and said to him, "*If we hear the Voice of the Eternal our G-d any more, then we shall die,*[517] for we have estimated our powers [and found] that we could not stand any more the burden of the word of the Eternal G-d." They had thought that G-d wanted to relate to them all the commandments [of the Torah], and therefore they said, *Go thou near, and hear all that the Eternal our G-d may say; and thou shalt speak unto us all that the Eternal our G-d may speak unto thee; and we will hear it, and do it.*[518] And the Holy One, blessed be He, agreed to their words, and He said, *They have well said all that they have*

---

(513) Psalms 114:6. See Pesachim 118 a that this verse refers to the time of the Giving of the Torah. (514) *Ibid.,* Verse 3. (515) Above 19:19. (516) See Daniel 10:16. (517) Deuteronomy 5:22. (518) *Ibid.,* Verse 24.

spoken,[519] for such was His desire to proclaim to them only the Ten Commandments, and their fear appeared correct to Him.

'VAYANU'U.' In the opinion of our Rabbis,[520] the term *nu'a* here can only denote reeling to and fro, and so it says, *The earth 'no'a tanu'a' (reeleth to and fro) like a drunken man.*[521] If so, the verse is stating [two things]: that the people were shaken up, and that out of their fear, they retreated farther backwards and stood afar off. But in the opinion of "the masters of the plain meaning of Scripture,"[522] *vayanu'u* means that " 'they moved' backwards from their place and stood from afar," the usage of the word being similar to: *'na' (a fugitive) and a wanderer shalt thou be in the earth,*[523] and so also: *'vay'ni'eim' (and He made them wander) in the wilderness.*[524]

16. BUT LET NOT G-D SPEAK WITH US. The Rabbi [Moshe ben Maimon] noted in the Moreh Nebuchim[525] that Onkelos translated *but let not G-d speak with us* as, "Let not aught be spoken to us from before G-d." However, he did not paraphrase in [a similar manner] in other such places, for he translated literally, *And G-d spoke all these words,*[526] and so also in all places where it says, *And the Eternal spoke unto Moses!*[527] Now the reason for Onkelos' paraphrasing it here, [according to Maimonides], was that even though all Israel heard the first commandment,[528] their capacity for comprehending it was unlike that of Moses our teacher.[529] But if [Maimonides' opinion is correct], why did

---

(519) *Ibid.*, Verse 25. (520) Mechilta on the verse here, and mentioned partly in Rashi. (521) Isaiah 24:20. (522) The allusion is to Ibn Ezra, who interprets it so. (523) Genesis 4:12. (524) Numbers 32:13. (525) Guide of the Perplexed, II, 33. (526) Above, Verse 1. (527) *Ibid.*, 6:10, etc. (528) Reference is to the first two commandments, for we heard both of them from the Almighty Himself, as explained above. See also above, Note 392. (529) Therefore, with reference to Moses, Onkelos translated literally, *And G-d spoke,* for Moses achieved the highest comprehension humanly possible in prophecy, and therefore he received the word of G-d directly. But where the people were concerned, since their comprehension was of a far lesser degree, Onkelos translated, "from before G-d."

Onkelos translate literally, *For I have talked with you from heaven,*[530] when he should have rendered it, "It was spoken to you from before Me!" Similarly in the Book of Deuteronomy, he translated literally: *These words the Eternal spoke unto all your assembly,*[531] [and he did not paraphrase it]! So also he translated literally their words, *and we have heard His Voice,* [532] which he rendered as follows: "we have heard the voice of His word; this day we have seen that G-d speaks with man!" Likewise he translated literally, *The Eternal spoke with you face to face.*[533] Moreover, [with reference to Moses] he translated, *And G-d answered him by a voice*[515] as "and from before G-d he was answered by a voice!" [Here Onkelos paraphrased it with regard to Moses himself, which according to Maimonides he should have translated literally!] In fact, such usage already occurs in the Torah with reference to Moses himself! Thus: *And he heard the Voice speaking*[534] *unto him,*[535] which Onkelos translated as "being spoken." So also in the verse, *The pillar of the cloud descended, and stood at the door of the Tent, and He spoke with Moses,*[536] which Onkelos translated, "and it was spoken!"

But the reason for Onkelos' translating here, ["Let not aught be spoken to us from before G-d"], is clear. In the entire Revelation, we find Israel hearing G-d's word only *out of the midst of the fire,*[532] and this is what they comprehended. Similarly, *that I have talked with you from heaven*[530] means, by way of the Truth, "from out of the midst of heaven," and it is identical with *out of the midst of the fire.*[532] The purport thereof has already been explained.[537] Now when Onkelos saw here the expression, *but let not G-d speak with us,* [which indicates *direct* revelation], and no "partition" is mentioned, he did not deem it fit to translate

---

(530) Further, Verse 19. Now here it refers to G-d speaking to the people, and yet Onkelos did not paraphrase it!   (531) Deuteronomy 5:19.   (532) *Ibid.,* Verse 21.   (533) *Ibid.,* Verse 5.   (534) The Hebrew is *midabeir,* not *m'dabeir* (speaking), and Rashi markedly comments that it means "uttering itself" and Moses heard it of himself. It is out of reverence for G-d that this expression is used.   (535) Numbers 7:89.   (536) Further, 33:9.   (537) Above, 19:20.

literally. [That would have implied that in their comprehension of the Revelation, they were equal to Moses], and since in his language [i.e., Aramaic] there is no epithet for the word *Elokim,* [538] he therefore negated here any direct communication to them, [and translated, "Let not aught *be spoken* to us *from before G-d*"].

Now the amazing thing in Onkelos' wisdom is that in the Revelation on Mount Sinai, he did not mention "the Glory of G-d," or "the word of G-d," but instead translated: "Behold, I will reveal Myself to you;" [539] "G-d will reveal Himself in the sight of all the people upon Mount Sinai;" [540] "because He revealed Himself upon it;" [541] "And G-d revealed Himself upon Mount Sinai." [542] He did not translate, "and the Glory of G-d revealed itself," as he translated the expression, *the mountain of G-d,* [543] at the beginning [of this book] as "the mountain upon which the Glory of G-d revealed itself." Likewise, Onkelos did so regarding this descent [upon Mount Sinai]; wherever the Proper Name of G-d [i.e., the Tetragrammaton] is mentioned, [he did not translate "the Glory of G-d"]. But when Scripture mentioned *Elokim,* such as *towards 'ha'Elokim,'* [544] he translated "towards the word of G-d." Similarly, he translated *'ha'Elokim' is come* [545] as "the Glory of G-d has revealed itself to you," and he did not render it "G-d has revealed Himself to you." Likewise, [he translated *where 'ha'Elokim' was* [546] as] "where the Glory of G-d was." And so also he translated [*'v'ha'Elokim' answered him by a voice* [547] as] "and from before G-d, he was answered with a voice." All this is clear and lucid to him who comprehends our words explained above. [548] Similarly, I have seen in carefully-edited texts of Onkelos that he

---

(538) Throughout his translation, Onkelos does not distinguish between *Elokim* and the Tetragrammaton. He translates both alike: *Ado-noy.*
(539) Above, 19:9. The verse reads: *Behold, I come unto thee.*
(540) Ibid., Verse 11. the verse reads: *the Eternal will come down.*
(541) Ibid., Verse 18. The verse reads: *because the Eternal descended upon it.* (542) Ibid., Verse 20. The verse reads: *And the Eternal came down.*
(543) Above, 3:1. (544) Ibid., 19:17. (545) Verse 17. (546) Further, Verse 18. (547) Above, 19:19. (548) Ibid., Verse 20. Also in Vol. I, pp. 550-552.

EXODUS XX, YITHRO

translated literally the verse, *And Moses went up into 'har ha'Elokim' (the mount of G-d).* [549] Since it was after the Giving of the Torah, [he translated even the name *Elokim* literally, and he did not render it, "and Moses went up into the mountain upon which the Glory of G-d revealed itself"], and so it is written, *And they set forward from the mount of the Eternal.* [550]

17. FOR G-D IS COME IN ORDER TO 'NASOTH' YOU. "I.e., to make you 'great' in the world, [to ensure] that you obtain a name amongst the nations [because of the fact] that He in His Glory revealed Himself to you. *Nasoth* is a term for 'exalting' and 'greatness,' just as in the verses: *Lift up a 'neis' (an ensign);* [551] *'k'neis' (as an ensign) on a hill,* [552] which is so called because it is high." Thus Rashi's language. But this is not correct. [553] Instead, it is possible that Moses is saying that "it is in order to get you 'accustomed' to have faith in Him that G-d is come. Since He has shown you the Revelation of the Divine Presence, your faith in Him has entered your hearts to cleave to Him, and your souls will never be separated from it forever. *And that His fear may be before you* when you see that He alone is G-d in heaven and upon the earth, you will have great fear of Him." It may be that Moses is saying that "the fear of *this great fire* [554] will be before you, and you will not sin because of your fear of it." And the word *nasoth* is similar in expression to the verses: *And he* [David] *assayed to go, but could not, for he had 'nisah' (tried) it. And David said unto Saul: I cannot go with these; for I have not 'nisithi' (tried) them,* [555] something like "accustomed."

The Rabbi [Moshe ben Maimon] has said in the Moreh Nebuchim [556] that Moses said to the people, "*Fear not,* because the purpose of that which you have seen is that when the Eternal

---

(549) Further, 24:13. (550) Numbers 10:33. (551) Isaiah 62:10. (552) *Ibid.*, 30:17. (553) Rashi connects *nasoth* with *neis* (ensign, banner). Ramban objects to this because in his opinion, the root of the word *nasoth* is *nasoh* (try, accustom). (554) Deuteronomy 5:22. (555) I Samuel 17:39. (556) Guide of the Perplexed, III, 24. The Hebrew text here follows Al Charizi's translation, and not that of Ibn Tibbon.

G-d, in order to demonstrate your faithfulness to Him, will test you by sending you a false prophet who will aim to reverse that which you have heard, your steps will never slide from the way of the truth, for you have seen the truth with your own eyes." But if so, the sense of the verse, [according to Rabbi Moshe ben Maimon], is that "in order to be able to prove you *in the future,* G-d came now so that you should remain faithful to Him in all trials."

In my opinion, the real "trial" is now, [and not as Rambam has it that "He now came in order to be able to prove you in the future"]. Moses is saying: "Now G-d wanted to try you whether you will keep His commandments,[557] since He has now removed all doubt from your hearts. From now on, He will see *whether ye do love Him,*[558] and whether you want Him and His commandments." So also does every expression of *nisayon* mean "test," such as: *I cannot go with these; for I have not 'nisithi' them,*[555] which means "I have never tried to walk with them."

It is possible that this "trial" is for the good [of the one who is being tried],[559] for the master will sometimes try his servant with hard work in order to know whether he will endure it out of his love for him. Sometimes he will do him good in order to know whether he will requite him with additional service and honor for the good he has done him. This is similar to what the Sages have said:[560] "Happy is the person who stands through his trials, for there is no man whom the Holy One, blessed be He, does not try. He tries the rich to see if his hand will be open for the poor; He tries the poor if he can bear suffering, etc." This is why Scripture says here: "G-d has been good to you in showing you His Glory, which *He hath not dealt with any nation,*[561] in order to prove you whether you will requite Him according to the good He has done to you *to be unto Him a people of inheritance,*[562] similar to what He said, *Do ye thus requite the Eternal?*[563] And it is said.

---

(557) See Deuteronomy 8:2. (558) *Ibid.*, 13:4. (559) See Vol. I, p. 275. (560) Shemoth Rabbah 31:2. (561) Psalms 147:20. (562) Deuteronomy 4:20. (563) *Ibid.*, 32:6.

"*You only have I known of all the families of the earth; therefore I will visit upon you all your iniquities,*[564] for the nations are not obligated to me as are you, whom I have known face to face."

19. YE YOURSELVES HAVE SEEN THAT I HAVE TALKED WITH YOU FROM HEAVEN. He commanded that Moses tell them: "Since you yourselves have seen that I have talked with you from heaven and that I am Master in heaven and upon the earth, do not combine *gods of silver or gods of gold*[565] with Me, for you have no need of another aid with Me." The purport of the verse is: *Ye shall not make with Me gods of silver,* and *ye shall not make unto you gods of gold*. In my opinion, the explanation of the verse is as follows: "Do not make gods of silver or gods of gold to be to you for gods with Him; *and ye shall not make them* altogether." Thus He warned against believing in them, and again warned against merely making them, similar to the verse, *Neither shall ye rear you up a graven image, or a pillar.*[566] By way of the Truth, [the mystic lore of the Cabala], the meaning of the word *iti (with Me)* is like the Expression *al panai* (before My face),[567] and I have already alluded to its explanation.[567]

Rashi wrote: "*That I have talked with you from heaven.* But another verse states, *And the Eternal came down upon Sinai!*[568] There comes a third verse to harmonize them: *Out of heaven He made thee to hear His Voice, that He might instruct thee; and upon earth He made thee to see His great fire.*[569] His Glory was in heaven, and His might was [manifest] upon the earth." Thus Rashi's language. But it is not precise.[570] The harmonizing of the

---

(564) Amos 3:2. (565) Verse 20. (566) Leviticus 26:1. There too He first admonished against believing in the idols — *Ye shall make you no idols,* i.e., to believe in them — and then He warned against the mere making of them. (567) Above, Verse 3. (568) *Ibid.,* 19:20. (569) Deuteronomy 4:36. (570) Ramban's intent, as is evident from the text which follows, is to this effect: The harmonizing of the verses is correct, for so it is stated in the Mechilta, but that which Rashi added: "His Glory was in heaven, etc.," is not precise, as will be explained that the Glory was upon Mount Sinai.

verses is indeed a Midrash of the Sages,[571] and it is true that G-d was in heaven, and His Glory was upon Mount Sinai,[572] for G-d was in the fire, and it is written, *Thou camest down also upon Mount Sinai, and spokest with them from heaven.*[573] All the verses in their various expressions are thus clear to all who know [the mystic teachings of the Cabala]. I have already explained it all above.[568] And Rabbi Abraham ibn Ezra wrote that he who has a discerning heart will understand the meaning thereof in the section of *Ki Thisa.*[574] *The words of a wise man's mouth are gracious.*[575]

21. AN ALTAR OF EARTH THOU SHALT MAKE UNTO ME. Rabbi Abraham ibn Ezra explained that He is saying: "*Ye shall not make with Me gods of silver, or gods of gold*[565] to receive power from heavenly creatures through them, that they be intermediaries between Me and you, for *in every place where I cause My Name to be mentioned I — I* in My Glory — *will come unto thee and bless thee.*[576] You have no need at all for an intermediary." And according to the opinion of the Rabbis concerning [the verses here, i.e., that they speak of] the altars that were made in the Tabernacle and in the Sanctuary,[571] He mentioned the commandment of the altars of earth and of stones[577] in order to say that they also make the altars for G-d alone and that there they shall sacrifice the burnt-offerings and the peace-offerings, and not to the demons in the open field.[578] In every place where they will mention His Name, He will come upon them in His Glory to make His Divine Presence dwell among them and to bless them.

---

(571) Mechilta on the verse here. (572) This is unlike Rashi, who wrote that "His Glory was in heaven." (573) Nehemiah 9:13. Thus, it is stated that He was in heaven and His Glory was upon Mount Sinai. (574) Further, 33:21. In harmonizing the above-mentioned conflicting verses, Ibn Ezra also suggests that His Glory came down upon Mount Sinai and the Voice was heard from heaven. This is identical with Ramban's explanation, and Ramban praises him for it. (575) Ecclesiastes 10:12. (576) Verse 21. (577) Verse 22. (578) Leviticus 17:5-7.

EXODUS XX, YITHRO

22. AND IF THOU MAKE ME AN ALTAR OF STONE. The meaning of the word *v'im* (and if) in an obligatory commandment[579] is: If the time comes that you will be worthy to inherit the Land and to build Me an altar of stone, beware that *thou shalt not build it of hewn stones*, for you may think to make it so to enhance the beauty of the structure. In his commentaries,[580] Rabbi Abraham ibn Ezra's opinion is that [the verse here refers] to the **altar** of the covenant [mentioned] in the section of *V'eileh Hamishpatim.*[581]

By way of the Truth, [the mystic lore of the Cabala], the verses are in methodical arrangement: *"Ye yourselves have seen that from heaven I have talked with you* with My Great Name, *and ye shall not make* before My face *gods of silver, or of gold.* But I permit you to make an altar to Me alone and to sacrifice thereon burnt-offerings, and also peace-offerings, *in every place where I cause My Name to be mentioned* for *I will come unto thee and bless thee – with blessings of heaven above, blessings of the deep that coucheth beneath."*[582] The word *azkir* (I will cause it to be mentioned) is associated with the expression: *He hath been mindful of us, He will bless.*[583]

FOR IF THOU LIFTETH UP 'CHARB'CHA'[584] (THY IRON TOOL) UPON IT THOU HAST PROFANED IT. This is to prohibit the touching of the stones of the altar with an iron tool, just as He said, *Thou shalt build the altar of the Eternal thy G-d of unhewn stones,*[585] *thou shalt lift up no iron tool upon them.*[586] He

---

(579) Since it is obligatory upon us to build an altar of stone in the Sanctuary, the question arises: Why does the Torah here use the word *v'im* (and if)? Ramban proceeds to answer this question. (580) Further, 24:4. (581) *Ibid.* The sense of the expression, *'and if'* thou make Me an altar of stone is thus as follows: "Make Me now an altar of earth, and if you will merit it, then you shall make Me an altar of stone for the altar of the covenant." See Ibn Ezra here. (582) Genesis 49:25. (583) Psalms 115:12. (584) Literally: "thy sword." The significance of it is explained further on in the text. (585) Deuteronomy 27:6. (586) *Ibid.*, Verse 5.

mentioned iron here by the term *cherev* (sword), because all iron tools that have sharp edges are called *cherev*. Thus it is said of a sword, *And Ehud made him 'cherev' (a sword) which had two edges;*[587] and of a blade it is said, *Take thee a sharp 'cherev' (sword).*[588] Of hatchet and hammers with which a building is demolished it is said, *And he shall break down thy towers 'b'charbothav' (with his axes).*[589] Similarly, an iron tool with which stones are cut is called *cherev*.

23. NEITHER SHALT THOU GO UP BY STEPS UNTO MINE ALTAR. Because He began the commandment of the altar, He therefore completed it and did not postpone it until He would command about the subject of the sacrifices in *Torath Kohanim*[590] This is proof to the words of the Sages,[591] which are not really in need of defense.

According to our Rabbis,[592] the reason for the commandment [against building an altar of stones which have been touched by iron] is the glorification of the altar: [It is not right] that that which shortens life [i.e., iron] is to be lifted up against that which prolongs life. Rabbi Abraham ibn Ezra said that this is in order that the chips of the stones should not remain in the dunghills, while part of them [i.e., the stones] is built into G-d's altar, or that the chips should not be taken to make an altar for the idols, since their worshippers might do so, hoping that perhaps this will bring them success. And the Rabbi [Moshe ben Maimon] wrote in *Moreh Nebuchim*[593] that this prohibition is an extraordinary

---

(587) Judges 3:16. (588) Ezekiel 5:1. (589) *Ibid.*, 26:9. (590) Literally: "Law of the Priests." Generally, it is another name for the Book of Leviticus. (591) Mentioned above in Verse 21, that the altars referred to here are those of the Tabernacle and the Sanctuary. Now since these altars were ascended by a ramp connecting them with the ground, this verse, which states that the altar should not be ascended by steps, fits in with the general subject. But if it is as Ibn Ezra wrote, (mentioned here in the text above, Verse 22), that the altar of stone referred to here was the altar of the covenant made at Mount Sinai the present verse does not fit in here because that altar had no ramp. (592) Mechilta on the verse here. (593) Guide of the Perplexed, III, 45.

precaution against making stones into certain shapes, thus being hewn stones, for such was the custom of the heathens [to build their altars with hewn stones].[594]

But I say that the reason for the commandment is that a sword is made out of iron and is the destroyer of the world. In fact, this is why it is called *cherev* (sword) [which is of the same root as *churban* (destruction)]. And since Esau whom G-d hated[595] is the inheritor of the sword — for to him it was said, *And by thy sword shalt thou live*[596] — and the sword is his power in heaven and upon the earth — for with [the power of] Mars and the stars [which influence] bloodshed, the sword succeeds, and with them Esau's might is shown — therefore it must not be brought into the House of G-d. It is this reason which Scripture mentions expressly: "You should not build [the altar] of hewn stones, for in lifting up any iron to make them, you have lifted up your murderous sword, and increased victims; and thus you have profaned it." It was for this reason that there was no iron in the Tabernacle, for even its pins, which would have been better if made of iron, were made of copper.[597] Similarly, in the Sanctuary[598] there were no vessels of iron except the ritual slaughtering-knives, for slaughtering [of the sacrifice] was not an act of "worship" [requiring a priest].[599]

Scripture prohibited only the building of an altar with hewn stones if touched by iron, for so it is clearly stated, *when thou lifteth up thy sword upon it thou has profaned it,* and still more clearly, *thou shalt lift up no iron tool upon it.*[586] But if he comes to chisel them with silver tools or the *shamir,*[600] which our Rabbis have mentioned,[601] it is permissible, even though the stones are not whole. This law will refute the reasoning of Rabbi

---

(594) Thus by prohibiting the building of an altar with stones which have been touched by iron, the Torah gave us an extraordinary precaution to guard against idolatry. (595) Malachi 1:3. (596) Genesis 27:40. (597) Further, 27:19. (598) Literally: "The Permanent House," a synonym for the Sanctuary in Jerusalem, which cannot be built in any other location. It stands in contrast to the Tabernacle, which could be moved from place to place. (599) Yoma 42 a. (600) A worm that pierced stones with its touch. (601) Sotah 48 b.

Abraham ibn Ezra.[602] The reason advanced by the Rabbi [Moshe ben Maimon] is also incorrect on account of this law.

Now [when building the Sanctuary], Solomon added a stricture in the commandment, i.e., that *no tool of iron was heard in the House while it was in building*[603] even though it was permissible, [the prohibition applying only to the altar]. Thus we were taught in the Mechilta:[604] *"Thou shalt not build it of hewn stones.* You are not allowed to build the altar of hewn stones, but you may build the Sanctuary and the Holy of Holies of hewn stones. And how do I explain the verse, *And there was neither hammer nor axe nor any tool of iron heard in the House, while it was in building?*[603] They were not heard 'in the House,' but outside of the House they were heard." What happened was thus as follows: They would remove the stones from their mountains with iron tools and chisel them there with iron, just as they also cut with iron the trees and the cypresses[605] which were in the House. And so it is written, *And they quarried great stones, costly stones, to lay the foundation of the House with hewn stone.*[606] When they brought them to the House to build the walls, they did not fix them with iron, nor did they lift up any iron tool upon them as is the custom of builders. And that which Scripture says, *It was built of whole stones from the quarry,*[603] does not mean that they were whole and complete; they were whole only insomuch as they had no notch deep enough for the nail to halt over on passing upon the edge,[607] but they were smooth and even. The meaning of the word *masa*[608] is "great"; for when they moved them from the mountain, they did not divide the rocks into many stones as is

---

(602) If, as Ibn Ezra suggested, the reason for the commandment is that the chips of the stones should not be on a dunghill while the stones be in the altar of G-d, why then is it permissible if the chiselling is done with a silver tool? The same question applies to Rambam's explanation that the commandment is a precautionary measure against idolatry. (603) I Kings 6:7. (604) Mechilta on the verse here. (605) *Ibid.*, Verse 31. (606) *Ibid.*, Verse 31. (607) Chullin 18 a. (608) *It was built of whole stones 'masa'* (I Kings 6:7) is generally translated "at the quarry." Ramban interprets *masa* to mean "great," and the sense of the verse is: "it was built of whole large stones."

the custom of the builders, and they did not fix them there, nor did they set them into the building with hammers or axes as any other building is built. Solomon did not want it to be built [with any iron tool], or that the sound of iron be even heard in the whole Mount of the House. All these strictures were for the purpose of removing iron from it. This is according to the opinion of Rabbi Yirmiyah in Tractate Sotah.[609] But according to Rabbi Yehudah, the hewn stones were for Solomon's own house, not for the Sanctuary. According to his opinion, the verse stating, *And they quarried great stones, costly stones, to lay the foundation of the house with hewn stone,*[606] means that they also quarried hewn stones which were for his own house. So also it appears from the plain meaning of Scripture, that he built the court with hewn stone, as it is written, *And he built the inner court with three rows of hewn stone,*[610] and he placed himself under restriction [to build with unhewn stone] only in the Sanctuary and the Holy of Holies. All this was for the sake of removing iron from the Sanctuary. And regarding *the iron without weight* which David prepared,[611] that was to make instruments of it [with which] to cut the trees and to quarry the stones.

The reason for [the prohibition against ascending the altar with] steps is that the fear of the altar and its enhancement is for the glory of G-d. Each of G-d's commandments has many reasons, there being many benefits in each for body and soul.

---

(609) Sotah 48 b. In our Gemara: Rabbi Nechemyah. (610) I Kings 6:36.
(611) I Chronicles 22:14.

Mishpatim

21 1. AND THESE ARE THE ORDINANCES WHICH THOU SHALT SET BEFORE THEM. The reason [why this whole section dealing with *mishpatim* — civil laws — is placed here, rather than being placed after the *chukim* — statutes — as is the order in the commandments given at Marah],[1] is that G-d wanted to explain to them first the civil laws. Thus we find that the first of the Ten Commandments dealt with the obligation of knowing of the existence of G-d, and the second one with the prohibition against idolatry, after which [following the giving of the Ten Commandments] He again instructed Moses, saying, *Thus shalt thou say unto the children of Israel: Ye yourselves have seen that I have talked with you from heaven,*[2] meaning that you, [Moses] should warn them again to take to heart that which they have seen, so that they will be careful to keep these precepts which I have commanded them. For *Ye yourselves have seen* corresponds to the commandment, *I am the Eternal thy G-d;*[3] *Ye shall not make with Me — gods of silver* etc.[4] — corresponds with *Thou shalt have no other gods,*[5] thereby completing the subject of idolatry; likewise, *And these are the ordinances* corresponds to *Thou shalt not covet,*[6] for if a man does not know the laws of house and field or other possessions, he might think that they belong to him and thus covet them and take them for himself. This is why He said, *thou shalt set before them* just ordinances,

---

(1) Above, 15:25: *There He made for them 'chock' (a statute) 'umishpat' (and an ordinance).* The "statutes" are the precepts for which the reasons are generally unknown. See Vol. I, p. 331. (2) Above, 20:19. (3) *Ibid.*, Verse 2. (4) *Ibid.*, Verse 20. (5) *Ibid.*, Verse 3. (6) *Ibid.*, Verse 14.

which they should establish amongst themselves, so that they will not covet that which does not legally belong to them. And thus did the Rabbis say in Midrash Rabbah:[7] "The whole Torah depends on justice; that is why the Holy One, blessed be He, gave the civil laws directly after the Ten Commandments." Similarly G-d explains in this section of *These are the ordinances* additional laws about idolatry,[8] the honor of parents,[9] murder,[10] and adultery [11] — which are all mentioned in the Ten Commandments.

The Rabbis have explained:[12] *"Before them,* but not before the Canaanites." This interpretation is based on the observation that it should have said, "which *tasim lahem"* ("thou shalt set *for them"*) just as He said, *There 'sam lo' (He set for them) a statute and an ordinance;* [13] thus since He said, *which thou shalt set 'liphneihem' (before them),* we interpret this to mean that they should be the judges, for it is with reference to a judge that this term [*liphnei* (before)] appears in Scripture: *And both the men, between whom the controversy is, shall stand before the Eternal, 'liphnei' (before) the priests and the judges;*[14] *Until he stand 'liphnei' (before) the congregation for judgment;* [15] *'liphnei' (before) all who know law and judgment.* [16] The Rabbis further explained: *"Before them,* but not before laymen." They interpreted [the verse in this way] because with reference to the ordinances it is written: *Then his master shall bring him unto 'ha'elohim;'* [17] *the cause of both parties shall come before 'ha'elohim;'* [18] and it is also written, *and he shall give 'biphlilim' (as the judges determine)*[19] — these terms referring to judges who are experts in the law, and who had received ordination [20] [in an unbroken chain from the time of

---

(7) Shemoth Rabbah 30:15. (8) Further, 22:19. (9) Further, Verses 15 and 17. (10) *Ibid.,* Verses 12-14. (11) *Ibid.,* 22:15-16. (12) Tanchuma *Mishpatim,* 6. (13) Above, 15:25. (14) Deuteronomy 19:17. (15) Numbers 35:12. (16) Esther 1:13. (17) Further, Verse 6. (18) *Ibid.,* 22:8. (19) Further, Verse 22. (20) The process of investiture with judicial rights and functions. Ordination was conferred by three Sages, only one of whom himself had to be duly ordained. Ordination was valid only if both the ordainers and the ordained were in the Land of Israel. Once received in the Land of Israel, however, the authority of ordination became effective outside the Land as well.

those who had been duly ordained] by Moses our Teacher. This is why He said here that these ordinances are to be set *before them,* meaning before the *elohim* [expert, ordained judges] that He will mention further on, but not before Canaanites, and not before one who is not a judge by the standard of the Torah, such as a layman in this respect. It is forbidden to appear before such a person to act as a judge, just as it is forbidden to bring it before the Canaanites, even if he knows that this layman knows the correct law and will render him a proper decision. Even so it is forbidden for the litigant to set him up as a judge and complain before him so that he orders the other party to come to court before him, and the layman himself is also forbidden to act as their judge. Now even though the Sages have mentioned these two groups [the layman and the Canaanite] together, there is a difference between them, in that if the two litigants are willing to come before an Israelite who is a layman, and accept him upon themselves, it is permissible for them to do so, and they must abide by his decision, but to come before the Canaanites to act as judges between them, is forbidden under all circumstances, even if the Canaanite laws are in that particular case the same as our laws.

2. IF THOU BUY A HEBREW SERVANT. G-d began the first ordinance with the subject of a Hebrew servant, because the liberation of the servant in the seventh year contains a rememberance of the departure from Egypt which is mentioned in the first commandment, just as He said on it, *And thou shalt remember that thou wast a bondman in the land of Egypt, and the Eternal thy G-d redeemed thee; therefore I command thee this thing today.*[21] It also contains a remembrance of the creation, just as the Sabbath does, for the seventh year signals to a servant a complete rest from the work of his master, just as the seventh day of the week does. There is in addition a 'seventh' amongst the years, which is the jubilee, for seven is the chosen of the days [to be the Sabbath], and of the years [to be the Sabbatical year], and of the [seven] Sabbaticals [to be the jubilee]; and they all point

(21) Deuteronomy 15:15.

to one subject, namely, the secret of the days of the world — from *bereshith (in the beginning)* till *vayechulu (and they were finished)*.[22] Therefore this commandment deserved to be mentioned first, because of its extreme importance, alluding as it does to great things in the process of creation.[23] This is why the prophet Jeremiah was very stringent about it and said, *Thus saith the Eternal, the G-d of Israel: I made a covenant with your fathers;*[24] *At the end of the seven years ye shall let go every one his manservant, and every one his maidservant.*[25] And on account of its violation, G-d decreed the exile,[26] just as the Torah decreed exile for the Sabbatical rest of the land which was not observed,[27] as I will yet write,[28] with the help of the Rock.

When He finished stating the ordinance of this [first] commandment as it applies to Hebrew servants, He began the ordinance of the commandment, *Thou shalt not murder,*[29] since it is the worst [sin] and then [He stated the ordinances of the commandments] to honor one's parents, and of *Thou shalt not steal,*[29] and then He went back to the ordinance of one who smites his fellow-man but did not kill him,[30] and then to the murder of a bondman, which is worse than the killing of an offspring,[31] and after that to [injury to] the limbs of Israelites

---

(22) Genesis 2:1. See Ramban Vol. I, pp. 61-64. (23) Ramban's reticent and challenging language is illuminated in an essay by I. Weinstock (B'maglei Haniglah V'hanistar, pp. 151-241) where he traces the development of this Cabalistic doctrine: The universe is subject to cycles of seven thousand years; after each six thousand years of growth and activity the seventh thousand is one of "rest" — destruction. This process repeats itself seven times — representing a total of forty-nine thousand years, the fiftieth thousand being the jubilee when all existence returns to its beginnings. This phenomenon applies to the planet on which we live as well as to the worlds above us. One can thus get a glimpse into the meaning of Ramban's words before us, that this commandment "alludes to great things in the process of creation." (24) Jeremiah 34:13. (25) *Ibid.*, Verses 14 and 10 (Ramban combined here parts of these verses). (26) *Ibid.*, Verses 17-22. (27) Leviticus 26:34-35. (28) *Ibid.*, 25:2. (29) Above, 20:13. (30) Further, Verses 18-19. (31) See further Verse 22 — that for killing an unborn child a fine is paid, while in the case of the bondman, if he did not survive for twenty-four hours after he was struck by the master, the master is liable to death (Verses 20-21).

and bondmen,[32] and then to cases of death inflicted by cattle which cause injury.[33] All the sections are thus arranged in logical sequence and in proper order.

3. THEN HIS WIFE SHALL GO OUT WITH HIM. Rashi commented: "But who brought her in, that Scripture need say that she shall go out with him? But [by saying this], Scripture tells us that he who acquires a Hebrew servant is obliged to provide for the food of his wife and children." This is a Midrash of the Sages.[34] Now [even though the children are not mentioned in this verse, but only his wife,] the Rabbis have included the children together with the wife in this duty of the master, on the basis of what is written further on, *Then he shall go out from thee, he and his children with him.*[35]

I am not clear on this law as to whether the earnings of the woman and children belong to the master during the time he is supporting them. It appears to me that the master takes the place of the husband [in this respect]. For the Torah had compassion on the wife and children, whose lives are hanging in suspense,[36] and who expect [to be supported from] the husband's earnings, since now that he is sold as a servant, they are in danger of being lost in their misery. Therefore the Torah commanded the master who is now entitled to the servant's labor, to act towards them as he [the servant] would. If so, the master only has to assume the responsibilities of the husband, [and no more]; thus he is entitled to their labor as is the husband, and in return he must feed and support them. This is the meaning of the expression, *then his wife shall go out with him,* since the servant's wife was together with him as a handmaid to his master, for the labor of both of them belongs to him, in return for which he is obliged to give them food. Thus the only difference between husband and wife is that the wife has a right to go away as she pleases, [and is not bound to work for her husband's master if she does not want to be supported by him, whilst the husband, who is the servant, is bound

---

(32) *Ibid.,* Verses 24-27. (33) *Ibid.,* Verses 28-32. (34) Mechilta on the Verse here. (35) Leviticus 25:41. (36) See Deuteronomy 28:66.

to the master]. Similarly, the master's obligation to support the children is limited to the time that the father is responsible for them, namely when they are minors, or as long as is customary to feed them, as Rashi explained in Tractate Kiddushin.[37] All this is out of G-d's compassion for them [the wife and children], and for the servant as well so that he should not die in his anguish, in the knowledge that whilst he is toiling in a strange house, his children and wife are neglected. Now even though he is not obliged by law of the Torah to support them, as has been explained in the Talmud, Tractate Kethuboth,[38] but since it is the normal way of life for a man to support his wife and small children, G-d in His mercies commanded the buyer [of the servant] to act to them as a merciful father. The meaning of the Sages in speaking of *banav* [literally: "his sons"] is both sons and daughters.

I have seen written in the Mechilta:[34] "I might think that the master is obliged to support the betrothed [of the servant] and the childless widow of his brother who is waiting for him to marry or reject her? Scripture therefore says, *his wife,* thus excluding the brother's childless widow who is waiting for him, since she is not yet his wife. *With him,* this excludes the betrothed who, [even though she is his wife], is not yet *with him.*" This Mechilta is a proof to the law which I have stated, for since it is not customary for the betrothed and the childless brother's widow to be supported by the man [in this case the servant], therefore the Torah did not impose their support upon the master either. And even if the brother-in-law or the bridegroom became liable by law at a certain time known in the Talmud[39] to support them, that obligation was in the nature of other debts they may have, and therefore the master did not become liable to support them.

---

(37) Kiddushin 22 a. See my Hebrew commentary p. 413.   (38) Kethuboth 49 a-b.   (39) According to a first [i.e., an older] Mishnah, if after such time as the law allows for the preparation of the wedding, the bridegroom postponed it, he is liable to support her, and she may eat from his goods, so that if she is an Israelite's daughter and betrothed to a priest, she may eat *terumah* (the heave-offering) as if she was already his wife. A later Mishnah though, ruled that a woman may not eat heave-offering until she has entered the bride-chamber (Kethuboth 57 b).

Again I have found in another Mechilta of Rabbi Shimon: [40] *"If he be married then his wife shall go out with him.* Just as the master is obliged to feed the servant, so he is obliged to feed his wife and children. Still I might say: if the servant had a wife and children before he was bought, then his master is obliged to feed them, because he bought him on that condition, but if he had a wife and children only after he was bought I might think that his master is not obliged to feed them. Scripture therefore says, *if he be married* [41] etc. There are thus two wives mentioned here, one referring to a wife that he had before his master bought him, and the other referring to a wife he had after he was bought. I might think that even if he had just a betrothed wife, or a childless brother's widow who is waiting for him, whom the servant himself is not obliged to feed, that nonetheless his master is obliged to support them, and proof for that argument I might find in the fact that the husband himself is not obliged [by law of the Torah, as explained above] to feed his own wife and children, and yet, the master of the servant is obliged to feed the wife and children of his servant; Scripture therefore says, *then his wife shall go out with him* — that wife who is *with him,* the master is obliged to feed, but he is not bound to feed a wife who is not *with him.* I might think that even if the servant's wife was one with whom it is not correct for him to continue living — such as a widow married to a High Priest, or a divorcee or profaned woman married to a common priest [42] — [that the master is bound to feed her]; Scripture therefore says, *then his wife shall go out with him* — one that is fit to live *with him,* but not this one etc. I might think that even if he married without the master's knowledge [the master is obliged to feed her]; Scripture therefore says, *if 'he' be married* — just as 'he' was acquired with the master's knowledge, so his wife [whom the master must support] means one taken with the master's knowledge. I might think that the earnings of his sons and

---

(40) In Hoffman's edition, p. 120. — See Vol. I, p. 603, Note 245, for explanation of the term "another." (41) Literally: "if he be the husband of a *wife,* then his *wife* shall go out with him." The word "wife" is thus mentioned twice, once to indicate etc. (see text). (42) See Leviticus 21:7:14.

EXODUS XXI, MISHPATIM 345

daughters belong to the master, and it is logical that it be so: for if we see in the case of a Canaanite bondman, whose master is not bound to feed him, that nonetheless the earnings of his sons and daughters belong to the master, then surely it is logical that in the case of a Hebrew servant, whose master is obliged to feed him, that the earnings of his sons and daughters should belong to his master! Scripture therefore says: *he (if 'he' be married)* — it is he whose earnings belong to his master, but not those of his sons and daughters. *Then his wife shall go out with him* — do not separate him from his wife; do not separate him from his children." Thus far the language of this Beraitha. [43]

Yet I continue to say [44] as I have written above, that if the servant's wife and children want to be supported by the master, that he may take their earnings, and this Beraitha quoted above intends only to tell us that they are not his by absolute right, as is the law of the Canaanite bondman, or as is the law of the Hebrew servant himself, [who must of necessity work for their master], but they [the wife and children of the Hebrew servant] can say to him: "We will not be fed by you, and we will not work for you." What is new in this Beraitha is that if the servant married without the consent of his master, he is not bound to feed the wife or her children, for since it is within the power of his master to give him a Canaanite bondmaid, he is not obliged to feed this Israelite woman. The Rabbis further interpreted the word *imo* (with him) to teach us that you are not to separate him from his wife and children, which means to say that the master cannot tell him: "Be together with the handmaid I gave you and sleep with her at night, and not with the Israelite wife," but the servant has the right to choose for himself.

---

(43) See *Seder Bo*, Note 209. (44) In spite of the fact that this Beraitha apparently contradicts what Ramban said above — namely, that during the time of the Hebrew servant's servitude the earnings of his wife and minor children belong to his master, since he is obliged to feed them, whereas here the Beraitha seems to be saying the opposite — "Yet I continue to say" writes Ramban, "as I have written above etc."

4. IF HIS MASTER GIVE HIM A WIFE. "Scripture is speaking of a Canaanite woman. Or perhaps this is not so; but Scripture here speaks only of an Israelite woman?! Scripture therefore says, *the wife and her children shall be her master's.* Consequently, it must be speaking of a Canaanite woman." This is the language of the Beraitha [43] taught in the Mechilta.[34] Now Rashi wrote [in explanation of this Mechilta]: "For a Hebrew maidservant also goes free at the end of six years [just as a Hebrew manservant does], or even before the end of six years if she shows signs of puberty, for it is said, *If thy brother, a Hebrew man, or a Hebrew woman, be sold unto thee, he shall serve thee six years.*" [45]

But this is not quite correct. For if we say [as the Beraitha above attempted to,] that the verse here speaks of an Israelite woman, it could no longer refer to the case of a father selling his minor daughter, about whom the law is given that when she shows signs of puberty she goes free, for how could the master give her as a wife to his Hebrew servant, since he has no power to hand her over to any other man [except to designate her to be his own wife, or that of his son — as is explained further in Verses 8-9]! [46] Similarly, the proof that Rashi mentioned, namely that she also goes free at the end of six years, is only so in accordance with his own words which he wrote [47] that a person who sells himself [on account of his destitution] is sold for a maximum of six years; but in the Talmud [48] these are the words of a single Sage [Rabbi Eliezer], but the accepted opinion is that one who sells himself can be sold for six years or more. Now if so, the case of a woman who goes free at the end of six years can only be when her

---

(45) Deuteronomy 15:12. "This teaches you that a Hebrew maidservant also goes free after six years' service" (Rashi). Consequently the verse here which states *the wife [and her children] shall be her master's* can only be speaking of a Canaanite woman.   (46) Accordingly, the Beraitha above that attempted to argue that Scripture here speaks of an Israelite woman [given by the master to his Hebrew servant], must refer only to a Hebrew woman *of age* who sold herself as a maidservant. So how then could Rashi support his argument [that if she were an Israelite woman, she would go free "if she shows signs of puberty]," when the Beraitha must of necessity be referring not to a minor but to a woman of age? (Mizrachi).   (47) Above, Verse 2, Rashi.   (48) Kiddushin 14 b.

EXODUS XXI, MISHPATIM

father sold her [as a minor, but in that case the master has no right to give her as a wife to his Hebrew servant, but only to designate her as his own wife or that of his son]! [49]

But that which the Rabbis have said [in the Beraitha above, on the basis of the verse, *the wife and her children shall be the master's*]: "Consequently, Scripture must be speaking of a Canaanite woman" — the meaning thereof is as follows: Since He stated, *the wife and her children shall be the master's* [it must be speaking only of a Canaanite woman], for the children of a Canaanite bondmaid are the master's since her child has the same status as she does, but in the case of an Israelite woman — even if she were of age [in which case her master could give her to his Hebrew servant as a wife], and even if we were to say that a woman may sell herself as a maidservant [50]— her children are the father's [not the master's].

6. THEN HIS MASTER SHALL BRING HIM UNTO 'HA'ELOHIM' — "to the court. The servant must take counsel with those who sold him." [51] [Thus is the language of Rashi.] And Rabbi Abraham ibn Ezra wrote that the judges are called *elohim* because they uphold the laws of G-d on earth.

In my opinion Scripture uses these expressions: *Then his master shall bring him unto 'ha'elohim;' the cause of both parties shall come before 'ha'elohim,'* [52] in order to indicate that G-d will be

---

(49) So both proofs of Rashi as to why Scripture cannot be speaking here of an Israelite woman, [1. that a Hebrew maidservant also goes free at the end of six years; 2. that even before the end of six years, she goes free if she shows signs of puberty], have no application here for reasons explained above. (50) A woman really cannot sell herself; as the Mechilta puts it: "*And if a man sell* (Verse 7) — a man can sell himself, but a woman cannot sell herself." But Ramban is writing only on the assumption that the Beraitha introduced this as a hypothesis finally to be disproved. See my Hebrew commentary pp. 515-516. (51) This section speaks here of one who was sold by the court for a theft which he had committed and was not able to pay for (further, 22:2). On refusing to go free at the end of his six years of service, the servant is to take counsel with his vendors [the court] "and they will advise him to go free, for when he is free he can serve G-d in more ways than he could as a servant etc." (Zeh Yenachmeinu — commentary on the Mechilta). (52) Further, 22:8.

with the judges in giving their judgment. It is He Who declares who is just, and it is He Who declares who is wicked. It is with reference to this that Scripture says, *he whom 'Elokim' (G-d) shall condemn.*[52] And so did Moses say, *for the judgment is G-d's;* [53] so also did Jehoshaphat say, *for ye judge not for man, but for the Eternal, and He is with you in giving judgment.*[54] Similarly Scripture says, *G-d standeth in the congregation of G-d; in the midst of 'elohim' (the judges) He judgeth,*[55] that is to say, in the midst of a congregation of judges He judges, for it is G-d Who is the Judge. And so also it says, *Then both men, between whom the controversy is, shall stand before the Eternal.*[56] And this is the purport of the verse, *For I will not justify the wicked,*[57] according to the correct interpretation. In Eileh Shemoth Rabbah I have seen it said: [58] "But when the judge sits and renders judgment in truth, the Holy One, blessed be He, leaves, as it were, the supreme heavens and causes His Presence to dwell next to him, for it is said, *When the Eternal raised them up judges, then the Eternal was with the judge.* [59]

AND HE SHALL SERVE HIM 'L'OLAM' (FOREVER). Our Rabbis interpreted [60] this to mean until the jubilee year. And Rabbi Abraham ibn Ezra wrote that "the meaning of *olam* in the Sacred Language is *'time.'* It hath been already, *'l'olamim'* which were before us means 'the times' [or 'the ages'] *which were before us.* [61] *And there he may abide 'ad olam'* [62] [cannot mean 'forever,' for Samuel did not stay all his life in Shiloh; it must therefore mean 'until a certain time,' i.e., until he comes of age]. This is why the Rabbis have said, *and he shall serve him l'olam* means up to the time of the jubilee year, for of all appointed seasons in Israel the jubilee year is the most remote, and the going out to freedom is as if the world was made anew for him. The sense of

---

(53) Deuteronomy 1:17. (54) II Chronicles, 19:6. (55) Psalms 82:1.
(56) Deuteronomy 19:17. (57) Further, 23:7. (58) Shemoth Rabbah 30:20. (59) Judges 2:18. (60) Mechilta here on the Verse.
(61) Ecclesiastes 1:10. (62) I Samuel 1:22.

the verse is then, that he should return to his status in his first time, when he was free." The student learned [in the mystic lore of the Cabala] will understand that *l'olam* is to be taken in its usual sense [i.e., forever], for he who works until the jubilee year has worked *all the days of old*. [63] In the words of the Mechilta: [60] "Rabbi [64] says: Come and see that *olam* cannot mean more than fifty years, for it is said *and he shall serve him 'l'olam,'* which means until the jubilee year." Now Rabbi Abraham ibn Ezra forgot that which he wrote with understanding in another place. [65]

7. SHE SHALL NOT GO OUT AS THE MENSERVANTS DO. This means that the Hebrew maidservant does not go out free "in consequence of the loss of a tooth or an eye, as Canaanite slaves do." [66] Thus is Rashi's language, and our Rabbis interpreted it likewise. [60] Indeed it is so, for a Hebrew servant is not called *eved* [67] without any further qualification.

But I wonder: why does Scripture find it necessary altogether to tell us this [that a Hebrew maidservant does not go out free because of the loss of a tooth or eye, as Canaanite bondmen do]? [68] Perhaps it is to tell us that we should not argue by

---

(63) Isaiah 63:9. See also above Note 23. (64) The epithet for Rabbi Yehudah Hanasi, the redactor of the Mishnah, or as he is often known *Rabbeinu Hakadosh*, "Our holy teacher," or simply "Rabbi." (65) In his commentary to Leviticus 25:40-41, Ibn Ezra wrote on the verses, *He shall serve with thee unto the year of jubilee. Then shall he go out from thee...*: "This is what the Rabbis have received by tradition concerning the verse, *and he shall serve him 'l'olam,'* " meaning that he is to serve him until the jubilee year." Thus Ibn Ezra did understand the verses there and found in them Scriptural proof that *olam* means fifty years, whilst here he wrote that it means "time." Apparently, "he forgot" — as Ramban puts it — "what he wrote with understanding elsewhere." (66) See further, Verses 26-27. (67) The Hebrew servant may be called *eved ivri* [as in Verse 2 here: *if thou buy an 'eved ivri'* — a Hebrew servant] but never just *eved*, which term by itself signifies a Canaanite bondman. Here in Verse 7 where it just says *ha'avadim* (menservants) it must therefore refer to the Canaanite bondmen. For a similar statement of Ramban see also further Verse 20. (68) For what reason might I have thought that she does go out free, so that Scripture should find it necessary to tell us that such is not the case?

applying the method of *kal vachomer* [69] from a Canaanite women, that a Hebrew maidservant goes out free because of the loss of a tooth or eye. This law is stated expressly in the case of a Hebrew woman, but such is also the law for a Hebrew man, who has been compared to her [thus he too does not go out free because of the loss of any of the chief external organs]. The author of the 'Hilchoth Gedoloth,' [70] wrote, however, that [the verse is not needed to exclude this *kal vachomer*, [69] for even if Scripture had not excluded it, we could not have argued that a Hebrew woman should go out free in consequence of the loss of a tooth or eye], because the going forth to freedom by slaves on account of the loss of a tooth or eye is a penalty [to the master], and you cannot derive a law by logical argument from penalties. The author of the 'Hilchoth Gedoloth' thus considered this verse a negative commandment[71] wherein G-d warns the master that if he wants to send her out free because of the loss of a tooth or eye, that he transgresses a prohibition; but instead he is to pay her

(69) See in *Seder Bo* Note 208. — The *kal vachomer* in this case would be as follows: A Canaanite bondwoman who does not go out free at the end of six years or in the jubilee year, does go out free because of the loss of any of the chief external organs. It is therefore only logical that a Hebrew maidservant, who does go out free at the end of six years or in the jubilee, should surely go out free because of the loss of any chief external organs. (70) Rabbi Shimon Kairo, who flourished in the second half of the eighth century — when the Gaonic period was at its height. Considered a most authoritative work on Rabbinic law, the 'Hilchoth Gedoloth' was a pioneer in the field of *Taryag* (613) Commandments, for in a preface to this work the author was the first scholar who attempted to define each separate commandment (see my foreword to "The Commandments," Vol. I pp. viii — ix). (71) As opposed to a mere "negation," where the verse just negates a certain law from being applicable, without constituting a prohibition. In his Book of the Commandments, Maimonides dedicated the eighth principle to the clarification of this distinction between a negation and a prohibition, and without mentioning the name of the author of the 'Hilchoth Gedoloth,' differs with him on the interpretation of this verse, which in his opinion merely states that there is no obligation on the part of the master to let her go free where he causes her the loss of one of her organs. [See in my translation, "The Commandments," Vol. II pp. 390-393.] In his notes to Maimonides' Book of Commandments, Ramban came to the defense of the 'Hilchoth Gedoloth.'

monetary compensation for the tooth or eye, and she shall stay with him up to the time [of six years, or before if she produces signs of puberty], to be designated as the master's wife [or his son's]. For it would be a great injustice if, after causing her the loss of a tooth in his anger and blemishing her thereby, he would then send her out of his house, when she had hoped to become his wife. Moreover, many times the monetary compensation for the damage done to the chief external organs, is more than the earnings for her labor if her days as a handmaid have nearly terminated. Therefore Scripture was strict upon the master and made a clear prohibition, so that he should not rob her of the monetary compensation due to her for the loss of any of her chief organs, even if he should want to let her go free on account of them. It may be that sending her to freedom is itself forbidden before the fixed time, for Scripture has obliged the master to support her and that she stay with him, in case she finds favor in his eyes and becomes his wife; just as He warned him with a prohibition that [after he marries her and takes another wife] *her food, her raiment, and her conjugal rights shall he not diminish*.[72] In accordance with this opinion [the author of the 'Hilchoth Gedoloth'] counted the verse, *She shall not go out as the menservants do* among the three hundred and sixty-five negative commandments.

8. 'L'AM NOCHRI' HE SHALL HAVE NO POWER TO SELL HER. "Neither her master nor her father has the right to sell her to another [Hebrew man].[73] *Seeing he hath dealt deceitfully with her* — if he [i.e. the master] intends to act deceitfully towards her and not to fulfill the commandment of designating her as his wife [or his son's]. So also did her father act deceitfully towards her, by selling her to this master." Thus far Rashi's language. And if so, *l'am nochri* would be like *l'ish nochri* (to a strange man), but we

---

(72) Verse 10. (73) Rashi thus interprets *l'am nochri* [literally: "unto a foreign people"] as signifying "unto a strange man," i.e., to another Israelite. Thus the verse is stating that neither the father nor the master has a right to resell her. Ramban will question this interpretation.

find in all Scripture no parallel to such a usage [that *am* (people) should be understood in the sense of "man"]. Perhaps the letter *lamed* in the word *l'am* draws along with it a similar letter in the next word, thus making it: *'l'am l'nochri'* he shall have no power to sell her, and the explanation thereof would be similar to the verse, *Thou gavest him to be food 'l'am l'tziyim' (to the folk inhabiting the wilderness)* [74] where the second word *l'tziyim* explains: who is *the folk?* — the men who inhabit the wilderness; so here too He says, *he shall have no power to sell her 'l'am'*, and He explains: who is *l'am?* — *l'nochri*, that is to say, to any stranger from the whole people [i.e., to another Israelite]. The term *nochri* here will then be similar in usage to the expressions: *and thy labors in the house of a 'nochri' (stranger)*, [75] which means in the house of another man; *even from the 'nochriyah' (the strange woman) that maketh smooth her words*, [76] meaning the woman who is not his wife. All this I have written in order to uphold the words of the Sages [77] who say that a man is not permitted to sell his daughter twice into the status of a handmaid, thus holding to the explanation: since he has once dealt deceitfully with her [by selling her to such a status of a handmaid], he has no more the right to sell her.

But I have seen in the Mechilta: [60] " *'L'am nochri'* he shall have no power to sell her, — this is a warning to the court that he [i.e., the father] should not sell her to an alien [i.e., a non-Israelite]." It would thus appear from their language that this verse is not meant as an admonition against the father reselling her to this Israelite master or to another one, but is a prohibition against her being sold altogether [even the first time] to a non-Israelite, so that a man may not sell his minor daughter to an idolator as a handmaid. [It was necessary for this to be stated] because in the case of a Hebrew servant He said, *and he sell himself unto the stranger who is a settler with thee, or to the offshoot of a stranger's family*, [78] therefore it had to say that this should not be

---

(74) Psalms 74:14. (75) Proverbs 5:10. (76) *Ibid.*, 2:16. (77) Rabbi Eleazar and Rabbi Shimon — in Kiddushin 18 a. (78) Leviticus 25:47.

EXODUS XXI, MISHPATIM 353

done to a woman. The reason for it is obvious.[79] This surely is the plain meaning of Scripture, that after the father — the vendor — redeemed her from her first master, he cannot sell her to an idolator, and the same law applies to the original sale. Scripture, however, [had to state this prohibition in the case of a re-sale], because sometimes a man may very much want to redeem his daughter from a master who did not take her as his wife, and will want to sell her to an idolator for a year or two with the intention of then taking her out from him; therefore Scripture warned him against doing this. Or it may be that this expression [i.e., *'l'am nochri' he shall have no power to sell her*] refers back to the beginning of this subject: *And if a man sell his daughter to be a maidservant* [80] — *he shall have no power to sell her to a foreign man*. If so, then the Rabbis' interpretation in the Talmud [77] that a man may not resell his daughter into the status of a handmaid, [even to an Israelite], is derived [not from *'l'am nochri' he shall have no power to sell her*, but] from the [apparently] superfluous expression: *seeing he hath dealt deceitfully with her*. For to a non-Israelite he never has power to sell her; so why did G-d say: *seeing he hath dealt deceitfully with her*, [since he cannot sell her even once to a foreign man], and the meaning of that expression is that since he acted once deceitfully with her by selling her into a status of a handmaid, he cannot do so another time? Therefore the Rabbis interpreted the verse thus: "*to a foreign people he shall have no power to sell her* [altogether], and *when he hath dealt deceitfully with her* [he also has no power to sell her] ;" that is to say, he shall have no power to sell her if he dealt deceitfully with her, for after he sold her once [to an Israelite], he cannot sell her again. There are many instances where the Rabbis interpreted the verses in such a manner. [Thus we find: *Unto the stranger that is within thy gates thou shalt give it that he may eat it, or thou mayest sell it unto a foreigner* [81] — which Rabbi Meir interpreted]: [82] "Read the verse thus: unto the stranger that is within thy gates thou shalt give it that he may eat it, or thou

---

(79) "That she not be exposed to the dangers of immorality." (Bachya).
(80) Verse 7. (81) Deuteronomy 14:21. (82) Pesachim 21 b.

mayest sell it; thou shalt give it that he may eat it or thou mayest sell it unto a foreigner." Similarly they interpreted here [83] *then shall she go out for nothing, without money,* [84] which, on account of the redundant language, ["for nothing," "without money"] they made the basis for two additional ways of the Hebrew maidservant regaining her freedom: *"she shall go out for nothing,* and *she shall go out without money;"* thus establishing that she goes out to freedom when she produces signs of puberty, or signs of fuller development if she had no signs of puberty — this being that maturity of the barren woman, [who is incapable of conception], as is stated in the beginning of Tractate Kiddushin. [83]

The plain meaning of Scripture in this section is as follows: *If a man sell his* minor *daughter to be a maidservant, she shall not go out as* these *menservants,* [i.e., the *Hebrew* menservants] mentioned [above in Verses 2-6,] who go out to freedom in the seventh year and in the jubilee year: for the master [85] can never send her away from his house if the maiden pleases him *and she obtains kindness of him,* [86] but he is to take her for a wife as is his will. *But if she pleaseth not her master,* who has not espoused her to be his wife — for he who buys an Israelite's daughter does so with the intention of taking her as his wife, thus she is under ordinary conditions designated for him; but now if her master does not desire her, *then shall* the father mentioned *redeem her,* for as soon as the master says: "I do not want to marry her," it is forbidden for the father to leave her any longer under his authority, nor may he sell her to a foreign people in case he comes to deal deceitfully with her, for it is deceit for a man to sell his daughter except to someone who can marry her. Or the meaning thereof may be that anyone who sells his daughter [even to an Israelite], deals deceitfully with her.

---

(83) Kiddushin 4 a. (84) Verse 11. (85) In the Tur who quotes Ramban: "the father." That is to say, if the maiden pleased the master and he wishes to marry her, the father cannot take her out from his house. (86) See Esther 2:9.

9. AND IF 'YI'ODENAH' (HE ESPOUSE HER) UNTO HIS SON, HE SHALL DEAL WITH HER AFTER THE MANNER OF DAUGHTERS. In line with the plain meaning of Scripture, it is possible that G-d is saying that if the buyer *yi'odenah* for his son, which means that he espoused her to him — for the term *yi'ud* is an expression of appointing, such as: *he tarried longer than the set time which 'y'ado' (he had appointed him)*[87] — then he shall do *unto her after the manner* that a man does *for* his own *daughters* — he is to give her of his own *according to the dowry of virgins.* [88] He thus commanded this as He did in the law of outfitting the emancipated servant,[89] and it is all an expression of His goodness, magnified be He! And in accordance with the interpretation of our Rabbis, which is the truth, the meaning of the verse is: *after the manner of daughters* whom parents marry off, *so shall* the son [of the master] *deal with her.* And then He explains [what is "the manner of daughters"] that *if he take him another wife, her food, her raiment, and her conjugal rights* — that is, of this one [the former maidservant] — *he shall not diminish.*[90] It is obvious that if he did not marry another woman he must not diminish her rights, but Scripture speaks of that which is usual. [91]

Now Rashi explained: "*sh'eirah* [90] means food; *k'suthah* is, as the literal sense of the word, raiment; *onatha* is the marital duty." And so did Onkelos render *sh'eirah: zivanah* (food). But in the Gemara [92] the Rabbis said with reference to the Sage who held this opinion [that *sh'eirah* means food]: "And this Tanna [93] holds that the alimentation of one's wife is a law of the Torah. For we have been taught: *sh'eirah* — this means her food, and so it says, *He caused 'sh'eir' (flesh) to rain upon them as the dust* [94] etc." And

---

(87) II Samuel 20:5. (88) Further, 22:6. (89) Deuteronomy 15:13-14. (90) Verse 10. (91) I.e., if he does marry another woman he is more likely to diminish the rights of this one; hence Scripture speaks of the case *'if'* he take him another wife. But this is by no means to be understood that it was "the usual" thing to take another wife. (92) Kethuboth 47 b. — For the meaning of the term Gemara see in *Seder Bo,* Note 204. (93) See in *Seder Yithro,* Note 451. (94) Psalms 78:27.

from the subject under discussion in that Gemara it is understood that this is the opinion of a single Sage, whilst the accepted law is that the alimentation of one's wife is a Rabbinical enactment. And even according to the plain meaning of Scripture, why should it mention food under the term *sh'eir* which means "flesh;" it should rather have mentioned *lachmah* (her bread), for man lives by bread [95] and his obligation towards her is [mainly] in that sustenance. Now Rabbi Abraham ibn Ezra thought to correct this, and so he explained *sh'eirah* as meaning food which builds up her *sh'eir,* namely her flesh. But there is no sense in Scripture saying that the "husband diminish not her flesh!"

Therefore I say that the meaning of *sh'eir* everywhere is flesh close and near to one's own, the root thereof being derived from the expression *sh'eir b'saro,* [96] that is his close flesh outside that of the flesh of his own body. Thus relatives are called *sh'eir: to any sh'eir b'saro' (that is near of kin to him);* [96] *they are 'sha'arah' (near kinswomen),* [97] this being associated with the expressions: *surely thou art my bone and my flesh;* [98] *of whom the flesh is half consumed.* [99] Similarly, *And I will cut off from Babylon a name, 'ush'ar' offshoot and offspring,* [100] means a child related to him. Likewise, *when thy flesh 'ush'eirecha' are consumed,* [101] which means "yourself and your children" who are the flesh closest to you. Thus meat is called *sh'eir — He caused 'sh'eir' to rain upon them as the dust* [94] — because meat when eaten is absorbed by the eater and becomes part of his flesh. It is possible that this is the meaning of the expression, *when thy flesh 'ush'eirecha' are consumed,* [101] meaning: when the original flesh of your body, and the nutriment of flesh which came from the food, will be consumed and will no longer be part of your flesh. Thus a woman in relation to her husband is called *sh'eir* — just as the Rabbis

---

(95) See Deuteronomy 8:3. (96) Leviticus 18:6. Generally translated: "that is near of kin to him." According to Ramban the literal meaning would be: "the flesh close and near to his flesh." (97) *Ibid.,* Verse 17. (98) Genesis 29:14. (99) Numbers 12:12. "The flesh" here refers to Miriam — Aaron's and Moses' sister. (100) Isaiah 14:22. (101) Proverbs 5:11.

interpreted: [102] *"except for 'lish'eiro,'* [103] *sh'eir means his wife;"* — the usage of the term being derived from the idea that G-d stated, *and he shall cleave unto his wife, and they shall be one flesh.*[104] Thus *sh'eira* here means "the nearness of her flesh;" *k'suthah* is "the cover of her bed," just as it is said, *for that is his only 'k'suthoh' (covering)... wherein shall he sleep?* [105] and *onathah* is "her time," that he come to her at times of love. And even if we say as some commentators do, that the meaning of *sh'eir* is like "his flesh," and the expression, *to any 'sh'eir' b'saro'* [96] is like "to any flesh of his flesh," just as it says, *for he is our brother, our flesh* [106] — in that case we would still explain *'sh'eirah'... he shall not diminish* as meaning that he shall not diminish from her her flesh; that is, the flesh due to her, namely, the flesh of her husband who with her is one flesh. Thus the meaning of the verse is, that G-d says that if the master takes another wife, he shall not diminish from this one the nearness of her flesh, the cover of her bed, and her time of love, for such is *the manner of daughters.* And the intention is that the other woman should not be sitting *upon a stately bed,* [107] and there *they shall be one flesh,* [104] whilst this one is to him merely like a concubine, with whom he lives only by chance, and upon the ground, just like one comes to a harlot. It is for this reason that Scripture has forbidden him to act in this way. And so did the Sages say: [108] *"sh'eirah* means the nearness of flesh, that he should not behave to her as is the custom among the Persians, who perform their marital rights in their clothes." This is a correct interpretation, for such is the style of Scripture always to mention sexual intercourse in clean and brief language. Therefore it mentions these duties by means of allusion: *sh'eirah k'sutha v'onatha,* referring to the three things which are usual when a man comes together with his wife. Thus the verse is properly explained in accordance with the accepted law, whilst alimentation of one's wife and provision of her raiment are duties put upon the husband by ordinance of the Rabbis.

(102) Yebamoth 22 b. (103) Leviticus 21:2. (104) Genesis 2:24.
(105) Further, 22:26. (106) Genesis 37:27. (107) Ezekiel 23:41.
(108) Kethuboth 48 a.

11. AND IF THESE THREE — designating her to himself as his wife, or to his son, or allowing her to be redeemed — HE DO NOT UNTO HER, then SHALL SHE GO OUT FOR NOTHING, WITHOUT MONEY, as do the menservants mentioned. [109]

15. AND HE THAT SMITETH HIS FATHER, OR HIS MOTHER, SHALL SURELY BE PUT TO DEATH. Our Sages have already taught [110] that his death is by strangulation. This is why He placed next to it, *And he that stealeth a man, and selleth him,* [111] for he too is punished by the same death. He separated it from the later verse, *And he that curseth his father or his mother,* [112] because his death is by stoning, as it is said concerning him, *he hath cursed his father or his mother; his blood shall be upon him,* [113] and whenever such an expression [*his blood be upon him*] is used about someone, his death is by stoning, this being derived from that which is written, *They shall stone them with stones; their blood shall be upon them.*[114] The reason why He was more severe as to the manner of death of the one who curses his mother or father than as to the manner of death of one who smites them, [115] is because the sin of cursing is more common, for when the fool gets angry *he frets himself and curses by his king* [116] and father and mother the whole day, and a crime that is frequently committed needs a greater punishment [than one rarely committed]. Or it may be that cursing involves a greater sin,

---

(109) I.e., at the end of six years, or the jubilee year. It is thus in contrast to Verse 7 above: *And if a man sell his daughter to be a maidservant, she shall not go out as the menservants do.* But if the master do not these three things to her [as explained], then she shall go out as the menservants do. See Ramban above at the end of Verse 8 ["The plain meaning of Scripture in this section etc."]. To this he now adds that if the master fails to do any of the three ways to ameliorate her condition, then she shall go out free for nothing, as menservants do. (110) Sanhedrin 84 b. (111) Verse 16. (112) Verse 17. (113) Leviticus 20:9. (114) *Ibid.,* Verse 27. (115) In the order of severity stoning is considered the most stringent of the four deaths that the court had power to inflict, and strangulation the least severe. Ramban's question is thus pertinent: why the most severe punishment for the curser, and the least severe one for one who smites? (116) Isaiah 8:21.

because he uses the Name of G-d, [117] and therefore he has to be punished for his sin against his father and mother, and also for taking G-d's Name in transgression and sin. Now the Gaon Rav Saadia [118] said, that the reason why He placed the matter of stealing a human being between that of smiting one's parents and cursing them, is because most people are kidnapped when they are young, and they grow up in a strange place unaware of who their parents are, and thus they may come to smite them or to curse them [not knowing that they are their parents]; therefore it is fitting that the thief too be punished by death as they are, since he is responsible for the punishment that is visited upon the child [who smites or curses either of his parents, and for that reason the verse dealing with the thief's punishment is mentioned between those dealing with smiting one's parents and cursing them].

16. AND HE THAT STEALETH A MAN, AND SELLETH HIM, AND HE BE FOUND IN HIS HAND — "previously, before the sale." This is Rashi's language. But I have not understood it. [119] If Rashi means that witnesses must have seen him [the stolen person] in the thief's possession before he had sold him — could it even enter your mind that the thief be subject to the death penalty without witnesses having seen him stealing and also seeing him selling! It would therefore have been sufficient if Scripture were to say: "and he that stealeth a man and selleth him". Further, his being found in the thief's possession is no real proof that he stole

---

(117) Shebuoth 36 a. Also in the Mechilta here: "One who curses his father or his mother is not liable to the death penalty unless he curses them by using the Divine Name." Needless to say cursing is strongly forbidden by itself, even without using the Divine Name. (118) Mentioned here in Ibn Ezra, Verse 16. — On Rav Saadia, see in *Seder Va'eira*, Note 229. (119) Ramban argues that since Rashi made his comment upon the phrase: *and he be found in his hand*, it would appear that the fact that the witnesses saw him in his possession constitutes their proof that the holder stole him. On this, Ramban asked: could you possibly think that the thief be subject to death without the witnesses having seen the actual theft and the sale? Their having seen him in the thief's possession is in fact no proof at all that he had stolen him (Nimukei Shmuel).

him! Rather, this verse is the source for that which we have been taught in a Mishnah: [120] "He that steals a person is not liable to the punishment unless he brings him into his own possession," and in a Beraitha the Rabbis have said: [120] "If he stole him but did not sell him, or if he sold him but he is still in his [the thief's], possession, he is free [from the death penalty]." The meaning of this is to teach us that the law applying to the thief of a human being is [in one respect] similar to that of thieves of other, i.e., monetary, matters; namely, that if a thief killed or sold [an ox or a sheep] within the domain of the owner, he is free [from paying five oxen for an ox and four sheeps for a sheep],[121] but if he lifted them up [thereby acquiring possession of them], or removed them from the domain of the owner, he is liable to pay. Similarly, this thief of a human being must first have brought the stolen person into his own domain [in order to be liable to death]. Likewise if he lifted the lad upon his shoulder, and sold him to another person, he is liable to the death penalty, because this too is called *if he be found in his hand,* since it is not logical that a man's ground should have a greater power of taking possession of a thing for the owner, than his own hand has. In a similar way, that which the Rabbis said [in the Beraitha mentioned above]: "or if he sold him but he is still in his [the thief's] possession etc.," means that the buyer did not remove him at all from the thief's domain, even though he paid him the money, and since he did not remove him from there, the thief is free [from the death penalty]. Now I do not know whether this is to say that [in order to make the thief of a human being liable to the death penalty] the buyer must perform a formal act of acquisition, as is the law in other transactions, that the buyer does not take ownership of the article until he draws it from the domain of the seller into a *simta,* [an alley adjoining an open place] or until he lifts it [even within the domain of the seller]— or it may be that it is a special Scriptural decree in the case of the sale of a stolen human being, that even if the sale has been finalized between them, and the buyer has taken

(120) Sanhedrin 85 b.   (121) Further, Verse 37.

ownership from the seller by lifting him or by drawing him along in ground which belongs to both of them, [in which case usually the act of drawing the purchased article is a valid act of acquisition even if not done in a *simta*], that the thief is nonetheless free from the death penalty until the stolen person goes out from his domain into the domain of the buyer. And so indeed it would appear to be [as the latter exposition].

Now Rashi in his commentaries there in the Gemara [120] explained [the phrase of the Beraitha]: "if he sold him but he is still in his possession" as meaning "if he is still *in the stolen person's* domain,[122] in which case the thief is free from punishment because there has been no real theft at all." But if so, nothing new has been established here which is unlike the ordinary law of theft in monetary matters! [123]

However, it may be, the words of the verse [to be interpreted properly, must be transposed as follows]: "and he that stealeth a man, and he be found in his hand, and he selleth him, he shall surely be put to death." But it is still possible that the verse may be explained properly in the order it is written in. Thus: *And he that stealeth a man, and selleth him, and he be found in the hand* of the buyer [*he* — the thief — *shall surely be put to death*]; for if he stole a human being and brought him to his house, and then he brought the buyer there and sold him without the buyer taking him out from there, the thief is not liable, because the sale has not been completed between them, or even if the sale has been completed, he is still free of the death penalty, as I have written above.

---

(122) Not as we have explained it heretofore, according to Ramban, that the reference is to *the thief's domain.* (123) But according to Ramban, as explained above, there is a new law established here: even if the thief brought the stolen person to his domain, and the buyer came there and the sale was completely finalized, [by the buyer lifting him, or drawing him into ground which belongs to both], the thief is nevertheless free from the death penalty as long as the buyer did not remove him from the seller's domain. In the case of theft of an ox or sheep under such circumstances, the thief would be liable to pay five oxen for an ox and four sheep for a sheep.

18. WITH A STONE OR 'B'EGROF' (WITH HIS FIST). Judging from certain expressions of the Rabbis, *egrof* is the hand closed tightly, with the fingers gathered into the palm for the purpose of striking someone with it. Thus they speak of *ba'alei egrofin* [literally: "men of fists," or men of power]; [124] "*egrofo* (the fist) of Ben Abtiach." [125] Similarly *'b'egrof' of wickedness* [126] means the hand of wickedness that strikes. Scripture thus mentioned two kinds of hitting — the hard one, with a stone, and the lighter one, with the fist, which in most cases does not cause death — in order to declare that in both cases an estimate [of the power of the stone or the fist with which he struck him] is needed, and the assailant is meanwhile imprisoned. If the assailed person dies, such as where he struck him a mortal blow, *he is a murderer; he shall surely be put to death*, [127] but if he does not die, the assailant has to pay him for the loss of his labor and for the cost of the healing.

In the Mechilta [we find the following text]: [128] "Rabbi Nathan says: He has likened the stone to the fist and the fist to the stone. Just as the stone can cause death, so also the blow of the fist must be such that it is capable of causing death. And just as the fist is something that can be identified [and measured for the power of its blow], so also the stone must be such as can be identified. But if the stone with which he struck him became mixed up with other stones, the assailant is free." This means if the stone became mixed up with other stones, they [e.i., the judges] estimate the lightest one and if it is incapable of causing death, they free the assailant.

Other scholars [129] have said that the word *egrof* means "a clod of earth," the term being derived from the expression: *the grains shrivel under 'megr'fotheihem' (their clods of earth)*, [130] and the letter *alef* [in the word *egrof* is redundant], as is the *alef* in the word *ezro'a* ["arm," where the word is really *zro'a*]. And this is the opinion of Onkelos who translated *b'egrof* — *b'churmeiza* (a

---

(124) Kiddushin 76 b. (125) Keilim 17:12. A giant who lived in the time of the Second Sanctuary. (126) Isaiah 58:4. (127) Numbers 35:16. (128) Mechilta here on the Verse. (129) Ibn Ezra and R'dak (in Sefer Hashorashim, root *goraf*). (130) Joel 1:17.

piece of white stone or glazed tile). He mentioned these things also in order to tell us that the assailant who hits him with a clod of earth is also liable to be put to death, if he struck him on a sensitive spot where it is capable of causing death. This is to distinguish the law of the sword from the stone and *egrof,* for no estimate [of a sword or weapon] needs to be taken [since even a minute piece of metal — such as a needle — can also cause death], as the Sages have mentioned.[131]

19. IF HE RISE AGAIN, AND WALKS ABROAD 'AL MISH'ANTO' — "in his former healthy state and vigor." This is Rashi's language. And Rabbi ibn Ezra said that the reason why this word [which means literally: "support"] is used, is to tell us that he must not be dependant upon others for the ability to walk, like an invalid, but must walk by himself;[132] only *then shall he that smote him be quit* from prison.

In my opinion, *mish'anto* is to be understood in its literal sense, [a staff], just as in the verses: *every man with 'mish'anto' (his staff) in his hand for old age;*[133] *'mish'eneth' (the staff) of this bruised reed.*[134] Scripture is thus stating that if the injured person's health improves sufficiently to enable him to go out walking as he wishes *in the streets and in the broad ways*[135] with his staff, like those healed from some prolonged disabling injury, *then shall he that smote him be quit;* and it further teaches us that even if the injured man is careless later about his health and dies after that in his weakness, the assailant is free from the death penalty. Scripture says *and he walketh abroad* because it speaks of the customary way of life, for injured men who were laid up in bed do not go out walking again until their wounds have healed and they are out of danger, this being the sense of the phrase, *and*

---

(131) Sanhedrin 76 b.　(132) Thus according to Rashi *mish'anto* is "his physical strength;" according to Ibn Ezra, it is "his leaning" or "support." Ramban will proceed to explain it in its literal sense — "on his staff." Almost all translations follow Ramban's interpretation.　(133) Zechariah 8:4. (134) II Kings 18:21.　(135) Song of Songs 3:2.

he walketh abroad, because if he just gets up and walks in his house on his staff, and then dies, the assailant is not free [from the death penalty].

In the words of the Mechilta:[136] "*If he rise again and walketh.* I might think this means within the house; Scripture therefore says, *abroad*. But from the word *abroad* I might think that even if he was wasting away [the assailant is still free from punishment]; Scripture therefore says, *if he rise again.*" This explanation too is very correct, that Scripture should be saying that if the injured man gets up completely from his bed and goes steadily outside — without having to go back to his bed when returning from outside, as is the way of those who continue to waste away — even though he is weak and has to lean upon a staff, the assailant shall be let off. In general all this is to be interpreted as being figurative, language expressing people's practical conduct, and the basic rule is that he must have been assessed as being capable of recovery. This is why Onkelos translated *al mish'anto: al boryeih* (in his healthy state).

Scripture states, *only he shall pay for the loss of his time, and shall cause him to be thoroughly healed,* but it does not say, "he shall pay for the loss of his time and his medical care." in order to tell us that he must pay the money for the doctors to heal him, and the injured person cannot demand that he should give him the compensation and he will do other things with it. Instead, the assailant must heal him under all circumstances.

20. IF A MAN SMITE HIS BONDMAN. Our Sages have already perforce derived from the expression, *for he is his money,*[137] that this verse speaks of a Canaanite bondman, and the plain meaning of Scripture is indeed as they say, for his countryman, a Hebrew man or woman, is not called plain *eved* or *amah* without any further qualifications.[138] Scripture states *'basheivet'* [with a *patach* under the *beth,* which indicates the definite article, thus

---

(136) Mechilta here on the Verse. (137) Verse 21. (138) See also Ramban above Verse 7, and Note 67.

EXODUS XXI, MISHPATIM

meaning] "with the rod": [*And if a man smite his bondman, or his bondwoman, with the rod*], because it is the custom of a ruler or master to keep in his hand a rod, and G-d therefore warned him that even if it be *a rod of correction*[139] and not a wooden cane, he should be careful with it and should not use it to hit even a Canaanite bondman *with a persecution that none restrained.*[140] This is the purport of the expression, *and he die under his hand,* meaning that he kept striking him until he died. It was not necessary for Scripture to state the punishment which he is liable to, but it just stated that he is not to go free merely because the bondman is his money, but *he shall surely be punished,* as is the punishment of anyone who strikes another person so that he dies, where Scripture has said, *he shall surely be put to death.* [141]

In line with the plain meaning of Scripture the intention of: *Notwithstanding, if a day or two 'ya'amod',* [137] [generally translated "he continues"], is that the bondman literally gets up "and stands" on his feet. This is why it was necessary for Scripture to say *a day or two,* the meaning thereof being that if on that day or on the following day the bondman will stand up on his feet, *he* [i.e., the master] *shall not be punished.* And the verse is to be understood as if it said: "notwithstanding, [if he stands up] '*bayom*' or '*bayomayim*' (*in* a day or *in* two) or '*l'yom*' or '*l'yomayim*' (*to* a day or *to* two). [142] There are many such cases [where the prefix *beth* or *lamed* is missing as it is assumed in the meaning of the word]. Thus, at first He had said, *and he die under his hand,* which might be taken to have meant that the bondman died immediately at the time he struck him; therefore He referred back and explained that if on the day he struck him he stood up on his feet, or even if he could not stand at all on that day, but

---

(139) Proverbs 22:15. (140) Isaiah 14:6. (141) Above, Verse 12. (142) The verse has it: *yom o yomayim* [literally: "a day or two"]. This fits in with the translation of *ya'amod* as "he continues," thus: *if he continues* [living] *a day or two.* Ramban who interprets *ya'amod* in its literal sense — "he stands up" — therefore concludes that the sense of the verse is: "notwithstanding, if *he stands up in* a day or *in* two etc." The opinion of the Rabbis mentioned further on will explain sufficiently why the Torah did write here *yom o yomayim.*

did so on the next day, the master is free from punishment. But if he did not stand up at all, the master is liable to punishment, even though the bondman only died on the second day, for that too is considered as if he died *under his hand.* It did not mention a case where he stood up on the third day, for if the bondman lived three days, the master is free from the death penalty, since this is no longer considered a case of *he die under his hand.*

In the opinion of our Rabbis [136] Scripture mentioned *yom o yomayim* ["a day or two," and not *bayom o bayomayim*, "in a day or in two"], in order to teach us that [for the master to go free] the bondman must have survived twenty-four hours, and the meaning of the expression used is: "*a* complete *day* [consisting, as it does, of twenty-four hours]; *or two days,* neither of which consists of a complete day, [but instead the period of twenty-four hours is made up of the parts of two separate days]." Had it said just "a day," the bondman would have had to continue living for a night first and then the following day, as is the "day" of the Torah mentioned at the creation [143] and in connection with the Sabbaths and festivals; [but now that it said, *a day or two* it means any period of twenty-four hours, as explained above]. The word *ya'amod* [in accordance with the opinion of the Rabbis] then means that "he continues to live." Similarly, *that they may 'ya'amdu' many days,* [144] means "continue to exist." And this is the correct and true interpretation of the verse.

22. AND IF MEN STRIVE TOGETHER, AND HURT A WOMAN WITH CHILD, SO THAT HER FRUIT DEPART, AND YET NO HARM FOLLOW, HE SHALL BE SURELY FINED, 'KA'ASHER' THE WOMAN'S HUSBAND SHALL LAY UPON HIM. "This means: 'when' [145] the husband will summon him before the court in order that they put a fine on him for it." Thus

---

(143) *And there was evening and there was morning, one day* (Genesis 1:5). (144) Jeremiah 32:14. (145) Rashi is thus explaining the letter *kaf* in the word *ka'asher* not in the sense of "as," indicating degree or extent ("according as"), but in the sense of "when" — when the woman's husband takes him to court.

EXODUS XXI, MISHPATIM 367

far Rashi's language. And it is correct [to interpret here the letter *kaf* in the word *ka'asher* as meaning "when", and not "as"]. A similar case is the expression, *'ka'asher' (when) it shall be well with thee,* [146] and there are many other such cases. And the intention of the verse is that the assailant has to pay compensation for the miscarriage when the husband takes him to court, not when the woman does so, as the compensation is not hers. Onkelos, however, translated: "according to the amount [that the woman's husband] shall lay upon him."

Rabbi Abraham ibn Ezra explained the verse as follows: *according as the woman's husband shall lay upon him,* or [147] *he shall pay as the judges determine,* as if to say that the assailant should come to agreement with the husband on a fixed sum, or he should pay compensation as the court will assess him. This is not correct, for what reason is there to mention this? [148]

In my opinion, since the damage done is one that is not discernible in the unborn children themselves — for who could know their fortune — therefore Scripture said, that although he cannot be made to pay a precise monetary compensation, he should nonetheless be fined as a sort of penalty in the form of a sum of money [149] which others [i.e., the judges] shall impose upon him. A similar usage [of the term *onesh* — punishment] is also found in these verses: *and he put the land to 'onesh' (a fine);* [150] *they drink the wine of them that have been 'anushim' (fined).*[151] Scripture is thus stating that the punishment be entirely *as the woman's husband shall lay upon him,* because he desires his children and they are important to him, but he [i.e., the husband] should fix the sum through the judges, in order that he

---

(146) Genesis 40:14. (147) The Hebrew word *v'nathan,* which is generally translated *"and he shall pay"* — *as the judges determine,* Ibn Ezra interprets to mean *"or* he shall pay," and the purport thereof is as explained in the text. (148) For surely if the parties voluntarily agree on a sum there is no necessity for them to go to court, and if they fail to agree on a sum it is self-understood that the court will have to assess the fine. (149) See my Hebrew commentary p. 424 for further elucidation of this phrase of Ramban "a sort of penalty." (150) II Kings 23:33. (151) Amos 2:8.

should not impose upon him an exorbitant sum. In the words of the Mechilta:[136], *"According as the woman's husband shall lay upon him.* I might think this to mean, whatever he pleases; Scripture therefore says, *and he shall pay as the 'pelilim' determine,* and *pelilim* always means judges."

24. EYE 'TACHATH' (FOR) EYE. It is known in the tradition of our Rabbis [136] that this means monetary compensation. Such usage [of the term *tachath* to indicate] monetary compensation is found in the verse: *And he that smiteth a beast mortally shall pay for it; life 'tachath' life,* [152] [in which case *tachath* surely indicates monetary compensation]. Rabbi Abraham ibn Ezra commented that Scripture uses such a term to indicate that he really is deserving of such a punishment, [that his eye be taken from him], if he does not give his ransom. For Scripture has forbidden us to take *ransom for the life of a murderer, that is guilty of death,* [153] but we may take ransom from a wicked person who cut off any of the limbs of another person. Therefore we are never to cut off that limb from him, but rather he is to pay monetary compensation, and if he has no money to pay, it lies as a debt on him until he acquires the means to pay, and then he is redeemed.

Proof for what the Sages have said [that *eye 'tachath' eye* means he pays him the value of his eye], is in what He has said above [with reference to one who injures another person], *only he shall pay for the loss of his time, and shall cause him to be thoroughly healed.* [154] But if we were to do to the assailant exactly as he has done to the injured man, why does he have to pay after that? He himself is in need of amends for the loss of his own time and costs of his own healing! And it would not be valid to argue that the assailant is to give the injured man [the difference in cost between a slow recovery and] a fast recovery,[155] since this is not the plain

---

(152) Leviticus 24:18.   (153) Numbers 35:31.   (154) Above, Verse 19.
(155) Thus, if the assailant had a fast recovery and the injured man a slower recovery, the assailant is to pay him the difference of expenses incurred in the loss of time and costs of healing. In that case, one could still argue that *eye 'tachath' eye* really means that the eye of the assailant be removed, and Verse 19 that deals with his obligation to pay for the loss of

EXODUS XXI, MISHPATIM

meaning of Scripture. Rather, Scripture speaks of all people, and even if his recovery [i.e., the assailant's] were to be fast, we would have long taken our punishment of him, in doing to him exactly as he did! [156]

If we explain the verses according to the literal interpretation of Scripture, there is no escape from this question, [157] unless they [158] will say that if someone maims his neighbor so that he deprives him permanently of some bodily member, such as an eye, hand, or foot, or causes a burn which leaves a permanent mark, then we are to do likewise to the assailant's body, this being the case of the verse which says, *As he hath caused a blemish in a man, so shall it be done to him,* [159] and in that case there is no monetary compensation paid for loss of time and cost of healing. But if he hits him with a stone or with his fist on his clothes, and he is laid up in bed but then is completely healed without any crippling effect remaining upon his body, in that case He said, *only he shall pay for the loss of his time, and shall cause him to be thoroughly healed.* [154] All the injuries specified in the verse, *burning for burning, wound for wound, stripe for stripe,* [160] are included,

---

time and cost of healing of the injured, applies to that difference as explained above. — This argument is actually mentioned in the Talmud (Baba Kamma 84 a.). But, argues Ramban, it is not the plain meaning of Scripture, for the simple meaning of Verse 19 is that it speaks of the assailant having to pay for the *whole* loss of time and costs of healing. Therefore it constitutes a proof that *eye 'tachath' eye* means monetary compensation, as explained above. (156) And why should he be burdened with the additional cost representing the difference in the recoveries [as explained above], after we have already taken our punishment of him by doing to him as he had done to others? Thus it is obvious that Verse 19 speaks of all men alike, and *eye 'tachath' eye* cannot be meant literally, but means the monetary value of the eye. (157) I.e., an apparent difficulty in the verses [if we interpret them in their plain meaning]: that in one verse it says *eye for an eye,* and in the other it speaks of the assailant's duty to pay for *the loss of his time and costs of healing,* and the question appears why he should pay this additional payment when we have already punished him. There is no escape from this question except by saying that etc. [see text]. Ramban will finally allude to why he mentions all this: it is to show what sophistry we have to display if we seek to follow only the plain meaning of Scripture! We thus have no recourse but to Tradition. (158) I.e., "those who pursue the plain meaning of Scripture" (the *rodfei ha'pshat*). See Vol. I, p. 154. (159) Leviticus 24:20. (160) Verse 25.

according to the plain meaning of Scripture, in this preceding general principle, for a wound and stripe may be completely healed. And as for that which Scripture states there, *And if a man cause a blemish in his neighbor, as he hath done so shall it be done to him,* [161] it too was meant to include all injuries, but He did not mention there at length the cases of wounding, striping, and burning [as He did here]. He used the term *mum* (blemish), for every wound causes at least a temporary blemish. Thus even if it is of the kind which heals, it is still called "a blemish," just as we say: "a passing blemish," [162] and the Torah calls *scabbed, or scurvy, or hath his stones crushed* [163] "a blemish" although they are temporary and can be healed,[164] and it is further written, *youths in whom there was no blemish.*[165] The general principle everywhere is that the Tradition is always true.[166]

29. AND ITS OWNER SHALL BE PUT TO DEATH. Our Rabbis have received by Tradition[167] that this death means by the hand of Heaven. Similar cases are these verses: *and the common man that draweth nigh shall be put to death;*[168] *and they die therein, if they profane it.* [169]

I have noticed that where the Torah speaks of those liable to be put to death by the court, it does not mention just *yumoth* (he shall be put to death), but always says, *moth yumoth* (he shall surely be put to death). Do not object to this rule from the verse, *and he that killeth a man 'yumoth' (shall be put to death),*[170] or

---

(161) Leviticus 24:19. (162) Bechoroth 37 b. (163) Leviticus 21:20. (164) See my Hebrew commentary, p. 425. (165) Daniel 1:3. The intention there is obviously that these youths who were to serve in the king's palace were free even of any passing blemish. (166) See above, Note 157. (167) Mechilta here on the Verse. (168) Numbers 18:7. Punishment for a non-priest who performs the Divine service in the Sanctuary is death by the hand of Heaven (Sanhedrin 83 a). (169) Leviticus 22:9. This is with reference to an unclean priest who ate clean heave-offering [which is forbidden to him as long as he remains in his state of uncleanness], and the punishment is death by the hand of Heaven (Sanhedrin 83 a). (170) Leviticus 24:21. In this case his punishment is death by the court, and yet it says only *yumoth*!

from the verse about the Sabbath, [171] or a prophet who misleads, [172] for in each of these cases He has already clearly explained elsewhere about them [that they are liable to death by the court, by using the phrase: *moth yumoth*]. [173]

Now I do not know the reason for Onkelos' rendering *yumoth* as *yithk'teil* ["he shall be killed", which indicates that his death is to be by the court, instead of by the hand of Heaven]. Perhaps his intention is to state that the owner, [who had been previously warned that his ox had gored three times, but still did not guard it, so that it went out and killed a man or woman], deserves to be put to death, but is instead made liable to the payment of a ransom. Or perhaps Onkelos means to explain that that which Scripture states, *and its owner also shall be put to death* means that the owner will perish in a similar manner to that by which the gored person was killed, for *his day shall come to die, or he shall go down into battle, and be swept away;* [174] *the Eternal will not hold him guiltless.* [175] Thus Onkelos wanted to teach us that the owner of the ox is liable, according to the view of Heaven, to die by the hand of a killer, and not by a natural death, something like it is said, *and I will kill you with the sword.*[176] In the verse, *and the common man that draweth nigh shall be put to death,* [168] Onkelos also translated *yumoth* as *yithk'teil* ["he shall be killed," indicating that his death is to be by the court], because he agrees with the opinion of Rabbi Akiba who said that a non-priest who performed the Divine service in the Sanctuary is put to death by strangulation. [177]

---

(171) Of the Sabbath it is said, *Whosoever doeth any work therein 'yumoth' (shall be put to death)* (further 35:2), and his punishment is death by the court!   (172) *And that prophet... 'yumoth' (shall be put to death)* (Deuteronomy 13:6), and there too his punishment is by the court (Sanhedrin 84 a).   (173) In the case of smiting a man — see above Verse 12; for the Sabbath, see further, 31:14. For a prophet who misleads, see Deuteronomy 13:10: *ki harog tahargenu (for thou shall surely kill him).*   (174) I Samuel 26:10.   (175) Above, 20:7.   (176) Further, 22:23.   (177) Sanhedrin 84 a. The Sages, however, are of the opinion that his death is by the hand of Heaven.

30. IF THERE BE LAID ON HIM A RANSOM, THEN HE SHALL GIVE FOR THE REDEMPTION OF HIS LIFE WHATSOEVER IS LAID UPON HIM. Since the redemption is a form of atonement [178] as are the offerings, and if the owner does not desire it we cannot force him to come before the court to impose the ransom on him, and even if the court ordered him to pay it, we cannot seize his goods as security, therefore He said: "if."

31. 'O' (OR) HE HAVE GORED A SON, OR HAVE GORED A DAUGHTER ACCORDING TO THIS JUDGMENT SHALL IT BE DONE UNTO HIM. Scripture uses the word *o* (*'or' he have gored a son*), because it adds to a phrase mentioned above, the meaning of the whole phrase thus being: "*and he hath put to death a man or a woman,* [179] *or he have gored a son, or have gored a daughter,* one ordinance shall be for them." Some scholars [180] say that the word *o* comes in the place of *im* (if). Similarly: *'o' (if) it be the carcass of an unclean beast;*[181] *'o' (if) I had dealt falsely against mine own life;* [182] *'o' (if) it be known that the ox was wont to gore.* [183] There are many such cases, in the opinion of these scholars.[180] But all these proofs are false witnesses; you will understand them all in their context.

According to our Rabbis,[184] Scripture had to detail the ordinance [in the case of an ox goring] minors, because it found it necessary to say above, *And if an ox gore a man or a woman,* [185] — in order to teach us that in all laws of the Torah concerning damages G-d has treated woman equally to man — thus I might have thought that one is only liable in the case of a grown man or woman; therefore Scripture says, *or he have gored a son,* to make him liable for the death of minors as for that of adults. The same

---

(178) "An atonement for the owner whose ox killed a man" (Rashi Makkoth 2 b).   (179) Above, Verse 29.   (180) Rashi in Leviticus 4:23, and R'dak in Sefer Hashorashim, root *o*.   (181) Leviticus 5:2.   (182) II Samuel 18:13.   (183) Further, Verse 36.   (184) Baba Kamma 44 a.   (185) Verse 28.

EXODUS XXI, MISHPATIM 373

method was followed by Scripture in the verse, *And he that smiteth any man mortally shall surely be put to death,*[186] as Rashi explained there.[187]

In line with the plain meaning of Scripture, [the ordinance concerning an ox goring minors is stated] because an ox that kills a grown-up person is extremely vicious, *as a bear robbed of her cubs*[188] in the wilderness, thus *if warning hath been given to its owner, and he hath not kept it in,*[179] he has committed a grave transgression, and deserves to be liable to death or to pay a ransom [for the redemption of his life]; but an ox that kills minors is not so vicious, for most oxen are not afraid of them, and one might therefore think that their owners are not liable [to the same punishment], therefore Scripture states that *according to this judgment shall it be done unto him.*

34. AND THE DEAD BEAST SHALL BELONG TO HIM — "to the one who suffered the damage. We make an estimation of the value of the carcass and he takes it in part payment and the one who caused the damage, [the owner of the pit], pays him in addition as much as makes up the value of his damage." This is Rashi's language. But he did not explain the law sufficiently. For there is no need for Scripture to tell us concerning this carcass that the one who suffered the damage must take it in part payment, when he brings it before the court to collect his damage; for even if the one who caused the damage had other carcasses that were carrion, or flesh that was *treifah*[189] in his possession, he can give it to him in part payment, it being already established[190] that restitution for damages need not be in money, but may "include

---

(186) Leviticus 24:17. (187) "Because it is said, *He that smiteth a man, so that he dieth, shall surely be put to death* (above Verse 12), I know only about a man. How do I know that the same applies to a woman and to a minor? Scripture therefore says, *kol nefesh adam (and he that smiteth 'any man')* — [literally: 'the soul of any human being']" (Rashi, Leviticus 24:17). (188) II Samuel 17:8. (189) Any animal suffering from a serious organic disease, whose meat is forbidden even if ritually slaughtered. (190) Baba Kamma 7 a.

anything of value, even bran." Rather, the meaning of the verse is to state that the carcass belongs to the one who suffered the damage and is considered his property; therefore if its value decreased after the damage was caused, or it was stolen, the one who caused the damage, [the owner of the pit], pays only the loss in value caused by the death of the animal. Thus if the ox that was killed was worth when alive one hundred *zuzim,* and upon its death became worth fifty, the one who caused the damage is liable to pay only fifty *zuzim,* and the other attends to his carcass [removing it from the pit], and keeps it for himself. [191] This law applies to all damages, and it is what the Sages call: "the loss in the carcass' value," and is explained in the Gemara. [192]

36. OR IF IT BE KNOWN THAT THE OX WAS WONT TO GORE IN TIME PAST, AND ITS OWNER HATH NOT KEPT IT IN, HE SHALL SURELY PAY AN OX FOR AN OX. It is known that if a *Tam* [193] too is properly guarded by its owner, but through an accident it so happened that it went out and caused damage, the owner is certainly not liable.[194] Thus the reason why He states only with reference to a *Muad,* [193] *and its owner hath not kept it in,* [when the same principle would apply to a *Tam* as well] is, according to that Sage in the Talmud [195] who says that a *Muad* needs better guarding than a *Tam,* as follows: Scripture states

(191) He may use its hide for leather, and its flesh to feed the animals, or he may sell it for such uses. (192) *Ibid.,* 34 a. [See in my translation of Hameniach, Shulsinger Bros., New York, 5729, p. 65.] (193) A *Tam* is an animal which has not injured, or killed [an animal] more than three times and whose owner has not been warned that it is dangerous and must be guarded. For whatever damages a *Tam* does, its owner pays only half the loss. The *Tam* is distinguished from a *Muad,* an animal which has killed or injured at least four times, and whose owner has been warned that it is dangerous and must be guarded. For whatever damage it does, the owner must pay in full. (194) But if so, the question arises why the Torah mentions the guarding of the animal only in the case of the *Muad,* (see Note above) since the same law applies to a *Tam* as well. Ramban proceeds to remove this difficulty. (195) Baba Kamma 45 b. See in my Hebrew commentary p. 426, that the reference is to Rabbi Meir.

EXODUS XXI, MISHPATIM

that *if the ox was wont to gore* and warning had been given to its owner, *and he hath not kept it in* and guarded it better in view of its dangerous nature, so that it went out and caused damage, the owner must pay the full damage. According to the opinion of that Sage [196] who holds that the degree of guarding necessary for both *Tam* and *Muad* [193] is alike, the meaning of the verse is as follows: If it be known to the owner *that the ox was wont to gore* and now too [i.e., at the fourth time] *he hath not kept it in,* he is liable to pay the full damage on account of his grave negligence.

AND THE DEAD BEAST SHALL BELONG TO HIM — "to the one who suffered the damage, and the one who caused the damage adds to it until he completes the amount, so that the one who was damaged will have been paid for his entire loss." This is Rashi's language, and is in accordance with the teaching of our Rabbis. [197] And if so, it is proper that we explain the verse as follows: *he shall surely pay ox for ox* "with" *the dead beast* which *shall, belong to him.* Similarly, *and Joseph was in Egypt,*[198] means: "with" Joseph who was in Egypt [they were seventy souls]. Likewise, *I cannot endure iniquity 'va'atzarah'*[199] [literally: "and the solemn assembly"] means *with the solemn assembly*, similar to that which He said, *I hate robbery 'b'olah'* — "with" *a burnt-offering.*[200]

According to the simple meaning of Scripture it is possible to explain the expression, *and the dead shall belong to him* — to the one who caused the damage, the verse thus stating: *he shall surely pay ox for ox,* but he may keep the carcass, so that in making monetary compensation he can turn it over to the one who suffered the damage as part payment. Thus according to both interpretations the law is alike — the owner of the dead animal attends to the carcass, and its value is determined as at the time of its death, [201] to be taken by him as part payment, according to the words of our Rabbis. [201]

---

(196) This is the opinion of Rabbi Eliezer ben Yaakov (*ibid.*). (197) *Ibid.*, 10 b. (198) Above, 1:5. (199) Isaiah 1:13. (200) *Ibid.*, 61:8. (201) If its value decreases after the time of its death, he must bear that loss alone (Baba Kamma 34 b).

2. IF THE SUN HAS RISEN UPON HIM. [202] "This is nothing but a metaphorical expression, [for did the sun rise upon him alone? Does it not rise upon the whole world? It means etc.] [203] But Onkelos who rendered the phrase *if the sun has risen upon him* as: 'if the eye of the witnesses fell upon him' chose a different way of interpreting the verse, which is as follows: if the witnesses found the thief before the householder came, and when the householder came to resist the thief, they warned him not to kill the thief, then *damim lo,* he is liable if he killed him, for since there were witnesses watching him, the thief had no thought of taking human life, and he would not have killed the householder." Thus is Rashi's language.

But I wonder! When He said above [in Verse 1], *there shall be no guilt of blood incurred for him,* thereby acquitting the householder for the murder of the thief, it must surely be speaking of a case where the witnesses warned him not to kill him, for no murderer is ever liable to death without prior warning. And if you say then that in stating: *there shall be no guilt of blood incurred for him,* Heaven permitted the thief's blood to be shed, that is to say, it is permissible to kill him — that is not true! [204] Rather, the first verse acquits the householder under all circumstances from the

---

(202) The verses read: 1. *If a thief be found breaking in, and be smitten so that he dieth 'ein lo damim' (there shall be no guilt of blood incurred for him).* 2. *If the sun be risen upon him 'damim lo' (there shall be guilt of blood incurred for him). He shall make restitution; if he have nothing, then he shall be sold for his theft.* (203) The Hebrew text shortens here Rashi's interpretation, since Ramban's intention here is not to comment on Rashi's own explanation, but upon Rashi's understanding of Onkelos. (204) I.e., such an interpretation cannot be the true meaning of *this* particular verse. For while the law itself is true [that the owner is permitted to kill him], but here the verse speaks of a case where he has already killed him! So how can you say that the intent of the verse is to give him permission to kill him, when he has already killed him! Moreover, since *damim lo* [in Verse 2] declares the householder culpable both by the court and at the hand of Heaven, then *ein lo damim* [in the preceeding verse, stating the opposite case], must as a counterpart free him from both, and the way Rashi interpreted Onkelos *ein lo damim* frees him only from punishment at the hand of Heaven! In other words, Verse 2 must be a case where there were witnesses, as is indicated by

EXODUS XXII, MISHPATIM 377

hand of Heaven, [where he had no prior warning], and from the court if he had prior warning, and the second verse [dealing as it does with another set of circumstances], holds him guilty by the law of both. Perhaps the Rabbi's intention [i.e., Rashi's intention in interpreting Onkelos' translation], was to say that if the witnesses found the thief before the householder came, and recognized him, and the thief knew of their presence, then the thief no longer could have intended to take human life, since he saw that the witnesses recognized him and knew that if he would kill, the witnesses would come to court and have him put to death. And this is the reason for the expression, *if the sun has risen upon him*, for at night, seeing that the witnesses did not recognize him, he would kill the householder and escape.

In my opinion Onkelos intended to say that if the thief has left the break-through, and the householder comes to court to say that he has witnesses that he was found breaking through, *damim lo* [literally: "he has blood"] as other living people do, and it is not permissible to kill him, and if the householder did kill him, he is to be put to death; but the thief is to pay if he took anything from there. Scripture uses the expression, *if the sun be risen upon him* because it speaks of the usual manner, for those who break into homes generally do so at night when no one recognizes them, and the one who kills them there is free and may do so with impunity. But if the thief stayed there until the sun had risen upon him, and then left in a stealthy manner and ran for his life, then if the householder comes to bring a charge against him with the help of witnesses, he [i.e., the thief] is not liable to death, neither by the hands of the court nor by the householder. If this is

---

the phrase *if the sun be risen upon him*, as Rashi understands Onkelos. In contrast Verse 1 speaks of a case where there were *no* witnesses, and hence it cannot refer at all to freeing him from the death by the court, for the court can never act anyway without witnesses; but instead it refers only to freeing him from death by the hand of Heaven. But in that case, the *ein lo damim* [of Verse 1] and *damim lo* [of Verse 2] are *not* in exact contrast: *ein lo damim* frees him only from punishment by Heaven, and *damim lo* holds him guilty in both! (Mizrachi). Rather etc.

so, then — according to the opinion of the Sage who says [205] that a thief who broke into a house and took some of its vessels and went out, is free from paying for them, because he acquired them with "blood" [206] — we must say that the second half of the verse which states, *he shall make restitution; if he have nothing, then he shall be sold for his theft,* refers back to a previous verse [i.e., Verse 37 in the preceeding chapter] : *if a man steal an ox* etc. A similar case is the verse, *And also unto thy bondwoman thou shalt do likewise.* [207]

The plain meaning of the verse is known to be as follows: If a thief dug through into a home at dark, and was found there at night, he may be killed; but if the sun shone upon the thief and someone saw him and recognized him, he may not be killed, but he must pay for what he stole and took from there at daytime. The meaning of the term *hashemesh* (the sun) is "in the sight of those who saw him." Similarly, *in the sight of this sun* [208] means "openly." The reason for this law is as we have mentioned, that one who comes at night will kill the householder, [and therefore the householder may kill him], whilst one who comes at daytime will flee from him [once he is recognized].

6. IF A MAN DELIVER UNTO HIS NEIGHBOR MONEY OR VESSELS TO KEEP. This section [Verses 6-8] speaks of an unpaid guardian, therefore He has freed him from payment in case the money or vessels are lost or stolen, as is the Tradition of our Rabbis. [209] Scripture mentioned it without specifying what the case is because those who guard money or vessels generally do so

---

(205) The opinion is that of Rav (Sanhedrin 72 a). (206) Had he been found by the householder while still in the house and he were killed by him, the householder would be free from punishment. (207) Deuteronomy 15:17. This is to be connected with Verse 14 there, which states that the master must present gifts to a manservant who goes out free, and here it states that the same must also be done to a maidservant. But it does not refer to the first half of that verse [17] which speaks of the piercing of the ear of a manservant, since that law does not apply to a woman. (208) II Samuel 12:11. (209) Baba Metzia 94 b.

without reward. The second section [Verses 9-12] speaking of a paid guardian mentions *an ass, or an ox, or a sheep, or any beast*, [210] because it is the customary way to give over cattle into the hands of shepherds who pasture them for payment.

AND IT BE STOLEN OUT OF THE MAN'S HOUSE. Rashi explained it as meaning that it was *stolen out of the man's house* "according to his statement," meaning that this is what the unpaid guardian claims.[211] Scholars have brought parallel cases in Scripture [as proof to Rashi's explanation]. Thus: *If there arise in the midst of thee a prophet;*[212] *Hananiah the son of Azzur the prophet,* [213] for he is not referred to by that epithet ["prophet"] as a true description, but only because he claimed to be so. But there is no need for this. For Scripture is stating that if it was really stolen out of the man's house and *the thief be found, he shall pay double;* and *if the thief be not found,*[214] they shall come to court and the guardian shall swear concerning the stolen article *whether he have not put his hand unto his neighbor's goods,* [214] and *he whom the court condemns* as the thief of this article *shall pay double,*[215] as the court will not convict anyone and make him pay double unless he stole it, since the law of twofold restitution applies only to a thief, as He said above, *If the theft be found in his hand alive... he shall pay double.*[216]

7. WHETHER HE HAVE NOT PUT HIS HAND UNTO HIS NEIGHBOR'S GOODS. In the opinion of Rashi this means that the guardian is to come before the judges to swear that he has not put his hand to his fellow-man's goods [i.e., that he is not guilty

---

(210) Verse 9. (211) It cannot mean that it was *admittedly* stolen, for then how could Scripture say in the next verse that if the thief was not found, the guardian must swear, since it is admitted that it was stolen from him? Hence the verse must mean that he claims it was stolen. (212) Deuteronomy 13:2. The case there speaks of a false prophet. The term "prophet" must therefore be understood as "one who claims to be a prophet." (213) Jeremiah 28:1. [The reasoning is as in the previous Note.] (214) Verse 7. (215) Verse 8. (216) Verse 3.

of embezzlement]. The correct interpretation is that he is to come before the judges to swear that it was stolen and thus substantiate his claim, but he can only swear thus if he did not *put his hand* to make use of *his neighbor's* goods, for he who puts to his own use what had been left in his keeping is answerable for it as if he were a robber, and is liable to make restitution even if it was lost through an unavoidable accident. [217]

8. WHEREOF ONE SAITH: 'THIS IS IT.' Rashi comments: "according to the literal sense it means: that which the witness will say *'this is it* — this is that article about which you have taken an oath [that it was stolen from you] but see, it is in your possession!' And our Rabbis have explained that the phrase *this is it* teaches us that an oath cannot be imposed [by the court on a defendant] unless he admits part of the claim, saying 'I owe you so and so much, but the rest was stolen from me.'" [218]

But this principle of partial admission which the Rabbi [Rashi] has written here, is in accordance with the opinion of certain individual Rabbis [in the Talmud],[219] but is not the accepted decision of the law, for guardians [to incur liability to an oath] need not partially deny and partially admit the claim,[220] but even if they claim that the whole article was stolen, they still have to take the oath of the guardians, [unlike debts, which, if the debtor denies completely, do not require an oath of the Torah]. Moreover, it has been explained in the Gemara [221] with convincing proofs, that when he denies the very fact that he ever became a guardian, such as where he says "you have never given me the

---

(217) Baba Metzia 41 a.   (218) But if he denied the claim altogether, he is free from having to take an oath of the Torah. The Rabbis, however, instituted a consuetude oath in such cases (Shebuoth 40 b).   (219) Rabbi Chiya bar Aba in the name of Rabbi Yochanan, and Rami bar Chama (Baba Kamma 106-107 a).   (220) In other words, while the principle of partial admission applies to claims of debts, in the case of claims in guardianship, the accepted decision of the law is that the guardians need not partially admit the claim in order to be liable an oath of the Torah. The above interpretation of Rashi agrees therefore only with the opinion of certain individual Rabbis, but is not the accepted opinion.   (221) Baba Kamma 107 a.

object to keep," in that case if he denied it totally, he is free from taking an oath, and if he admitted it partially he is obliged to take an oath, this being the opinion of all Rabbis in the Talmud,[222] even though the Rabbi [Rashi] has not written so in his commentaries to the Gemara. [221] If so, we may say that the phrase [*this is it* — from which we derive the principle of partial admission, as explained above], speaks according to the interpretation of the Sages of a case where the guardian's defense is: "He never gave me anything to keep," in which case if he denied it totally he is free of an oath, and if he partially admitted it and partially denied it, he is liable to take an oath.[223] Thus the verses are to be explained as follows: *If the thief be not found, then the master of the house shall come near unto the judges*[214] — *for every* claim *of trespass* which he may claim against him, such as: "You were negligent in your guarding it," or where the guardian says: *"this is it,* — this is what you have deposited with me, and you did not deposit any more with me" — then the one with whom the article was deposited *that the judges will condemn,* [upon testimony given before them that he embezzled it], *shall pay double unto his neighbor.* Thus, both [the debtor and the guardian] pay, but double restitution is only where the guardian

---

(222) Ramban is here making an important distinction [in accordance with the teaching of the masters of the Tosafoth — see my Hebrew commentary, p. 430]: If the guardian sets up the kind of defense which can apply to cases of guardianship, such as where he says "an unavoidable accident happened to it" [such a defense has no place naturally where one is sued for a plain debt], then there is no distinction between total and partial admission — he is liable to an oath in either case. But where he puts up the kind of defense which can apply also to a debt, such as where he says, "You have never given me the object to keep" [which can apply to a debt as well: "You have never lent me"], then the law of partial admission applies to a guardian as well as to a debtor: if he denies it totally he is free of an oath, and if he admits it partially he is subject to an oath. — A re-reading of Ramban's words ["Moreover, etc."] will yield this thought clearly. (223) Such as where the claimant said, "I gave you two vessels to keep," and he replies, "You gave me one to keep, but the other you never gave to me." Had the defendant claimed so on both vessels, he would be free of an oath of the Torah. However, if his defense had been that an unavoidable accident happened, even if he claimed so on both of them, he would have had to swear [see preceding Note].

claims falsely that it was stolen, and the rule concerning the plea of partial admission applies to all claims, even to loans, robbery and other matters. In all these laws the verses of Scripture are few and the rules many. But there is no need to explain them here, except in order to interpret the verses.

12. IF IT BE TORN IN PIECES — "by a wild beast. 'Y'VIEIHU EID' — let him bring witnesses that it has been torn in pieces by accident, and then he will be free from paying." This is the language of Rashi.

But one may wonder. Why did Scripture mention specifically here [in the case of the animal being torn to pieces by a wild beast], the necessity of having witnesses, since in this [very same section of the law of the paid guardian] it has already said above, [in the cases where the animal dies, or is hurt, or captured], *The oath of the Eternal shall be between them both* [224] [i.e., between the owner of the animal and the guardian], and the law in all cases is alike: if there are witnesses that the animal died, or was hurt, or captured, he is free from paying and so also if it was torn in pieces by a wild beast, and if there are no witnesses he must take an oath in all cases, and if he does so, he does not pay? Perhaps Scripture speaks of the customary manner, for when an animal dies in *his master's crib* [225] or it goes up to the top of a crag and is hurt, *there is* usually *no man seeing it;* so also if it was captured by armed bandits who came upon it and took it from the flock and went away [there are usually no witnesses]. But when a lion or bear attacks, *a multitude of shepherds is called forth against it,* [226] and therefore Scripture says that he should bring the shepherds to court, and [upon their testimony] he will be freed from the liability of payment.

Or we may explain that Scripture intends to establish the law enunciated by Isi ben Yehudah, [227] who says, "*No-one seeing it* — he is free [from payment but he must swear]; but if there are witnesses who could testify in this matter, let him bring the

(224) Verse 10.   (225) Isaiah 1:3.   (226) *Ibid.,* 31:4.   (227) Baba Metzia 83 a.

witnesses and only then will he be free." And the explanation thereof is as follows: If the accident happened [to the animal entrusted to his guardianship] in a place where people are present the whole day, we do not rely upon his oath but instead he must bring witnesses, and where an animal is torn in pieces by a wild beast, it is generally the case [that other people are present besides the guardian], and therefore Scripture required him to bring witnesses.

Rabbi Abraham ibn Ezra explained: *y'vieihu eid* — "let him bring part of the torn animal as witness, *two legs, or a piece of an ear* [228] in proof of his statement." And I have seen it explained thus in the Mechilta of Rabbi Shimon ben Yochai: [229] "Aba Shaul said, he should bring the carcass, as it is said, *Thus saith the Eternal, as the shepherd rescueth out of the mouth of the lion, two legs* etc." [228]

15. AND IF A MAN 'Y'FATEH' — "speaks to her emotions [until she submits to him]. And so did Onkelos render it *arei y'shadeil*, the term *shidul* in Aramaic being like *pitui* [persuasion, seduction], in the Sacred Language. 'MAHOR YIMHARENAH' (HE SHALL SURELY PAY A DOWRY FOR HER) TO BE HIS WIFE — he shall assign her a marriage portion as is the manner of a man to his wife by writing her a *kethubah* (marriage contract), and he shall marry her." Thus far is Rashi's language.

But this is not correct, for the term *pitui* [does not mean "speaking to her feelings," as Rashi put it], but winning over another person's will by falsehood. A similar usage of the term is found in these verses: *'yifteh l'vavchem' (your heart will be deceived);* [230] *'vayift' (and he seduced) my heart secretly;* [231] *if my heart 'niftah' (have been enticed) unto a woman.* [232] This is why people whose minds are not adroit in discriminating matters, and whose hearts can be easily bent by a few words at the

---

(228) Amos 3:12.   (229) In Hoffman's edition of that Mechilta, p. 147. — See Vol. 1. p. 603, Note 245.   (230) Deuteronomy 11:16.   (231) Job 31:27.   (232) *Ibid.*, 9.

beginning of a discussion, are called *p'ta'im* (simple-minded ones), just as it is said, *'peti' (the simple-minded) believeth every word*,[233] and he who seduces a virgin in order to have sexual relations with her, bends her will to his desire by words of falsehood, and is therefore called *m'fateh* (seducer).

Onkelos, however, divided the term *pitui* into two meanings. Thus here he translated it: *y'shadeil*, which is an expression for cunning and effort that a person exercises towards another in order to do with him as he pleases, regardless of whether this effort is by means of words or deeds. Thus Onkelos translated: *'vayei'aveik'* a man with him [234] — *v'ishtadeil* (and a man 'wrestled craftily' with him). And Yonathan ben Uziel [235] translated: *'v'shovavticho' (and I will turn thee about), and put hooks into thy jaws* [236] — *'v'ishtadlinoch.'* And in the Targum of the Scroll of Ruth we find: *Where hast thou gleaned to-day? 'v'anah asit' (and where wroughtest thou)?* [237] — *'u'lan ishtadalt l'me'bad' (and where have you 'endeavored' to work)?* — *And she said: The man's name with whom 'asithi' (I wrought) to-day is Boaz,*[237] is translated in the Targum: *'d'ishtadalith imei'* (with whom I 'endeavored'). For all effort involving skill, with which a person attempts to achieve something, is called *hishtadluth* (endeavoring). Thus the Rabbis have said in the Mishnah:[238] "And where there are no men, *hishtadeil* (strive) to be a man." And in the Gemara [239] we find: "A man should always *yishtadeil* (strive) to go out to welcome kings of Israel." And in Scripture it is written: *and he* [i.e., the king] *'mishtadar' (labored) to rescue him,* [240] — employing every skill [to save Daniel].

---

(233) Proverbs 14:15. (234) Genesis 32:25. See Vol. 1, pp. 404-405 where Ramban discusses in brief the same theme as here. (235) See Vol. 1, p. 127 Note 152. (236) Ezekiel 38:4. (237) Ruth 2:19. It is of interest to note that Ramban refers to "the Targum of the Scroll of Esther" instead of ascribing it as he had done in the preceding reference to the Targum on the Book of Ezekiel. This indicates that Ramban held them to be of different authorship. Such indeed is the prevailing opinion in modern scholarship (see P. Churgin, Targum Kethuvim, pp. 140-151). (238) Aboth 2:5. (239) Berachoth 58 a. (240) Daniel 6:15.

EXODUS XXII, MISHPATIM 385

In my opinion, associated with this term [*hishtadluth* — striving] is the expression, *rebellion 'v'eshtadur' (and sedition) have been made therein,* [241] meaning, rebellion and "much striving." For even in the Sacred Language these letters [the *lamed* and the *reish* of *y'shadeil, y'shadeir*] interchange. Thus we find: *mazaloth* (constellations) [242] and *mazaroth;* [243] *niml'tzu* (sweet), [244] and *nimr'tzu* (forcible); [245] *'mifl'sei' (the balancing of) the clouds,* [246] and *'mifr'sei' (the spreadings of) the clouds.* [247] Similarly in Aramaic: *va'alu* (and behold), [248] and *va'aru.* [249] *Sharshereth* (chain) [250] is termed by the Sages *shalsheleth.* [251] There are Mishnaic texts where it is written, "*hishtadeir* [instead of *hishtadeil* — both terms meaning 'strive'] to be a man."[238] It is for this reason that Onkelos renders *ki y'fateh — arei y'shadeil* (he will endeavor); he will attempt by devious means to invest the virgin with a sense of trust in him, by many ruses, until she submits to him. And since seduction may be achieved in many ways — sometimes with words, sometimes with money, sometimes by falsehood to mislead her, and sometimes even by truth, as when he really wishes to marry her — therefore Onkelos did not use a precise term for it, but rendered it as an expression of "endeavor." However, in the verse, *lest your heart be 'yifteh,'*[230] he used the other meaning and translated it: *'dilma yit'ei,'* for there it means, "perhaps you will be misled."

And that which the Rabbi [Rashi] explained: "*'Mahor yimharenah' (he shall surely pay a dowry for her) to be his wife* — he shall assign her a marriage portion as is the manner of a man to his wife, by writing her a *kethubah* (marriage contract)" — this is not correct, for if the seducer marries her, he pays no penalty,[252] and if he divorces her after the marriage, there is no monetary obligation upon him by law of the Torah, since a *kethubah* is a matter of Rabbinic ordinance. Rather, *mohar* means gifts — the

---

(241) Ezra 4:19. (242) II Kings 23:5. (243) Job 38:32. (244) Psalms 119:103. (245) Job 6:25. (246) *Ibid.,* 37:16. (247) *Ibid.,* 36:29. (248) Daniel 7:8. (249) *Ibid.,* Verse 7. (250) Further, 28:14. (251) Mikvaoth 10:5. (252) Verse 16, and Kethuboth 39 a.

gifts which a man sends to his betrothed, *jewels of silver and jewels of gold* [253] and clothes for the wedding ceremony and marriage, these being called *sivlonoth* in the language of the Rabbis. [254] Thus they said: "*Mohari* go back [upon the death of the wife]." [255] And Onkelos rendered the verse, *And Shechem said... Multiply upon me greatly 'mohar' and gift* [256] — "multiply upon me greatly *moharin* [in the plural] and gifts," and Shechem would not have vowed to write Dinah many *kethuboth*. Instead, *mohar* means gifts, as I have explained. It is possible that the word is derived from the expression *'m'heirah chushah' (hasten, stay not)*, [257] because the *mohar* is the first thing which hastens the wedding, as the groom hurries and sends these presents ahead of him in eager haste and then he comes to his father-in-law's house to make the wedding or the feast, just as the Sages have spoken of "parties of *sivlonoth*" (when presents are presented to the betrothed). [258] The meaning of *'mahor yimharenah' to be his wife* is then, that the seducer should send her presents and necessities for the wedding in order to become his wife. There is thus a hint here that both the seducer and the seduced can prevent the marriage, since Scripture uses such language rather than saying expressly that he should take her to him as his wife; for there is no commandment upon him to marry her unless he so desires, and if he does not want her to begin with, he is to pay fifty shekels of silver. [259] After that Scripture states [260] that if the father *refuses to give her unto him, he shall pay* him *money according to the 'mohar'* which men give *to virgins* whom they marry. The reason for this fine is that the seducer has spoiled her reputation in the eyes of young men, thus the father will have to give her many presents and they will not give her any dowry, therefore it is right that the seducer should pay it. Our Rabbis have said [261] that the

---

(253) Genesis 24:53.   (254) Kiddushin 50 a.   (255) Baba Bathra 145 a. This applies to a case where the marriage was not consumated (Even Ha'ezer 50, 4).   (256) Genesis 34:12.   (257) I Samuel 20:38.   (258) Pesachim 49 a.   (259) Deuteronomy 22:29. As explained further on in Ramban, this fine [stated in the case of a violator] applies also to a seducer — if he or she refuses marriage.   (260) Verse 16 here.   (261) Mechilta here in the verse, and Kethuboth 10 a.

amount of this *mohar* was determined by Scripture in the case of the violator to be fifty shekels of silver, [262] the law of the violator and of the seducer being alike in this respect. Scripture, however, did differentiate between them in that in the case of the violator it says, *and she shall be his wife... he may not put her away all his days,* [262] the reason [for this distinction between the violator, who must marry the maiden whom he has raped, and is forbidden to divorce her ever, and the seducer, who does not have to marry the seduced girl, but may instead pay the penalty mentioned in the Torah], is that usually it is *handsome young men* [263] who seduce virgins, and the beautiful daughters of prominent families, [in the hope of marrying them]. But since it is not proper that he should gain from his sin, [i.e., that the girl should have to marry the seducer], therefore He explained that he cannot marry her against their will [hers and that of her father], but instead must pay them. Also, because she too sinned in this matter, He did not impose it on him to have to marry her against his will, but instead it is enough if he pays the penalty [of the fifty shekels of silver], and if he marries her with her consent and that of her father, she has the same status in relation to him as all women, having no claim to a *kethubah* from him by law of the Torah [but only by Rabbinic ordinance]. Similarly, it is usually the sons of prominent families who rape the daughters of those less-known families who have no power against them. Therefore He said in the case of the violator, *and she shall be his wife* [262] — against his will. And in the opinion of our Rabbis, [264] there too [in the case of the violator] the maiden and her father can withhold consent, as it would not be correct that he should marry her against her will, and thus do her two evils. Sometimes she may be of a more honorable family than he, and it is inconceivable that she should be further disgraced by his sinful act. The fair law is thus that the decision as to the marriage of the raped maiden be left to her discretion and that of her father, and not to the violator; instead, [if she desires it] he must marry her against his

(262) Deuteronomy 22:29.   (263) Ezekiel 23:6.   (264) Kethuboth 39 b.

will,[265] in order that violent men should not take liberties with the daughters of Israel.

Now this law of seduction only applies to a *na'arah*,[266] as does the law of violation [which applies only to a girl between the ages of twelve years and a day, and twelve and a half], for there Scripture expressly stated, *if a man find a 'n'arah' that is a virgin,*[267] but here He did not mention *na'arah*. The reason for this is that the term *na'arah* mentioned there [in the case of a violator], is used in order to exclude the *bogereth* [a woman who has passed the stage of maidenhood], who is considered an adult woman, whereas a girl who is a minor [between the ages of three years and a day and twelve years and a day], is also included under the terms of the law of violation. But here [in the case of seduction], it was not necessary to exclude a *bogereth,* for it is self-understood that one who seduces a *bogereth* pays nothing, as he did it with her mature consent. Besides, a father has no rights at all in his daughter after the days of her maidenhood, as it is written, *'bin'ureihah' (in her maidenhood) in her father's house,* [268] and here He said, *If her father utterly refuse to give her unto him,*[260] thus indicating that he [the father] can give her to him as a wife, seeing that he has the authority to take her betrothal-money, and this applies only when she is a minor or a *na'arah,* [266] just as the Rabbis interpreted:[269] "All benefits which accrue during maidenhood belong to her father." [270] But in the case of a violation it was necessary to write *na'arah,* in order to exclude a *bogereth* [266] from that law, because we might have

---

(265) "Even if she be lame, even if she be blind, and even if she is afflicted with boils" (*ibid.*, 39 a). (266) A *na'arah* is a maiden between the age of twelve years and a day and twelve and a half. After that she counts as a *bogereth* — past her maidenhood. The period of *yalduth* (childhood) is from three years and a day to twelve years and a day. (267) Deuteronomy 22:28. (268) Numbers 30:17. (269) Kiddushin 3 b. (270) There was no need for Scripture here to write *na'arah* to exclude a *bogereth* from the law of seduction, since the verse *if her father utterly refuse* etc. could not possibly speak of a *bogereth*. Hence it is self-understood that the section deals here with a *na'arah,* and there was no need to mention it. But in the case of violation etc.

thought that if she were a *bogereth* he should pay the fifty shekels of silver to her, [instead of to her father; it was therefore necessary to state] that it is a Scriptural decree [that if she is a *bogereth* he is free from that penalty], the reason being that since she is in full control of herself, she should guard herself against such a mishap.

Now Rabbi Abraham ibn Ezra explained *mohar* as being an expression of "binding" [that he should bind her to him as a wife], similar in usage to the verse, *Let the idols of them be multiplied 'acheir maharu' (who bind themselves to another god).* [271] But this is not correct; instead, the meaning of *mohar* is as I have explained it on the basis of the words of our Rabbis, of blessed memory. And in my opinion *acheir maharu* [271] means, "those who are 'hasty' in thought, [from the root *maheir* — fast] and follow another god precipitately, without consideration and without knowledge." In the writings of the grammarians [272] [*acheir maharu* is explained as meaning]: "those who give *mohar* (gifts) to another god," meaning that they bring him sacrifice and offering.

17. THOU SHALT NOT SUFFER A SORCERESS TO LIVE. In connection with all those who are guilty of death, He has said above: *moth yumoth (he shall be surely put to death),*[273] meaning he is liable to death, and it is a positive commandment upon us to slay him, based upon the verse which says, *And thou shalt put away the evil from the midst of thee,* [274] or it may be that this obligation on us is derived from the very expression *yumoth* (he

---

(271) Psalms 16:4. It is generally translated: "that make suit unto another." According to Ibn Ezra: "that bind (or connect) themselves with another god." Ramban's own interpretation of that verse follows later in the text. (272) R'dak in Sefer Hashorashim, root *acheir*. (273) Above 21:15-17. (274) Deuteronomy 17:7. Ramban is here intimating that this verse is the basis for the *one* commandment of the execution of all four modes of death penalties. Rabbi Moshe ben Maimon (Rambam) counted them as *four* separate commandments. See my translation, "The Commandments," Vol. I, p. 240.

shall be put to death) which He used in these cases.[275] But here, however, He did not say, "a sorceress shall be put to death," but in this case He warned us in a stricter manner by means of a negative commandment, that we should not suffer her to live.[276] The reason for this is that the sorceress is *defiled of name and full of tumult,* [277] and fools are mislead by her, therefore He was more stringent and admonished us with a prohibition. We find a similar severity in relation to all those who cause snares for many people, such as that which He said in the case of the misleader after idols, *neither shalt thou spare, nor shalt thou conceal him,* [278] and in the case of a murderer He said, *And ye shall take no ransom for the life of a murderer, that is guilty of death.* [279]

19. HE THAT SACRIFICETH 'LO'ELOHIM YOCHARAM' (SHALL BE UTTERLY DESTROYED). "*Lo'elohim* means to the idols, for since the word is voweled with a *patach,*[280] it means *those* gods which in another place you have been warned not to worship." This is Rashi's language. Rabbi Abraham ibn Ezra commented that in accordance with the plain meaning of Scripture, this command is not directed to Israel, as they had already been warned in the second of the Ten Commandments against the worship of idols. Instead it was said to "the stranger" mentioned in the following verse, that he may live in our land only on condition that he should not sacrifice to his gods as he was wont to do. — But *he* [i.e., Ibn Ezra] *openeth his mouth in vanity.* [281] For in the Ten Commandments He warned against idolatry by a prohibition, and here He explained the punishment

---

(275) This opinion corresponds closely to that of the author of 'Hilchoth Gedoloth' which Rambam in his Sefer Hamitzvoth criticised, and Ramban in his notes to that work defended. See "The Commandments," Vol. II, p. 420. (276) See *ibid.,* pp. 285-286. (277) Ezekiel 22:5. (278) Deuteronomy 13:9. (279) Numbers 35:31. (280) The *patach* and *kamatz* are in this sense alike, as both indicate the definite article — "*those* gods which in another place you have been forbidden to worship." The word *lo'elohim* is voweled with a *kamatz.* (281) Job 35:16. Here in the sense of "worthless" or "unsubstantial."

EXODUS XXII, MISHPATIM

and the law that we are to apply to he who transgresses that commandment, just as He did in the case of *Thou shalt not murder; Thou shalt not commit adultery*,[282] for *these are the ordinances* which He set *before them* [with respect to these commandments].[283] Thus He is hereby declaring that one who sacrifices to idols is guilty of death, for the term *yocharam* means death by the court. Similarly we find, *All 'cheirem' that may be 'yocharam' of men may not be ransomed; he shall surely be put to death.* [284] He uses the term *yocharam* [of the root *cheirem* — unlawful, anathema], because he who sacrifices to that which is anathema, deserves destruction, similar to that which is said in the verse, *And thou shalt not bring an abomination into thy house, and be 'cheirem' (accursed) like unto it; thou shalt utterly detest it, and thou shalt utterly abhor it; for it is an accursed thing.*[285]

It is possible that the verse includes the slaughterer and the animal slaughtered, to tell us that they both go to *cheirem* (destruction), thus hinting that it is forbidden to derive any benefit from that which has been offered to the idols. It mentioned sacrificing, but the same law applies to bowing down before the idol, and to all other acts of worship performed in the Sanctuary,[286] but other acts of worship — such as sweeping it, or besprinkling it, or putting his arms around it, or kissing it — are not punishable by death, provided that the idol is not usually worshipped in that manner, but if it is the customary way of worshipping it, he is liable to death under all circumstances, even if excreting to Baal Peor.

The correct interpretation of the term *lo'elohim* with the *lamed* voweled with a *patach*, [or a *kamatz* as in this instance], is that it

---

(282) Above, 20:13.   (283) See Ramban above 21:12 (towards the end) for further explanation.   (284) Leviticus 27:29. See Ramban there for full explanation. But here he merely brings proof from this verse that the word *yocharam* signifies death by the court.   (285) Deuteronomy 7:26. (286) Such as offering incense and libation. Since these acts are performed in the worship of G-d, they come under the terms of this law, so that he who performs them in the worship of the idols is liable to death by the court.

refers to the angels of above who are called *elohim* in many places of Scripture, as it is written: *There is none like unto Thee among 'elohim,' O Eternal;* [287] *He is G-d of 'elohim' and Lord of lords;* [288] *Bow down to him, all ye 'elohim.'* [289] They are also called *eilim* (the mighty ones), [290] as I have already mentioned. [290] And He said here, *save unto the Eternal only*, because those who sacrifice to His angels think that thereby they do His will, and that the angels will be the intermediaries to obtain His favor for them, and that it is as if they sacrifice to G-d and His ministers; therefore He said [that sacrifices must not be brought] *save unto the Eternal only*. [291] Inherent in this interpretation is also a profound secret, from which one can understand the concept of offerings, and the student learned in the secrets of the Cabala can understand it from that which we have written elsewhere. [292] Onkelos hinted at it here. [293] We shall yet allude to it in *Torath Kohanim* [294] with the help of G-d, may His Name forever be blessed to all eternity.

20. AND A STRANGER SHALT THOU NOT WRONG, NEITHER SHALT THOU OPPRESS HIM; FOR YE WERE STRANGERS IN THE LAND OF EGYPT. There is no reason why all strangers [from countries outside the land of Egypt] should be included here because of our having been strangers in the land of Egypt! And there is no reason why they be assured for ever against being wronged or oppressed because we were once strangers there! Now Rashi explained that this is a reason for the prohibition against annoying a stranger. G-d warned against vexing him with words, for "if you vex him he can also vex you, by saying to you, "You also descend from strangers.' Do not reproach your fellow man with a fault which is also in you." Rabbi Abraham ibn Ezra

---

(287) Psalms 86:8. (288) Deuteronomy 10:17. (289) Psalms 97:7. (290) Above, 15:11. (291) See also Ramban above, 20:3. (292) In *Seder Shemoth* 5:3. and *Seder Yithro* 18:13. (293) Onkelos rendered the verse thus: "save unto the *name of the* Eternal only." With this translation Onkelos indicated that the intention of the sacrifice is to the proper Name of G-d (Abusaulah, and Ma'or V'shamesh). (294) Leviticus 1:9. — For the term *Torath Kohanim* see *Seder Yithro* Note 590.

explained the verses: "Remember *that ye were strangers* as he is now." But there is in all these comments no real reason for the law.

The correct interpretation appears to me to be that He is saying: "Do not wrong a stranger or oppress him, thinking as you might that none can deliver him out of your hand; for you know that you were strangers in the land of Egypt *and I saw the oppression wherewith the Egyptians oppressed*[295] you, and I avenged your cause on them, because *I behold the tears of such who are oppressed and have no comforter, and on the side of their oppressors there is power,* [296] and I deliver each one *from him that is too strong for him.*[297] Likewise *you shall not afflict the widow and the fatherless child,*[298] for I will hear their cry,[299] for all these people do not rely upon themselves but trust in Me." And in another verse He added this reason: *for ye know the soul of a stranger, seeing ye were strangers in the land of Egypt.*[300] That is to say, you know that every stranger feels depressed, and is always sighing and crying, and his eyes are always directed towards G-d, therefore He will have mercy upon him even as He showed mercy to you, just as it is written, *and the children of Israel sighed by reason of the bondage, and they cried, and their cry came up unto G-d by reason of the bondage,*[301] meaning that He had mercy on them not because of their merits, but only an account of the bondage [and likewise He has mercy on all who are oppressed].

21. ANY WIDOW — even a rich one of quite considerable wealth — YE SHALL NOT AFFLICT, for her tears are frequent and her soul is depressed. He states, *If thou afflict 'otho'* [299] ["him" in the singular], meaning any one [who is a widow or a fatherless child]. Therefore it is written after that, *and your wives shall be widows,* [302] in punishment for your causing the cry of the widow, *and your children fatherless,*[302] in punishment for the cry of the orphan.

(295) Above 3:9. (296) Ecclesiastes 4:1. (297) Psalms 35:10. (298) Verse 21. (299) Verse 22. (300) Further, 23:9. (301) Above, 2:23. (302) Verse 23.

This punishment [*And My wrath shall glow, and I will kill you with the sword* etc.] [302] is not counted by our Rabbis amongst those brought upon people who are liable to death by the hand of Heaven, as listed in the Beraitha, [303] "These are the people who are liable to death by the hand of Heaven" taught in Tractate Sanhedrin. [304] The reason for this is that the death mentioned here is unlike the usual death of people by the hand of Heaven, of whom it is said, *and they die therein, if they profane it;* [305] *and ye die not.* [306] But here the punishment is that they will die by the enemy's sword, *or he shall go down into battle, and be swept away* [307] without anyone knowing it, and their wives will thus have to remain forever widows, and their children always be fatherless.

22. IF THOU AFFLICT HIM IN ANY WISE. "This is an elliptical verse; it threatens, but does not explain the punishment needed to complete the sense of the verse. It is like the verse, *therefore, whosoever slayeth Cain,* [308] which does not explain what the punishment is. Here too, *if thou afflict him in any wise,* is an expression of determination to inflict punishment, as if to say: 'In the end you will get your deserts. Why? For *if he cry unto Me* I will hear him, and I will avenge him.'" This is Rashi's language. But it is not correct [to interpret a verse on the basis of such a long omission, in order to complete the sense]. The witness he brings [i.e., the verse about Cain] also does not testify to that [kind of long omission]. But it is possible that the word *ki* [generally translated "for"], here means "if," for this is one of the usages of the word *ki,* [309] and the verse thus states: "if if he cry at all unto Me, I will surely hear his cry," the repetition of the word

---

(303) See *Seder Bo* Note 209.   (304) Sanhedrin 83 a.   (305) Leviticus 22:9.   (306) Numbers 18:32.   (307) I Samuel 26:10.   (308) Genesis 4:15. (309)   Rosh Hashanah 3 a. The verse here reads: *ki im tza'ok yitzak,* and is generally translated: *"for* if he cry." But with the word *ki* understood as "if", the verse would read: "if if he cry," as explained further on in the text.

EXODUS XXII, MISHPATIM

"if" being used in order to show the gravity and importance of the matter, similar in usage to these phrases; *hamiblie ein k'varim* [generally translated: "Was it because there were no graves...?" — but literally: "was it because there were 'no no' graves...?"] ; [310] *harak ach b'Mosheh* [generally translated: "hath the Eternal indeed spoken only with Moses", but literally: " 'only only' with Moses]." [311]

The correct interpretation appears to me to be that He is stating: "*If thou afflict him in any wise, if he will* only just *cry at all unto Me I will* at once *hear his cry:* he does not need anything else at all, for I will save him and avenge his cause from you. And the reason for this is that you oppress him because [you think] he has no one to help him against you, but behold he has more help than anyone else. For other people will try to find saviors to save them, and helpers to avenge their cause, and perhaps *they cannot profit nor deliver,* [312] while this one will be saved by the Eternal merely through his crying out, and He will take vengeance from you, for *The Eternal is a jealous and avenging G-d.*" [313] There are many verses to a similar effect. Thus, that which He said, *Rob not the weak, because he is weak, neither crush the poor in the gate; for the Eternal will plead their cause,* [314] means: "rob not the poor merely because he is poor and has no helpers, nor crush the poor in your gates, for the Eternal will plead on their behalf." Similarly He said, *And enter not into the fields of the fatherless, for their Redeemer is strong;* [315] *the Eternal of hosts is His Name,* [316] for they have a Redeemer Who is stronger and closer to them than all people have. Here also He said, that just by his cry, the fatherless will be saved. Likewise: *For as the rain cometh down and the snow from heaven, and returneth not thither, except it water the earth, and make it bring forth and bud, and give seed to the sower and bread to the eater; so shall My word be that goeth*

---

(310) Exodus 14:11. (311) Numbers 12:2. (312) I Samuel 12:21. (313) Nachum 1:2. (314) Proverbs 22:22-23. (315) *Ibid.,* 23:10-11. (316) Jeremiah 50:34: *Their Redeemer is strong, the Eternal of hosts is His Name.*

forth out of My mouth; it shall not return unto Me void, except it accomplish that which I please.[317] In both phrases [*except it water — except it accomplish*] He is stating that they[318] will do nothing else other than to water the earth immediately, and so also will *My word* do that which I please. Thus the meaning of the word *ki* [*ki im hirvah — ki im asah*: except it water — except it accomplish] has the sense of "but." And so also: '*ki im*' *(but) I will depart to mine own land, and to my kindred.* [319]

24. THOU SHALT NOT BE TO HIM AS AN EXACTOR — that is, a creditor. He is saying that the lender should not behave to the borrower like a creditor who is a sort of lord over the borrower, as it is written, *and the borrower is a servant to the lender,*[320] but instead you should behave to him exactly as if he had never borrowed from you; neither shall you lay upon him interest, whether *interest of money, interest of victuals.*[321] Rather, the loan to him should be an act of goodness; you should not take from him any mark of honor because of it, nor are you to derive any monetary benefit from it.

26. AND I WILL HEAR FOR I AM GRACIOUS — showing favor and accepting everyone's supplication even though he is unworthy, the word *chanun* (gracious) being derived from the word *chinam* (for nothing). And the meaning of the verse is that you should not think: "I will not take the righteous man's garment as a pledge, but the garment of a man who is not righteous I will take as a pledge and not return to him, for G-d will not hear his cry." Therefore He said, *for I am gracious* and I hear the cry of all who beseech Me.

27. THOU SHALL NOT CURSE 'ELOHIM.' Onkelos translated it as referring to a judge, that one is not to curse him if he should hold him guilty in a lawsuit. *Lo takeil* [Onkelos' rendition of the Hebrew *lo t'kaleil* — thou shalt not curse], is the Aramaic

---

(317) Isaiah 55:10-11. (318) I.e., the rain and the snow. (319) Numbers 10:30. (320) Proverbs 22:7. (321) Deuteronomy 23:20.

expression for "cursing." Thus: *"Meikal l'hu* (they curse him): *May the Eternal cut off to the man that doeth this, him that calleth and him that answereth."* [322] There are many similar expressions, in the language of the Talmud Yerushalmi.

NOR CURSE A 'NASI' OF THY PEOPLE — *nasi* means the one who is "lifted up" above his people, namely, the king. He thus mentioned that one is not to curse him in case he declares him guilty in a trial before him.

In the opinion of our Rabbis in the Gemara,[323] *Thou shalt not curse 'Elokim,'* constitutes an admonition against blaspheming the Name of G-d, even by one of the substituted names [such as: Gracious and Merciful etc.].[324] Thus He warned against cursing the King on high, blessed be He, and also the monarch that reigns on earth. The Rabbis have also said in the Gemara [323] that included in the term *Elokim,* is *the Glorious Name,* [325] as well as the judge who sits *in the seat of G-d* [326] on earth. But it has not been explained whether the term *nasi* includes the head of the Great Sanhedrin,[327] who is called *nasi* in the Gemara.[328] Harav Rabbi Moshe ben Maimon said [329] that he is included under the term of this prohibition. And so it also appears to me, on the basis of a question that Rabbi Yehudah Hanasi [330] asked about himself: [331]

---

(322) Malachi 2:12. — Yerushalmi Shabbath III, 7. (323) Sanhedrin 66 a.
(324) See Mishneh Torah, Mada, Hilchoth Yesodei Hatorah 6:5.
(325) Deuteronomy 28:58. — I.e., the Tetragrammaton. (326) Ezekiel 28:2. (327) The Great Sanhedrin consisted of seventy-one judges, and sat in the court of the Sanctuary. A small Sanhedrin of twenty-three judges was to be found in every city. (328) Sanhedrin 19 b. (329) In his Book of the Commandments, Negative Commandment 316 (See Vol. II of my translation, p. 290). (330) Rabbi Yehudah Hanasi, the redactor of the Mishnah, was Chief of the Sanhedrin of his generation. — The question he asked concerning himself was whether he had, in the eyes of the Law, the status of a *nasi* so that [in the time of the Sanctuary] the law of a special sin-offering for the prince (see Leviticus 4:22-26) applied to him as well, since he was the *nasi* of the Sanhedrin, or perhaps because he had his counterpart in the Diaspora — the Exilarch — his authority was no longer unique as that of a king, and therefore his sin-offering is to be like that of any individual Israelite. It is thus obvious that the office of the Chief of the Sanhedrin as such is included under the term *nasi*. (331) Horayoth 11 b.

"A person in my status, am I to bring a *sa'ir* [332] etc.?" If so, He is stating: "Do not curse any ruler of the people, who holds a position of supreme authority over all Israel, whether that position be in the secular sphere of government or in the rule of Torah," for the head of the Sanhedrin is the highest position in the authority of the Torah.

28. 'M'LEIATHCHA V'DIM'ACHA' (OF THE FULNESS OF THY HARVEST, AND OUT OF THE OUTFLOW OF THY PRESSES) THOU SHALT NOT DELAY TO OFFER. We find the word *m'leiah* with reference to seed, thus: *lest there be forfeited 'ham'leiah' (the fulness) of the seed which thou hast sown,*[333] and again: *'v'kamleiah' (and as the fulness) of the winepress,*[334] meaning wine and oil, just as it is said, *and the vats shall overflow with wine and oil.*[335]

It appears to me in connection with these terms, that fruits of the field and vineyard are called *t'vuah* [of the root *bo* — come in] because the farmers "bring" the whole crop in together to the homes. It is also called *asif* (the ingathering): *'osef' (the ingathering) shall not come;*[336] *and the feast of 'ha'asif' (the ingathering).*[337] This is why produce is called *m'leiah* (fulness), because a gathering-together into one place of a mass of material or people is called *milui* (fulness): *though there be called forth against him 'm'lo' (a multitude of) shepherds;*[338] *even they are 'malei' (in full) cry after you;*[339] *together against me 'yitmalo'un'*[340] — they gather themselves and come. Similarly, *and his seed shall become 'm'lo' nations*[341] — means an assembly and multitude of nations.

It is further possible that produce is called *m'leiah* (full) as a substitute term for a blessing — that *the granaries shall be full of*

---

(332) A male goat. See Leviticus 4:23. The individual Israelite brings a female goat as a sin-offering (*ibid.*, Verse 28). (333) Deuteronomy 22:9. (334) Numbers 18:27. (335) Joel 2:24. (336) Isaiah 32:10. (337) Further, 23:16. (338) Isaiah 31:4. (339) Jeremiah 12:6. (340) Job 16:10. (341) Genesis 48:19.

EXODUS XXII, MISHPATIM

corn, and the vats shall overflow with wine and oil,[342] and the reaper fills his hands, and the binder of sheaves his bosom,[343] and gathers grapes in the vintage. For when *their portion is cursed*[344] Scripture says, *Let them be as the grass upon the housetops, which withereth afore it springeth up; wherewith the reaper filleth not his hand, nor he that bindeth sheaves, his bosom,*[345] but when their portion is blessed, it is called *m'leiah* (full). And in that case *dim'acha* [literally: "your tear"] is an allusion to wine and oil, a usage borrowed from *dim'ath ha'ayin* (tear of the eye), because the drops from the grape and olive resemble the tear of the eye. Or it may be that all moisture that falls in globules — even drops of water — are called *dim'ah* (tear), such as: *and mine eyes shall run down 'dim'ah' (with tear),*[346] and it is not a term used only for tears. And the intention of the verse is, that when you gather in the crops of the field, and *the granaries will be full of corn,*[342] and you press the grapes and olives to extract their juice, *and the vats shall overflow with wine and oil,*[342] you should not delay them in your possession, but right at the beginning you are to give your tithings to Me, just as He said, *The first fruits of thy corn, of thy wine, and of thine oil... shalt thou give him* — [i.e., the priest].[347]

In the opinion of our Rabbis,[348] of blessed memory, *thou shalt not delay* means that: "you are not to set aside last what should be first, [and set aside first what should be last]." Now here He did not explain [the correct order of the gifts], for here He mentions the commandments in a general way, and afterwards He explained them in detail. The Rabbis arranged the order of the gifts as follows: first-fruits, the heave-offering, the First Tithe, and the Second Tithe.[349] This order they established on the basis of

---

(342) Joel 2:24. (343) See Psalms 129:7. (344) Job 24:18. (345) Psalms 129:6-7. (346) Jeremiah 13:17. (347) Deuteronomy 18:4. (348) Mechilta here on the Verse. (349) The first-fruits are brought to the Sanctuary and then given to the priest. The heave-offering is given to the priest, the First Tithe to the Levite, and the Second Tithe is eaten by the owner in Jerusalem. See "The Commandments," Vol. II, pp. 145-146, for full discussion of this commandment.

the following interpretation with reference to these gifts, just as we have been taught: [350] "How do we know that first-fruits come before the heave-offering, being that this one is called by Scripture *terumah* (heave-offering) and *reshith* (the first), and the other is also called *terumah* and *reshith*?[351] First-fruits have priority because they are the first [to grow] of all produce. The heave-offering comes before the First Tithe, because it is called *reshith* (the first),[351] and the First Tithe comes before the Second Tithe because it contains in it *reshith*" [since the Levite who receives the First Tithe must give a tenth of it as *terumah* to the priest].

Onkelos translated *m'leiathcha v'dim'acha:* "*bikurach* (your first fruit), *v'dim'ach.*" [352] And Rashi explained: "*M'leiathcha* — this means the duty which falls upon you when your crop becomes fully ripened, and it refers to the first-fruits. *V'dim'acha* means the heave-offering. But I do not know what the term *dim'a* means." It is similarly stated in the Mechilta:[348] "*M'leiathcha* means the first-fruits which are taken from the full crop, and *dim'acha* means the heave-offering." Perhaps in the same way that according to the Rabbis the first-fruits are called in this verse *m'leiah* (fulness), because they are taken from the full crop, so the heave-offering is called *dim'ah* [literally: "tear" or "outflow," as explained above], because it is set aside from wine and oil, [as liquids], not from the fruit. Scripture mentioned only these two kinds of produce, [wine and oil], in order to hint at the law that the heave-offering only has to be set aside from them when in the form of wine and oil, there being no obligation upon the owner to anticipate and set it aside when they are still grapes and olives.

---

(350) Terumoth 3:7. (351) Deuteronomy 12:6 speaks of first-fruits as *terumath yedchem* (the heave-offering of your hand); they are called *reshith* in this Scriptural section (further 23:19). The heave-offering is called *terumah* in Numbers 18:8, and is called *reshith* in Deuteronomy 18:4. (352) Onkelos thus left the Hebrew word *v'dim'acha* untranslated. As explained further it is a term denoting the priest's share of the produce — in other words, the *terumah* [or the heave-offering]. According to Onkelos the verse thus refers to the first-fruits and the heave-offering.

EXODUS XXIII, MISHPATIM

Thus He only mentioned these commandments here by way of allusion, as if to say, "Be careful to keep these commandments about which I will command you further," in a similar manner to that which He said above, *and I will appoint thee a place whither he may flee.* [353] This was in order to write down these commandments in *the book of the covenant* [354] which He mentions in a subsequent section, and Scripture explains them all again in another place, [each one in detail].

30. AND YE SHALL BE HOLY MEN UNTO ME. The reason for the expression in this verse is that until now He mentioned only the ordinances and admonished them about repulsive matters, [355] but now when He is about to begin the law of forbidden food, He prefaced it by saying, *And ye shall be holy men unto Me.* For in order to preserve his physical life man should [be able to] eat anything which serves that purpose, and the prohibitions concerning certain foods are only a means of guarding the purity of the soul, in order that one should eat clean things which do not give rise to harshness and coarseness in the soul. Therefore He said, *And ye shall be holy men unto Me,* that is to say: "I want you to be holy men so that you will become suitable for Me, to cleave to Me, for I am Holy; therefore do not defile your souls by eating abominable things." And similarly He said, *Ye shall not make yourselves detestable with any swarming thing that swarmeth, neither shall ye make yourselves unclean with them, that ye should be defiled thereby. For I am the Eternal your G-d; sanctify yourselves therefore, and be ye holy; for I am Holy.* [356] Swarming things thus make the soul detestable, but the *treifah* [357] is not detestable, however abstention from eating it adds holiness.

23   11. BUT THE SEVENTH YEAR 'TISHM' TENAH U'N'TASHTAH' (THOU SHALT LET IT REST AND LIE FALLOW). "*Tishm'tenah* — by not tilling it. *U'n'tashtah* by not

---

(353) Above, 21:13. (354) Further, 24:7. (355) Such as those described above in Verses 17-21. (356) Leviticus 11:43-44. (357) See above, Note 189.

eating of its produce after 'the time of removal.' [358] Another interpretation: *Tishm'tenah* — from real work, such as plowing and sowing; *u'n'tashtah* — from hoeing or manuring it." This is Rashi's language. But it is not correct, for according to the law of the Torah we have only been warned against plowing and sowing in the seventh year, but hoeing and manuring, and even weeding, hoeing under the vines, and cutting away thorns, and all other forms of agricultural work, are not forbidden by law of the Torah. This is the conclusion that the Rabbis came to [after a discussion of this matter] at the beginning of Tractate Moed Katan in the Chapter *Mashkin*;[359] that the Merciful One forbade only plowing and sowing in the seventh year, but did not prohibit secondary kinds of work [such as hoeing, manuring, etc.], which are all forbidden only by Rabbinic ordinance, and the verse mentioned [there in the Talmud] in connection with these secondary kinds of work is a mere support in the Scriptural text.[360] Similarly, the law of "removal" [358] is not derived from this verse [as Rashi explained here].

Rabbi Abraham ibn Ezra wrote: "*Tishm'tenah* means: every creditor *'shamot' (shall release)* that which he hath lent unto his neighbor.[361] — *U'n'tashtah* means that you should not sow your field." But it is not a correct comment. Instead, [the true explanation is that] Scripture first said, *six years thou shalt sow and gather in the increase thereof,*[362] *but the seventh year 'tishm'tenah'* — you should not sow your land; *u'n'tashtah* — you should not gather in its increase, but instead you are to leave it so that the poor of your people and the beasts of the field may eat the fruits of the tree and the produce of the vineyard. In a similar

---

(358) See Leviticus 25:6-7. The produce of the Sabbatical year which grows of its own accord may be eaten by humans and animals in the house, as long as the wild beasts are able to eat of that produce in the field. But when it is no longer found by the wild beasts in the field, the food has to be "removed" from the house and made available to all alike. (359) Literally: "We may water" [an irrigated field...]. — Moed Katan 2 b-3 a. (360) See in *Seder Yithro* Note 449. (361) Deuteronomy 15:2. (362) Verse 10.

EXODUS XXIII, MISHPATIM

sense is the verse, *'v'nitash' the seventh year,* [363] [which thus means: "and we will not gather in the increase of the field in the seventh year"].

12. 'L'MA'AN' (THAT) THINE OX AND THINE ASS MAY HAVE REST. Because the word *l'ma'an* is like *ba'avur* ("in order that"), we must explain [364] that the verse is stating: "Six days you shall do all your work in the house and in the field, in order that the ox and the ass may have rest on the seventh day. *And the son of thy handmaid, and the stranger, may be refreshed* — in order that they all be witnesses to the Creation." The verse here is then similar in meaning to: *Bake that which ye will bake.*[365] Similarly He said, *Six days shalt thou labor, and do all thy work,*[366] as I have explained there.

13. AND IN ALL THINGS THAT I HAVE SAID UNTO YOU TAKE YE HEED. Rashi explained: "This verse is intended to bring every positive commandment also under the term of a prohibition, [367] for wherever the term *shmirah* (taking heed) or *shvithah* [368] is used in the Torah, it signifies an admonition in the place of an express prohibition."

---

(363) Nehemiah 10:32. (364) Ramban's intention is as follows: It cannot be said that the command here is directed to the owner himself, that he should rest on the Sabbath, since it says clearly *'in order that'* thine ox... *may have rest;* neither can it be referring to a case where the owner works together with the animal, for if that were so, why does the Torah not mention that the reason is that he himself should have rest? Hence Ramban explains the verse in the following way: "*Six days thou shalt do thy work* in such a manner as if it were all completed by the Sabbath-day, so that the animal can have rest by itself on that day." (365) Above, 16:23. In other words, bake on the sixth day double in order that you should not have to bake on the Sabbath. Here likewise a similar thought is expressed: do all your work in six days so that the animal can have rest on the seventh day. (366) *Ibid.*, 20:9. (367) So that if one fails to fulfill a positive commandment [as e.g. taking the *Lulav* on the festival of Succoth] he has also violated thereby a negative commandment as expressed in the verse before us. (368) "Or *shvithah*" is not found in our Rashi. And correctly so, for the term *shvithah* can indicate a *positive* commandment, such as: *and on the seventh day 'tishboth'* (thou shalt rest) — Verse 12.

Now according to his explanation, Rashi will have to say that this verse is a *lav sh'bichlaluth* [a negative admonition expressed in general terms, so that violation of any or all of the prohibitions included under it does not render one liable to punishment].[369] For if that were not so, the court would have to administer whipping to anyone who fails to fulfill any of the positive commandments of the Torah; but in such a prohibition which includes many matters without mentioning specifically any particular transgression, everyone would agree that no whipping is incurred on account of its breach. But [if so, there is the following difficulty with Rashi's explanation]: the Rabbis have already said [370] that the term *hishamer* (take heed) used in connection with a positive commandment, carries the force of an additional *positive* commandment; in that case, He has added here [not a *negative* commandment as Rashi has it], but a mere positive one [since the statement, *and in all things that I have said unto you 'tishameru' (take ye heed)*, refers to the *positive* commandments mentioned in the preceding Verses 10-12]! In the Mechilta the Sages differed as to the explanation of this verse and interpreted it in many ways.

In accordance with the plain meaning of Scripture, the explanation of the verse is: "*and in all things that I have said unto you* concerning other gods *take ye heed,*" for the verse is to be connected with its continuation, [which states: *and make no mention of the name of other gods, neither let it be heard out of thy mouth*]. Thus He is stating: Of all the many admonitions that I have said to you concerning other gods, take great heed; do not worship them, nor bow down to them, condemn to death anyone who sacrifices to them, and make no graven image, nor any manner of likeness. Moreover, take heed not to mention the name

---

(369) This term is applied to a verse which covers many different prohibitions, none of which is specifically indicated, and therefore the court does not administer punishment for violation thereof. — See "The Commandments," Vol. II, p. 11, Note 1, for full explanation of this term.
(370) Erubin 96 a. The opinion is that of Rabbi Ilai.

of their gods, such as *Chemosh the god of Moab, and Milkom the god of the children of Ammon,* [371] and Ashima the god of Hamath. [372] *Neither let there be heard out of thy mouth* their name, even without the epithet of deity, such as merely mentioning Milkom or Ashima; instead you are to mention them in a manner of condemnation: "the abhorrent thing of Moab," "the abomination of the children of Ammon." Or, the expression *lo yishama (neither let there be heard),* means: let it not be heard from its worshipper through your dealings with him, similarly to that which our Rabbis have said, [373] that one should not make a business–partnership with an idolator, for it might lead to him swearing by his deity.

It is possible that *lo tazkiru (make no mention)* is transitive, meaning: do not mention the name of other gods to their worshippers, such as saying, "By your god! deal kindly with me." *Neither let there be heard out of thy mouth* the mention of his name at all. It is this which is said in the Book of Joshua, *Neither make mention of the name of their gods, nor cause to swear by them, nor serve them.* [374] He added prohibitions in that verse, in order to explain that the admonition here covers not mentioning or causing anyone whomsoever to swear by the foreign gods.

16. AND THE FEAST OF HARVEST, THE FIRST-FRUITS OF THY LABORS, AND THE FEAST OF INGATHERING AT THE END OF THE YEAR. I do not know why Scripture mentions the names of the festivals with the definite article since He has not yet commanded about or mentioned them at all till now, and it ought to have said first: "and you shall keep a feast of harvest, the first-fruits of your labors," just as He said in the Book of Deuteronomy, *And thou shalt keep a festival of weeks unto the Eternal thy G-d.* [375] But perhaps because He had already said, *Three times thou shalt keep a feast unto Me in the year,* [376] and further explained, *The feast of unleavened bread shalt thou keep...*

---

(371) I Kings 11:33. (372) II Kings 17:30. (373) Sanhedrin 63 b.
(374) Joshua 23:7. (375) Deuteronomy 16:9. (376) Verse 14 here.

in the mouth of Aviv,[377] meaning that you are to make sure that the Passover festival is observed at the beginning of the month of Aviv, He referred back [to these verses] and said, "And as for the other festival, make sure that it be *the feast of harvest, the first-fruits of thy labors,* and as for the third one, make sure that it be *the feast of ingathering, at the end of the year.* Now all these festivals are thus named with reference to man's activities in the field, in order that he give thanks for them to G-d who guards *the ordinances of heaven,*[378] and brings forth bread out of the earth [379] to satisfy *the longing soul, and the hungry soul He hath filled with good.* [380] This is Scripture's intention in using here the expression: *el pnei Ha'adon Hashem (three times in the year shall all thy males appear — 'before the Master, the Eternal'),*[381] for He is the Master who provides the needs of His servants, and when they take their part from before Him, they come to Him to see what He commands them to do. Thus the expression *el pnei* is like *'liphnei'* ("before") — *before the Master.* But by way of the Truth, [the mystic teachings of the Cabala], the word *pnei* is derived from the term *panim* [literally: "face"], and I have already alluded to the explanation of *panim* in the Ten Commandments. [382] This is why He said *Ha'adon Hashem (the Master, the Eternal),* just as He said the second time, *the Master, the Eternal, the G-d of Israel.* [383] Similarly: *Behold, the ark of the covenant of the Master of all the earth;* [384] *Tremble, thou earth, 'miliphnei' (at the presence) of the Master.* [385]

---

(377) Verse 15. — *Aviv* [literally: "maturity"] means the month when the grain becomes full in its ripe state (Rashi). It is the month of spring. (378) Jeremiah 33:25. (379) See Psalms 104:14. (380) *Ibid.,* 107:9. (381) Verse 17 here. (382) Above, 20:3. (383) Further, 34:23. — Ramban's intention is to suggest that *el pnei Ha'adon* here is not in the grammatical form of construct with the word *Hashem;* this is evident from the same expression which occurs a second time [in 34:23] where it is written *Hashem Elokei Yisrael,* thus indicating that here too the word *Hashem* is not in construct with *Ha'adon* (Abusaula). (384) Joshua 3:11. (385) Psalms 114:7. The allusion is here to the word *'miliphnei'* which is suggestive of *panim,* as mentioned above (Abusaula).

EXODUS XXIII, MISHPATIM

18. THOU SHALT NOT OFFER THE BLOOD OF MY SACRIFICE WITH LEAVENED BREAD. "You shall not slaughter the Passover-offering on the fourteenth day of Nisan before you have removed the leavened bread [from your possession]." This is Rashi's language.

Do not interpret the meaning of this statement of Rashi to refer to the removal of unleavened bread, [and that the verse tells us] that this must take place before the time of slaughtering the Passover-offering, just as is mentioned in the first chapter of Tractate Pesachim: [386] "The Merciful One has declared a time for the slaughtering of the Passover-offering for all alike" — for this interpretation is not the real point of the verse in accordance with the final decision of the law mentioned there. For there is no *prohibition* [387] according to the law of the Torah requiring the removal of unleavened bread on the day before Passover, not even is there a prohibition against eating it [but the violation of a

---

(386) Reference is to the question that was asked in the Gemara Pesachim [4 b-5 a]: how do we know that unleavened bread is forbidden by law of the Torah after six hours on the fourteenth day of Nisan? To this Rava answered that we derive it from the verse, *Thou shalt not slaughter...* (further 34:25), which means: "do not slaughter the Paschal-lamb while the leavened bread is still there." And since the time for the slaughtering of the Paschal-lamb begins after the sixth hour, we therefore deduce that unleavened bread is forbidden from that time on. When the Gemara further asked: "Perhaps the Torah meant a separate time for each individual, [so that if he slaughtered it on the ninth hour of the day, he would not be in violation of the law against keeping unleavened bread till such time]? To this the answer is given: "The Merciful One has declared a time for the slaughtering of the Passover-offering [for all alike, and He did not distinguish between one person and another]. — Ramban is now writing that Rashi's explanation was *not* prompted by this text of the Gemara, for reasons explained further on. (387) Ramban's point is that the duty of removing from one's possession unleavened bread on the fourteenth day of Nisan, is a matter of a *positive* commandment, thus one who failed to remove it from his possession after the sixth hour of that day, has thereby violated a *positive* commandment. But there is no *negative* commandment to cover this matter. Hence the verse before us which is a *negative* commandment cannot be establishing the time for the removal of unleavened bread, since that is covered only by a positive commandment. This is the intention of Ramban's words.

positive commandment].³⁸⁸ But the subject of the verse as established according to the final decision of the law, is an admonition against slaughtering the Passover-offering *with leavened bread,* meaning that none of the company who have been counted to eat of this Passover-offering, may have leavened bread remaining in their possession at the time it is slaughtered. And so Rashi explained it in the section of *Ki Thisa.*³⁸⁹ Now the verse should have read, "Thou shalt not slaughter with unleavened bread My sacrifice" [omitting the word: *dam* — blood], for the blood is not "slaughtered." But in the opinion of our Rabbis³⁹⁰ this comes to include the sprinkling, so that the priest who sprinkles the blood of the offering is also forbidden to have leavened bread in his possession. The verse thus states: "Do not slaughter the Passover-offering with unleavened bread, and neither [sprinkle] the blood of My sacrifice," That is, and neither let the blood of My sacrifice be with unleavened bread. It is an elliptical verse.

20. BEHOLD, I SEND AN ANGEL BEFORE THEE. "Here they were informed that they would sin [by worshipping the golden calf] and that the Divine Glory would be saying to them, *For I will not go up in the midst of thee.*³⁹¹ 21. FOR MY NAME IS IN HIM. This is connected with the beginning of this verse: *Take heed of him,* for My Name is associated with him. Our Rabbis explained³⁹² that the angel referred to is Mattatron³⁹³ whose name in numerical value is equal to that of his Master, for the sum

---

(388) Here too Ramban's opinion is that there is no *negative* commandment of the Torah covering it, but one who eats it violates thereby a *positive* commandment, since he had failed to destroy the unleavened bread beforehand. See, however, "the Commandments," Vol. II, p. 196, where Rambam differs on this point and counts a specific negative commandment, wherein we are forbidden to eat unleavened bread after the middle of the fourteenth of Nisan. (389) Further, 34:25. "This is an admonition addressed to him who slaughters the offering, as well as to him who sprinkles its blood [on the altar], or to one of the company [that joined together to eat the Paschal-lamb]" (Rashi). (390) Mechilta here on the Verse. (391) Further, 33:3. (392) Sanhedrin 38 b. (393) See Ramban above, 12:12 [beginning: *I will execute judgments*].

EXODUS XXIII, MISHPATIM

of the letter-numbers of the name Mattatron is equal to that of *Sha-dai* (Almighty)." [394] All this is the language of Rashi. In *Eileh Shemoth Rabbah* [395] I have likewise seen that one of the Sages interprets the verse in this way, referring to the worshipping of the calf.

But one must ask that [we find that] this decree of *I send an angel before thee* did not actually take place, for the Holy One, blessed be He, had said to Moses, *And I will send an angel before thee... for I will not go up in the midst of thee,* [396] but Moses pleaded for mercy on this and said, *If Thy presence go not, carry us not up hence. For wherein now shall it be known that I have found grace in Thy sight, I and Thy people? is it not in that Thou goest with us?* [397] And the Holy One, blessed be He, consented to him and told him, *I will do also this thing that thou hast spoken.* [398] Thus also did the Rabbis interpret it: [392] "Even as a guide we refused to accept him, as it is written, *If Thy presence go not, carry us not up hence.*" [397]

The answer according to this opinion of the Rabbis is that this decree was not fulfilled in the days of Moses, and it is with reference to this that Moses said, *So that we are distinguished, I and Thy people,* [399] and G-d answered him, *For thou hast found grace in My sight, and I know thee by name,* [398] and He further said, *And all the people among which thou art shall see the work of the Eternal* [that I am about to do]; [400] however, after the death of Moses our Teacher He did send with them the angel. It is with reference to this that Scripture states: *And it came to pass, when Joshua was by Jericho, that he lifted up his eyes and looked, and, behold, there stood a man over against him with his sword drawn in his hand, and Joshua went unto him, and said unto him: 'Art thou for us, or for our adversaries? 'And he said: 'Nay, but I am captain of the host of the Eternal; I am now come.'* [401] And

---

(394) The number of each is three hundred and fourteen. (395) Shemoth Rabbah 32:7. (396) Further, 33:2-3. (397) *Ibid.*, Verses 15-16. (398) *Ibid.*, Verse 17. (399) *Ibid.*, Verse 16. (400) *Ibid.*, 34:10. (401) Joshua 5:13-14.

there you will see that Joshua asked him, *What saith my lord unto his servant?* [402] Now the angel did not command Joshua anything in connection with his appearance to him, but merely told him, *Put off thy shoe from off thy foot,* [403] nor did he explain why he came. But the vision was for the purpose of informing Joshua that from now on there would be an angel sent before them to go out in the host in battle. It is with reference to this that he said, *I am now come.*[401] And so did the Sages say in the Tanchuma: [404] "The angel said to Joshua: 'I am he who came in the days of Moses your master, and he pushed me away and did not want me to go with him.'" The Rabbis have also said expressly: [405] "The promise that Israel would not be turned over to 'a captain' all the days of Moses now became void; thus as soon as Moses died 'the captain' returned to his position, for Joshua saw him, as it is said, *And it came to pass, when Joshua was by Jericho... And he said, 'Nay, but I am captain of the host of the Eternal; I am now come.'* [401] This is why it is said, *Behold, I send an angel before thee.*"

By way of the Truth, [the mystic teachings of the Cabala], this angel they were promised here is *the redeeming angel* [406] in whom is the Great Name, *for in Y-a-h the Eternal is an everlasting Rock.* [407] This is [what He meant when] He said, *I am the G-d of Beth-el,* [408] for it is the custom of the King to dwell in His Palace. He is called *mal'ach* (angel) because the whole conduct of this world is by that attribute. And our Rabbis have said [392] that this is Mattatron, a name which signifies "the guide of the road" — I have already explained this in *Seder Bo* [393] — and this is the sense of the phrase here, [*Behold, I send an angel before thee,*] *to keep thee in the way.* — *And to bring thee into the place which I have prepared,* referring to the Sanctuary, as it is written, *the Sanctuary, O Eternal, which Thy hands have established.* [409] The meaning of

---

(402) *Ibid.*, Verse 14. (403) *Ibid.*, Verse 15. (404) Tanchuma *Mishpatim*, 18. (405) Shemoth Rabbah 32:4. (406) Genesis 48:16. See Ricanti (*ibid.*, 31:13) where he quotes this text of Ramban, and explains that the reference is to the *Shechinah* (the Divine Glory). See in the text Note 419. (407) Isaiah 26:4. (408) Genesis 31:13. (409) Above, 15:17.

EXODUS XXIII, MISHPATIM

the expression: *which I have prepared,* is "for Myself, to be My holy and beautiful house,"[410] for there the Throne is perfect. I will yet mention[411] the Rabbis' meaning in saying that Mattatron's name [in the sum of letter-numbers] is even as the Name of his Master. His voice is thus the voice of the living G-d, and it is mandatory upon us to hearken to His voice by the mouth of the prophets. Or the meaning may be that "they should not mutilate the shoots" of faith[412] and thus come to abandon the Oral Torah, just as the Rabbis have interpreted:[413] *"And they have spurned the word of the Holy One of Israel*[414] — this refers to the Oral Torah." Thus the explanation of the expression, *and hearken unto his voice,*[415] is "to My words." Similarly He said, *But if thou shalt indeed hearken unto his voice, and do all that I speak.*[416] Onkelos hinted at this, for he translated [*'ki sh'mi b'kirbo'* — *for My Name is in him*]: "for in My Name is his word," as he speaks with it. He said, *Then I will be an enemy unto thine enemies,*[416] for even with the attribute of mercy I will be an enemy to them; *and an adversary unto thine adversaries* — through him, [the angel], through the attribute of justice. Hence He explained, *For Mine angel shall go before thee, and bring thee in unto the Amorite etc. and the Canaanite etc. and I will cut him off,*[417] when he will bring you to them, that we may know that it is He [through the attribute of justice] that will cut them off. He mentioned them in the singular ["and I will cut *him* off], for He will cut them all off as if they were one man. Now when this angel dwelled in the midst of Israel, the Holy One, blessed be He, would not have said, *For I will not go up in the midst of thee*[418] — [for He said] *for My Name is in him,* so He was in the midst of Israel! But when they sinned by worshipping the golden calf He wanted to remove His Divine Glory[419] from their midst, and that one of His angels should go before them as His messenger, and Moses

---

(410) See Isaiah 64:10. (411) Further, 24:1 (towards the end). (412) See Vol. I, p. 155. (413) P'sichta Eichah Rabbathi, 2. (414) Isaiah 5:24. (415) Verse 21. (416) Verse 22. (417) Verse 23. (418) Further, 33:3. (419) See above Note 406.

pleaded for mercy, and He again caused His Divine Glory to dwell amongst them as before. There I will explain the verses, with the help of G-d.

The Rabbis have also hinted to this in Midrash Rabbah [420] in that section. Thus they said: *"Behold, I send an angel.* The Holy One, blessed be He, said to Moses: 'The one who guarded the fathers will guard the children.' And thus you find with Abraham, that when he blessed Isaac he said, *He will send His angel before thee.* [421] In the case of Jacob we find [that he blessed Joseph's sons by saying], *The angel who hath redeemed me* etc. [422] He said to them: 'He redeemed me from the hand of Esau; He redeemed me from the hand of Laban; He fed me and sustained me in the years of famine.' Said the Holy One, blessed be He, to Moses: 'Now too, the one who guarded the fathers will guard the children,' as it is said, *Behold, I send an angel before thee."* Again the Rabbis have said there clearly:[423] "The Holy One, blessed be He, said to Israel: 'Be heedful of the messenger, for he does not go back on his mission; he is the attribute of justice, *be not rebellious against him,* etc.' " [415]

In any case, according to all authorities the Midrash I have mentioned is true, that as long as Moses lived the angel who was *captain of the host*[402] did not go with them, for Moses filled his place, similarly to that which is said, *And it came to pass, when Moses held up his hand, that Israel prevailed.* [424] And in the days of Joshua it was necessary that the angel *captain of the host of the Eternal*[402] come to him to fight their battles, this being Gabriel who fights for them, and this was why Joshua saw him *with his sword drawn in his hand,*[425] because he came *to execute vengeance upon the nations, and chastisements upon the peoples.*[426]

---

(420) Shemoth Rabbah 32:8. (421) Genesis 24:7. The words were actually addressed by Abraham to Eliezer — but the goal of Eliezer's mission was for Isaac's blessing. (422) *Ibid.*, 48:16. (423) Shemoth Rabbah 32:4. (424) Above, 17:11. (425) Joshua 5:13. (426) Psalms 149:7.

For he will not pardon your transgression; for My Name is in him. [415] He is saying: *"Be not rebellious against him, for he will not pardon your transgression* if you rebel against his word, for he who rebels against him, rebels against the Great Name which is in him, and he deserves to be cut off by the attribute of justice." It is possible that the expression *My Name is in Him,* is connected to the above verses: hearken to his voice, for My Name is in him, and his voice is the voice of the Supreme One.

24. THOU SHALT NOT BOW DOWN TO THEIR GODS, NOR SERVE THEM. The Torah has warned against idolatry in many places, and even though there are excessive verses on this subject, the redundancy is not a matter to be concerned about, for because the matter is so stringent — since he who acknowledges the divine nature of the idols, thereby denies the whole Torah [427] — therefore the Torah warns against it again and again, like one who says to his servant: "remember continually and do not forget the great principle which I have commanded you, since everything depends on it." It is possible that in the Ten Commandments He warned against making an idol and worshipping it, and now He warned that if they find a ready-made idol which is worshipped by the nations in the land, that they should not worship it at all, but they should uproot it from the land.

NOR DO AFTER THEIR DEEDS. This may possibly be an admonition against adopting the "ways of the Amorites" [i.e., superstitious practices] which the Sages have enumerated,[428] just as He warned against them in another place, saying, *Neither shall ye walk in their statutes,* [429] on which the Rabbis commented: [430] "These statutes refer to the 'ways of the Amorites' which the Sages have enumerated." A more all acceptable interpretation is that He is warning here against worshipping an idol in the particular manner in which it is ordinarily worshipped, even if it is

---

(427) Sifre *R'ei,* 54. (428) Shabbath 67 a. See "The Commandments," Vol. II, pp. 28-29. (429) Leviticus 18:3. (430) Sifra *ibid.*

a disgraceful act [such as excreting to Baal Peor], just as the Rabbis have interpreted [431] the verse, *Take heed... that thou enquire not after their gods, saying: 'How used these nations to serve their gods? Even so will I do likewise.'* [432] Thus the meaning of the verse here is as follows: He said, [in the Ten Commandments 20:5], *Thou shalt not bow down to their gods, nor serve them,* "serving" usually being an act of honor that a servant does to his master, and then He said, additionally that even if that act is not one of honor but is disgusting, such as in connection with Baal Peor which one worships by excreting before it, or throwing a stone at Merkulis,[433] nonetheless if that is the customary manner of worshipping them, you may not do such acts at all. Similarly the Rabbis have said:[434] "Even if he intends to worship Peor in this ignominious way, and even if he intends to throw a stone to Merkulis in a contemptible manner [he is still liable]."

25. AND YE SHALL SERVE THE ETERNAL YOUR G-D, AND HE WILL BLESS THY BREAD, AND THY WATER. The intention of this verse is as follows. Most idolaters acknowledge and know that the revered G-d is *G-d of gods, and Lord of lords,*[435] and they do not intend to worship the idols themselves, but they think that because of these acts of worship they will have success in their endeavors. Thus when they worship the sun it is because they have found it to have a beneficial power over their crops, and they find the moon to have influence over fountains and all deep waters, and similarly [they attribute powers] to all the hosts of heaven. They are even more inclined to think that they will be greatly benefitted by worshipping the angels, since they are invested with dignity through ministering before the Great G-d. Therefore this verse states that only through the worship of the Holy One, blessed be He, can you have success and protection, and the uprooting of idolatry [436] will not cause damage; on the

---

(431) Sanhedrin 61 b. (432) Deuteronomy 12:30. (433) I.e., Mercury, the Roman divinity, who was worshipped by throwing stones to his statue. (434) Sanhedrin 64 a. (435) Deuteronomy 10:17. (436) As commanded in Verse 24.

EXODUS XXIII, MISHPATIM

contrary, it will add goodness and blessing to you, for the Holy One, blessed be He, will bless your "bread," this being a term which includes all manner of food, and will bless your "water," which is a generic term for all liquids that people drink. The blessing referred to means increase, so that you will have an exceeding abundance of them.

AND I WILL TAKE SICKNESS AWAY FROM THE MIDST OF THEE. That is to say, through them [the bread and water that I will bless], I will free you from disease, for when your food and drink are good and healthy, they do not cause sicknesses but, on the contrary, heal you. And He states[437] furthermore that there will not be amongst you a woman that miscarries, *a miscarrying womb*[438] nor one barren of the womb *and with dry breasts,*[438] for when food and drink and the air are blessed, human bodies become healthy and the organs of reproduction are able to function properly. The verse[437] singles out women because they are liable to miscarriage, and sterility too is more common amongst them than amongst men. It is possible that [male sterility] is included in the expression, *and I will take sickness away from the midst of thee,* for barrenness is a sickness in bodies. He addresses Himself without specifications to men, and afterwards He mentioned the women, as He said, *there shall not be male or female barren among you.* [439] The meaning of the expression *in thy land,* [*None shall miscarry, nor be barren, in thy land*], [437] is to include also the animals, just as He said there, *or amongst your cattle.*[439] *The number of thy days I will fulfill*[437] means that one will not die prematurely in battle, nor through an epidemic caused by a change in the atmosphere, but only at a ripe age, whatever happens to be the normal span of life during that particular generation, such as seventy or eighty years as in the generation of King David. [440] I have already mentioned [441] that these are all miracles, G-d showing *wonders in the heavens and in the earth* [442]

---

(437) Verse 26. (438) Hosea 9:14. (439) Deuteronomy 7:14. (440) See Psalms 90:10. (441) Above at the beginning of *Seder Va'eira,* and on Genesis 17:1 (Vol. I, p. 215). (442) Joel 3:3.

for the sake of those who do His will. And then He said that just as He will do on their behalf *a sign for good*,[443] so will He do to their enemies for bad; He will give them *a trembling heart*,[444] *and in the chambers terror.*[445] Moreover, He will send the *tzir'ah* amongst them, [446] this being a certain kind of hornet of the family of the bee. The Sages mention it continually:[447] "Bees' honey, hornets' honey." The meaning of the verse is that He will send this plague through the atmosphere of their land, like the locust that He had sent in Egypt: *the canker-worm, and the caterpillar, and the palmer-worm, His great army*[448] which came in the days of Joel. The meaning of the expression, *and she* [the hornet] *will drive out the Hivite* etc.,[446] is that this will be the cause of their being driven out of the land, for since the hornets *will cover the face of the earth*[449] and darken it, they will not be able to go into battle. Moreover, it will eat up all their produce in the field, similar to that which is said in the imprecations, *Thou shalt carry much seed out into the field, and shalt gather little in; for the locust shall consume it,* etc.;[450] *All thy trees and the fruit of thy land shall the locust possess.*[451] Similarly He said here that He will do such things to our enemies.

Scripture mentioned here *the Hivite, the Canaanite, and the Hittite,*[446] [and not the other four nations as well], because it adopted here a shortened form, and the intention is to all those mentioned above.[452] The correct interpretation appears to me to be that the majority of these three nations [mentioned here] did not go out to battle and thus avoided being killed by the sword, because they remained strongly enclosed in their fortified places. It is against them that He sent only this form of death [through the

---

(443) Psalms 86:17. (444) Deuteronomy 28:65. — Ramban derives this from the phrase written here: *I will send My terror before thee* (Verse 27). (445) *Ibid.,* 32:25. — Ramban derives this from the expression here: *And I will cause discomfort to all the people to whom thou shalt come.* (446) Verse 28. (447) Machshirin 6:4. (448) Joel 2:25. (449) Above, 10:5. (450) Deuteronomy 28:38. (451) *Ibid.,* Verse 42. (452) Verse 23. See Ramban above, 3:8 as to why the Girgashite [the seventh one] is omitted.

EXODUS XXIII, MISHPATIM

hornet], in a similar manner to that which is said of Egypt, *And thy houses shall be filled, and the houses of all thy servants, and the houses of all the Egyptians.* [453] It is this which He said in the Book of Deuteronomy: *Moreover the Eternal thy G-d will send the hornet amongst them, until they that are left, and they that hide themselves, perish from before thee,* [454] and it is this hornet that crossed the Jordon with Joshua.[455] So did the Rabbis conclude in Tractate Sotah,[455] saying that the hornet injected a poison into them which caused their death, and indeed there is nowadays also in the hornet a poisonous substance which harms or even kills the victim. And it is written in the Book of Joshua: *And ye went over the Jordan, and came unto Jericho; and the men of Jericho fought against you, the Amorite, and the Perizzite, and the Canaanite, and the Hittite, and the Girgashite, the Hivite and the Jebusite; and I delivered them into your hand,* [456] and it is further written there, *And I sent the hornet before you, which drove them out from before you, even the two kings of the Amorites; not with thy sword, nor with thy bow.* [457] The phrase *which drove them out* [457] refers to *those that are left* [454] amongst them, for after I delivered into your hand all the nations mentioned, *I sent the hornet* to drive out *those that are left and they that hide themselves.* He mentioned *the two kings of the Amorites,* [457] meaning Sichon and Og whom He had referred to earlier. All this you have done *not with thy sword, nor with thy bow.* [457]

Rabbi Abraham ibn Ezra wrote that the *tzir'ah* refers to a disease in the body, the word being of the root *tzara'ath* (leprosy). But there is no need for this interpretation.

And ye shall serve the Eternal your G-d [458] means that service [by offering or prayer] is to be devoted to the Proper Name [i.e., the Tetragrammaton]. The verse stating *and He will bless... and I will take,* [thus changing from the third-person pronoun to the

---

(453) Above, 10:6. (454) Deuteronomy 7:20. (455) Rashi's statement that the hornets did *not* cross the Jordan but merely "placed themselves on the east bank of the Jordan and from there injected the poison against them" applies to the hornet of the days of Moses. The one in the days of Joshua did cross the Jordan. This distinction is made in Sotah 36 a. (456) Joshua 24:11. (457) *Ibid.,* Verse 12. (458) Verse 25.

first-person pronoun], is similar to the verse *and thou wilt keep all His statutes... for I am the Eternal that healeth thee.* [459] I have already explained it, and the person learned [in the mystic lore of the Cabala] will understand the verse here from what I have written there.

32. THOU SHALT MAKE NO COVENANT WITH THEM, NOR WITH THEIR GODS. He warned here against making a covenant *with them* [the seven nations] to save them and keep them alive; *nor with their gods,* this being a warning against making a covenant with the nations to leave them their idols, but instead we are to destroy them and break their pillars in pieces.[460] It is possible that the verse is stating that we are not to make a covenant with them and their gods together, but we are to destroy them and break their idols in pieces, and the intention is to state that as long as they worship their gods we are not to make any covenant with them, but if they accepted upon themselves not to worship the idols, we may leave them unharmed.

33. 'KI' (FOR) THOU WILT SERVE THEIR GODS, 'KI' (FOR) THEY WILL BE A SNARE UNTO THEE. "Both words *ki* here have the meaning of *asher* (that),[461] and we find this in many places. This is the meaning of the [Aramaic word] *ie* which is one of the four usages of the word *ki* as we find in many places,[462] and this [Aramaic word *ie* is the Hebrew] *im* which in many verses has the meaning of *asher* (that), etc." Thus far is Rashi's language. But it is not so.[463] Instead, the meaning of the verse is: "They

---

(459) Above, 15:26. In that case too the pronouns change. (460) Verse 24. (461) Rashi's interpretation of the verse is thus as follows: "The idolators shall not dwell in your land lest they make you sin against Me 'that' you serve their gods 'that' it be a snare against you." Ramban will explain the word *ki* as meaning "for," as explained further on. — The J.P.S. translation using the words "for" follows thus Ramban's interpretation. (462) See Rosh Hashanah 3 a, Rashi, and Gittin 90 a. (463) For according to Rashi the first *ki* would mean "when that," and the second *ki* would mean only "that" — thus: "lest they make you sin against Me *when that* you serve their gods *that* will be a snare against you" (Mizrachi). The two identical Hebrew words thus have different meanings in the same verse.

EXODUS XXIV, MISHPATIM

shall not dwell in thy land for they will be a snare unto thee lest they make thee sin against Me, for you will serve their gods." Similarly He said, *Take heed to thyself, lest thou make a covenant with the inhabitants of the land whither thou goest, lest they be a snare in the midst of thee.* [464] The meaning of this verse is that their dwelling in your land will be a snare unto you and a source of stumbling, lest they make you sin against Me through their evil ways and their corrupt doings, for you will serve their gods when they will persuade and beguile you to do so.

24   1. AND UNTO MOSES HE SAID: 'COME UP UNTO THE ETERNAL etc.' "This section was told to Moses before the giving of the Ten Commandments, on the fourth day of Sivan." This is Rashi's language. "*And the Eternal said unto Moses: 'Come up to Me into the mountain, and be there'* [465] — this was said to Moses after the Giving of the Torah." These too are Rashi's words. But if so, the sections of the Torah are not in chronological order, nor even in their ordinary sense! Moreover, it is written here, *And Moses came and told the people all the words of the Eternal, and all the ordinances,* [466] which are these ordinances written above, concerning which He said, *And these are the ordinances which thou shalt set before them.* [467] For it is not correct to interpret the expression: *and all the ordinances,* [466] to mean [as Rashi wrote], the ordinances which "the sons of Noah" [468] were commanded, or the laws which were given to the Israelites in Marah [469] which they had already heard and knew, and besides, the word *vayesapeir (and he told)* [466] always indicates new things which one tells!

But Rabbi Abraham ibn Ezra has already grasped this subject correctly, in explaining the verses to be in their proper order, when he commented: [470] "Up to here is the Book of the Covenant." On the basis of this statement it can be seen that all the sections of the Torah are in methodical arrangement. For after the Giving of

---

(464) Further, 34:12. (465) Verse 12 (further in this section).
(466) Verse 3. (467) Above, 21:1. (468) See Vol. I, p. 417, Notes 147-8. (469) See above, 15:25. (470) On the preceding Verse (23:33).

the Torah immediately on the same day G-d said to Moses, *Thus shall you tell the children of Israel: Ye yourselves have seen that I have talked with you from heaven,* [471] and He began to warn them again against idolatry, by saying, *Ye shall not make with Me* etc., [472] and He continued to command him, *Now these are the ordinances which thou shalt set before them,* [467] and all the commandments following that, and finally He finished with the admonition against the worship of idols which they find in the Land, and against making a covenant with their worshippers. He then said to Moses, "After you have commanded them this, *come up unto the Eternal, thou and Aaron.*" The section mentions that Moses did according to the command of G-d, and came to the camp *and told the people all the words of the Eternal* [466] as He had commanded him, *Thus shall you tell the children of Israel: Ye yourselves have seen* etc.; [471] *and all the ordinances,* [466] as He had commanded him, *Now these are the ordinances which thou shalt set before them.* [467] The people received everything with joy and said, *All that the Eternal hath spoken will we do,* [473] meaning that all these things which G-d has told you we will do, for we believe in your words; just as he narrated in the Book of Deuteronomy [that the people said to him], *and thou shalt speak unto us all that the Eternal our G-d may speak unto thee; and we will hear it, and do it,* [474] and then Moses wrote them down. Thus on that day he wrote down in a book all that he had been commanded — the statutes, the ordinances, and the laws — and he *rose up early in the morning* [475] of the following day to make a covenant with them concerning all this. He built the altar and offered the sacrifices, [475] and put half of the blood upon the altar of G-d, and half of it he put in basins [476] [in order to sprinkle upon the

(471) Above, 20:19. (472) *Ibid.*, Verse 20. (473) Above 19:8. See though my Hebrew commentary, p. 447, where it is pointed out that since this verse relates to an event *before* the Revelation and Ramban is now discussing the events *after* the Revelation, we must perforce understand his use of that verse, in a stylistic manner, namely, that the people joyfully accepted upon themselves the duty of observing all of G-d's commandments. (474) Deuteronomy 5:24. (475) Verse 4. (476) Verse 6.

people],[477] and he took the book which he had written the day before and read it in their hearing,[478] and they accepted upon themselves to make the covenant with Him, saying. *All that the Eternal hath spoken will we do, and hearken* [478] to you and to whatever you will command in His Name. Then he sprinkled upon them half of the blood [which he had put in the basins], for this is the sign of a covenant, when two things [479] come in equal parts. Now after he finished what he did with them, he had to fulfill the word of G-d which He told him, *Come up... thou and Aaron,* etc. and it is with reference to this that it is said, *Then went up Moses, and Aaron, Nadab, and Abihu* etc.[480] He completed that which he had been commanded,[481] by coming near alone unto the Eternal. It is with reference to this that it is said, *And Moses entered into the midst of the cloud* etc.[482] Thus the act of the covenant took place on the day after the Giving of the Torah, and on that day was the ascent, when Moses went up into the mountain and he stayed from then on for forty days. It is with reference to this that Scripture explains, *and on the seventh day He called unto Moses out of the midst of the cloud,* [483] [i.e., *the seventh day* of the month Sivan, which was the day after the Giving of the Torah], and it is said, *And Moses entered into the midst of the cloud.* [482] All this is correctly and clearly explained.

Now I have seen in the Mechilta[484] That the Rabbis differed on this matter. Some say [485] that the making of the covenant took place before the Giving of the Torah — on the fifth day of Sivan — and Moses said to them: "Now you are bound, held and tied;

---

(477) As explained further in Ramban, (also in Rashi). For the reason of exact division into two equal parts see further in the text of Ramban and also in Note 479. (478) Verse 7. (479) By putting half of the blood upon the altar of G-d and the other half upon the people, Moses indicated that "the two [parties to the covenant] come into equal parts." See Deuteronomy 26:17-18, and also Vayikra Rabbah 6:5, where the equal division of the blood is explained as signifying that G-d swore to Israel never to exchange it for another nation, and Israel swore eternal fidelity to G-d. (480) Verse 9. (481) I.e., *And Moses alone shall come near unto the Eternal* (Verse 2). (482) Further, Verse 18. (483) *Ibid.,* Verse 16. (484) Mechilta above, 19:10. (485) This is the opinion of Rabbi Yishmael.

tomorrow come and accept upon yourselves all the commandments." But Rabbi Yosei the son of Rabbi Yehudah says: "All these acts were done on one and the same day," that is to say all these acts were performed on the same day, namely the day after the Torah was given — all that Moses told the people and the writing of the Book of the Covenant — all as we have explained. And to this one [i.e., Rabbi Yosei the son of Rabbi Yehudah] we listen, since he has spoken according to the accepted opinion.[486]

And unto Moses He said. The reason for this kind of expression [when it should have said, as elsewhere, *And the Eternal spoke unto Moses*], is that up till now the commandments and the ordinances were addressed to the children of Israel, therefore Scripture said here that this particular commandment was given to Moses, that he alone should do it; thus He commanded him: "After you have set before them the commandments and the ordinances, and have made with them the covenant, come up to Me." This was why Moses fulfilled the first command [i.e., of telling the people the section beginning with *Ye yourselves have seen* — above 20:19 — up to *for they will be a snare unto thee* — 23:33], on the sixth day of Sivan, [following the Revelation which took place on that morning], and on the seventh he rose up early in the morning and made with them the covenant, and after that he went up into the mountain, he and those that were asked to come, [487] as they were commanded.[488]

Come up to the Eternal. In line with the simple meaning of Scripture, the reason for this expression [when it should have said: "Come up unto Me"], is because it is the Scriptural style to mention the proper name instead of the pronoun, such as: *And Lemech said... Ye wives of Lemech;*[489] *and the Eternal sent*

---

(486) See Peah 4:1 for origin of this expression ["to this one we listen etc."]. (487) I.e., Aaron, Nadab and Abihu, and seventy of the elders of Israel (Verse 1). (488) I.e., just as at the time of the Giving of the Torah Moses had a place designated for himself, Aaron a place designated for himself, and the people a place designated for themselves (see Ramban above 19:19), so here too Moses approached closer than Aaron, etc. (489) Genesis 4:23. It should have said: "My wives."

EXODUS XXIV, MISHPATIM

Jerubaal and Bedan and Jephthah and Samuel.[490] A similar case is the verse, *and cause Thy face to shine upon Thy Sanctuary that is desolate, for the Eternal's sake.*[491] In the Talmud,[492] however, we find that they [493] asked, "It should have said, 'come up to Me,'" and therefore they said, "this refers to Mattatron, whose name is even as the Name of his Master." [494] That is to say, "*And unto Moses He* — the Divine Name mentioned at the beginning of this subject, namely, *And the Eternal said unto Moses* [495] — said, come up to Mattatron, for My Name is in him." The meaning is thus: "Come up to the place of the Glory where the great angel is," and the intention was that Moses should come *into the midst of the cloud* [482] where the Glory of G-d was, but he should not come right up to the Proper Divine Name, *for man shall not see Me, and live.* [496] The intention of our Rabbis is thus not at all as Rashi had written above.[497] In Tractate Sanhedrin also the Rabbi [Rashi] turned the subject around.[498] Now I have already mentioned [499] the Rabbis' intention concerning this name [Mattatron], and all their words are true. In that homily, however, [related in Tractate Sanhedrin, concerning the infidel's question to Rav Idie],[493] the Sages spoke in an abstract manner, since Rav Idie did not want, Heaven forbid, to reveal to that infidel who asked him the question, the matter of the great Mattatron and its

---

(490) I Samuel 12:11. Since Samuel was the speaker, he should have said: "and myself." (491) Daniel 9:17. It should have said: "for Thy sake." (492) Sanhedrin 38 b. (493) "They" — the Rabbis, asked. To understand, however, the following references in Ramban it is necessary to know that the question was addressed by a *min* [a Jewish infidel], to Rav Idie for sectarian purposes. The answer here quoted was given by Rav Idie. (494) See Ramban above, 23:20. (495) Above, 20:19. (496) Further, 33:20. (497) 23:20. — Ramban refers to what Rashi wrote there, that the verse mentioned further on [after the sin with the golden calf], *and I will send an angel before thee* (33:2) has reference to Mattatron. That is not correct, for Moses did not consent that the angel mentioned there should go with them (Abusaula). See also Ramban above 23:20 for a full discussion. (498) In Sanhedrin 38 b, Rashi commented: "This is Mattatron. It was he who said *Come up unto the Eternal.*" Ramban's opinion, as explained above, is that the Eternal said, "Come up to Mattatron." (499) Above, 23:20, and in *Seder Bo* 12:12.

secret! Instead, he mentioned to him that the verse speaks of the angel who is "the guide of the road" of the world below; and hence he told him, that "even as a guide we refused to accept him, for it is written [that Moses said], *If 'panecha'* — [literally: 'Thy face' or 'Thy presence'] *go not up, carry us not up hence,"* [500] for we accepted no messenger, only the Revered G-d. I have already explained [501] clearly the secret of *panim* (face) and the whole subject to those learned in the secret lore of the Cabala, in the section of the Giving of the Torah.

2. AND MOSES ALONE SHALL COME NEAR UNTO THE ETERNAL. In the opinion of Rabbi Abraham ibn Ezra this too is a case where a proper name is used instead of a pronoun, for after the expression, *Come up unto the Eternal,* it should have said, "and you alone shall come near," but such is the Scriptural style, as I have mentioned.[502] Similarly: *And the Eternal caused to rain upon Sodom and upon Gomorrah brimstone and fire from the Eternal,* [503] which means "from Him;" *And Moses said unto Hobab, the son of Reuel the Midianite, Moses' father-in-law,* [504] which means "his father-in-law." Also: *And the Eternal sent Jerubaal, and Bedan, and Jephthah, and Samuel,* [490] and similarly: *Then Solomon assembled the elders of Israel, and all the heads of the tribes... unto King Solomon.* [505]

The correct interpretation here appears to me to be that this commandment was addressed also to Aaron, and he too heard the Voice of G-d saying to Moses, *Come up unto the Eternal, thou, and Aaron, Nadab and Abihu, and seventy of the elders of Israel; and worship ye afar off.* [506] And if so, it was necessary that the name of the one who was to draw near [i.e., Moses] be expressly mentioned, for it was he alone who was to come near [and not Aaron]. And even if [we were to explain that when G-d said, *Come up unto the Eternal* etc.] He spoke to Moses directly [and

---

(500) Further, 33:15. (501) Above, 20:3. (502) Above, Verse 1. (503) Genesis 19:24. (504) Numbers 10:29. (505) I Kings 8:1. The meaning is: he gathered them "to himself." (506) Above, Verse 1.

Aaron did not hear it], it would still be necessary to explain that "you Moses alone shall come near unto the Eternal," and the mere pronoun "thou" would not have sufficed.[507] Therefore He said, *And Moses alone shall come near; but they shall not come near.* This is the reason for the word *l'vado* (alone), to exclude Aaron who had been included previously with Moses as far as the commandment [to "come up"].

3. AND MOSES CAME AND TOLD THE PEOPLE ALL THE WORDS OF THE ETERNAL. At the time that this whole commandment mentioned here was given, Moses was at the place where *he drew near unto the thick darkness where G-d was,*[508] and now he came to that "far off" place where the people had been at the time of the Revelation,[508] and told them all that he had been commanded [i.e., beginning with *Ye yourselves have seen* — above 20:19 — up to the end of all the commandments and ordinances, 23:33], and they listened to his voice. Scripture does not say here: "and he came down from the mountain," for they were all then *at the lower part of the mountain,*[509] and not at the top where the Glory of G-d was; [the difference] was only that Moses was near the place of *the thick darkness,* whilst the people *stood from afar* at the time of the giving of the commandments, as I have explained.[510] When Moses left his place and began coming towards the people, all the heads of their tribes and their elders came up to the place where *the priests that come near to the Eternal*[511] stood, and said to him, *Now therefore why should we die? for this great fire will consume us;*[512] *Go thou near, and hear* etc.,[513] for they thought that the Revered G-d Himself would tell them all the commandments of the Torah just as He had told them the Ten Commandments. Then Moses came together with the

---

(507) For since Aaron's name was after all mentioned in the command [in Verse 1], it was already necessary that Moses' name be designated in Verse 2, so that he would know that it was he who was to come near, otherwise it would have included Aaron as well. Therefore etc. (508) Above, 20:18. (509) *Ibid.,* 19:17. (510) *Ibid.,* 19:19, and 20:15. (511) *Ibid.,* 19:22. (512) Deuteronomy 5:22. (513) *Ibid.,* Verse 24.

heads of the tribes and the elders to the place where the people were standing and told all of them all the words of G-d, and they said, "*We will do* all that He has commanded us in the Ten Commandments, and *we will hearken* [514] to your voice in everything that you have commanded, or will command in His Name, exalted be He." When Moses went back afterwards to the edge of the mountain with the elders, as G-d had commanded him, [506] then G-d said to him again, *Come up to Me into the mountain, and be there.* [515] It was at that time that He informed him, *I have heard the voice of the words of the people, which they have spoken unto thee; they have well said all that they have spoken,* [516] and He commanded him: *Go say to them: Return ye to your tents. But as for thee, stand thou here by Me, and I will speak unto thee all the commandment, and the statutes, and the ordinances, which thou shalt teach them.* [517] It is with reference to this that He said here, *And I will give thee the Tablets of stone, and the law and the commandment,* [518] meaning, that to you alone I will give the law and the commandments which you will teach them, and they will keep them as they have undertaken to do.

5. AND HE SENT 'NA'AREI' (THE YOUNG MEN OF) THE CHILDREN OF ISRAEL. These were the firstborns, as Onkelos rendered it, for it was they who used to offer the burnt-offerings and the peace-offerings. But I do not know why Scripture designates the firstborns by the term *na'arei* (the young men)? Perhaps it is because Scripture mentioned the elders who are *the nobles of the children of Israel,* [519] therefore it called the firstborns *ne'arim* (young men), for in relation to the elders they were young. It thus indicates that Moses sent them to offer the sacrifices not because of their status in wisdom, for they were not yet advanced in age, but only an account of the birthright, through which they were set aside to offer sacrifices.

(514) Verse 7. (515) Verse 12. (516) Deuteronomy 5:25. (517) *Ibid.,* Verses 27-28. (518) Verse 12. See Vol. I, p. 7 for Ramban's interpretation of each term mentioned. (519) Further, Verse 11.

In line with the plain meaning of Scripture, *the young men of the children of Israel* were the youth of Israel who had not tasted of sin, [520] and had never come near a woman, for they were the most select and holy of the people, in a similar manner to that which the Rabbis have said:[521] "The young men of Israel who have not tasted of sin [522] are destined to give forth a fragrance like the Lebanon etc." [523]

OXEN UNTO THE ETERNAL. The reason they brought oxen is that as long as Israel was in the wilderness they feared the attribute of justice, this being indeed the source of their mistake at the incident of the golden calf — as I will mention there.[524] And so they now offered burnt-offerings and sacrificed peace-offerings all of oxen, for a similar reason to that of the bullock brought by the anointed priest [for a sin-offering], [525] and the bullock which the court brings for an erroneous decision [which contradicts in part what the Torah enjoins],[526] and the bullock for idolatry, [527] as well as the Red Heifer. [528]

6. AND MOSES TOOK HALF OF THE BLOOD AND HE PLACED IT 'BA'AGANOTH.' These are vessels made unlike the shape of the regular basins of the altar. Hence Scripture states that half of the blood of the sacrifices which Moses intended to sprinkle on the people, he put into these vessels, and the other half he sprinkled upon the altar from the regular basins in which he had received the blood, as is the customary way with all offerings.

---

(520) Erubin 21 b. (521) Berachoth 43 b. (522) "Who have not tasted of sin" is not found in our Gemara, but it is present in manuscripts of the Talmud and other early works (see Dikdukei Sofrim, *ibid.*, Note 6). (523) "As it said, *His branches shall spread, and his beauty shall be as the olive-tree, and his fragrance as Lebanon (Hosea 14:7)*" (*ibid*). The word Lebanon [of the root *lavan* — white] is an allusion here to the Sanctuary which "whitens" [atones for] the sins of Israel. The thought suggested then is that these young men who have not tasted of sin are as beneficial to Israel as the Sanctuary (Maharsha). (524) See Ramban further, 32:1. (525) Leviticus 4:3. (526) *Ibid.*, Verse 14. (527) Numbers 15:24. (528) *Ibid.*, 19:2. See Ramban there: "Its redness alludes to the attribute of justice, etc."

But Rabbi Abraham ibn Ezra said that *ba'aganoth* served for both halves, [and thus the word signifies the regular basins of the altar]. Such is also the opinion of Onkelos, who translated *ba'aganoth* as *b'mizr'kaya* [a term referring to the regular basins].

10. AND THEY SAW THE G-D OF ISRAEL. Rabbi Abraham ibn Ezra explained: "They saw Him in a prophetic vision, this being similar to the verse: *I saw the Eternal standing beside the altar.*[529] — *And there was under His feet the like of a paved work of sapphire stone.*[530] This is identical with what the prophet Ezekiel saw: *as the appearance of a sapphire stone was the likeness of a throne.*[531] — *And the like of the very heaven for clearness,*[530] means that they saw under the paved work of sapphire stone the likeness of the very heaven for clearness, which is identical with *the firmament, like the color of the terrible ice, stretched forth*[532] over the heads of the living creatures [that Ezekiel saw]. Now here it is written, *And they saw the G-d of Israel,* and there it is written, *This is the living creature that I saw under the G-d of Israel.*[533] [In saying that he saw the living creature *under the G-d of Israel,* the prophet Ezekiel] used a shortened expression, for the living creature was under the firmament which was under the throne, and all this was under the Glorious Name." [Thus far is Ibn Ezra's language.]

In line with the simple meaning of Scripture the expression *the G-d of Israel* is used here to indicate that the merit of their father Israel [Jacob] was with them, and it was through his merit that they beheld this vision. And by the way of the Truth, [the mystic doctrine of the Cabala], it is because Scripture mentioned at the Giving of the Torah, *and G-d spoke,*[534] this being identical with the verse, *Behold, the Eternal our G-d hath shown us His glory and His greatness, and we have heard His voice out of the midst of the fire,*[535] therefore Scripture explained here that they saw *the G-d*

---

(529) Amos 9:1. (530) Continuing Verse 10 before us. (531) Ezekiel 1:26. (532) *Ibid.*, Verse 22. (533) *Ibid.*, 10:20. (534) Genesis 1:3. (535) Deuteronomy 5:21.

EXODUS XXIV, MISHPATIM

of Israel. It does not say as it does in all other places, *the Eternal, the G-d of Israel,* [536] but mentioned this [*the G-d of Israel*] in order to say that the seventy elders perceived in this vision more than the rest of the people who saw upon the earth *His great fire,* [537] because the people saw through a partition of *cloud and thick darkness.* [538] Onkelos hinted at this, for he translated here, "and they *saw* the Glory of the G-d of Israel," but did not render it, "and the Glory of G-d *revealed* itself to them," as is his way of translating in other places. [539]

11. AND TO 'ATZILEI' (THE NOBLES OF) THE CHILDREN OF ISRAEL. These are Nadab, and Abihu, and the elders mentioned above. [540] They are called *atzilim* [of the root *atzal,* to emanate] because the spirit of G-d emanated upon them. Similarly, *I have called thee 'mei'atzilehah'* [541] — from those upon whom His spirit has emanated, or the great people upon whom honor has descended from royalty.

The meaning of the expression *He laid not His hand,* is that since He had said, *But let not the priests and the people break through to come up unto the Eternal, lest He break forth upon them,* [542] therefore He let it be known here that they had been careful to observe that command and that He did not break forth upon them, and that the nobles of the children of Israel were worthy of that which they saw in this vision; thus the meaning of the verse is that *they beheld G-d* but they did not break through *to come up unto the Eternal.* [542]

And they did eat and drink. This means that they ate there the peace-offerings at the lower part of the mountain before G-d previous to their returning to their tents, for peace-offerings have

---

(536) Above, 5:1, etc. (537) Deuteronomy 4:36. (538) *Ibid.,* 5:19. (539) E.g., in Numbers 16:19, where it states, *And the Glory of the Eternal appeared unto all the congregation,* Onkelos translated: "and the Glory of the Eternal *revealed* itself..." Here, however, he wrote "and they saw," in order to indicate that they achieved a greater insight in this vision than the rest of the people. (540) Verse 1. (541) Isaiah 41:9. (542) Above, 19:24.

to be eaten within an enclosure; in Jerusalem they were eaten within the wall of the city, [543] in Shiloh [544] they could be eaten within sight of Shiloh, [543] and here they were eaten before the altar at the lower part of the mountain, and not in the camp. The meaning of the expression *and they drank,* is that they made it an occasion for rejoicing and festival, for such is one's duty to rejoice at the receiving of the Torah, just as He commanded when they finished writing all the words of the Torah upon the stones, *And thou shalt sacrifice peace-offerings, and shalt eat there; and thou shalt rejoice before the Eternal thy G-d.* [545] And with reference to Solomon it is written, *Wisdom and knowledge is granted unto thee etc.,*[546] and immediately after that, *he came to Jerusalem... and made a feast for all his servants.*[547] "Said Rabbi Eleazar: [548] From here you learn that we make a feast at the finishing of the Torah." With reference to David, Solomon's father, it is likewise said that when the people gave of their free-will towards the building of the Sanctuary, *And they offered sacrifices unto the Eternal, and offered burnt-offerings unto the Eternal etc., and they did eat and drink before the Eternal on that day with great gladness.*[549] Similarly, here too on the day of the "wedding" of the Torah, [550] they did likewise.

12. AND THE ETERNAL SAID UNTO MOSES: 'COME UP TO ME INTO THE MOUNTAIN.' This is the same command which He had said to him on the preceeding day [i.e., on the sixth of Sivan], *Come up unto the Eternal;*[551] *and Moses alone shall come near unto the Eternal,*[552] and now on the seventh day of Sivan He said additionally to him, *and be there, and I will give thee the*

---

(543) Zebachim 112 b. (544) The Tabernacle stood in Shiloh, in the territory of the tribe of Ephraim, for three hundred and sixty-nine years. After Shiloh was destroyed by the Philistines, the Tabernacle stood in Nob and then in Gibeon — a period of fifty-seven years — and then finally the Sanctuary was built by King Solomon in Jerusalem. (545) Deuteronomy 27:7. (546) II Chronicles 1:12. (547) I Kings 3:15. (548) Shir Hashirim Rabbah 1:9. (549) I Chronicles 29:21-22. (550) Taanith 26 b. (551) Verse 1. (552) Verse 2.

Tablets of stone etc., for Moses was to stay on the mountain until He would give him *the Tablets of stone, and the law and the commandment.* The expression *which I have written* refers back to *the Tablets of stone; that thou mayest teach them* relates to *the law and the commandment.* Thus the meaning of the verse is: "and I will give thee the Tablets of stone which I have written, and the law and the commandment that thou mayest teach them." This is identical with what He said in the Book of Deuteronomy, *And I will speak unto thee all the commandment, and the statutes, and the ordinances, which thou shalt teach them.*[553]

Rashi wrote: "*Which I have written* in the Tablets of stone.[554] *That thou mayest teach them,* for all the six hundred and thirteen commandments are implicit in the Ten Commandments."[555] And Rabbi Abraham ibn Ezra commented: "*The law,* this refers to the first and second commandments; *and the commandment* refers to the other eight mentioned." It is a comment of no value, since the verse in Deuteronomy mentioned above, *And I will speak unto thee,* etc.[553] testifies that He is speaking about all the commandments. In accordance with the opinion of our Rabbis it is possible that the expression *which I have written* is a hint that the whole Torah was written before Him before the creation of the world, as I have mentioned at the beginning of the Book of Genesis.[556]

13. AND MOSES ROSE UP, AND JOSHUA HIS MINISTER. "I do not know in what capacity Joshua was serving here. But it appears to me that the disciple was accompanying the master as far as the place where the limits of the mountain were marked out, for beyond them Joshua was not permitted to go, and from there *Moses went up* alone *into the mountain of G-d,* while Joshua

---

(553) Deuteronomy 5:28. (554) This sentence is not found in our Rashi. (555) Our Rashi adds: "And Rabbeinu Saadia Gaon listed in his 'Azharoth' [Exhortations — liturgical poems treating of the Divine Commandments] the commandments which may be associated with each of the Ten Commandments." — See further in my Foreword to "The Commandments," Vol. I, pp. VIII-X. (556) Vol. I, pp. 8, 14-15.

pitched his tent there for the whole of the forty days. Thus we find that when Moses came down from the mountain it is written, *And Joshua heard the noise of the people as they shouted,* [557] from which we learn that Joshua was not with them in the camp" [at the time of the making of the golden calf]. Thus far is Rashi's language.

In my opinion, Joshua was one of the seventy elders [who were asked to ascend the mountain], for there was nobody more worthy amongst the seventy elders of Israel to approach G-d than he, and when Moses separated from them [to ascend higher], Joshua accompanied his master up to the border [beyond which he was not permitted to go]. Now do not object to my explanation on this point from what the Rabbis have said [558] concerning the punishment of these elders at Taberah, [559] for they said so concerning all of them except Joshua, for he was indeed worthy to see visions of G-d and to receive prophecy.

14. AND UNTO THE ELDERS HE SAID: 'TARRY YE HERE FOR US.' The meaning of this is that when Moses parted from them with his minister, he commanded them that they should tarry there. It does not mean that they were to stay there day and night until their return, for he said, *and behold, Aaron and Hur are with you; whosoever hath a cause, let him come near unto them,*

---

(557) Further, 32:17.   (558) Tanchuma *Beha'alothcha*, 16. Rashi in Verse 10 here brings part of the Midrash with reference to Nadab and Abihu. (559) Numbers 11:3. The place was called Taberah (which means "burning") *because the Eternal burnt among them* — that is, among the most distinguished and prominent ones among them, namely the elders (see Rashi *ibid.*, Verse 1). Now the reason why the elders were singled out for punishment at that time is stated by the Rabbis as follows: Since at the time of the Giving of the Torah they gazed more intently than they were permitted to, behaving as if they were eating and drinking (see here Verse 11), they were liable to death. But since G-d did not wish to disturb the joy caused by the Giving of the Torah, He waited with their punishment till Taberah. — Now on the basis of this Midrash you might think that Joshua, too, was like the elders and unworthy of seeing Divine visions. But, concludes Ramban, this was not the case with Joshua.

and it is in the camp that parties to a dispute would be found, since that was where the seat of justice was, and he had already told everybody, *Return ye to your tents.*[560] But the meaning of *tarry ye here* is that they should stay at that place, and should not break through to come up to them, even to the place where Joshua was, until he [Moses] would come back to them.

In my opinion it is possible that the explanation of the verse is as follows: "Sit [561] in our place and serve as a substitute for us in the camp; *Aaron and Hur are with you,* and *whosoever hath a cause* — one of those hard causes that they would bring to me [562] — *let him come near unto them* in my place." He said *unto them* as a special recognition to Aaron and Hur, for they were to come before all the elders and they would all be assembled at one place, just as he said *Aaron and Hur are with you.* Thus Moses commanded that the elders together with Aaron and Hur should sit as a court, just as he himself did, over the officers of thousands and hundreds, until he returns, since he knew that he would tarry in the mountain. He said: *for us* [*tarry ye here 'for us'*] as a mark of honor to his disciple, just as he said to Joshua, *Choose us out men.*[563] This is a correct interpretation. But Rashi wrote: "*And unto the elders he said* — when he left the camp, *Tarry ye here for us* — stay you with the rest of the people so as to be ready to judge each man's dispute." But this is impossible, for they were not at that moment in the camp, and what sense would there be for him to tell them so when they were in the camp and had already been appointed as judges!

---

(560) Deuteronomy 5:27. (561) Ramban thus takes the Hebrew word *sh'vu* [translated as "tarry"] in its literal meaning: "sit" — sit in court in our place and act as a substitute for us. (562) See Deuteronomy 1:17. (563) Above, 17:9.

Terumah

25 1. Now that G-d had told Israel *face to face*[1] the Ten Commandments, and had further commanded them through Moses some of the precepts which are like general principles to the [individual] commandments of the Torah — in the same way that our Rabbis were accustomed to deal with strangers who come to be converted to the Jewish faith[2] — and now that the Israelites accepted upon themselves to do all that He would command them through Moses and He made a covenant with them concerning all this, from now on they are His people and He is their G-d[3] This is in accordance with the condition He made with them at the beginning: *Now, therefore, if ye will indeed hearken unto My voice, and keep My covenant, then ye shall be Mine own treasure,*[4] and He said further: *and ye shall be unto Me a kingdom of priests, and a holy nation.*[5] They are now holy, in that they are worthy that there be amongst them a Sanctuary through which He makes His Divine Glory dwell among them. Therefore He first commanded concerning the Tabernacle, so that He have amongst them a house dedicated to His name, from where He would speak with Moses and command the children of Israel. Thus the main purpose of the Tabernacle was to

---

(1) Deuteronomy 5:4. (2) Yebamoth 47 a: "We inform him of some of the light commandments and of some of the weightiest ... " The convert to Judaism is thus not taught the whole Torah prior to his conversion but only some of the essentials thereof, which is followed by his total commitment to observe whatever the Torah will command. Ramban's language clearly indicates that the procedure of the Rabbis with converts followed the pattern of events at Sinai. (3) See Leviticus 26:12. (4) Above, 19:5. (5) *Ibid.*, Verse 6.

contain a place in which the Divine Glory rests, this being the ark, just as He said, *And there will I meet with thee, and I will speak with thee from above the ark-cover.*[6] Therefore He first gave the commandment about the ark and the ark-cover, for they are first in importance. Next to the ark He gave the commandment about the table and the candelabrum, which are vessels just like the ark, and because they indicate the purpose for which the Tabernacle was made. Moses, however, preceded to mention in the section of *Vayakheil: the Tabernacle, its Tent, and its covering,*[7] and in that order Bezalel made them [first the Tabernacle and then the ark],[8] because from the practical end it is proper to build the house first [and then make its vessels].

The secret of the Tabernacle is that the Glory which abode upon Mount Sinai [openly] should abide upon it in a concealed manner. For just as it is said there, *And the glory of the Eternal abode upon Mount Sinai,*[9] and it is further written, *Behold, the Eternal our G-d hath shown us His glory and His greatness,*[10] so it is written of the Tabernacle, *and the glory of the Eternal filled the Tabernacle.*[11] Twice is this verse, *and the glory of the Eternal filled the Tabernacle*[11] mentioned in connection with the Tabernacle,[12] to correspond with *His glory and His greatness.*[10] Thus Israel always had with them in the Tabernacle the Glory which appeared to them on Mount Sinai. And when Moses went into the Tabernacle, he would hear the Divine utterance being spoken to him in the same way as on Mount Sinai. Thus just as it is said at the Giving of the Torah: *Out of heaven He made thee to hear His voice, that He might instruct thee; and upon earth He made thee to see His great fire,*[13] so it is written of the Tabernacle, *and he heard the voice speaking unto him from above the ark-cover...from between the two cherubim; and He spoke unto him.*[14] The expression "speaking unto him" is mentioned here twice in order to indicate

---

(6) Further, Verse 22. (7) *Ibid.*, 35:11. And then in the following verse mentioned: *the ark...* (8) *Ibid.*, 36:8-38. 37:1-9. (9) Above, 24:16. (10) Deuteronomy 5:21. (11) Further, 40:34. (12) *Ibid.*, and in Verse 35. (13) Deuteronomy 4:36. (14) Numbers 7:89.

that which the Rabbis have said in the Tradition[15] that the Voice would come from heaven to Moses from upon the ark-cover, and from there He spoke with him; for every Divine utterance with Moses came from heaven during daytime,[16] and was heard *from between the two cherubim,*[14] similar to what is said, *and thou didst hear His words out of the midst of the fire.*[13] It is for this reason that the two cherubim were made of gold.[17] And Scripture so states: *where I will meet with you, to speak there unto thee;*[18] *and it shall be sanctified by My glory,*[19] for there [in the Tabernacle] will be the appointed place for the Divine utterance, *and it will be sanctified by My glory.*[19]

Now he who looks carefully at the verses mentioned at the Giving of the Torah, and understands what we have written about them,[20] will perceive the secret of the Tabernacle and the Sanctuary [built later by King Solomon]. He will also be able to understand it from what Solomon in his wisdom said in his prayer in the Sanctuary: *O Eternal, the G-d of Israel,*[21] just as is said at Mount Sinai: *And they saw the G-d of Israel.*[22] Solomon however added the Name *the Eternal* because of a matter which we have alluded to above;[22] for *the G-d of Israel sitteth upon the cherubim,*[23] just as is said: *And the glory of the G-d of Israel was over them above. This is the living creature that I saw, under the G-d of Israel by the river Chebar; and I knew that they were cherubim,*[24] and David said, *and gold for the pattern of the chariot, even the cherubim, that spread out their wings, and covered the ark of the covenant of the Eternal.*[25] Solomon also always mentions that the Sanctuary is to be *for the name of the Eternal,*[26] or *for Thy name,*[27] and at each and every section of the prayer he says, *then hear Thou in heaven*[28] — with the

---

(15) Bamidmar Rabbah 14:22. (16) Vayikra Rabbah 1:3: "But to the prophets of Israel the Holy One, blessed be He, revealed Himself at daytime." (17) Further, Verse 18. — In order to resemble "the fire" that was on Mount Sinai. (Tziyoni). (18) Further, 29:42. (19) *Ibid.,* Verse 43. (20) See above, 20:16, 24:10, and further here, Verse 21. (21) I Kings 8:23. (22) Above, 24:10. (23) II Kings 19:15. (24) Ezekiel 10:19-20. (25) I Chronicles 28:18. (26) I Kings 5:19. (27) *Ibid.,* 8:44. (28) *Ibid.,* Verse 32 etc.

attribute of mercy. And it is further written: *If Thy people go out to battle against their enemy... and they pray unto the Eternal toward the city which Thou hast chosen, and toward the house which I have built for Thy name, then hear Thou in heaven,*[29] and in explanation Solomon said: *But will G-d in very truth dwell with man on the earth? Behold, heaven and the heaven of heavens cannot contain Thee.*[30] And it is written concerning the ark, *And David arose... to bring up from thence the ark of G-d, whereupon is called the Name, even the Name of the Eternal of hosts that sitteth upon the cherubim,*[31] and in the Book of Chronicles it is written: *to bring up from thence the ark of G-d, the Eternal, Who sitteth upon the cherubim, whereon is called the Name*[32] — for it is G-d Who sitteth upon the cherubim.

3. 'V'ZOTH' (AND THIS) IS THE OFFERING. By way of the Truth, [the mystic lore of the Cabala], this is like the expression, *And the Eternal gave Solomon wisdom.*[33] It is also written: *'v'zoth' (and this) is it that their father spoke unto them and blessed them;*[34] *'v'zoth' (and this) is the blessing;*[35] *the Eternal's doing is 'zoth' (this).*[36] The Rabbis have already alluded to this in Bereshith Rabbah on the basis of the verse, *I understand from the elders.*[36] The discerning student will understand.

And in Eileh Shemoth Rabbah[37] the Rabbis have said: *"And this is the offering which ye shall take of them* — this refers to the congregation of Israel, which is the heave-offering, as it is said, *Israel is the Eternal's hallowed portion, His first-fruits of the increase."*[38] And it is also said there:[39] "The Holy One, blessed be He, said to Israel: I have sold you My Torah; and I, as it were, was sold with it, for it is said, *'v'yikchu li terumah'"* [which the Midrash takes to mean: "and they shall acquire Me as an

---

(29) *Ibid.*, Verses 44-45. (30) II Chronicles 6:18. (31) II Samuel 6:2. (32) I Chronicles 13:6. (33) I Kings 5:26. — See my Hebrew commentary p. 454 that in the word *zoth* Cabalists saw an allusion to the Divine Glory. (34) Genesis 49:28. (35) Deuteronomy 33:1. (36) Psalms 118:23. — Bereshith Rabbah 100:12. (37) Shemoth Rabbah 49:2. (38) Jeremiah 2:3. (39) Shemoth Rabbah 33:1.

offering"]. For the offering shall be Mine, and I am with it, similar to: *My beloved is mine, and I am his.*[40] Similarly, He said, *according to all that I show thee,*[41] for it is I who show [the pattern of the Tabernacle, and the pattern of all its vessels]. The statement, *it hath been shown to thee,*[42] also alludes to the word "I"; similarly, *which is being shown to thee.*[43] And so did David say, *All this [do I give thee] in writing, as the Eternal hath made me wise by His hand upon me,*[44] for the hand of G-d was upon David [to show him the pattern of the Sanctuary and of all its works].

6. SPICES FOR ANOINTING OIL AND FOR INCENSE OF 'HASAMIM' (AROMATICS). Some scholars[45] say that this is an elliptical verse,[46] the sense being: "spices for anointing oil and aromatics for incense of aromatics." And other scholars[47] say that the verse is to be understood as if it were inverted: "and for incense of aromatics they shall bring aromatics." Scripture mentions them with the definite article [*hasamim*], in order to indicate that it is referring to those aromatics that are good as incense, for there also [i.e., further in the section of the Torah dealing with the incense — 30:34] He did not explain [fully the compound forming the incense].[48] And Rabbi Abraham ibn Ezra wrote that the verse is to be taken in its simple sense, that spices be taken for both — for the anointing oil and for the incense, for included in the compound of the incense were these spices: spikenard and saffron and cinnamon, according to the words of

---

(40) Song of Songs 2:16. (41) Further, Verse 9. (42) *Ibid.*, 27:8. (43) Further, Verse 40. (44) I Chronicles 28:19. (45) I have not been able to identify these scholars. (46) These scholars are of the opinion that *b'samim* (spices) and *hasamim* (aromatics) are two different terms. And since it says further on that for the incense *take unto thee 'samim' (aromatics)* (30:34), the word *b'samim* cannot refer also to the incense mentioned here. Hence they complete the sentence thus: "spices for anointing oil, *and aromatics* for incense and aromatics." (47) Mentioned in Ibn Ezra in the name of "contemporary scholars." I found this in Chizkuni. (48) Hence He referred to them here by the definite article — *hasamim* — the aromatics that are known. See Ramban further 30:34 for full discussion of this subject.

our Rabbis.[49] It was not necessary for Scripture to mention "spices and aromatics for the incense," because it said *the incense of aromatics*, just as it did not say "oil for the anointing oil." This is the correct interpretation.

All these opinions are necessary because according to the view of the linguists [*samim* and *b'samim* connote two different things]: *samim* are curative herbs which are not edible, such as frankincense and galbanum,[50] while *b'samim* are those that are edible, and are called *mis'adim* (props)[51] because they have a strengthening power by their fragrant odor.

However, in the opinion of Rashi *samim* is identical with *b'samim*. And such is the meaning of our Rabbis in the Midrash[52] in saying: "Eleven *samonin* (ingredients) were told to Moses on Mount Sinai" [which form the incense, and among them were spikenard and saffron and cinnamon which are *b'samim*, thus proving that they are all called by the term *samim*]. Onkelos also translates in both cases *busmin* ["*busmaya* for the anointing oil, and for incense of *busmaya*"]. This is correct in the understanding of this verse. But because Scripture changed the terms [calling one *b'samim* and the other *samim*] we might possibly say that the most important of aromatics and spices are called *b'samim*, a term which signifies the choicest and most famous of the spices, just as He said, '*b'samim rosh*' (the chief spices).[53] '*b'rosh kol bosem*' *(with chief of all spieces)*.[54] We are also correct in saying that the words *b'samim* and *bosem* are composite words: *bo sem, bo samim* ("in it is spice," "in it are spices"). Proof to the words of the Rabbis [that the term *b'samim* includes also *samim*] is the verse, *Take thou unto thee 'b'samim rosh' (the chief spices) of flowing myrrh*,[53] and myrrh is counted among the *samim* since it is a curative, not an edible herb. Scripture further says, *Spikenard and saffron, calamus and cinnamon, with all trees of frankincense*,[55]

---

(49) Kerithoth 6 a. (50) Further, 30:34. (51) This was a Medieval medicinal term for spices which were given to the sick to restore their vigor. See Hebrew dictionaries, under the term *mis'ad*. (52) Shir Hashirim Rabbah 1:61. (53) Further, 30:23. (54) Ezekiel 27:22. (55) Song of Songs 4:14.

and the verse there continues: *myrrh and aloes, with all the chief 'b'samim' (spices).* And with reference to all of these Scripture says, *Awake, O north wind; and come, thou south; blow upon my garden, that 'b'samov' (the spices thereof) may flow out.*[56] A further proof [to the opinion of the Rabbis that *b'samim* includes also *samim*] is the verse, *and the princes brought... the 'bosem' and the oil for the light and for the annointing oil and the incense of aromatics,*[57] but it does not mention that they brought *samim*, from which we may conclude that they are all included in the *bosem*.

7. 'AVNEI SHOHAM' (ONYX STONES) 'V'AVNEI MILU'IM' (AND STONES FOR SETTING). "Because they used to make a setting for the stone in gold — a kind of indentation — and they placed the stone there to fill the indentation, they are called *avnei milu'im* (stones for filling-in), and the place of the indentation is called *mishbetzet* (setting). FOR THE EPHOD AND THE BREASTPLATE. The onyx stones were for the *ephod,* and the stones for setting were for the breastplate." This is Rashi's language. Similarly Rashi explained: "*They shall be inclosed in gold in their settings,*[58] — surrounded by gold settings of such a depth that each setting shall be filled by the thickness of the stone. This is the meaning of the word *milu'otham* (their filling),[58] and this is the meaning of every expression of *milui* (filling) mentioned in this connection."

But it does not appear to me to be at all correct to say that Scripture calls them already now *avnei milu'im*, because in some time as yet in the future He was to command that the indentations made for them were to be filled with these stones! Moreover, the onyx stones were also *enclosed in settings of gold,*[59] and yet He did not call them *milu'im*. Again, our Rabbis have already said in

---

(56) *Ibid.,* Verse 16. Thus it is clear that the term *b'samim* (spices) includes also *samim* (aromatics), since it speaks of all of them as *b'samim* and lists amongst them myrrh, which is one of the *samim*. (57) Further, 35:28. (58) Further, 28:20. (59) *Ibid.,* Verse 11 — in the case of the ephod.

EXODUS XXV, TERUMAH 441

the Gemara: [60] "These stones [61] are not incised with a chisel, [62] for it is said *b'milu'otham* [58] (in their filling)." Now if the explanation *b'milu'otham* would be, [as Rashi has it], that they fill the indentations with the stones, there would have been no proof at all from this verse that they should not incise the names [of the tribes] on them with a chisel. Besides, the manner of the setting of the stones which the Rabbi [Rashi] mentioned, namely that it was made in a kind of indentation, is not correct. Instead, it is as Onkelos rendered it: [*meshubatzim zahav* — inclosed in gold] *meramtzan didhav*,[58] which means that they made at the bottom a gold setting according to the measure of the stone, and from it they projected a fork-like shape of three prongs which would hold the stone. [The word *meramtzan* mentioned by Onkelos] is similar to the expressions of the Sages: "and they take it out *beramtza* (with a pointed tool) made of iron;"[63] "as when he bored a hole in it *beramtza* (with a pick) made of iron." [64] This is how they also do it today when they set precious stones in rings, in order that they be seen from all angles and that their beauty and splendor should not be hidden in the indentations. You may know that this is so, for the two gold chains inserted in the two rings of the breastplate were attached to the *mishb'tzoth* on the shoulder-pieces of the *ephod*.[65] Now if *mishb'tzoth* were [as Rashi said] frames for the setting of the stone, how would they attach to them the chains? And even [if there were there other *mishb'tzoth* not for the setting of the stone but for the purpose of inserting the chains] how would the indentations serve that purpose [as they were not perforated for the chains to go through]? Rather, the *mishb'tzoth* are the fork-like prongs as we have said and the holes for the chains were made in them. Associated with the word *mishb'tzoth* is, in my opinion, [Saul's

---

(60) Sotah 48 b. (61) The onyx stones for the ephod, and the stones for setting in the breastplate. Ramban will later suggest that the reference perhaps is only to the stones for setting in the breastplate. See further, Note 76. (62) For the purpose of writing the names of the tribes upon the stones (further, 28:12, and 21). (63) Niddah 62 a. (64) Shabbath 103 a. (65) Further, 28:24-25.

expression, *Slay me*] *for 'hashabatz' hath taken hold of me*[66] — these being the men who hold spear-like weapons with mounted forks on top to catch those that flee the battle-field, just as it is said, *and lo, the chariots and the horsemen pressed hard upon him.*[67]

And the meaning of *musaboth mishb'tzoth*[68] is that he should fix the gold prongs "around it." And in the opinion of Onkelos who translated [*musaboth* as] *meshak'on* [literally: "depressed," "sunk"], the stones were sunk into the frames from which came forth prongs surrounding them above and holding them in place.

But the sense of the word *milu'im* is that the stones be whole as they were created, and that they should not be hewn stones which were cut from a large quarry, or from which anything has been chipped off. It is also known in the natural sciences that the complete powers of precious stones and the particular qualities that distinguish them, exist only when in their natural state, as when smooth stones are taken from the river. This is why Onkelos translated [*avnei milu'im* — *avnei*] *ashlamutha* (stones of perfection). But the term *milui* (filling of) vessels or an indentation [Onkelos] translates literally, — thus: *'va't'malei' (and she filled) her pitcher,*[69] Onkelos translated: *u'mleiah* (and she filled), and similarly in all other cases — but here he translated the term *milui* to mean *shleimuth* (perfection). Similarly, he translated the verse, *'milei' (He filled) them with wisdom of heart*[70] — *ashleim* ("He perfected" them with wisdom of heart), as wisdom is not something that you can fill a vessel with, but instead it denotes perfection, that they [i.e. Bezalel and Oholiab — who did the workmanship of the Tabernacle] were perfect in wisdom. This is the intent of the verse, *and in cutting of stones 'l'maloth'*[71] — that they knew how to engrave like the engravings of a signet upon stones in their [natural] perfect state.

Now in the case of the stones of the ephod it is said, however, *with the work of an engraver in stone, like the engravings of a*

---

(66) II Samuel 1:9. (67) *Ibid.*, Verse 6. (68) Further, 28:11. (69) Genesis 24:16. (70) Further, 35:35. (71) *Ibid.*, 31:5.

signet, shalt thou engrave the two stones, according to the names of the children of Israel [59] [but it does not say here *b'milu'otham* — "in their perfect state"], because they made an incision in them when writing the names [of the tribes upon them] as stone engravers do, and thus the stones were no longer in their [natural] perfect state. But in the case of the stones for the breastplate it is written, *'umileitha' in it 'miluath' of stone,* [72] and again it is written of them, *they shall be 'b'milu'otham;'* [73] *and the stones* [of the breastplate] *were according to the names of the children of Israel, twelve, according to their names* [74] — not the work of engravers [who make incisions upon the stones]. Therefore Moses our teacher could find no way [of inscribing the names of the tribes of Israel upon the twelve stones in the breastplate] except by means of the *shamir* [a worm that cuts stones with its glance] which our Rabbis mentioned, just as they have said in Tractate Sotah: [75] "These stones [76] are not written upon with ink, for it is said, *like the engravings of a signet*,[77] and they are not incised with a chisel, for it is said *b'milu'otham* (in their perfect state). [78] But instead [Moses] brought the *shamir* and showed it the stones and they split of their own accord." Now the word *b'milu'otham* is said only in connection with the stones of the breastplate. Do not be troubled by what is mentioned in the Agadah (homily, tradition) that the Rabbis said to Solomon:[79] "There is the *shamir* with which Moses cut the precious stones of the *ephod*." [From this you might argue that the stones of the *ephod* also had to be *b'milu'otham* — in their perfect natural state — which would be contrary to what we have said above, that this applied only to the stones of the breastplate! Do not be troubled by this statement,] for the breastplate is called ephod by the Rabbis by way of metaphor, because the breastplate is attached thereto. It is also

---

(72) *Ibid.*, 28:17.   (73) *Ibid.*, Verse 20.   (74) *Ibid.*, 38:14.   (75) Sotah 48 b.   (76) I.e. the stones of the breastplate. See above Note 61. (77)   Further, 28:21. "And this means carving" (Rashi, *ibid.*, Sotah). — The verse is mentioned in connection with the stones of the breastplate. (78)   *Ibid.*, Verse 20. — Also in connection with the stones of the breastplate.   (79) Gittin 68 a. In preparing to build the Sanctuary, Solomon asked the Rabbis: "How shall I accomplish the cutting of the stones without using iron tools?" They replied: "There is the *shamir* etc."

written, *Bring hither the ephod*,[80] and it was of the breastplate that they asked [for guidance].[81] Thus the explanation of the verse before us is as follows: "*onyx stones* three — two for the ephod[82] and one for the breastplate;[83] and *stones of 'milu'im'* for the breastplate." And in case the opinion of our Rabbis was that the stones of the ephod also had to be in their full natural state [as the stones of the breastplate], then both *the onyx stones and the stones of 'milu'im'* were for both, *for the ephod and for the breastplate.*[84]

9. AND SO SHALL YE MAKE IT — [also] "in future generations. If one of the vessels is lost, or when you make[85] the vessels of the Sanctuary of Jerusalem,[86] such as the tables,[87] the candelabrums,[88] the lavers,[89] and the bases[90] which Solomon made — after the pattern of these you shall make them. If, however, this [part of the verse] were not connected with the preceding part [which reads: *According to all that I show thee, the pattern of the Tabernacle, and the pattern of all the vessels*], Scripture should not have written: *'and' so shall ye make it*, but: "so shall ye make it," and then it would be speaking of the making of the Tent of Meeting[91] and its vessels." Thus is Rashi's

---

(80) I Samuel 23:9.   (81) See Ramban further, 28:30.   (82) Further, 28:9.   (83) *Ibid.*, Verse 20.   (84) In other words, if that be the opinion of the Rabbis that the stones of the ephod also had to be *b'milu'otham* (in their full natural state), then they derived it from this verse as explained in the text. For — the ephod and the breastplate — had both the onyx stones and the stones of *milu'im*. Of the ephod it is clearly written that it had two onyx stones (further, 28:9), and according to the Rabbis these were also *b'milu'otham* (in their full natural state). In the case of the breastplate *b'milu'otham* is clearly mentioned (*ibid.*, Verse 20) and so is the onyx stone (*ibid.*). Thus the verse before us, *stones of onyx and stones of 'milu'im'* means that both were *for the ephod and for the breastplate.*   (85) "Make." In our Rashi: "make Me."   (86) The Hebrew is *beith olamim* — "the Eternal House." See in *Seder Yithro* Note 598.   (87) II Chronicles 4:8: *And he made ten tables.*   (88) *Ibid.*, Verse 7: *And he made the ten candelabrums.*   (89) *Ibid.*, Verse 6: *And he made ten lavers.*   (90) I Kings 7:27-39: *And he made the ten bases...*   (91) And not of the Sanctuary of Jerusalem and its vessels. But now that Scripture says *'and' so shall ye make it*, the expression is not set apart from the preceding part of the verse but is connected with it, thus: "and" so shall you make the pattern of all the furniture of the Sanctuary.

language. But I do not know if this is true, that Solomon was bound to make the vessels of the Sanctuary of Jerusalem [86] after the pattern of these vessels [of the Tabernacle]. The altar of brass which Solomon made was twenty cubits long and twenty wide! [92] And Rabbi Abraham ibn Ezra wrote: *"And so shall ye make* — the vessels, [93] for at the beginning He said, *And let them make Me a Sanctuary.*" [94]

In line with the plain meaning of Scripture there is no need for all this. Rather, the duplication [*and so shall ye make it*] has the purpose of expressing emphasis and eagerness. Thus He said: "*And let them make Me a Sanctuary*[94] — a house and vessels — as a Royal Sanctuary and seat of Majesty, *that I may dwell in the midst of them* in the house and on the Throne of Glory which they will make for Me there. *According to all that I show thee the pattern of this Tabernacle* of which I have said that I will dwell in the midst of them, *and the pattern of all the vessels thereof.* He repeated, *and so shall ye* all *make it* with eagerness and diligence. This is similar to the repetition found in the verse, *and the children of Israel did according to all that the Eternal commanded Moses, so did they.* [95] Here, because the verse speaks of a command, it says, *and so 'shall' ye make it,* [whereas in the other verse the repeat states *so 'did' they*, because it speaks of a deed accomplished].

10. AND THEY SHALL MAKE AN ARK. The plural [*and 'they' shall make*] refers back to *the children of Israel* mentioned above.[96] But afterwards Scripture states: *And thou shalt overlay it,*[97] *And thou shalt cast for it* [98] — all in the singular, as Moses is the leader of all Israel. It is possible that [in using the plural — *and*

---

(92) II Chronicles 4:1. The altar of the Tabernacle was five cubits long and five cubits broad (further, 27:1).   (93) The expression *and so shall ye make it* thus refers only to *the pattern of all the furniture* (mentioned right above), but does not refer to *the pattern of the Tabernacle* since the term "making" was already stated with reference to it, namely, *and let them 'make' Me a Sanctuary.*   (94) Above, Verse 8.   (95) Further, 39:32.   (96) Above, Verse 2.   (97) Verse 11.   (98) Verse 12.

they shall make] He is indicating His wish that all Israel should share in the making of the ark because it is *the holiest dwelling-place of the Most High*,[99] and that they should all merit thereby [a knowledge of] the Torah. Thus the Rabbis have said in Midrash Rabbah:[100] "Why is it that with reference to all the vessels it says, *and thou shalt make*, and in the case of the ark it says, *and they shall make?* Said Rabbi Yehudah the son of Rabbi Shalom: The Holy One, blessed be He, said, Let all the people come and engage themselves in the making of the ark, so that they should all merit [a knowledge of] the Torah." The "engaging themselves" of which the Rabbi speaks means that they should each offer one golden vessel [for the making of the ark, in addition to their general offering for the building of the Tabernacle], or that they should help Bezalel in some small way, or that they should have intent [of heart in the making thereof].[101]

12. AND THOU SHALT CAST FOUR RINGS OF GOLD FOR IT, AND PUT THEM IN THE FOUR 'PA'AMOTHAV' (CORNERS THEREOF). "The word *pa'amothav* is to be understood as the Targum rendered it: 'corners thereof.' It was on the upper corners near to the cover of the ark that the rings were placed. *And two rings shall be on the one side of it, and two rings on the other side of it*. These are the very four rings which are mentioned at the beginning of the verse, but here Scripture explains that two of these rings were placed on one side [and the other two on the other side]." Thus did Rashi explain, and he explained it well. But I do not know why Rashi wrote that "on the upper corners near to the cover" the rings were placed. For in that case, the weight [of the ark and the tables of law hanging down from the staves] would be very much heavier. Moreover, the respectful way is that

---

(99) Psalms 46:5. (100) Shemoth Rabbah 33:3. (101) Thus even the desire to help Bezalel in the making of the ark was already accounted as an act of helping in the making thereof (Kli Chemdah). It may also hint that a mere genuine craving for Torah is praiseworthy before the Creator.

EXODUS XXV, TERUMAH 447

the ark be lifted up, resting high upon the shoulders of the priests [102] [when carrying it].

Rabbi Abraham ibn Ezra wrote: "I have searched in all Scripture and I have not found the term *pa'am* to mean 'corner' but only 'foot.' Thus: *How beautiful are p'amayich' (thy feet);* [103] *the feet of the poor, 'pa'amei' (the feet of) the needy.* [104] Therefore I felt bound to explain that the ark had feet to it [upon which it rested]." And so Ibn Ezra explained the meaning of the verse to be that there were altogether eight rings, the four bottom ones [105] being those through which the staves were inserted to carry the ark with, whilst the four upper rings were purely for ornamental purposes. His words are, however, not at all correct. For if, as he said, *pa'am* means foot, then Scripture is commanding that the rings should be in the lower corners upon which the ark rests, and these bottom corners are called "feet" because the Sacred Language adapts all forms according to the image of man. Thus it calls the upper part of any object *rosh* (head), and the bottom part *regel* (foot). [Accordingly there is no need to say as did Ibn Ezra that the ark had feet to it upon which it rested, since Scripture

---

(102) In Numbers 7:9 it is clearly stated that it is the Levites the sons of Kohath who carried the ark, not the priests. See, however, "The Commandments," Vol. I, pp. 43-44, that in reality the fulfillment of this commandment, bearing the ark upon the shoulders, devolves upon the priests, but in the wilderness the duty was laid upon the Levites because of the limited number of priests then available. This is Rambam's position. For Ramban's opinion see my Note there, p. 44. (103) Song of Songs 7:2. The J.P.S. translation "steps" follows Ramban's interpretation, explained further on. (104) Isaiah 26:6. In J.P.S. translation: "steps," as Ramban explains it. (105) See my Hebrew commentary p. 459, that our Ibn Ezra texts have here a different version, and that it is *only* according to that different version that Ramban's questions on Ibn Ezra can be understood. Principally Ramban differs with three points that Ibn Ezra made: 1. That there were eight rings to the ark; 2. that the staves for carrying the ark were inserted in the *upper* rings; 3. that the ark had feet. — It is on this second point that the texts differ. It must then be remembered that Ramban is directing his criticism on Ibn Ezra holding that it was the *upper* rings that were for carriage. Ramban's opinion is that the lower rings were for the insertion of the staves with which the ark was carried. Ramban will also differ with Ibn Ezra on the other two points.

calls the bottom corners "feet."] And this is indeed true, that the rings for the purpose of carriage were at the bottom corners, and the ark was thus lifted up above the staves, as I have explained above.

But in my opinion *pa'am* does not mean "foot" but is a term meaning "step." *How beautiful are 'p'amayich'* [103] — your steps. This usage is similar to the phrase in the Talmud: [106] "How beautiful are the steps of this maiden." Similarly: *why tarry 'pa'amei' (the steps of) his chariots?* [107] The word *pa'amothav* here is Scripture's reference to the steps of the priests [102] that carry the ark, thus hinting at two things: that the rings be in the corners right at the bottom, near the seat of the ark, and that the whole length of the ark should interpose between the two rings. For, assuming that the length of the ark was placed in an east-west position, then there were two rings on its north side, one at the eastern head and one at the western, and likewise two rings on the south side of the ark [similarly placed], and the steps of the priests moved between the rings with their faces towards one another. In the Mishnah of the Tabernacle[108] we have learned: "There were four gold rings affixed in the ark, two to the north thereof and two to the south, and in them the staves were inserted and were never moved therefrom etc."

21. AND IN THE ARK THOU SHALT PUT THE TESTIMONY THAT I SHALL GIVE THEE. "I do not know why this is repeated, for it has already been stated [in Verse 16], *And thou shalt put into the ark the Testimony which I shall give thee?* One

---

(106) Abodah Zarah 18 a. (107) Judges 5:28. Translated: *why tarry 'the wheels' of his chariots?* (108) This is the Beraitha on the work of the Tabernacle. (Otzar Midrashim, Eisenstein, p. 301; Ish Shalom's scientific edition, Breslau 1915.) For the name Beraitha see in *Seder Bo*, Note 209. — In the Holy of Holies the length of the ark was in a north-south position i.e., to the width of the holy place while the width of the ark was in an east-west position i.e., to the length of the holy place (Mishneh Torah, Hilchoth Beth Habchirah 3:13). When carrying the ark they carried it face to face, with their backs turned outward, and their faces set towards the ark (*ibid.* Hilchoth Klei Hamikdash 2:13). A reference to this point is found here in the text of Ramban.

EXODUS XXV, TERUMAH 449

may answer that it intends to teach us that while the ark was still by itself, without its cover, he should first place the Testimony into it and then place the cover on it [for the first time]. Thus we find also when Moses set up the Tabernacle that Scripture says, *And he put the Testimony into the ark,* [109] and after that it says, [109] *and he put the cover of the ark above.*" This is Rashi's language.

But if this be a command [as Rashi has it], the sense thereof would rather seem to be that after he puts the cover on the ark as G-d had commanded, [he should then remove the cover and] put the Testimony into the ark, for the term "ark" applies also when there is a cover on it. Moreover, one can also ask why did Scripture repeat the phrase *from between the two cherubim which are upon the ark of the Testimony,* [110] when it is known already from the preceding verses that the cherubim are upon the ark of Testimony? And what need is there to explain this again, seeing that He has already stated, *from above the ark-cover, from between the two cherubim?* [110] But the explanation thereof is as follows: Because He had commanded that *the cherubim shall spread out their wings on high,* [111] but had not said why they should be made altogether, and what function they should serve in the Tabernacle, and why they should be in that form, therefore He now said, *and thou shalt put the ark-cover* with the cherubim, for they are all one, *above upon the ark,* because *in the ark thou shalt put the Testimony that I shall give thee,* so that there be for Me a Throne of Glory, for there will I meet with thee and I will cause My Glory to dwell upon them, *and I will speak with thee from above the ark-cover, from between the two cherubim* because it is *upon the ark of the testimony.* [110] It is thus identical with the Divine Chariot which the prophet Ezekiel saw, of which he said, *This is the living creature that I saw under the G-d of Israel by the river Chebar; and I knew that they were cherubim.* [112] This is why He is called *He Who sitteth upon the cherubim,* [113] for they spread out their wings on high in order to teach us that they are the

---

(109) Further, 40:20. (110) Verse 22. (111) Verse 20. (112) Ezekiel 10:20. (113) I Samuel 4:4.

Chariot who carry the Glory, just as it is said, *and gold for the pattern of the chariot, even the cherubim, that spread out their wings, and covered the ark of the covenant of the Eternal,* [114] as I have mentioned.

In the opinion of our Rabbis [115] the cherubim had the forms of a human being, the word being of the Aramaic language which calls a lad *ravya*. In that case the letter *kaf* in the word *k'rubim* (cherubim) is not part of the root of the word, but merely serves in a comparative function [meaning "as lads"], the name indicating their substance. If you will further contemplate as to why their faces were turned one to another,[111] and why they were *of beaten work,*[116] you will be able to know that it was proper for them that they be *spreading out their wings on high,*[111] for they are the throne of the Supreme One, sheltering the Testimony.which is *the writing of G-d.*[117] *This is the meaning of the expression, the pattern of the chariot,*[114] for the cherubim which Ezekiel saw carrying the Glory are the pattern of the cherubim [on high], these being the Glory and the *tipheret* (beauty); and the cherubim which were in the Tabernacle and in the Sanctuary were of a likeness to them, *for one higher than the high watcheth, and there are higher than they.*[118] And this is the meaning of *and I knew*[112] [and not "and I saw"], for Ezekiel saw one and knew the other [on high]. This is why he said "they" [*and I knew that 'they' were cherubim*]. The student learned in the mysteries of the Cabala will understand.

24. A CROWN OF GOLD ROUND ABOUT. "This is a symbol of the crown of royalty, for the table represents wealth and prominence, just as the Rabbis say [119] 'the royal table.'" This is Rashi's language. And this explanation is indeed the truth, for in this lies the secret of the table [in the Tabernacle]. For since the time that the world came into existence, G-d's blessing did not

---

(114) I Chronicles 28:18.   (115) Chagigah 13 b.   (116) Verse 18. (117) Further, 32:16.   (118) Ecclesiastes 5:7.   (119) Yebamoth 24 b: "He who becomes a proselyte for the sake of 'the royal table.'"

create something from nothing; instead, the world follows its natural course, for it is written, *and G-d saw every thing that He had made, and behold, it was very good.*[120] But when *the root of the matter* [121] already exists, the blessing descends upon it and increases it, just as Elisha said, *tell me; what hast thou in the house?* [122] and then the blessing came upon the pot of oil that she already had, and she filled all the vessels from it.[123] And in the case of Elijah it is said, *The jar of meal was not spent, neither did the cruse of oil fail.* [124] And so also was the case with the showbread on the table; upon it rested the blessing, and from it came abundance to all Israel. That is why the Rabbis have said: [125] "Every priest who received even only as much as the size of a bean [of the showbread] ate it and was satisfied."

29. AND THOU SHALT MAKE 'KE'AROTHAV VEKAPOTHAV UKSOTHAV UMENAKIYOTHAV.' Rashi explained: "*Ke'arothav* are the forms [the moulds that were made to fit the shape of the bread]; *vekapothav* are spoons in which the incense was put;[126] *uksothav* are rods in the shape of halves of hollow canes [which were put between one loaf and another so that they would not become mouldy]; *umenakiyothav* are the trestles which were notched in [five places] to support the canes." These vessels [that Rashi referred to] are indeed mentioned in the Gemara.[127] And the Rabbi further said: "The word *mechilathei* [which Onkelos used for the Hebrew *menakiyothav*] means 'bearers,' similar to the expressions: *and I weary myself 'kalkeil' (to bear it);*[128] *I am weary 'hachil' (bearing it).*[129] Now the Sages of Israel have differed on this. For some say that *ksothav* are the trestles, and *menakiyothav* are the hollow canes. But Onkelos who translated *menakiyothav* by [the Aramaic] *mechilathei* was of the same opinion as he who says that *menakiyoth* are the trestles [supporting pillars attached to the table]." These are Rashi's words.

---

(120) Genesis 1:31. (121) Job 19:28. (122) II Kings 4:2. (123) *Ibid.*, 6. (124) I Kings 17:16. (125) Yoma 39 a. (126) See Leviticus 24:7. (127) Menachoth 97 a. (128) Jeremiah 20:9. (129) *Ibid.*, 6:11. The beginning of the verse reads: *Therefore I am full of the fury of the Eternal.*

But I do not find them to be correct. for the word *mechilathei* [of Onkelos] in the Aramaic language is but a term meaning measures, such as ephahs and the like. Thus Onkelos rendered, *eiphath tzedek* [130] — *mechilon dikshot* (a true measure); *Thou shalt not have in thy house 'eiphah v'eiphah'* [131] — thou shalt not have *mechilta umechilta (diverse measures)*. In a similar sense it is found whenever mentioned in the Talmud and in the Sages' words: *kayal meikal* (he was measuring); [132] *bimchilta d'kayil inish ba mitkil* (with the measure that one measures others, with that he is measured). [133] Similarly, *I am weary 'hachil'* [129] means "I am weary of being a holding measure" [of G-d's fury], and it is associated with these expressions: *alpayim bath yachil (it held two thousand baths);* [134] *v'chol bashalish aphar ha'aretz (and He comprehended the dust of the earth in a measure);* [135] *too little 'meihachil' (to receive) the burnt offering.* [136] Similarly, *I am weary 'hachil'* [129] is in my opinion not an expression of "bearing" but is instead a form of that very same meaning of "holding," thus saying, "I am weary of holding" [G-d's fury], similar in usage to these expressions: *the land is not able 'l'hachil' (to hold) all his words;* [137] *the spirit of a man 'y'chalkeil' his infirmity,* [138] meaning that he will be able to hold the pain within himself and not become weary [and broken in spirit] because of it. *Behold, heaven and the heaven of heavens cannot 'y'chalelucha'* [139] — they cannot hold and contain the greatness of Your exaltedness, for there is no limit and measure to You — *how much less this house that I have built!* [139] *'Y'chalkeil' his words rightfully* [140] means that he is not *a fool* who *spendeth all his spirit,* [141] but holds his words within himself when necessary, and uses them as necessary. *'Vay'chalkeil Yoseiph'* [142] means that Joseph gave them as much food as they could hold; he gave neither too much nor

---

(130) Leviticus 19:36. (131) Deuteronomy 25:14. (132) Menachoth 53 b: *ka kayol*. (133) Targum Yerushalmi Genesis 38:26. (134) I Kings 7:26. (135) Isaiah 40:12. (136) I Kings 8:64. (137) Amos 7:10. (138) Proverbs 18:14. (139) I Kings 8:27. (140) Psalms 112:5. (141) Proverbs 29:11. (142) Genesis 47:12.

too little, but *bread according to the want of their little ones.* [143] And such is the explanation of all [other similar expressions].

But Onkelos' opinion [who translated *umenakiyothav — umechilathei*] is not clear. Perhaps *menakiyothav* is in the opinion of Onkelos a term for measures, since they had [in the Tabernacle and later in the Sanctuary] a measure holding two tenth parts [of an ephah] flour, with which to measure one cake, [144] and they did not measure it twice with the one tenth measure of the meal-offering. We must then say that Onkelos differs from the Mishnah which teaches: [145] "There were two dry-measures in the Sanctuary: the tenth, and the half-tenth" [of an ephah], and in his opinion there were three dry-measures: the tenth, the half-tenth, and the two tenths.

The correct interpretation of Onkelos' opinion appears to me to be that *mechila* is the form (mould) made for the dough, just as the Rabbis have said: [146] "There were in the Tabernacle three moulds [for the showbread]: he placed it in a mould whilst it was still dough; when baked in the oven it was put in another mould, and when he took it out he placed it in a [third] frame so that it should not spoil." [147] This [third] frame which was used so that it should not spoil did not have to be shaped to the form of the bread and its size; instead, it was made like a sort of dish to support the sides of the bread, this being the *ke'arothav* mentioned in the verse. But the first mould for the dough was shaped to the form of the bread and its size, namely, ten [handbreadths] long and five wide, and its horns [148] seven fingerbreadths [high]. Into this mould the dough was put, measured and shaped to fit its form, and for this reason it was called *mechila* because it was made

---

(143) See Ramban on Genesis 41:48 (Vol. I, p. 507) that Joseph had gathered all food essential to life "even figs, fresh and dried, etc." Now of this kind of food he gave his family abundantly, but bread he gave them *according to the want of their little ones* (Genesis 47:12). (144) Leviticus 24:5. (145) Menachoth 87 a. (146) *Ibid.*, 94 a. (147) The first and third moulds were made of gold; the one for the oven was an iron mould. (148) Small pieces of dough were put on the four corners of each of the breads (Menachoth 96 a).

to "the measure." The term *menakiyoth* then [according to Onkelos] is a name just like ephah and *s'ah* [a third of the ephah measure is a *s'ah*], similar, to *ke'arothav* and *ksothav* and other nouns which are not descriptive. Perhaps those just measures which are called *a just ephah, and a just hin*, [149] and termed *menakiyoth* [of the root *naki* — clean] because they are clean of any falsehood, and thus they clear their owners of any cheating and sin. And *ksavoth* is a general term covering the canes [which were put between one loaf and another] and the trestles [notched in five places upon which the canes separating the loaves rested]. Perhaps because of their notches they were so called [*ksavoth*], with the letter *tzade* [*ktzavoth* — sides, corners] being used instead of the letter *sin* [*ksavoth*], this word [*ksavoth*] being similar to [the word *ktzavoth* found in the following verse]: *so that they that dwell in 'ktzavoth' (the uttermost parts) stand in awe of Thy signs*, [150] by interchanging the letter *tzade* with the *sin*, just like in the word *s'chok* ["laughter," which is the word *tzchok*].

Rabbi Abraham ibn Ezra wrote: "There is an error in Chronicles, [151] for in speaking of the vessels of the table in place of *ke'aroth* [mentioned here] it writes *mizrakoth* (basins); in place of *kapoth* [mentioned here] it writes *kiporim* (bowls); *ksavoth* is mentioned there as here; and in the place of *menakiyoth* it speaks of *mizlagoth* (forks). And all these were made of gold for the purpose of the table [and yet we do not find the *mizrakoth, kiporim*, and *mizlagoth* mentioned here in connection with the table in the Tabernacle]! Perhaps these were other vessels which

---

(149) Leviticus 19:36. (150) Psalms 65:9. (151) I Chronicles 28:17. The verse there reads: *'v'hamizlagoth' (and the forks), 'v'hamizrakoth' (and the basins), 'v'haksavoth' (and the jars), of pure gold; 'v'lichphorei' (and the bowls of) gold by weight 'lichphor uchphor' (for every bowl); 'v'lichphorei' (and for the bowls of) silver by weight 'lichphor uchphor' (for every bowl).* — Ibn Ezra's comment is to the effect that there are new vessels here mentioned for the table in the Sanctuary that are not found here in the Torah in connection with the table in the Tabernacle. — Ramban will point out that Ibn Ezra erred in thinking that this Verse 17 refers back to the tables of showbread mentioned above in Verse 16, since it really refers back to Verse 13, as explained in the text.

EXODUS XXV, TERUMAH

David commanded to be placed on the tables [152] which his son Solomon would make, but the table in the Tent of Meeting did not have these vessels." The error, however, is in Rabbi Abraham's words, [not in the Book of Chronicles], for that which Scripture states, *and the forks, and the basins, and the jars of pure gold; and for the golden bowls by weight for every bowl,* [151] is not connected only with *the tables of showbread* [153] [mentioned in the preceding verse], but it reverts back to that which Scripture stated [several verses above], *and for all the work of the service of the house of the Eternal, and for all the vessels of service in the house of the Eternal.* [154] And then it continues, *of gold, for all vessels of every kind of service,* [155] and then it mentioned, *and the forks, and the basins* [151] which are vessels of the altar, *and the jars* for the table, and *the bowls* for the altar. And finally it stated, *and for the altar of incense refined gold by weight,* [156] concluding: *All this [do I give thee] in writing, as the Eternal hath made me wise by His hand upon me, even all the works of this pattern.* [157] Thus David [in speaking to his son Solomon] included all needs of the Sanctuary.

30. 'LECHEM PANIM' (SHOWBREAD). "It is called *lechem panim* [which literally means 'bread of faces'] because it had 'faces' [surfaces] looking in both directions towards the sides of the House [Tabernacle or Sanctuary]. The loaf was set lengthwise across the breadth of the table with its sides standing up exactly in a line with the edge of the table." This is the language of Rashi. This conforms with the language of the Mishnah: [158] "Ben Zoma says: *lechem panim* — [it is so called] because it is to have surfaces" [looking in both directions]. But all this is in accordance with the opinion of the Sage [159] who says: "How did they make the showbread? Like a case broken open." [160] But according to

---

(152) II Chronicles 4:8. (153) I Chronicles 28:16. (154) *Ibid.*, Verse 13. (155) *Ibid.*, Verse 14. (156) *Ibid.*, Verse 18. (157) *Ibid.*, Verse 19. (158) Menachoth 96 a. (159) Rabbi Chanina (*ibid.*, 94 b). (160) "With its cover and two of its opposite sides removed, thus leaving the bread the two sides [facing each other] and the bottom underneath" (Rashi *ibid.*). The figure thus is: ⊔.

the Sage [161] who says that it was shaped "like a rocking boat," [162] then it could not have been [called *lechem panim* because of the parallel surfaces looking in both directions, as it had none]! And Rabbi Abraham ibn Ezra wrote that it is called *lechem panim* because it is *before Me always*. [163]

By way of the Truth, [the mystic lore of the Cabala], when you will understand the word *l'phanai* (before Me) [164] you will understand its name [i.e., why it is called "the bread of *panim*"] and its secret, for because of that [the table] was placed on the north side [of the Tabernacle], [165] seeing that *the blessing of the Eternal maketh rich*, [166] similar to what is said, *in every place where I cause My name to be mentioned I will come unto thee and bless thee*. [167] I have already alluded to this. [168]

Where shall be found the wisdom embodied in the candelabrum, its cups and knops and flowers, seeing that it is so *hidden from the eyes of all living!* [169] But as to the reason for its being of beaten work, with the six branches coming out of the seventh, and upon them *the lamp of G-d* [170] *and all* [six lamps] *to give light over against it* [171] — all this you can understand from our words that we have written in another place. [172] This is the intent of the saying of the Sages [173] that Moses found difficulty with the candelabrum. [174]

---

(161) Rabbi Yochanan (*ibid*). (162) The sides of which narrowed downwards until there was but a fingerbreadth at the bottom and it had no covering on top (Rashi *ibid*.). The figure is: V. (163) The word *panim* meaning "face" is thus explained by *l'phanai tamid (before Me always):* it is *lechem panim* literally: "bread of the face" because it is *before Me always.* (164) Literally: "to My face." (165) Further, 26:35. (166) Proverbs 10:22. (167) Above, 20:24. (168) *Ibid*., 20:3. — So explained in Bachya. (169) See Job 28:20-21. (170) I Samuel 3:3. (171) Further, Verse 37. (172) I have not been able to identify that "other place." The basic concept though is explained by Abusaula that it is an allusion to the lower six emanations all being *one beaten work* (Verse 36), symbolizing a perfect Unity, with *the lamp of G-d*, alluding to the Supreme One, above them. (173) Menachoth 29 a. (174) Meaning, that he found it perplexing to understand the secret of its cups and knops and flowers, for it is extremely hidden from the eyes of all living (Abusaula).

39. OF A TALENT OF PURE GOLD SHALL HE MAKE IT WITH ALL THESE VESSELS. This means "that its weight together with all its vessels shall be exactly one talent, neither less nor more." This is Rashi's language. And such indeed is the simple meaning of Scripture. But if that be so, there is here a point which is greatly to be wondered about, namely that Scripture should not specify at all how much of the talent of gold should go into the candelabrum itself! For in that case half of the talent or even more could then go into the making of the tongs and the snuffdishes [175] which are vessels separate from the candelabrum, while the candelabrum itself could be made of less than half the talent, or perhaps the candelabrum would be made of the entire talent less one *maneh* [a sacred talent consisted of one hundred and twenty *manoth*] and all these vessels would be made of the one *maneh*! Moreover, what reason is there that the total weight of the candelabrum with its many separate vessels should be given as one talent, and why was it not explained how many tongs and snuffdishes should be made from it?

But the opinion of our Rabbis is not as the Rabbi [Rashi] stated it, for thus did the Sages teach in Tractate Menachoth:[176] "The candelabrum and its seven lamps [177] came from the talent, but not its tongs and snuffdishes. And if you ask how will I then explain, [*Of a talent of pure gold shall he make it,*] *with all these vessels*? Then I reply that this includes the lamps. These are the words of Rabbi Yehudah. Rabbi Nechemyah says: the candelabrum [alone] came from the talent but not its lamps, tongs, and snuffdishes. And if you ask how will I then explain the expression, *with all these vessels*? I answer that it teaches that they all be made of gold [aside of the talent mentioned]." There in Tractate Menachoth the Rabbis have further said, that according to Rabbi Yehudah [who says that the lamps came from the talent], the lamps were also of beaten work together with the candelabrum; yet Scripture calls them *these 'vessels,'* because they are receptacles

---

(175) Verse 38. (176) Menachoth 88 b. (177) Verse 37. — These were a kind of small receptacle into which the oil and the wicks were put (Rashi).

for the oil, known by a name of their own, since in all other candelabrums they are separate from them [although here they were hammered out of the same talent of gold from which the whole candelabrum was made]. And according to Rabbi Nechemyah [who says that the lamps did not come from the talent, the Rabbis] have said there that the lamps were not of beaten work together with the candelabrum. Thus according to Rabbi Yehudah included in the weight of the talent — with that which was of beaten work with it — is only the candelabrum itself but none of the separate vessels thereof. And according to Rabbi Nechemyah the Rabbis have said there: "And if you ask how will I then explain the expression, *with all these vessels*? I answer, it teaches that they all be made of gold, this being necessary to be stated because of the mouth of the lamps." [178]

According to the simple meaning of Scripture the verse states: "*Of a talent of pure gold shall he make it; all these vessels* he shall [also] make of pure gold," since He did not explain at first that the lamps [179] should be of gold. Similarly, Scripture relates at the time of the making of the candelabrum, *And he made the lamps thereof, seven, and the tongs thereof, and the snuffdishes thereof, of pure gold,* [180] the expression *of pure gold* referring only to the tongs and the snuffdishes [but not to the lamps], and therefore He explained it further and said, *Of a talent of pure gold he made it, and all the vessels thereof,* [181] the meaning being that all its vessels he [i.e., Bezalel] made of pure gold, not that he made them out of the talent of gold. Included in the expression *all the vessels thereof* are the oil vessels, for he made with the candelabrum many vessels besides those mentioned, just as it is said during the journeyings,

---

(178) One might think that the mouth of the lamps where the wicks burn and become blackened should not be made of pure gold, since the Torah cares for the wealth of Israel; therefore Scripture let it be known that even the mouth of the lamps be made of pure gold (Rashi, Menachoth 88 b). (179) That the tongs and snuffdishes are to be made of pure gold is clearly stated in Verse 38. However, concerning the lamps He did not mention at all (in Verse 37) that they be made of pure gold. Hence the reverting to them in Verse 39 before us. (180) Further, 37:23. (181) *Ibid.,* Verse 24.

EXODUS XXV, TERUMAH

And they shall cover the candelabrum of the light, and its lamps, and its tongs, and its snuffdishes, and all the oil vessels thereof, wherewith they minister unto it.[182] And the verse which states, *unto the base thereof, and unto the flowers thereof, it was beaten work,*[183] likewise indicates according to its plain sense that only the candelabrum itself was of beaten work but not its lamps. All this is in accordance with the line of teaching of the Gemara.

But in the Beraitha of the work of the Tabernacle [184] it is taught in another way. "The candelabrum which Moses made in the wilderness was made of gold. It had to be made by a process of beating, and had to have cups, knops, and flowers, for it is said, *And thou shalt make a candelabrum of pure gold.*[185] I might have thought that [the cups etc.] may be made separately and then soldered on to the candelabrum; Scripture therefore states, *they shall be of one piece with it.*[186] How do we know that this includes lamps, so that they must also be made of one piece with it? Scripture therefore says, [*Of a talent of pure gold*] *he shall make.*[187] I might think this also includes its cups, knops, and flowers? Scripture therefore says, *it* [*he shall make 'it'*]. Now how do you know that you are to include its lamps and exclude its cups, knops and flowers? Since Scripture has here used a term of amplification and followed it by a term of limitation,[188] I reason as follows: I include its lamps because they have to be made with the candelabrum, and I exclude its cups, knops and flowers because they do not always have to be made with it.[189] And how

---

(182) Numbers 4:9. (183) *Ibid.*, 8:4. (184) See above, Note 108. (185) Above, Verse 31. (186) Verse 36. (187) Verse 39 before us. (188) A literal translation of the text here reads: "After it included its lamps Scripture limited." I have followed on this point Ish Shalom's text (see Note 108). The thought conveyed would seem to be identical in both versions. (189) The intent, as explained further on, is as follows: even if the candelabrum is made of any other metal beside gold it must also contain the branches. But cups, knops, and flowers are to be made only if the candelabrum is made out of gold. — When the Hasmonean kings recaptured the Temple from the hands of the Greeks the candelabrum was first made of iron, then of silver and finally when the people could afford it, they made it of gold (Menachoth 28 b). Now when it was made of iron or silver it did not need cups, knops etc.

do I know that I am to include its *malkocheha*[190] and *machtotheha*?[191] Scripture therefore says, [*of beaten work*] *shall it be done.*[185] I might think I am also to include the *tzvatim* (tongs) and the snuffers; Scripture therefore says, [*Of a talent of pure gold he shall make*] *it.*[187] And how do you know that you are to include the *malkocheha* and *machtotheha* and exclude the tongs and the snuffers? Since Scripture has here used a term of amplification and followed it by a term of limitation, I reason as follows: I include the *malkocheha* and *machtotheha* because they are used with the candelabrum, and I exclude the tongs and the snuffers because they are not used with it. Rabbi Yehoshua the son of Korcha says: *It* [i.e., the candelabrum] is made of the talent, but not its vessels, for it is said, *Of a talent of pure gold he shall make 'it.'*[187] And if you ask how will I then explain the expression, *and all its vessels*? Then I reply that it means that they should be made of pure gold [but not of the talent]." Thus far is the text of the Beraitha.

It appears from that which the Rabbis, of blessed memory, have said, that the lamps, the *melkochayim*, and the *machtoth* were all made of beaten work together with the candelabrum; since the *melkochayim* were not tongs [as we understood the word till now][192] but they were rather golden lids which were made on the rim of the lamps for opening and closing, and would cover them so that nothing fell into the oil, in the same way that they make

---

(190) Up to this point we have followed all standard commentators — Rashi, Onkelos, etc. as well as all translations — that *melkochayim* are "tongs." But from this point on it is clear [and Ramban will so clarify it further] that *melkochayim* are a sort of cover-like part for each of the lamps so that no impurities fall into the lamp while it is burning. Ramban's comment that "in the same way they make today in candelabrums for kings" is obviously a reference to what he had personally seen in the royal palace of the Kingdom of Aragon which as the recognized leader of the Jews he often visited.   (191) The same change applies to *machtoth* which we have translated till now as "snuffdishes." But it is clear that Ramban interprets it now as meaning that underneath each lamp there was a small receptacle for the sparks to fall into.   (192) And as Rashi and Onkelos interpreted *melkochayim* to mean "tongs."

today in candelabrums for kings. This usage [of the word *melkochayim*] is associated with the expression, *and my tongue cleaveth 'malkochay'* [193] — the palate and bottom parts of the mouth being called *melkochayim* [of the root *loko'ach* — "taking"] because they "take in" the tongue between them. [194] The *machtoth* are receptacles under each lamp to catch the sparks of fire which might fall from them. The *melkochayim* and the *machtoth* were all of one beaten work with the candelabrum and were made out of the talent of gold. But the tongs and the snuffers, which were not used in the candelabrum itself but were instead vessels separate from it and not attached thereto, did not come from the talent at all. Similarly this Beraitha excluded its cups, knops and flowers, so that if he wanted to make them not of beaten work together with the candelabrum he was so permitted, the reason according to the Beraitha being "because they are not made with it," that is to say, they do not invalidate the candelabrum. For if he made it of any other metal besides gold, it did not come with cups, knops and flowers, but the [six] branches [with the central shaft] always invalidated the candelabrum if lacking therefrom.

According to this Beraitha then, the Scriptural expression, *and all the vessels thereof* [181] means that Bezalel made of gold all vessels needed for the proper use of the candelabrum and appropriate to it — these being the tongs and the snuffers that are necessary in the use of all candelabrums. Similarly, *All the instruments of the Tabernacle in all the service thereof* [195] means all instruments needed for [erecting] the Tabernacle. These He did not explain but mentioned only that they were to be made of brass. But the verse before us which states, *Of a talent of pure gold shall he make it, with all these vessels*, refers to those vessels mentioned [in the preceding verse, namely, *malkocheha* and *machtotheha*], and they were all of beaten work with it. It is possible that the statement which Scripture uses at the

---

(193) Psalms 22:16. (194) The above-mentioned verse from the Psalms would then mean: "and my tongue cleaveth to the roof and bottom of my mouth." (195) Further, 27:19.

construction, namely, *and all the vessels thereof,* [181] alludes to these vessels [the *malkocheha* and *machtotheha*] mentioned there in the preceding verse, so that they were all to be made with the candelabrum of beaten work, as is the plain meaning of Scripture. But *the vessels of oil* [182] were not mentioned at the construction just as they were not mentioned at the command [for making the candelabrum], but they made them on their [196] own accord. Perhaps Bezalel did not make them but certain individuals made them and dedicated them to the public.

In summary, the candelabrum itself came from the talent, but nothing outside of it came therefrom, according to the words of all authorities.

17. TWO TENONS SHALL THERE BE IN EACH BOARD. Rashi wrote: "He cut out the lower part of the board in the middle to a height of one cubit, and he left one quarter of its width on the one side and one quarter of it on the other side. These [pieces on each side] are the *yadoth* (the tenons). The part cut out between the tenons was one half of the breadth of the board, and these tenons they fixed into the sockets which were hollowed out. The sockets were one cubit in height, forty of them fitting closely one to the other. The tenons of the boards which were fixed into the sockets were cut away on three sides, the width of the portions cut away being equal to the thickness of the rim of the sockets, so that when the boards [were fitted into the sockets, the wood of the board] would cover the entire top of the socket. For if this were not so [if the same thickness were not cut away from the tenons], there would have been a space between one board and the other equal to the thickness of the rims of the two sockets which would have separated them. This is what is meant when it is said, *And they shall be coupled together beneath,* [197] meaning, that they should cut away the sides of the tenons so that the boards should fit closely one to the other." So I found the language of the Rabbi.

(196) I.e., Bezalel and Oholiab.   (197) Verse 24.

But I wonder! If the part cut away in the middle was half of the breadth of the board [as Rashi has it] — measuring four and a half handbreadths [198] — it follows that the thickness of the rim of each socket must be the same as a fourth of the breadth of the board, which is two handbreadths and a thumb, in order that the thickness [of the rims] of the two sockets should cover the part cut away in the middle, which is half of the breadth of the board, and thus there would be no space between one socket and the other. But if so, if you cut away the boards [199] on three sides in that way, there would be nothing left [for the tenons], since the rims of the sockets were alike on all sides! Moreover, the Rabbi [Rashi] brought proof further on in Verse 20, stating: "Thus it is taught in the Mishnah of 'The structure of the Tabernacle:' The order of arranging the boards for making the Tabernacle was as follows: He made the sockets hollow and cut away from [200] the board at the bottom a quarter of its width on one side and a quarter on the other, and the cut-away portion in the middle totalled one half of its width. Thus they made for each board two tenons like two rungs of a ladder, and these they fixed into the two sockets." But if one takes this Beraitha too in its ordinary sense, it would result in something exceedingly astonishing. For if he cuts away from the board a quarter on each side, and in the middle he cuts away half of the breadth of the board, then the

---

(198) The whole breadth of the board was a cubit and a half (Verse 16) which are nine handbreadths, and a half thereof is four and a half. (199) "The boards." In Mizrachi quoting Ramban: "the tenons." This is correct. The Hebrew text before us also means the same, except that the term "boards" is here used in a general sense. (200) The text in Rashi states *v'choreitz* (and he cuts away) — "and he cuts away a quarter on one side and a quarter on the other side." Ramban will then ask: if in addition to these two quarters which he cuts away at the sides he also cuts away in the middle half of the width of the board — then there is nothing left for the tenons! Mizrachi answers that Rashi's understanding of the Beraitha was that the expression "a quarter on one side etc." does not refer to the cutting away but to what is "left" at the sides of the board as tenons. The translation would then be: "and he cuts the board at the bottom, [leaving] a quarter on one side and a quarter on the other." To understand the text of Ramban though requires the first translation as above.

whole bottom part [to the height of a cubit] is cut away, and nothing is left of it at all [to serve as a tenon]! In my opinion, however, this Beraitha did not specify the size of the amount cut away, since the Torah also gave no measurements for the thickness of the rims of the sockets. Therefore what the Rabbis [in this Beraitha] said is that he cut away a quarter of the total amount of the board on one side in order to cover one rim of the socket, and another quarter he cut away on the other side; and in the middle of the board he cut away *half* of the total amount cut away from the whole board, in order to cover the rims of the two sockets.

But according to all opinions it still needs to be clarified further, because the Tabernacle at the bottom to the height of a cubit was not wide ten cubits, [201] since the thickness of the two sockets, one on each side, reduced its size! Perhaps there is no objection to that. And in the words of Rashi we read: "He cut away from the thickness of the tenons inside, out of the board which was a cubit thick, according to the thickness of the rims of the sockets". This is correct, but it is not mentioned in the Beraitha.

'MESHULAVOTH ISHAH EL ACHOTHAH' (SET IN ORDER ONE TO ANOTHER). "*Meshulavoth* means made like *shlivoth* (rungs of) a ladder. *One to another,* this means that they should correspond exactly one to the other, and should be separated from each other, and so planed at their ends that they may be inserted into the hollow of the sockets, just like a rung enters the holes of a ladder's uprights; further, that the portions cut away [from the boards] in their fronts and backs should be alike, one identical to the other, in order that there should not be two tenons, one of which extends towards the front and the other towards the back in relation to the thickness of the board which was one cubit." This is Rashi's language. [202]

---

(201) That is to say, Scripture states that the height of each board was to be *ten* cubits (Verse 16). But because of the cutting away at the bottom to the height of a cubit for the tenons, its size was reduced to *nine* cubits high, as it lay on top of the sockets! (202) It should be noted that the version of Rashi here in Ramban is somewhat different in the order of the phrases from the standard editions of Rashi.

Thus according to Rashi the word *meshulavoth* refers back to the tenons, that they be planed at their ends so that they enter the hollow of the sockets, and *ishah el achothah (one to the other)* refers only to the boards, that they be fitted close together. But the Hebrew word *krashim* (boards) is masculine, and therefore it should have rather said *ish el achiv* ["one to the other" — in the masculine form]! [203] Perhaps [Rashi] will interpret *ishah el achothah* as meaning that the *shlivoth* [literally: "the rungs" but here referring to the *yadoth*, the tenons — a feminine form] correspond exactly one with the other, and the thickness of wood cut away from each of the tenons be exactly alike, for in that way the boards will fit closely together. Now the tenons were not planed in a sloping fashion, for the hollow of the sockets was alike in each of them; they were cut only on their sides in order that the boards fit closely one to another.

But in the Beraitha on the work of the Tabernacle I found the following text: "Two *sanin* ('pegs') [as explained further] projected from the boards, two from each of them, fitting into corresponding holes, for it is said, *meshulavoth ishah el achothah*. These are the words of Rabbi Nechemyah. For Rabbi Nechemyah says: It should not have said *meshulavoth*; what does Scripture teach us then by using that word? It is to teach us that he make them like the rungs of an Egyptian ladder." Now the meaning of the word *sanin* is similar to the device they make in chests to tighten and hold the boards together, a sort of wooden peg, somewhat like that which we have been taught in the Mishnah of Keilim: [204] "If [two boards] were fastened together with *sanin* (pegs) or joints they need not be plastered in the middle." [205] In the Talmud [206] they likewise speak of "reeds and *sanin*." Accordingly it would appear that Scripture is telling us that he is to make a projection on the side of the board, like a sort of "male shafts," [207] and on the opposite side of the board next to it he is

---

(203) And not *ishah el achothah* — which is in the feminine form. (204) Keilim 10:6. (205) Since the pegs or joints hold the boards together tightly they need not be plastered in the middle to afford protection from corpse uncleanness. (206) Baba Metzia 117 a. (207) Succah 12 b.

to make a corresponding cavity into which the arrow-head is set. The same he is to do on the other board, thus dovetailing each board twice [one on each side]. *Meshulavoth ishah el achothah* is thus a reference to these *shlivoth* (pegs) themselves [and not to the tenons as Rashi has it], and is here properly in the feminine form [*ishah el achothah*, because of the word *shlivah* which is feminine]. And so did the Sages make mention of this term in the feminine: "The *shlivah* (rundle) slipped from under him;" [208] "In a ladder it depends on the material of *shlivothav* (its steps)." [209] And even though we find the plural of this word in the masculine form — *between 'hashlabim' (the stays)* [210] — it is like *nashim* (women) and *pilagshim* (concubines) whose plural form is in the masculine.

'KEIDMAH MIZRACHAH' (ON THE EAST SIDE EASTWARD). [211] The reason for this expression is that the Sacred Language calls the east *kedem*, just as it is said, *And ye shall measure without the city for the side of 'keidmah' (east) two thousand cubits,* [212] and calls the west *achor* (back), just as it is said, *Behold, I go 'kedem' (forward), but He is not there, v'achor (and backward), but I cannot perceive Him.* [213] Similarly: *As far as 'ha'achron' (the hinder) sea,* [214] which means the western sea. Both [*kedem* and *achor*] are borrowed terms, as the Sacred Language adopts these substitute forms from the standpoint of a person who turns to the light of the sun [thus calling the east *panim*, "face," because his face is turned eastward to the rising sun, and the west

---

(208) Makkoth 7 b. (209) Shabbath 60 a. And if the steps are of metal the whole ladder is susceptible to uncleanness. (210) I Kings 7:28. (211) Further, 27:13. — At this point Ramban begins to explain the significance of the Hebrew terms for "east, west etc.," which are mentioned in connection with the arrangement of the boards. The word *kedem* (east) is not found in connection with the boards, as the Tabernacle on that side had only a curtain. Hence Ramban chose a verse from the following chapter which mentions *kedem*, and then he will revert to the theme of the boards, and explain the terms *negbah, teimanah* (the south side, southward) mentioned here in the following Verse 18. (212) Numbers 35:5. (213) Job 23:8. (214) Deuteronomy 34:2.

achor, "back," because his back is then to the west]. Similarly it says, *and they went l'achor (backward) and not 'l'panim' (forward).* [215] And the south is called *negev* (dry, parched) because the land is dried up on account of the heat. At times Scripture mentions the borrowed term and then explains it by name. Thus it says *keidmah,* a term which is borrowed, and explains it by saying *mizrachah* (eastward), [211] which is the name itself. Similarly, it says *negbah,* which is the borrowed name, and explains it by its proper name — *teimanah* (southward). [216] And the west is called by the substitute name *yam* [which also means "sea"] because the language adopted it from the standpoint of the people living in the Land of Israel to whom the Great Sea is on the west. The north on the other hand has no by-name, and is so called *tzaphon* [which means "hidden"] because the sun never appears on that side. The south is called *darom,* just as it is said, *The wind goeth toward 'darom' (the south), and turneth about into the north.* [217] It is really a double word [*dor rum* — "it abides in the height," a reference to the sun that always reaches its greatest height on that side], with one letter *reish* missing because of the combination of two similar letters: *dor rum,* which means that the sun [always] moves at its highest point on that side. The south is also called *yamin* [which means "right"] and the north is called *smol* [meaning "left"] with reference to a man who turns eastward [to face the light of the rising sun, in which case his right hand is to the south, and his left to the north], as I have mentioned.

The secret of these names is known from the mystic speculations on the Chariot on high [i.e. the vision of Ezekiel of the Divine Chariot]. Likewise, [the secret of] the name for the west which is *yam* (sea) is known from that which the Rabbis have said: [218] "The Divine Glory is in the west," for the *yam* alludes to "the wisdom of Solomon," just as the Rabbis have said in the

---

(215) Jeremiah 7:24. According to Ramban the sense of the verse is: they went away from the light [the word of G-d] and did not go towards it.
(216) Verse 18 (here in Chapter 26 before us). See above Note 211.
(217) Ecclesiastes 1:6. (218) Baba Bathra 25 a.

Midrash:[219] "*Yam* always signifies Torah, as it is said, *and broader than 'yam' (the sea).*"[220] I intend to mention this in the section of *V'zoth Habrachah*[221] on the verse, *possess thou 'yam' (the sea) and the south,*[222] if my Creator will bless me to reach there.

24. AND THEY SHALL BE COUPLED TOGETHER ABOVE THE HEAD OF IT UNTO THE ONE RING. According to Rashi's interpretation this verse goes back to explain that all the boards should be coupled together beneath, where the boards were cut away on their sides, and they all should be *coupled together about the head of it*, meaning "of each board." Or it may be that *rosho (the head of it)* refers to the top of the Tabernacle. Similarly, [according to Rashi] the expression *unto the one ring* means of each of the boards. Likewise he explained, *thus shall it be for them both,*[223] for the two end boards [for the board at the end of the north side and for the adjacent board in the western wall].

But if this is so, I do not know why Scripture does not explicitly tell us about these rings, saying "and you shall make twenty gold rings" [instead of saying, *unto the one ring*, which means of each board], seeing that it mentions the cut which he is to make in all the boards.[224] Moreover, how could Scripture say *unto the one ring* with the definite article [when it has not mentioned it previously]? Perhaps because it is the customary manner with all houses made of boards to attach them at the top with one ring, Scripture shortened the explanation and said *the ring* — meaning the one which is known to him and customary. Similarly it said of the bars, *and thou shalt make their rings of gold for places for the bolts,*[225] which means the customary [rings] being known to them. A similar case is the expression, *their hooks shall be of gold.*[226]

---

(219) The exact source is unknown to me. See, however, in my Hebrew commentary p. 468, Note 52 for a similar thought in Yerushalmi Shekalim VI, 1.   (220) Job 11:9.   (221) Deuteronomy 33:1.   (222) *Ibid.*, Verse 23.   (223) In the second half of Verse 24 (before us).   (224) Verse 17.   (225) Verse 29.   (226) Verse 37.

I have found in the Beraitha on the work of the Tabernacle [the following text]: "He cut away the board at the top, a fingerbreadth on one side and a fingerbreadth on the other side, and he placed them [i.e., the two adjacent boards] inside one gold ring in order that they should not move apart from each other, for it is said, *And they shall be coupled together beneath, and they shall be coupled together above the head of it unto the one ring.* Now it need not have said, *unto the one ring;* and what does it teach us by saying it? It is to teach us that this is the place where the bolts were inserted." Accordingly, the verse stating: *and they shall be coupled together above the head of it,* refers to the head of the board where it was cut away until the place of the upper ring of the bolts, for the incision in the board was to extend as far as the place of the ring. Now Scripture was not particular [concerning these upper parts of the boards] how they should be attached, whether with rings of silver or gold, fixed ones or moveable, or with connecting rods. But the Beraitha states that Moses made rings for that purpose. However, in line with the plain meaning of Scripture this verse refers only to the endboards.

33. AND THOU SHALT BRING IN THITHER WITHIN THE VEIL THE ARK OF THE TESTIMONY. He did not now command Moses to do it in this particular order, to hang up the veil under the clasps and only afterwards to bring in the ark inside the veil, for the commandment now does not refer to the erection of the Tabernacle but to the making thereof. Similarly, *And thou shalt put the ark-cover upon the ark of the Testimony in the most holy place,*[227] does not mean that he is to put the ark-cover upon the ark of the Testimony when the ark has already been brought into the Holy of Holies [screened by the veil].[228] But the purport of the verse is to command Moses to hang up the veil under the clasps in order that the ark be there within the veil, and the veil

---

(227) Verse 34.   (228) On the contrary, at the charge for the erection of the Tabernacle it is said, *And thou shalt put therein the ark of the Testimony* (further 40:3), *and* then *thou shalt screan the ark with the veil (ibid.).* It is so explained in the Tur based upon Ramban's words further on.

will thus divide *between the holy place and the most holy.* Similarly He says, *And thou shalt put the ark-cover upon the ark of the Testimony in the most holy place,*[227] in order to inform us that the ark-cover with its cherubim on the ark should all be there in the Holy of Holies mentioned, which means within the veil. But when He came to command the erection of the Tabernacle He said, *And thou shalt put therein the ark of the Testimony, and* afterwards, *thou shalt screen the ark with the veil.*[229] Similarly, at the actual construction it is said, *and he put the ark-cover above the ark. And he brought the ark into the Tabernacle, and* afterwards, *he set up the veil of the screen.*[230]

(229) Further, 40:3. (230) *Ibid.*, 20-21.

Tetzaveh

27 20. Scripture states here, *and thou shalt command* [and does not say, "command the children of Israel"], because He always said with reference to the Tabernacle *and thou shalt make*,[1] which means by your command [i.e., "you Moses command them to do it"]. Therefore He said here "and you yourself command them that they bring to you the oil for the light." [It says *that they bring* and not "that they make"] because they had no way of making the oil in the wilderness; [therefore they were told] to bring it if they had it in reserve. Actually it were the princes that brought it.[2] The meaning of the word *eilecha* (unto thee) — [*that they bring 'unto thee' pure olive oil*] is that they were to bring it to Moses and he would see if it was pure and beaten properly. A similar intent is present in the verse, *Command the children of Israel, that they bring unto thee* [*pure olive oil beaten for the light*].[3] The meaning of the expression *of the children of Israel*,[4] is that they bring you the oil from the children of Israel, from whoever has it in his possession, just as He said, *of every man whose heart maketh him willing*.[5] Similarly He said, *And bring thou near unto thee Aaron thy brother, and his sons with him*,[6] meaning that you yourself are to call them and give them the tidings of this distinction. *And thou shalt make* them *holy garments*[7] means by commanding the wise men who wrought the work as was done with *all the work of this pattern*.[8] Likewise,

---

(1) Above, 25:11, etc. (2) Further, 35:27-28. (3) Leviticus 24:2. (4) Verse 21. (5) Above, 25:2. (6) Further, 28:1. (7) *Ibid.*, Verse 2. (8) I Chronicles 28:19.

And thou shalt speak unto all that are wise-hearted [9] means that Moses himself is to speak to them, for he will recognize their qualifications and know which is the work that ought to be given over to each of them. Now because He said, *And bring thou near;*[6] *And thou shalt make,*[7] it was necessary that He explain, *And thou shalt speak unto all that are wise-hearted* [...*that they make Aaron's garments*],[9] for it was by the command of Moses that they were to make the garments,[10] as was the case with the rest of the work of which it is said, *See, I have called by name Bezalel etc.*[11]

TO CAUSE A LAMP TO BURN 'TAMID' (CONTINUALLY). "Doing something each and every night is called *tamid* (continually), just as you say, *olath tamid (a continual burnt-offering)*[12] and yet it was brought only from day to day. Similarly in the case of the meal-offering made on the griddle [brought every day by the High Priest] it is said *tamid*,[13] and yet it was brought only *half of it in the morning, and half thereof in the evening*.[13] However, the word *tamid* used in connection with the showbread[14] signifies [the whole period without interruption] from Sabbath to Sabbath." Thus is Rashi's language.

But the Midrash [interpretation] of our Rabbis is not so. Instead they taught in the Sifre as follows:[15] "*The seven lamps shall give light.*[16] I might think that they are to burn always; Scripture therefore says, *from evening to morning.*[17] I might then think that they are to burn from evening to morning and then he

---

(9) Further, 28:3. (10) For one might have thought that since Verse 1 [*And bring thou near unto thee*...] means that Moses himself is to speak to Aaron and his sons, as explained above, Verse 2 following [*And thou shalt make holy garments for Aaron*...] also means that Moses himself is to make them; hence it was necessary to explain in Verse 3 [*And thou shalt speak unto all that are wise-hearted... that they make Aaron's garments*], meaning that they are to be made in the same way as the rest of the work. (11) Further, 31:2. (12) Numbers 28:6. (13) Leviticus 6:13. (14) Above, 25:30. (15) Sifre, beginning of *Seder Beha'alothcha.*— For meaning of "Sifre" see *Seder Yithro*, Note 52. (16) Numbers 8:2. (17) Leviticus 24:3, and Verse 2 here.

EXODUS XXVII, TETZAVEH

is to extinguish them; Scripture therefore says, *the seven lamps shall give light.* — How is this to be understood? *The seven lamps shall give light from evening to morning. Before the Eternal continually*[17] — this refers to the *neir ma'aravi*[18] which is to burn perpetually, since the candelabrum was lit from it in the evening." In the Torath Kohanim[19] the Rabbis have likewise said: "*To cause a lamp to burn continually* — this means that 'the western light' should burn perpetually." They have further taught there: "If [the priest who came into the Sanctuary in the morning to trim the candelabrum] found that it had gone out, he cleaned it out and kindled it from [the fire upon] the altar of the whole-offering." Thus it is clear that even at daytime he kindled the *neir ma'aravi*, for that lamp always burnt regularly [and not as Rashi has it that the candelabrum was lit only in the evening]. And in Tractate Tamid[20] we have been taught as follows: "[The priest] who was privileged to clean out the candelabrum [during the morning service] entered [the Sanctuary], and if he found the two easternmost lamps burning, he cleaned out the rest [leaving them to be lit during the evening service], but the two easternmost lamps he left burning as they were. If he found that [the two easternmost lamps] had gone out, he cleaned them out and kindled them from those that were still burning, and then cleaned out the rest" [leaving them to be kindled during the evening service].[21] Now this anonymous Mishnah conforms to the opinion of Rabbi[22] who says that the lamps of the candelabrum were

---

(18) Literally: "the western light." It is this light which is considered as being *before the Eternal*, and therefore is to burn *continually*, for it is to that particular light that the expression *before the Eternal continually*, applies. See further Note 23 as to which of the seven lamps in the candelabrum the term *neir hama'aravi* has reference to. (19) Sifra *Emor* 13:7. — Torath Kohanim is another name for the Sifra, which is the Halachic Midrash of the Tannaim on the Book of Leviticus. (20) Tamid 3:9. (21) This text again shows that there were lamps burning in the candelabrum the whole day. — In case the priest found that all the lights had gone out it has already been mentioned above in Ramban's text quoting the Torath Kohanim that the *neir ma'aravi* was then kindled from the fire upon the altar of the burnt-offering which stood outside in the Sanctuary Court. (22) Rabbi Yehudah Hanasi. See in *Seder Mishpatim* Note 64.

placed in an east-west direction, and the *neir ma'aravi* (the western light) in his opinion is the second light from the east side.[23] It is called *ma'aravi* (western) because it is to the west of the first, and since he has to kindle the western light to fulfill therewith the Divine command *before the Eternal continually,* [17] he must kindle also the easternmost lamp, for the second lamp cannot be called "western" until there be an "eastern" next to it.[24] But according to the opinion of the Sage [25] who says that the candelabrum was placed in a north-south direction, the *neir ma'aravi* was the middle one — on the central shaft of the candelabrum — and that light alone he kindled in the morning [for since none of the lamps were "outside" of it towards the east it was not necessary that another lamp be lighted].[26] Thus the principle is clear that the expression *before the Eternal continually* applies to "the western light," which burns regularly day and night.

(23) For since the candelabrum was standing with its six branches extending in an east-west direction, the first [the easternmost] light could not be considered as being *before the Eternal,* since that expression implies that there is one light still further away from the Holy of Holies [where the Divine Glory abided]. Hence the first lamp of which it might be said that it is *before the Eternal* is the second from the east, and since we must not pass over an occasion for performing a religious act, the second light from the east becomes affixed as being *before the Eternal,* and that is the *neir ma'aravi* (the western light). — There is, however, another opinion [mentioned further on in the text] that the candelabrum was placed in a south-north direction, and the term *neir ma'aravi* was given to the middle lamp, because the three lamps on each side turned towards the center one. — Menachoth 98 b. See also Shabbath 22 b, Rashi. (24) Hence if the ministering priest found that the two easternmost lamps had gone out, he trimmed them and kindled them both. For although the command regarding the perpetual lamp [burning day and night] applied essentially to the second — the western — light, yet since it could not be called "western" unless there was an "eastern" in front of it, the priest lit both. (25) This is Rabbi Eleazar the son of Rabbi Shimon (Menachoth 98 b). (26) Thus there appears an important difference as to the number of lights that burned a whole day in the candelabrum. According to Rabbi who holds that the candelabrum was placed in an east-west direction, the two easternmost lamps burned a whole day [for reasons explained in Note 24]. But according to Rabbi Eleazar the son of Rabbi Shimon who says that the candelabrum was placed in a north-south direction, only the middle lamp burned a whole day.

28 1. AND THOU BRING THOU NEAR AARON THY BROTHER, AND HIS SONS WITH HIM ... THAT THEY MINISTER UNTO ME IN THE PRIEST'S OFFICE, EVEN AARON, NADAB AND ABIHU, ELEAZAR AND ITHAMAR, AARON'S SONS. The reason for mentioning *Nadab and Abihu, Eleazar and Ithamar* [when it mentioned already "and his sons"] is that Moses should not think that by anointing the father to minister as priest, his sons would automatically become priests; instead he had to initiate them personally into the priesthood. Thus Phinehas [the son of Eleazar] and others already born were excluded [from the priesthood], for only these four sons who were anointed with Aaron, and their children born to them henceforth, were appointed as priests.

2. AND THOU SHALT MAKE HOLY GARMENTS FOR AARON THY BROTHER FOR SPLENDOR AND BEAUTY — this means that he be distinguished and glorified with garments of distinction and beauty, just as Scripture says, *as a bridegroom putteth on a priestly diadem.*[27] For these garments [of the High Priest] correspond in their forms to garments of royalty, which monarchs wore at the time when the Torah was given. Thus we find with reference to the tunic, *and he made him a tunic of 'pasim'*[28] — meaning, a cloth woven of variegated colors, this being *the tunic of chequer work* [mentioned here], just as [Ibn Ezra] explained, which clothed him *as a son of ancient kings.*[29] The same applies to the robe and the tunic, as it is written, *Now she* [Tamar] *had a garment of many colors upon her; for with such robes were the king's daughters that were virgins apparelled,*[30] which means that a garment of many colors was seen clearly upon her, for such was the custom that the virgin daughters of the king wore robes with which they wrapped themselves; thus the coat of many colors was upon her as an upper garment. It is for this reason that it says there, *and she rent her garment of many colors*

---

(27) Isaiah 61:10. (28) Genesis 37:3. (29) Isaiah 19:11. (30) II Samuel 13:18.

that was on her.[31] The mitre [mentioned here] is to this day known among kings and distinguished lords. Therefore Scripture says with reference to the fall of the kingdom [of Judah], *The mitre shall be removed, and the crown taken off.*[32] Similarly it is written, *and a royal diadem.*[33] Scripture also calls them *the ornamented high caps,*[34] and it is further written, *They shall have linen ornamented* [caps] *upon their heads,*[35] which are for the beauty and glory of those that are adorned with them. The ephod and the breastplate are also royal garments, just as it is written, *and thou shalt have a chain of gold about thy neck.*[36] The plate [around the forehead, which the High Priest wore], is like a king's crown. Thus it is written, *'yatzitz nizro' (his crown will shine).*[37] Furthermore, [the High Priest's garments] are made of *gold, blue-purple, and red-purple*[38] [which are all symbolic of royalty]. Thus it is written, *All glorious is the king's daughter within the palace; her raiment is of chequer work inwrought with gold,*[39] and it is further written, *thou shalt be clothed with purple, and have a chain of gold about thy neck.*[36] As for the blue-purple, even to this day *no man will lift up his hand*[40] to wear it except a king of nations,[41] and it is written, *And Mordecai went forth from the presence of the king in royal apparel of blue and white, and with a great crown of gold, and with a 'tachrich' (robe) of fine linen and purple*[42] — the *tachrich* being a robe in which the wearer wraps himself.

By way of the Truth, [the mystic teachings of the Cabala,] majesty is to *kavod* (glory) and to *tiphereth* (splendor),[43] the verse thus stating that they should make *holy garments for Aaron* to minister in them to the Glory of G-d Who dwells in their midst, and to the Splendor of their strength, as it is written, *For Thou art*

---

(31) *Ibid.,* Verse 19. (32) Ezekiel 21:31. (33) Isaiah 62:3. (34) Further, 39:28. (35) Ezekiel 44:18. (36) Daniel 5:16. (37) Psalms 132:18. — Ramban thus associates the word *tzitz* (plate) with the expression *yatzitz nizro* (his crown will shine), thus suggesting that the *tzitz* of the High Priest is a sort of royal crown. (38) Further, Verse 5. (39) Psalms 45:14. (40) Genesis 41:44. (41) See Isaiah 14:9. (42) Esther 8:15. (43) Cabalistic terms for certain Emanations.

the Glory of their strength,[44] and it is further stated, *Our holy and our beautiful house, where our fathers praised Thee,*[45] meaning ["the house of] our Holy One" which is the Glory, and "of our Splendor" which is the Splendor of Israel. And it is further stated, *Strength and beauty are in His Sanctuary,*[46] and similarly, *To beautify the place of My Sanctuary, and I will make the place of My feet glorious*[47] — meaning, that the place of the Sanctuary will be glorified by the Splendor, and the place of His feet, which is the place of the Sanctuary, will be honored by the presence of the Glory of G-d. *And in Israel will He glorify Himself*[48] also means that in Israel He will show and designate His Splendor. Likewise He says further with respect to the garments of all of Aaron's sons, that they are *for splendor and for beauty.*[49] Of the sacrifices He also says, *they will come up with 'ratzon' ('will' — acceptance) on Mine altar, and I will glorify My glorious house.*[50] Thus the altar is His Will and the house of His Glory is the Splendor.

The [priestly] garments had to be made with the intention to be used for that purpose. It is possible that in making them, intent of heart [for what they symbolize] was also needed on the part of their makers. It is for this reason that He said, *And thou shalt speak unto all that are wise-hearted, whom I have filled with the spirit of wisdom*[51] — who will understand what they will do. And the Rabbis have already said [of Alexander the Great, that when asked by his generals why he descended from his chariot to bow before the High Priest Simon the Just, he answered]:[52] "His image glistened before me whenever I had a victory."

---

(44) Psalms 89:18. (45) Isaiah 64:10. (46) Psalms 96:6. (47) Isaiah 60:13. (48) *Ibid.,* 44:23. (49) Further, Verse 40. (50) Isaiah 60:7. (51) Verse 3. (52) Yoma 69 a. The story told there is that when Alexander the Great conquered the Land of Israel the Samaritans petitioned him to destroy the Temple in Jerusalem. Thereupon a procession of notables went out from Jerusalem headed by Simon the Just, the High Priest, who was attired in the high priestly garments. They walked a whole night with torches in their hand until dawn. In the morning as soon as Alexander saw Simon the Just, he descended from his chariot and bowed down to him. When the Samaritans said to him, "Such a great king as thou art dost thou bow thyself to that Jew?" He replied, "His image etc."

5. AND THEY SHALL TAKE THE GOLD. Now up to this point all the commands were directed to Moses himself: *and thou shalt make,*[53] *thou shalt make,*[54] but now He commanded that He should speak *unto all that are wise-hearted* that they make the garments. It is for this reason that He said, *and they shall take the gold and the blue-purple,* meaning that they are to receive the free-will gifts directly from the public, and make with them the garments. The purport thereof is to state that the gifts should not be weighed out to them, nor be counted, for they are trustworthy people, similarly to that which is said, *Moreover they reckoned not with the men, into whose hand they delivered the money to give to them that did the work; for they dealt faithfully.*[55] And just as this is said with reference to the garments, the same applied to the whole work of the Tabernacle. Only on the first day [of its construction] is it written, *and they received of Moses,*[56] and even then they took everything from him without an accounting. But on the other days the people brought the gifts directly to those who did the work. Therefore it is written, *And they spoke unto Moses, saying: The people bring much more than enough*[57] — for it was to them that the people brought the free-will gifts, not that they gave them to Moses for him to weigh it out to them. However, after the workers had collected everything, they did count and weigh it out, and told it to Moses, as it is written, *and the gold of the offering was twenty and nine talents* etc.[58]

28. AND THE BREASTPLATE SHALL NOT BE 'YIZACH' (LOOSENED) FROM THE EPHOD. "*Yizach* is an expression of 'breaking away'. It is an Arabic expression, as Dunash ben Labrat explained."[59] This is Rashi's language.

---

(53) Verse 2.   (54) Above, 26:1.   (55) II Kings 12:16.   (56) Further, 36:3.   (57) *Ibid.,* Verse 5.   (58) *Ibid.,* 38:24.   (59) A pupil of Saadia Gaon, he was grammarian, exegete and poet. He wrote a criticism of Menachem ben Saruk's Machbereth (see Vol. I, p. 156, Note 347), whose contemporary he was. He was born in Baghdad and ultimately settled in Cordova where, like Menachem, he was a protege of Hasdai ibn Shaprut. He flourished in the middle of the tenth century.

It appears likely to me, however, that *yizach* is like *yisach* (break away), which is associated with the expressions: *The Eternal 'yisach' (will pluck up) the house of the proud;*[60] *and the faithless 'yis'chu' (shall be plucked up) out of it*[61] — referring to breaking and plucking, and the letter *samech* (in *yisach*), is interchanged with the letter *zayin* (of *yizach*), just as in the verses: *let the saints 'ya'alzu' (exult) in glory;*[62] *'nithalsa' (let us solace ourselves) with loves;*[63] *'v'nitatztem' (and ye shall break down) their altars;*[64] *'nathsu' (they break up) my path.*[65] Similarly, *and they shall keep the watch of the house 'masach'* [66] — from being torn away; he [Jehoiada the priest] thus warned the guard that not one of them should leave his position and thus cause the watch to be broken. Perhaps the following verse can also be explained on this basis: *'ulmeizach' wherewith he is girded continually,*[67] which means "for separation and breaking," the verse stating that the wicked shall always be girded with the curse until they will be destroyed and broken up by it, just as others gird themselves with a girdle. *There is no 'meizach' any more*[68] — there is no more separation, the prophet [Isaiah] telling the people of Tyre: "overflow with the people of your land as the Nile to the land of Tarshish your trafficker; there will be no more separation and scattering for you — for not one will be separated from you there [in the hope of returning to his city], since he will not return to Tyre, because it will have been destroyed completely." The term *horeis* applies to one who separates himself from the station of his colleagues, just as in the expression, *let them not 'yehersu' (break through) towards the Eternal to see,*[69] and it is written, *and from thy station 'yehersecha' (shalt thou be pulled down).*[70] Similarly: *He looseth 'meziach aphikim'*[71] — He abates the destruction of the

---

(60) Proverbs 15:25. (61) *Ibid.*, 2:22. (62) Psalms 149:5. — Here *ya'alzu* is with a *zayin*. (63) Proverbs 7:18. — Here the same root appears with a *samech*. (64) Deuteronomy 12:3. (65) Job 30:13. In this case the *tzade* interchanges with the *samech* of the above verse. See in this connection Vol. I, p. 485. (66) II Kings 11:6. (67) Psalms 109:19. (68) Isaiah 23:10. (69) Above, 19:21. The beginning of the quote here comes from Verse 24 there. (70) Isaiah 22:19. (71) Job 12:21.

aphikim, which are flooding rivers that inundate mountains and valleys. The term *meizach* [68] is in the same form as *meitzach* (forehead), both of them having the letter *nun* missing,[72] *as [meitzach]* is of the root *nitzuach* (enduring, victory), for the strength of the head is in the forehead.

30. AND THOU SHALT PUT IN THE BREASTPLATE OF JUDGMENT THE URIM AND THE THUMMIM. Rabbi Abraham ibn Ezra thought to display wisdom in the matter of the Urim and the Thummim, by saying that they were made by a craftsman from gold and silver, and he continued his discussion of them in this vein, for he thought that they were akin to the forms which the astrologers make in order to know the thoughts of the one who comes to ask of them [about the future]. But what [Ibn Ezra] said is of no import. Rather, the Urim and the Thummim are as Rashi has written: "This was an inscription of the Proper Name of G-d which was placed between the folds of the breastplate." It was for this reason that the breastplate had to be double [73] [i.e., made of a material that was folded in order to form a sort of bag, into which the Urim and the Thummim — the sacred Names of G-d, as explained further on, — were placed by Moses]. The proof for this is that in the work of the craftsmen the Urim and the Thummim are not mentioned at all, neither in the command nor in the [description of the] making thereof. Now concerning the garments He details: *And he made the ephod*,[74] *and he made the breastplate*,[75] but it does not say, "and he made the Urim and the Thummim." And if it were the work of a skilled engraver He would have dealt with it in greater length than with all [the garments]. Even if perhaps He desired to shorten the discussion about them on account of their profundity, He would at least have said here, "and thou shalt make the Urim and the

---

(72) As Ramban will explain, *meitzach* (forehead) is of the root *nitzuach* (victory), since the strength of the head is in the forehead. Likewise the word *meizah* is of the root *nosach* or *nozach* which means pull or tear away. (73) Verse 16. (74) Further, 39:2. (75) *Ibid.*, Verse 8.

EXODUS XXVIII, TETZAVEH

Thumim as it has been shown to you in the mount; of pure gold — or purified silver — you shall make them." moreover, you will notice that He did not use the definite article in connection with any of the vessels [of the Tabernacle] which had not been previously mentioned. Instead, He said, *and they shall make an ark;*[76] *and thou shalt make a table;*[77] *and thou shalt make a candelabrum*,[78] and thus too in connection with all of them. In the case of the Tabernacle, however, He said, *And thou shalt make 'the' Tabernacle*,[79] because He had already mentioned it [in saying], *And let them make Me a Sanctuary.*[80] Now with reference to the Urim and the Thummim He said, *And thou shalt put in the breastplate of judgment 'the' Urim and 'the' Thummim.* He did not command him as to the making of them, and yet Scripture mentions them with the definite article! Moreover, Scripture mentions them with reference to Moses only, saying by way of command, *and thou shalt put in the breastplate of judgment...;* similarly, at the time of making them it says, *and in the breastplate he put the Urim and the Thummim*,[81] since they were not the work of craftsmen. Neither craftsmen nor the congregation of Israel had any part whatsoever in their making or in their donation, for they were a secret transmitted by the Almighty to Moses, and he wrote them in holiness. They[82] were thus of heavenly origin, and therefore they are referred to without any specification and with the definite article, in a similar usage to that which we have in the verse, *and He placed at the east of the garden of Eden the cherubim.*[83] Now Moses took the inscription of the Urim and the Thummim, and placed them in the breastplate of judgment after he had clothed Aaron with the ephod and the breastplate, as it is said, *And he put the ephod upon him, and he girded him with the skilfully-woven band of the ephod... And he placed the breastplate upon him; and in the breastplate he put the*

---

(76) Above, 25:10. (77) *Ibid.*, Verse 23. (78) *Ibid.*, Verse 31. (79) *Ibid.*, 26:1. (80) *Ibid.*, 25:8. (81) Leviticus 8:8. (82) In Ricanti [quoting the language of Ramban]: "Or they were..." (83) Genesis 3:24. Here too Scripture uses the definite article ['*the*' *cherubim*] and yet nowhere previously do we read concerning them (Bachya).

Urim and the Thummim.[84] For only after [Aaron was already clothed with the ephod and the breastplate] did Moses place the Urim and the Thummim between the folds of the breastplate.

Thus the Urim and the Thummim were the holy Names of G-d, and it was by virtue of the power residing in these Names that the letters inscribed upon the stones of the breastplate would light up before the eyes of the priest who inquired of their judgment.[85] For example, when they inquired, *Who shall go up for us first against the Canaanites, to fight against them,*[86] the priest fixed his thoughts on those Divine Names which were the Urim [literally: "lights"], and the letters forming the name *Yehudah* lighted up before his eyes, and [for the word *ya'aleh* — "he shall go up"] the letter *yod* lighted up from the word *Levi,*[87] the *ayin* from *Shimon,* the *lamed* from *Levi,* and the *hei* from *Avraham* which was also written there, according to the opinion of our Rabbis,[88] or perhaps the *hei* from *Yehudah* lighted up a second time. Now when the letters lighted up before the eyes of the priest, he did not yet know their arrangement [that is, how these letters were to be grouped together into words], for from the letters forming the words *Yehudah ya'aleh* (Judah shall go up), it is possible to form the words: *hoy heid alehah,*[89] or *hie al Yehudah,*[90] and very many other words. But then there were other sacred Divine Names [in the fold of the breastplate] called Thummim [literally: "perfection"], through whose power the priest's heart was made perfect to understand the meaning of the letters which lighted up

---

(84) Leviticus 8:7-8. (85) Numbers 27:21. (86) Judges 1:1. — Scripture continues [in Verse 2]: *And the* Eternal *said: 'Yehudah ya'aleh' (Judah shall go up).* (87) The twelve stones in the breastplate bore the names of the twelve tribes of Israel. Since there was no letter *tzade* amongst these names, the patriarchs' names [*Avraham, Yitzchak* and *Yaakov*] were also inscribed upon the stones. Finally to include the letter *tet* the words *shivtei Y-ah* ("the tribes of G-d") were also written upon them (Yoma 73 b). The answer given to the priest who inquired of the Urim and Thummim was through the gleaming forth of the letters written upon the stones. Thus when the tribes asked, *Who shall go up for us first against the Canaanites?* the name *Yehudah* gleamed forth, and as for the word *ya'aleh,* the *yod* of *Levi* lighted up etc. (88) Yoma 73 b. See Note above. (89) "The echo of woe upon it." (90) "Lamentation upon Judah."

EXODUS XXVIII, TETZAVEH

before his eyes. Thus, when he fixed his thoughts on the Divine Names in the Urim, and the letters lighted up, he would then immediately turn and fix his thoughts on the Divine Names in the Thummim, whilst the letters [of the Urim] were still lit up before him, and then it came to his mind that they combine to form the words *Yehudah ya'aleh* (Judah shall go up). This knowledge [of how to combine the letters that lit up in the breastplate into words], is one level of the degrees of *Ruach Hakodesh*.[91] It is lower than prophecy, and higher than the *Bath Kol*[92] which served [Israel] in the Second Sanctuary after prophecy had ceased, and after the Urim and Thummim had ceased, just as our Rabbis have mentioned.[93] It is possible that after Moses placed the sacred Names of the Urim and Thummim in the breastplate, they became known to the great Sages of Israel, having been transmitted to them from Moses together with the secrets of the Torah. Hence we find that David possessed an ephod[94], which was similar to the ephod of Moses, and together with it was a breastplate similar to the holy breastplate [in the Tabernacle]. It appears, however, that [instead of being made of gold, blue-purple etc.] it was made of linen, just as it says of Samuel that he was *a child, girden with a linen ephod*,[95] and of Nob, the city of priests, it is said, *fourscore and five persons that did wear a linen ephod*.[96] They would clothe a priest who was of *the sons of the prophets*,[97] and inquire of him [regarding certain events] and at times they were answered, just as Rabbi Abraham ibn Ezra thought on this point. However, as far as that which he [Ibn Ezra] said, that if [Rashi] had seen the responsum of Rabbeinu Hai,[98] he would not have explained as he

---

(91) Literally: "The Holy Spirit." See Moreh Nebuchim II, 45, beginning: "second degree of prophecy." (92) Literally: "echo" or "reverberating sound." It is here used in the sense of a Divine Voice which on certain occasions was heard coming forth from the Holy of Holies (Sotah 33 a). (93) Yoma 21 b. (94) I Samuel 23:6. (95) *Ibid.*, 2:18. (96) *Ibid*, 22:18. (97) II Kings 4:1. A term denoting the disciples of the prophets, or those who sought the prophetic gift. (98) The last of the Gaonim. He was a son of Rabbeinu Sherira Gaon (see Vol. I, p. 97, Note 477). — Rabbeinu Hai Gaon wrote in a responsum that by invoking the Proper Name of G-d, or the names of the angels, one could not predict future events. Using this

did, [that the Urim and Thummim were inscriptions of the Proper Name of G-d] — now we have already seen that responsum and have considered it, and we know [for a certainty] that it was Rabbi Abraham whose opinion [shows that he] did not grasp it.

31. 'ME'IL' (ROBE). Rashi commented:[99] "This was a kind of shirt, and so also was the *k'thoneth,* except that the *k'thoneth* was worn next to the body and the *me'il* is a term for the upper [outer] shirt." But this is not so, for the *me'il* is a garment in which one wraps oneself, just as Scripture says, *and he* [Samuel] *is covered with a 'me'il',*[100] and it is further written, *'y'atoni' (He hath covered me) with 'me'il' (the robe) of righteousness,*[101] and the term *atiyah* (enwrapping) does not apply to a shirt, but to a garment with which one covers oneself, as it is said, *'oteh' (Who coverest Thyself) with light as with a garment,*[102] it being associated with the term *atoph* (enveloping onself). And so we find: *and his upper lip 'ya'teh' (he shall cover up,*[103] [which Onkelos renders] *yitatoph.*[104] This is identical with the word *kardunin*[105] from the Targum of Jonathan ben Uziel which the Rabbi [Rashi] mentioned [as his translation of the word *me'il*], for this *kardunin* is used for enwrapping oneself, something akin to the form of the ephod with which [the High Priest] envelops the half of his body that is towards his feet. But if a *me'il* was a kind of shirt [as Rashi said], then *me'il* and *kardunin* would not be alike at all. Another proof is the verse, *and he seized the skirt of 'me'ilo' (his robe), and it rent.*[106] Thus the *me'il* has skirts and is not a kind of shirt. Rather, the *me'il* is a garment which enwraps

---

responsum as a basis, Ibn Ezra commented that if Rashi had seen this responsum he would not have written that the Urim and Thummim were inscriptions of the Proper Name of G-d etc. [as quoted above]. — To this comment of Ibn Ezra, Ramban answers caustically: "We have already seen this responsum of Rabbeinu Hai and have pondered its meaning, and we do know that it was Ibn Ezra's understanding that did not grasp it." (99) On Verse 4 above. (100) I Samuel 28:14. (101) Isaiah 61:10. (102) Psalms 104:2. (103) Leviticus 13:45. (104) This shows that *atiyah* and *atoph* are identical terms. (105) In our Rashi: *kardutin.* (106) I Samuel 15:27.

EXODUS XXVIII, TETZAVEH

the whole body from the neck downwards to the feet of the person, and has no sleeves at all. Now in other *me'ilim* there is a piece of garment for the neck, covering the whole of it, and sewed on [with a needle], this garment being called *pi me'il* (the hole of the robe), but with reference to this *me'il* Scripture commanded that it be woven together with the robe.[107] The *me'il* is entirely slit frontwise till the bottom, and he put his head through the hole on top; thus the neck [of the priest] is enwrapped with the hole of the *me'il*, and in front of him are the two skirts with which he covers or uncovers himself at will — something like [our] cloak which has no head-tire. Now since the seam divides the front part of the *me'il* and separates it all the way downwards, therefore the term *atiyah* (enwrapping) is always used in connection with it [as explained above].

Nor do I know either[108] why the Rabbi [Rashi] made the bells independent objects, stating that there was one bell between every two pomegranates.[109] For if so, the pomegranates served no purpose. And if they were made just for ornament, why were they made like hollow pomegranates? Let him rather make them like golden apples! Moreover, Scripture should have explained with what the bells should be hung, and whether rings should be made on which to hang the bells. Instead, [we must say that] the bells were inside the pomegranates themselves, for the pomegranates were hollow and made in the shape of small pomegranates that have not yet burst open,[110] and the bells were hidden inside but visible through them. Now Scripture has not specified their number. But our Rabbis have said[110] that there were seventy-two bells and within them there were seventy-two clappers; he hung thirty-six on one side and thirty-six on the other side, as is found in Tractate Zebachim, in the chapter The Altar Sanctifies.[110] From here also you may learn that the *me'il* was not a sort of shirt or *kthoneth* [as Rashi wrote], but instead it had skirts [front

---

(107) Verse 32. (108) I.e., "in addition to that which I did not understand in Rashi's definition of the *me'il* [as explained above], I also do not know why etc." (109) Rashi, Verse 33. (110) Zebachim 88 b.

and back, and therefore the Rabbis speak of "one side" and "the other side" of the *me'il*].

Similarly Rashi wrote[99] that "the *mitznepheth* (mitre) is a kind of domed helmet, for in another place[111] the verse calls it *migba'oth*, which we translate in the Targum *kov'in* (helmets)." This also is not correct, for the Rabbis have said[112] that the *mitznepheth* was sixteen cubits long. Thus it was a sort of turban with which the head is wrapped, as he wound it around and around his head, fold upon fold. Moreover, the *mitznepheth* of the High Priest is nowhere called *migba'oth* [as Rashi said]. It is only with reference to the ordinary priests that Scripture calls the head-dress *migba'oth*,[113] and these too were a sort of turban,[114] except that they were set upon[115] the head and the folds came up like a sort of [conical] helmet which is the *kovei'a*, as Onkelos rendered it. For *migba'at* is like *mikba'at*, as I have said in *Seder Mikeitz*,[116] as the letter *gimmel* serves here as *kuph*, excepting that the *migba'at* was also wound like a *mitznepheth*. It is for this reason that the Sages always mention in Torath Kohanim[117] the

---

(111) Verse 40. (112) The source is not known. See my Hebrew commentary, p. 476. (113) Further, 39:28. [*And they made... the 'mitznepheth' (mitre) of fine linen, and the ornamented 'migba'oth' (head-tires) of fine linen.* — Thus Scripture distinguishes between the two garments, since the *mitznepheth* was made for Aaron and the *migba'oth* for Aaron's sons. So how did Rashi write of the *mitznepheth* that in another place Scripture calls it *migba'oth*? (114) Ramban's intent is as follows: Even if we were to say that Rashi intended to state that the head-dress for the High Priest here called *mitznepheth* is for the common priest elsewhere called *migba'at*, that too, continues Ramban, would not be correct; since the head-dress for the common priest is also called *mitznepheth*, as explained in the text (Gur Aryeh). Thus according to Ramban the head-dress for the common priest is called both *mitznepheth* and *migba'at*, while that of the High Priest is called only *mitznepheth*. (115) The difference between the two attires is thus clear. The head-dress of the High Priest — i.e., the *mitznepheth* — was wound *around* his head in several folds like a turban, and the one for the common priest was also wound in folds (hence its name *mitznepheth*) but set *upon* his head and came up like a conical helmet [hence its other name — *migba'at*]. See also Ramban further on Verse 37, and 29:7. (116) Genesis 41:47 (Vol. I, pp. 505-506). (117) Sifra Tzav, 2:1. — For the term Torath Kohanim see above Note 19.

EXODUS XXVIII, TETZAVEH

mitznepheth both in relation to the High Priest and the common priest. And in Tractate Yoma[118] we have been taught [in a Mishnah]: "A High Priest ministers [the Divine Service] in eight garments, and a common priest in four — in tunic, breeches, *mitznepheth* (mitre), and belt. To these the High Priest adds the breastplate, the ephod, the upper garment, and the frontplate."[119]

35. THAT HE DIE NOT. "From this negative statement you infer the positive: if these garments are upon him, he will not incur death, but if he enters [the Sanctuary] lacking one of these garments he is liable to death [by the hand of Heaven]." This is Rashi's language. But it does not appear to me to be correct, for if so He should have written this verse after having mentioned all eight garments [of the High Priest], and why did He mention it after three garments — the breastplate, the ephod, and the robe — before mentioning the frontplate, the upper garment, the mitre, the belt and the breeches! Furthermore, [the verse reads here,] *and when he cometh out* [of the Sanctuary], *that he die not*. But the act of going out [from the Sanctuary] is no function for which he should incur death if lacking the [proper number of] garments!

Similarly Rashi commented on the verse: "*And they shall be upon Aaron and upon his sons*[120] — *they* means all these garments; *upon Aaron and upon his sons,* those which are proper to him, and those specified for them. [*That they bear not iniquity,*] *and die*[120] — thus you learn that he who ministers [the Divine Service] lacking any of these garments incurs death [by the hand of Heaven]." And so indeed it appears from the simple meaning of Scripture. But according to the conclusion reached on these subjects in the discussions in the Gemara,[121] it would appear

---

(118) Yoma 71 b. (119) Thus it is clear that the term *mitznepheth* applies to the head-dress of both the High Priest and the common priest. As to why the head-dress of the common priest is also called *migba'at*, see Note 115 above. (120) Verse 43. (121) For meaning of the term Gemara see in *Seder Bo*, Note 204. The particular texts here referred to are mentioned further on.

that this does not conform to the opinion of our Rabbis, for to them this commandment applies to all alike, to Aaron and his sons, but it refers only to the breeches, and the punishment [of death by the hand of Heaven for lacking them] likewise applies [only] to them [i.e. the breeches]. For He had commanded that they be made, [as it is said,] *And thou shalt make them linen breeches,*[122] and then He commanded concerning their being worn [by the priests, saying,] *And they shall be upon Aaron, and upon his sons.*[120] As to the rest of the garments, He had already given the command above concerning the making of them and wearing them, [as it is said,] *And thou shalt put them upon Aaron thy brother, and upon his sons with him.*[123] If so, this command *[And they shall be upon Aaron, and upon his sons]*[120] refers wholly to the breeches, and the punishment likewise refers [only] to them.

We learn this from what the Rabbis have said in Tractates Sanhedrin[124] and The Slaughtering of Sacrifices:[125] "Whence do we know that a priest who ministered [the Divine Service] lacking the [proper number of] garments is liable to death [by the hand of Heaven]? Said Rabbi Abohu in the name of Rabbi Yochanan, and they arrived in the chain of tradition up to 'in the name of Rabbi Eleazar the son of Rabbi Shimon:' *And thou shalt gird them with belts, Aaron and his sons, and bind head-tires on them; and they shall have the priesthood by a perpetual statute,*[126] the interpretation of which is: 'So long as they wear their [appointed] garments, they are invested with their priesthood; when they do not wear their garments, they are not invested with their priesthood, and they become laymen, and it has been said that a layman who ministers [in the Sanctuary] incurs the penalty of death [by the hand of Heaven]." Now if this verse [*that they bear not iniquity, and die*][120] were held by the Rabbis to apply to all the garments [of the priests], as the Rabbi [Rashi] said, they could have found in it an expressly stated punishment for one who ministers lacking all the garments, [and why did they need to base

---

(122) Verse 42. (123) Verse 41. (124) Sanhedrin 83 b. (125) Zebachim 17 b. (126) Further, 29:9.

EXODUS XXVIII, TETZAVEH

it upon an inference from another verse]! Rather, this verse refers only to the breeches, and the other verse to the rest of the garments, where the breeches are not mentioned at all. Proof to what the Rabbis have said [that this verse, *And they shall be upon Aaron, and upon his sons... that they bear not iniquity, and die,* [120] refers only to the breeches], is that further on when the order of putting on the garments is mentioned, [127] the breeches are not referred to at all, for having declared here the punishment if they are lacking [when ministering in the Sanctuary], there was no more need to mention them again further on, as it is understood already that he would wear them.

And that which He said above [i.e., in Verse 35 before us], *and the sound thereof shall be heard when he goeth in unto the holy place before the Eternal, and when he goeth out, that he die not,* is [not as Rashi has it that from here we learn that if he enters the Sanctuary lacking one of these garments he incurs death at the hand of Heaven, but is] in my opinion an explanation for the commandment of the bells [upon the robe], since there was no need to wear them, nor are they customary amongst dignitaries. Therefore He said that He commanded that they be made in order that the sound thereof be heard in the Sanctuary, that the priest enter before his Master as if with permission. For he who comes into the king's palace suddenly, incurs the penalty of death according to the court ceremonial, just as we find in the case of Ahasuerus.[128] It thus alludes to what the Rabbis have said in Yerushalmi Tractate Yoma: [129] "*And there shall be no man in the Tent of Meeting when he goeth in to make atonement in the holy place* [130] — even those [heavenly beings] of whom it is written, *As for the likeness of their faces they had the face of a man,* [131] they too are not to be then in the Tent of Meeting." Therefore He commanded that [the ministering High Priest] make a sound be

---

(127) *Ibid.*, Verses 5-9. (128) Esther 4:11. *All the king's servants... do know, that whosoever... shall come unto the king... who is not called, there is one law for him, that he be put to death.* (129) Yerushalmi Yoma I,5. — On Jerusalem Talmud see in *Seder Bo*, Note 204. (130) Leviticus 16:17. (131) Ezekiel 1:10.

heard, as if crying out, *'Cause everyone to go out from before me,'* [132] so that he can come to minister before the King alone. Similarly, when going out from the Sanctuary his sound is heard in order to leave with permission, and that the matter be known so that the King's ministers can go out before Him. In the Chapters of the Palaces [133] this subject is known. Thus the reason [for the bells upon the robe of the High Priest] is that he should not be encountered by the angels of G-d. He gave this warning concerning the High Priest [134] on account of his high position. This is Scripture's intent in saying, *when he goeth in unto the holy place before the Eternal,* for it is the High Priest who passes[135] before Him so that He cause His Divine Glory to rest upon his service, *for he is the messenger of the Eternal of hosts,*[136] even though the common priests also enter the Sanctuary to burn the incense and to kindle [the lamps].[137]

Now I have seen in the Midrash Shemoth Rabbah[138] with reference to the stones upon the breastplate: "For what reason were the stones? It was in order that the Holy One, blessed be He, observe them in the garments of the priest when he enters on the Day of Atonement,[139] and He be gracious to the tribes [whose

---

(132) Genesis 45:1. (133) Pirkei Heichaloth, 31. — This is an Agadic Midrash on "The Seven Palaces of Heaven." See Wertheimer's ed. of Batei Midrashoth Vol. I, p. 67. (134) Since the common priests also entered the Sanctuary in the regular daily service, the question arises why were these bells not necessary upon their garments so that their sound be heard when they come into the Sanctuary? Ramban's answer is that this was on account of the high position of the High Priest. "For the greater the person the more are the powers of strict judgment stirred up against him" (Bi'ur Ha'lvush to Ricanti who quotes the language of Ramban). (135) Another reading: "ministers." (136) Malachi 2:7. (137) Yet the High Priest is more distinguished; hence the bells were necessary upon his garments and not upon those of the common priests, as explained above (see Note 134). (138) Shemoth Rabbah 38:10. (139) When the High Priest on the Day of Atonement entered the Holy of Holies he did not wear the eight garments [amongst which was the breastplate], but instead, he wore the four linen garments [as prescribed in Leviticus 16:4]. The meaning of the Midrash must perforce be as follows: The merit of the High Priest wearing the breastplate all the year round when ministering in the Sanctuary, stood by him when he entered the Holy of Holies on the Day of Atonement, although at that moment he did not wear it.

EXODUS XXVIII, TETZAVEH

names were inscribed upon the stones in the breastplate]. Rabbi Yehoshua in the name of Rabbi Levi says: This may be compared to a king's son, whose tutor came before the king to speak in his defense, but was afraid of those standing there lest they strike him. What did the king do? He dressed him in his purple cloak in order that they see it and be afraid of him. In the same way Aaron entered at all times[140] the Holy of Holies, and were it not for the many merits that entered with him and helped him, he could not have entered. Why? Because of the ministering angels who were there. What did the Holy One, blessed be He, do? He gave him a likeness of His sacred garment, as it is said, *And He put on righteousness as a coat of mail.*"[141] Thus far is the language of this Agadah. Now even though the High Priest did not enter into the innermost part of the Sanctuary [i.e., the Holy of Holies] with these garments, yet on the Day of Atonement he needed these [garments] even in the Tent of Meeting, for it is written, *And there shall be no man in the Tent of Meeting.*[142]

37. AND THOU SHALT PUT IT ON A BLUE-PURPLE STRING. "But in another place in Scripture it states, *And they put upon it a string of blue-purple*[143] [which indicates that the frontplate was beneath the string, not upon it as is here commanded]! Moreover, here it is written, *and it shall be upon the mitre,* and further on it says, *And it shall be upon Aaron's forehead!*[144] In the Tractate on the Slaughtering of Sacrifices[145] we have been taught: 'The High Priest's hair was visible between the frontplate and the mitre, whereon he placed the phylacteries.' From this we learn that the mitre was above on the crown of the head [and was not so large that it covered the entire head right

---

(140) Reference here is to the four times that the High Priest entered the Holy of Holies during the special service for the Day of Atonement (Peirush Maharzav on Midrash Rabbah). (141) Isaiah 59:17. (142) Leviticus 16:17. Therefore when the High Priest came into the Sanctuary during the service preceding his entrance into the Holy of Holies, he also had to wear these garments as his protection against those powers assailing him because of his high position. (143) Further, 39:31. (144) Verse 38. (145) Zebachim 19 a-b.

down to the forehead], and the frontplate was beneath it [with a space between them], and the strings were in holes and hung from the frontplate at its two ends and in its middle — six in these three places:[146] one string on top [of the frontplate], one outside and one inside [between the frontplate and the forehead]. He tied the ends of the three strings behind the neck, and thus it came to be that the length of the frontplate and the strings at its ends encompassed his whole skull. The middle string which was on top was tied together to the ends of the two strings [at the extremities of the frontplate], and passed over above the breadth of the head. Thus it came to be that [the frontplate with the strings] formed a kind of helmet. Now it is with reference to the middle string that Scripture states, *and it shall be upon the mitre,* for he placed the frontplate [together with the strings tied in the above manner] upon his head [as a kind of helmet, passing it over the mitre], and tightened it through the middle string so that it would not fall. Thus the frontplate hung in front of his forehead. All these verses are thus reconciled: the string was on the frontplate, and the frontplate upon the string, and the string on the mitre above." All this is Rashi's language.

But I wonder concerning Rashi's words, for Scripture commands the making of only one blue-purple string, and he makes six! Moreover, Rashi combined the verses which tell of the command to make [the frontplate] with those which tell of the making thereof,[147] increasing the strings with the number of verses! One could count in such manner in the case of the ark, the table, and the candelabrum [two of each, since they are mentioned once in the command to make, and again in the narrative when they were actually made]! Furthermore, if Scripture commanded that they put the frontplate on a blue-purple string, how did they [do the

---

(146) For, as the center of each string rested at the bottom point of the hole, the three strings became six. (147) The verse mentioned by Rashi [*And they put upon it a string of blue-purple*] is found further (39:31) in connection with the actual making thereof. So how can the string mentioned in that verse be added to the one that is stated in the verse commanding the making of the frontplate?

opposite and] put a blue-purple string on it? Where were they commanded to do so? And why did they need the strings in the middle, since the frontplate was tied behind the neck, as are all frontplates which are worn by men and women?

Indeed, the matter is not as the Rabbi [Rashi] said. For there was only one string there; the plate reached from ear to ear and was pierced at its two ends and the blue-purple string was put through the two holes, the plate being thus tied behind the neck. Thus he wound the *mitznepheth* (mitre) around the head, not at all upon the forehead, but on the head where the hair grows. And according to the opinion of our Rabbis[148] that he also left [uncovered] part of the hair of his head towards his face for the phylacteries, he wound [the *mitznepheth*] high above on the crown of the head, opposite the middle of the brain, covering the whole head at the back. Thus the *mitznepheth* lay above on the slope of the head opposite the brain, and the frontplate rested opposite his forehead from ear to ear, there being nothing intervening between his forehead and the frontplate. Thus the *mitznepheth* lay on the back of his head from ear to ear, opposite the whole neck, and the string which was tied to the frontplate was upon the *mitznepheth*. It is with reference to this that Scripture says, *And thou shalt put it on a blue-purple string,* meaning that he should put the string through the holes of the frontplate; *and* the string *shall be upon the mitre* behind his ears opposite the neck; *towards the front of the mitre it shall be* — that is, the frontplate, which shall be upon the forehead opposite the front part of the mitre. This is Scripture's intent in stating, *And thou shalt set the mitre upon his head,*[149] that is to say, above on the crown of the head, unlike the *migba'oth* of which it is said, *and thou shalt bind head-tires upon them,*[150] binding the head like one whose head hurts and he binds it for the purpose of strengthening the head. It further states, *and thou shalt put the holy crown upon the mitre,*[149] for it was upon the mitre that [the frontplate] was tied at the back. This is so stated: *And they put*

---

(148) Zebachim 19 a.   (149) Further, 29:6.   (150) *Ibid.*, Verse 9.

upon it a string of blue-purple, to fasten it upon the mitre above, [143] for there upon [the mitre] the string [of the frontplate] was tied. Similarly, *and upon the mitre, in front, did he set the golden plate,* [151] means that he tied upon the front of the mitre the golden frontplate. Thus the term "placing" in all the verses refers to putting [the string of the frontplate] upon the mitre, for it was there that it was tied; the frontplate itself, however, was on the forehead opposite the mitre. There is then no difference between the expression *And they put upon it a string of blue-purple,* [143] and [in the verse before us] *and thou shalt put it on a blue-purple string* [unlike Rashi who distinguished between them], for in both cases it is as if it said, "and thou shalt place it *with* a blue-purple string," "and thou shalt put a blue-purple string," similar in usage to the expression, *and thou shalt put them 'on' one basket,* [152] which means "in" the basket. Likewise, *escape 'on' thy life* [153] [which means "with your life," as long as your life is in you, or "escape for your life"]. Or it may be that the word *al* ('on' — *on a blue-purple string*) here serves as *el* (to), thus stating: "and you shall put it *to* a blue-purple string," "and they put a blue-purple string *to* it," for the string was put [to the frontplate, and the frontplate was put] to it, for it rested on it for support. In essence, the meaning of the verses is only that they should place a string in the holes of the frontplate, and in that way it also came about that the frontplate was upon the string and the string upon the frontplate. Similarly, *And they shall bind the breastplate by the rings thereof to the rings of the ephod with a string of blue-purple,* [154] from which Rashi brought a proof [155]

---

(151) Leviticus 8:9. (152) Further, 29:3. (153) Genesis 19:17. (154) Above, Verse 28. (155) In Rashi's exposition of the frontplate he had explained (as mentioned above) that there were three double strings attached to it. To answer the question why Scripture speaks only of "a thread of blue-purple" in the singular, Rashi wrote (further 39:31). "Do not be puzzled because it does not say '*threads* of blue-purple,' for we find the same thing in the case of the breastplate and the ephod, of which it is said, *And they shall bind the breastplate by the rings thereof with a string of blue-purple* (above, Verse 28), and you must admit that there could not have been less than two strings, for at the two ends of the breastplate were the two

[that there were three double strings in the frontplate], also refers to only one string, which they put through the rings of the breastplate and the rings of the ephod opposite them; so also on the other side there was one string, for these were two [separate] places, and in each place they tied [the breastplate by the rings thereof] with one string [of blue-purple to the rings of the ephod].

41. AND THOU SHALT PUT THEM UPON AARON THY BROTHER AND UPON HIS SONS WITH HIM — "those which are mentioned in connection with them." This is Rashi's language. The meaning of *with him* is that they were all clothed with the priestly garments and anointed on the same day.

AND THOU SHALT ANOINT THEM 'UMILEITHA ETH YADAM' [literally: "and fill their hands"]. "Every expression of 'filling the hand' denotes installation, when one enters for the first time into an office which one is to hold from that day onwards." This is Rashi's language. But I have not understood his words. How does the expression of "filling the hand" come to mean "installation?" And as to that which the Rabbi said that "in the [old] French language — when a person is appointed to be in charge of any matter, the ruler puts into his hand a leather glove which they call *gant*, and by means of that glove gives him the right to that matter, and it is this which is called 'filling the hand,' " — I do not know whether the Rabbi's intent is to state that because of that glove the installation is called "filling the hand," and to this he brought proof from a custom [in France]! Know that this custom they derived from the Torah, as to them this form of taking possession is [what is meant by] the

---

rings of the breastplate, and on the two shoulder pieces of the ephod were two rings opposite them. Now according to the way the breastplate was tied on, there were four threads, and under any circumstance it could not have been less than two [and yet Scripture speaks only of *'a string'* of *blue-purple*]!" — To this proof of Rashi, Ramban answers that reference is only to one string, as explained in the text.

acquisition by exchange mentioned in connection with Boaz, for so they translated: [*Now this was the custom in former time in Israel concerning redeeming and concerning exchanging...*] *a man drew off 'na'alo' (his shoe)*[156] — "a man drew off his *gant*," and they say[157] that it was the near kinsman that gave it to Boaz. This custom of theirs is mentioned in the books of their scholars. Thus we have engaged in vain talk!

The correct interpretation of *milui yadayim* in the Torah is that it is an expression of perfection, similar in usage to these verses: *'ki malu yamai' (for my days are completed);*[158] *'ubimloth' hayamim ha'eileh' (and when these days were fulfilled);*[159] *until the days 'm'loth'*[160] — be fulfilled. Similarly, *'b'keseph malei'*[161] means "for the full price." And the reason for this expression is that one might say of a stranger [i.e., a non-priest] who cannot perform the offering for his cleansing, or of any person who is not empowered to perform some royal service, that his hand misses that function; and when he becomes empowered to do it, his hand has thereby been perfected and made fit for all kinds of work and service. Thus, *'milu yedchem hayom'* [162] [generally translated: *consecrate yourselves today*] means that: "now your hands are full with the whole service of G-d, *for even every man upon his son, and upon his brother*[162] have you served Him [that day]." Or it may be that Moses was hinting to the sons of Levi that by virtue of this merit they would be chosen to perform the Divine Service in the Tabernacle, as it is said, *At that time the Eternal separated the tribe of Levi.*[163] Similarly King David said to Israel on the occasion of the donations for the House

---

(156) Ruth 4:7. (157) Our accepted law is that acquisition by exchange is accomplished with something that originally belongs to the buyer. Hence it was Boaz [the buyer] who "drew off his shoe" and gave it to the near kinsman. But "they say" differently, that it was the near kinsman [the seller] that gave it to Boaz. Hence they derived the custom that it is the prince [who is in the position of the bestower or seller] who pulls off his *gant* and gives it to the recipient. (158) Genesis 29:21. (159) Esther 1:5. (160) Leviticus 8:33. (161) Genesis 23:9. (162) Further, 32:29. (163) Deuteronomy 10:8.

EXODUS XXVIII, TETZAVEH

[of G-d], *Because I have set my affection on the house of my G-d, seeing that I have a treasure of mine own of gold and silver, I give it into the house of my G-d,*[164] and then he continued saying, *Who then offereth willingly 'l'maloth yado' this day unto the Eternal?*[165] — meaning "to perfect his hand [this day unto the Eternal]," for by doanting towards the building of the House [of G-d] their hands become full with all the sacrifices and all manner of services, for Israel's worship of G-d is only a complete one in the Sanctuary. Similarly, *the ram of 'milu'im'* mentioned in this section[166] is so called because the filling of the priests' duties was accomplished through this offering, for the sin-offering and the burnt-offering[167] were to effect atonement, and this ram was to fill the priest's hand with [the right to] sacrifice. I have also found that in Targum Yerushalmi *the ram of 'milu'im'* is translated: *d'ashlamutha,* (of perfection);[168] similarly also in all expressions of *milui yadayim* it translated "perfection." Onkelos, however, [in translating *umileitha eth yadam* — 'and you will bring their sacrifices'[169]] followed the sense of the subject and was not pedantic as to the literal language, as is his custom in many places. Some scholars[170] explain *umileitha eth yadam* as meaning that he will fill their hands [with the gifts] from the sacrifices. Similarly: *whosoever would, he* [Jeroboam] *'yemalei eth yado'*[171] means that he could fill his hands at will from the sacrifices. But the correct interpretation [of the term *milui yadayim*] is as I have explained. And the meaning of the expression, *whosoever would, 'yemalei eth yado' that he might be one of the priests of the high places*[171] is that he would bring for himself an offering of installation *as he devised of his own heart,*[172] in order to initiate

---

(164) I Chronicles 29:3. (165) *Ibid.,* Verse 5. (166) Further, 29:22. (167) *Ibid.,* Verse 5. (168) This translation I found in Targum Yonathan ben Uziel to Leviticus 8:22. (169) On the seven days of installation it was Moses who acted in the role of the priest and performed the rites of the sacrifices. Hence Onkelos' translation: "and you [i.e., Moses] will bring their sacrifices," as during these seven days of installation you will be the priest to offer their sacrifices. (170) Found in R'dak's Sefer Hashorashim, root *male.* (171) I Kings 13:33. (172) *Ibid.,* 12:33.

himself into his office, and thereby he became one of the priests of the high places, for they acted in a manner similar to the ways of the Torah. [173]

3. AND THOU SHALT BRING THEM IN THE BASKET. This is connected with the following verse [... *unto the door of the Tent of Meeting*],[174] Scripture thus stating that he [Moses] shall bring the bread in the basket, the bullock, the rams, and Aaron and his sons, to the door of the Tent of Meeting. *And thou shalt wash them with water*[174] — that is, Aaron and his sons. A more correct interpretation is that the expression *and thou shalt bring them in the basket* leaves the matter unspecified, for without further explanation it is known that he should bring them to the place where He commands the priests to come [it being sufficient if they come before the door of the court of the Tabernacle]. And the second verse speaks only of Aaron and his sons, and therefore He says [*thou shalt bring unto the door of the Tent of Meeting*] *and thou shalt wash them with water.*[174]

7. THEN SHALT THOU TAKE THE ANOINTING OIL, AND POUR IT UPON HIS HEAD. Rabbi Abraham ibn Ezra wrote that this was before the setting of the mitre upon his head [mentioned in the preceding verse], for it is upon the head itself that Moses was to pour the oil. But this does not appear to me to be correct. For at the actual installation also, Scripture says, *And he set the mitre upon his head* etc.,[175] and afterwards it says, *And Moses*

---

(173) See Leviticus 6:13. This is also applied to the ordinary priest who brought a meal-offering when he officiated for the first time. Ramban's intent is thus that in the days of Jeroboam when the king installed a new group of priests in the kingdom of Israel to officiate at the sacrifices on the *Bamoth* (high places) he adopted the ways of the Torah as explained, in order to give the appearance of his remaining loyal to the commandments of the Torah. (174) Verse 4. Ramban is thus taking the phrase, *unto the door of the Tent of Meeting* from Verse 4 and transposing it to Verse 3, thus meaning: "and thou shalt bring them in the basket — unto the door of the Tent of Meeting." Under "the more correct interpretation" Ramban will explain that the phrase rightfully belongs in Verse 4, teaching that the washing of Aaron and his sons must be done in the Sanctuary Court. (175) Leviticus 8:9.

took the anointing oil, and anointed the Tabernacle,[176] and subsequently it states, *And he poured of the anointing oil upon Aaron's head.*[177] But the correct interpretation is that he wound [the *mitznepheth*] around and around the head, but left the middle of the head uncovered, and it was on that place that he poured the oil. But if the anointing was upon the entire head as Rashi said,[178] then [we must say] that the pouring of the oil was upon the place where the phylacteries lay, which was left uncovered, and from there he joined [the oil with his finger to the drop between his eyebrows] in the form of an X.

9. AND THOU SHALT GIRD THEM WITH BELTS. This alludes to Aaron and his sons, and then Scripture reverts and explains, *Aaron and his sons.* This is similar to the expressions: *let him bring it, the Eternal's offering;*[179] *the kingdom which will not serve him, Nebuchadnezzar.*[180] Such are the words of Rabbi Abraham ibn Ezra. But if so, [the following phrase in the verse before us,] *and thou shalt bind 'migba'oth' on them* refers only to some of them [mentioned before, namely, Aaron's sons], for Aaron's head-dress was not of the *migba'oth,* and besides, the *mitznepheth* is already on his head [as mentioned in Verse 6]. It is possible that the explanation of the verse is: "and thou shalt gird them with belts, *and* Aaron and his sons." The verse is thus stating that he should gird Aaron's sons mentioned with belts, and Aaron himself should be girded with his sons. For since the belt was alike for all of them [for Aaron and his sons], it was not mentioned above among the particular garments of Aaron; therefore it now became necessary to say that he should gird Aaron too with a belt

---

(176) *Ibid.,* Verse 10. (177) *Ibid.,* Verse 12. (178) Rashi here in Verse 7: "This anointing was in the form of an X. He put a drop of oil on his head and another drop between his eyebrows and joined them with his finger." In that case he could not have put the drop of oil on top of the head, for the mitre would then intervene between it and the drop of oil between his eyebrows. Ramban concludes that according to this comment of Rashi we must say, that the pouring of the oil etc. (179) Further, 35:5. The word *it* alludes already to *the Eternal's offering,* but then Scripture itself reverts and explains it. The same principle applies in the next example. (180) Jeremiah 27:8.

like his sons. The breeches were not mentioned here as it was not necessary, as I have explained.[181] And the reason why the breeches were singled out from the rest of the garments [by not being mentioned here] is that it was Moses who clothed them with all the garments, as G-d commanded, *and thou shalt clothe them*.[182] But the breeches which were *to cover the flesh of their nakedness,* [183] they themselves put on in privacy. Therefore He did not mention them here among the garments — *and thou shalt take the garments, and clothe Aaron...*[184] and therefore He separated them [from the other garments] in command and in punishment, as I have mentioned above. [181]

10. AND THOU SHALT BRING THE BULLOCK BEFORE THE TENT OF MEETING; AND AARON AND HIS SONS SHALL LAY THEIR HANDS UPON THE HEAD OF THE BULLOCK. Rabbi Abraham ibn Ezra commented, that the meaning of it is that when you will bring the bullock before the Tent of Meeting, Aaron and his sons shall lay their hands upon it, for [the bringing of the bullock] has already been mentioned above. [185] The correct interpretation appears to me to be as I have explained, [185] that above He commanded to bring them but did not explain "to the Tent of Meeting," but only that he bring them; the purport being that he bring them to the place of the priests so that they be ready [for sacrifice], thus it would be sufficient that they be before the door of the court of the Tabernacle. But now He required that they be brought before the Tent of Meeting, to the door of the Tent, as He will explain in connection with the slaughtering thereof, [186] for it is there that the laying of hands will take place.

13. AND THOU SHALT TAKE ALL THE FAT THAT COVERETH THE INWARDS. "This is the membrane upon the

---

(181) Above, 28:35. "For having declared there [above] the punishment for lacking them there was no more need to revert and mention them [here], as it is understood already that he would wear them." (182) Verse 8. (183) Above, 28:42. (184) Verse 5. (185) Verse 3. (186) Verse 11.

EXODUS XXIX, TETZAVEH

maw which is called *tele* [in old French]." This is Rashi's language. In my opinion, the expression *the fat that covereth the inwards* is indeed a reference to the membrane [upon the maw]. But when it says [as it does here], *'all' the fat that covereth the inwards,* it alludes to two kinds of fat which are there: to the fat of that membrane, and to the heavy fat which is upon the inwards, as it is said in *Seder Vayikra: the fat that covereth the inwards, and the fat that is upon the inwards.*[187] Thus it is clear that there are two kinds of fat upon the inwards — at times Scripture mentions them both, and at other times it includes them as one under the term "all" [as it says here]. Thus by saying here, *all the fat that covereth the inwards,* He already included the fat that is upon the inwards. Similarly in the actual fulfillment of this command He says, *And he took all the fat that was upon the inwards, and the lobe of the liver,*[188] thus including [the two kinds of fat upon the inwards] in the phrase, *'all' the fat that was upon the inwards.* But further in this section He says, *And thou shalt take of the ram the fat, and the fat tail, and the fat that covereth the inwards.*[189] Here the first "fat" mentioned without explanation, means the fat upon the inwards.

14. THOU SHALT BURN WITH FIRE WITHOUT THE CAMP; IT IS A SIN-OFFERING. "We do not find any outside [190] sin-offering that was to be burnt except this." Thus is Rashi's language. It was a temporary, special legislation, according to the words of our Rabbis.[191] The reason for this is, that everything

---

(187) Leviticus 3:3. (188) *Ibid.,* 8:16. (189) Further, Verse 22.
(190) An *inner* sin-offering was one the blood of which was sprinkled within the Sanctuary — upon the veil in front of the Holy of Holies and the golden altar; that kind of a sin-offering was burnt completely outside the camp (Leviticus 6:23). Such a sacrifice, for example, was the sin-offering of the High Priest (*ibid.,* 4:3-12). An *outside* sin-offering was one the blood of which was sprinkled upon the outer altar that stood in the court of the Tabernacle [or Sanctuary]. Of such a sin-offering only certain fats were burnt on the altar, and the meat eaten by the priests. Since the sin-offering mentioned here was an *outside* sacrifice, and yet it was to the burnt wholly outside of the camp, it must have been a temporary, special legislation.
(191) See Rashi to Leviticus 9:11.

being foreseen by Him, this sin-offering was to effect forgiveness for the making of the golden calf, and it was the sacrifice of the anointed priest;[192] and there [in the Book of Leviticus] He was to command that the blood of the sin-offering [of the High Priest] be brought within [the Tent of Meeting and sprinkled in front of] the veil,[193] [and the sacrifice be burnt outside the camp[194]]. At present, however, He did not wish to mention that [the blood be brought] within the Tent, for there [in the Book of Leviticus] He says in discernment, [that he sprinkle the blood] *in front of the holy veil,*[193] and at this point [the Tabernacle] had not yet been sanctified, and the Divine Glory did not yet dwell upon it, that it be called "the holy veil." Thus the outside sin-offering [mentioned here] was like the inner one [of the anointed priest]. The laying of hands was [also] by Aaron's sons, [although if it was deemed to be Aaron's sin-offering the laying of hands should have been done only by Aaron], because *He was angry with Aaron to have destroyed him,* [195] which means the extermination of his children, therefore they too needed atonement by this sin-offering. The reason for burning [such a sin-offering outside the camp] is the same as the reason for burning the Red Heifer there,[196] and the secret thereof is known from [the text concerning] the goat sent to Azazel.[197]

26. OF THE RAM OF CONSECRATION WHICH IS AARON'S. He did not mention here Aaron's sons, although the ram was for the consecration of all of them. The reason for this is that Scripture commanded [in the first part of the verse before us], *And thou* [i.e., Moses] *shalt take the breast* of the wave-offering *of the ram of consecration* because it is *Aaron's,* since the breast of the offering is by right not Aaron's, for it does not belong to the owner of the animal [but to the priest,[198] and since on this

---

(192) A reference to Aaron's role in that affair (see further 32:35) (Ricanti). (193) Leviticus 4:6. (194) *Ibid.*, Verse 12. Hence He commanded here — in advance — that that sin-offering was to be burnt. (195) Deuteronomy 9:20. (196) Numbers 19:3, 5. (197) Leviticus 16:10. See Ramban there on Verse 8. (198) *Ibid.*, 7:31.

EXODUS XXIX, TETZAVEH

occasion Aaron and his sons were the owners of the ram of consecration, and Moses the officiating priest, the breast in this instance belonged to Moses]. Now having stated the reason why it does not belong of right to Aaron, there was no need any more to declare that it does not belong to his sons, for they follow him in their rights [and where it does not belong to him, it likewise does not belong to them]. Further, however, He does say, *And thou shalt sanctify the breast of the wave-offering... of the ram of consecration, even of that which is Aaron's, and of that which is his sons',* [199] for the intent is to state: "just as he [Moses] takes of the offering which belongs to them all, the breast and the shoulder, [200] so shall they — the father and the sons [High Priest and common priests] — take of the future [peace-] offerings which they [the children of Israel] will offer up."

29. 'L'MOSHCHAH BAHEM' (TO BE ANOINTED IN THEM). "*L'moshchah* means to be raised to dignity by means of them, for the term *m'shichah* (anointing) is sometimes used in the sense of 'authority,' just as in these expressions: *unto thee have I given them 'l'moshchah' (as a distinction);*[201] *touch not 'bimshichai' (My noble ones).*"[202] This is Rashi's language. Perhaps it is so. For because authority in Israel belonged to those who were anointed — the king and the High Priest — they used the term ["anointing"] metaphorically for all kinds of authority. Similarly, when it says, *thou shalt anoint Hazael to be king over Aram... and Elisha the son of Shaphat of Abel-meholah shalt thou anoint to be prophet in thy stead,*[203] [the term "anoint" is used metaphorically — "appoint" or "designate"]. Here, however, the correct interpretation of *l'moshchah bahem* is to anoint with the garments the High Priests above their sons, and to consecrate them to offer the sacrifices. Likewise, *unto thee have I given them 'l'moshchah'*[201] means that I have given them [i.e., the priestly

---

(199) Verse 27.   (200) "And the shoulder," is merely an expression, for it is clearly stated in Verse 22 that the shoulder was also burnt on the altar, and Rashi also so states it clearly.   (201) Numbers 18:8.   (202) Psalms 105:15. (203) I Kings 19:15-16.

gifts] because I have anointed you *to minister unto Me.*[204] Similarly, *touch not 'bimshichai'*[202] means that he who touches them touches the anointed ones of G-d [i.e., the kings] who are destined to come from them, as He said, *and kings shall come out from thy loins;*[205] *kings of peoples shall be of her.*[206]

It is even possible that we say that the expression *thou shalt anoint Hazael to be king over Aram*,[203] means that he [i.e., Elijah] is to send him oil to be anointed as king, in order to inform him that this was the command of G-d; and Elisha [his disciple] did so in accordance with the charge of his master when he told Hazael that he will rule as king.[207] Now even though it is not written there, [he yet actually anointed him as king], and [so did Elijah] anoint Elisha as a prophet [in accordance with G-d's command to him]. Perhaps they[208] also did so to Cyrus [king of Persia] whom they anointed like the kings of Israel, in order that he would know that it was a prophet in Israel who prophesied that he would reign, and [generations before his birth] he even called forth his name, for [the glory of] G-d. Therefore [Isaiah] said, *to His anointed, to Cyrus,*[209] upon which our Rabbis have commented:[210] "And was Cyrus the anointed one? etc."[211] Thus all these verses speak of real anointing. However, the verse stating, *The spirit of the Eternal G-d is upon me; because the Eternal 'mashach' me to bring good tidings unto the humble,*[212] is by way of metaphor, comparing the holy spirit which came to rest upon the prophet with precious oil, similar to that which is said, *A good name is better than precious oil.*[213]

---

(204) Above, Verse 1. (205) Genesis 35:11. (206) *Ibid.*, 17:16. (207) II Kings 8:13. (208) The prophets who lived in the time of Cyrus. (209) Isaiah 45:1. (210) Megillah 12 a. (211) "Rather, the Holy One, blessed be He, said to the Messiah: "I complain to you about Cyrus. I said he will build My house and gather My exiles, but he said, *Whosoever there is among you of all His people... let him go up.*" (Ezra 1:3) — From this text it would appear that the Rabbis understood the verse to mean that Cyrus was really anointed [for otherwise there would have been no place at all for their question], except that he later became impaired in character. (212) Isaiah 61:1. (213) Ecclesiastes 7:1.

EXODUS XXIX, TETZAVEH

31. AND THOU SHALT SEETHE ITS FLESH IN A HOLY PLACE. We do not know whether this was a temporary, special legislation that the flesh of [the ram of] consecration be seethed only by a priest, [who in this case was Moses] or — as Rabbi Abraham ibn Ezra has it — that the expression *and thou shalt seethe* means by commanding [another person to do it], it being similar in usage to these verses: *and thy rod wherewith thou smotest the river;*[214] and *Solomon built the house*[215] [by commanding the builders to build it].

The seething had to be done *in a holy place,* since they [216] were like the peace-offerings of the congregation which were to be eaten within the hangings of the court, the same day and evening until midnight. [217]

36. AND EVERY DAY SHALT THOU OFFER THE BULLOCK OF SIN-OFFERING 'AL HAKIPURIM' — "for atonement, to atone for the altar for anything strange [i.e., unholy] and abominable [that may happen to be brought upon it]. And in the Midrash of Torath Kohanim [218] it says: 'atonement for the altar was necessary in case a person had donated for work in connection with the construction of the Tabernacle and [the sacrifices brought upon] the altar something he had acquired by robbery'" [or other unlawful means]. This is the language of Rashi. The correct interpretation of *al hakipurim* is, however, [that he is to bring the bullock of sin-offering] in addition to the two rams [219] which were an atonement for Aaron and his sons, as He said here, *And they shall eat those things wherewith atonement was made,* [220] and surely the [bullock] sin-offering was for the purpose of atonement.

---

(214) Above, 17:5. Since it was Aaron who smote the river (*ibid.*, 7:19), the verse must mean: "*thy rod wherewith thou smotest the river* — by commanding Aaron." (215) I Kings 6:14. (216) I.e., the seven rams of consecration, one brought on each of the seven days of consecration. (217) Zebachim 54 b. (218) Sifra *Tzav,* Milu'im 1:15. (219) One was a burnt-offering (Verses 16-18) and the other — the ram of consecration — was a peace-offering, as explained by Ramban above in Verse 31. (220) Verse 33.

And it is further written, *As hath been done this day, so the Eternal hath commanded to do, to make atonement for you.* [221] Such are the words of Rabbi Abraham ibn Ezra.

46. 'L'SHOCHNI B'THOCHAM' [222] — "on condition that I dwell in the midst of them." This is Rashi's language. But the usage of the letter *lamed* [*l'shochni*] for a condition of this kind is not found [elsewhere in Scripture]! It is possible that He is stating: "and they shall know 'when' I dwell among them that I am the Eternal their G-d that brought them forth out of the land of Egypt, for they will [then] know My Glory and believe that I brought them forth from the land of Egypt." It is similar in usage to the verses: *And David had great success 'l'chol drachav'* [223] [which is like *b'chol drachav* — "in all his ways"]; *that thou hast chosen 'l'ben Yishai'* [224] [which means *b'ben Yishai* — "the son of Jesse"]; *because ye rebelled against My word 'l'mei Meribah'* [225] [which means *b'mei Meribah* — "in (or 'at') the waters of Meribah"], and similar cases.

But Rabbi Abraham ibn Ezra explained [the verse to mean that] the purpose of My bringing them forth from the land of Egypt was only that I might dwell in their midst, and that this was the fulfilment of [the promise to Moses], *you shall serve G-d upon this mountain.*[226] He explained it well, and if it is so, there is in this matter a great secret. For in the plain sense of things it would appear that [the dwelling of] the Divine Glory in Israel was to fulfill a want below, but it is not so. It fulfilled a want above, being rather similar in thought to that which Scripture states, *Israel, in whom I will be glorified.*[227] And Joshua said, [*For when*

---

(221) Leviticus 8:34. This verse shows that all three sacrifices [the bullock sin-offering, the ram burnt-offering, and the ram peace-offering] brought on each of the seven days of consecration were for the purpose of making atonement. Thus it is seen that there was atonement in all the three sacrifices. (222) Literally: "to dwell among them." (223) I Samuel 18:14. Literally: "*to* all his ways." (224) *Ibid.*, 20:30. Literally: "*to* the son of Jesse." (225) Numbers 20:24. Literally: "*to* the waters of Meribah." (226) Above, 3:12. (227) Isaiah 49:3.

EXODUS XXX, TETZAVEH 507

the Canaanites... hear of it... and cut off our name from the earth,] and what wilt Thou do for Thy Great Name?[228] There are many verses which express this thought: *He hath desired it* [i.e., Zion] *for His habitation;*[229] *Here I dwell; for I have desired it.* [230] And it is further written, *and I will remember the land.* [231]

30   1. AND THOU SHALT MAKE AN ALTAR TO BURN INCENSE UPON. Now the altar of incense being one of the articles in the inner part of the Sanctuary, it should have been mentioned with the table and the candelabrum together with which it was placed, as indeed they are mentioned at the actual construction in the section of *Vayakheil.*[232] But the reason for mentioning it here after the Tabernacle and all its vessels and the sacrifices [for the seven days of consecration], is because of what He said at the completion of them all, *and the Tent shall be sanctified by My Glory;*[233] *and I will dwell among the children of Israel.*[234] Therefore He now said that they will yet be obliged to make an altar for the burning of incense — to burn it for the glory of G-d. This was a secret which was transmitted to Moses our Teacher,[235] that the incense checks the plague.[236] For the incense is of the attribute of justice, as it is said, *they shall put incense 'b'apecha',* [237] which is of the root *v'charah api (My wrath shall wax hot).* [238] It is for this reason that He said of strange incense, *and before all the people I will be glorified,*[239] meaning that they will know My glory, *for He will not pardon your transgression.*[240] For this reason too He said here [of the altar of

---

(228) Joshua 7:9.   (229) Psalms 132:13.   (230) *Ibid.*, Verse 14. (231) Leviticus 26:42. "That is to say, the land is remembered in mercy. *And I will remember* is of the root *The Eternal hath been mindful of us*" (Psalms 115:12) (Ricanti).   (232) Further, 37:25 — next to the making of the candelabrum.   (233) Above, 29:43.   (234) *Ibid.*, Verse 45. (235) Shabbath 89 a.   (236) Numbers 17:11-13.   (237) Deuteronomy 33:10. It is generally translated: "before Thee," but Ramban suggests that *b'apecha* is of the root *aph* (anger).   (238) Above, 22:23.   (239) Leviticus 10:3.   (240) Above, 23:21.

incense], *And thou shalt put it before the veil that is by the ark of the Testimony, before the ark-cover that is over the Testimony, where I will meet with thee.*[241] For why is it necessary to speak at length of all these matters, and why did He not say briefly, "and thou shalt put it before the ark of the Testimony in the Tent of Meeting," as He said in the section of *Vayakheil?*[242] But the extended form of the verse here indicates the purport [of the altar of incense].

7. AND AARON SHALL BURN THEREON INCENSE. This commandment [of burning the incense] did not devolve upon the High Priest alone, but was also incumbent upon the common priests, as is the law of the lighting of the lamps mentioned right beside it, [*every morning, when he dresseth the lamps*], although of that too it says, *And when Aaron lighteth the lamps,*[243] and yet it does not apply to the High Priest alone, as He said above, *Aaron and his sons shall set in order.*[244] Therefore I do not know why He mentioned Aaron in both of them, and did not say "the priest" [which would signify any — even a common-priest]. Perhaps it is because of Scripture's statement further, *And Aaron shall make atonement upon the horns of it once in the year,*[245] which was done by Aaron only, [because the reference there is to the Service on the Day of Atonement which could be performed only by the High Priest — therefore He also mentioned the name of Aaron in the verse before us and in the following verse]. Or it may be that He hinted that it was to be Aaron who [at the first time] was to begin the burning of the incense and the lighting of the lamps. Similarly at the end of *Seder Emor el hakohanim* He said, *Aaron shall set in order,*[246] and He did not mention his sons, because it was Aaron who performed it first. The phrase *a statute forever* mentioned there,[246] refers to the commandment [of kindling the lamps, and does not mean that it is *a statute forever* that only the High Priest do it].

(241) Verse 6. (242) It is found in the section of *Pekudei* (further, 40:5). (243) Verse 8. (244) Above, 27:21. (245) Further, Verse 10. (246) Leviticus 24:3.

EXODUS XXX, TETZAVEH

9. YE SHALL NOT BRING UP 'KTORETH ZARAH' (STRANGE INCENSE) THEREON — "any incense brought as a freewill offering; for all [offerings of incense] are 'strange' to [this altar] except this one [prescribed here]." This is Rashi's language. But Onkelos rendered *ktoreth zarah: ktoreth busmin nuchra'in* ("the burning of aromatics which are of strange components,") and he did not translate it *nuchritha* "strange incense" [as Rashi interpreted it]. By this translation Onkelos wanted to explain that the sense of the verse is that he should not offer an incense of any other components except those prescribed as He commanded. [247] Similarly, if one were to add to the prescribed composition any other components one would transgress this negative commandment.

---

(247) This is identical with Ibn Ezra's interpretation of the verse. Ramban, however, called attention to Onkelos' text because it required an explanation as mentioned.

Ki Thisa

12. The Holy One, blessed be He, commanded Moses that when he takes a census of the children of Israel, they should each give a soul's ransom — half a shekel; and He further told him, *And thou shalt take the atonement-money* [1] mentioned, *and shalt give it for the service of the Tent of Meeting.* [1] From this Moses would understand that he was to count them now. And so indeed he did, as Scripture says, *And the silver of them that were numbered of the congregation was a hundred talents* etc. [2] It was thus not necessary to state at length, "and now you should take their census and give the silver for the service of the Tent of Meeting," for it is self-understood that he should count them now. The reason that He generalized the commandment — saying "when you will take their census you should do it in the prescribed way" — is in order to include in this general principle any time when a census was decided upon.

It appears to me that now [at this census, Moses] did not have to come to the people's tents and count them, as he did in the census spoken of in the Book of Numbers,[3] but he did it as our Rabbis have said through the [half] shekels they brought for the sacrifices; for he commanded them that all who know themselves to be *from twenty years old and upward* [4] should give that sum,

---

(1) Verse 16. (2) Further, 38:25. (3) In connection with that census the Midrash says specifically that when the enumeration of the Levites was taken "Moses went and stationed himself at the entrance of each tent etc." (Tanchuma *Bamidbar*, 16). Ramban is here suggesting that the same was done with the other tribes as well. (4) Verse 14.

EXODUS XXX, KI THISA

and they brought him the ransom as a voluntary offering together with all the other voluntary offerings every morning.[5] That is why He said only, *And thou shalt take the atonement-money,*[1] that is to say, "Behold, I have commanded you that when you count them they shall give their ransom, and now they will voluntarily give it and you should appoint it *for the service of the Tent of Meeting.*"[1] This is the reason why it was not necessary now that Aaron and the princes [of the tribes] be present with Moses [at the taking of the half-shekels, as was required in the census spoken of in the Book of Numbers[6]]. Do not object on account of the verse, *This they shall give, every one that passeth among them that are numbered*[7] [from which you might think that here too, Moses actually counted the people], for the meaning thereof is "those that are eligible to pass."

Now because it has not been explained here whether this is a commandment binding for all time or only for that particular period of when Moses was in the wilderness, David erred and counted the people without shekels, and on account of this a plague broke out amongst them.[8] He confessed about this [sin], as it is said, *And David said unto G-d, I have sinned greatly, in that I have done this thing.*[9]

Our Rabbis have derived[10] from the many expressions [of "offering"] mentioned here,[11] [an indication] that there were three [separate] offerings.[12] And so it appears from what Scripture says, [*And the king called for Jehoiada the chief, and said unto him:*] *'Why hast thou not required of the Levites to bring in out of Judah and out of Jerusalem the tax of Moses the*

---

(5) Further, 36:3. (6) Numbers 1:3-4. (7) Verse 13. (8) II Samuel 24:1-15. (9) I Chronicles 21:8. (10) Yerushalmı Shekalim I, 1. (11) *Half a shekel for an offering to the Eternal* (Verse 13); *he shall give the offering of the Eternal* (Verse 14); *when they give the offering of the Eternal* (Verse 15). (12) One was for the making of the sockets of the Tabernacle (further 38:26-27). The second was after the erection of the Tabernacle and the money was used for purchasing the public sacrifices. Both of these offerings were compulsory, each person giving a half-shekel. The third was voluntary and was used for the building of the Tabernacle. See also further on in the text.

servant of the Eternal, and of the congregation of Israel, for the Tent of Testimony?'[13] From this it would appear that the tax of Moses was enjoined for all time — and that it was to be brought for the repair of the Temple even though no census was to be taken. Likewise the offering for [buying the public] sacrifices [was enjoined for all time] as the Sages have said, and it is so written [of Ezra and Nehemiah]: *Also we made ordinances for us to charge ourselves yearly with the third part of a shekel for the service of the house of our G-d; for the showbread, and for the continual meal-offering and for the continual burnt-offering, of the Sabbaths, of the New Moons, for the appointed reasons, and for the holy things, and for the sin-offerings to make atonement for Israel, and for all the work of the house of our G-d.*[14] Here it is clearly stated that they used to bring shekels every year for the sacrifices and for the Temple repair. Scripture states that the levy was *the third part of a shekel* [whereas here it is stated that it is to be half a shekel]; this was because in the days of Ezra they added to the value of a shekel, so that the third of a shekel was then ten gerahs [the equivalent of a half a shekel in the days of Moses].[15]

In Tractate Shekalim we are taught:[16] "When Israel came up from [the Babylonian] exile they used to pay the [half-] shekel in *darics* [a Persian silver coin, each one giving one *daric,* as will be explained further]. Then they changed, and paid it in *s'laim* [each one giving one *sela*]. Again they changed and paid the shekel in *tibin* [each one giving one *tiba*], and they finally sought to pay it in *denars* [but these were not accepted of them]." The meaning of this Mishnah is as follows: When Israel came up from the exile and large funds were needed for the Temple repair, they paid the shekel in *darics,* which were larger than the *s'laim,* each one giving one *daric.* Then they changed and began paying in whole *s'laim* [each one giving one *sela* — since there was a decrease in the needs

---

(13) II Chronicles 24:6. (14) Nehemiah 10:33-34. (15) *The shekel is twenty gerahs* (Verse 13). In the days of Ezra a shekel was worth thirty gerahs; hence a third was ten gerahs. (16) Shekalim 2:4.

of the Temple repair]. Again they changed it to *tibin* — in the Yerushalmi [17] it is explained that a *tiba* is half a *sela*. [18] When they sought to pay it in *denars* [each one giving one *denar*] [19] they did not accept it of them, for although the public can increase the levy to more than half a *sela*, provided only that everyone pays alike, as we have been taught in the Mishnah of Tractate Shekalim, [16] yet no one is permitted to decrease it and give less than half of a *sela*, be it one person or many people, for "the ransom of a soul" is not less than that [i.e. a half-*sela*], as it is written, *This they shall give* etc. [7] In the Yerushalmi [17] the Rabbis have said with reference to what is written [that in the days of Ezra and Nehemiah they ordained that each one is to give] *the third part of a shekel,* [14] "from here you learn that a person is responsible for shekels three times a year. [20] From here you also learn that we must not impose on the public more than three times a year" [for the Temple treasury].

Now Rashi wrote: "there are three offerings hinted at here [11] — one was for the making of the sockets, for Moses counted them when they began to contribute towards the building of the Tabernacle after the Day of Atonement in the first year [of the exodus], — each one giving half of a shekel, and the total amounting to a hundred talents, as it is said, *And the silver of*

---

(17) Yerushalmi *ibid*. (18) A *sela* was the exact equivalent of the shekel that was in the days of Moses. Hence a *tiba* which is half a *sela* is the same as the half-shekel which the Torah commanded to be given by each Israelite. (19) There are four *denars* to a shekel [or *sela*]. Hence to give one *denar* only would be half of a half-shekel, and as will be explained further on that less than a half-shekel cannot be given. (20) According to the Yerushalmi the meaning of the verse (Nehemiah 10:33) is thus as follows: *"we made ordinances for us to charge ourselves* each *third part* of the year with *the shekel* mentioned in the Torah." For by law of the Torah they were enjoined to give it only once; but because the needs for the Temple repair were so great [as explained above], they took it voluntarily upon themselves to donate it three times a year. Since three *s'laim* [or shekels of the Torah] make one *daric*, it is now clear why the Mishnah quoted above states that when Israel came up from the exile they paid the shekel in *darics*, and as Ramban clearly states, "each one giving a *daric* " which was equivalent to three shekels of the Torah.

them that were numbered was a hundred talents etc. [21] The second [offering] was also levied through a census, for he counted them after the Tabernacle was erected, this being the census referred to in the Book of Numbers: *on the first day of the second month in the second year,* [22] each one giving a half-shekel for purchasing the public sacrifices. And if you ask: How is it possible that on both of these occasions the number of Israelites was exactly the same — 603,550? [23] Were these two censuses not taken in two [different] years; [24] thus it is impossible that there were no people aged nineteen at the time of the first census, [who accordingly were not counted], who became twenty years old [by the time the second census was taken, and thus must have added to the total]! The reply to this question is as follows: As far as the years of people's ages are concerned, the two censuses were taken in one year, but counting from the exodus from Egypt, they were held in two years. For when we count from the exodus from Egypt, we calculate from Nisan, but when we count the years of man's ages we count according to the era of the creation of the world, which begins with Tishri. In that way, the two censuses were in one year: the first census was in Tishri after the Day of Atonement, when the Holy One, blessed be He, became reconciled to Israel and they were commanded about the construction of the Tabernacle, and the second census took place [in the same year] on the first day of Iyar." All these are the Rabbi's words.

But I wonder! How is it possible that the number of deaths amongst such a great assemblage of people in a period of half a year did not run to the hundreds and thousands! For according to the words of the Rabbi [Rashi], they remained for about seven months [from about the middle of Tishri to the beginning of Iyar] without one fatality, and yet it is written, *But there were certain*

---

(21) Further, 38:25. (22) Numbers 1:1. (23) Further, 38:26. Numbers 1:46. (24) The first census was taken in the month of Tishri [after the Day of Atonement in the *first* year of the exodus]. The second census — on the first day of Iyar — was seven months later. But since we calculated the beginning of a new year [in the count after the exodus] with Nisan, the second census was therefore in the *second* year. Thus the two censuses were in two years!

EXODUS XXX, KI THISA

men, who were unclean by the dead body of a man.[25] I have also another difficulty: The years of men's ages are not counted according to the era of the creation of the world which begins with Tishri, but are counted in astronomical years beginning with the day of one's birth. It is for this reason that it says with reference to the people counted, that they are to be *from twenty years old and upward,*[26] meaning that they are to be a full twenty years old. Similarly, all countings of the Torah with respect to people's ages are calculated in astronomical years, just as the Rabbis have said in Tractate Arakhin:[27] "The 'year' mentioned in connection with the hallowed offerings,[28] and dwelling-houses in a walled city,[29] the two 'years' mentioned in connection with a field which is the owner's by inheritance [which, if sold, he may not redeem until after two years],[30] the six 'years' mentioned in connection with a Hebrew servant,[31] a son and daughter [explained further on], are all reckoned in astronomical years. Whence do we know this of the hallowed offerings? Scripture says, *keves ben shnatho*[28] [literally: "a lamb of his year"] — his year, and not the year counted according to the era of the creation of the world etc." Then [the Gemara] explains there: "In connection with what law does this principle affect 'the son and daughter' [mentioned above]? Said Rav Gidal, It is in connection with Valuations."[32] And the reason for this is because [in the case of Valuations] it says, *and upward,*[33] and in all censuses of the wilderness it is also written *and upward.*[34] The calculation of years

---

(25) Numbers 9:6. This happened in Nisan in the second year after the exodus. Thus it is clear that before the month of Iyar when the second census took place, there was at least one death in the camp. (26) *Ibid.*, 1:3. (27) Arakhin 18 b. (28) Such as *a he-lamb of the first year* (Leviticus 12:6). (29) If sold, these houses can be redeemed within the space of a full year (Leviticus 25:30). (30) Leviticus 25:15, and Arakhin 29 b. (31) Above, 21:2. (32) If a person vows to give to the Sanctuary his "Valuation," the sum is fixed by the Torah on the basis of years for a male and for a female (Leviticus 27:1-7). These years then are not counted according to the era of the creation of the world, but are calculated astronomically. (33) Leviticus 27:7: *And if it be from sixty years old and upward...* (34) Numbers 1:3: *from twenty years old and upward.* Similarly, *ibid.*, 26:2.

in the census taken in the wilderness was thus alike in every respect to the calculation in the Valuations, as the Rabbis have said in [Tractate] Baba Bathra:[35] "The analogy is established on the basis of the identical phrase *and upward* [which is stated in the censuses taken in the wilderness, and its precise meaning is] derived from that mentioned in the law of Valuations." And if so, all people born between Tishri and Iyar completed an astronomical year in the interim, thus between the two censuses there was bound to be a great number of people added to the total! But it would be more correct if we were to say that it so happened that the Israelites at the time of the first census [in Tishri] were 603,550 people, and in the following seven months many of them died, as is natural, and those who were twenty years old completed their twentieth year between Tishri and Iyar, and it so happened [36] that their number corresponded exactly to that of those who died.

In my opinion, however, these identical numbers [of the two censuses] present no difficulty at all. For in the first census the tribe of Levi was counted together with the other tribes, since they had not yet been selected and were therefore not separated from the people, but at the second census Moses was told, *Only thou shalt not number the tribe of Levi, and neither take the sum of them among the children of Israel.*[37] Now the number of those whose twentieth year was completed between the two censuses was close to twenty thousand[38] [thus making up for the tribe of Levi which was not counted in the second general census]. This is clearly established [that the tribe of Levi was counted in the first census]. For since Scripture found it necessary to say at the second census, *Only thou shalt not number the tribe of Levi, and neither take the sum of them,*[37] it is proof that until then they

---

(35) Baba Bathra 121 b. (36) By way of miracle (L'vush Ha'orah). (37) Numbers 1:49. (38) In the separate count that was taken of the Levites they numbered twenty-two thousand (*ibid.*, 3:39). But since they were numbered from the age of a month upward, Ramban rightly assumes that the Levites who were twenty years old and upward were "approximate to twenty thousand." Their numbers [not included in the figures of the second census], were made up by those Israelites who completed their twentieth year between the two censuses.

were counted with the other tribes of Israel; and only now was the tribe of Levi selected and numbered by itself, in order to become "the legion of the King." [39] Now when Israel left Egypt they were *'about' six hundred thousand 'g'varim' (men) on foot* [40] — not "six hundred thousand;" of these there died a number of people corresponding to the number of young men whose twentieth year was completed [in the next six months between the exodus, which was in the middle of Nisan, and the first census which was taken in the middle of Tishri, when the number was 603,550]. Perhaps the term *g'varim* [40] does not denote men of twenty years of age, but all those who had reached puberty — including all those from thirteen years old upwards — and that term [*g'varim*] is only used in order to exclude women and children, as it says, *beside little ones.* [40]

It also appears to me that of the three offerings here alluded to, the one designed for purchasing the public sacrifices is not the one taken through a census and mentioned in the Book of Numbers, as the Rabbi [Rashi] said, for there it is said, *Only thou shalt not count the tribe of Levi,* [37] and all the Sages agree that the Levites too were liable to give the shekels for the sacrifices; and in accordance with the words of the Sages, even the priests had to give it, [41] and such is the established law as is explained in Tractate Shekalim. [41] Moreover, the duty of giving the [half-] shekel for the sacrifices was not dependent upon a man being twenty years old or more, [as is mentioned in the case of the second census], but as soon as he could produce two [bottom] hairs he became liable to give the shekel. It is so clearly stated there [in Tractate Shekalim]. [42] Rather, Scripture commanded that they bring for the work of the Tabernacle an offering of a half-shekel, *every one that passeth among them that are numbered, from twenty years old and upward,* [4] and it hinted: *The rich shall not give more, and the poor shall not give less, than the half-shekel... to make atonement for your souls,* [43] for all who need atonement — that is, all who have

---

(39) Numbers 1:49, Rashi. (40) Above, 12:37. (41) Shekalim 1:4.
(42) *Ibid.*, 1:3. See also my Hebrew commentary p. 491. (43) Verse 15.

reached the stage of being obligated to observe the commandments [which is at thirteen years and a day, corresponding to the period of puberty], shall being one half-shekel for the sacrifices [in addition to the half-shekel given for the work of the Tabernacle].

13. HALF OF A SHEKEL AFTER THE SHEKEL OF HOLINESS. Moses our Teacher instituted a silver coin in Israel, for he was a great king.[44] He called it "shekel" [literally: "weight"] because that whole coin was a perfect weight, it had nothing defective in it and the silver contained no dross. And since the standard shekel of Valuations[32] and the redemption of the firstborn,[45] which are holy matters, were given in that coin, as also all shekels mentioned in connection with the Tabernacle, and all moneys the amount of which is exactly specified in the Torah,[46] therefore Scripture calls it *the shekel of holiness*.

I hold that this is the same reason why our Rabbis call the language of the Torah "the Sacred Language,"[47] because the words of the Torah, and the prophecies, and all words of holiness[48] were all expressed in that language. It is thus the language in which the Holy One, blessed be He, spoke with His prophets, and with His congregation [when He said], — *I am the Eternal thy G-d*, etc.[49] and *Thou shalt have no other gods before Me*,[50] and the other communications of the Torah and prophecy — and in that tongue He is called by His sacred names: *E-il, Elokim, Tze-baoth, Sha-dai, Ya-h,* and the Great Proper Name [i.e., the Tetragrammaton]. In that tongue He created His world,[51] and called the names *shamayim* (heavens),[52] *eretz* (earth)[53] and all that is in them, His angels and all His hosts — *He called them all by name*.[54] The names of Michael and Gabriel are in this Sacred

---

(44) See Deuteronomy 33:5. See also Ramban above, 15:25. (45) Numbers 18:16. (46) Such as thirty shekels if an ox kills a slave (above, 21:32), etc. (47) Sotah, 32 a. (48) A reference to the third section of the Bible which contains the Writings. (49) Above, 20:2. (50) *Ibid.*, Verse 3, and Makkoth 23 b. (51) Bereshith Rabbah 18:4. (52) Genesis 1:8. (53) *Ibid.*, Verse 10. (54) Isaiah 40:26.

Language.[55] In that language He called the names of *the holy ones that are in the earth:* [56] Abraham,[57] Isaac,[58] Jacob,[59] Solomon,[60] and others.[61]

Now the Rabbi [Moshe ben Maimon] has written in the Moreh Nebuchim:[62] "Do not think that our language is called the Sacred Language just as a matter of our pride, or it be an error on our part, but it is perfectly justified; for this holy language has no special names for the organs of generation in male or female, nor for semen, nor for urination or excretion, excepting in indirect language. Be not misled by the word *sheigal* [to take it to mean the act of intercourse; this is not the case,] but it rather denotes a female ready for intercourse. It says *yishgalenah*[63] in accordance with what has been written on it, and it means that 'he will take the woman as a concubine.' "[64] Now there is no need for this reason [why Hebrew is called the Sacred Language], for it is clear that the Hebrew language is most holy, as I have explained. And the reason [Rabbi Moshe ben Maimon] mentioned is in my opinion not correct. The mere fact that [the masters of the Masorah] have circumscribed the word *yishgalenah* [to be read as] *yishk'venah* (he will lie with her), shows that the word *mishgal* is the term for sexual intercourse itself. Similarly the fact that they circumscribed the expression, *to eat 'et choreihem'*[65] [to be read *eth tzo'atam* — "their dung"] shows that *choreihem* is an indecent

---

(55) Michael [*mi kamocha E-il*] signifies "who is like unto Thee, O G-d." Gabriel [*gabri E-il*] means "my strength is from G-d." (56) Psalms 16:3. (57) Genesis 17:5: *but thy name shall be Abraham, for the father of a multitude of nations have I made thee.* (58) Ibid., Verse 19: *and thou shalt call his name Isaac* [of the Hebrew root meaning "to laugh"]. (59) Ibid., 25:26: *and He called his name Jacob* ["one that takes by the heel"], the word *vayikra* (and He called) referring to G-d (Rashi quoting the Midrash). (60) II Samuel 12:25: *And he called his name Jedidiah, for the Eternal's sake.* (61) See I Kings 13:2: *Josiah will be his name.* (62) Guide of the Perplexed III, 8. Ramban is following the text of Al Charizi's translation [and not that of Ibn Tibbon]. (63) Deuteronomy 28:30. In Tibbon's translation there is here a completely different text. (64) I have found this interpretation in Jonah ibn Ganach's Sefer Hashorashim (under the root: *shin, gimmel, lamed*): "The most appropriate of the interpretations on it is that it is used in reference to a concubine." (65) II Kings 18:27.

term. And if the reason were indeed as the Rabbi [Moshe ben Maimon] has said, they should have called [the Hebrew language not "the Holy Language" but] "the modest langauge," similarly to that which we have been taught [in a Mishnah]: [66] "until he grows a beard — the lower one and not the upper one [is meant], except that the Sages spoke in modest language." The Rabbis have further said: [67] "*Save the bread which he did eat,*[68] — this is a refined expression [for it refers to his wife]," and so also in many places.

Now Scripture explained that *the shekel is twenty gerahs,* of silver. Onkelos translated gerahs as *mo'ah,* for the gerah was, in his opinion, a name for a coin which in Aramaic is called *mo'ah.* And so did Yonathan ben Uziel translate *la'agorath keseph* (a piece of silver):[69] *l'mo'ah d'chsaph* (for a *mo'ah* of silver). So also did Onkelos translate *after the shekel of holiness* as *sil'o,* for such is the name of the [shekel] coin in Aramaic, and its measure is also known in the Talmud.

Rashi wrote:[70] "A shekel weighs four gold coins, making half an ounce according to the correct weight of Cologne." Now when the Rabbi [Rashi] found it clearly written in the Gemara [71] that a [silver] *sela* [which is equivalent to the shekel] is four [silver] *denars,* he deduced [that a gold shekel is also equivalent to four gold *denars*], for the weight of the silver *denars* is as the weight of the gold *denars.* Thus he wrote in his commentary to the Gemara of Baba Kamma:[72] "A [silver] *denar* weighs as much as a gold [*denar*], and in Constantinople they even call the gold coin *denar.*" All this is correct. But as to the Rabbi's estimation, that in terms of the gold coins found in his generation and in our generation the shekel is equivalent to half an ounce, as he mentioned — that is not so, for the kings of the peoples have lessened [the weight of] the gold coins. We find it already mentioned in the words of the author of Hilchoth Gedoloth [73] and

---

(66) Sanhedrin 68 b.   (67) Bereshith Rabbah 86:6.   (68) Genesis 39:6.
(69) I Samuel 2:36.   (70) In *Seder Mishpatim* 21:32.   (71) Baba Metzia 34 b; Shebuoth 43 a.   (72) Baba Kamma 36 b.   (73) See in *Seder Mishpatim* Note 70.

EXODUS XXX, KI THISA 521

the first Gaonim,[74] that the *denar* mentioned throughout the Talmud is the *denar shashdang*,[75] and it is so written in Tractate Kiddushin in the Halachoth (Laws) of our Rabbi [Rabbi Yitzchak Alfasi] who said that "[the *zuz*[76] *shashdang*] is the gold *denar* of the Arabs." Now according to these estimations found in the words [of the Hilchoth Gedoloth and the Halachoth of Alfasi], the *denars* of the Talmud were larger than the gold coins current in our times by almost a third, and the shekel weighed three fourths of an ounce according to the weight of that country [and not as Rashi wrote that the shekel weighed four gold coins, making *half* an ounce etc.], and that is "the ounce" that the Rabbi [Rashi], of blessed memory, mentioned.[77]

Know that the shekels [mentioned in] the Torah are these *s'laim* [mentioned in the Talmud], each *sela* being four *denars*. But the shekel mentioned in the words of the Sages — such as that which we have been taught in a Mishnah:[78] ["if a man lent his fellow money on a pledge, and the pledge was lost, and the borrower said,] 'You have lent me a shekel on it and it was worth a *sela* [and therefore you owe me two *denars*],' or [the lender said,] 'I lent you a *sela* on it and it was worth a shekel [and therefore you still owe me two *denars*]' " — [this shekel] is two *denars*, half of a *sela*. The reason for this [change in the meaning of the term shekel — the shekel of the Torah being four *denars* whilst the shekel of the Sages is two *denars*], is that the people called the half-*s'laim* [which were each two *denars*] "shekels," since they used them every year to pay the [half-] shekel to the

---

(74) Following the close of the Talmud [in the year 500 of the Common Era] the recognized spiritual heads of Jewry were the heads of the Sura and Pumbeditha academies in Babylon. The recipients and interpreters of the traditions of the Rabbis of the Talmud, the Gaonim were active for over a period of five hundred years — during the height of the Moslem empires. (75) A small coin (Kohut, Aruch Hashalem). (76) A *zuz* is the same as a *denar* (ibid., *zuz*). (77) At this point see the Addendum which Ramban added to the end of his commentary after he arrived at Acco and found some ancient Hebrew coins which when he weighed them he found that the result corroberated Rashi's explanation. (78) Shebuoth 43 a.

Sanctuary. And so it was adopted by the Sages in the style of the Mishnah. Therefore a man would say to his friend, "You have lent me a shekel," that is, the "shekel" which Israelites give to the Sanctuary. [79] It is possible that in the time of the Second Sanctuary they actually made a silver coin of two denars, so that it should be available to be given to the Temple treasurer, and they would not have to give an allowance [for exchanging the full shekel of the Torah into two half-shekels]. That coin they called "shekel," and the shekel of Moses which is the shekel of the Torah they called *sela,* as Onkelos translated it. Some scholars [80] say that the reason [they called the shekel of Moses *sela*] is because of what the Rabbis have said:[81] "The maneh [82] of the Sanctuary was double [as much as the common maneh]," and so also were all the coins. But this is not correct, for the [thirty] shekels that the owner of an ox who killed a slave must pay [83] and the [fifty] shekels that the violator [84] and seducer [85] must pay, were not connected with the Sanctuary.

15. THE RICH SHALL NOT GIVE MORE, AND THE POOR SHALL NOT GIVE LESS. The meaning of this is that they should all bring the specified amount of money in equality. It would appear from this verse that if the poor man gave as his shekel-dues less than the half-shekel [prescribed by the Torah], he transgresses this negative commandment, since this verse constitutes a prohibition. For even if we were to say that the phrase *the rich shall not give more* constitutes a mere negation,[86] meaning that it is enough for him to give the half-shekel, we could not so interpret *and the poor shall not give less.* If so, they must both be

---

(79) Thus the shekel of the Torah is really four *denars,* but since the Torah enjoined the giving of a half-shekel, that half-shekel came to be called "shekel," as that was the coin the people gave yearly to the Sanctuary, and hence the Sages adopted the usage of that term — so that when people say "shekel" they really mean a coin worth two *denars.* (80) I have not identified them. (81) Bechoroth 5 a. (82) The maneh is a weight equal to the sixtieth part of a talent. (83) Above, 21:32. (84) Deuteronomy 22:29. (85) Above, 22:16. See Ramban here. (86) See in *Seder Mishpatim,* Note 71.

prohibitions: thus if the individual rich man gave more, or the poor man gave less, he transgressed this negative commandment. Perhaps the reason why the Temple-officers used to take up the shekel-dues in baskets [out of the shekel-chamber], with the intention also to cover the shekels lost and those still to be collected, [87] was to rectify this matter, for if the poor gave less, the balance was destined to be collected from him, but as for the rich who gave more, the Temple-officers would not "take up" his surplus, for they would not take possession of these surpluses [on anyone's behalf]. However, I have noticed that neither the author of the Hilchoth Gedoloth nor all other scholars who counted the commandments [including the Rambam in his Sefer Hamitzvoth], have mentioned this as one of the negative commandments.

19. AND AARON AND HIS SONS SHALL WASH THEIR HANDS AND THEIR FEET THEREAT. This washing was out of reverence for Him Who is on high, for whoever approaches the King's table to serve, or to touch *the portion of the king's food, and of the wine which he drinks,* [88] washes his hands, because "hands are busy" [89] [touching unclean things automatically]. In addition He prescribed here the washing of feet because the priests performed the Service barefooted, and there are some people who have impurities and dirt on their feet.

By way of the Truth, [the mystic teachings of the Cabala], these parts of the body had to be washed because the extremities of the person's body are his hands and feet, for when the hands are upraised they are higher than the rest of the body, and the feet

---

(87) Kethuboth 108 a. When the shekels were collected they were put in a chamber. Three times in the year the officers of the Temple would take up three basketfuls out of the chamber for the purpose of purchasing the public sacrifices. And in order to cover every Jew, even those living in the remote parts of the Diaspora, [whose shekel contribution has not arrived yet], or to cover anyone whose shekel was lost, the officers in taking up the shekels would do it also on behalf of those people whose shekels were lost and those whose shekels were yet to arrive. Ramban on the basis of the verse before us suggests an additional reason for this procedure. (88) Daniel 1:5. (89) Succah 26 b.

are the lowest point. They allude in the human form to the Ten Emanations, with the whole body between them, just as the Rabbis have said in Sefer Yetzirah:[90] "He made a covenant with him [i.e., Abraham] between the ten fingers of his hands and the ten fingers of his feet, with the protrusive part of the tongue and with the protrusive part of the nakedness." Therefore the ministers of the One on High were commanded to wash their hands and feet, this washing being for the sake of holiness, as Onkelos translated here, *l'rochtzah* (to wash): *l'kidush* (to sanctify).[91] It is on the basis of the idea of this commandment that our Rabbis have instituted the washing of hands before prayer,[92] in order that one should direct one's thoughts to this matter, just as in the uplifting of hands by the priests when blessing the people.[93]

It is the washing which is the essence of the commandment, but He commanded [the making of] the laver only in order that the water should be ready in it. Thus the absence of the laver does not invalidate the washing, neither is there any duty [to do the washing specifically from the laver]; thus on the Day of Atonement the High Priest washed his hands and feet from a golden jug[94] which they made in his honor. However, what we do learn from the laver [that the Torah mentions], is that the washing [of the hands and feet by the priests] must be performed from a vessel.

23. 'MOR DROR' (FLOWING MYRRH) FIVE HUNDRED SHEKELS. The commentators[95] — including Harav Rabbi Moshe [ben Maimon][96] — have agreed that *mor* is that perfume which is

---

(90) Sefer Yetzirah (Book of Creation), 6:4. (91) But in all other places (such as Genesis 18:4) Onkelos renders the term *rochtzah* (washing) literally. (92) Berachoth 60 b. (93) When reciting the Benediction for the washing of hands one must lift up the hands. This is comparable to the raising of the hands of the priests in order to bring down the blessings from on High; so also the washer raises his hands for that purpose. (94) Yoma 43 b. (95) Ibn Ezra quoting Rabbeinu Saadia Gaon. (96) Mishneh Torah, *Hilchoth Klei Hamikdash*, 1:3: "*Mor* is the blood gathered up [in the abdomen] of a certain animal in the land of India known to all, which is used in perfumery."

called musk [an animal perfume]. [97] But Rabbi Abraham ibn Ezra objected to this interpretation, since [musk] is not a spice [as are *the sweet cinnamon* and *the sweet calamus* mentioned here in the same verse], even though it has a pleasing odor. Perhaps this is why Scripture separated it from the spices." And then [Ibn Ezra] asked: "But is it not written, *I have gathered 'mori' (my myrrh)*, [98] which shows that *mor* is something gathered [like spices], while those who bring musk say that it is a substance gathered in a glandular sac under the skin of the neck of the deer? [99] Moreover, the verse states, *and my hands dropped with myrrh*, [100] [and musk does not drop]. But perhaps it does do so, due to its moistness." [Thus far are Ibn Ezra's words].

It is possible that we say that Scripture states *I have gathered 'mori'* [98] because *mor* is the blood gathered up in the abdomen of an animal of the hind species known in the land of India; when it walks between the shrubs on very hot days it scratches against the sac and the blood comes out in thickened mass, which is then gathered from the reed-grass. It states *and my hands dropped 'mor,'* [100] because Scripture imagines its odor to be such that one's hands drop globules of water because of it.

Others [101] have argued: how could there be included in the incense [102] and the sacred oil the blood of an unclean animal? This too is no question, for that moisture gathered up in the animal because of its abundant blood, which drops from [the animal] whilst still alive, is not susceptible to uncleanness, nor is it repulsive.

---

(97) See Jastrow: *muskin* and *mor*. (98) Song of Songs 5:1. (99) In other words, this proves that *mor* is not musk as Saadia Gaon said, for the verse speaks of *mor* being gathered while musk is not "gathered." (100) Song of Songs 5:5. (101) Reference is to Rabbi Abraham ben David [Rabad] who commented on Rambam's language (see Note 96): "My opinion does not accept this, that there should enter into sacred things the blood of any animal in the world, and all the more the blood of an unclean animal." (102) Among the eleven components of the incense was *'mor'* (myrrh, cassia, spikenard etc.) (Kerithoth 6 a).

The word *dror* they [103] have explained to be of the expression, *and ye shall proclaim 'dror' (liberty)*, [104] here meaning that it should be free from any imitation or adulteration. Perhaps we might say that Scripture requires it to be gathered when free, meaning that it should be taken from that deer whilst it is free, wandering between the beds of spices and enjoying itself at will, because once it is captured and held in the possession of man, it produces but little *mor* (musk) and it does not have such a pleasant odor. This is clear.

Yet despite all this [that we have written to justify the opinion of Rabbeinu Saadia Gaon and Rabbi Moshe ben Maimon, that *mor* mentioned here is musk], it appears to me from the words of our Rabbis that *mor* is not musk, for they have said in Midrash Chazita: [105] "*Mor* [106] means *inmirinon*" [an unguent scented with Arabian myrtle], while musk is so called even in the language of the Sages, just as it is said in Tractate Berachoth: [107] ["Over all spices put on coals one recites the Benediction: 'Blessed... Who createst diverse kinds of spices'], except over musk, because it is derived from an animal." In the Yerushalmi there [108] they likewise say, [with respect to this Benediction]: "excepting *muskin*," and the author of the Aruch [109] wrote that it is also so called in Greek. In Midrash Chazita it furthermore says: [110] "*My beloved is unto me a bag of 'hamor'* [111] — this refers to Abraham. Just as the *mor* is the chief of all kinds of spices, [112] so was

---

(103) R'dak, in his Book of Roots, under the root of *dror*. (104) Leviticus 25:10. (105) Shir Hashirim Rabbah 4:29. See Vol. I, p. 292, Note 73, for explanation of the name "Chazita." (106) Song of Songs 4:14. (107) Berachoth 43 a. (108) Yerushalmi Berachoth VI, 6. (109) Rabbi Nathan ben Yechiel of Rome [flourished in the middle of the eleventh century] was a contemporary of Rashi. His work the "Aruch" is not only a complete dictionary of Talmudic and Midrashic language but is also a veritable storehouse of explanations of Rabbinic texts. It is thus both a dictionary and commentary. It has had a lasting influence on Jewish learning. — The particular reference here is to the Aruch, under the term: *mushk*. (110) Shir Hashirim Rabbah 1:58. (111) Song of Songs 1:13. (112) Ramban will further on explain that the intent thereof is, that in the verse before us where the spices [for the making of the Oil of Anointment] are listed, the myrrh heads the list, or it may mean that for aromatic purposes it is the best of all spices.

EXODUS XXX, KI THISA

Abraham the chief of all righteous people. Just as this *mor* exudes only through the fire, so Abraham's deeds were not known until he was thrown in the fiery furnace.[113] And just as with this *mor* [we see that] whoever gathers it with his hands develops bad sores, so did Abraham cause himself to be distressed and afflicted with suffering" [for the sake of his love of G-d.] Now the musk exudes its odor [spontaneously], without being put upon the flame! Moreover, we have been taught [in a Mishnah]:[114] "These interpose in vessels:[115] pitch and *mor* etc. on a packsaddle. Rabban[116] Shimon ben Gamaliel says: [They interpose only] if they are as big as an Italian *issar* [a Roman coin]." And it further teaches there:[117] "This is the general principle: Anything about which a person is particular, interposes [and invalidates the immersion]; anything about which he is not particular that does not interpose." Now musk is not something which sticks [to a vessel or to a garment] so that it should interpose [and invalidate the immersion, and so, if *mor* is musk, why does the Mishnah state that it does interpose]! And even if perhaps they fix it in such a way that it does attach to vessels, a person is not particular about it, so that it should interpose even on a packsaddle! Moreover, the verse *'mor va'aholoth k'tzioth' are all thy garments*[118] [Yonathan ben Uziel] translated: *'mura,' aloe-wood and cassia.* [Thus it is clear that *mor* is not musk, for *mura* is myrrh.]

It is likely that *mor* is so called in Arabic as there are diverse kinds of it — *mur achmar ve'abitz*. It is used for incense, and when burned produces a sweet odor. Thus all languages — Hebrew, Aramaic, and also Arabic — are alike in the usage of this term. And in the language of the Agadah [quoted above][119] — be it Persian or Greek[120] — it is a similar expression: *inmirinon*. In Latin as well it is called *myrrha*. The consensus of the languages

---

(113) See Vol. I, p. 160. (114) Mikvaoth 9:5. (115) When immersing an unclean vessel in an Immersion-pool to be cleansed, for the immersion to be valid there must be nothing interposing between the body's surface and the water of the pool. (116) The title "Rabban" [instead of "Rabbi"] signifies that he was the *Nasi* (Prince) of the Sanhedrin. (117) Mikvaoth 9:7. (118) Psalms 45:9. (119) See the text from the Midrash Chazita, at Note 105. (120) In Kohut's Aruch Hashalem [and in Jastrow's Dictionary] *inmirinon* is explained as a word of Greek origin.

on this term would thus indicate that [the *mor* of the Torah] is indeed that substance [called myrrh or its equivalent in the above-mentioned languages — and not the musk mentioned by Saadia Gaon], and it is counted among the spices.

And as to that which the Rabbis said above, [121] that "the *mor* is the chief of all kinds of spices," they mean that [in the verse before us where the spices are listed] the Torah mentioned it first, or it may mean that for aromatic purposes it is the best of all spices. Possibly amongst its diverse kinds there may be a still more aromatic one, and that is called *dror,* and the one who gathers it [as the Midrash quoted above said], develops bad sores on his hands, because it is bitter as wormwood. And the Rabbis have taught in the Sifra: [122] "Things which cannot be recognized, such as a mixture of water into wine, or of gum in myrrh," for this is how they falsify the myrrh, by putting into it a certain gum which resembles it, called *tzemeg* in Arabic. This is why He said *mor dror,* meaning that it be clear of any of these usual adulterations. It is possible that the term *dror* always indicates "clean" (or "pure"). Similarly, *and ye shall proclaim 'dror' throughout the land unto all the inhabitants thereof,* [104] means that all people of the land be "clean" from servitude, and from all subjection attaching to their persons or lands, similar to the expression, *and the owner of the ox shall be quit.*[123] And as to that which Scripture says, *And my hands dropped with 'mor', and my fingers with flowing 'mor,'* [100] it is possible that the meaning is as follows: "and my hands dropped with *oil* of myrrh," for it is customary to apply it also to the hands in order to make them gentle and soft, as it is written, *six months with oil of myrrh,*[124] which our Rabbis have explained to be: "the oil of olives that have not reached a third of their growth, because that makes the hair fall out and improves the complexion." And the purport thereof is that that oil was prepared with myrrh and therefore it was so called ["oil of myrrh"]. This then is the meaning of *'natphu'*

---

(121) See the text from Midrash Chazita mentioned above at Note 110. (122) Sifra, *Vayikra Chova* 22:7. (123) Above, 21:18. (124) Esther 2:12.

(dropped with) 'mor', [100] [the dropping being not from the myrrh but from the oil put in it]. I hold this to be the *inmirinon* mentioned in the Midrash [quoted above, [105] namely that it is identical with *the oil of myrrh* mentioned in the Scroll of Esther], for similarly the Rabbis in the Yerushalmi [125] call "oil of *v'rad*" (roses): *vardinun* [and in the same way they called "the oil of *mor*" — *inmirinon*]. Such is the customary usage for names of oils in the various languages of the nations. [Finally,] it is also possible that they extract oil from the myrrh, as is done with gum mastic and other kinds of gums. Thus it is correct to call it "myrrh," and "oil of myrrh."

'V'KINMON BESEM' (AND OF CINNAMON SPICE) HALF SO MUCH. "Since cinnamon is the bark of a tree [and it is of two kinds], one which has a good taste and fragrance, whilst the other is just like [any other] wood, therefore Scripture had to say: *kinmon besem* — of the good kind." This is Rashi's language. And Harav Rabbi Moshe [ben Maimon] said [126] that it is *"kesher salichah."* [127] Other scholars [128] hold that it is that precious tree called *itib*. But none of these interpretations is correct, for the Rabbis have said in Bereshith Rabbah [129] and in Midrash Chazita: [130] " '*kinmon*' grew in the Land of Israel, and goat and deer ate of it." Thus it is like the grass of the field from which the sheep pasture. In my opinion *kinmon besem* is the aromatic grass called in Arabic *adbar*, and in Latin *ascinant*, [131] which is an

---

(125) Yerushalmi Demai I, 3. (126) In his commentary to the Mishnah, at the beginning of Tractate Kerithoth. See, however, in my Hebrew commentary p. 497, Note 8, that this definition that Ramban quotes in the name of Rambam on *kinmon besem*, is in our texts of Rambam's commentary found on a different name altogether. The term mentioned here is in Arabic since Rambam wrote his commentary to the Mishnah in Arabic. See also following note. (127) In Joseph Kapach's new Hebrew translation of Rambam's commentary in Arabic, he comments on this term that it is "Cinnamonum Zeylanicum" (Kerithoth, p. 229, Note 49). (128) Mentioned by Ibn Ezra [in his short commentary on Exodus] in the name of Rabbeinu Saadia Gaon. (129) Bereshith Rabbah 65:13. (130) Shir Hashirim Rabbah 4:29. See Vol. I, p. 277. (131) See Dictionary under "ascidium."

important spice, called in the vernacular, *saika domika,* and where it grows it is used as fodder for camels. Our Rabbi [Yitzchak Alfasi] wrote in [his Halachoth on Tractate] Pesachim,[132] [in connection with the spices put into *charoseth* in memory of the straw from which the Israelites in Egypt made the bricks]: "such as *kinmon* and *sanbal,* which are similar to straw."

Kidah[133] is known from the Aramaic language, [as Onkelos rendered it] *k'tziah* (cassia). It is also so in Arabic.

25. AND THOU SHALT MAKE IT A HOLY ANOINTING OIL, A PERFUME COMPOUNDED AFTER THE ART OF THE PERFUMER. In line with the simple meaning of Scripture, the preparation of the Oil of Anointment was in accordance with the view of Rabbi Yehudah, who said [134] that they first soaked the spices in water in order that they would not absorb the oil which was poured upon them Now this soaking [of which Rabbi Yehuda speaks] was not mere soaking in water alone. Rather, they put ground spices in a vessel full of water and then they poured upon them *a hin of olive oil.* [135] Then they placed this vessel upon another vessel full of water, and put it over a low flame with embers, and boiled it until the water [in the upper vessel] evaporated, and they retained the oil which was upon it. Such indeed is the way that perfumers make all aromatic oils. This is why Scripture shortened the explanation and commanded merely that they make this oil *a perfume compounded after the art of the perfumer,* without explaining the process by which it is to be made, for the way of the perfumers was known among them. And so I found in Tractate Shekalim of the Yerushalmi:[136] "Rabbi Yehudah says: They boiled [the spices] in water and put the oil on top of it; as soon as [the oil] retained the odor [of the spices] they would take off the oil, just as druggists do, for it is said, *And thou shalt make it a holy anointing oil, a perfume compounded after the art of the perfumer."*

(132) In the Chapter *Arbei Pesachim.* (133) Mentioned in Verse 24. (134) Kerithoth 5 a. (135) Verse 24. (136) Yerushalmi Shekalim VI, 1.

EXODUS XXX, KI THISA

33. OR WHOSOEVER PUTTETH ANY OF IT UPON A 'ZAR'... — "When it is not required [for anointing a person] into the [high-] priesthood or kingship." This is Rashi's language. But Rabbi Abraham ibn Ezra retorted that *zar* in this connection means anyone who is not of the seed of Aaron and his sons mentioned, [137] just like the verse, *and the 'zar' that draweth nigh shall be put to death*, [138] which means any stranger not included in those mentioned. Similarly: *There shall no 'zar' eat of the holy thing*, [139] [which means anyone not of the seed of Aaron]; *to the end that no 'zar' that is not of the seed of Aaron, draw near...* [140] It is for this reason that [Ibn Ezra] thought that the anointing of Solomon [141] which was done by Zadok [the priest] taking *the horn of oil out of the Tent*, [141] — which refers to the Oil of Anointment [which Moses prepared] — was a special, temporary decree by authority of prophecy [permitting the oil to be used upon one who was not of the seed of Aaron]. But this is not the opinion of our Rabbis. [142]

And I say that [the opinion of our Rabbis is borne out by the language of the verse]. For Scripture states, *This shall be a holy anointing oil unto Me throughout your generations,* [143] and it would have been correct if it were to say instead, "This shall be a holy anointing oil for Aaron and his sons throughout their generations," just as He said in the case of the garments, *And the holy garments of Aaron shall be for his sons after him;* [144] or that

---

(137) For since He mentioned first (in Verse 30): *And thou shalt anoint Aaron and his sons*, it follows that the expression, *or whosoever putteth any of it upon a 'zar'* means that anyone who is not of the seed of Aaron is a *zar* (a stranger). So why did Rashi say that the oil may also be used for the anointing of a king? (138) Numbers 1:51. "*Shall be put to death* — by the hand of Heaven" (Rashi). (139) Leviticus 22:10. (140) Numbers 17:5. (141) I Kings 1:39. (142) For according to the Talmud (Kerithoth 5 b) every High Priest who would be appointed was to be anointed with this oil, as were also some of the kings. Generally an heir to the throne of Israel did not have to be anointed, though in order to avoid disputes over the royal succession [as was the case with Solomon] anointing was resorted to. See further on this topic "The Commandments," Vol. I, p. 45. (143) Verse 31. (144) Above, 29:29.

He say, "And thou shalt anoint Aaron and his sons, and sanctify them, that they may minister unto Me, and it shall be a statute forever to them throughout their generations." But now that He mentioned only them, [*And Aaron and his sons thou shalt anoint*] and then continued by saying that it should not be put upon any *zar*, it could mean that [the prohibition extends] to all people [even High Priests after Aaron] except those mentioned specifically [i.e., Aaron and his sons]! Similarly He said, *Upon the flesh of man shall it not be poured*,[145] [which might be taken to mean upon anyone's flesh — even that of the High Priests after Aaron], and yet Scripture explicitly states, *And the anointed priest that shall be in his* [Aaron's] *stead, from among his sons!* [146] But such is the explanation: He commanded that at the moment Aaron and his sons should be anointed with this oil, and then He continued, *This shall be a holy anointing oil unto Me*,[143] — to anoint with it My holy anointed ones whom I will choose — *throughout your generations*,[143] and it shall not be put upon a *zar* (stranger) whom I have not designated unto Me. It is for this reason that kings and High Priests were anointed with this oil, for both of them are "the anointed ones of G-d." Thus it is written, *I have found David My servant; with My holy oil have I anointed him* [147] — meaning, with the oil which is *the holy anointing oil unto Me*. And the meaning of the verse, *Upon the flesh of man shall it not be poured*,[145] is as an admonition to all men [even to Aaron and his sons after they have been anointed with it], since He did not say, "upon the flesh of a *zar* shall it not be poured." Thus the purport thereof is that he [Moses] is to pour of the oil upon Aaron's head in order to anoint him, and then he is to anoint also his sons, but he is not to pour this oil upon any man, even upon the anointed priests, merely as people apply good oils to their bodies in order to scent themselves with hands soaked in

---

(145) Verse 32. (146) Leviticus 6:15. This shows that it is impossible to say that the High Priests after Aaron should not be anointed with this oil. And if so, the question appears why did Scripture use here language which might indicate the opposite, as explained above? But such is the explanation etc. (147) Psalms 89:21.

EXODUS XXX, KI THISA

oil, after bathing, something like it is said, *Wash thyself and anoint thee;*[148] *Then I washed thee with water... and I anointed thee with oil.*[149] This is the plain meaning of the verse and its intention. And so did our Rabbis say:[150] "How do we know that if the High Priest took some of the oil of anointment which was upon his head and put it upon his stomach, that he is liable [to punishment]? Scripture therefore says, *Upon the flesh of man shall it not be poured.*"[145]

34. TAKE UNTO THEE 'SAMIM' (AROMATICS), STACTE, AND ONYCHA, AND GALBANUM; 'SAMIM' (AROMATICS) WITH PURE FRANKINCENSE. Rabbi Abraham ibn Ezra commented that by way of the plain meaning of Scripture the interpretation of the verse is: "take unto you the aromatics which are stacte, onycha and galbanum; these spices [you are to take], and pure frankincense with them." But it is not correct that Scripture should just repeat the word *samim* [in such a short verse], for it is not the normal way of Scripture to repeat words unless there is some lengthy interpolation[151] or in order to indicate that it is a continuing thing.[152] The truth is as our Rabbis have said,[153] that the second word *samim* refers to other aromatics.

Now Rashi wrote: "*'Samim'* — the least number of aromatics implied by the plural form of this word is two. *Stacte, and onycha, and galbanum,* make together five. *'Samim'* adds a similar number to those already prescribed, thus making ten. *With frankincense,* makes eleven [altogether]."

But one wonders! Why did Scripture not mention them explicitly? Perhaps Scripture is saying: *"Take unto thee aromatics, stacte, and onycha, and galbanum,* many *aromatics with pure frankincense,"* thus insisting only on these four spices, for they were the ones that caused *the cloud of* the smoke of *the incense*[154] to ascend; but He commanded that they add to them

---

(148) Ruth 3:3. (149) Ezekiel 16:9. (150) Kerithoth 7 a. (151) See Ramban above, 4:9. (152) See Ramban above, 15:6. (153) Kerithoth 6 b. (154) Leviticus 16:13.

many other aromatic spices in order that the pillars of smoke [of the incense] should be fragrant. This is why He did not explain [in the case of the incense] the weight of each component [as He did in the case of the Oil of Anointment], nor how much of it should be burnt [daily], since He insisted only that these four [spices mentioned] should be alike [in weight], and that he should add to them other good spices for the burning. The reason for this is that just as He had said with reference to the Oil of Anointment that they make it in accordance with the art of the perfumer, and did not specify how it was to be made but relied upon it [that they knew how to make it], so He said in respect of this incense that he take an equal weight of these four [mentioned] aromatics, and add to them other aromatics and make out of all the components one incense, done *after the art of the perfumer*,[155] [which implies by] using spices known to blend well with these [four] and by preparing them through the process by which they are usually prepared. It is of this incense that he had to put before the Testimony,[156] so that its pillar of smoke should go up, as was the custom to put spices on coals before kings. In the same way He shortened the account of how to make the incense, and did not mention it when He referred to all the other spices. In a similar vein the Rabbis have said in the Gemara:[153] "Resh Lakish said: What is the meaning of the word *k'toreth*? It is something which circles and rises."[157] Thus the Torah only commanded in connection with the incense to use those spices the smoke of which circles and rises, in a way similar to the art of the perfumers. Perhaps it was explained to Moses on Sinai by word of mouth which spices are best for that purpose, as well as the whole process of making the incense, for the process of making the Oil of Anointment was likewise explained to him in this manner, even though Scripture made it dependent upon the art of the perfumers. Or it may be that He insisted only on those [four spices] expressly mentioned in the verse, commanding that he perfume them with

(155) Verse 35. (156) Verse 36. (157) The word *k'toreth* (incense) is thus of the root *kateir* (surrounding, circling), because the smoke of the burning incense circles and rises.

EXODUS XXX, KI THISA 535

other spices after the art of the perfumers. And so the Rabbis have said in Midrash Chazit:[158] "The Sages investigated and found no more fitting components for the incense than those eleven spices."

It is also possible that *samim* (aromatics) and *b'samim* (spices) denote the same thing, as I have mentioned,[159] and these three components[160] which He specified are not spices, for *'nataph'* and *'chel'bnah'* are saps, and *shcheileth* is the onycha which comes from the ocean.[161] And Scripture states: "Take unto you the mentioned *samim* [i.e., all components mentioned above[162] in the preparation of the Oil of Anointment — namely, the flowing myrrh, the cinnamon, the calamus, and the cassia — as all these *b'samim* also went into the incense, as will be explained], and the *nataph*, and *shcheileth* and the *chel'bnah*, and other *samim* [in addition, as will be explained], with pure frankincense, and make of them a perfumed incense, after the art of the perfumer." For the *samim* mentioned above in connection with the Oil [of Anointment] — flowing myrrh, cinnamon, and cassia — also went into the incense. And the *knei bosem* [mentioned among the components of the oil][163] is in my opinion the *kiluphah* mentioned by the Sages,[164] called *dratzini* in Arabic, and so also in the language of the Gemara,[165] which is a cane [of sweet spices] resembling reeds. And the *samim* which He commanded to add [to all those mentioned above] are: spikenard and saffron and the costus, in accordance with that which the Sages have taught.[164] Perhaps Scripture only insisted on these nine[166] which

---

(158) Shir Hashirim Rabbah 3:7. (159) Above 25:6. (160) I.e., *Nataph ushcheileth v'chel'bnah'* These are generally translated as being various kinds of fragrant spices: "stacte, and onycha, and galbanum." But Ramban will now question the two terms [stacte and galbanum]. (161) Onycha... supposed to be the operculum of a marine gastropod (Dictionary). (162) Above, Verses 23-24. (163) Verse 23. Generally translated "sweet calamus." (164) Kerithoth 6 a. (165) Shabbath 65 a. In connection with what is taught in the Mishnah there that a woman may go out on the Sabbath with "anything that she puts in her mouth" [to have a good breath], the Gemara explained, "such as *dartzuna*," which Rashi explained as "cinnamon." (166) "Nine." The reading should be "eight" (as explained above): the four

He mentioned, but was not particular as to [the nature of] those included by means of the repetition of the word *samim*, except inasmuch as they are to be sweet, so that they may make a perfumed incense. Thus He shortened the account of the making thereof, as well as of the weights of the other components [except for the four mentioned in the making of the oil, where the weights are prescribed], [162] because He commanded that they make it *after the art of the perfumer.*

It appears to me that the Sages chose three spices [spikenard, saffron, and costus] because they are mentioned in the Song of Songs: *Spikenard and saffron... and 'oholoth,'* [167] which is the costus. Its name is in the plural from [*oholoth*] because there are two kinds of it, the sweet and the bitter. Now Scripture mentioned there, *calamus and cinnamon... frankincense,* and *myrrh* [167] together with these three [spikenard, saffron, and costus], and then said, *with 'all' the chief spices,* so as to include cassia. Thus you have there all [168] the components of the incense. Now before that Scripture mentioned there: *'k'pharim im n'radim' (henna with spikenard plants).* [169] This is to include *nataph ushcheileth v'chel'bnah* [mentioned here in the verse] which are saps, for *k'pharim* is of the root *'v'chapharta othah' (and thou shalt pitch it),* [170] it being an adhesive sap. And the Targum Yerushalmi rendered: *myrrh and 'oholoth'* [167] — [pure myrrh and] *aksi lalu'an,* [171] which is that precious tree called in Latin *linga lubin* as *aksi* means "tree" in Aramaic, and *lalu'an* is the name of the

---

components mentioned in the making of the Oil of Anointment [myrrh, cinnamon, *kanah* — the cane of sweet spice — and cassia], and the four expressly stated in the making of the incense [*nataph, shcheileth, chel'bnah,* and frankincense]. With the three components [spikenard, saffron, and costus] added by the second word *samim* they form the eleven components of the incense. (167) Song of Songs 4:14. (168) I.e., eight components: spikenard, saffron, costus, calamus, cinnamon, frankincense, myrrh, and cassia. Three more will follow. Thus Ramban found the eleven components of the incense mentioned in the Song of Songs. (169) Song of Songs 4:13. (170) Genesis 6:14. (171) "A tree of bitter aloe wood." Ramban will further on explain that *aksi* means tree. See also Jastrow under the term *aksiloliyon.*

tree. In Greek it is actually so called: *aksiluin,* [172] and so it is called in Arabic — *al urtib.* But Onkelos rendered: *'ka'aholim' planted of the Eternal* [173] — *k'busmaya* (as spices), without specifying a particular name [for *oholim,* as did the Targum Yerushalmi mentioned above].

'NATAPH' — is *tzori* (balsam). Now in Rashi's commentary it is written: "The balm itself is called *triga,* [174] but because it is merely the sap which 'drips' from the wood of the balsam it is called *nataph* (dripping)." But I do not know whether this is the scribe's mistake, or the one who so told Rashi misinformed him. For theriac [the *triga* mentioned by Rashi] is not one ingredient but is a compound of many ingredients, containing leaven and honey, the flesh of forbidden animals and reptiles, for the powder of dried scorpions and the flesh of the viper go into it, this being the reason why it is so called [theriac], for "poison" in Greek is called *theriac.* So also in the language of the Talmud: [175] *"Torkai* (stung by) a serpent." Similarly this compound is mentioned in the language [of the Rabbis]: [176] "as theriac is good for the whole body." And Heaven forbid that there should be in the incense the flesh of forbidden animals and reptiles, leaven and honey, for it is written, *for ye shall make no leaven, nor any honey, smoke as an offering made by fire unto the Eternal.* [177] Rather, the *tzori* is the oily sap which drips from the balsam tree, called in the language of the Sages *k'taph.* It is this which we have been taught: [164] "Rabban [116] Shimon ben Gamaliel says: The *tzori* [required for the incense] was the sap which exuded from the *k'taph* (balsam) tree." Perhaps it is called *k'taph* (plucking off) because they break off its branches on days in the hot season, and the balm runs down from the place where it is broken. In the Gemara of Chapter *Bameh Madlikin* [178] it is stated: "Rabbi Shimon ben Eleazar says:

---

(172) See Jastrow *(ibid.)* for the Greek term. (173) Numbers 24:6.
(174) In our Rashi: *theriaque.* — To this term Ramban will object, since a theriac is an electuary [a medical compound] composed of many ingredients.
(175) Shabbath 109 b. (176) Nedarim 41 b. (177) Leviticus 2:11.
(178) "With what may they light" [the Sabbath lamp]? — Shabbath 26 a.

We do not light [the Sabbath lamp] with *tzori*, and so did Rabbi Shimon ben Eleazar [179] say: The *tzori* [required for the incense] was the sap exuding from the balsam tree." And there in the Gemara [180] the Sages explained the reason [why that balm is not used for the Sabbath lamp], because its fragrance spreads and he may come to use it as food [and taking off oil from a burning lamp is considered the same as extinguishing it]. Thus it is clear that the *tzori* mentioned [for the incense] is that good oil mentioned [in the above Gemara].

And I wonder! For Onkelos translated: *'n'choth' (spicery) 'u'tzri' (and balm) and labdanum* [181] — *sh'aph u'ktaph*. Similarly he rendered: *a little 'tzori' (balm)* [182] — *k'taph*. But *nataph* [here in this verse] he translated *n'tupha*, and did not translate it as he did in the case of the word *tzori!* [183] And Yonathan [ben Uziel] translated everywhere *tzori* as *sh'aph*, which is a term for an anointing oil in the language of the Talmud, such as in their saying: [184] "[for him whose eyes hurt] they make *shipha* (an ointment of various components) in a vessel," the word *shipha* being short of the letter *ayin*, which would make it *she'ipha*. A similar example is: [185] "*D'sha'yeiph* (he anoints) him with the same kind he gave him" to eat. Here too, the word *d'sha'yeiph* is like *d'sha'iph* [with the letter *ayin*].

It appears from their opinions [186] that both the balsam tree and its fruit are called *tzori* in the Sacred Language, just like *t'einah* (fig), *rimon* (pomegranate), *ethrog*, and many other names like them. The term *n'choth* [181] is thus, according to them, [Onkelos and Yonathan], a generic name for all notable and fragrant oils.

---

(179) In Ramban manuscripts: "Rabban Shimon ben Gamaliel." So also in some manuscripts of the Talmud (see Dikdukei Sofrim, Shabbath, p. 48 Note 1). (180) *Ibid.*, 25 b. (181) Genesis 37:25. (182) *Ibid.*, 43:11. (183) For since Onkelos translated (in Genesis 37:25) the Hebrew *tzori* as the Aramaic *k'taph*, he should have translated likewise here the Hebrew *nataph*, for as said above *nataph* is *tzori*, and so why did he translate it as *k'topha*? (184) Chullin 111 b. (185) Beitzah 16 a. (186) From Onkelos who translated (in Genesis 37:25) *tzori* as *k'taph*, and from Yonathan who translated it as *sh'aph*.

EXODUS XXX, KI THISA

That is why Scripture states, *and he* [Hezekiah] *showed them all the house 'n'chothoh'* (of his treasure),[187] because the treasure-house where the precious oil is stored is called by that name, seeing that it is the choicest of all treasure, and there in fact it is also written, *and the precious oil.*[187] Therefore Onkelos said in the case of the present that Jacob sent to Joseph, that they brought him *sh'aph* [which is the Aramaic translation for the Hebrew *n'chot*],[182] which is the term for that notable oil. And they further brought [in the present for Joseph] from the branches of the *tzori*-tree called *k'taph*.[188] In other places where Scripture mentions *tzori* alone, speaking of it as a beneficial medicine — such as in the verse, *Is there no 'tzori' in Gilead?*[189] — Yonathan translates it as referring to the oil called *sh'aph*. Onkelos translated [here] *nataph* as *netupha,* which is an oil called by that name because it "drips" from the broken branches. There is no justification here to translate *nataph* as *sh'aph,* for the incense did not contain any ointment.

Now I have seen that Harav Rabbi Moshe [ben Maimon][190] included in the incense the bark of a tree called in Arabic *od balsan*. From this it would appear that he was of the opinion that Rabban Shimon ben Gamaliel who said:[164] "The *tzori* [required for the incense] was the sap which exuded from the *k'taph*-tree" thereby intended to differ with the Sages [who counted the *tzori* among the eleven components of the incense], and to say instead that *tzori* was not one of the ingredients of the incense, since *tzori* is nothing but a sap, and it was not the sap [of the *k'taph*] that was put into the incense, but the [bark of the] *k'taph* itself.

35. 'MEMULACH' (SEASONED WITH SALT), PURE AND HOLY. This means that it be seasoned with salt of Sodom, just as the Rabbis have said:[164] "Of salt of Sodom, the fourth part of a *kab*." Onkelos translated [*memulach* as] *m'areiv* (mixed together).

---

(187) II Kings 20:13. (188) This explains Onkelos' translation in Genesis 43:11. (189) Jeremiah 8:22. (190) Mishneh Torah, *Hilchoth Klei Hamikdash* 2:4.

By this he intended to say that *memulach* means "rubbed out" — that the ingredients should all be so well-ground and mixed so thoroughly together, that their identity is "rubbed out" and none of the [individual] ingredients can be recognized. This is of the expression: *For the heavens 'nimlochu' (shall vanish away) like smoke.* [191] Similarly: *'u'vloyei m'lachim'* (and worn rags); [192] *A fruitful land 'limleichah' (into a salt waste).* [193] These are all expressions of destruction and annihilation.

And Rashi explained that the term *memluach* means that it be thoroughly mixed together in the grinding of the ingredients one with another. To this interpretation Rashi brought proof from the verse similar in meaning: *'malachayich' (thy mariners) and thy pilots,* [194] who are so called "because they turn over the water with the oars when they propel the ship, like a person who stirs up beaten eggs with a spoon in order to mix them thoroughly."

In my opinion mariners are called *malachim* [of the root *melach* — salt] because they know the "taste" of the sea, as if they could feel if it is "salty" or "sweet;" that is to say, they know when it will be sweet and pleasant for those travelling by sea, and when it will be bad and bitter for them. It is not those who hold the oars [propelling the ship] who are called *malachim* [as Rashi said], for it is written on Tyre, *The inhabitants of Sidon and Arvad were thy 'shotim' (rowers);* [195] *The elders of Gebal and the wise men thereof were in thee thy calkers; all the ships of the sea 'u'malacheyhem' (and their mariners) were in thee.* [196] For it is the older captains who know the sea that are called *malachim*. And it is further written, *And all that handle the oar, 'malachim' (the mariners), and all the pilots of the sea, shall come down from their ships, they shall stand upon the land.* [197] Thus three categories are mentioned: those that handle the oar, the mariners, and the pilots [which proves that *malachim* — the mariners — are not those that handle the oar].

(191) Isaiah 51:6. (192) Jeremiah 38:11. (193) Psalms 107:34.
(194) Ezekiel 27:27. (195) *Ibid.,* Verse 8. (196) *Ibid.,* Verse 9.
(197) *Ibid.,* Verse 29.

Similarly, *a fruitful land 'limleichah'* [193] means "to a salt land," for in a salt land nothing will grow, just as is written of Sodom, *The whole land thereof is brimstone, and salt, and a burning, that it is not sown, nor beareth,* [198] and it is further written, *and he sowed it with salt.* [199] It is possible that the letter *lamed* is redundant in the verse, *for the heavens 'nimlochu' like smoke,* [191] the intent thereof being as in the word *nimchu* (erased), which would make it similar to these cases: *ba'l'umim;* [200] wholly *'shalanan' (at ease) and quiet.* [201]

36. AND THOU SHALT PUT OF IT BEFORE THE TESTIMONY IN THE TENT OF MEETING, WHERE I WILL MEET WITH THEE. We may possibly explain that Scripture mentions here all the [various] regulations concerning the burning of the incense. It thus states that he should burn of it *before the Testimony* in the Holy of Holies, which refers to the incense burnt on the Day of Atonement, and that he should also burn of it *in the Tent of Meeting,* [referring to that burnt] every day. The phrase, *where I will meet with thee* refers back to [*before*] *the Testimony* [from where He spoke to Moses]. It is possible that He refers to the putting of the incense on the inner altar which is set *before the* ark of the *Testimony,*[202] as He says in the section of *Vayakheil.* [203]

31   2. SEE, I HAVE CALLED BY NAME BEZALEL THE SON OF URI, THE SON OF HUR. G-d said to Moses, *See, I have called by name,* and Moses said to Israel, *See, the Eternal hath called by*

---

(198) Deuteronomy 29:22.   (199) Judges 9:45.   (200) Psalms 44:15. The structure of the word is *ba'umim* (among the nations).   (201) Job 21:23. The structure of the word is *shanon* (ease).   (202) In this way the phrase *before the Testimony* does not allude to the incense burnt on the Day of Atonement in the Holy of Holies, as explained above, but is instead to be understood as follows: "*and thou shalt put of it* [daily] on the inner altar which is set in the Tent of Meeting *before the Testimony* in the Holy of Holies."   (203) It is in the section of *Pekudei* (40:5): *And thou shalt set the golden altar for incense before the ark of Testimony.*

name. [204] The reason for this is because Israel in Egypt had been crushed under the work *in mortar and in brick*,[205] and had acquired no knowledge of how to work with silver and gold, and the cutting of precious stones, and had never seen them at all. It was thus a wonder that there was to be found amongst them such a great wise-hearted man who knew how to work with silver and gold, and in cutting of stones [for setting] and in carving of wood, a craftsman, an embroiderer, and a weaver. [206] For even amongst those who study before the experts, you cannot find one who is proficient in all these crafts. And even those who know them and are used to doing them, if their hands are continually engaged in [work with] lime and mud, lose the ability to do with them such artistic and delicate work. Moreover, he [i.e. Bezalel] was a great Sage *in wisdom, and in understanding, and in knowledge,*[207] to understand the secret of the Tabernacle and all its vessels, why they were commanded and to what they hinted. Therefore G-d said to Moses that when he sees this wonder he should know that *I filled him with the spirit of G-d,*[207] to know all these things in order that he would make the Tabernacle. For it was His Will to make the Tabernacle in the wilderness, and He created him for His glory, [208] for it is *He that called the generations from the beginning,*[209] it being similar in meaning to the verse, *Before I formed thee in the belly I knew thee, and before thou camest forth out of the womb I sanctified thee.*[210] The same type of expression we find in the verse, *See that the Eternal hath given you the Sabbath; therefore He giveth you on the sixth day the bread of two days.* [211]

(204) And the question appears: Why was that special designation called for? The answer is that it was needed because etc. (205) Above, 1:14. (206) See further, 35:35. (207) Verse 3. (208) See Isaiah 43:7. And in Chapter *Kinyan Torah:* "Whatsoever the Holy One, blessed be He, created in His world He created it but for His glory." Bezalel thus was born for that sacred purpose, as the thought continues to be unfolded by Ramban. (209) Isaiah 41:4. — See Vol. I, p. 59, Note 240, for important note on this topic. (210) Jeremiah 1:5. (211) Above, 16:29. Here too the sense of the verse is: "See the wonder..."

Our Rabbis have on this topic a Midrash:[212] "G-d showed Moses the book of the first man and told him: 'Each person I have given a role from that moment on, and Bezalel too I have given a role already then, as it is said, *See, I have called by name Bezalel.*" This is similar to what I have explained. The Rabbis have also said:[213] "Bezalel knew how to combine the letters with which heaven and earth were created." The purport of this saying is that the Tabernacle alludes to these matters [heaven and earth], and he knew and understood its secret.

10. AND THE GARMENTS OF 'HA'SROD.'[214] I do not know why He did not command the making of these garments at the beginning, as He did concerning all the [rest of the] work of the Tabernacle and the garments of Aaron and his sons, for it would have been proper that He say to Moses, "and thou shalt make cloth of blue-purple to cover with it the ark,[215] and a red-purple cloth to cover with it the altar,[216] and a cloth of scarlet to cover with it the table," and now when charging Moses about those who were to make these things, He should have included these garments with the rest of the work. Perhaps there was no insistence on how they were to be made, and they could have made these garments of *srod* of one kind alone, but they made them of blue-purple, red-purple and scarlet. They did not want to make them of linen, as that is not distinguished, as are those other colors. After they made them, G-d willed that the blue-purple cloth be for the ark, the red-purple for the altar, and the scarlet for the table. Therefore, it was sufficient to command them in brief [here] when He gave the command about those who were to do all the work, for these *garments of 'ha'srod'* were to be made according to their understanding.

Now it is not befitting that a garment made to cover [the sacred vessels] should have many holes in it, as Rashi has said. Rather,

---

(212) Shemoth Rabbah 40:2.   (213) Berachoth 55 a.   (214) Rashi explains it as "the garments of net-work" [with which the sacred vessels were covered during the journeyings]. Ramban will differ with this interpretation. (215) Numbers 4:6.   (216) *Ibid.*, Verse 13.

the word *ha'srod* is of the term *sarid* (a lone survivor), because all these garments were of one kind,[217] as Rabbi Abraham ibn Ezra said.

All this I have written in accordance with the line of thought of Rashi. *Yet all this availeth me nothing.*[218] For what meaning is there in the Holy One, blessed be He, saying to Moses that they should make "garments of *kela*,"[219] or "garments of *s'ridah*," without explaining to him how many of them there should be, two or a hundred, how long and wide they should be, and why they should be made altogether, since the matter cannot be understood at all from this communication [stated here]? Moreover, why are they mentioned always before the garments of Aaron?[220] Besides, what is the meaning of the phrase, *the garments of 'ha'srod', for ministering in the holy place,*[221] for this seems to refer to the sacrificial rites in the holy place, just as He says, *or when they come near to the altar to minister*[222] in the holy place. Similarly, *even he who cometh into the Tent of Meeting to minister in the holy place*[223] does not refer to outer work, or the carrying of the holy vessels. Furthermore, it is written, *and they will make all that I commanded thee: the Tent of Meeting* etc., *and the garments of 'ha'srod'* etc., *and the incense of sweet spices; according to all that I have commanded thee shall they do.*[224] But He had not commanded him before about *the garments of 'ha'srod'* at all!

What appears from the words of our Rabbis is that *the garments of 'ha'srod'* are the actual garments of the priesthood.

---

(217) I.e. wool, excepting that they were colored differently: blue-purple, red-purple, and scarlet. (218) Esther 5:13. (219) The Hebrew word *kla'im* (hangings) (above 27:9) Onkelos translates *s'radin*. Similarly he translates the Hebrew word *michbar* (grate) (*ibid.*, Verse 4) as *s'rada*. On the basis of these translations of Onkelos, Rashi suggests here that the word *ha'srod* is an Aramaic term, which means "garments of net-work," because they were made with many holes. — It is with reference to this basis for Rashi's explanation that Ramban says, "garments of *kela*." (220) In the verse before us: *And the garments of 'ha'srod,' and the holy garments for Aaron* etc. — Likewise further, 35:19, and 39:41. (221) Further, 35:19. (222) Above, 30:20. (223) *Ibid.*, 29:30. (224) Verses 6-11.

EXODUS XXXI, KI THISA

This is mentioned in Tractate Yoma.[225] If that is so, it is correct that we translate *the garments of 'ha'srod'* as "the garments of uniqueness," that is to say, the garments which when worn designate the outstanding one of the people, *the highest among his brethren.*[226] Similarly, *'u'basridim' whom the Eternal shall call*[227] means the remnants of those who have survived, [the word being] of the root, *escape 'v'sarid' (and remain).*[228] [*The garments of 'ha'srod'*] thus allude to the garments of Aaron, which are so called ['unique'] because only one of the generation may wear them — Aaron in his lifetime, and after him *the priest that is highest... upon whose head the anointing oil is poured, and that is consecrated to put on the garments.*[226] And Scripture always mentions Aaron's garments in a way of honor, as it says: *for splendor and for beauty;*[229] *holy garments;*[230] *the golden plate, the holy crown.*[231] It is for this reason that they are called *the garments of 'ha'srod'* — garments of royalty. This is the meaning of the verse, *And the garments of 'ha'srod'* (the High Priest) *to minister in the holy place, and the holy garments for Aaron the priest,* Scripture thus reverting [in the second half of the verse] to explain [that the garments of *ha'srod* are for Aaron]. Similarly it is mentioned in the section beginning, *And they brought the Tabernacle unto Moses.*[232] And the reason why in this section of *See, I have called by name*[233] it says, *And the garments of 'ha'srod,' 'and' the holy garments for Aaron the priest* [when the second half of the verse should have been without the connective *vav* which signifies "and," since, as explained, it is in apposition to

---

(225) Yoma 72 a-b. "What is the meaning of the verse, *the garments of 'ha'srod' for ministering in the holy place* (further 35:19)? If not for the garments of the priesthood [which are worn during the service which brings atonement to Israel], there would not have been left a survivor [a *sarid*] of Israel's enemies." The final expression is a euphemism. But the whole quotation shows that *the garments of 'ha'srod'* refer to the actual garments of the priests. (226) Leviticus 21:10. (227) Joel 3:5. (228) Jeremiah 44:14. (229) Above, 28:2. (230) *Ibid.*, Verse 4. (231) Leviticus 8:9. (232) Further, 39:33. In Verse 41 there it is stated: *the garments of 'ha'srod'... the holy garments for Aaron the priest.* (233) Verse 2.

the first [234]], is to indicate that these garments are superior in two qualities: they are garments of *ha'srod* [the High Priesthood], and they are garments of holiness. This is in order to tell us that only the outstanding one among the people should wear them, [and only] when he comes in to minister in the holy place. And seeing that He did not mention here the phrase, *to minister in the holy place*, [223] He added in explanation that they are garments of *s'rod* and garments of holiness. Besides, there are many cases in Scripture where a redundant *vav* occurs. And the reason why Scripture states, *And of the blue-purple, and red-purple, and scarlet, they made garments of 'srod,'* [235] is because it comes to explain *These are the accounts of the Tabernacle,* [236] giving an accounting — because of their importance — of the gold, silver and brass, how much of them the Israelites brought and what they did with them; therefore it then said afterwards that *of the blue-purple, and the red-purple, and scarlet* which were brought to them they made *the garments of 'srod'* (the High Priest), neither more nor less. Thus it did not mention the linen because it is not as costly a matter [as the rest]. Perhaps they brought so much [of the linen] that it was left over [and therefore Scripture did not mention it]. Then Scripture there refers back and explains [what they did with the blue-purple, the red-purple, etc.] and says, *and they made the holy garments for Aaron, as the Eternal commanded Moses,* [235] *And he made the ephod of gold,* [237] and then finished the [whole] subject.

13. 'ACH' (BUT) YE SHALL KEEP MY SABBATHS. "Even though you may be anxious [238] to do the work promptly, do not set aside the Sabbath on its account. All [Scriptural expressions containing] the words *ach* (but) or *rak* (only), intimate limiting

---

(234) See also Note 232; further in 39:41 the connective "and" is not used by Scripture. The question then appears why is it mentioned here. (235) Further, 39:1. And if, as explained above, *srod* is a term referring to the garments of the High Priest, why then does the verse not mention the linen, of which the garments of Aaron were also made? This is because etc. (236) *Ibid.*, 38:21. (237) *Ibid.*, 39:2. (238) Our Rashi adds: "and alert."

qualifications; [in this case] it is to exclude the Sabbath from [the days on which] the work of the Tabernacle may be done." This is Rashi's language. But I have not been able to explain it. For according to the method used by our Rabbis to interpret the words *ach* (but) and *rak* (only), it should limit the scope of Sabbath-observance [and permit the work of the Tabernacle on the Sabbath], for the limiting qualifications [of *ach* and *rak*] everywhere apply to the subject of the commandment itself [and since the verse here speaks of Sabbath-observance, the word *ach* should be restricting its application]. Thus if we are to interpret [and apply] the limiting nature of the word *ach* to the subject of the work of the Tabernacle, it should follow that it is allowed to be done on the Sabbath! Rather, the limiting nature of the word *ach* here applies to circumcision [on the eighth day of the child], or to the saving of human life, and similar instances, [to tell us] that they set aside the Sabbath. And so the Rabbis said in Tractate Yoma:[239] "And whence do we know that even in a doubt whether life is in danger, the Sabbath may be set aside? Rabbi Abohu said in the name of Rabbi Yochanan: *'Ach' ye shall keep My Sabbaths* — [the word *ach*] has a limiting qualification." And the reason why the work of the Tabernacle does not override the Sabbath [is not on account of the word *ach*, but] because He warned [about keeping the Sabbath] here [right next to the subject of the making of the Tabernacle, thus indicating that the Sabbath is not to be set aside on account of it]. And in line with the plain meaning of Scripture the verse states as follows: "You shall do the work of the Tent of Meeting, but My Sabbaths you shall keep forever." And in the Torath Kohanim[240] [the Rabbis have said as follows]: "I might think that the building of the Sanctuary overrides the Sabbath? Scripture therefore says, *Ye shall keep My Sabbaths, and reverence My Sanctuary: I am the Eternal.*"[241]

(239) Yerushalmi Yoma VIII, 5. (240) Sifra *Kedoshim* Section 3, 7:7. (241) Leviticus 19:30. This teaches that "all of you are obligated to keep My honor" (Yebamoth 6 a), and as the Meiri explains it: "you and the Sanctuary are obligated to keep My honor." Thus the building of the Sanctuary does not override the Sabbath.

Now the reason for the word *Shabtothai* [in the plural] is because the Sabbaths of the year are many. By way of the Truth, [the mystic lore of the Cabala], He commanded here [the keeping of the "Sabbaths"] by *zachor* [242] and *shamor*, [243] as I have hinted with reference to their secret, [244] this being the reason for the plural — *My Sabbaths*. Of the two of them [*zachor* and *shamor*] He says, *for it is a sign* [when He should have said "for *they* are a sign," this is in order to indicate] that "it" [the Sabbath] is the sign *between Me and you... that ye may know.* [245] He states, *Ye shall keep the Sabbath,* [246] and declares that those that profane it are liable to extinction, [246] for *the spirit returneth unto G-d who gave it,* [247] but the soul of that one [who profanes the Sabbath] will be cut off from there. [248] He states concerning the seventh day that it is *a Sabbath of solemn rest holy to G-d,* [249] because it is the foundation of the world; of the Sabbath He also says that it is *a perpetual covenant,* [250] and then He states again that *it is a sign between Me and the children of Israel* [251] meaning that the Sabbath is the sign on the seventh day, and the purport thereof is that the [seventh] day itself is a sign, and [its sanctification as] the Sabbath is the sign forever. [252] This is also the purport of the expression, *He ceased from work and rested,* [251] this being an allusion to "the extra [Sabbath] soul" which comes from The Foundation of the world, *in Whose hand is the soul of every living thing.* [253] Thus the chapter is explained. I have already hinted at its meaning in [my commentary to] the Ten Commandments. [244] The student learned [in the Cabala] will understand.

---

(242) *'Remember' the Sabbath-day* (above 20:8). (243) *'Observe' the Sabbath-day* (Deuteronomy 5:12). (244) Above, 20:8. (245) See my Hebrew commentary here, p. 505, for the mystic interpretation thereof. (246) Verse 14. (247) Ecclesiastes 12:7. (248) "It is measure for measure. On the Sabbath everything is in perfect Unity. But he who desecrates the Sabbath shows that he does not believe in that Unity, and therefore he deserves to be cut off from it" (Ma'or V'shamesh). (249) Verse 15. (250) Verse 16. (251) Verse 17. (252) The allusions are Cabalistic. According to Ricanti [here] reference is to the thoughts mentioned above in *Seder Mishpatim,* Note 23. (253) Job 12:10.

EXODUS XXXII, KI THISA

18. AND HE GAVE UNTO MOSES. This is connected with the end-part of the verse, where the word "G-d" is mentioned, thus meaning: "and G-d gave unto Moses." Just as Scripture mentioned concerning G-d's communicating with Moses, *And G-d spoke all these words,* [254] and with reference to the work of the Tablets of Law and the writing thereon it says, *And the Tablets were the work of G-d, and the writing was the writing of G-d,* [255] so also it says concerning the giving, *and G-d gave to Moses.*

32 1. MAKE US A GOD WHO 'YEILCHU' (SHALL GO — in the plural) BEFORE US. "They wished to have many gods. FOR THIS MOSES, THE MAN THAT BROUGHT US UP OUT OF THE LAND OF EGYPT, and used to show us the way we were to go, WE KNOW NOT WHAT IT BECOME OF HIM. Now we need many gods which shall go before us." This is Rashi's language.

But his language does not fit [the verse, since Scripture indicates only that they wanted a leader in place of Moses, but not gods]. Rather, this verse is the key to understand the incident of the golden calf, and the thought of those who made it. For it is known that the Israelites did not think that Moses was a god, and that he did for them the signs and wonders through his own power. So what sense is there in their saying, "since Moses is gone from us, we will make ourselves gods?" Moreover, they clearly said, *make us, 'elohim' who shall go before us* — and not a deity who should give them life in this world or in the World to Come. Instead, they wanted another Moses, saying: "Moses, the man who showed us the way *from Egypt until now,* [256] being in charge of the journeyings *at the commandment of the Eternal by the hand of Moses,* [257] he is now lost to us; let us make ourselves another Moses who will show us the way at the commandment of the Eternal by his hand." This is the reason for their mentioning, *Moses, the man that brought us up,* rather than saying "the G-d who brought them up," for they needed *a man of G-d.* [258] You

---

(254) Above, 20:1. (255) Further, 32:16. (256) Numbers 14:19. (257) *Ibid.,* 9:23. (258) Deuteronomy 33:1.

can also understand this matter from Aaron's answer to Moses our Teacher, when he asked him, *What did this people do unto thee, that thou hast brought a great sin upon them,*[259] to which Aaron replied, *And they said unto me: Make us a god* etc. *And I said unto them: Whosoever hath any gold, let him break it off; so they gave it to me; and I cast it into the fire.*[260] Now Aaron was apologizing to Moses and saying to him, *Let not the anger of my lord wax hot,*[261] and yet here he was speaking as if adding *rebellion unto his sin,*[262] saying that they asked of him an idol and he made it for them with his hands! So why should Moses' anger not burn against him! What greater sin than this is there?

But the matter is as I have stated, that they did not want the calf to be for them in place of a god *who killeth and maketh alive,*[263] whom they would take upon themselves to serve as a deity; instead, they wanted to have someone in place of Moses to show them the way. And this was the apology of Aaron. He argued that "they merely told me that I should make them *elohim* who would go before them in your place, my lord, because they did not know what had happened to you and whether you would return or not. Therefore they needed someone who would show them the way as long as you were not with them, and if perchance you would return they would leave him and follow you as before." And so indeed it happened, for as soon as the people saw Moses, they immediately left the calf and rejected it, and they allowed him to burn it and scatter its powder upon the water,[264] and no one quarrelled with him at all. Similarly you will note that he did not rebuke the people nor say anything to them, and yet when he came into the camp *and he saw the calf and the dancing,*[265] they immediately fled from before him; and he took the calf and burnt it [and scattered its powder upon the water] and made them drink of it, and yet they did not protest at all. But if the calf were to them in place of a god, it is surely not normal that a person

(259) Further, Verse 21. (260) *Ibid.*, Verses 23-24. (261) *Ibid.*, Verse 22. (262) Job 34:37. (263) I Samuel 2:6. (264) Further, Verse 20. (265) Verse 19.

should let his king and god be burnt in fire. Lo, if one burn their abominations before their eyes, would they not stone him? [266] Now it was Aaron who brought forth this shape, for they did not tell him what he should make, whether *a bullock, or a sheep, or a goat*, [267] or other forms. It is this which is the intention of the saying of the Sages who said, [268] "The verse teaches us that they wished to have many gods," For they did not know what to choose and which one would be best for them.

Now Aaron's intention was as follows. Because Israel was in a wilderness, a desolate wasteland, and destruction and everlasting desolation come from the north, as it is written, *Out of the north the evil shall break forth upon all the inhabitants of the land,* [269] the reference being not merely to the king of Babylon, as can be seen clearly from Scripture, [270] but rather [the intent of the verse is to state] that the attribute of justice comes to the world from the left, [271] to requite upon all the inhabitants of the land according to their evil; and since in the account of the Divine Chariot it is said, *and the four of them had the face of an ox on the left side* [272] — therefore Aaron thought that the destroyer [the ox, which was to the left, i.e. the north] points to the place of destruction where its great power is centered, and when worshipping G-d through there *the spirit will be poured from on high,* [273] just as it was put upon Moses. It is for this reason that Aaron said, *Tomorrow shall be a feast to the Eternal,* [274] meaning that the services and the sacrifices would be to the Proper Name of G-d in order to obtain His favor upon the power [symbolized by] this image, [275] for, it being before them, they would direct their thoughts towards the purport thereof [and thus would be able to mitigate the destructive forces of the wilderness].

---

(266) See above, 8:22. (267) Leviticus 22:27. (268) Sanhedrin 63 a. (269) Jeremiah 1:14. (270) *Ibid.*, Verse 15: *For, lo, I will call all the families of the kingdoms of the north* etc. (271) As one faces the east, his left hand is to the north. (272) Ezekiel 1:10. (273) Isaiah 32:15. (274) Verse 5. (275) I.e., "the ox" which is on the left side of the Divine Chariot, and denotes the attribute of justice. See my Hebrew commentary, p. 507.

It is our Rabbis who have taught us this interpretation, and it is they who have revealed the secret thereof. Thus they have said: [276] *" 'Ra'oh ra'ithi' (I have surely seen) the affliction of My people.* [277] Said the Holy One, blessed be He, to Moses: 'Moses, you see them in one appearance, and I see them in two appearances.[278] You see them coming to Sinai and accepting My Torah, and I see them contemplating Me and how I came forth in My 'travelling coach' to give them the Torah, as it is said, *The chariots of G-d are myriads, even thousands upon thousands,* [279] and they will unhitch one of My *tatromulin,*[280] of which it is written, *and the face of an ox on the left side,* [272] and bring Me to anger with it." *Tatromulin* means "four mules," for *tetra* in Greek means "four," just as the Rabbis have said, [281] ["If a person vowed, 'I will be a *Nazir*] *tetragon,*' he becomes [a *Nazir* for a period of] four times;" *mulin* means "mules," just as in the expression, "The *mula'oth* (mules) of Rabbi's house [282] [used to go out with their bits on the Sabbath]." The word *tatromulin* is thus used as a symbol of the four *chayoth* (living creatures) who carried the Divine Chariot.[283] And in Vayikra Rabbah [10:3] [we find the Midrash stating] that Aaron said, "Since I am building the altar, I will build it to the Name of the Holy One, blessed be He, as it is said, *and Aaron made a proclamation, and said, 'Tomorrow shall be a feast to the Eternal.'* [274] It is not written here, 'Tomorrow shall be a feast to the calf,' but *to the Eternal.*"

Rabbi Abraham ibn Ezra wrote that *elohim* in this case [*Arise, make us 'elohim'*] means that Aaron should make them

---

(276) Ramban is quoting here a composite of Midrashim in Shemoth Rabbah — 3:2, 42:5, 43:8. (277) Exodus 3:7. (278) Hence the double expression: *Ra'oh ra'ithi,* translated "I have surely seen." (279) Psalms 68:18. This whole psalm is interpreted in Midrash Tehilim with reference to the Revelation on Sinai. (280) This is a Greek word [as Ramban will explain further on] which denotes "four mules." Here it is used in reference to the four *chayoth* (living creatures) in the Divine Chariot as described by Ezekiel (Chapter 1), which, as stated in Psalms quoted above, were also seen at the Revelation on Sinai. The sense here is thus that "they will unhitch one of the four *chayoth* (creatures) in My Chariot, and worship it." (281) Nazir 8 b. (282) Shabbath 52 a. (283) Ezekiel 1:5.

"something visible and corporeal on which the glory would rest. And if you will pay attention to the first journey,[284] you will understand this." But this does not appear to me to be correct, since the calf was not made according to the manner of those proficient in the art of the constellations, so that the glory or some spiritual influence should dwell upon it; rather, the figure was made so that when the people would worship it they would direct their thoughts to the purport thereof [as explained above]. Now I have already explained[285] the secret of the first journey, and far it be from Aaron that he should want to be likened to him. Instead, his desire was merely to take of [the *tatromulin,* as explained above] so that their journeys [in the wilderness] should be on the side of that attribute. The student learned [in the mysteries of the Cabala] will understand.

2. PULL OFF THE GOLDEN RINGS. He selected gold and not silver, because gold indicates the attribute of justice, its appearance being *as the appearance of fire,*[286] just as the Rabbis have said,[287] "gold of *parvayim,* gold which is like the blood of bullocks." It is for this reason that the House where the sacrifices were brought was made wholly of gold, as also the altar of incense[288] and the cherubim,[289] and the Rabbis have interpreted [the verses to mean][290] that "if they made them of silver [and not of gold] they are like gods of silver and gods of gold." Even the form for the calf they made of gold rather than of silver.

4. AND THEY SAID, THESE ARE THY GODS, O ISRAEL, WHICH BROUGHT THEE UP OUT OF THE LAND OF EGYPT. This verse also will teach you [that they had no intention of worshipping it as an idol], for there is no fool in the world who would think that this gold which was in their ears[291] is that which

---

(284) Above, 14:19. *And the angel of G-d, who went before the camp of Israel* etc. (Bachya). (285) Above, 13:21. (286) Ezekiel 1:27. (287) Yoma 45 a. The Biblical expression (gold of *parvaim*) is found in II Chronicles 3:6. (288) Above, 30:3. (289) *Ibid.,* 25:18. (290) Mechilta *ibid.,* 20:23. (291) Verse 3.

brought them up out of the land of Egypt. Rather, they said that the power of that figure brought them up out of there. Thus you will find that in no place does it say of the calf, "which brought us 'out' of Egypt," for they acknowledged Him Who said, *I am the Eternal thy G-d, who brought thee 'out' of the land of Egypt,* [292] and that it was by His Great Name that He delivered them from there. Instead, they said in many places *who brought thee 'up,'* for they took it to be in place of *the great hand* [293] — *that dried up the sea, the waters of the great deep; that made the depths of the sea a way for the redeemed to pass over.* [294] It is with this intention that Scripture says, *Thus they exchanged their Glory for the likeness of an ox that eateth grass,* [295] and there it is said, *They forgot G-d Who had delivered them, Who had done great things in Egypt; wondrous works in the land of Ham, terrible things by the Red Sea.* [296] They forgot His word which He commanded them. Thus they transgressed the prohibition, *Thou shalt have no other gods before Me,* [297] as I have hinted there, and you will understand this.

5. AND AARON SAW. The meaning of this verse is that Aaron saw them set on evil, intent upon making the calf, and he arose and built an altar and proclaimed, *Tomorrow shall be a feast to the Eternal,* [274] so that they should bring offerings to the Proper Name of G-d upon the altar which he built to His Name, and that they should not build *altars to the shameful thing,* [298] and that their intent in the offerings should be [to none] *save unto the Eternal only.* [299]

It is possible that Aaron said, *Tomorrow* [*shall be a feast*], in order to delay them, thinking that perhaps Moses would come in the meantime and they would abandon the calf. But they rose up early in the morning *and offered burnt-offerings, and brought peace-offerings.* [300] Now Scripture does not say "and they offered

---

(292) Above, 20:2. (293) *Ibid.,* 14:31. (294) Isaiah 51:10. (295) Psalms 106:20. (296) *Ibid.,* Verses 21-22. (297) Above, 20:3. (298) Jeremiah 11:13. (299) Above, 22:19. (300) Verse 6.

burnt-offerings to it, and brought peace-offerings to it." The reason for that is that there were some people amongst them who intended them to be for the Name of the Holy One, blessed be He, as Aaron had said, but some of them became corrupted and sacrificed them to the calf. It is with reference to this latter group that the Holy One, blessed be He, said to Moses, *they have worshipped it, and have sacrificed unto it,* [301] for it is they who were the sinners. And even if it was perhaps Aaron who performed the sacrifical rites, Scripture used an indefinite expression — saying, *they offered burnt-offerings and brought peace-offerings* [300] — in order to suggest that Aaron's intention was directed towards the Name of the Eternal, whilst they set their mind towards the calf which they had made, and thus the owners [of the sacrifices] invalidated them.

6. AND THE PEOPLE SAT DOWN TO EAT AND TO DRINK. This means that they all sat down together to eat and drink inordinately, as they would do at feasts and on festivals, and afterwards *they rose up to make merry* with their idols and indulge in revelry. Scripture tells us this on account of what Moses [later] said, *the noise of them that sing do I hear,*[302] for Moses found them acting riotously in front of him *and his heart was lifted up in the ways of the Eternal,*[303] to take it from before them and to burn it in their presence [and scatter its powder upon the water] and make them drink of it.

Now Scripture first completed the account of everything they had done with the calf, and afterwards told of what the Holy One, blessed be He, said to Moses, *Go, get thee down.*[304] This communication, however, was given to Moses early that morning, when they worshipped the calf and sacrificed to it. When Moses came down from the mountain they had *sat down to eat and to drink, and rose up to make merry,* [300] and he found them in revelry. This also is proof to what I have explained [that at first their intent was not to worship idols]. since it was not said to

(301) Verse 8. (302) Verse 18. (303) II Chronicles 17:6. (304) Verse 7.

Moses, *Go, get thee down, for thy people have dealt corruptly* [304] on the day that Aaron made the [golden] calf and the altar, [for had they been made for the purpose of idolatry, Moses] would have come down immediately. Instead, it was only when the people sacrificed to it and worshipped it that He told Moses to go down.

7. FOR THY PEOPLE HAVE DEALT CORRUPTLY. G-d said to Moses that *they have committed two evils.* [305] One is that *thy people have dealt corruptly.* The meaning of the term *hashchathah* (corruption) is destruction of a structure, similar to that which is said, *every man with his weapon of 'mashchetho' (destruction) in his hand;* [306] *behold, I am against thee, 'hamashchith' (O destroying) mountain* [307] — Babylon — which destroyed every wall and tower [of the fortified cities]. And the meaning of "the destruction" here is that which our Rabbis have called [308] "mutilating the shoots," [of faith, by seeking to undermine the principle of the Unity]. Secondly, *they have made them a molten calf, and have worshipped it, and have sacrificed unto it.* [301] Now as regards the first transgression it was known only to G-d, for it is *He Who knoweth the secrets of the heart,* [309] but the second one, [the open disregard of the Law] was by the sinners amongst them, as I have explained, [in bringing sacrifices to the golden calf; and that was a matter known to all]. Now most of the people shared in the sin of the incident of the calf, for so it is written, *And all the people pulled off the golden pendants.* [291] And were it not for this [participation of theirs in the incident], the anger [of G-d] would not have been directed against them to destroy them all. For even though the numbers of those who were killed for this sin [310] and those smitten by G-d [311] were few [in comparison to the total number of the people, this was because] most of them

---

(305) Jeremiah 2:13. (306) Ezekiel 9:1. (307) Jeremiah 51:25. (308) Chagigah 14 b. See Vol. I, p. 155. — The "mutilating of the shoots" consists of separating any of the Ten Emanations and worshipping it independently (see Ha'emunah Vehabitachon, Chapter 3, in my Kithvei Haramban, Vol. II, p. 362). (309) Psalms 44:22. (310) Verse 28: *there fell of the people that day about three thousand.* (311) Verse 35.

shared in the sin only in their evil thought [and not in action], as I have explained.

THAT THOU [i.e., Moses] BROUGHTEST UP OUT OF THE LAND OF EGYPT. This is to be understood in the light of the verse, *And Moses led Israel onward from the Red Sea.*[312] Or it may be that G-d wanted to tell it to Moses in the same way as the people had said it — *for as for this Moses, the man that brought us up out of the land of Egypt.*[313] Similarly, in the Book of Deuteronomy, He said, *thy people that thou hast brought forth out of Egypt,*[314] meaning that through you [Moses] they have gone out of Egypt, as they say. But in his prayer Moses said, *that Thou hast brought forth out of the land of Egypt with great power and with a mighty hand,*[315] meaning that You alone are the One Who took them out of Egypt, for Yours is the might and the power; for it was with great power that *Thy right hand, O Eternal is glorious in power,*[316] and with a mighty hand *Thy right hand, O Eternal dasheth in pieces the enemy.*[316] Similarly it is said, *by Thy great power and by Thy outstretched arm,*[317] as I have hinted at[316] in connection with the secret of the attribute of the Arm.

10. NOW THEREFORE LET ME ALONE, THAT MY WRATH MAY WAX HOT AGAINST THEM. The meaning of this cannot be "*let Me alone* and I will become angry," for if His anger had not been aroused yet, why should it wax hot as soon as Moses leaves Him alone? But in line with the plain meaning of Scripture the meaning thereof is: "leave Me, *and I will consume them* in My burning anger," similar in thought to the expression, *let Me alone, and I will destroy them.*[318]

By way of the Truth, [the mystic lore of the Cabala], the verse means: "My mercy will subside, and My attribute of justice will wax hot against them *and I will consume them* with it, for with

---

(312) Above, 15:22. (313) Verse 1. (314) Deuteronomy 9:12. (315) Verse 11 here. (316) Above, 15:6. (317) Deuteronomy 9:29. (318) *Ibid.*, Verse 14.

Me [i.e. when the attribute of mercy is before Me], it [319] has no power over them." This is the meaning of the expression, *And Moses besought the face of the Eternal his G-d,* [320] being similar in usage to the expression, *the face of the Lord Eternal G-d, the G-d of Israel.* [321] And so Moses mentioned [in his prayer] in the Book of Deuteronomy, *O G-d Eternal* [322] — first the name of G-d with *Aleph Dalet,* [323] followed by the name of *Yod Hei.* [324] It is possible that the word *vay'chal* (and he besought) is of the root *t'chilah* (beginning). [325] Understand it and you will know.

11. ETERNAL, WHY DOTH THY WRATH WAX HOT AGAINST THY PEOPLE? Now when Moses prayed about this great sin, it would have been fitting that he do so by way of confession and supplication, similar to what he said later on, *Oh, this people have sinned a great sin,* [326] and just as Ezra prayed and confessed [327] *because of the faithlessness of them of the captivity,* [328] and there is no reason why he should say, *why doth the Eternal* etc.? Our Rabbis, prompted by this [difficulty], have in various homiletic ways [329] tried to mention several reasons for Moses' minimizing the sin before Him.

By way of the Truth, [the mystic lore of the Cabala], Moses is saying: "Why do You give permission to the attribute of justice to hold sway over Your people, for You have taken them out of the land of Egypt for the sake of Your Name with the attribute of

---

(319) I.e., the attribute of justice has then no power. — So it is clearly explained in Abusaula's commentary on the mystic passages in Ramban. See Vol. I, Preface, xii, Note 21.   (320) Verse 11. The word *pnei* ("face of") alludes to the attribute of justice (Bachya).   (321) Further, 34:23. (322) Deuteronomy 9:26.   (323) *Ado-noy* which alludes to the attribute of justice.   (324) The Tetragrammaton which alludes to the attribute of mercy.   (325) "Since Moses prayed that the attribute of justice be withheld from the people, Scripture therefore uses the word *vay'chal* [of the root *t'chilah*, meaning "beginning" or "first"], because [in the order of the attributes as they are arranged from lowest to highest, the one of justice] is nearest to us" (Ricanti). See also Bachya, in my edition, Vol. II, p. 332. (326) Further, Verse 31.   (327) Ezra 10:1.   (328) *Ibid.*, 9:4.   (329) See Shemoth Rabbah 43:7-10.

EXODUS XXXII, KI THISA

mercy ruling over them, and with the attribute of justice upon their enemies."

Now this prayer — *Why doth the Eternal... Wherefore should the Egyptians speak*[330] — appears really to be the very same prayer he mentioned in the Book of Deuteronomy, *And I prayed unto G-d and I said: O Eternal G-d, destroy not Thy people*,[331] for the purport of the prayer is alike in both cases, the difference being only that here Scripture mentioned the prayer before it told us that he came down from the mountain, and there Moses mentioned it after it tells us that he came down from the mountain. But Rabbi Abraham ibn Ezra's opinion is that Moses did not pray for Israel as long as the idol was among them;[332] but only when G-d told him, *Let me alone, that I may destroy them,*[318] and he realized that the fate [of the people] was dependent upon him, did he go down the mountain and destroy the calf, and then he returned to pray for forty days, there being no strict chronological order in the narrative of the Torah. But I do not agree with this opinion. For the prayer he recited upon his return to the mountain [after he had cleansed the camp of the idol] is the one which he mentions, *Oh, this people have sinned a great sin.*[326] And if it is all one prayer[333] which Moses said during the forty days after he returned to the mountain, why does Scripture divide it, mentioning here [in Verses 11-13] part of it, and after he had come down, mentioning the other part [in Verses 31-32]? Rather, these are two separate prayers. Therefore it appears that when G-d told him *Let Me alone, that My wrath may wax hot against them,*[334] Moses immediately *besought the face of the Eternal* and did not delay at all, for he was afraid lest the wrath go out from G-d and the plague would begin[335] and

---

(330) Verses 11-12. (331) Deuteronomy 9:26. (332) Hence the prayer recorded in Verses 11-13 was really not recited by Moses until after his descent from the mount and his cleansing the camp of the idolatrous worship, mentioned in Verses 15-29. — Ramban will differ with this interpretation of Ibn Ezra. (333) I.e., if the prayer mentioned in Verses 11-13, and the one in Verses 31-32, were both said at the same time, as Ibn Ezra would have it, namely during the forty days after he returned to the mountain, then why etc. (334) Verse 10 here. (335) See Numbers 17:11.

consume them in a moment,[336] therefore at once he said, *Eternal, why doth Thy wrath wax hot against Thy people?* Similarly I found it in Eileh Shemoth Rabbah:[337] "Said Moses: 'If I leave Israel [to their fate] and go down the mountain, they will never have a restoration again. Instead I will not move from here until I seek mercy for them.' Immediately Moses began pleading on their behalf etc." Thus he prayed for them and G-d *repented of the evil which He said* [338] to kill them and destroy them. That does not mean that He was [completely] reconciled with them, but at least He said, "I have repented, I will not destroy them." And now that Moses had time, he went down the mountain and burnt the calf, and punished its worshippers, and afterwards he said to the people, *I will go up unto the Eternal, perhaps I shall make atonement for your sin,*[339] so that He should entirely forgive you. However, in the Book of Deuteronomy Moses narrated the account in another order, stating that after G-d had told him, *Let Me alone, that I may destroy them,* [340] he said, *So I turned and came down.* [341] The reason [for this change in the account of the narrative] is that Moses was listing to them there all their transgressions, and the pains he took for them. Thus he told them of the golden calf they had made in Horeb, [342] on account of which he had to break the Tablets of the Law and to pray for them forty days and forty nights, and also for Aaron, [343] and how he was put to the trouble of burning the calf. Then he continued to tell what they had done *at Taberah, and at Massah, and at Kibroth-hattaavah,*[344] *And when the Eternal sent* them *from Kadesh-barnea;* [345] and after he finished, *Ye have been rebellious against the Eternal from the day that I knew you,*[346] he went back to the matter of his prayers which he had mentioned, and set down in order the two prayers, saying, *So I fell down before the Eternal the forty days and forty nights that I fell down; because the Eternal had said He would destroy you* [347] — until I prayed, *destroy not Thy people.*[348] It

---

(336) *Ibid.,* Verse 10. (337) Shemoth Rabbah 42:1. (338) Verse 14. (339) Verse 30. (340) Deuteronomy 9:14. (341) *Ibid.,* Verse 15. (342) *Ibid.,* Verse 8. (343) *Ibid.,* Verse 20. (344) *Ibid.,* Verse 22. (345) *Ibid.,* Verse 23. (346) *Ibid.,* Verse 24. (347) *Ibid.,* Verse 25. (348) *Ibid.,* Verse 26.

was not necessary for him to mention the second prayer [349] because he had already said there that he prayed for them forty days, and even here it does not mention [all the prayers he recited], for who can write down the many supplications and entreaties that he prayed for them during the forty days. And if you will understand what I have explained, then you will really comprehend that there were [here] two prayers, for at first he *besought the face of the Eternal his G-d,* and at the end [i.e., after he came down the mountain and burnt the golden calf etc. and then returned to the mountain], he *fell down before the Eternal for forty days,*[347] as it is explained in the section, *and Moses returned unto the Eternal.*[350]

Now in the Book of Deuteronomy he mentioned, *Moreover the Eternal was very angry with Aaron... and I prayed for Aaron also at the same time.*[351] This he did not mention here at all for the sake of Aaron's honor, for Moses did not want to mention in Aaron's lifetime that he had been dependent upon his prayer, in order that he should not feel ashamed.[352] But there [in the Book of Deuteronomy] after Aaron's death, he informed us of the truth. This is the correct order in these Scriptural sections.

16. AND THE TABLETS WERE THE WORK OF G-D. It would have been proper for Scripture to mention everything connected with the work of the Tablets of the Law in the verse, *And He gave unto Moses [... the two Tablets of the Testimony],*[353] as He said [there], *written with the finger of G-d.*[353] It is, however, mentioned here in order to tell of their high distinction [that they were *the work of G-d*], thus stating that despite all this Moses did not hesitate to break them, because he was angered upon seeing that evil sight and he could not restrain himself from breaking them. Or the matter may be as our Rabbis have mentioned,[354] that the writing vanished from the Tablets as he approached the

---

(349) I.e., the prayer mentioned here in Verses 31-32: *Oh, this people have sinned a great sin,* etc. (350) Verse 31 here. (351) Deuteronomy 9:20. (352) Of the grief he had caused (Abusaula). (353) Above, 31:18. (354) Shemoth Rabbah 46:1.

border [of the camp] where the calf was, the place of defilement and transgression.

18. THE NOISE OF THEM THAT SING DO I HEAR.[355] The meaning of this is not that Moses knew the matter to be so, for in that case he would have said, "It is the noise of them that sing" [instead of saying, "do I hear"]. Rather, its meaning is that since Moses was the father of wisdom,[356] and recognized the musical character of all sounds, he said that it was a noise of singing which was being heard by him. The Rabbis have likewise said in an Agadah[357] that Moses told Joshua, "Is it possible that one who is destined to be the leader of Israel cannot distinguish between the different kinds of sounds?" Now Moses in his great humility did not tell Joshua the cause of the noise, as he did not want to speak of the disgrace of Israel, and so instead he told him that it was a noise of merriment.

20. AND HE STREWED IT UPON THE WATER, AND MADE THE CHILDREN OF ISRAEL DRINK IT. After grinding the golden calf to a fine powder, he scattered it on the surface of the stream which came down from the mountain, and made the people drink of those waters. It is possible that gold burnt in fire does not melt, but instead when placed therein is charred and can be ground to powder, as Rabbi Abraham ibn Ezra mentioned.[358] This powder was *light upon the face of the waters*,[359] and therefore it floated, and he made them drink of it. Or it may be that he scattered it upon the stream in small quantities, and then drew the water and made them drink it before the gold powder sank in the stream. Or perhaps it was a miraculous event. Thus he wanted to

---

(355) In the Tur it is correctly marked as a new paragraph. In all Hebrew editions of Ramban, however, it is connected with the above. As the subject is clearly independent of the preceding matter, I have followed here the order of the Tur for the sake of clarity.   (356) Sifre *Devarim* 1. See also in Vol. I, pp. 9-10.   (357) Koheleth Rabbah 9:11.   (358) "There is a certain substance which, if put with gold into the fire, will cause the gold to become charred to dust and never return to its former properties" (Ibn Ezra). (359) Job 24:18.

disgrace their deeds by grinding their god to powder and bringing it into their bellies to issue as excrement, something like it is said, *Thou shalt put them* [i.e., the graven images] *far away as one unclean; thou shalt say unto it: 'get thee hence.'* [360] In the opinion of our Rabbis [361] he also intended to put them to the test in the same way that faithless wives were tried,[362] [so that those guilty of having worshipped the golden calf] would have their bellies swell and their thighs fall away. [363] This is the truth.

21. WHAT DID THIS PEOPLE UNTO THEE, THAT THOU HAST BROUGHT SO GREAT A SIN UPON THEM? "How many pains did you endure, and how much suffering did they inflict on you, before you brought this sin upon them?" This is Rashi's language. But it does not appear to me to be correct. For this transgression [of idolatry] is of the kind for which one must sacrifice one's life and submit to death rather than transgress it [and from Rashi's words it would appear that if Aaron had suffered much it was permissible for him to make it]. Perhaps Moses told him so in order to magnify his guilt.

The correct interpretation appears to me to be that this is like the verse, *What have I done? what is mine iniquity? and what is my sin before thy father, that he seeketh my life?* [364] Moses is thus saying: "What hatred did you have for this people, that you have [almost] brought about their destruction and annihilation?" Moses told him this because Aaron had served them in the function of one who reproves [365] and atones for them, and he should have had compassion and mercy on them [and should have made them desist from their course of conduct]; thus the meaning is: "You conducted yourself towards them as an enemy who desires to see their calamity, when they had neither sinned nor transgressed against you." Now the proper order would have been for Moses to blame him firstly for the sin which he himself had

---

(360) Isaiah 30:22. (361) Abodah Zarah 44 a. (362) Numbers 5:16-22. (363) *Ibid.*, Verse 27. (364) I Samuel 20:1. (365) This is a reference to what the Rabbis have said that Aaron served as prophet while Israel was yet in Egypt. See commentaries to I Samuel 2:27.

done, and then to charge him for the sin which he brought upon the people, saying: "how did you do this great sin against G-d, causing also many people to trespass, and bringing a great sin upon them?" Moses, however, in his humility showed respect towards his elder brother, and only mentioned to him the stumbling of the people. It is possible that Moses' *heart was steadfast, trusting* [366] in the righteousness of his brother [and he assumed] that his intention was not a bad one, [and therefore he did not reprove him for his own conduct]; but for the people's guilt he did blame him, for he should have reproved them, and thus they stumbled because of him, — and Aaron replied that they deceived him with their words.

22. THOU KNOWEST THE PEOPLE, THAT THEY ARE SET ON EVIL. Aaron is saying: "They proceeded along the path of evil. They told me to make them a guide in the place of my lord until he returns to me, for perhaps he will return, and then they gave me the gold *and I cast it into the fire*[367] and behold there came out this calf for them, for they had an evil intention as to the gold, [and wanted] to worship it and sacrifice to it." But because Aaron did not want to speak at length about their corruption, he spoke briefly and said, *and there came out this calf,* [367] meaning, "there came out for them this evil matter that my lord sees."

25. AND MOSES SAW THAT THE PEOPLE WERE 'PHARUA' (BROKEN LOOSE). The meaning of this is that although Aaron defended himself and said that he was not at fault with them, yet Moses knew in his heart that the people were broken loose — *For they are a nation void of counsel, and there is no understanding in them.* [368] It is similar to the expression, *'vatiphr'u' (and ye have set at nought) all my counsel,*[369] and similar also to the verse, *for 'hiphria' (he had cast away restraint) in Judah, and acted treacherously against the Eternal.* [370] [Thus the verse is stating that

---

(366) Psalms 112:7. (367) Verse 24. (368) Deuteronomy 32:28.
(369) Proverbs 1:25. (370) II Chronicles 28:19.

Moses saw] that Aaron had let the people loose, and left them without any counsel and instruction, so that they became like sheep scattered upon the mountains [371] without counsellor and guide. Scripture stated this [especially] because they had thought that the calf would be their guide, but in fact they appeared as if they had no counsel, not knowing *the way wherein they must walk, and the deeds they must do,* [372] for some of them intended it for the good, according to their way of thinking, and others intended it for real evil [i.e., outright idolatry], and thus each one went his own way.

'L'SHIMTZAH B'KAMEIHEM' (FOR A DERISION AMONG THEIR ENEMIES). This means that even those who had no evil design [in the affair of the golden calf] will be slandered throughout the generations by the evil report of their enemies, who will say that the whole people were bereft of counsel and instruction; some [of the nations] will say it for a purely evil purpose, and others will merely say it *in the lips of the talkers, and the evil report of the people.*[373] Moses said this with reference to Aaron, meaning that he sinned towards all [i.e., even towards those who did not really intend to sin in the matter of the golden calf]. This is in accordance with the opinion of Onkelos who translated *l'shimtzah b'kameihem* — "to give them a bad name in their generations." However, since Onkelos rendered it "in their generations," [374] it would seem that his intention was to explain that the calf which they made will become a cause of evil talk throughout the generations of Israel, for they will say: "It was not in vain that our fathers made the calf and worshipped it, for they knew that it was this which brought them up out of the land of Egypt, and they found worshipping it to be to their benefit, so we will do likewise, it being better for us to serve it ;" as indeed

---

(371) See I Kings 22:17. (372) Above, 18:20. (373) Ezekiel 36:3. (374) In other words, Onkelos' translation of *l'shimtzah* as meaning "for an evil report" is in agreement with the above interpretation. However, that which Onkelos said "in their generations" shows that his intent is that even throughout the generations *in Israel* this affair will become a source of evil, as is explained further on.

happened in the case of Jeroboam who said, *Ye have gone up long enough to Jerusalem; behold thy gods, O Israel, which brought thee up out of the land of Egypt.* [375] Moses thus saw how the incident of the calf would remain a cause for sin throughout the generations.

Now *shimtzah* according to Onkelos means "evil report," it being a common term in the language of our Rabbis, such as "a *shemetz* (a blemish of) descent." [376] Perhaps according to their [377] opinion, that which Scripture states, *and mine ear received a 'shemetz' thereof,* [378] also means that his [i.e., Eliphaz the Temanite's] ear received knowledge of man's blemish and imperfection, saying, *Behold, He putteth no trust in His servants, and His angels He chargeth with folly; how much less them that dwell in houses of clay, whose foundation is in dust.*[379] Similarly, *and what 'shemetz davar' is heard of Him*[380] means that of all His ways there is nothing deserving of reproach or censure, but only praise and adoration.

In line with the plain meaning of Scripture *shemetz* means "little." Thus [*and mine ear received a 'shemetz' thereof* [378] means] that his ear received but a whisper thereof. *And what 'shemetz davar' is heard of Him*[380] means that whatever is heard and said about G-d's strength and His powers, is but a minute amount in relation to the greatness of His deeds. Similarly, *l'shimtzah b'kameihem* means that Aaron had uncovered the people, thus enabling their enemies to diminish them, for this great sin would lessen them in the eyes of their enemies, or reduce their merits when coming to battle with the enemy, something like that which is said, *and I shall diminish them, that they shall no more rule over the nations,*[381] or as it is said, *O Eternal, correct me, but in measure; not in Thine anger, lest Thou diminish me.* [382]

---

(375) I Kings 12:28. (376) Pesachim 3 b. (377) Onkelos' and that of the Rabbis, as mentioned above. (378) Job 4:12. (379) *Ibid.,* Verses 18-19. (380) *Ibid.,* 26:14. (381) Ezekiel 29:15. (382) Jeremiah 10:24.

26. AND MOSES STOOD IN THE GATE OF THE CAMP. This is connected with what is said in the preceding verse, thus stating that when Moses saw that the people would be a source of derision and disgrace amongst their enemies, and would thereby profane the Name of G-d, he stood in the gate of the camp and called out loudly, *Whoso is on the Eternal's side, let him come unto me;* and they killed publicly all those who worshipped the calf, so that the matter be heard about amongst their enemies, and G-d's Name would thus be sanctified, in place of the profanation that they had caused.

27. THUS SAITH THE ETERNAL, THE G-D OF ISRAEL. The reason for this expression [383] is that since the worshippers of the calf had intended to sacrifice to the G-d of Israel, therefore the attribute of justice extracted punishment from them, because they "mutilated the shoots" [of faith], [384] and besides, *for the judgment is G-d's.* [385] It is for this reason that he [Moses], said of the Levites, *for the G-d of Israel hath separated you from the congregation of Israel,* [386] for the Service is to the G-d of Israel, and to His Name they were separated by virtue of this meritorious deed.

PUT YE EVERY MAN HIS SWORD UPON HIS THIGH. Since there were many worshippers of the calf, and they could not have all been brought to the court, therefore Moses commanded all the sons of Levi to put on their swords, in a similar way to that which our Rabbis have said, [387] that if you cannot administer to the guilty the specific kind of death mentioned for his case, you may execute him by any means that you can. Now this procedure was a decision only for an emergency, in order to sanctify G-d's Name, since those who worshipped [the calf] had not been forewarned [of the death penalty], for who had warned them beforehand?

---

(383) *'Elokei' (the G-d of) Israel* — the Divine Name which denotes the attribute of justice. (384) See Note 308 above. (385) Deuteronomy 1:17. (386) Numbers 16:9. (387) Sanhedrin 45 b.

The sons of Levi, however, recognized those whom they killed as the worshippers of the calf. And in the opinion of the Sage who says [388] that if there were witnesses [to the act of idolatry] and forewarning of the penalty, the offender's death was by hand of man, as Rashi wrote,[389] then we shall interpret the meaning of the verse to be that Moses commanded the sons of Levi to put on their swords and take hold of the offenders by force and bring them to court before Moses or before the Sanhedrin. Those who were found to have worshipped the calf in the presence of witnesses and with forewarning, were then put to death by stoning, as is the punishment of those who worship idols, or perhaps their death was by the sword, as is the punishment of a whole city gone astray.[390] Thus all the sons of Levi remained loyal to G-d, and it was they who had warned the people not to worship the calf or sacrifice to it, seeing that Aaron had only commanded to hold a feast to the Eternal alone, as I have explained.[391]

The correct interpretation[392] is in accordance with the opinion of the Sage who says:[388] "Those who slaughtered or burnt the sacrificial portions [to the calf] were punished by the sword;[393] those who embraced and kissed it, were punished with death [by the hand of Heaven]; those who merely rejoiced in their heart, were afflicted with dropsy," as is stated in Tractate Yoma.[388] Thus it was all a decision under circumstances of emergency, because embracing or kissing an idol does not make one liable to death [by the hand of Heaven] in all future generations.

AND SLAY EVERY MAN HIS BROTHER. This means that they were not to spare nor conceal[394] brother, friend, or relative.

---

(388) Yoma 66 b. The Gemara there brings this opinion in the name of one of two Amoraim, Rav and Levi. Hence Ramban writes anonymously: "in the opinion of the Sage who says..." (389) Verse 20 here. (390) Deuteronomy 13:13-16. (391) Above, Verse 5. (392) Ramban now goes back to his original thesis, that this whole procedure was a decision under emergency. (393) Even though such an offense makes the offender liable to stoning according to Torah-law, but since the law of the four kinds of death had not been declared yet, the offenders were treated under the law of "the sons of Noah" to whom its form of punishment is applicable (Rashi Yoma 66 b). (394) See Deuteronomy 13:9.

And the meaning of the expression, *Thus saith the Eternal, the G-d of Israel: [Put ye every man his sword...]* is not [as Rashi has it, a command] based upon the verse, *He that sacrificeth unto the gods shall be utterly destroyed,* [395] since these worshippers of the calf were not strictly liable to death [as has been explained above], but it was a command said to Moses by the Almighty which was not written in the Torah; for when *the Glorious Name* [396] *repented of the evil,* [397] He commanded Moses, "Since you do not want Me to destroy them, you should slay its worshippers by the sword," similar to that which is said, *Take all of the chiefs of the people, and hang them up unto the Eternal in face of the sun, that the fierce anger of the Eternal may turn away from Israel.* [398] This commandment is thus similar to the one in connection with the manna, where it is said, *This is the thing which the Eternal hath commanded: Let an omerful of it be kept* etc. [399] I have already mentioned [400] similar instances.

32. YET NOW, IF THOU WILT FORGIVE THEIR SIN. Rashi comments: "If You forgive their sins — well and good, and I do not say to you 'Blot me out.' *But if not, blot me out.* This is thus an abbreviated verse. There are many cases similar to it. *Out of Thy book* — this means out of the whole Torah; so that people should not say about me that I was not worthy [successful] to seek mercy for them." But if so, what was the answer that the Holy One, blessed be He, gave to Moses — *Whosoever hath sinned against Me, him will I blot out of My book* [401] — since there was no one else to be blotted out of His book [i.e. the Torah, since they are not mentioned therein to begin with]? Perhaps [Rashi] will interpret it thus: "I shall only blot out [from My Torah] those who have sinned against Me, and you have not sinned against Me." But this is not correct.

Rabbi Abraham ibn Ezra wrote that the expression *out of Thy book which Thou hast written* is like, *The judgment was set, and*

---

(395) Above, 22:19. (396) Deuteronomy 28:58. (397) Verse 14. (398) Numbers 25:4. (399) Above, 16:32. There too the original command given to Moses is not written in the Torah. (400) *Ibid.,* 10:2, and 11:1. (401) Verse 33.

the books were opened,[402] "the books" in Ibn Ezra's opinion being the dispositions of the heavenly bodies upon which the fate of the lower creatures depends. And G-d answered, *Whosoever had sinned against Me, him will I blot out from My book,*[401] which means: "I will not blot you out, but I will blot out from among the people those sinners who have sinned against Me in their thoughts, and were not killed by the sons of Levi." It is with reference to this that it is said, *And the Eternal smote the people.*[403] — This interpretation [of Ibn Ezra] does not appear to me to be correct, for besides those killed by the sword of the sons of Levi and those who died in the plague, most of the people had sinned against Him, as I have written.[404]

In my opinion [the interpretation of the verse is as follows]: Moses said, "*Yet now, if Thou wilt forgive their sin* in Thine mercies [— well and good]; *but if not, blot me out* in their place *from the book* of life, and I will share their punishment," it being similar to what Scripture says, *But he was wounded because of our transgressions, he was crushed because of our iniquities; the chastisement of our welfare was upon him, and with his stripes we were healed.*[405] And the Holy One, blessed be He, answered Moses: "I will erase from My book [of life] whosoever sinned, but not you, for you have not sinned."

34. AND NOW GO, LEAD THE PEOPLE. [G-d is saying here:] "Since I have repented from destroying them, lead them *unto the place of which I have spoken unto thee* — to the place of the Amorite, the Canaanite, etc." However, He did not want to mention this expressly, for this was said in a manner of anger, as if to say: "What I have said to you, I shall do in your honor, but I will not forgive them their sin, for *in the day when I visit, I will visit their sin upon them* — I will visit it upon them even after they come to the Land." This was an allusion to the time of the exile, or to what our Rabbis have said [406] that "No punishment [ever comes upon Israel] in which there is not a small part for the sin of the golden calf."

(402) Daniel 7:10. (403) Verse 35. (404) Above, Verse 7. (405) Isaiah 53:5. (406) Shemoth Rabbah 43:3.

EXODUS XXXII, KI THISA

35. AND THE ETERNAL SMOTE THE PEOPLE. Scripture does not state how many died in this plague, as it stated the number of those that fell by the hand of the sons of Levi,[407] and as it mentioned in the case of the plague *about the matter of Korah,*[408] and in connection with the Baal of Peor,[409] the reason perhaps being that those here did not all die in one plague, but they were smitten and died prematurely, something like it said, *but the Eternal shall smite him, or his day shall come to die.*[410] Perhaps Scripture did not bother to number them, for similarly it did not number those that died in the plague at Taberah,[411] and at Kibroth-hattaavah, where it says, *and the Eternal smote the people with a very great plague.*[412] Those that fell, however, through the sons of Levi He counted in their honor, thus saying that they slew many of the people but yet they did not fear them, for they trusted in the Eternal.

BECAUSE THEY MADE THE CALF. This means that they were not amongst those who worshipped it or sacrificed to it,[413] but they were the men who "made" it, that is to say, they were the ones who gathered around Aaron and brought him the gold. Now since Scripture states that they were punished *for making the calf,* not for worshipping it, and in reality they did not make it, it explains further, *which Aaron made,* meaning that Aaron made it at their command.

But Onkelos translated [the expression, *because they 'made' the calf*], "because they 'worshipped' the calf which Aaron made." By this Onkelos intended to explain that the ones who died in the plague were those who embraced and kissed it, and were pleased with the calf. Now [although the same term *asah* ("did") is mentioned in both cases, *because they 'made' the calf, which Aaron 'made'*], Onkelos did not feel obliged to translate both alike [but instead he translated: "because they 'worshipped' the calf,

---

(407) Above, Verse 28: *and there fell of the people that day about three thousand men.* (408) Numbers 17:14: *Now they that died by the plague were fourteen thousand and seven hundred.* (409) Ibid., 25:9: *And those that died by the plague were twenty and four thousand.* (410) I Samuel 26:10. (411) Numbers 11:3. (412) Ibid., 33. (413) Above, Verse 8.

which Aaron 'made' "]. A similar case [of Onkelos' rendition] is the verse, *and whatsoever they 'did' there, he was the 'doer' of it,* [414] which he translated: "and whatsoever they did there 'was done' by his command." [415]

This plague occurred after Moses had punished the worshippers and prayed for Israel, saying, *and if not, blot me, I pray Thee, out of Thy book.*[416] For because Moses had shown his readiness to give his life for them, the Holy One, blessed be He, had mercy upon them, and told him to bring them up to the Land, and that He would send an angel before them;[417] but since He wanted to take away from them part of the great sin, in order that they should be worthy [to go up to the Land], He sent upon them this plague. Or it may be that He had decreed this plague upon them [before Moses' prayer] and the plague had already begun, and after that He said again to Moses, *Go up hence, thou and the people,* [418] meaning, that the plague will not blot out their sin from before Me so that I should again dwell in their midst. He mentioned though, *unto the land of which I swore unto Abraham, to Isaac, and to Jacob,* [418] and further said, *and I will drive out the Canaanite,* etc.; [417] for on account of the plague which He brought or decreed upon them, part of their sin was blotted out, and He was partially appeased to them, in remembering the merit of the patriarchs, and [promising] that He would fulfill to them the oath He had taken to bring them *unto a good land, a land flowing with milk and honey.* [419] Thus He hinted to Moses that the earth [i.e., the land of Canaan] would not become corrupt [420] nor would it be *defiled under the inhabitants thereof* [421] on account of their sin, and that He would drive out all the six nations whose land they were originally promised. [422] And He also said by way of pacification, *for I will not go up in the midst of thee,* [423] this being to your benefit, *lest I consume thee in the way,* [423] because of your stiff-neckedness.

---

(414) Genesis 39:22. (415) Thus Onkelos translated the same form of the verb once in the active tense and once in the passive. (416) Verse 32. (417) Further, 33:2. (418) *Ibid.,* Verse 1. (419) Above, 3:8. (420) See Genesis 6:11. (421) Isaiah 24:5. (422) Above, 3:8. (423) Further, 33:3.

Thus there were here two punishments for Israel: firstly, that He would not cause His Divine Glory to dwell amongst them, and secondly, that He would send an angel before Moses until the nations would be driven out; but He did not promise them after they would inherit the Land even an angel to help them, for this is why He mentioned *in the way* [*lest I consume thee 'in the way'*]. It is with reference to all this that Scripture says, *And when the people heard these evil tidings, they mourned; and no man put on him his ornaments* [424] — just as mourners. But G-d is merciful, abounding in compassion, and when He saw that they mourned, He said again by way of mercy, *Say unto the children of Israel* etc., [425] for up till now He had used the terms, *thy people,* [426] and *the people,* [418] but now He mentioned them by their beloved name, and He commanded Moses to tell them that it was to their benefit that He would not go up in their midst, in order that He should not consume them in one moment. However, they have done well in repenting and mourning for their sin. So should they always do, *and I will know what to do unto* them. [425] That is to say, I will visit their sin in accordance with My knowledge of their mourning and repenting their sin, since it is I Who tries the heart and searches the kidneys. [427]

By way of the Truth, [the mystic teachings of the Cabala], the expression, *that I may know what to do unto thee* [425] means that He will do unto them in the knowledge of mercy, similar to what is said, *and if not, I will know,* [428] as I have already explained. [429]

33 6. AND THE CHILDREN OF ISRAEL STRIPPED THEMSELVES OF THEIR ORNAMENTS. The meaning of this is that when they heard this declaration, they stripped and divested themselves of all their ornaments, even more so than they had done before. Now Onkelos who translated the word *edi* (ornament) as "the equipment of armor," was in agreement with the opinion of the Sage [430] in Bereshith Rabbah [431] who said "He tied them

---

(424) *Ibid.*, Verse 4. (425) *Ibid.*, Verse 5. (426) Above, 32:7. (427) See Jeremiah 17:10. (428) Genesis 18:21. (429) *Ibid.*, Verse 20. Vol. I, p. 245. (430) Reference is to Rabbi Shimon ben Yochai. (431) I have not found it in Bereshith Rabbah, but in Shemoth Rabbah 45:1.

with belts." That is to say, at the time of the Giving of the Torah the Holy One, blessed be He, girded them with weapons of armor to save them from all mishaps and the angel of death, just as the Rabbis have interpreted:[432] *" 'charuth' (graven) upon the Tablets*[433] — *'cheiruth'* (freedom) from the angel of death" [was given to the Israelites together with the Tablets of the Law], these [weapons of armor] being the Names of the Holy One, blessed be He.[434] Thus Israel now accepted upon themselves death from their own free will as a form of punishment for the incident of the calf. This was indeed an expression of great repentance and regret for their sin.

7. NOW MOSES TOOK THE TENT AND WOULD PITCH IT WITHOUT THE CAMP. Rashi wrote: "This was practiced by Moses from the Day of Atonement until the Tabernacle was set up [five and a half months later — on the first day of Nisan], but not afterwards. For on the seventeenth day of Tammuz the Tablets of the Law were broken, on the eighteenth he burnt the calf and brought the sinners to judgment, and on the nineteenth he ascended the mountain and stayed there for forty days. On the first of Ellul it was said to him, *and come up in the morning*[435] to receive the second Tablets. There he spent another forty days [which terminated on the tenth day of Tishri]. On the tenth of Tishri the Holy One, blessed be He, became reconciled with Israel, and He handed over to Moses the second Tablets, whereupon Moses came down the mountain and began to command them concerning the work of the Tabernacle. This occupied them till the first of Nisan, and from that time on, since the Tabernacle was set up, G-d only communicated with him from there." This also is the opinion of Rabbi Abraham ibn Ezra, that all this [narrated here in Verses 7-11] took place after Moses brought down the second Tablets [the account of which is narrated further on in 34:1-10], there being no strict chronological order in the narrative of the Torah.

(432) Erubin 54 a. (433) Above, 32:16. (434) And as long as they were in possession of that knowledge they were above the power of the angel of death. Now, however, that they were divested of this knowledge they became subject to the decree of death as all human beings are (Bachya, Vol. II, p. 340, in my edition). (435) Further, 34:2.

EXODUS XXXIII, KI THISA

But it does not appear to me to be correct, for what reason is there to mention this [practice of Moses] here in the middle of the section? The words of our Rabbis in all Midrashim are also to the effect that Moses did this on account of their sin with the calf. Thus they explained [436] [that Moses said], "One who is excommunicated from the master, is also excommunicated from the disciple," and as Rashi mentioned [that G-d said to Moses], "I am angry and you are angry; if so, who will bring them near to Me?" Now if the removal of the Tent was after the Day of Atonement [as Rashi and Ibn Ezra have it], the Holy One, blessed be He, as well as Moses, was already in [complete] reconciliation with them! Rather, it appears that on the day that he came down from the mountain — on the seventeenth of Tamuz — he burnt the calf and punished the worshippers. [437] On the next day, [i.e., on the eighteenth of Tammuz] he told them that he would go up to G-d to seek atonement for them, [438] and so he went up to the mountain where the Glory was. This is the sense of the verse, *And Moses returned unto the Eternal,* [439] and prayed briefly: *Oh, this people have sinned a great sin,* [439] and G-d answered him, *Whosoever hath sinned against Me,* etc.; [440] *And now go, lead the people,* [441] and the plague began. [442] Then He commanded him, *Depart, go up hence, thou and the people* etc., [443] and Moses told this to Israel, *and they mourned, and stripped themselves of the ornaments.* [444] Then Moses realized that the matter was a very long one, and did not know what the end thereof would be, therefore he took the tent and pitched it outside the camp so that the Divine Glory would communicate with him from there, for it was no longer dwelling in the midst of the people, and if the tent were to be in the midst of the camp, He would not communicate with him from there. Scripture continues, *and it came to pass, that every one that sought the Eternal...,* [445] meaning that everyone

---

(436) Shemoth Rabbah 45:3. (437) And not, as Rashi has it, that the burning of the calf and the punishing of the sinners took place on the eighteenth of Tammuz. (438) Above, 32:30. (439) *Ibid.,* Verse 31. (440) *Ibid.,* Verse 33. (441) *Ibid.,* Verse 34. (442) *Ibid.,* Verse 35. (443) Verse 1 here. (444) Verses 4-6. (445) In Verse 7 here.

who sought the Eternal used to go out to him.[446] Then Scripture [in Verse 8-11] completed the narrative of all that happened whilst the tent was there until the Tabernacle was set up, which was, according to the opinion of our Sages, from the Day of Atonement until the first day of Nisan.[447]

I have seen in Pirkei d'Rabbi Eliezer [the following text]:[448] "Rabbi Yehoshua ben Korcha says: "[After the Revelation] Moses spent forty days on the mountain, studying the Written Law at daytime, and the Oral Law at night. After the forty days he took the Tablets and came back to the camp. On the seventeenth of Tammuz he broke the Tablets and killed the sinners of Israel, and then stayed in the camp forty days until he burnt the calf and ground it like dust of the earth. Thus he eliminated idolatry from Israel, and established each tribe in its place. On the first of Ellul the Holy One, blessed be He, said to him, *come up unto Me into the mount* [449] [to be given the second Tablets]. Then the ram's horn was sounded throughout the camp, announcing to the people that Moses was going up the mountain, so that [they might not be alarmed by his absence] and not be misled anymore after idols. [On that day] the Holy One, blessed be He, was exalted by the sound of that ram's horn, as it is said, *G-d is gone up amidst shouting, the Eternal amidst the sound of the horn.*[450] And thus likewise the Sages ordained that we blow the horn every year on the first day of Ellul."[451] Thus far are the words of this Agadah. And if this is so, then the whole section from: *Moses took the tent,* applied to the time from the eighteenth of Tammuz till the end of the forty days [i.e., up to the first of Ellul], and from the Day of Atonement till the first of Nisan [when the Tabernacle was set up]. But this exposition does not fit in well with what

---

(446) Ramban interprets the Hebrew *yeitzei* (the imperfect — "was going out") as *yotzei* (a participle — taking of the nature of both a verb and an adjective — "used to go out"). Rashi explained it likewise. (447) See Ramban further, 40:2. (448) Chapters of Rabbi Eliezer, Chapter 46. (449) Deuteronomy 10:1. (450) Psalm 47:6. "For by the sound of this horn Israel vowed eternally never again to be deceived by the idols" (R'dal; see my Hebrew commentary, p. 518). (451) The Shofar is now sounded in the synagogue every morning during the whole month of Ellul, except on the Sabbaths and on the day before the New Year.

Scripture says, *And I fell down before the Eternal, as at the first, forty days and forty nights; I did neither eat bread etc.,*[452] and it is further written there, *So I fell down before the Eternal the forty days and forty nights that I fell down; because the Eternal had said He would destroy you,*[453] and it is impossible that all this refers to the last forty days [i.e., between the first of Ellul and the Day of Atonement], since He told him, *Hew thee two Tablets of stone... and come up unto Me into the mount,*[449] thus these last forty days were already those of G-d's good-will, after He had already nullified the decree that *He would destroy you!*[454]

11. AND HIS MINISTER JOSHUA, 'BIN' (THE SON OF) NUN, 'NA'AR' (A LAD). Rabbi Abraham ibn Ezra wrote: "Joshua lived a hundred and ten years,[455] and the Sages say[456] that it took him seven years to conquer the Land [of Israel] and seven years to apportion it amongst the tribes. If so, he was now fifty-six years old,[457] and how does Scripture call him *na'ar* (lad)? We must therefore say that this is the meaning thereof: *and his minister Joshua the son of Nun* rendered him such service as can be given only by a youthful attendant."

In my opinion it is the way of the Sacred Language to call any attendant [regardless of age] *na'ar*, for the person of high office is called *ish* (man),[458] and [with respect to him] his attendant is called *na'ar*. Thus: *Gehazi 'na'aro' (his attendant);*[459] *Let*

---

(452) Deuteronomy 9:18. (453) *Ibid.*, Verse 25. (454) From all this it is thus obvious that there was an intervening period of forty days [i.e. from the eighteenth of Tammuz to the twenty-ninth of Ab] when Moses was on the mountain interceeding for Israel. So how could the Pirkei d'Rabbi Eliezer hold that there were only two ascents of forty-day periods of Moses? — In his commentary to that Midrash, Rabbi David Luria answers Ramban's question by suggesting that the phrase *He would destroy you* does not refer to the beginning of that verse, *so I fell down before the Eternal*, but reverts to the very beginning of the incident of the calf, when G-d had said He would destroy them. The verse itself can still apply then to the final forty days, which culminated on the Day of Atonement. (455) Joshua 24:29. (456) Arakhin 13 a. (457) The forty years of the wilderness plus the fourteen years in the Land of Israel, make a total of fifty-four years. Subtract these from a hundred and ten, and you are left with fifty-six. Yet Scripture calls him *na'ar* (lad)! (458) See Ramban Genesis 9:20, Vol. I, p. 141. (459) II Kings 4:12.

'ha'ne'arim' (the attendants), I pray thee, arise and play before us.[460] Similarly, *and ten 'ne'arim' (attendants) that bore Joab's armor,*[461] and Joab [David's commander-in-chief] would surely only turn over his armor to valiant men who stood near him! And it is also written, *And Joshua said unto the two 'men' that had spied out the land,*[462] and yet it is written there, *and 'ha'ne'arim' the spies went in* etc!*[463] [Thus we must say that the] term [*ha'ne'arim*] is used because they were servants of the congregation, acting for them as spies. There are many similar instances. So also, *the 'na'arei' of the king that ministered unto him,*[464] [the second half of the phrase being in apposition,] explaining that they were the servants who attended the king personally, and not the attendants of the court. And if so, our verse is stating: *and his minister Joshua the son of Nun* was always in attendance, and never departed out of the tent.

The reason for the form *'bin' Nun* [instead of *'ben' Nun*] is that the vowel *chirik* comes sometimes in place of the *segal* [which would have made it "ben Nun"]. Similar cases are: *The words of Agur 'bin' (the son of) Jakeh;*[465] *'she'bin lailah hayah' (which came up in a night) 'u'bin lailah avad' (and perished in a night);*[466] *'im bin hakoth harasha' (if the wicked man deserve to be beaten).*[467]

Yet despite all this I wonder! Why [of all the times that Joshua the son of Nun is cited in the Scriptures] is the name of this righteous man not once mentioned properly [i.e., *'ben'* Nun]? Therefore I think that they used to call him in this way as a mark of honor, since he was the greatest of the disciples of Moses our teacher, and so they called him *binun,* meaning "the understanding one," since there was *none so discreet and wise* as he.[468] Or it may be that the meaning of it is: "Joshua, whom understanding

---

(460) II Samuel 2:14.   (461) *Ibid.*, 18:15.   (462) Joshua 6:22. (463) *Ibid.*, Verse 23.   (464) Esther 2:2.   (465) Proverbs 30:1. Normally it should have been *ben.*   (466) Jonah 4:10. Here too the words should have been: *she'ben, u'ben.*   (467) Deuteronomy 25:2. Here likewise the sense of the verse is: "*ben hakoth* — a person deserving to be beaten, because he hit his friend." So clearly explained in Ibn Ezra *ibid.*   (468) Genesis 41:39.

begot;" they thus used the term *nun* as in the expression, *may his name 'yinon' (be continued) as long as the sun.*[469]

12. AND MOSES SAID UNTO THE ETERNAL: 'SEE, THOU SAYEST UNTO ME: BRING UP THIS PEOPLE.' This happened on Mount Sinai, when Moses went up there on the nineteenth of Tammuz. It was not necessary though for Scripture to say, "and Moses went up to G-d, and he said to him, 'See, Thou sayest unto me, etc.,' " for it is known that as long as the Glory dwelled upon Mount Sinai, all communications [to Moses] took place there. Similarly Moses said, *and now I will go up unto the Eternal,*[470] and it is also said, *And Moses returned unto the Eternal,*[471] meaning that he returned *to the place where he had stood before the Eternal.*[472]

AND THOU HAST NOT LET ME KNOW WHOM THOU WILT SEND WITH ME. "And that which You said to me, *Behold, I send an angel before thee,* [473] — that is not 'letting me know,' for I am not satisfied with it." This is Rashi's language. But it is not correct to fit this thought into the language of the verse. Besides, why should Moses have said this only now [that he was not satisfied with the angel], and when the matter was communicated to him he remained quiet? Did Moses think to gain because of the incident of the calf? Instead, the purport thereof is as follows: The Holy One, blessed be He, had told Moses here, *and I will send an angel before thee,* [474] and Moses told Him, *Thou has not let me know* who is that angel *whom Thou wilt send with me,* and whether it is that first angel in whom is Thy Name. [475] This is the sense of the expression, *Yet Thou hast said: I know thee by Name,* meaning that You have known me and exalted me by [the knowledge of] Your Name. And so also did Rabbi Abraham ibn Ezra explain the verse here. In his opinion [476] the angel he [i.e., Moses] wanted was Michael. With his good sense [Ibn Ezra] understood the verses to imply that the first angel was pleasing to

---

(469) Psalms 72:17. (470) Above, 32:30. (471) *Ibid.*, Verse 31. (472) Genesis 19:27. (473) Above, 23:20. (474) Above, Verse 2 (in this chapter). (475) *Ibid.*, 23:21. (476) So explained by Ibn Ezra above 23:20 (towards the end).

Moses and to Israel. He could not, however, know the truth, since he neither heard it [from others] nor did he prophesy it [on his own].[477]

14. 'PANAI' (MY PRESENCE) SHALL GO. In the opinion of all commentators this means, "I myself will go." And they brought a parallel expression to this from the verse, *'upanecha' (and thine own person) shalt go to battle.*[478] AND HE [Moses] SAID UNTO HIM: IF 'PANECHA' (THY PRESENCE) GO NOT WITH ME, CARRY US NOT UP HENCE. The meaning thereof according to Rashi is as follows: "This is what I desired, for if it be by an angel, rather do not carry us up from here." But G-d forbid! that Moses should say, *If Thy presence go not,* after he had already been promised, *My presence shall go!*

And Rabbi Abraham ibn Ezra explained that G-d said to Moses: "I Myself will go, and only you will I give rest, for only with you will I go [but I will not dwell in the midst of the people]." But Moses replied: "If Your presence does not go with the whole nation, *carry us not up hence.*" This is why Moses used the plural, "carry us up." But this interpretation too, does not fit the verses properly. For Moses said at first, *Thou hast not let me know whom Thou wilt send with me*[479] — in the singular. Now even at the time of G-d's good-will, before the sin [with the golden calf occurred], He also said, *Behold, I send an angel before thee, to keep thee by the way, and to bring thee into the place which I have prepared,*[473] [and yet this promise too is expressed in the singular — to Moses]! And if you will say that the singular there [*before 'thee', to keep 'thee'* etc.] refers to Israel [as one unit], then here also it could be explained to refer to all Israel! Besides, if it is so [as Ibn Ezra interpreted], that Moses requested of G-d that He inform him who is the angel He would send with him, then we see that Moses was satisfied with the angel, concerning

---

(477) This is a veiled criticism of Ibn Ezra who neither received the mystic traditions of the Cabala from others, nor studied them by himself. As Ramban will explain in the following verse, this whole subject can be understood only through "the way of Truth."   (478) II Samuel 17:11.   (479) Verse 12.

whom it is said, *for My Name is in him*, [475] and G-d answered him with a double, and redoubled, beneficence, over and above that which he had asked for — that He Himself would go!

But this section of Scripture cannot possibly be grasped by one who has not heard the secrets of the Torah. The following is its meaning by way of the Truth. Moses said, and *Thou hast not let me know* who is the angel *Thou wilt send with me,* and he requested that He fulfill two things He had said to him: firstly, that *I know thee by Name,* meaning [G-d said to Moses] that "I will be known to you by My [Great] Name, for your sake" [and this was now Moses' request, that he be not divested of this highest degree of prophecy on account of the incident of the calf]. It is possible that the phrase, *yet Thou hast said,* [*I know thee by Name*], is based upon what He had said to Moses [with reference to the patriarchs], *but by My Name the Eternal I made Me not known to them,* [480] as I have explained [there]. And secondly Moses had been told: *and thou hast also found grace in My sight,* meaning that he will find grace, which is the cleaving of knowledge.[481] And Moses continued, *Now therefore, I pray Thee, if I have found grace in Thy sight,*[482] in the attribute of justice, *show me now* the paths of the ways [483] even as Thou art known by Thy Name, *that I may know Thee* to declare Thy Unity, *to the end that I may find* the great *grace; and consider that this nation is Thy people* — Thou art their Father, and they are Thy children. It is this that Onkelos intended in translating the verse thus: "make me then know the path of Thy goodness to the end that I may know Thy mercy." Then the Holy One, blessed be He, answered him, *My presence shall go* — the messenger of the covenant, whom ye delight in, [484] for in him My presence will be seen, since it is with reference to him that it is said, *in an acceptable time have I answered thee;* [485] *for My Name is in him.* [475] '*Vahanichothi lach*' (*and I will give thee rest*) through

---

(480) Above, 6:3. But to Moses He did reveal Himself by His Great Name, as explained there. (481) That G-d always be with them in the wilderness *face to face* (Abusaula). (482) Verse 13. (483) "The paths of goodness with which You conduct Your world, and by which You are known" (Bachya). (484) Malachi 3:1. (485) Isaiah 49:8.

him, that he should not conduct himself towards you with the stringent attribute of justice but with the measure which is inclusive of the attribute of mercy, the usage [of the word *vahanichothi*] being associated with the expression, *Therefore it shall be 'b'haniyach' (when) the Eternal thy G-d (hath given thee rest) from all thine enemies.*[486] This is similar to that which is said, *Thus shall Mine anger spend itself, 'vahanichothi' (and I will satisfy) My fury upon them.*[487] Then Moses answered, *If Thy presence* — Thou Thyself and in Thy Glory — *go not, carry us not up hence,* for Thou art to be with us *face to face,*[488] for such were the conditions [as mentioned] in the section of *Va'eira.*[489] Likewise Moses mentioned above, *with great power and with a mighty hand,*[490] and so now too he asked that He bring them to the Land *with great power and with a mighty hand,* just as He took them out with them from Egypt.

16. 'V'NIPHLINU' (SO THAT WE BE DISTINGUISHED) I AND THY PEOPLE. This means that our portion be that which is unique, something which is not to be found amongst *all the people that are upon the face of the earth.*

17. I WILL DO THIS THING ALSO THAT THOU HAST SPOKEN. Perhaps this manifestation of G-d's good-will was at the end of the second [period of] forty days, in accordance with the opinion of our Rabbis,[491] when the Holy One, blessed be He, became completely appeased with him, and He said to him, *Hew thee two Tablets of stone like unto the first.*[492]

18. AND HE [Moses] SAID: 'SHOW ME, I PRAY THEE, THY GLORY.' Moses desired that he should actually see in clear sight the Glory of G-d. It is possible that *Thy Glory* here means the

---

(486) Deuteronomy 25:19.   (487) Ezekiel 5:13.   (488) Deuteronomy 5:4.   (489) Above, 6:6-8.   (490) *Ibid.*, 32:11.   (491) See above in Verse 7 where Ramban quotes the Pirkei d'Rabbi Eliezer, that Moses went up to the mountain for forty days only twice, the second time culminating on the Day of Atonement. This is Ramban's intent in writing here "at the end of the *second* forty days according to the opinion of our Rabbis." Rashi, quoted there, holds that there were three such periods.   (492) Further, 34:1.

EXODUS XXXIII, KI THISA

Great Glory — the clear vision.[493] And G-d answered him, *I will make* the measure of *all My goodness pass before thee*,[494] that you will comprehend and understand all My goodness more than all men, but the vision of the Presence that you have asked for, you will not be able to see.

19. AND I WILL PROCLAIM THE NAME OF THE ETERNAL BEFORE THEE. I will proclaim before you the Great Name, for you will not be able to see Him. AND I WILL BE GRACIOUS [through it] TO WHOM I WILL BE GRACIOUS, AND WILL SHOW MERCY [through it] TO WHOM I WILL SHOW MERCY. This means that by this proclamation you will know the attributes of graciousness and mercy, by which people are shown grace and mercy through My name and through My goodness. It is with reference to this [knowledge received by Moses] that G-d said of him, *he is trusted in all My house*,[495] for a man's goodness is in his house.

20. FOR MAN SHALL NOT SEE ME AND LIVE. This does not mean that man could see Him, but must immediately die; it means that before he could grasp the sight, his soul would depart from him, for even of the vision of the angels it is said, *by reason of the vision my pains are come upon me*, [*and I retained no strength*].[496]

21. BEHOLD, THERE IS A PLACE BY ME — on this mountain, where My Glory resides. AND THOU SHALT STAND UPON THE ROCK — which was upon the mountain, as it is said, *Behold, I will stand before thee there upon the rock in Horeb.*[497]

23. BUT MY FACE SHALL NOT BE SEEN — meaning the clear countenance, as I have explained.[498] It is possible that the word *achorai (My back — and thou shalt see 'My back')* is of similar

---

(493) See Vol. I, p. 229. (494) Verse 19. (495) Numbers 12:7.
(496) Daniel 10:16. (497) Above, 17:6. (498) Above, Verse 18.

usage as in the verse, *Thou hast hemmed me in behind and before*, [499] in accordance with the opinion of our Rabbis. [500]

34

3. AND NO MAN SHALL COME UP WITH THEE. None of the elders of Israel at all should go up with you, as they had done at the first Tablets of the Law. [501] NEITHER LET ANY MAN BE SEEN THROUGHOUT ALL THE MOUNT — even at the foot of the mountain, where Israel had stood at first [during the Revelation]. NEITHER LET THE FLOCKS NOR HERDS FEED BEFORE THAT MOUNT — in front of it. For at [the giving of] the first Tablets they had been warned only, *no hand shall touch it* [i.e., the mountain] ... *whether it be beast or man,* [502] and now they were still under that admonition, for the Glory was always on the mountain until the last Tablets of the Law were given. However, at the giving of these Tablets He was now more stringent than at the first Revelation [in requiring that none of the elders accompany Moses]. The reason for all this was that at the first Tablets the Revelation was for all Israel, whereas this one was only for Moses, because of his merit and his prayer, and the Glory revealed on the mountain for [the giving of] the last Tablets would be greater than that of the first ones.

5. AND HE STOOD WITH HIM THERE. That is, the Eternal stood — something like it is said, *And the Eternal came, and stood* [503] — with Moses, meaning, that Moses entered into the cloud as he had done at first. [504]

6. AND THE ETERNAL PASSED BY BEFORE HIM. This means that He fulfilled His promise to Moses, *I will make all My goodness pass before thee.* [494]

AND HE PROCLAIMED: 'HASHEM HASHEM E-IL' (THE ETERNAL, THE ETERNAL, G-D). These three words are sacred

---

(499) Psalms 139:5. (500) Based on this verse in Psalms the Rabbis have said (Berachoth 61 a) that Adam was originally created with two faces (see Vol. I, p. 76). Ramban's application here of this saying of the Sages is Cabalistic. (501) Above, 24:9. (502) *Ibid.,* 19:13. (503) I Samuel 3:10. (504) Above, 24:18: *And Moses entered into the midst of the cloud.*

EXODUS XXXIV, KI THISA

Names of G-d which the Sages call *midoth* (attributes), being that they constitute the attribute of the Lord of repentance, the attribute of His mercies and that of His goodness.[505] The Proper Name of G-d [i.e. the Tetragrammaton], however does not lend itself to any plural form.[506] And the attributes which are perceived in human terms are ten: *merciful and gracious,* etc. Thus on one side they are all attributes, and on the other, there are the three which denote the Names of His essence, whereas the Ten are attributes. Now the attributes also represent Names of G-d, for *merciful and gracious, long-suffering* etc. are all with reference to the essence of G-d the Most High. Therefore it does not say "the G-d Who has mercy, grace, and is long-suffering," for [that would have meant that these are His ways with the lower creatures; instead it says, *merciful and gracious, long-suffering,* indicating] that these actions emanate from G-d's attributes, [which are His essence].[507]

And abounding in goodness and truth; keeping mercy upon the thousandth generation — these three denote the attribute of mercy, since He increases the goodness over His strength and might and the truth in His mercies. *And 'notzeir' (keeping) mercy unto the thousandth generation,* for *He hath remembered His mercy and His faithfulness toward the house of Israel.*[508] Or it may be that the word *notzeir* means "sprouting," of the root, *'v'neitzer' (and a twig) shall grow forth out of his roots.*[509] And in His goodness He is *'nosei' (forgiving) iniquity and transgression and sin.* This is of the expression, *I have made, and I 'esa' (will bear).*[510]

The two phrases, *and that will by no means clear the guilty,* and *visiting the iniquity of the fathers upon the children,* are an

---

(505) See my Hebrew commentary, p. 522, for some elucidation of these Cabalistic terms. — It is noteworthy that Ramban here follows a long line of authorities who count *Eternal, Eternal* as separate attributes. See, however, Guide of the Perplexed, Vol. I, p.193, Note 5, in Friedlander's translation. (506) Ramban's intent here is to stress the perfect Unity, regardless of the various attributes. This is why he stresses that the Proper Name of G-d [and as stated here: *Hashem, Hashem*...] does not lend itself to any plural form, in spite of the fact that the various attributes are here cited (Abusaula). (507) Abusaula. (508) Psalms 98:3. (509) Isaiah 11:1. (510) Isaiah 46:4.

explanation to the one of *forgiving iniquity* [mentioned before]. It is called an "attribute" [511] because He clears the sinner by this visitation. And because this act of forgiving is not equal for iniquity, transgression and sin, but instead in each category has its own form of clearing the sinner, it is called in each case "one attribute." [512]

Now Moses bowed his head to G-d Who passed by before him, and prayed that G-d should always go in their midst and forgive their iniquity and their sin [513] in whatever they might do, and that He cause them to inherit the Land. Moses, however, did not ask that G-d forgive "our transgressions," since it is not possible that G-d forgive transgressions, which are sins of a rebellious nature; in those cases He is only to bear them [through visitation] and not to destroy them. It will not be concealed from you why these two Names [*If now I have found grace in Thy sight, O Lord, let the Lord, I pray Thee, go in the midst of us...* [513]] are written with *Aleph Daleth* [instead of in the letters of the Tetragrammaton]; [514] it is for this reason that G-d said, *Behold, I make a covenant,* [515] until [*all people shall see...*] *the work of the Eternal that it is tremendous.* [515]

9. FOR IT IS A STIFFNECKED PEOPLE. This is to be understood in its literal sense. G-d is to go in their midst because

---

(511) Thus it is now clear that Ramban counts the thirteen attributes as follows: 1. The Eternal. 2. The Eternal. 3. G-d. 4. Merciful. 5. Gracious 6. Long-suffering. 7.-8. Abounding in goodness and truth. 9. Keeping mercy unto the thousandth generation. 10.-11.-12. Forgiving iniquity, transgression and sin. 13. That will by no means clear the guilty, visiting the iniquity etc. — See Tosafoth Rosh Hashanah 17 b that such is also the opinion of Rabbeinu Tam. Ibn Ezra likewise follows generally this interpretation. (512) "And the expressions, *and that will by no means clear the guilty; visiting the iniquity of the fathers* etc., also constitute an independent attribute, for the 'clearing' done in this form of forgiving is by visitation, it being another way of forgiveness of sin, that He will not forgive it outright, but visit it upon the generations etc." (Abusaula). (513) Verse 9. (514) As Moses now prayed for the perfect Unity to go in the midst of Israel. At such time it is as if all is in the *Aleph Daleth*. Thus the first Name is in place of the Tegragrammaton, and Moses prayed that the Lord [written in *Aleph Daleth*] go in our midst in the absolute perfection of the Unity of the two Names (Abusaula). (515) Verse 10.

they are a stiffnecked people, for now that the Holy One, blessed be He, became reconciled with them, His Presence amongst those who are stiffnecked would be better than that of the angel. For He will want to increase their blessings more, since they are His people and His inheritance.[516] And just as at the time of anger it was better for them that He send before them an angel, because they are a stiffnecked people, just as He said, *lest I consume thee in the way,*[517] so at the time of good-will it is better for them that the Divine Glory go with them, because they are a stiffnecked people, and He would more readily show grace and mercy upon His servants. And G-d answered him that He would do so, that He would make the covenant and do marvels because of it, just as Moses had asked for, *so that we are distinguished, I and Thy people.*[518] He said, *before all thy people I will do marvels... and all the people amongst which thou art shall see,* because all these great and tremendous things He would do with Moses and for his sake, and the people would merely be in the covenant. It is not possible, however, to explain that G-d was promising that He would now do with Israel wonders *such as have not been wrought* before and *in all the earth, nor in any nation,* for [we do not find] that after this [statement] there were any wonders done for them, greater than those which had been wrought for them at the beginning in Egypt and at the sea; on the contrary, at first there were wrought and done for them greater things. Rather, the purport thereof hints at the dwelling of the Divine Glory amongst them, and at G-d being with Moses, *for splendor and for beauty*[519] in hidden and wondrous matters, as he said, *'v'niphlinu' (so that we are distinguished)*[518] [which is of the root *peleh* — wonder], and as I have explained. May the Holy One, blessed be He, show us wonders in His Torah.

11. OBSERVE THOU THAT WHICH I AM COMMANDING THEE THIS DAY. Of all the commandments mentioned previously He did not say *I am commanding thee.* Therefore we must explain

(516) See Deuteronomy 9:29 and 32:9. (517) Above, 33:3. (518) *Ibid.,* Verse 16. (519) *Ibid.,* 28:2.

the meaning of His words as follows: "Observe the commandments which I command you today, and do not treat them as you have treated those which I commanded you at first, when you violated everything by worshipping the idols." Now He promised here to drive out from before them the peoples [of the Land], and He warned them against their idols and against making a covenant with them, just as He had done in the section of *Behold, I send an angel before thee,*[520] thus going over the first conditions again. However, He added here, *Thou shalt make thee no molten gods,* [521] meaning that they should not do as they had done with the calf, even if their thoughts are directed to Heaven, to make themselves a guide. He restated here the subject of the three festivals,[522] that they *appear before the Eternal G-d, the G-d of Israel,*[522] as He had mentioned it there.[523] The reason [for the restatement] is known, since it comes after the admonition against idolatry. I have already explained it at the end of [*Seder*] *Vayishma Yithro.*[524]

15. AND THOU EAT OF THEIR SACRIFICE. "You might think that there is no punishment for eating thereof, but I will account it to you as if you agreed to its idolatrous worship." This is Rashi's language.[525] But I say in accordance with the opinion of our Rabbis that this constitutes an admonition against eating of the sacrifices to idols, which they said [526] is forbidden by law of the Torah, and we find no verse concerning it except this one. And the following is the meaning of the verse: "*Lest thou make a covenant with the inhabitants of the land, and they go astray after their gods,* for they will always be sacrificing to them, *and lest they call thee and thou eat of their sacrifice,* which he will

(520) *Ibid.,* 23:20.　(521) Further, Verse 17.　(522) *Ibid.,* Verse 23. (523) Above, 23:17.　(524) *Ibid.,* 20:21.　(525) In our text of Rashi the text concludes: "Because through this [partaking of his meals] you will come to take of his daughters to your sons" (as mentioned in the following Verse 16). Rashi thus connects Verse 15 with the following verse, as if to say that the danger of partaking of his meals (mentioned in Verse 15) is that it will lead to the taking of his daughters to your sons (mentioned in Verse 16). Ramban will differ with this interpretation, and hold that Verse 15 constitutes an independent prohibition.　(526) Abodah Zarah 29 b.

EXODUS XXXIV, KI THISA

sacrifice to his gods in his going astray after them, *and* lest *thou take of their daughters unto thy sons.*" Thus they are all admonitions following the first prohibition, concerning which He said, *lest thou make a covenant.*[527]

21. IN PLOWING TIME AND IN HARVEST THOU SHALT REST. In line with the plain meaning of Scripture He mentioned plowing and harvesting [as works forbidden on the Sabbath] because they are the mainstay of man's life. He mentioned the Sabbath between the holidays, putting it next to the feast of unleavened bread and the sanctification of the firstborn,[528] because they are all a reminder of the act of Creation, for in the exodus from Egypt itself there is a sign and wonder referring to the Creation, as I have explained in the Ten Commandments.[529] Besides, Scripture states that in the Sabbath likewise there is a reminder of the exodus from Egypt, as it says in the second Ten Commandments, *And thou shalt remember that thou wast a servant in the land of Egypt, and the Eternal thy G-d brought thee out thence [by a mighty hand and by an outstretched arm]; therefore the Eternal thy G-d commanded thee to keep the Sabbath-day.*[530] There I will explain it, with the help of G-d, blessed and exalted be He.

25. NEITHER SHALL THE SACRIFICE OF THE FEAST OF THE PASSOVER BE LEFT UNTO THE MORNING. In line with the plain meaning of Scripture this admonition applies to the whole [Passover-] offering, [the sacrificial portions burnt on the altar, and the flesh eaten by the Passover celebrants]: that one should not leave over of the flesh unto the morning, for that which remains of it until the morning shall be burnt with fire,[531] and also the fat of it should be burnt on the altar only until the morning. Onkelos, however, translated the verse as applying [only] to the fat which had to be taken up to be burnt on the altar,[532]

(527) In Verse 15 before us. (528) Verses 19-20. (529) Above, 20:2. (530) Deuteronomy 5:15. (531) Above, 12:10. (532) Thus Onkelos translated: "There shall not remain [overnight] away from the altar till the morning the fat of the sacrifice of the feast of the Passover."

for this "feast" [mentioned there] is explained there, *neither shall the fat of My feast remain all night until the morning,* [533] since all these commandments [mentioned here] are based upon those cited there.

Now Rashi wrote: "*Neither shall [the sacrifice of the feast of the Passover] be left unto the morning.* This is to be understood as the Targum renders it [namely, that it refers to the fat, as explained above]. An offering left overnight is not invalidated if it was placed on top of the altar [during the night, even though it was not burnt at night; and it may be burnt on the altar the following day], neither is it invalidated until the dawn of morning [i.e., if at that time it is not on top of the altar, it is deemed to have been 'left-over']. *The sacrifice of the feast of the Passover.* This refers to the sacrificial portions. From here you derive the law concerning the burning of all fats and limbs of sacrifices [which were burnt on the altar]." In the section of *Tzav* [534] I will explain this with the help of G-d. And with regard to what Rashi wrote about an offering left overnight if it was placed on top of the altar [during the night it is not invalidated] — there is a difference of opinion on this matter in the Gemara, [535] and in the opinion of Raba it does become invalidated even if on top of the altar; thus if limbs of a sacrifice were left there [on top of the altar] overnight, and then by accident they were taken down [from the altar to the pavement], they may no longer be taken up. On the other hand, if they were not taken down, then even those limbs that had been left over on the pavement of the Court for many days, and by accident were taken up, do not need to come down [and are burnt upon the altar], as is found in the Chapter "The Altar." [535]

26. THE CHOICEST FIRST-FRUITS OF THY LAND THOU SHALT BRING INTO THE HOUSE OF THE ETERNAL THY G-D. Because He mentioned that they should bring *the first-ripe*

---

(533) Above, 23:18.   (534) Leviticus 6:2.   (535) Zebachim 87 a.

EXODUS XXXIV, KI THISA 591

fruits of all that is in their land [536] to the house of G-d, He placed next to it, *Thou shalt not seethe a kid in its mother's milk.* For at the time of bringing the first-fruits of the earth they would also take along all firstlings of cattle, goats and sheep, and at that season the goats have grown up and begin giving milk. Thus they would often bring up the mother with its firstborn whilst it was still a suckling, in order that it should not die. Now those who came to celebrate the festival would enjoy eating the firstlings amongst all tasty foods, together with the priests. That is why He mentioned the prohibition [against seething the kid in its mother's milk] together with the precept of the first-fruits. In the Book of Deuteronomy, however, He mentioned this commandment together with the laws of prohibited foods,[537] after He cited the laws of unclean cattle, fish, and unclean fowl, and carrion, for that is the fitting place to mention it, since it is a prohibition concerning eating, and not merely a prohibition against seething it alone, as those wanting in faith and devoid of knowledge think.[538]

27. WRITE THOU THESE WORDS. G-d commanded Moses that he write *a book of covenant* and read it *in the hearing of the people,*[539] and they should accept it upon themselves by saying, *we will do and we will obey,*[539] as they had done at first; for He wanted that the whole procedure with the first Tablets should now be repeated with the second Tablets. There is no doubt that Moses actually did repeat it; however, Scripture did not want to prolong the account by saying, "and Moses did so," as I have shown you in many places.[540]

The correct interpretation appears to me to be, that since Israel had sinned and violated the [first] covenant, the Holy One, blessed be He, had to renew the covenant with them, so that He should

---

(536) Numbers 18:13. — Ramban's intention of course is to the verse here before us, but as a matter of style he uses similar language referring to that commandment found elsewhere in Scripture. This can be observed in countless instances. (537) Deuteronomy 14:21. (538) Reference is to the Karaites. See Ibn Ezra who writes in a vein similar to that of Ramban. — See also Vol. I, p. 22, where Ramban uses a similar reproof to those who scoff at the words of our Rabbis. (539) Above, 24:7. (540) *Ibid.,* 10:2, etc.

not nullify His covenant with them, and so He told Moses to write the conditions [of the renewed covenant]. This is the sense of the verse, *for after the tenor of these words I have made a covenant with thee and with Israel.* The meaning of *with thee* is that for your sake I have done it with them, and it will not be necessary for them to bring themselves *into the bond of this covenant.* [541] However, G-d, blessed be He, had to make with them a covenant on the forgiveness that He extended to them [for their sin with the calf], and so [Moses] wrote the forgiveness, and the conditions [of the new covenant].

28. AND HE WAS THERE WITH THE ETERNAL FORTY DAYS AND FORTY NIGHTS... AND HE WROTE UPON THE TABLETS THE WORDS OF THE COVENANT, THE TEN WORDS. The verse is stating that Moses was on top of the mountain for forty days and forty nights, and he wrote there upon the Tablets. And in the opinion of our Rabbis [542] the meaning of the verse is that Moses was there with G-d for forty days and forty nights, [543] during which time He wrote on the Tablets the words of this second covenant. But he had stayed there for another forty days [544] prior to these to pray for all his requests, as is narrated in the section beginning, *See, Thou sayest unto me: Bring up this people;* [545] and with reference to these days it is said in the Book of Deuteronomy, *So I fell down before the Eternal the forty days and forty nights that I fell down; because the Eternal had said He would destroy you.* [546] Here, however, Scripture did not explain how many days were the duration of this period of supplication and prayer, for it is known that it was from the time he went up to the mountain until he came down to hew the second Tablets. [547] But it said that the matter of the second

(541) Ezekiel 20:37. (542) Shemoth Rabbah 47:12. (543) From the first of Ellul to the tenth of Tishri, which is the Day of Atonement. (544) From the nineteenth of Tammuz to the twenty-ninth of Ab. (545) Above, 33:12. (546) Deuteronomy 9:25. (547) This was on the first day of Ellul (see Ramban above, 33:7). Having hewn the Tablets, he went up to the mountain and stayed until the tenth of Tishri. From this we learn that the forty-day period of prayer preceded it, which brings it to the days between the nineteenth of Tammuz and the twenty-ninth of Ab.

EXODUS XXXIV, KI THISA 593

Tablets was like that of the first in every respect — the writing of G-d, and the number of days he stood before G-d, so that he should not think that he had already learned the Torah during the first time, and that therefore it would not be necessary for him to stay there many days.

'Va'yichtov' upon the Tablets — this means that G-d wrote, and does not refer back to Moses [mentioned in the preceding phrase, *he did neither eat bread, nor drink water*], for so He said, *and I will write upon the Tablets.*[548] Similarly, in the Book of Deuteronomy it says, *and I hewed two Tablets of stone like unto the first, and went up into the mount, having the two Tablets in my hand. And He wrote on the Tablets, according to the first writing.*[549] And since it says *according to the first writing*, we know that they were written with the finger of G-d.[550] Thus the meaning of the expression, *and I will write*[548] means "with the finger," and you know [already] the meaning of "finger" from that of "the hand."[551]

31. 'VA'YEDABEIR MOSHEH' (AND MOSES SPOKE) TO THEM. "This whole section denotes a [continuing] present action [thus making the sense of the verbs: 'and Moses used to speak...' 'and they used to come near...']. 32. AND AFTERWARDS ALL THE CHILDREN OF ISRAEL CAME NIGH. After Moses had taught the elders, he would again teach the section or the specific law to the Israelites." All this is Rashi's language. But it is not so [that this section describes a continuing occurrence — whenever Moses spoke to Israel]. Rather, Scripture is stating that when all Israel went forth to meet him [upon his descent from the mountain with the second Tablets], they saw the beams of glory streaming from his face, *and they were afraid to come nigh him*[552] and stepped backwards. Perhaps they thought that the Glory of G-d was there, or that the angels of Him on high were with him, and they feared *lest the Eternal break forth upon*

(548) Above, Verse 1. (549) Deuteronomy 10:3-4. (550) Above, 31:18.
(551) *Ibid.*, 14:31. See Ramban there. (552) Verse 30.

them. [553] Then *Moses called unto them; and Aaron and all the princes,* who walked before them *returned unto him,*[554] and Moses spoke to them *words of peace,*[555] and told them the tidings of the forgiveness of their sin and of the Tablets he brought down. *And afterwards* when all the children of Israel saw that he was speaking with the princes of the congregation, they all came near to him, and then he commanded them *all that the Eternal had spoken with him in Mount Sinai,*[556] these being the second Ten Commandments that He gave him, and all that was said to him from the beginning of, *Observe thou that which I am commanding thee this day,*[557] to the end of the section; for he told them that G-d had commanded him to make a covenant with them *after the tenor of these words.*[558] Scripture, however, shortened the account and narrated the matter in general terms. Then Scripture says that *when Moses had done speaking with them* the whole subject mentioned, *he put a veil upon his face,*[559] for he understood that upon his return [from the mountain] *the skin of his face sent forth beams,*[560] or perhaps they told it to him. Finally, after having told the account of the events of that day, Scripture states, *But when Moses went in before the Eternal* etc. [561] It is this part of Scripture that represents the continuing action, meaning that so did Moses conduct himself with them all the days. [562]

(553) Above, 19:22. (554) Verse 31. (555) Esther 9:30. (556) Verse 32. (557) Above, Verse 11. (558) *Ibid.,* Verse 27. (559) Verse 33. (560) Verse 29. (561) Verse 34. (562) But not, as Rashi put it, that this *whole* section (from Verses 31 to 35) represents a frequentative action. According to Ramban this applies only to Verses 34-35.

Vayakheil

35   1. AND MOSES ASSEMBLED ALL THE CONGREGATION OF THE CHILDREN OF ISRAEL. The expression *all the congregation of the children of Israel* includes the men and women, for all donated to the work of the Tabernacle. Thus Moses, after having commanded Aaron, and the rulers and *all the children of Israel* — the men — *all that the Eternal had spoken with him in Mount Sinai*,[1] following the breaking of the Tablets, and after he had put the veil on his face[2] [as all this is narrated in the preceding section], again commanded that the people be assembled, whereupon the whole congregation gathered to him — men, women, and children.

It is possible that this occurred on the day following his descent from the mountain, and he told all of them the subject of the Tabernacle which he had been previously commanded, before[3] the breaking of the Tablets. For since the Holy One, blessed be He, became reconciled with them and gave Moses the second Tablets, and also made a new covenant that G-d would go in their midst,[4]

---

(1) Above, 34:32.   (2) *Ibid.*, Verse 33.   (3) Ramban follows [here as elsewhere] the natural sequence of Scripture which tells of the command to build the Tabernacle [in Chapters 25-30] before the people's sin with the calf [in Chapter 32]. The actual building thereof was delayed until after Moses' intercession and the complete reconciliation of G-d with Israel. Rashi, however, following the principle that there is no strict chronological order in the narrative of the Torah, clearly writes: "The incident of the golden calf happened a considerable time before the command regarding the building of the Tabernacle was given" (Rashi above, 31-18). See my Hebrew commentary, p. 526, for further elucidation of this point.   (4) See Ramban above, 34:9.

He thereby returned to His previous relationship with them, and to the love of their "wedding,"[5] and it was obvious that His Presence would be in their midst just as He had commanded him at first, even as He said, *And let them make Me a Sanctuary, that I may dwell amongst them.*[6] Therefore Moses now commanded them all that he had been told at first.

THESE ARE THE THINGS WHICH THE ETERNAL HATH COMMANDED, THAT YE SHOULD DO THEM. 2. SIX DAYS SHALL WORK BE DONE. The expression, *these are the things which the Eternal hath commanded* refers to the construction of the Tabernacle,[7] all its vessels and all its various works. He preceded [the explanation of the construction of the Tabernacle] with the law of the Sabbath, meaning to say that the work of *these things* should be done during the six days, but not on the seventh day which is *holy to G-d.* It is from here that we learn the principle that the work of the Tabernacle does not set aside the Sabbath, and not from the interpretation of the word *ach (but — 'but' you shall keep My Sabbaths),*[8] as I have explained in the section of *Ki Thisa.*[8]

3. YE SHALL KINDLE NO FIRE THROUGHOUT YOUR HABITATIONS UPON THE SABBATH DAY. The meaning of this verse is clearly to prohibit also on the Sabbath doing any work necessary for the preparation of food, since He said, *whosoever doeth work therein shall be put to death,*[9] and He further explained that they *should* also *not kindle fire,* in order to bake bread and boil meat, for fire is needed in the preparation of all food. This had to be stated because He did not say here: "whosoever doeth 'any manner' of work," just as He said in the Ten Commandments, *thou shalt not do any manner of work,*[10]

(5) See Jeremiah 2:2. (6) Above, 25:8. (7) And not as Ibn Ezra explains [in his short commentary on the Book of Exodus], that *these are the words* refers to the law of the Sabbath, it being mentioned in the plural "words" because the Sabbath is as important as all the other commandments. But according to Ramban, the reference is to the building of the Tabernacle, and the plural is used because the allusion is also to all its vessels, etc. (8) Above, 31:13. (9) Verse 2. (10) Above, 20:10.

but instead He merely said "work" without specifying any type. Therefore we might have excluded from the general statement [*whosoever doeth work* ...] all activity necessary for the preparation of food, for we find it said about the feast of unleavened bread, *thou shalt not do work therein*,[11] and yet the preparation of food is not included [in the scope of its prohibition]. It is for this reason that here He mentioned expressly that the preparation of food is also forbidden on the Sabbath.

I have found a similar text in the Midrash:[12] "Rabbi Nathan says: *Ye shall kindle no fire throughout your habitations upon the Sabbath-day.* Why is this said? Because it is stated, *And Moses assembled all the congregation of the children of Israel.*[13] I might think that one should be allowed to light a candle, to put away food to be kept warm, and to make a fire on the Sabbath. Therefore Scripture says, *Ye shall kindle no fire throughout your habitations upon the Sabbath-day.*" This corresponds closely to that which we have said, that these works [mentioned in the Mechilta], since they are of direct benefit to the body, were not included in the first prohibition. Thus Rabbi Nathan wanted to say that the purpose of the verse here is not to prohibit baking, cooking, and the rest of the activities involved in the preparation of food, for these have already been prohibited to them by the verse, *Bake that* [on the sixth day of the week] *which ye will bake* [i.e., which ye intend to bake on the Sabbath], *and seethe that which ye will seethe.*[14] But yet I might think that all activities which benefit man in such a way that the benefit is only to the body — such as lighting a candle, making fire, or washing one's whole body in hot water — should be allowed, for these are part of the delight of the Sabbath.[15] Therefore it says, *Ye shall kindle no fire* — to prohibit all [mentioned activities even if done for these purposes].

(11) Deuteronomy 16:8. (12) Mechilta here. (13) Verse 1. — Reference here in the Mechilta is of course to Verse 2: *whosoever doeth work therein...*, and as Ramban explained above. The insertion of the word "etc." at the end of the verse mentioned in the text of Ramban, would clarify the matter completely. It is present in texts of the Mechilta. (14) Above, 16:23. (15) See Isaiah 58:13.

Our Rabbis in the Talmud [16] have yet another Midrash on this verse, because it does not say: "whosoever doeth any manner of work therein shall be put to death," or: "whosoever kindles fire throughout your habitations shall be put to death." Therefore they said that the kindling of fire was singled out in order to make it punishable in a less stringent manner, [namely by stripe], since it is a mere negative command, [whereas violation of the Sabbath by doing any of the other kinds of work is punishable by death]. But another Sage [17] holds that it was singled out in order to separate it, since it was included in the prohibition, *thou shalt not do any manner of work.*[18]

5. 'Y'VI'EHA' (LET HIM BRING IT), THE ETERNAL'S OFFERING. This is like "*yavi* (let him bring) the Eternal's offering." But Scripture mentions a pronoun and then returns to explain it. Similarly: *And she opened and saw him, the child;*[19] *when he went in, the man;*[20] *the nation and the kingdom which will not serve him, Nebuchadnezzar;*[21] *which I do give to them, the children of Israel.*[22] There are many similar instances.

(16) Shabbath 70 a. (17) This is Rabbi Nathan. (18) Above, 20:10. It was thus singled out to indicate a general principle: just as in the case of kindling, which is specifically mentioned although it is included in the prohibition, *thou shalt not do any manner of work in it*, one becomes liable to punishment for transgressing it alone, so also in the case of all the other thirty-nine categories of forbidden work on the Sabbath, one becomes liable upon transgressing each one of them by itself. For otherwise we might have thought that only if one has done all thirty-nine main classes of "work" he is liable to punishment; therefore kindling of fire was singled out in order to teach that the punishment applies even if he has done but one kind of "work" (Rashi, Yebamoth 6 b). For it is one of the thirteen rules of interpretation of the Torah: "If anything is included in a general proposition and is then made the subject of a special statement, that which is predicated of it is not to be understood as limited to itself alone, but is to be applied to the whole of the general proposition." Similarly we might have thought that if one has done all thirty-nine main classes of "work" on the Sabbath through error he is liable to bring but one sin-offering, therefore kindling of fire was singled out to teach that he is liable to bring such an offering for each of the main classes of "work" he has done. (19) Above, 2:6 (20) Ezekiel 10:3. It should have said: *b'vo ha'ish* — when the man went in. (21) Jeremiah 27:8. (22) Joshua 1:2.

By way of the Truth, [the mystic lore of the Cabala], the phrase here is like "let him bring it 'with' the Eternal's offering," meaning that he is to bring the higher offering as alluded to in the secret of *and they take for Me an offering*.[23] I have already explained it.[24] Our Rabbis have a Midrash [25] on the verse, *and she opened and saw him, the child*,[19] that she saw with him the Divine Glory.

Now it was necessary for Moses to tell the whole congregation all the work which G-d had commanded him, in order to let them know that they had to bring large donations, for *the work is great*.[26] That is why he told them, *The Tabernacle, its tent, and its covering* etc., [27] mentioning all in a general way. The reason for the definite article in *'eth hamishkan' (the Tabernacle)*,[27] *'eth ha'aron' (the ark)*,[28] *'eth hashulchan' (the table)*,[29] and all those mentioned with the definite article, is as if to say: "the Tabernacle and the vessels which we will explain to the wise men doing the work in their details and measurements," but speaking now to the whole congregation, he told them only their names in general.

21. AND THEY CAME, EVERY ONE WHOSE HEART STIRRED HIM UP. This is said with reference to the wise men who did the work, for we do not find the use of this phrase, "the stirring up of the heart," in connection with those who merely brought the donations; Scripture rather mentions "generosity of heart" with reference to them. Now the reason for using such a phrase, *whose heart stirred him up*, is because they undertook to do the work, although there was no one amongst them who had learned these crafts from an instructor, or had trained his hands at all to do them. Rather, a person who felt in his nature that he knew how to do such skills, *his heart was lifted up in the ways of the Eternal* [30] to come before Moses and say to him, "I will do all that my lord speaks." I have already mentioned this in another section.[31] Thus Scripture is stating that there came before Moses

(23) Above, 25:2. (24) *Ibid.*, Verse 3. (25) Sotah 12 b. (26) I Chronicles 29:1. (27) Verse 11. (28) Verse 12. (29) Verse 13. (30) II Chronicles 17:6. (31) Above, 31:2.

every one whose heart stirred him up to undertake the work, *and every one whom his spirit made willing* brought the offering. Then Moses said to all of them that *G-d had called by name Bezalel,* [32] *and Oholiab.* [33] Afterwards Moses called them *and every wise-hearted man* [34] to come before him, and he gave them the whole donation [brought by the people so that they could proceed to do the work].

22. AND THE MEN CAME 'AL HANASHIM' (WITH THE WOMEN). The meaning of this expression is that because donations of ornaments were more common amongst women, and they all had these jewels [cited in the verse: *nose-rings, and ear-rings, and signet-rings, and golden beads, all jewels of gold*], therefore they immediately pulled off their ear-rings and signet-rings and were the first to come to Moses, and [afterwards] they brought with them those men with whom they found ornaments. For the phrase *al hanashim* indicates that they were there first, while the men joined them later. Similar usage of the word *al* is found in these verses: *Aram is confederate 'al' Ephraim,* [35] for that war [against Judah] was mainly led by Ephraim [i.e., the kingdom of Israel]; *and he did not put them 'al' (unto) Laban's flock;* [36] *'v'alav' (and next unto him) shall be the tribe of Manasseh.* [37] There are other similar instances. Thus Scripture is stating that all — men and women — came with *nose-rings, and ear-rings, and signet-rings, and golden beads,* and with *all jewels of gold,* such as bracelets and ear-rings, as all of the people found some jewelry to bring. It further states that some of them *brought an offering of gold,* in some broken form or as coin.

And every man, with whom was found blue-purple and red-purple. [38] The reason for this expression is that these items were found only amongst a few of the people. Then Scripture states again, *and every man, with whom was found acacia-wood,* [39] because the people who had this kind of wood were still fewer in number. It states, *Every one that did set apart an offering of silver*

(32) Further, Verse 30. (33) *Ibid.,* Verse 34. (34) *Ibid.,* 36:2. (35) Isaiah 7:2. (36) Genesis 30:40. (37) Numbers 2:20. (38) Verse 23. (39) Verse 24.

EXODUS XXXVI, VAYAKHEIL 601

and brass,[39] because most people had silver and brass in coins or vessels. Scripture, however, did not mention this above together with *all jewels of gold,* because it mentioned there the women, and they did not have silver and brass ornaments but gold ones, just as Aaron said, *Pull off the golden rings, which are in the ears of your wives.*[40]

And every man that 'heinif tenufath' (brought an offering of) gold. This is so phrased because the number of these people was not as great as those who brought silver and brass. Thus the amount of gold brought was not as much as that of silver and brass. It is for this reason that the gold donation is called *tenufah* (waving), whilst that of silver and brass is called *terumah* (offering),[41] for one who brings gold waves it with his hand to show the importance of the donation, or it may be that those who take it from him wave the gold to show up the donor in a praiseworthy light for having brought such a donation. However, in the section of *Eileh Pekudei* Scripture calls the donations of both gold and brass *tenufah,*[42] because there it does not mention at all *terumah* (free-will offering,) but only *the silver of them that were numbered.*[43] It is possible that brass also was called *tenufah* because it was more important to them than silver, since they did not have much of it. Or it may have been very important on its own merit, similar to that which is said, *and two vessels of fine bright brass, precious as gold.*[44]

36 3. AND THEY TOOK FROM BEFORE MOSES ALL THE OFFERING. In one day they brought all this donation to the Tent of Meeting where Moses was,[45] and the wise men took it from Moses on that very same day and on the following day, early in the morning. On the second day, too, the people still continued to

(40) Above, 32:2. (41) Thus in Verse 24: Every one that *'meirim terumath'* (set apart an offering of) silver and brass... (42) Further, 38:24: *And the gold of 'hatenufah'...* And in Verse 29: *And the brass of 'hatenufah'...* (43) *Ibid.,* Verse 25. And since everyone had to give the half-shekel in order to be counted, it is not called *terumah* which indicates a free-will offering. See Ramban above at beginning of *Seder Ki Thisa.* (44) Ezra 8:27. (45) See above, 33:7.

bring the donation to Moses' tent and he commanded them to bring it to the craftsmen, until they told him that *the people bring much more;* [46] thus there was *sufficient [for all the work to make it], and too much.* [47] The surplus, however, was not a sufficiently important amount to warrant Moses' telling in the section of *Eileh Pekudei* what they did with it. Perhaps it remained in the tent to repair the breaches of the Tabernacle, or to make with it vessels used in the Tabernacle service, as they used to do with the surpluses in the Sanctuary. [48] Scripture mentions, *the people bring much more than enough,* [46] in order to praise the people who brought with such generosity, and to glorify the wise men for their honesty. The one who was in charge principally over them [namely Moses], also comes in for praise for having *caused it to be proclaimed throughout the camp* [49] that the people should stop bringing, telling us that he had no desire for their silver and gold, as do other rulers over peoples, in a similar way to that which it says, *I have not taken one ass from them.* [50]

6. LET NEITHER MAN NOR WOMAN MAKE ANY MORE 'MLACHAH' (WORK). Money [and possessions] are called *mlachah.* Similarly: *whether he have not put his hand 'bimlecheth' (the goods of) his neighbor;* [51] *according to the pace of 'hamlachah' (the cattle) that are before me;* [52] *'v'chol hamlachah' (but everything) that was of no account and feeble, that they destroyed utterly.* [53] Thus the meaning of this verse is that they should not bring anything more for the sacred work. Scripture, however, states, *Let them not make any more 'mlachah'* [using the verb "to make"] in order to include therein the women, that they should no longer spin the goats' hair. [54] Thus even the act of bringing is here referred to as "making," and [it was now Moses' wish] to restrain them altogether [from bringing more donations, and from making any work in their homes, as explained].

(46) Verse 5.   47) Verse 7.   (48) Shekalim 4:4.   (49) Verse 6.   (50) Numbers 16:15.   (51) Above, 22:7.   (52) Genesis 33:14.   (53) I Samuel 15:9.   (54) Above, 35:26.

8. AND EVERY WISE-HEARTED MAN AMONG THEM THAT WROUGHT THE WORK, MADE THE TABERNACLE OF TEN CURTAINS. The Torah has repeated the [description of the] work of the Tabernacle five times.[55] It mentions the whole of it at the time of the command in detail, and in general terms. First it says, "and you shall make it thus," "and you shall make it thus," and then it mentioned all things in a general way, *and they will make all that I have commanded thee: the Tent of Meeting, and the ark of the Testimony,*[56] until *according to all that I have commanded thee shall they do.*[57] The reason [why the command is repeated in a general way], is that G-d commanded Moses that he should tell Bezalel and Oholiab and all the wise men about the work in general terms, and only afterwards should they begin to do it, for they would not be suited for the sacred work until they had heard the scope of the whole undertaking and understood it all, and only then could they accept it upon themselves, when they know how to finish it. At the time of its actual construction he described it to them first in the general way as mentioned here, saying, *let every wise-hearted man among you come, and make all that the Eternal hath commanded: the Tabernacle, its tent,* etc.[58] The statement of the details is, however, missing here; for surely Moses had to say to the wise men who did the work: "make the Tabernacle of ten curtains, each curtain of such-and-such a length and such-and-such a width," and so on with the whole work. This procedure [of Moses' telling the workers the exact details of the measurements] Scripture does not mention, for it is understood that he told them everything in order, since they made each part exactly as prescribed. And the reason why Scripture does not

---

(55) 1. When commanding to make it — designating each part specifically [in the section of *Terumah* — Chapters 25-27, and in parts of *Tetzaveh*]. 2. In a general way [in the section of *Ki Thisa* — 31:6-11]. 3. At the time of the actual making thereof — in a general way [at the beginning of this section — 35:10-19]. 4. Specifically at the time of construction. For even though this is not mentioned expressly, yet Moses surely told them details, such as that the curtains should be of such and such a length, etc., as will be explained by Ramban further on. 5. The specific account of how each part was made [beginning with our verse here]. (56) Above, 31:6-7. — This is the second time it is mentioned (see above, Note 55). (57) *Ibid.,* Verse 11. (58) *Ibid.,* 35:10-11. This is the third time (see Note 55).

mention it is that it was not necessary for Moses to go with them into the smallest details as they are mentioned at the command and the construction; instead, he told it to them briefly, as if to say that they should make the Tabernacle of ten curtains, five opposite five, and they themselves understood that they had to make loops corresponding to clasps of gold in order to couple the curtains together. Similarly with the rest of the work, he hinted to them the matter in brief, and they understood everything. It is for this reason that Scripture does not dwell at length on this detail [of Moses' instruction to the workers], since its hints [at the same time] at their wisdom, understanding, and good sense. After this Scripture describes again the whole work in a specific way as at first, stating, *And every wise-hearted man among them that wrought the work made the Tabernacle; and he made curtains of goats' hair;* [59] *and he made the boards* etc. [60]

Now it would have been sufficient in this whole subject for Scripture to have said, "and Moses told the whole congregation of the children of Israel all the work which G-d had commanded him," and then say, "and the children of Israel did *according to all that the Eternal had commanded Moses,* [61] *so did they. And Moses saw all the work, and behold they had done it, as the Eternal had commanded, even so had they done it. And Moses blessed them."* [62] Scripture, however, wanted to state that Moses mentioned to the whole congregation of the children of Israel and the wise men who were there all the work in general, for he intended thereby to stir the people to donate sufficiently for the large work, and in order also that the wise men should hear [the entire scope of the work] and would know if they could undertake to do everything as he had been commanded. Then Scripture mentions in detail the whole work in order to tell us that all the wise men worked on the Tabernacle. It is with reference to this that Scripture states here, *And every wise-hearted man among them that wrought the work made the Tabernacle of ten curtains.* The verses stating, *and he made curtains of goats' hair,*[59] *and he*

(59) Further, Verse 14. (60) *Ibid.,* Verse 20. (61) *Ibid.,* 39:42. (62) *Ibid.,* Verse 43.

made the boards,[60] mean: "and every wise-hearted man made the curtains of goats' hair," [not Bezalel alone].

In the case of the ark, however, Scripture mentions specifically, *and Bezalel made the ark,*[63] in order to say that the greatest craftsman amongst them made the ark alone. The reason for this is because he was filled *with the spirit of G-d, in wisdom, and understanding, and in knowledge,*[64] so that he could contemplate its meaning and make it with the proper intention. For in the actual making of the ark there was no great craftsmanship entailed, there being amongst the other work things which required greater skill than that of the ark. [Hence we must conclude that Bezalel was required to make the ark on account of its great significance.]

Then Scripture again states without elaboration, *and he made the table,*[65] *and he made the candelabrum.*[66] In the opinion of Rabbi Abraham ibn Ezra,[63] this alludes to Bezalel who made all the sacred vessels. But this is not my opinion, for in the case of the court of the Tabernacle it likewise says, *and he made the court.*[67] Rather, this refers back to every *wise-hearted man* as mentioned in the making of the Tabernacle.[68]

After Scripture completed the account of the construction of the Tabernacle in general and particular terms, it mentions their bringing it to Moses in a general way, stating, *And they brought the Tabernacle unto Moses, the Tent, and all its vessels* etc.,[69] in order to tell of their wisdom, in that they brought everything in order and no one brought his work to Moses until the whole work had been completed, as Scripture says, *Thus was finished all the work of the Tabernacle of the Tent of Meeting.*[70] After it was finished they all gathered and showed it to Moses in order, saying at first: "Our Rabbi, here is the Tent and there are its vessels," and afterwards they said, "Here is the ark and here are its staves," and so on with everything.

(63) *Ibid.,* 37:1.   (64) Above, 31:3.   (65) Further, 37:10.   (66) *Ibid.,* Verse 17.   (67) *Ibid.,* 38:9. And it would not be reasonable to say that Bezalel alone made the court.   (68) Mentioned here in the verse before us (36:8), and as explained above.   (69) Further, 39:33.   (70) *Ibid.,* Verse 32.

Now [in this whole section of *Vayakheil*] Scripture does not state that the Tabernacle and its vessels were made "as the Eternal commanded Moses." But in the next section of *Eileh Pekudei,* with reference to the garments of priesthood, it mentions such a statement at each item. The reason for this is that the whole work of the Tabernacle is included in the verse mentioned at the end, *And Bezalel the son of Uri... made all that the Eternal commanded Moses.*[71] Perhaps it is because of the change of the order, as our Rabbis have mentioned.[72]

In general, then, all this repetition in the account of the Tabernacle is a sign of love and distinction, showing that G-d desires the work, and He mentions it in His Torah many times in order to increase the reward of those who engage themselves in its study. This is similar to what the Rabbis have said in the Midrash:[73] "The ordinary conversation of the servants of the patriarchs' homes is more pleasing to the Holy One, blessed be He, than even the Torah-discourses of their children, for the section about Eliezer [as he recounts his journey],[74] comprises two or three columns in the Torah, [whereas many important principles of the Torah are derived from only slight references in the text]."

29. AND HE MADE THE HOLY ANOINTING OIL, AND THE PURE INCENSE OF SWEET SPICES. Scripture did not explain these as it did with the others, for according to the way it writes about the others it should have said, "and he took the chief spices, of flowing myrrh etc.,[75] and he made them into the holy anointing oil; and he took sweet spices, stacte, and onycha etc.[76] and he made them into an incense compounded after the art of the perfumers." But the reason [for Scripture not saying so] is because He did not state the whole process of the making of the

---

(71) *Ibid.*, 38:22. (72) Berachoth 55 a. Moses told Bezalel to make "the ark, vessels and the Tabernacle." But Bezalel said to him, "It is the way of the world first to build a house and then to place in it its various utensils. Perhaps G-d told you to make the Tabernacle, and then the ark and vessels." Moses consented, and Bezalel made them in this order. (73) Bereshith Rabbah 60:11. (74) Genesis 24:34-48. (75) Above, 30:23. (76) *Ibid.*, Verse 34.

oil of anointment when He gave the command for them, as I have explained there.[76] In the making of the incense likewise it does not mention all the spices, but relied on them [the craftsmen who made the Tabernacle] by saying that it should be made *after the art of the perfumer,* [77] and therefore when they made it Scripture only mentioned that they made it according to the way of the perfumers. This is the sense of the expression, *holy... pure, after the art of the perfumer.*

38   8. OF THE MIRRORS 'HATZOVOTH' (OF THE SERVING WOMEN). "The women of Israel possessed mirrors of brass which they used to look into when they adorned themselves, and even these they did not withhold [from donating to the Tabernacle]. But Moses was reluctant to accept them because they were made to arouse sensual desires. Said the Holy One, blessed be He, to Moses: 'These are dearer to Me than all [other donations], for by means of them the women raised many hosts in Egypt, etc. For this reason the laver was made from these mirrors, because it was used in order to bring peace between husband and wife; for it was out of this laver that they took the water which they give to drink to a woman who was warned by her husband not to meet a certain man privately and who had nevertheless associated with him."[78] This is Rashi's language.

The meaning of this Midrash is that in the whole work of the Tabernacle they accepted ornaments from women, as it is written, *And they came, both men and women... and brought nose-rings, and ear-rings, and signet-rings 'v'chumaz'* [79] — the *chumaz,* according to its Midrashic interpretation, being even more undesirable.[80] There, however, all the donations became mixed together, whereas here they were to make one specific vessel purely from ornaments [i.e., the mirrors] which were made to arouse sensual desire. Therefore Moses did not consent at first [to accept them] until he was told to do so by the Almighty.

(77) *Ibid.,* Verse 35.   (78) Numbers 5:17-24.   (79) Above, 35:22. (80) In Shabbath 64, the *chumaz* is explained as an ornament worn by women on their pudendum.

But I do not know how to explain according to this Midrash the phrase — *that did service at the door of the Tent of Meeting* — [since the Tent of Meeting had not yet been put up]. Perhaps it can be said that the women brought this donation to Moses' tent, which he called the Tent of Meeting,[81] and he himself received it from them by word of G-d, since the tent of the Tabernacle had not yet been made. Onkelos' translation, "women that came to pray at the door of the Tent of Meeting," accords approximately to the words of Rabbi Abraham ibn Ezra, who said that these women worshipped G-d, and turned away from the desires of this world and gave their mirrors as a donation, coming each day to the door of the Tent of Meeting to pray and to hear instruction about the commandments.

In line with the plain meaning of Scripture, it is also possible to say that Moses *made the laver and its base for the mirrors* of the women who came in a great crowd,[82] *and assembled at the door of the Tent of Meeting* in order to give their mirrors in the generosity of their hearts. Now the brass of the mirrors was *burnished brass*,[83] resplendent and very beautiful. It is for this reason that he set aside this brass from the beginning for the making of this vessel. Upon seeing this [that Moses accepted it from them], the women gathered and came in many hosts, all of them wanting to give their mirrors for the making of the whole laver and its base. It is also correct to explain that they had in mind right at the start to offer them for the laver because of its use in connection with the suspected adulteress [as explained above], and they accepted the law [of the suspected adulteress] upon themselves with joy, and offered to give all their mirrors.

(81) Above, 33:7. (82) Ramban thus interprets the word *tzavu* as being from the root *tzava* (a host). *Of the mirrors 'hatzovoth'* would thus mean "of the mirrors of the hosts of women" who assembled at the door of the Tent of Meeting. (83) Ezekiel 1:7.

Pekudei

21. THESE ARE THE ACCOUNTS OF THE TABERNACLE, THE TABERNACLE OF THE TESTIMONY. Scripture uses this expression because the term "Tabernacle" means the curtains of fine-twined linen, which are so called both when the command was given [1] and at the construction of the Tabernacle, [2] while "the Tabernacle of the Testimony" includes the entire building, which is the Tabernacle made to house the Tablets of the Testimony.

In the opinion of many scholars [3] the phrase *these are the accounts of the Tabernacle* refers back to all the things mentioned above, the verse stating that the Tabernacle and its vessels, namely, the house and the court and all that was made for them, constituted the service entrusted to the Levites at the command of Moses *by the hand of Ithamar* [whose duty it was to hand over to each family the service that devolved upon it]. But the holy vessels — the ark, the table, the candelabrum, and the altars — are not included in the term "Tabernacle," for they were in the hands of Eleazar. [4] But this is not my opinion, for why should Scripture mention the entrusting of those things given to Ithamar, and not mention that of Eleazar, which was the more honored one? Rather, *these are the accounts of* hints at those things that Scripture mentions in the section further on, thus stating that *the silver of them that were numbered of the congregation was a*

---

(1) *And thou shalt make the Tabernacle of ten curtains* (above, 26:1). (2) *And every wise-hearted man... made the Tabernacle of ten curtains (ibid.,* 36:8). See also Ramban further on, 39:33. (3) Rashi and Ibn Ezra. (4) Numbers 3:32. The verse refers to the time of the journeying through the wilderness.

hundred talents etc.,[5] — from which were made the sockets, the hooks for the pillars, the overlaying of their capitals and their fillets.[6] And *the brass of the wave-offering,* which was seventy talents, from which were made the brazen altar and its grating and all its vessels, and the sockets of the court and the pins[7] — all these Moses gave over by number and weight through the hand of Ithamar. Now the section does not say what was done with the gold, for that was partly in the charge of Ithamar, namely, that used for covering the boards and the bars, and part of it was in the charge of Eleazar — the ark and the cover, the candelabrum, the table, and the golden altar. Now since one cannot know exactly how much gold went into the covering of each of these vessels, Scripture did not say that Moses gave it over to them by number and weight. It is for this reason that Scripture did not mention here the entrusting of the things given to Eleazar, for its intention here is only to speak of the work of the Tabernacle, not of that involved in the journeyings. Do not object [to this explanation] because Scripture mentions here *the brazen altar,*[8] which was in the charge of Eleazar,[9] for Scripture had to state that they made it out of the brass of the wave-offering, therefore it was not particular to exclude this one item from the general list of objects of which it said that they were *by the hand of Ithamar,* this being the way of Scripture in many places.

Scripture does not mention in this section the laver and its base [which were also made of brass, and were under the charge of Ithamar], because it was not made according to a specified weight; instead, he put into it all the mirrors that the women brought together [10] and thus Moses did not know its weight. It is possible that these were not under the charge of Ithamar [and therefore they are not mentioned], but they come into the category of that which Scripture says [of the children of Kohath, whose work was under the charge of Eleazar], *and their charge was the ark, and the table, and the candelabrum, and the altars, and the vessels of the*

---

(5) Further, Verse 25. (6) *Ibid.,* Verses 27-28. (7) *Ibid.,* Verses 29-31. (8) *Ibid.,* Verse 30. (9) Numbers 3:31-32. (10) see Ramban above, 38:8, towards the end.

EXODUS XXXVIII, PEKUDEI 611

Sanctuary wherewith the priests minister, [11] for through the laver and its base the priests were enabled to minister at the altar. Thus they do not come into the listing given in this section.

22. AND BEZALEL THE SON OF URI, THE SON OF HUR, OF THE TRIBE OF JUDAH, MADE ALL THAT THE ETERNAL COMMANDED MOSES. The meaning of this is that everything was done through his direction, for he acted as instructor to all the wise men, and they all did heir work in his presence and showed him all that they had done, just as it is said, *And He hath put in his heart that he may teach.* [12] But all the wise-hearted men also did the work, as it is said, *and every wise-hearted man among them that wrought the work made the Tabernacle.* [13] In the opinion of our Rabbis, [14] this verse is intended to praise Bezalel, and to say that even these things that his master Moses did not tell him, he understood through his own mind in exactly the same way that they had been told to Moses on Sinai. [15] Thus the intention of Scripture is not to state that Bezalel did all the work, but that in all which was done through him, he fulfilled *all that the Eternal commanded Moses.* It is for this reason that Scripture does not state in connection with anything that was done until now: "as G-d spoke to Moses," for this would have implied: "as Moses said by the word of G-d," and he [i.e., Bezalel] changed their order from that which Moses had told him. Therefore Scripture stated everything in general terms, and said that Bezalel did everything as G-d had said, as I have written above. [16]

27. THE SOCKETS OF THE SANCTUARY, AND THE SOCKETS OF THE VEIL. Scripture calls the Tabernacle "the Sanctuary," and mentioned the veil separately, because it divided *between the holy place and the most holy.* [17] Thus it is as if it said, "the sockets of the holy place and the sockets of the most holy."

(11) Numbers 3:31. (12) Above, 35:34. (13) *Ibid.*, 36:8. (14) Yerushalmi Peah I, 1; and quoted here by Rashi. (15) See in *Seder Vayakheil* Note 72. Moses agreed that originally G-d had told him to do it as Bezalel said it should be done. (16) Above, 36:8 (towards the end). (17) *Ibid.*, 26:33.

3. AND THEY BEAT THE GOLD INTO THIN PLATES. In all the sacred work that was done, Scripture did not add an explanation as to the method of execution except for here. It should rather have said: "and they made the ephod of gold, and blue-purple etc., the work of a skilful workman; they made shoulder-pieces for it etc.," for such is the way it describes all of them. It is possible that Scripture relates here [how it was made] because of the original thought that they had to put into making the gold threads, for they were greatly astonished [to be told] that the gold should be spun and twined as is done with wool or linen, for no-one ever heard of doing such a thing until that day.

24. AND THEY MADE UPON THE SKIRTS OF THE ROBE POMEGRANATES OF BLUE-PURPLE AND RED-PURPLE, AND SCARLET, AND TWINED LINEN. This means [18] that they made the pomegranates in order to put them around the bottom of the skirts of the robe, and they made bells of pure gold, [19] and then they put the bells inside the pomegranates before they put them on the robe. Thus the bells were within the pomegranates whilst they were still detached, and they put the pomegranates on the skirts of the robe round about while the bells were within them [i.e., the pomegranates]. This is why Scripture mentions the phrase *within the pomegranates* twice, [20] in order to indicate that the bells were within the pomegranates from the beginning, and also when they hung them upon the skirts of the robe round about. This too is proof to what we have explained in *Seder V'atah Tetzaveh.* [21]

27. AND THEY MADE THE TUNICS OF FINE LINEN OF WOVEN WORK FOR AARON, AND FOR HIS SONS. It appears from here that the tunics were identical for father [Aaron] and

---

(18) Since the pomegranates were not made upon the robe, but instead were made separately and then attached to the robe, Ramban found difficulty in the language of the verse, *And they made upon the skirts of the robe pomegranates.* Hence his interpretation: "This means, etc." (19) Verse 25. (20) *Ibid.: and they put the bells within the pomegranates upon the skirts of the robe round about, within the pomegranates.* — The repetition of the phrase is in order to indicate etc. (21) Above, 28:31.

sons. For even though in the case of the tunic made for Aaron it says, *And thou shalt make the tunic of chequer-work from fine linen,* [22] and in speaking of those made for his sons it just says, *thou shalt make tunics* [23] [without specifying that they should be of chequer-work], the intention is: *"thou shalt make tunics* similar to the one mentioned." And thus it is written, *a breastplate, and an ephod, and a robe, and a tunic of chequer-work, a mitre, and a belt; and they shall make holy garments for Aaron thy brother, and his sons, that they may minister unto Me,* [24] for the expression *for Aaron... and his sons* refers back to the tunic of chequer-work, the mitre and the belt, which were alike for all of them. Similarly, that which Scripture says here, *and the mitre of fine linen, and the beautiful head-tires,* refers to those of both Aaron and his sons, since the *mitznepheth* (mitre) and the *migba'ath* (the head-tire) were made in the same way, except that Aaron wound it [around his head, fold upon fold], and his sons set them upon their heads tightly, as I have explained. [25]

28. 'PA'AREI HAMIGBA'OTH.' The term (the beautiful head-tires) means that these head-dresses rose upon the head like turbans, similar to the expressions, *'hap'eirim' (the head-tires) and the armlets;* [26] *'pa'arei' (tires of) linen they shall have upon their heads.* [27]

Scripture explained with reference to the belt [in the following verse], that they made it *of fine-twined linen, and blue-purple, and red-purple, and scarlet.* This, however, was not explained at the command, except for that which it said briefly about the belt, *that thou shalt make it the work of the weaver in colors,* [22] from which

---

Ramban there discusses Rashi's opinion that the bells were hung separately on the skirts of the robe alongside the pomegranates. On this point he differs and holds that the bells were within the pomegranates. The proof to his opinion Ramban finds in the repetition of the phrase: *within the pomegranates,* which indicates that they were so to begin with and also when attached to the robe. But according to Rashi the repetition is redundant. — It should be noted that the J. P. S. translation of *b'thoch harimonim*: "between the pomegranates" [instead of "within the pomegranates"], follows Rashi's interpretations. (22) Above, 28:39. (23) *Ibid.,* Verse 40. (24) *Ibid.,* Verse 4. (25) *Ibid.,* Verse 31 (towards the end) and Verse 37. (26) Isaiah 3:20. (27) Ezekiel 44:18.

it is known that it was to be woven of these four kinds, as it said with reference to the screen, *And thou shalt make a screen for the door of the Tent, of blue-purple, and red-purple, and scarlet, and fine-twined linen, the work of the weaver in colors.*[28] This belt referred to was also for both Aaron and his sons, in accordance with the opinion of the Sage who says[29] that the belt of the High Priest was made in the same way as that of the common priest. In the opinion, however, of the Sage who says[30] that the High Priest's belt was not the same as that of the common priest, [for that of the common priest was merely of plain linen, whilst the High Priest's was of the above-mentioned four kinds — blue-purple, red-purple, scarlet, and twined linen], Scripture explained with reference to the belt of Aaron that it should be *the work of the weaver in colors,*[22] but it was not even necessary to mention that the one for his sons should be made of linen, just as it said, *And for Aaron's sons thou shalt make tunics, and thou shalt make for them belts, and head-tires shalt thou make for them,*[23] [and it is self-understood] that all of them should be made of linen just like the tunics.

33. AND THEY BROUGHT THE TABERNACLE UNTO MOSES, THE TENT, AND ALL ITS VESSELS. The translation of this verse is as if it were written with the connective *vav* [which indicates "and"], thus making the sense of the verse: "and they brought the Tabernacle unto Moses, 'and' the tent and all its vessels," for it was the curtains of fine-twined linen that are called "Tabernacle," as it is said, *And thou shalt make the Tabernacle with ten curtains of fine-twined linen,*[31] and then it continues, *and thou shalt couple the curtains... that the Tabernacle may be one whole.*[32] The "tent," however, means the curtains of goats' hair, as Scripture says with reference to them, *And thou shalt make curtains of goats' hair for a tent over the Tabernacle;*[33] *and thou shalt couple the tent together, that it may be one.*[34] Similarly, *the*

---

(28) Above, 26:36. (29) Yoma 12 a. The opinion is that of Rabbi Dosa (*ibid.*, b). (30) The opinion is that of Rabbi Yehudah Hanasi. (31) Above, 26:1. (32) *Ibid.*, Verse 6. (33) *Ibid.*, Verse 7. (34) *Ibid.*, Verse 11.

EXODUS XXXIX, PEKUDEI

Tabernacle, its tent, and its covering [35] means "and its tent." So also here the meaning of the verse is, "and they brought the Tabernacle unto Moses, and the tent, and all its vessels," as Scripture mentions here [in this section] the names of all its parts. At times the whole house is called "the Tent of Meeting," as He said, *and they shall make all that I have commanded thee: the Tent of Meeting, and the ark of the Testimony,*[36] for "the Tent of Meeting" is the house in its totality, where He would meet with Moses.[37] Similarly, *all the vessels of the service of the Tabernacle of the Tent of Meeting* [38] [refers to the building as a whole].

37. THE LAMPS THEREOF, EVEN THE LAMPS TO BE SET IN ORDER. It is possible that there are candelabrums with lamps on them purely for decorative purposes, or that they should give additional light if more is required. But this was not the case with the candelabrum of the Sanctuary, for it only had seven lamps. Therefore He explained, *even the lamps to be set in order,* for they were always set in order at dusk.

42. ACCORDING TO ALL THAT THE ETERNAL COMMANDED MOSES, SO THE CHILDREN OF ISRAEL DID ALL 'HA'AVODAH' (THE WORK) — all the work of the Tabernacle. Scripture calls it *avodah* [a term which means also "the Service" to G-d], in order to indicate that they did it for the service of the Glorious Name, it being similar to that which is said, *'v'avad'tem' (and ye shall serve) the Eternal your G-d;* [39] and Him *'ta'avodu' (shall ye serve).*[40] It is possible that the phrase *all the 'avodah'* refers here also to all the vessels, similar to the expression, "all the vessels of the *'avodah'* (service) of the Tabernacle."[41] Thus Scripture first mentioned the vessels, in order to say that even in making the vessels they were careful to do them exactly as they were commanded, and afterwards it states, *And Moses saw all the work...* [42]

---

(35) *Ibid.*, 35:11. (36) *Ibid.*, 31:6-7. (37) *Ibid.*, 30:6. (38) Further, Verse 40. (39) Above, 23:25. (40) Deuteronomy 13:5. (41) The source is unknown to me. (42) Verse 43.

40 2. ON THE FIRST DAY OF THE FIRST MONTH SHALT THOU SET UP THE TABERNACLE OF THE TENT OF MEETING. In the opinion of our Rabbis [43] who say that this was on the eighth day of the installation [of the priests into their sacred office], [44] the meaning of the verse is: "you are to put up the Tabernacle and it should remain so; do not dismantle it and do not put it up again, for when the camps will move, the Levites will dismantle it and put it up." It was not necessary that G-d should command Moses now about the putting up of the Tabernacle during the first seven days, since He had told him at the start, *And thou shalt set up the Tabernacle according to the fashion thereof which hath been shown thee in the mountain.*[45] Now since He explained to him here that *On the first day of the first month* the setting up of the Tabernacle would be of a permanent nature, Moses thus understood that during [each of] the seven days of installation it would be necessary for him to put it up and to dismantle it. Perhaps this was done in order to train the Levites how to do it, for they would see how he did it and would do likewise. Or it may be that this was done in order to crown the eighth day with this special crown [that the Tabernacle was for the first time not dismantled on that day].

It would appear according to the opinion of the Rabbis that on the first seven days Moses put up the Tabernacle each morning, and it remained standing all day and all the following night, and at each dawn he would dismantle it and put it up again immediately, for Scripture says, *And at the door of the Tent of Meeting shall ye abide day and night for seven days,*[46] and there could be no "door" to the Tent of Meeting except at the time when it was

---

(43) Sifra, beginning of *Seder Shemini*. (44) On the first seven days of the installation the Tabernacle was put up and taken apart each day. But on the eighth day it was put up and no longer dismantled until they moved away from the encampment at Mount Sinai. Accordingly, since in the opinion of the Rabbis the first day of Nisan was the eighth day of the installation, the expression *thou shalt set up the Tabernacle* must mean "set it up permanently etc.," (45) Above, 26:30. (46) Leviticus 8:35.

EXODUX XL, PEKUDEI

erected.[47] The Sages have already interpreted:[48] *"he shall bring it to the door of the Tent of Meeting* [49] — at the time when it is open, and not when [the Tent of Meeting] is taken to pieces." Similarly, the Rabbis have said:[50] "Peace-offerings which have been slaughtered before the doors of the Sanctuary were opened are invalid, because it is said, *and he shall slaughter it at the door of the Tent of Meeting* [51] — at the time it is open, and not when it is locked." Similarly, "at the Tabernacle, [peace-offerings which were slaughtered] before the Levites put up the Tabernacle, or after the Levites had dismantled it, were invalid."[50] Moreover, [during the first seven days of installation, Moses] used to sacrifice the Daily Offering of the evening and kindle the lamps at night. And in Vayikra Rabbah [52] I have seen [the following text]: "Moses used to put up the Tabernacle and dismantle it twice every day. Rabbi Chanina the Great says: three times every day, for [the phrase 'putting up' of the Tabernacle] is mentioned three times: *thou shalt put up;* [53] *the Tabernacle was put up;* [54] *and Moses put up the Tabernacle.* [55] Once it was put up for the Daily Offering of the morning, and once for the special offerings of the installation, and once for the Daily Offering of the evening." It is possible that all this was done for the sake of practice, so that they would know the procedure for putting it up, and which order to follow, but they never left it in a dismantled state at all [during the seven days of installation].

And that which Scripture states here, *And the cloud covered the Tent of Meeting, and the Glory of the Eternal filled the Tabernacle,* [56] in the opinion of the Rabbis it refers to the eighth day, for Scripture says, *So Moses finished the work,* [57] and when he had completed this erection on the first of Nisan, the cloud

---

(47) Thus since Scripture states that during the first seven days of the installation Aaron and his sons had to sit *at the door of the Tent of Meeting,* we must therefore conclude that the Tabernacle was dismantled at dawn and put up again immediately. (48) Sifra *Vayikra, parshata* 4. (49) Leviticus 1:3. (50) Zebachim 55 b. (51) Leviticus 3:2. (52) I have not found this quotation in Vayikra Rabbah, but in Tanchuma *Pekudei,* 11. (53) In Verse 2 before us. (54) Further, Verse 17. (55) *Ibid.,* Verse 18. (56) *Ibid.,* Verse 34. (57) *Ibid.,* Verse 33.

covered the Tabernacle. Now Rashi has already mentioned the interpretation of the Rabbis: "*And they came out and blessed the people.*[58] During all the seven days of installation when Moses was putting up the Tabernacle, and officiating therein, and dismantling it,[59] the Divine Glory did not rest upon it, and the Israelites felt ashamed, and they said to Moses: 'Our master! All the trouble which we have taken was only so that the Divine Glory would dwell amongst us, and that we would know that the sin of the calf has been atoned for!' Then Moses said to them: 'My brother Aaron is more worthy and meritorious than I am, and it is through his offerings and service that the Divine Glory will rest upon us.'"

And in the *Parshath Hamiluim*[60] (the Chapter of the Installation) we find written: "I might think that the Tabernacle was put up on the first of the month of Nisan, and that the Divine Glory did not rest thereon until the eighth day of the month. Scripture therefore says, *And on the day that the Tabernacle was put up, the cloud covered the Tabernacle, even the Tent of Meeting.*[61] This teaches us that on the day the Tabernacle was put up, the Divine Glory rested thereon through the service of Aaron." Thus the Rabbis are clearly saying that the cloud covering the Tabernacle was on the eighth day of the installation, which was on the first day of Nisan.

If this is so, then this whole chapter, in the opinion of the Rabbis, took place on the eighth day of the installation. This is indeed so, because Scripture describes the sequence of events as follows: G-d commanded Moses that the final putting up of the Tabernacle should be *on the first day of the first month,* and then it states that Moses did so and finished the whole work [57] [of the seven days of installation], and then [on the eighth day] *the cloud covered the tent,*[56] and so it was always [henceforth whenever they journeyed and put up the Tabernacle at their new place of encampment]. Then Scripture goes back to the beginning of the communication which came to Moses from the Tent, saying, *And He called unto Moses.*[62] All this is now in proper order.

(58) Leviticus 9:23. (59) Our Rashi adds: "every day." (60) Sifra, beginning of *Seder Shemini*. (61) Numbers 9:15. (62) Leviticus 1:1.

EXODUS XL, PEKUDEI

A kind of proof to what the Rabbis have said, [that during the seven days of installation the Tabernacle was dismantled every day], is what Scripture says, *And it came to pass on the day that Moses had made an end of setting up the Tabernacle.* [63] Now if he did not dismantle it, what sense is there to the expression, *the day that he 'made an end' of setting up the Tabernacle,* since he began and finished all the work in one day? In that case it should rather have said: "and it came to pass on the day that Moses set up the Tabernacle." Moreover, it says there [with reference to the eighth day], *This is the thing which the Eternal commanded that ye should do;* [64] *and the Glory of the Eternal appeared unto all the people.* [65] The implication of these verses is that the cloud had not yet covered the Tent of Meeting, and the Glory of the Eternal did not yet fill the Tabernacle.

However it may be, from the first day of the installation G-d communicated to Moses from the Tabernacle all the sections from the beginning of the Book of Leviticus until *And it came to pass on the eighth day.* [66] But the cloud did not cover the Tabernacle, and the people therefore thought that the communication from there to Moses was directly from heaven, just as it was in the land of Egypt. But in the Midrash Chazit [67] I have found the following text: "*And it came to pass on the eighth day.* [66] This really should have been the beginning of the Book of Leviticus. Why then was it written here? Because there is no strict chronological order in the narrative of the Torah." Now if this is so, then the chapter beginning *And He called unto Moses... out of the Tent of Meeting* [62] happened after *and the Glory of the Eternal appeared unto all the people. And there came forth fire from before the Eternal, and consumed upon the altar;* [68] and the communication addressed to Aaron, *drink no wine or strong drink,* [69] took place on the following day, for it is impossible that G-d should speak to Aaron from the Tent of Meeting before He had spoken to

---

(63) Numbers 7:1. (64) Leviticus 9:6. (65) *Ibid.*, Verse 23. (66) *Ibid.*, 9:1. (67) I have not found it in Shir Hashirim Rabbah (Midrash Chazit), but in Koheleth Rabbah 1:31. (68) Leviticus 9:23-24. (69) *Ibid.*, 10:9.

Moses.[70] But I do not know whether this Midrash represents the unanimous opinion of all the Sages, or whether they are the words of a single Sage, for they are mentioned there in the Midrash with reference to Rabbi Yishmael.

THOU SHALT SET UP THE TABERNACLE OF THE TENT OF MEETING. G-d did not explain to Moses in this command the order of putting it up, as it is clearly set forth in the actual construction: *and he laid its sockets, and set up the boards thereof* etc.[71] The reason for His not explaining it here is because He had already shown it to him visually, as He said, *And thou shalt put up the Tabernacle according to the fashion thereof which hath been shown thee in the mountain.*[72] Similarly, He shortened the account here, saying, *And thou shalt put therein the ark of the Testimony,*[73] and did not mention *and in the ark thou shalt put the Testimony,*[74] for since He used the phrase: *the ark of the Testimony,* Moses would understand this, since the ark is only termed "the ark of the Testimony" when the Tablets of the Testimony are in it, and they were already commanded at the beginning, *And thou shalt put the ark-cover above upon the ark; and in the ark thou shalt put the Testimony that I shall give thee.*[74] It was necessary here to mention it only in order to tell him the order of priority, namely that the putting of the ark with the Tablets [into the Tabernacle] should precede the setting up of all other vessels. Similarly He shortened the account of the table and the candelabrum, since He had already commanded him in what place of the Tabernacle they were to be set up.[75] He also shortened the subject of the dressing of Aaron and his sons, saying merely, *And thou shalt put upon Aaron the holy garments,*[76] and with reference to Aaron's sons He said, *and thou shalt put tunics upon them,*[77] for He had already told and commanded Moses in detail about the order of putting on their garments.[78] Here the

---

(70) But if we say, as Ramban does, that G-d already spoke to Moses from the Tent of Meeting on the first day of the installation, then the communication to Aaron, *drink no wine nor strong drink,* took place on the eighth day of the installation. (71) Further, Verse 18. (72) Above, 26:30. (73) Verse 3. (74) Above, 25:21. (75) *Ibid.,* 26:35. (76) Further, Verse 13. (77) *Ibid.,* Verse 14. (78) Above, 29:5-9.

intention was only to fix the time of the dressing in its correct order, namely, after the whole Tabernacle had been set up. Of the priestly garments He mentioned only the tunics, because it is with them that the dressing began.

3. AND THOU SHALT SCREEN 'AL' THE ARK. The word *al* (upon) is in place of the word *el* (to), for the word *v'sakotha* (and thou shalt screen) is derived from the term *masach* (curtain, screen). [79] Similarly, *and he set up the veil of the screen, and screened 'al' the ark of the Testimony* [80] [carries the same interpretation as the verse before us].

10. AND THE ALTAR SHALL BE MOST HOLY. Since they would also sacrifice on it the most holy offerings, Scripture describes the altar as "most holy," even though it stood in the court of the Tabernacle. Of the Tabernacle, however, Scripture says, *and it shall be holy*,[81] because the term "most holy" is used usually only with reference to the place where the ark rests, just as it is said, *and the veil shall divide unto you between the holy place and the most holy.*[82] It is possible that He said of the altar "most holy," because it sanctifies other things, just as He said, *whatsoever toucheth the altar shall be holy.*[83]

17. AND IT CAME TO PASS IN THE FIRST MONTH. . . ON THE FIRST DAY OF THE MONTH. In the opinion of our Rabbis [who hold, as mentioned above,[84] that the eighth day of the installation was on the first of Nisan], Scripture stated that the Tabernacle was first put up on a permanent basis on the first day of the first month, as He had commanded.[84] It states, *And Moses put up the Tabernacle,*[85] in order to tell us what he did when putting it up from the first day that he began to do so, which was

---

(79) Thus the sense of the verse is not: "and thou shalt screen 'upon' the ark," but: "thou shalt screen the ark." By putting up the veil in front of the ark, the ark will be screened. (80) Further, Verse 21. (81) Verse 9. (82) Above, 26:33. (83) *Ibid.*, 29:37. See also Ramban above in *Seder Ki Thisa* 34:25, towards the end, for the specific explanation of how the altar sanctifies whatever touches it. (84) Above, Verse 2. (85) Verse 18.

on the twenty-third day of Adar. Scripture does not mention here the anointing of the Tabernacle and its vessels, nor the anointing of Aaron and his sons and the offerings of the installation, since Moses did not do these until he had finished putting up the Tabernacle [on each of the seven days of the installation],[86] and was commanded thereon a second time, *Take Aaron and his sons,*[87] as is explained in the section of *Tzav.*[87] Now the Tabernacle and its vessels were only sanctified for the Divine Service through their anointing, just as it is said, *and thou shalt anoint the Tabernacle, and all that is therein, and shalt hallow it, and all the vessels thereof.*[88] Therefore the meaning of the verses, *And he set a row of bread upon it,*[89] *And he lighted the lamps,*[90] must be that he did so at the time that was appropriate for them, that is, after they were anointed [on each of the seven days of the installation], and the sense of the verses is that such was their ultimate purpose [i.e., he put the table in the Tent of Meeting so that he would later on be able to set a row of bread upon it; he put the candelabrum so that he would be able to light the lamps]. And that which Scripture states above, *And thou shalt bring in the table, and set in order the bread that is upon it,*[91] also means that he is to set the bread upon it after the anointing of the table. The same meaning applies to the verse, *And thou shalt set the golden altar for incense.*[92] Similarly, *and he offered upon it the burnt-offering and the meal-offering*[93] means at its proper time, for the court around the Tabernacle had not yet been put up,[94] and no sacrifices can be brought without the hangings of the court, for that would be considered slaughtering outside [the Tabernacle].[95] But all these mean that they were done at their proper time.

And he took and put the Testimony into the ark. The meaning of this is that he took the Tablets from the wooden ark in Moses' tent which they were in, and brought them to the Tabernacle.[96]

---

(86) See my Hebrew commentary p. 538, where I have shown that this is perforce the meaning of Ramban. (87) Leviticus 8:2. (88) Above, Verse 9. (89) Further, Verse 23. (90) *Ibid.,* Verse 25. (91) Above, Verse 4. (92) *Ibid.,* Verse 5. (93) Further, Verse 29. (94) For that is only mentioned further, in Verse 33. (95) A matter strongly forbidden in Leviticus 17:1-9. (96) Verse 20.

EXODUS XL, PEKUDEI

27. AND HE BURNT THEREON INCENSE OF SWEET SPICES. All the seven days of the installation Moses burnt the incense on the golden altar, and even though he was not specifically told to do so when he was commanded, [97] he did so nonetheless, for he understood that he was to do so from all the other acts of service, since G-d had commanded him here that he should set the bread [91] and kindle the lamps. [91] Similarly, *and he offered upon it the burnt-offering and the meal-offering* [93] means that Moses was the one who offered them, for thus he was commanded, *Now this is that which thou shalt offer upon the altar,* [98] meaning that he was to begin to do this when performing the Service during the days of the installation, for all commands there [about the burnt- and the meal-offering] [99] refer to Moses' service. Afterward, it says, *It shall be a continual burnt-offering throughout your generations,* [100] meaning that the priests shall do throughout the generations as Moses now did. Therefore in the section of *Pinchas* it says about this Daily Offering, *It is a continual burnt-offering, which was offered in Mount Sinai,* [101] meaning that Moses began doing it there. Thus Moses our Teacher was the first priest in all these acts of service, therefore he also burnt the incense. Perhaps this is included in the words, *and thou shalt put the golden altar for incense,* [92] meaning that he should immediately burn the incense on it. And that which is said at the time of the command, *And thou shalt put it before the veil... and Aaron shall burn thereon the incense of sweet spices,* [102] refers to the proper time, from the day that Aaron begins his service and forever afterwards, [and does not exclude Moses' service during the seven days], for so He said, *And when Aaron lighteth the lamps at dusk,* [103] and he only lit them from that day on, for here Moses was clearly commanded: *and thou shalt light the lamps thereof.* [104]

---

(97) In Verse 5: *And thou shalt set the golden altar for incense...* (98) Above, 29:38. (99) *Ibid.*, Verses 39-41. (100) *Ibid.*, Verse 42. (101) Numbers 28:6. (102) Above, 30:6-7. (103) *Ibid.*, Verse 8. (104) Above, Verse 4. Accordingly, the verse here in this chapter must refer to the seven days of the installation when Moses acted as the priest, and the verses above (30:6-8) refer to the time when Aaron would take charge of the service.

Now in Rashi's commentary I have seen this text: [105] *"And he* — Aaron — *burnt thereon incense (of sweet spices)* morning and evening, as it is said, *every morning, when he dresseth the lamps, he shall burn it. And when Aaron lighteth the lamps at dusk* etc." [106] But I do not know if this is the scribe's mistake. [107]

34. AND THE CLOUD COVERED THE TENT OF MEETING etc. Scripture is stating that the cloud covered the Tabernacle from all sides, with the result that the building was covered and hidden in it. AND THE GLORY OF THE ETERNAL FILLED THE TABERNACLE, this means that it was filled completely with the Glory, for the Glory rested within the cloud inside the Tabernacle, just as it is said with reference to Mount Sinai, *unto the thick darkness where G-d was.* [108] It states further on that *Moses was not able to come into the Tent of Meeting* [109] — even to the door, because the cloud covered it, and he was not permitted to come into the cloud. Moreover, *the Glory of the Eternal filled the Tabernacle,* [109] so how could he enter it? The reason for this was so that Moses should not go in without permission, but instead G-d would call him and then he was to come into the midst of the cloud, just as He had done at Mount Sinai, as it is said, *and He called unto Moses on the seventh day out of the midst of the cloud,* [110] and then it says, *And Moses entered into the midst of the cloud.* [111]

In line with the plain meaning of Scripture, it is because it is said, *and the Eternal spoke unto him out of the Tent of Meeting* [112] that Moses did not enter the Tabernacle, but G-d called him from the Tent of Meeting and he stood at its door and He spoke to him. But our Rabbis have said: [113] "One verse states, *And Moses was not able to enter into the Tent of Meeting,* [109] and

---

(105) It is not found in our texts of Rashi. (106) Above, 30:7-8. (107) For, as explained above, the verse here speaks of Moses doing the service, and not Aaron, since the account here is of what happened during the seven days of the installation. (108) Above, 20:21. (109) Verse 35. (110) Above, 24:16. (111) *Ibid.*, Verse 18. (112) Leviticus 1:1. (113) Sifra, Introduction, 8.

another verse states, *and when Moses went into the Tent of Meeting* [114] [thus the two verses appear to be contradictory]! The matter is decided by the passage, *because the cloud abode thereon.*" [115] For in the opinion of the Rabbis, the phrase *and when Moses went into the Tent of Meeting,* [114] means that he went inside of his own accord without being called. Or it may be that because Scripture states there, *and he heard the Voice speaking unto him from above the ark-cover,* [114] therefore it appeared to the Rabbis that Moses stood within the Tent before the ark-cover. Now as long as the Glory of G-d filled the Tabernacle, Moses did not enter it. Therefore they say that he only would enter after the cloud withdrew, meaning after it withdrew from covering the whole Tent, and the Glory no longer filled the Tabernacle. That was only on the eighth day of the installation when the Glory descended there,[116] and as for the call that came to Moses, of which it is said, *And he called unto Moses,* [112] that happened, in the opinion of the Rabbis, before [the eighth day, namely, on the first day of the installation], as I have explained above. [117] It is possible that the verse before us which repeats, *and the Glory of the Eternal filled the Tabernacle* [when it had already stated, *and the cloud covered the Tent of Meeting*], alludes to the Glory that dwells within it.

(114) Numbers 7:89. (115) Here in Verse 35. "From this you learn that as long as the cloud was there, Moses was not able to enter; when the cloud withdrew, Moses entered and He spoke with him" (Sifra *ibid.*). (116) Leviticus 9:23-24. (117) Above, Verse 2.

Thus is completed the Book of Redemption,

In which *the Eternal, the G-d of Israel, hath entered* [118]

Even for the children of Israel, a people near unto Him. [119]

He saved him from the hand of him that hated him,

And redeemed him from the hand of his enemy. [120]

And blessed be G-d

Who delighted in the peace of His servant, [121]

Who has helped him to come thus far, [122]

Who renews his youth [123] in his old age,

Who satisfies his hunger with His Torah,

And He made him to suck honey [124] and the fat thereof.

For he set his whole heart [to seek G-d], [125]

And to His Name he offers blessings morning and evening.

Blessed be He of Whose bounty we have partaken,

And through Whose goodness we live. [126]

(118) Ezekiel 44:2. In the Book of Exodus Israel first appears as a people. Hence Ramban uses this expression: *The Eternal the G-d of Israel hath entered.* (119) Psalms 148:14. (120) See *ibid.*, 106:10. (121) *Ibid.*, 35:27. (122) The reference may be personal: "Blessed be G-d Who has helped me to reach so far in my commentary on the Torah." Or again, it may be that these concluding verses Ramban wrote when already in the Land of Israel. In that case the words assume a literal meaning: "Who has helped him to come thus far," which is, as he continues, the place where his youth is renewed in his old age. See in "Hamayon," Tammuz, 5728, pp. 32-6, where I defended this explanation at length. (123) See Psalms 103:5. (124) Deuteronomy 32:13. (125) See II Chronicles 30:19. (126) Berachoth 50 a.

Additional Note by Ramban[1]

G-d has blessed me till now, so that I have had the merit to come to Acco, and I found there in the possession of the elders of the Land a silver coin engraved like the engravings of a signet, with a pattern like *a rod of an almond tree*[2] on one side, and on the other side a pattern like a jar, and around the two sides was an engraved writing written very clearly. The writing was shown to the Kuthiim[3] and they read it at once, for that was the Hebrew script which was left to the Kuthiim,[3] as is mentioned in Tractate Sanhedrin.[4] On one side they read: *the shekel of shekalim,* and on

---

(1) Ramban arrived in the Land of Israel in the early part of the summer 1267 C. E. at the port of Acco — the city where some fifty-three years earlier a great part of the three hundred French and English Rabbis had settled. Although he wanted to press on and continue the journey to Jerusalem, he was advised against it because of the hardships of the road. He finally set foot in the Holy City on the ninth of Ellul of that year (5027-1267). The intervening months which he spent in Acco were not lost to him, as is clearly indicated by this note. Of special interest in this connection is an object which has come to light only recently (in the winter of 5732-1972) when the seal of Ramban was found in Tel-Kisan — a high mound in the Acco plain, which Ramban undoubtedly passed along on his trips through the Land. The seal (cast in copper) encloses four lines of Hebrew script, meaning: "Moses — son of Rabbi Nachman — of restful soul of Gerona — be strong." See the brochure of the Israel Museum, "The Seal of Nahmanides" by Isaiah Shachar, the finder of this important and rare Ramban memorabilia. Ramban added this note to the end of his commentary, at the end of the Book of Deuteronomy. In view of the fact that it concerns a topic discussed in *Seder Ki Thisa* (30:13 — see there Note 77), we have placed it here at the end of the Book of Exodus. (2) Jeremiah 1:11. (3) A term for the Samaritans. (4) Sanhedrin 21 b. Reference is to the old Hebrew alphabetical symbols [*kthav l'bono'ah* — which are now the Samaritan characters], and which reappeared on the coinage during the Hasmonean rulers. Our alphabet is known as the *kthav ashurith* — or *kthav meruba* ["quadratic"].

the other side: *Jerusalem the holy*. They further said that the figures represent the rod of Aaron with its flowers and almonds,[5] and the second figure represents the jar of manna.[6] We weighed it at money changers and it weighed ten silver *astralinash*,[7] and they are equivalent to "the half an ounce" which Rashi mentioned. Similarly I have seen an identical coin, with the same figures and the same script as the first, but half of its weight, this being the half-shekel that they donated for the offerings. Thus the words of Rabbeinu Shlomo [Rashi] have been supported with a strong proof. For according to the words of our great Rabbi [i.e., the author of the Hilchoth Gedoloth],[8] and the Gaonim,[9] the *perutah* [mentioned throughout the Talmud] is a half of a *chakah*,[10] but a *denar* is a *chakah*,[10] and they say that the *denars* each weigh ninety-six barley grains, this being the *denar* which they call in Acco "Bizand Saradint,"[11] for such is its weight precisely. This is the *shashdang*[12] which the Gaonim mentioned, and which those who speak in the various European languages refer to.[13] And so they call "the Bizand [Saradint]" the "Tyrian *denar*." Similarly they write in their documents: "Tyrian *denars*," for they used to mint them in Tyre which is near Acco. The weight of this *denar* is three *istatlinish*. Thus a *sela* [which consists of four *denars*] is twelve *istatlinish* according to their words. But since, as is the opinion of Rashi,[14] they only weigh ten, we must conclude that the nations have added a sixth thereto. Perhaps the small pieces weighed with "the Bizand" are the additions, and the basic coin itself weighs twenty dry grains [of barley].

Completed and finished. Praise be to G-d, Creator of the world.

(5) Numbers 17:23. (6) Above, 16:33. (7) See my Hebrew commentary (Vol. II, p. 507) that the word is used by Rashba in one of his responsa. It would seem that the word is related to the English word "sterling." (8) See in *Seder Ki Thisa* Note 73, and in corresponding text in Ramban. (9) See *ibid.*, Note 74. (10) "A grain of barley," as is explained in the text further on. (11) This is the "Byzantinus Saracinatus" — a coin issued by the Latin Kingdom of Jerusalem which had an Arabic legend on it. Hence the two names: Byzantinus Saracinatus. A picture of it is found in Joshua Prawer's (Hebrew) History of the Latin Kingdom of Jerusalem, Vol. II, p. 354. (12) See in *Seder Ki Thisa* Note 75, and in corresponding text in Ramban. (13) This is probably a reference to the various peoples who resided at that time in Acco. (14) Rashi Bechoroth 49 b.

Index

OF NAMES, PLACES, BOOKS AND SUBJECTS

Index

A

Aaron,
- when born, 9, 18.
- why his birth not recorded in Scripture, 13.
- his joy at Moses' birth, 14.
- to speak on Moses' behalf to people and to Pharaoh, 50, 73, 75.
- told by Moses the Divine Names revealed to him, 57.
- his role in the mission to Pharaoh, 74-75.
- the mark of honor to him at the Song of the Red Sea, 207.

Aaron,
- Moses' special recognition to him, 433.
- in the affair of the golden calf, 550-553, 563-565.

Acquisition, custom in —, 495-496.
Adultery, 319-320.
Ahasuerus, 489.
Aleinu prayer, 215.
Alexander the Great, 477.
Alimentation of one's wife, 355-357.
Altars, 332-337.
- reason for prohibition of building it with stones touched by iron, 334-337.
- to burn incense thereon, 507-509.
- why they were regarded as "most holy," 621.

Numbers refer to pages. Names and subjects in the Commentary appearing in place of the Biblical text, are not listed.

Abraham Ibn Ezra, Shemoth Rabbah, Mechilta, Onkelos and Rashi, because of their constant occurrence, are not listed.

Amalek,
- his hatred of Israel, 178.
- war of –, 242-248.
- why Moses feared the Amalekites, 243.
- time for fulfulling the commandment to blot out – did not come until reign of Saul, 246.
- reason why punishment was meted out to him more than other nations, 248.

Amram and Jochebed, 12-13.
- the meaning of the goodliness Jochebed saw when Moses was born, 14.
- G-d associates His Name with Amram, 26.
- the tradition Amram received from his father about the way to recognize the true redeemer, 41.
- worthy to be spoken of (Kohath and Amram) as the fathers of the world, 76.
- the miracle that happened to Jochebed, 76.

Angels, 25, 26, 27, 70, 80, 129-131, 141-143, 179, 185-187, 201, 226, 292, 392, 408-413, 414, 423, 579, 587.

Animal,
- if it kills a person, 370-373.
- if it causes damage, 373-375.

Apostate, 160.

Ark, 445-450.
- His wish that all Israel should share in making of the –, 446; reason for it, 446.
- why Bezalel alone was fit to make the –, 605.

Aruch, 526.
Asmachta, 133.
Atlantic Ocean,
- the fogs over – as testified by Abraham ibn Ezra, 109.

B

Babylon,
- why we adopted names of months of –, 117-118.
- the memorial to our coming up from Babylonian exile, 117-118.
- donations for the Sanctuary after the Babylonian exile, 512-513.

Bath Kol, 483.
Benedictions,
- the secret of –, 206.
- why – contain two different pronouns, 214-215.
- *Sh'moneh Esreh*, 215 (Note 270).
- over spices, 526.

Beraitha, 133, (Note 209).
Bereshith Rabbah, 26, 529, 573.
Bezalel,
- miracle of his craftsmanship and nature of his wisdom, 542-543.
- why – alone was fit to make the Ark, 605.
- Scripture speaking in his praise, 611.

Bitter herbs, 127-128.
"Bizand Saradint," 628.

INDEX

Book of Chronicles, 6-7.
— Ibn Ezra's remark with respect to a certain item in — and Ramban's refutation, 454-455.

"Book of the Covenant," 419, 422, 591-592.

Book of Creation, 322.

Book of Exodus,
— scope and contents, 3-5.
— why it concludes with building of Tabernacle, 5.
— the Book of Redemption, 626.

Book of Ezra, 6-7.

Book of Genesis,
— scope and contents, 3.

Book of Leviticus,
— when first sections of — were declared, 619.

"Book of the Wars of the Eternal," 245-246.

C

Cabala, 25, 31, 33, 39-40, 57, 67, 68, 70, 170, 190-191, 194-195, 214, 245, 248, 273, 284, 290-291, 318, 331, 349, 406, 418, 424, 428, 437, 450, 456, 476-477, 523-524, 548, 557-559, 573, 581-582, 599.

Canaanite Bondman, 349, 364-366.

Candelabrum,
— why Moses found difficulty with —, 456.
— making thereof, 456-462.

Candelabrum,
— how lit, 472-474.
— Aaron to light it at first time, 508.

Census,
— how to be taken, 510-511.
— when taken, 513-517.

Chananel, Rabbeinu,
— has written in his commentary on the Torah, 106.

Chapters of the Palaces, 490.

Circumcision, 52-53, 155, 158, 170, 301-302, 547.

Cologne,
— "the correct weight of —," 520.

Commandments,
— general principle in reason of many —, 171-175.
— significance of commandments which are a memorial to the exodus, 173.
— why a positive commandment overrides a negative one, 309-310.
— why a positive commandment is "greater" than a negative one, 309.
— the — have many reasons, there being many benefits in each for body and soul, 337.
— as opposed to a mere negation, 350.
— negative admonition expressed in general terms, 404-405.
— some of the precepts which are like general principles to the — of the Torah, 434.

Compassion,
— G-d's — for servant's wife and children, 343.
— for maidservant, 354-355.
— for helpless, 392-395.

Constantinople, 520.
Converts to Judaism,
— called by another name, 19.
— circumcision and immersion, 161 (Note 360).
— those who foreswear only idolatry, 160-161.
— righteous proselytes, 317.
— proper way to deal with —, 434.
Court,
— constituted in Egypt, 140.
Creation,
— the wondrous miracles point to principle of —, 172.
— acknowledging —, 174.
— "the first Creation," 174.
— exodus evidence of —, 285.
— the perpetual remembrance of —, 306, 312.
— allusion to great things in process of —, 341.
— witnesses to —, 403.
Creator,
— His existence never doubted in Israel, 38.
— the great duty of man to acknowledge— and be thankful to Him for having created him, 174.
— why His Sovereignty is stated in a future tense at end of Song at Red Sea, 206.
— the rule for mentioning His Sovereignty in benedictions, 214-215.
— the positive commandment to believe that the Eternal exists, 285.
Cursing,
— parents, 358-359; why punishment more severe than in smiting, 358.

Cursing,
— those of supreme authority, 396-398.
Cyrus, king of Persia, 6-7, 131.
— if anointed, 504.

D

Dathan and Abiram, 235.
David,
— provided all needs for the Sanctuary in Jerusalem, 455.
— reason for his error in census, 511.
Day,
— the names for various divisions of the —, 120-125.
— why days of week have no individual names, 116-117, 313.
— the allusion in the six days of creation, 318.
— the secret of the days of the world, 340-341, 341 (Note 23).
— day of "wedding" of Torah, 430.
Day of Atonement, 261-262, 508.
— when the High Priest performs the Service on —, 490-491.
Death,
— life after — of body, 65.
"Divine Chariot," 5, 449-450, 467, 551-552.
Divine Names, 33-40, 44, 57, 58, 60, 64-70, 186, 193-194, 246-247, 282-283, 397, 408-413, 584-586.

INDEX

E

Egyptian Bondage,
- the decree to drown the Israelite children, and when revoked, 9, 13.
- scope of the affliction, 11-12, 31, 71.
- beating and cursing, 11.
- worked in levies in the royal building-projects, 8, 11, 59.
- why the slavery was not imposed upon tribe of Levi, 59-60.
- the length of —, 150-156.
- spiritual condition of Israel in Egypt, 24, 156.
- why Egyptians were punished, 259-260.

Eliezer,
- his recounting his journey, 606.

Elijah, 244.
- the miracle with the jar of meal, 451.

Elisha, 211.
- the miracle with the pot of oil, 451.
- when anointed as prophet, 504.

Ephod, see: Garments, priestly.

Ephraim,
- children of — who went out from Egypt before Moses came, 157.

Esau,
- the inheritor of the sword, 335.

Exile,
- Egyptian — when begun and when completed 4-5, 6, 150-156.
- Babylonian —, 117-118.
- in — of Edom, 244.

Exodus, see: Redemption from Egyptian Bondage.

Ezra, 512-513, 558.

F

Faith,
- "the whole foundation of the —," 169, (Note 410).
- opinions in matter of — that fell into error, 171-172.
- how miracles confirm three basic principles of —, and of whole Torah, 172-173.
- importance of making a memorial of — which we have seen, 172-173.
- all the fundamentals of —, creation, providence, and prophecy, 312.

Festival-offering, 164 (Note 383).

Firstborn, redemption of, 167.
- the firstborns at the Giving of the Torah, 426.

First fruits, 163, 399, 400, 590-591.

Foods,
- purport of prohibitions concerning certain —, 401.

G

Gaonim, 521 (Note 74), 628.
Garments, priestly, 475-487.
– correspond to garments of royalty, 475-476.
– had to be made with intention to be used for that purpose, 477.
– breastplate and ephod, 440-444.
– Urim and Thummim, 480-484.
– Robe, 484-485, 612.
– head-dress, 486-487, 491-495, 613.
– when lacking these –, 487-491.
– reason for these –, 490-491.
– frontplate, 491-495.
– nature of their uniqueness, 544-546.
– belt, 613-614.
Gemara, 132, (Note 204).
Generation of the wilderness,
– status of their spiritual attainment, 227-228.
Golden Calf,
– nature of sin in this affair, 549-555.
– the evil repercussions thereof, 565-566.
– the punishment for the sin in the affair of –, 567-573.
– series of events between affair of – and final forgiveness, 574-577.
– when tidings of the forgiveness of the sin was brought, 599.
Guardians, law of four –, 378-383.
Gzeirah shavah, 136 (Note 217).

H

Halachoth of Rabbi Yitzchak Alfasi, 521, 530.
Harav Rabbi Moshe [ben Maimon], 524, 526, 529, 539.
– see also: "The Rabbi" (Rambam).
Hazael, king of Aram,
– anointed as king, 504.
Health, 213-214.
– conditions for people to be healthy, 415.
Heave-offering, 399, 400.
Hebrew, see: Sacred Language.
Hilchoth Gedoloth, 350, 351, 520, 523, 628.
Hillel the Elder, 311, 313.
Husband and wife,
– duties of husband to wife, 355-357.

I

Idolatry,
– scope of prohibition of second of Ten Commandments, 289-290, 295-296.
– the three kinds of –, 292-295.
– punishment imposed on a sinner and felt up to fourth generation applies only to –, 300.
– why a warning of punishment is needed in case of –, 321.

INDEX

Idolatry,
— slaughtering to idols, 390-392, 404-405.
— the forbidden modes of worship, 391.
— mentioning names of idols, 405.
— severity of worshipping idols, 413,588.
— "ways of the Amorites," 413-414.
— destruction of idols, 418-419.

Immersion,
— as necessary in conversion, 161, 279.

Incense,
— the compound forming the —, 438-430, 525, 533-541.
— altar to burn —, 507-509.
— all regulations concerning burning of —, 541.

India, 515.

Injuries to person, 362-364, 366-370.

Inquiring of the Urim and Thummim, 482-483.

Installation of Priests, 495-506, 616-621.
— when was "the eighth day" of —, 616, 621-622.

Israel,
— love of G-d for —, 8.
— elders of — never doubted existence of Creator, 38-39.
— praiseworthiness of — at preparation for Passover, 145.
— duration of stay in Egypt, 150-156.
— stay in wilderness, 156.
— meaning of term "children of —," 182.
— the preferred of all — for leadership, 266.
— no power delegated to rule over —, 274.

Israel,
— never doubted prophecy, 277.
— when became worthy that there be amongst them a Sanctuary, 434.
— the dwelling of the Divine Glory in — fulfilled a want above, 506-507.
— accepted upon themselves freely a form of punishment for incident of the golden calf, 574.

J

Jealousy,
— the term — when applied to G-d, 291-292, 322.

Jeroboam,
— his investiture of new priests, 497-498.
— when instituting the worship of the calves, 566.

Jethro,
— his various names and reasons for, 19-20.
— the most likely explanation that — came before the Revelation, 251-254.
— Scripture speaking in praise of —, 254.
— when did his return to his land take place, 255.
— his return to Israel — 255-256.
— became converted through circumcision, etc., 260.

Jethro,
- on day of his conversion he was "as a newly-circumcised child," 261.
Jonathan ben Uziel, 384, 484, 527, 538, 539.
Joseph,
- the tradition he handed over to Levi, 41.
- how his sons were blessed by Jacob, 412.
Joshua, 27.
- the six nations that assembled to fight -, 29.
- established customs and ways of civilized society upon people entering the Land, 210.
- when was his original name Hoshea changed to -, 242.
- why he was charged to fight Amalek, 242.
- the angel that appeared to him at Jericho, 409-412.
- at Moses' ascent to Mount Sinai, 431-432.
- the uniqueness in his name and reason for it, 578.
Jubilee Year, 340, 348-349.
Justice, administration of,
- necessary qualification of judges, 266-269, 339-340.
- a layman acting as judge, 340.
- Divine participation in -, 348.

K

Kaddish prayer, 206 (Note 229).
Kal Vachomer, 133 (Note 208).
Kethubah, 385-387.
Kiddush, 309, 313-315.
Kingdom of Heaven,
- obligation to take upon oneself yoke of -, 286, 321.
Kuthiim, 627.

L

Land of Israel,
- meaning of "a land flowing with milk and honey," 30.
- those who live in - and give their lives for the commandments, 301.
Languages,
- the Sacred Language, 26-27, 45, 518-520, 538, 577.
- the masters of -, 45, 168, 439.
- Greek, 131, 526, 527, 537, 552.
- Arabic, 527, 528, 529, 530, 535, 537.
- Persian, 527.
- Latin, 527, 529, 536.
Leaders,
- qualities that make for leadership, 266-268.

INDEX

639

Leaven.
- the prohibition against ownership and possession of - on Passover, 134-138.
- the prohibition against eating, 139.
- removal of - on day before Passover 407-408.

Love,
- greater than fear, 309.

"Lovers of G-d," 300-302.

M

Maidservant, Hebrew
- her rights to freedom, 349-354.
- her rights after espousal, 355-357.

Manna,
- where and when it began falling, 217-219.
- nature of "trial" in connection with -, 221-223.
- the wonder inherent in -, 225-231.
- a product of the "Higher Light," 227, 230-231.
- description of -, 231-234.

Marah,
- nature of the statute and ordinance given at -, 208-210, 419.

Mars, 335.

Mashiach ben Yoseph, 244 (Note 462).

Mattatron, 130-131, 408-413, 423.

Mechilta of Rabbi Shimon ben Yochai, 186, 311 (Note 433), 344, 383.

Mezuzah,
- spiritual significance, 173.

Midian,
- Moses' sojourn there, 22-23.
- Moses' return there from Egypt, 62.

Midrash Agadah, 36.

Midrash Chazita, see: Shir Hashirim Rabbah.

Midrash of Rabbi Nechunya ben Hakanah, 25, 215, 308.

Midrash Yelamdeinu, 131, 211, 268.

Miracles,
- hidden and open, 65-66, 174-175, 219.
- remembering of - in connection with exodus, 116, 157.
- how - confirmed three foundations of faith: creation, providence, and prophecy etc. - 172.
- most outstanding wonder of all wonders, 180.
- how the Red Sea split and why, 188-189.
- miracle within a miracle 211.
- G-d will not make wonders in every generation for sake of some heretic, 172.
- Scripture disposed to be silent on hidden -, 219.

Miriam,
- the advice to her father, 12.
- her joy at Moses' birth, 14.

Miriam,
- her prophecy before Moses' birth, 14.
- why her genealogy is connected to Aaron in Song at the Red Sea, 207.

Mishnah of the Tabernacle, 448, 463, 465.

Months,
- why Nisan is the first of —, 116-118.
- origin of names of —, 117-119.
- why — have no individual names in the Torah, 116.

Moreh Nebuchim, 37, 48, 222, 291, 326, 329, 334, 519.

Moses,
- his birth prophesied by his sister, 14.
- the unique quality his mother saw in him at once, 14.
- why the princess had compassion for him, 16-17.
- desires to see his brethren "because they were his brethren," 17-18.
- why and how he killed the Egyptian who was smiting the Hebrew, 18-19.
- his anger aroused because of injustice to Jethro's daughters, 21.
- in the days when he was a fugitive from Pharaoh, 22-23.
- how old when he became a fugitive from Pharaoh, 22.
- when he married Zipporah, 22.
- at the burning bush, 27.
- his gradual reaching highest degree of prophecy, 27.
- reasons why he refused to go to Pharaoh, 31-32, 46-49, 73.

Moses,
- at the burning bush he was already "the father of wisdom etc.," 34.
- why he was torn up from his father's house, 41.
- why — had to be shown signs by G-d before going to Pharaoh, 44.
- rebuked by G-d, 44, 69.
- his natural defective speech, 46-48, 49, 72.
- why he took his wife and children from Midian to Egypt, 51-52; why they returned, 53, 62.
- his two sons, 52-53, 257-258.
- reason for his complaint to G-d, 60-62.
- nature of his prophecy, 67.
- Egyptians' admiration of his greatness, 75.
- treated his older brother with respect, 56.
- achievement he merited by his humility, 75.
- the doubt people had about — at the Red Sea, 183.
- established customs for the people as they came into the wilderness how to regulate their lives, 209-210.
- at the Giving of the Torah, 281-282, 324-325, 424-426.
- the officiating priest during the Seven days of installation, 503, 623-624.
- instituted a silver coin, 518.
- prayers of — in the affair of the golden calf, 559-561.
- his great humility when speaking to Joshua, 562.

INDEX

Moses,
- his request after incident of calf, 581-583.
- when G-d spoke to him in Tabernacle, 624-625.

Mount Sinai,
- where Israel achieved its true redemption, 4-5.
- whole mountain became sanctified at time of the burning bush, just as at Giving of the Torah, 27.
- length of journey from Egypt, 33.
- coming into wilderness of — was an occasion of joy for the people for they knew they would receive the Torah there, 269.
- at the Revelation, 324-325.

Mountains of Darkness, 108.
Murder, 319-320, 341-342.
Myrrh, 524-529.

N

Nasi, 397-398.
Nebuchadnezzar,
- why people worshipped him as a god, 294.

Night-time, domain of, 141-143.
Noachides,
- seven laws of, 316, 419.

O

Offerings,
- secret of —, 57, 392.
- when dedicating beasts as —, 303.
- sin-offering, 427, 502, 505-506.
- peace-offerings, 429-430, 617.

Oil for the light, 471-472.

Oil of the Anointment,
- authority in Israel belonged to those who were anointed with —, 503.
- composition of —, 524-530.
- making of —, 530-533.
- on whom to be used, 503-504; 531-533.

Onkelos,
- variant texts of —, 104-105.
- amazing thing in Onkelos' wisdom in his understanding of the Revelation on Mount Sinai, 328-329.
- translates both Elokim and Tetragrammaton alike, 328.

Ordination, 339 (Note 20).

P

Parents,
- honoring — and reward thereof, 318-319, 322.
- smiting — 358-359.

Parents,
- why punishment for cursing — is more severe than smiting, 358.
- anyone who sells his daughter as a maidservant deals deceitfully with her, 354.

Parshath Hamiluim, 618.

Partial Admission, law of —, 380-382.

Passover,
- how the first night is to be sanctified to G-d's Name, 157.
- to be observed only in month of Aviv, 162, 406.
- first and seventh days, 165.
- reason for reading the Song at the Red Sea on seventh day of —, 180.

Passover-offering,
- buying thereof, 115.
- reason for, 118-119.
- time of slaughtering, 119-126.
- how eaten, 127-128, 141.
- "ordinance of the Passover," 158-160.
- of the generations, Egypt, and wilderness, 128, 159.
- and leavened bread, 407-408.
- offering thereof, 589-590.

Patriarchs,
- the "counsel of G-d" which was upon their tents, 4.
- constituted the "Divine Chariot," 5.
- when their children returned to their status, 4.
- reason why "the G-d of" is mentioned with each one, 28.
- nature of their prophecy, 34, 64-67.
- length of Egyptian bondage as revealed to Abraham, 150-156.

Patriarchs,
- way Abraham learned the Torah, 209.
- why Abraham called "the friend of G-d," 301-302.
- Abraham in relation to the prophets, 302.
- the merit of Jacob at the Revelation, 428.
- when Abraham's deeds were made known, 527.

"Permanent House", 335.

Pharaoh,
- reason why he did not order the outright slaying of the Hebrews, 8-9.
- a very wise man, 58.
- why he did not impose slavery upon tribe of Levi, 59.
- his relationship to Moses and Aaron, 59, 82.
- why his heart was hardened, 78-80, 95, 100, 114, 179-180, 198.
- looked upon himself as a god, and why people worshipped him, 294.

Phylacteries,
- reason for commandment 168-171, 173.
- "the sign of —," 170.
- we have received their form from the holy fathers who saw the prophets and the ancient ones up to Moses, 168.
- as worn by High Priest, 491.

Pirkei d'Rabbi Eliezer, 242, 576.

Plagues, the ten
- initials written on the rod that Moses held, 56.

INDEX

Plagues, the ten
- the role of the magicians in the first two plagues, 87-88.
- why magicians could not bring forth gnats, 87, 89.
- why was there a forewarning only in certain —, 89-90, 96.
- where the warnings were given, 90-91.
- where Moses prayed that the plagues cease, 97.
- the intervals between —, 102-103.
- the uniqueness of the — of locusts, 105-107.
- nature of — of darkness, 108-109.
- when the Divine communication was given to Moses about the slaying of the firstborn, 113-114.
- Pharaoh's dread of last —, 114
- nature of final judgmen executed upon Egypt, 129-131 146.

Prayer,
- purpose of Service in Synagogues as well as merit of public —, 174.
- reason for formula of benedictions, 214.
- the *Kaddish*, 206 (Note 229).
- the *Aleinu* —, 215.
- *Sh'moneh Esreh*, 215 (Note 270).
- for more than three hours, 244.
- devotion in —, 417-418.
- Moses' prayers in the affair of the golden calf, 559-561.

Priests,
- anointing of —, 475.

Priests,
- garments of High Priest and common priest, 487.
- installation of —, 495-506.

Prophecy,
- the principle of the truth of 172.
- the children of Abraham never doubted truth of —, 277-278.
- of the fundamentals of faith, 312.
- on Sabbath we are to go to Sages and prophets to hear the words of G-d, 312.

Prophets of the Babylonian Era, 118.

Proselytes, see: Converts to Judaism.

Providence,
- principle of —, 172-173, 312.

Q

Quail, 223-224, 230-231.

R

Rabbeinu Hai, 483-484.

Rabbeinu Hakadosh, see: Rabbi Yehudah Hanasi.

"The Rabbi" (Rabbeinu Chananel), 106.

"The Rabbi" (Rambam), 37, 38, 48, 49, 222, 291, 326, 329, 334, 336, 519.
- see also: Harav Rabbi Moshe.

"The Rabbi" (Rashi), 45, 106, 120, 160, 380, 381, 385, 423, 441, 485, 488, 493, 495, 514, 517, 520, 521.
— Rabbeinu Shlomo, 528.
Rabbi Yehudah Hanasi (Judah the Prince), 26, 132, 133, 349, 397.
Ramban,
— reference to his age, 626.
— his arrival in Acco, 627.
Ram's Horn,
— at the Giving of the Torah, 280.
— to be blown every year on first day of Ellul, 576.
Ransom, 372.
Red Heifer, 208, 427, 502.
Redemption from Egyptian Bondage
— the many reasons for —, 24-25.
— when finally achieved, 4-5.
— the expression with which it was to be announced, 40-41.
— the meaning of *g'ulah* (redemption), 69.
— nature of final judgment executed upon Egypt, 129-131.
— memorial of — in the counting of months, 116-118.
— when — took place, 147-148, 161.
— children of Ephraim who went out of Egypt before coming of Moses, 157.
— importance of the memorial we are to make of —, 172-173.
— went out with mirth and song, 181.
— some of the commandments which are a memorial to —, 173, 340.

Redemption from Egyptian Bondage
— evidence for creation of world, His infinite power and His Unity, 285.
Religious Persecutions, 301-302.
Revelation on Mount Sinai.
— the Divine name by which the Torah was given, 35, 282-284, 327-329.
— the order of events at —, 324-325, 419-422.
— purpose of — that we never slide from way of truth, 330.
Reward and Punishment
— miraculous nature of —, 65.
— doctrine of, 169, 174-175.
— nature of punishment which is felt to fourth generation and to what sin it applies, 296-300.
— the mercy shown to those who keep the commandments, 300-302.
— those who worship G-d without intent of receiving reward, 301-302.
Rome,
— from — came our present exile, 244.
— Hadrianic persecutions, 301 (Note 369).

INDEX

S

Saadia Gaon, 37, 99, 275, 359, 526.
Sabbath,
— in counting the weekdays we always remember the —, 116-117, 313.
— "the sign" of —, 170, 548.
— at Marah, 208.
— preparation for —, 236.
— the perpetual remembrance that G-d created everything, 306, 589.
— scope of the commandment to remember —, 306-315.
— welcoming the —, 309.
— *Kiddush*, 309, 313-315.
— purport of — that we turn away from our mental preoccupations, etc, 312.
— on — we testify to all fundamentals of faith, 312, 322.
— prohibition of work on —, 316-317.
— when life is in danger, 547.
— reason for special prohibition against kindling fire, 596-598.

Sacred Language,
— style of — to use one term in the same instance with two different meanings, 26-27.
— Rabbis of Talmud are the true Hebrew linguists, 168.
— certain letters interchange, 385.

Sacred Language,
— adapts all forms according to image of man, 447, 466.
— adopted from standpoint living in Land of Israel, 467.
— why so called, 518-520.

"Sanctification of the New Moon," 116.

Sanctuary,
— reference to building thereof in Song at Red Sea, 204.
— strictures of Solomon when building the —, 336-337.
— a non-priest who performs the Divine Service in —, 371.
— secret of — built by Solomon, 436-437.
— number of donations necessary 511-513.

Sanhedrin, the Great, 397.
— head of — is highest position in authority of Torah, 398.

Saul, 246-247, 251, 255.

Scripture, customary ways of —,
— connection of books, 6-7.
— to repeat words for emphasis and significance, or for some lengthy intervening phrase, 45.
— to mention names of mothers of kings, 77.
— shortens a narrative sometimes at one point and other times at another, 101, 111.
— to repeat the phrase *so did they* in order to explain etc., 145.
— hints and deals briefly with hidden matters, 130.
— reason why — uses past and future tenses interchangeably, 192.

Scripture, customary ways of,
- words are repeated in order to indicate that such will always be the case, 196.
- disposed to be silent on hidden miracles, 219.

Scroll of Esther, 118.
Secret Arts of the Egyptians, 80-81, 85, 87.
Seder Olam, 150.
Seduction, 383-389.
Sefer Yetzirah, 524.
Self-defense, right to, 376-378.
Sennacherib, 294.
Separate Intelligences, 292, 296.
Servant, Hebrew
- why the ordinances begin with subject of —, 340-341.
- duties of master to him and his family, 342.

Seven Nations
- why only six nations were first mentioned to Moses, 29-30.
- which land of these nations was "flowing with milk and honey," 29, 163-164.
- the three nations that did not go out to battle, 415-417.

Seventh Year, 340, 402.
Sickness, 212-213, 415.
Simon the Just, 477.
Shamir, 443.
Shammai the Elder, 311, 313.
Shashdang, 75, 628.
Shekel,
- weight and equivalent thereof, 520-522.
- found by Ramban in Acco, 627-628.

Shiloh, 430.
Shir Hashirim Rabbah, 56, 62, 526, 529, 535.

Sh'moneh Esreh Prayers, 215 (Note 270).
Shmuel ben Chophni, Gaon Rav, 84.
Sifra, 287, 528.
    See also: Torath Kohanim.
Sifre, 131, 163, 255 (also Note 52), 472.
Solomon,
- when building the Sanctuary, 336-337, 436-437.
- what — in his wisdom said in his prayer in the Sanctuary, 436.
- anointing of — 531.

Sorcery,
- reason for stringency of the law, 389-390.

Soul,
- why Torah does not explain assurances of — in life after death of body, 65.

Stealing,
- of a human being, 320, 359-361.
- of goods, 379.

Stones, precious, 440-444, 490-491.
Stranger, 392-393.
Synagogues,
- purpose of service in —, 174.

T

Tabernacle,
- why Book of Exodus concludes with building of —, 5.
- main purpose 434-435, 506-507.
- secret of —, 435-437.
- continuation of Mount Sinai, 435-436.

INDEX

Tabernacle,
- miracle of craftsmen involved in making thereof, 542-543, 599.
- when work was begun, 595-596.
- why work of — repeated five times in Torah, 603-606.
- women's share in building of —, 600-601, 607-608.
- meaning of various terms —, 609, 614-615.
- order of events when erected and dedicated, 616-624.
- when was "the eighth day of installation," 616, 621-622.

Table, in Tabernacle
- secret thereof, 450-451.
- various vessels, 451-455.
- showbread, how made, 455-456.

Tablets of the Law
- how the Ten Commandments were written on them and why, 322-323.
- correspond to heaven and earth, 323.
- when given, 430-431.
- their high distinction, 561.
- series of events between breaking of first — and giving of second —, 574-577.
- how second — were given, 584.
- when were second — written, 592-593.

Taking G-d's Name in vain, 302-306.
- the punishment for, 322.

Targum Yerushalmi, 497, 536.

Ten Commandments,
- why all — addressed to individual, 287.
- the three kinds of idol-worship, and scope of prohibition, 292-296.

Ten Commandments,
- difference in how we heard the first two commandments, 304-306.
- the order of the —, 319-322.
- why He mentioned the recompense in some of —, 321-322.
- how written on the two Tablets and why, 322-323.
- all — further explained in *Seder Mishpatim,* 338-342.
- all 613 Commandments implicit in —, 431.

Theriac, 537-539.

Thirteen attributes of G-d, 584-586.

Tithes, 399-400.

Torah,
- coming into wilderness of Sinai was an occasion for joy to Israel because they knew they would receive — there, 269.
- people's consent to receive the —, 275.
- preparation for receiving the —, 279.
- order of events at the giving of the —, 281-284.
- Written and Oral, 223, 411.
- duty to rejoice at giving of —, and at finishing of —, 430.
- whole — written before creation, 431.
- all people should merit a knowledge of the —, 446.

Torath Kohanim (Sifra), 473, 486, 547.

Trial,
- nature of — with manna, 221-222.
- nature of — at the Revelation on Mount Sinai, 329-330.

U

Unleavened bread, 127-128, 149.
Ur of the Chaldees, 301.
Urim and Thummim, 480-484.

V

Vayikra Rabbah, 617.

W

Washing,
— of hands and feet by priests, 523-524.
— of hands before prayer, 524.
— the High Priest on Day of Atonement, 524.

Water,
— which came from the rock in Horeb, 239-241.

"Ways of the Amorites," 413-414.

Widow and orphan, 393-396.

Wife,
— rights of —, 355-357.

Women,
— with respect to observance of commandments, 308.
— share in building of Tabernacle, 600-601, 607-608.

Work, forbidden — on Sabbath and Festivals, 131-134.

World,
— follows its natural course, and since creation His blessing did not create something from nothing, 450-451.

"World to Come," 65 (Note 12), 227, 274, 319,
— how the righteous inheriting — will be sustained, 228.
— in Messianic era, 179.

"World of Souls," 65, 227 (Note 346).

Z

Zalzalah, (Earthquake) 324.
Zodiac, 118.